P9-CMA-880

Origin of the

LAND TENURE SYSTEM

in the United States

Origin of the
LAND TENURE SYSTEM
in the United States

By

MARSHALL HARRIS

Head, Land Tenure Section
Bureau of Agricultural Economics
U. S. Department of Agriculture

Ames: The Iowa State College Press

 Composed and printed by The Iowa State College Press, Ames, Iowa, U. S. A.

Library of Congress Catalog Card Number: 52-13802

To my wife

Katherine Franklin Harris

Preface

SOME OF THE MOST IMPORTANT INFLUENCES in the politico-economic development of the thirteen original colonies were those which surrounded the evolution of the system of land tenure. Yet, these influences largely have escaped the scrutiny of historians, economists, and other social scientists.

Colonial reliance upon agriculture as a means of securing a living, together with the unsatisfactory European land tenure system from which many of the colonists fled, made control over land a vital consideration throughout the period. Especially was this true during and immediately following the struggle for independence and freedom. Emphasis on rights in land grew out of the close relationship between the land tenure system and economic opportunity in those early days, and also out of the dependence of political democracy upon economic democracy — a dependence clearly recognized by many of the colonial leaders.

The early settlers, many of whom came to America to escape the rigors of the feudal system, used every opportunity to get their land on as easy terms and under as secure and free tenure as possible. The founding fathers also were on the alert to prevent the development in America of a landed aristocracy similar to that existing in contemporary Europe. On the other hand, many of the colonizing agencies (with land grants from European sovereigns) and private parties saw in America a place where the dying feudalism of England could be made to flourish again with new vigor. The English Crown also hoped to develop a subservient colonial empire upon which the mother country could depend for raw materials and to which she could send manufactured products. These currents and crosscurrents in the evolution of the national land tenure system must be examined to understand the manner in which land is held in the United States today.

During the last half century federal and state governments have become increasingly concerned with the tenure under which the American farmer occupies and uses the land. This concern has resulted in national and state legislation to improve obvious shortcomings growing out of the present farm tenure system and pattern of land occupancy. Agricultural research and extension education to expedite needed tenure adjustments have been expanded greatly in recent decades. The objective is to prevent internal decay which would lead to a weakening of American civilization. A review of the deliberations of national, regional, state, and county tenure committees, however, indicates a serious lack of usable information about the forces that influenced the evolution of the present tenure system. Little information is available on why we have the present tenure system and pattern of land occupancy. Several excellent studies have been published on developments during the Colonial era, but many of the writings regarding the land system are concerned chiefly with the post-Colonial period, and confined largely to the last few decades. Numerous exhaustive treatises have been prepared on the historical antecedents of the legal system governing real estate, as exemplified in English feudal tenures and common and civil law. Many excellent spot studies indicate the tenure status of American farmers and home owners. But these studies have not told how basic tenure principles were developed. This information is needed, for proposed action to improve the present tenure system will be influenced by the history of its development.

This book is designed to fulfil in part that need, by helping to determine the processes through which the land tenure system of the United States became what it was at the time of its emergence just prior to 1800. Thus, the book deals chiefly with tenure processes during the two centuries of the Colonial era. It focuses special attention on: (1) changes made in the land tenure system prior to establishment of the national government; and (2) forces, factors, conditions, and situations that brought about these changes and finally secured their formal recognition.

The major principles which undergird the whole land tenure structure were established by the time of the formation of the national government. The present-day tenure system, therefore, is largely an outgrowth of the concepts that the English colonists brought with them to America, as changed during the Colonial period. The influence of the French and Spanish grew out of the fact of their presence and competition for trade and territory, rather than their peculiar tenure system.

A record of everything — including minor happenings — that affected the land tenure system is not available. Even if complete information were available it would be impossible here to report such a mass of data. It would be necessary to select only the crucial items. Fortunately, some data on most of the decisive events have been recorded. It is the author's purpose to trace simultaneously four separate, yet related, types of phenomena: (1) processes of slow modification (evolutionary); (2) events that marked significant changes (revolutionary); (3) specific adjustments in the tenure system; and (4) the economic, social, religious, and political philosophies and theories that brought about slow modification and eventually resulted in formalized change.

The author considers the whole system of land tenure as a complex scheme for distributing or assigning rights in land. It should be emphasized that *rights,* and not *men* nor *land,* are the basic considerations. By and large, the rights to be dealt with are qualitative and not quantitative. No endeavor is made to indicate qualitative evaluations or to pass value judgments upon the wisdom of the various changes that were made and the tenurial arrangements that were evolved.

The central question is: *What events brought about significant change or prevented change?* Did change depend upon the tenure concepts the colonists brought with them to America? Was it influenced by the kind of people who came to the New World? Was the land tenure system an outgrowth of the American frontier? What were the influences of contemporary thinking outside of the colonies, particularly in England and on the Continent? Did differences in soil, climate, and topography have an influence? Was the tenure system influenced by the new Christianity, the emerging democracy, and the rising capitalism? What events encouraged the evolutionary process, and what events made for revolutionary adjustments?

The basic data for a major part of the study were available chiefly in the fragmentary records of the Colonial period. The incomplete records of the early colonizing companies and the sketchy proceedings of many of the local governing bodies were available. More complete data, however, were found in the statutes and records of the colonial assemblies. Constitutional guidance was completely absent in Colonial days. The nearest thing to a constitution was Magna Carta, and it was extremely far removed from the colonies. It was four centuries old and 3,000 miles of water separated the colonial possessions from the mother country. Court decisions were not recorded generally except for the occasional case that was brought to the attention of one of the assemblies.

Many of the state historical societies have made invaluable contributions by preserving a wide range of information in their publications. Much of the information, however, was generally scattered throughout many volumes which were either indexed with other purposes in mind or not indexed at all. Although there apparently were many blind spots in all of the records, tribute must be paid to our forefathers who wrote down so completely the events as they took place, and to the historical societies that have preserved so well the record of colonial development.

Nearly all of the objective evidence is from original sources, although the findings of other writers have been accepted where the ground was well covered. Several excellent monographs have been written on particular aspects of the subject, and many volumes have been published on general phases of the evolving land system. If it seems that scant attention has been paid to them, it is not because of oversight or lack of appreciation of their value, but rather because it is endeavored in this volume to present a fairly complete sketch, which precludes the possibility of covering in detail each event and the happenings leading up to it.

The author is grateful for the cooperation of numerous organizations and individuals who have aided him in collecting and evaluating information for this book. Permission was granted by the University of Illinois for the full use of material in the author's dissertation on the subject. A leave of absence was granted by the United States Department of Agriculture, during which time much additional material was collected. The General Education Board, through Duke University, made the leave of absence granted by the Department of Agriculture financially possible. It should be emphasized that these organizations have made no effort to control the findings. The author alone assumes full responsibility for the results.

It would be impossible to list here all of the persons who contributed to this study. However, special mention is due those who were of major help on the project. Among those who inspired the study and offered sound advice in laying out its bounds were L. C. Gray and M. M. Kelso, formerly of the Bureau of Agricultural Economics, United States Department of Agriculture, and H. C. M. Case and C. L. Stewart of the Department of Agricultural Economics, University of Illinois. Technical help on legal aspects of the study was rendered by James Leavy, formerly of the Bureau of Agricultural Economics, and by members of the Office of the Solicitor, United States Department of Agriculture.

The Library of Congress unstintingly made available its extensive facilities, and its well-qualified staff facilitated the study in numerous ways. The study could not have been completed without the constant assistance of Katherine Franklin Harris, who spent many days in searching for pertinent facts, in organizing the material, and in standardizing the citations. Marie B. Harmon assisted in editing the manuscript, in proofreading, and in preparing the index. Elizabeth Cashell Dunlevy, Josephine Adamson, Ann D. Defrin, and Esther C. Wirth rendered invaluable assistance in typing and assisting with mechanical details.

Grateful acknowledgment is made to the following publishers for permission to use selections from their copyrighted publications: to Alfred A. Knopf, Incorporated, for a selection from *The British Empire*

Before the American Revolution . . . , by Lawrence Henry Gipson; to Cambridge University Press, for a selection from *The History of English Law Before the Time of Edward I,* by Sir Frederick Pollock and Frederick W. Maitland; to Columbia University Press, for a selection from *The Patroon's Domain,* by Samuel G. Nissenson; to Henry Holt and Company, for certain maps from *The Foundations of American Civilization,* by Max Savelle; to Houghton Mifflin Company, for selections from *The First Republic in America,* by Alexander Brown; to Little, Brown and Company, for a selection from *The Rule Against Perpetuities,* by John C. Gray; to Longmans, Green and Company, for selections from *The Institution of Property,* by Charles Reinold Noyes; to the Macmillan Company, for a selection from *Select Charters Illustrative of American History,* by William MacDonald; to the University of Wisconsin Press, for a selection from *Colonial Precedents of Our National Land System As It Existed in 1800,* by Amelia Clewley Ford, and for selections from *English Common Law in the Early American Colonies,* by Paul S. Reinsch; to Yale University Press, for a selection from *Labaree's Essays in Colonial History Presented to Charles McLean Andrews . . .*;to Wide World Photos, Inc., for an Associated Press selection from the Evening Star, of March 15, 1948, Washington, D. C.; and to the publishers whose copyrighted selections are acknowledged in the Literature Cited.

MARSHALL HARRIS

July, 1953

Contents

1. The Nature of Land Tenure 1

Definition of land tenure. The bundle of rights concept. Principal forms of tenure. Distribution of tenure rights. Some characteristics of land tenure.

2. Development of English Feudal Tenures 21

Developments prior to the Norman Conquest. Development of feudalism. Major tenure types in feudal England. Minor types of tenure. The English manor. Tenures of Kent and Durham.

3. Adjustments in English Feudal Tenures 40

Magna Carta. Laws regarding waste. Alienation of freehold estates. Alienation of copyhold estates. Inheritance in feudal England. Leasehold interests. Bondmen and laborers. Later legislation.

4. Conflicting Claims to the Land of the New World . . . 62

Conflicting claims of sovereigns. Rights of Indian tribes. Conflicting claims.

5. Nature of Colonial Grants of Land and Government . . 71

Nature of charters. Presettlement charters. Power to govern and rights in land. Settlement agencies' rights in land. Landed rights and governmental control.

6. Two Royal Colonies 82

The three Virginia charters. New York under Dutch and English control.

7. Three Corporate Colonies 98

New England Council. Maine and New Hampshire territory. Massachusetts and Plymouth. Rhode Island and Providence plantations. Connecticut and New Haven.

8. Three Proprietary Colonies 117

Maryland and the Lords Baltimore. William Penn and Pennsylvania. Delaware-Pennsylvania relations.

9. Five Composite Colonies 127

New Hampshire. New Jersey — East and West. The two Carolinas — North and South. Oglethorpe's Georgia.

10. Relation of Original Grants to Tenure System 141

Power to govern. Rights in land. Territorial overlapping of grants. Power to grant land. Organizational difficulties. Kentish tenure clause.

11. Acquisition of Indians' Land 155
General processes employed. Restraints placed upon alienation. Purchase by the white man. Gifts from the Indians. Treaty as a means of acquisition. Abandonment by the Indians. Acquisition by seizure. Leases with the Indians. Land reserved for the Indians. Interpretive summary.

12. Transfers to Financial Supporters of the Trading Companies 179
Transfer of land for shares. Treasury right grants. Dutch and Swedish trading companies. Interpretive summary.

13. Headright System of Granting Land 194
The headright system in Virginia. Headright grants in New York. Headrights under the Lords Baltimore. Headrights in Pennsylvania-Delaware. Headright grants in New Jersey. Headright system in the Carolinas. Oglethorpe and headrights.

14. Disposition of Land by Sale 237
Penn's system of selling land. Sale of land in New Jersey. Transfers by sale in Virginia. Land sales in the Carolinas. Disposal by sale in Maryland. Sale of land in New York. Sale of land in Georgia. Interpretive summary.

15. Special-Purpose Grants to Settlers 255
Grants for military purposes. Grants for meritorious service. Glebe land grants. School lands. Grants to encourage industry.

16. The New England Land System 273
The Council and the Company. The New England town system. Interpretive summary.

17. Land Companies 289
Early Colonial land companies. Pre-Revolutionary land companies. Post-Revolutionary land companies.

18. Emergence of the National Land System 310
Colonial land tenure system characteristics. The right to alienate by sale. Inheritance in Colonial America. Reservations of quitrent. Recording transfers of land rights. Survey inaccuracies and difficulties. Leasing in Colonial America.

19. Some Forces That Influenced the Evolving Land System . . 345
Imprint of religion. Common law influence. Economic and political considerations.

20. Adjustments During the Revolutionary Period 367
Treason and confiscation. Property acquisition—pursuit of happiness. Barring entails and outlawing primogeniture. Taxes and quitrent. Minor adjustments. State land offices. Cessions to the federal government. Territorial ordinances.

21. Some Antecedents of Public Land Policies and the Tenure System 394
Contributions to general land policy. Contributions to the system.

Bibliography 413

Biographical Index 425

Geographic Index 429

Subject Index 433

Origin of the
LAND TENURE SYSTEM
in the United States

CHAPTER 1

The Nature of Land Tenure

A STUDY OF THE ORIGIN and development of the land tenure system of the United States is conditioned heavily by what are conceived to be its principal forms and fundamental characteristics. Thus, we might ask such questions as these:

What was the substance and content of the land tenure system handed down by the founding fathers? What was its basic structure? How did the various parts fit together into a unified whole? What were the principles that undergirded the system and gave it cohesiveness? What procedures gave the structure vitality, vitality to meet the test of time as the young nation moved toward its destiny?

DEFINITION OF LAND TENURE

The concept "land tenure" refers to the manner in which and the period for which rights in land are held. The term "tenure," most authorities agree, means the holding of property, especially real estate, of or by reference to a superior. Inherent in the word "held" is the idea of exclusion, that is, to set aside and keep as one's own by shutting out or excluding others. Another indispensable dimension of tenure is the period of time for which the property is held.

In a hopeless endeavor to describe definitively rights in land, the definition often includes one or more additional ideas, such as "enjoyed" and "used" and "possession" and "disposition." If the former terms are used, the last phrase in the definition may read: "rights in land are held and enjoyed" or "held and used." The inclusion of either of these terms, however, appears to mislead and to confuse. All holders of rights in land do not at all times receive pleasure from that which they possess. Also, many parties hold rights in land without exercising the privilege of using them. In some cases, the landholder exercises but one of the many rights that he holds — that of disposition by devise or bequeath. He may even leave disposition up to the state, and as a consequence never exercise by outward action any right that he holds. He merely holds numerous rights that make up private property in land.

The term "land" in this definition merits brief attention. It includes not only the soil surface but the air, water, sunlight, minerals, and vegetation and animals which are "free gifts of nature." The commonly accepted version of "land," however, needs a dash of law to give it a slightly different flavor. Under the Anglo-American legal concept (and it is this concept that must be used), land is "whatever is a parcel of the terrestrial globe," including everything that is "permanently affixed to such parcel." But this is not all that is included in the common law concept of land, for "tenements" and possibly "hereditaments" must be included. The former has been defined as anything which is subject to common law tenure and includes not only land but "incorporeal things real." "Hereditaments" include that which passes by law to the heir and not to the administrator upon the death of an owner without a will. Tenements and hereditaments are not easily distinguished, for they include things such as the rights *to use* and the right *to the profits of* another's land. An example is an easement or right-of-way, which is the right to make limited use of the land of another without removing any of the substance or taking possession of the land. The rights to hunt and to fish in a particular district are also classified in the same category.

The right of a landowner to the natural flow of water in a stream along the land is a part and parcel of the land itself. The landowner, however, does not own the water until he has appropriated it for his own use. The natural flow of water is incident to and annexed to the land and is transferable with the land. It is like land itself and in most cases may be taken away from the owner only by exercise of the right of eminent domain. The theory is that the owner is entitled to have the water flow as it is accustomed to flow, and since other owners have the same right, he cannot interfere with the flow to any material extent.

There is no property and consequently no land tenure in a Crusoe economy. In such a situation, rights in land cannot be assigned or distributed and there is no need for protection against the encroachment of others, for there is no one to receive any right and no one to intrude upon any right. Use is present, but exclusion and disposition are absent. Contrary to some popular usage, property is concerned with relations among men, and not physical objects. Property is *rights,* not *things.* The things are property objects, and tenure is concerned with rights in these things. To be sure, in a Crusoe economy there can be physical objects or natural forces of tremendous use value, but these objects cannot be spoken of as property, they are only property objects. There can be no property relation between a Crusoe and the objects with which he sustains life; he has no tenure in the things. Who is he going to exclude? Against whom is he going to hold it? To whom will he dispose of it?

This position has been defined by philosophers and others. Kant says, ". . . if a man were alone in the world he could properly hold or acquire nothing as his own; because between himself, as person, and all other outward objects, as things, there is no relation." (*Noyes. Institution, 290, quoting Kant. Rechtslehre, I, 2.*) In the *Restatement of the Law of Property* the word "property" is used ". . . to denote legal relations between persons with respect to a thing." (*Amer. Law Inst. Restatement, 3.*)

As soon as more than one person appears upon the scene, property comes into being, regardless of its form and structure. In the tooth and fang economy of early society, however, the system of land tenure was doubtless crude. It was based principally upon the idea that might made right, and consequently the strong had dominion over all things that could be held by the sword. As social organization became more complex, law rather than might became the basis for rights in land. The more socialized man became, the more important became the role that law played in the distribution of rights in land among all members of society. Individual rights based upon might were restricted and rights based upon equity and the general welfare were expanded.

The legalistic concept of tenure never has taken root extensively in the United States. From a purely legalistic point of view, the tenure concept covers only those relationships established between individuals, or between an individual and society, when a lesser estate than that enjoyed by the grantor is created in land. This concept grew out of the doctrine of tenure deeply rooted in our feudal heritage, dating back at least to the Norman Conquest of England. One of the fundamental principles of the feudal system was that all land was held of the king, and that it could be granted successively from one subject to another to be held in turn of the last grantor. The relationship was one of lord and tenant. The king was the paramount lord and the last grantee was the lowest tenant. "Tenure" was the term used to describe the relationship between the lord and the tenant. It was possible for this relationship to be changed without directly affecting the relationship between the grantor and his lord or any of the others higher up the hierarchy.

Land that is held of another is commonly spoken of as feudal land, in contrast with allodial land, which is possessed by a man in his own right. He is not dependent upon another, and does not owe obligations of rent or service. For centuries, the holder of allodial land was not regarded as having tenure. There was no status — the land was not held of another.

Common usage, however, sanctions the use of the term "tenure" to describe the relationship among men in regard to the holding of rights in land. The earlier usage in its strictest sense was lost in the gradual evolution from the pure feudal land system of the Middle Ages to the relatively free system of holding land described by the phrase "fee simple absolute." Land tenure, as the term is commonly used today, includes " . . . all the relations established among men, determining their varying rights in the use of the land." (*Wehrwein. Res. in Agr. Land Ten., 2.*) These relations are nothing more or less than property in land.

THE BUNDLE OF RIGHTS CONCEPT

Tenure of land has been described as a "bundle of rights." The bundle is made up of many heterogeneous, complex, highly flexible sticks. The complete quota of rights covers all sorts of relations. It is a mass of claims, privileges, powers, and immunities, all of which are illustrated in the relation of landlord and tenant under a typical tenancy agreement. *Claims* are concerned with the duty on the part of another or others. For example, a lease involves a claim on the lessee for rent. *Privileges* are just the opposite. They indicate the absence of a claim by others. For example, unless otherwise prohibited (which rarely happens) the lessor can transfer the property to another through sale or otherwise without the consent of the lessee, thereby substituting a new lessor. This is the lessor's privilege. *Powers* involve liability upon another and may be illustrated by the right of distraint which is a liability upon the lessee. *Immunities* are disabilities in others. For example, the lessor generally does not have to accept a new lessee. The orginal lessee under most lease agreements is unable to substitute a new lessee for himself unless the lessor is agreeable, except perhaps in case of death. (*Noyes. Institution, 290.*)

All rights are relations, negative or positive, between persons, and only between persons. Some of these rights belong to all citizens by virtue of their citizenship. Others are gained by particular individuals as a result of arrangement among men. Still others arise when an existing right is infringed. In other words, rights in land may pre-exist a wrong or may arise only because of a wrong. In general, they are promised liberties from interference by others.

Rights in land held by a private party are spoken of as an estate in land. A private party may hold only one right or he may hold all rights not reserved by society. He may hold these rights for long or short periods of time, and his rights may attach immediately or at some time in the future. Thus, the quantity, permanence, and timing of rights in land are important considerations.

The largest and most exclusive estate in land that a private party may hold consists of all of the sticks in the bundle of rights except those reserved by society. This is spoken of as a fee simple estate. The holder of such an estate is commonly called the owner, and his tenure is described by the word "ownership." In Colonial America, many estates in land were less than fee simple, for the holders could not alienate them freely. They passed to the lineal descendents of the original grantor. That is, they were entailed, and were known as fee tail estates. The strong reaction against entailed estates, however, brought about their downfall.

Still lesser estates in land are those that run only for life, that is, life estates. Probably the most common life estate is the one created by a will which conveys the deceased husband's real property to his wife so long as she may live. Similar estates can be held by the husband in real property owned by his deceased wife.

The tenant under a typical lease agreement holds a still lesser estate in land. He usually holds for a year, or a term of years, or some indefinite period subject to determination in the future. Tenancies at will and tenancies at sufferance are still more restrictive, since their permanence or duration is subject to the will of one of the parties. Estates of expectancy may also be created, and the holder of such an estate has to wait until some future time to assert his right.

Thus, the fee simple owner holds the largest possible quantity of rights under our system of private property. He holds them for the longest period of time, and his rights begin immediately. All other estates are conditioned by some disability as to quantity of rights, as to permanence, or as to how soon the rights are effective.

Society always reserves at least three specific sticks out of the bundle of rights in land — the rights to tax, to condemn, and to police. The first of these is probably the best known. It can be exercised by units of government over all of the privately held land under their jurisdictions. Even though this right may not be exercised by a particular unit of government, it does not disappear or revert to some other party or unit of government. Furthermore, even within one taxing unit the right to tax can be exercised with regard to selected parties while it may not be imposed upon others. Or, it may apply with unequal weight and unequal rates upon different parties, as in homestead tax exemption and the graduated land tax or the graduated inheritance tax.

Although the exercise of the right to condemn privately held land for public or quasi-public use is not as universally applied as taxes, the right applies to all parcels of land held privately. This reserved right is not expressly authorized in the United States Constitution, but it needs no sanction, for it stems from the nation's right to carry on essential functions of government. It may lie dormant for years and then be exercised at the most unexpected place and inopportune time.

Privately held land may be condemned for a road, a park, a public building, a military post, a munitions plant, a home for a landless family, or for conservational purposes. The rights held by private owners, however, are safeguarded since these rights cannot be taken except through due process of law and for the general welfare.

Most mortgagor-mortgagee, landlord-tenant, and employer-employee regulations are established under the police power. The nature and extent of the rights in land reserved by society under this power are exceedingly vague. Although it is clear that privately held rights cannot be adjusted, whether expanded or restricted, without due process of law, it is equally clear that society may restrict the freedom with which the owner uses his land where necessary to protect and promote the public health, safety, morals, and general welfare.

Under the police power, minimum standards may be established, the maintenance of which is required of the individual. The very vagueness of the due process and the public welfare clauses leave the nature and magnitude of the police power difficult to assess. It should be explained, however, that many of the rules and regulations imposed under the police power, or under the inherent right of society to make adjustments in the tenure system, or under the interstate commerce clause, are pliable and easy to act upon. Many of the laws and regulations covering transfers, for example, make it possible for the parties to gain their desires with a minimum of effort. The standardization and recordation of farm mortgages is a good example. Some rules, on the other hand, help one party and restrict another party. An example is the landlord's lien. It restricts the freedom with which the tenant can dispose of the produce of the rented land and it makes easier the collection of rent by the landlord.

In addition, the regulations may be either directory or mandatory. Any law that the two parties can contract around is merely directory or permissive, while any right that cannot be changed by contract is mandatory. For example, England tried to introduce compensation for improvements into her tenancy system by providing that the tenant should be permitted to claim such compensation, but later found it necessary to make the adjustment mandatory despite provisions in the contract. (*Harris. Legal Aspects, 175.*)

Society maintains an additional control over land use and occupancy through its spending power. "The power of the purse," to use the words of Justice Stone, is a fourth right that government may exercise in regard to land. The power of the purse is more indirect than direct. The right of the fee simple owner to use his land as he pleases is reduced only by the spending power; no right is taken away. Various payments made under the soil conservation and crop adjustment programs are examples of purchasing control over land.

In the famous Hoosac Mills case Justice Stone, in dissenting, laid down the following argument. "The spending power . . . is in addition to the legislative power and not subordinate to it. This independent grant of the power of the purse, and its very nature . . . presuppose freedom of selection among divers ends and aims, and the capacity to impose such conditions as will render the choice effective." (*U.S. v. Butler.*) Actually the spending power is in its infancy insofar as control of rights in land is concerned. Its full nature and scope is yet to be determined.

The rights to tax, to condemn, to police, and to spend appear simple and straightforward when viewed individually. But when considered collectively they are more complex and their possibilities become more potent. Taxation may be used to make a certain police power regulation effective and the taxes thus collected may be used through the spending power to obtain specific land tenure objectives, which may necessitate the use of the power of eminent domain. Consider this case: The Congress of the United States provided that no corporation could hold more than 500 acres of land in Puerto Rico. But this police power regulation to improve land tenure was ineffective for forty years until taxes made funds available to purchase the land in excess of 500 acres held by corporations. To make the spending power effective the power of eminent domain was specifically given to the agency administering the spending program. Congress established the 500-acre rule, taxes were levied, revenues were spent, and land was acquired under the power of eminent domain. This procedure of combining rights reserved by society in attaining changes in land occupancy and use has been sanctioned by the Supreme Court of the United States.

Society, represented by federal, state, and local government units, cannot transfer all of its rights in land. The government specifically reserves three rights in all land owned by private parties, but another right – the right of escheat – cannot be transferred and consequently no reservation is necessary. A unit of government is free to grant its land to a private party under whatever terms are mutually acceptable, but always it must take back the rights which constitute ownership whenever the private party does not choose to maintain them. That is, land escheats automatically to some unit of government when certain conditions develop. This universal principle in the land tenure system is one of its peculiar characteristics.

The transfer of rights in land from private parties to the state may take place in at least three ways: first, through failure of the grantee to meet conditions specified in the grant; second, through tax delinquency and forfeiture; finally, in the absence of an heir to claim the land when the grantee deceases intestate. In addition, an owner may cause his land to revert to society by deserting it. Thus, as Kelso put it, "Society through its government can, then, grant rights in land, can retake rights in land, but it can also have rights thrust upon it." (*Kelso. Needed Research, 293.*)

Rights transferred to private parties give these parties considerable freedom in the use of their land. In the administration and disposition of all publicly held land the government, under the land ordinances and otherwise, transferred to private parties all rights in land except the three mentioned above, and the inalienable interests referred to as escheat and the spending power. The tenure established in such a procedure is called "fee simple absolute." The rights of the fee simple tenant may be classified as use, exclusion, and disposition. More specifically the *owner* as he is called holds the exclusive right to use or abuse as he sees fit, to sell, to bequeath, to will, to subdivide, to consolidate, to mortgage, to lease, to exclude all others, to grant easement, or to create any other type of lesser estates, except those specifically prohibited by law. When a lesser estate is transferred the private party receives only those rights explicitly stated or definitely implied in the instrument or agreement of transfer. He also may exercise the right to vacate or desert the land and thereby thrust it upon some unit of government.

A landowner has rights against other owners of land in the neighborhood. These rights may be put into four groups: first, the right of freedom from interference of possession, as by trespass; second, the right to demand of the other owners that they exercise due care not to damage the land; third, the right of absolute immunity from physical damage of a relatively permanent nature by reason of some condition created on the neighbor's land; and, fourth, the right to demand that the owner of neighboring land shall not utilize it so as to create a "nuisance," that is, interfere with the use of the owner of the land.

The legal, economic, and social setting in which these land tenure principles evolved emphasized rights and ignored responsibilities. At the end of the Colonial period a landed right usually was thought of as any title to or interest in any land that was enforceable by law. The same is true today. This concept fails to emphasize responsibility on the part of the owner, except that in theory any right presupposes a corresponding responsibility. The owner need not execise the right of use at all, or he may destroy the land's productive qualities by misuse. He need not exercise his right of exclusion, or he may demand that his fellow-man observe the letter of the law. And, he need not dispose of his rights in any way whatsoever, for he may leave to society the distribution of the land among his heirs, or in the absence of natural heirs his rights in land may be left to escheat to the state.

Classical economic doctrine assumed that if a private party were given fee simple title to land he would in pursuing his own best interests automatically fulfil any responsibilities that he might owe society. Arthur Young's adage that the "magic of property turns sand into gold" is an example of what was anticipated of the fee simple owner. Freedom of action without personal responsibility was the basic principle of the land tenure system. Freedom to make economic decisions, it was reasoned, would assure full utilization of the land; its improvement and conservation would likewise be guaranteed; economic forces would establish optimum size farm units; and all of these would provide for efficient production, which would result in widespread wealth and income. Thus, the landowner's responsibility to society would be fulfilled automatically, and attention to or concern over the responsibility of the private owner could be ignored with impunity.

However, the wide disparity between immediate private self-interest and long-time public general welfare was not envisaged at that time. The enormous divergence between full freedom of private contract and full personal responsibility in the social contract (or compact), so widely discussed at that time and so prominent in the first state constitutions, was not taken into account. The economist's theory and the policymaker's practice of laissez faire complemented the legalist's championing of freedom of contract. Laissez faire and freedom of contract went hand in hand. Working together they tended strongly to emphasize private rights and to disregard both public and private responsibility. The old maxim, *caveat emptor,* let the buyer beware, is an example of a principle of law that gives power to freedom of contract.

PRINCIPAL FORMS OF TENURE

Ownership is the fundamental form of land tenure. It is the highest tenure form, and is usually evidenced by title. It is the foundation and cornerstone of the whole land tenure structure. From a purely legalistic viewpoint, title is a necessary emblem of ownership, except in certain jurisdictions. Yet many persons claim ownership without title. This usually is the case when a claim to title cannot be denied if certain conditions are met, as under a sales contract or a trusteeship.

The owner of the land may hold all of the rights not reserved by society or he may hold only one — the right of reversion as among private parties. He may transfer, however, all of his rights except that of reversion. He may assign all profits to another, grant various types of easements, pledge the land as security for a loan, rent it to a tenant, and condition the title by covenants running with the land, and his rights may be further reduced by the operation of law through police power regulations, taxation, statutory liens, etc. But the moment he loses the legal right to repossess the land at the end of a grant he is no longer the owner — ownership has passed to another.

Title and ownership are of little consequence, except psychologically, if all other rights are held by another party or by society. Henry George recognized this powerful psychological influence, for he would not expropriate title, although he would take all income assignable to land. (*George. Prog. and Pov., Bk. VIII, ch. II.*) The psychological power of ownership is one of the two major factors making it the fundamental form of land tenure in the United States. The other factor is the right of reversion.

Tenancy is the second most common tenure form in this country. The terms "tenant" and "tenancy" were derived directly from the feudal tenure system, and the tenancy system follows many of the principles involved. The two most important of these are that the property is held of a superior, and that services or payments are to be rendered. Owner operatorship is significantly different.

One of the chief attributes of land tenure is *possession.* The owner operator has possession and retains possession so long as he maintains the status of owner operator. When property is leased, possession passes to the tenant operator, and the landlord loses his possession. Another major characteristic is *use.* The owner operator holds the use right and so does the tenant, but not the landlord. A third quality is the right to the *produce.* The owner operator has this right unless he has assigned all or part of the produce to another party, while the landlord and the tenant generally share the produce, under a share-tenancy or standing-rent agreement. Where the rent is to be paid in cash it is more difficult to maintain that the produce of the land — at least that of the current year — is shared by the two parties. Within limits, however, when rents are paid in a fixed amount of produce, and even in a fixed amount of cash, the produce of the land is shared by the two parties.

The owner is the only one who has the right to *waste,* that is, to use up. The landlord cannot waste the rented property since he does not have the use right, while the tenant, at common law and usually by statute, is responsible, at least theoretically, for waste, and the landlord may stop wastage through court action. This does not deny the tenant the right to usual wear and tear. For instance, a tenant might use up a building or a particular plant food element in the soil and not commit waste.

Another characteristic of land tenure is *disposition.* The owner has the unqualified right, the landlord's right is subject to the tenant's right of possession and other conditions in the lease agreement, while the tenant does not have the right of disposition through subleasing, unless it is specifically granted and except where statutes, contracts, or custom confer the right. The tenant generally does not have the right, at the end of his lease, to sell or remove improvements which he added to the land during his occupancy. The right to *exclude* others from interference with the property — trespass — resides in the owner and passes to the tenant in typical leasing arrangements. In the absence of a provision in the contract or local custom, even the landlord may be excluded from his land if the tenant so desires.

Society's rights are not changed by transfer of certain rights from landlord to tenant. The impact of society's rights, however, shifts slightly. Escheat remains in society. The right to tax remains the same since the landlord generally has no claim on the tenant for taxes, for the landlord's claim is for rent. The incidence of the power of eminent domain and the police power are divided between the landlord and tenant.

In the distribution of the more formalized legal rights as between landlord and tenant, three other distinctions should be mentioned. Probably the most basic economic trait under the capitalistic system is change in the price of property in response to unpredictable influences, and not as a result of structural changes above or below ground, or as a result of high quality or low quality farming. The landlord usually retains completely this so-called unearned increment or gain – if there is one. He also must risk loss of value due to fluctuation. Another distinguishing characteristic that has an important economic impact under our short-term leasing system is security of tenure. The difference in the expectancy of continuous possession as between the three types of holders of rights in land seems obvious. The third important economic distinction is the status of improvements added to the land. If an owner operator adds improvements he takes full risks and reaps full benefits. If the landlord adds improvements, the current benefits are divided with the tenant, but their unexhausted value returns to the landlord when the tenancy terminates. But if the tenant makes improvements that become affixed to the land, the current benefits are usually divided with the landlord and, in most jurisdictions, they remain as a part of the landlord's property when the tenant vacates. Here the famous legal maxim, *quicquid plantatur solo, solo cedit,* a heritage of bygone days, is a powerful influence, for "that which is attached to the premises becomes the property of the owner." This dictum was powerful in early England, it remained in full force throughout Colonial America, and is still recognized in the United States, although it has been outlawed in England for a century.

Ownership and tenancy, however, are not the only forms of tenure. The other forms are "share-cropping" and "hired man." Here we part company somewhat with the legalist, but law usually follows rather than precedes customary ways of doing things. Share-cropping was practiced in Colonial America and still is a well-recognized system under which the owner of land and the operator co-operate in the production of crops, particularly cotton and tobacco. Share-cropping is not confined to the production of crops, for the "partido" system of producing livestock in the Southwest, particularly sheep, is not unlike the share-cropping of cotton and tobacco. Indeed, it has been called "share-cropping sheep."

The legal position of the share-cropper is problematical. In one state a statute declares that the relation of landlord and tenant is established. In some others the statutory implications are that the relation is that of employer and employee. In still others the courts decide each case in light of the circumstances involved.

The position of the hired man is still less clear. Where he occupies a part of the farm, typically the house and garden plot, and has a right to certain farm-produced food for home consumption, and where the income fluctuates with the income of the farm under some sort of profit-sharing agreement, the relation has many of the attributes of tenancy. But generally it is held that a tenure relation does not exist in the commonly accepted meaning of the word. However, some court decisions have recognized rights of labor that are very similar to property rights. Apparently, the sit-down strike decision in the Fansteel case is undergoing significant adjustments.

DISTRIBUTION OF TENURE RIGHTS

Society distributes to all members rights in some parcels of land. To every person, whether citizen or not, some right in land is allowed. The most humble person, along with the multimillionaire, is granted access to highways and streets, and to public parks and buildings. No pauper is denied a plot for burial, while in some jurisdictions the right to hunt or fish on the property of others is recognized. Certain types of rights are more far-reaching. Any member of society, for example, has the right to fly over the land of another.

Thus, there is a blending of the rights of the public and those of private parties. On the one hand, society may own a parcel of land and a private party, as a member of that society, may have certain rights in that land. On the other hand, a private party may own a piece of land and other private parties as members of society or the public in general may enter upon (or over) and use the land for specific purposes.

Special rights may be granted to some private parties in certain parcels of land. Alienations of this type may be put in two general classes: Those involving transfer of the entire fee and those involving the granting of lesser estates. The former is the procedure used in the transfer of those parts of the public domain which are now in the hands of private owners. This was outlined in the Ordinances of 1785 and 1787. The latter usually involves a lease or patent whereby the government transfers only a temporary use right. This procedure was not followed widely in Colonial America for most public land was at that time alienated in fee simple to those who desired to use it.

These use rights need not be absolute. They can be restricted as to the nature of the use, whether for cultivation, grazing, or taking of specified natural resources; they can be restricted as to the intensity of the use, witness the many and specific grazing regulations on the public domain, and the rules covering lumbering in the national forests; or they can be granted individually or in common, an example of the latter being the co-operative or collective grazing of range land in certain western states.

Between the two extremes, the granting of fee simple title and of restricted and temporary use rights, any combination of rights in land can be created. Of course, early Americans determined against the creation of feudal estates, common in Europe and existing in parts of America at the time of the establishment of the national land system. Many rules and regulations also have been developed governing the alienation of the public domain. Granting "complete property" in family-sized units to bona fide owner operators has been the guiding principle ever since the beginning of the national land policy.

Specified rights may be withheld from certain classes of persons. There is no assurance that all members of society will be treated the same. Although the common law restraint upon the right of aliens to acquire property has been relaxed, constitutional and statutory provisions in some of the Pacific Coast states imply that Chinese and Japanese foreigners, at least, cannot legally acquire title to certain types of land within their jurisdictions. The legality of such laws has been tested in court action, and the implications of the Constitution have been upheld. Most states, however, make no effort to block alien landholding by statute. Aliens can hold land the same as native citizens, except in the case of nonresident aliens, who are barred from tenure in some states. Usually the rights of aliens in regard to the holding of land, whether acquired by inheritance or otherwise, are outlined in a treaty between the United States and the homeland of the alien. (*Tiffany. Treat. on Real Prop., 907.*)

Rights in land granted private parties may vary, within limits, from one jurisdiction to another. When title — the badge of ownership — has been granted in fee simple without specified restrictions, the owner is relatively (but not absolutely) free in the use, exclusion, and disposition of the land. Such control as society imposes may be different from time to time and from area to area. The present tenure laws in the forty-eight states and Alaska vary considerably, and a variety of arrangements are found. Some of the more recent devices adding flexibility to the system are federal and state laws favoring co-operative grazing associations, and state laws for zoning and for soil conservation districts.

Much is left to the discretion of local residents. Some of the variations from state to state result from the wide range of principles followed in regulating mortgagor-mortgagee relations, e.g., in some states a mortgage vests the title in the mortgagee, while in others the title remains in the hands of the mortgagor. Regulations covering foreclosure, redemption, and deficiency judgments are other examples. There is an equally wide divergence in the rules controlling landlord-tenant relations. The landlord's lien in some areas may be inclusive and severe, while in an adjoining state the landlord may not be in a preferred position among the several creditors of the tenant. Again in some jurisdictions the share-cropper may be a tenant by the operation of a specific statute, while in an adjoining state he may be merely a wage worker. Many other illustrations of this type could be cited.

Rights in land are established by society and are subject to adjustment by society under principles laid down in the basic laws. Rights held by private parties are established and maintained for social purposes. The group has the power to shift these rights any time the majority believes the general welfare can be served better, whether these rights are concerned with relations between private parties or between private parties and the public.

The maxim *cujus est solum ejus est usque ad coelum* — he who owns the soil owns to the sky — was one of the foundation stones of the theory of land tenure. With the advent of the airplane, however, outmoded theory gave way to the necessity of the age. As Tiffany has said, "The conclusion reached is that despite the maxim there is a right to fly over another's land for legitimate purposes if this is done in a reasonable manner at such a height as not unreasonably to interfere with the owner's use and enjoyment and in compliance with federal and state regulations." (*Tiffany. Treat. on Real Prop., 394.*)

All land in this country is held under some form of tenure, either public or private. Whether the land is held publicly or privately, however, is not always clear and definite. In tax delinquency cases, for example, it is frequently uncertain whether all of the rights of the private owner have been taken over and whether the new owner has a clear title. Regardless of these uncertainties, the land always is held under some form of tenure.

Also, private parties may be given use rights in publicly held land through leasing, licensing, or patenting. Usually, when this is done the form of tenure is clear and definite. Frequently, however, private parties use publicly held land without a definite arrangement with a unit of government and without the payment of a fee for its use. In such cases the rights of the private party, whether as between the user and other private parties or as between the user and the public, are not always clear. A similar situation arises when a parcel of the public domain is transferred to a private party and all the conditions of the transfer have not been fulfilled by the private party.

Another hazy situation may exist where a private party has agreed to purchase land under a sales contract. Generally, the party would be classified as an owner although he does not possess title, the badge of ownership. Title is transferred only when the conditions of the sales contract have been met. Another situation that confuses many persons is a credit transaction. Generally, title passes to the purchaser and he would be classed as an encumbered owner. In some states, however, the land title is held in trust in behalf of the purchaser and title does not pass to the owner until the final payment has been made. In these situations it usually is possible to determine the rights of the several parties in the land; however, the particular tenure form may have special and restricted meaning. Much of the confusion arises out the difficulty of outlining acceptable classifications, because of the wide freedom allowed private parties and units of government in establishing tenurial arrangements.

Public ownership may be complete, while private ownership always is conditional. Public ownership basically is complete, that is, the unit of government generally holds all the rights in its land, unless it has granted a lesser estate through leasing, licensing, or some similar device. The particular unit of government may hold all of the rights insofar as private parties or lower units of government are concerned. But it may have to yield some rights to higher units of government. Society has complete ownership, although its members may use in common the land for particular purposes. Society does not have the power to alienate all its rights. The right of escheat always remains with the public, even though the unit of government may not immediately assert it. Private parties may have relatively complete ownership as against other private parties, but as against the public there is no completeness in the rights of ownership. The private party always shares his land with society since it is always subject to regulation in the public interest.

The concept of completeness is rooted deeply in the allodial property system established in ancient Rome and in pre-Norman England. A spear or a piece of land was owned completely by one person or tribe. It was not owned in part by several persons or tribes. Property could not be separated into a bundle with distinct and separate rights. The Roman concept of completeness remains in the minds of landowners in the United States even though it was never entirely substituted for the derivative property system of feudal England. The freedom with which society permits private parties to use and abuse their land and the freedom with which they may contract away their rights are powerful influences in keeping this attitude alive.

SOME CHARACTERISTICS OF LAND TENURE

Land may be held privately by individuals, partnerships, corporations, or co-operatives. Most privately held land at the present time, as was true in Colonial America, is in the hands of individuals under the qualified type of ownership previously discussed. But land also may be held by the various types of business organizations recognized by law. Very little agricultural land is held by true partnerships since this type of association has disadvantages not present in the corporate form. Consequently, much of the land not held by individuals is held by corporations. The land merchandising companies were examples of early corporations that held land in Colonial America. Also, corporate ownership has long been common in western grazing lands, and in forest and mineral lands. Some of the lands occupied by certain agricultural enterprises, such as citrus fruits and vegetables and other crop specialties, for decades have been in corporate ownership to a significant degree. An important recent development in corporate ownership of land arose out of foreclosure of mortgages by corporate lending agencies during the agricultural depression between World War I and World War II.

Co-operative ownership has not been important in any part of the country. Co-operative grazing associations in certain states of the Great Plains and the Intermountain region have been authorized to acquire and hold land, but they have not yet become extensive landholders. Probably of more immediate significance has been the co-operative holding of land in government sponsored resettlement projects.

The holder of rights in land may be an occupier resident on the land or an absentee. One of the early American ideals was that "every farmer should sit under his own vine and fig tree." In other words, America should be a land of resident occupiers — of family farmers. In striving to become free from the last shackles of feudalism the newly formed states went far in establishing relatively free tenures. The pendulum of freedom may have swung too far, for much land in Colonial America was held by absentee operators and landlords, both individual and corporate. Although many did not look with favor upon absenteeism, it was not outlawed, for freedom of the individual was deemed more important at that time.

All rights in land attach to parcels of land measured on the earth's surface. Rights usually are concerned not only with surface space but with the resources that may be above or beneath the earth's surface. In public ownership these parcels may be roads, parks, forest reserves, wild life refuges, etc. In private ownership they are customarily spoken of as ownership or operating units.

Two general systems are used in the United States in marking off units of space upon the earth's surface: (1) metes and bounds and (2) rectangular survey. The former follows natural boundaries or peculiar local conditions. The latter is based on meridians of longitude and parallels of latitude. The metes and bounds system was used almost exclusively in the thirteen original colonies and in parts of the other six nonpublic land states. The rectangular system was used in the twenty-nine public land states.

Ownership and operating units of land may be held in single parcels or in noncontiguous parcels. Some of the land held by the federal government is in exceptionally large single ownership units. National parks and forests are examples. On the other hand, the federal government probably holds more separate parcels than any other landowner in the country. Some corporations still hold land allotted to them under the "checkerboard system" of granting land for the building of railroads. These too are examples of large holders of land in many separate units. Each single ownership parcel is frequently spoken of as an ownership unit whether it is operated as a complete operating unit, as a part of an operating unit, or subdivided into several operating units.

The reverse of this situation exists where many separate ownership units are brought together, through leasing, licensing, and other means, into one operating unit. In these situations are found the most heterogeneous and complex tenurial arrangements. Some of the western cattlemen hold land in large separate units through ownership (mortgaged and unmortgaged), under sales contract, through leasing from numerous types of individuals and owners, as a permittee of one or more government agencies, and as a trespasser on other land. Thus one operating unit may be composed of several score ownership units and held under any variety of arrangements with the several owners.

Ownership and operating units may or may not be coterminous. In many areas of the country the usual pattern is for ownership and operating units to be coterminous, or to have the same limits. The most prevalent of these is the full owner-operated unit, although there are many tenant-operated units that encompass a complete ownership unit. These types of units are prevalent in the Corn Belt, the northeastern section of the country and in the semisubsistence, self-sufficing areas of the Appalachian Mountains and the border territory separating the Corn and Cotton Belts.

In much of the Great Plains, where often part of an operating unit is rented and part is owned, the operating units do not have a common boundary line with the ownership units. In this area many operating units are made up of numerous separate ownership units. One operator may have several landlords. Still another situation exists particularly in the southern plantation areas and in other parts of the country. Here the ownership units are cut up into numerous operating units and one landlord may have many tenant operators.

Land may be held in any size parcel—whether in ownership or operating units. There was no restriction in this country after the Revolutionary War on the quantity of land that could be held by a unit of government or a private party. The limitation in Georgia had long since been removed, and other colonies gave little attention to restricting the amount of land that one party could hold. No restriction exists today in the continental United States. Government may subdivide and parcel out the land in units of any size, although the practice as in Colonial America favors the family-sized farm.

Much of the public domain was granted to private parties in family-sized units of 160 acres. As settlement continued westward into the semiarid areas the units were increased in size to 320 acres and to 640 acres. However, in many areas these larger sizes were still too small for successful operation. Many of the land problems in the western states emphasize this fact. At the same time and in the same areas, however, private parties accumulated land in units sufficiently large to sustain scores of families.

On the other hand, segmenting into uneconomic units may take place, frequently through inheritance and also through sale. The outlawing of exclusive right of inheritance to the first-born and the substitution of equal division among the several heirs has been a powerful influence. This practice is widespread geographically and is common in the disposition of many estates. It is most obvious where it causes the most serious problems, as in the southern Appalachians and the Ozarks, where the operating units are much too small to sustain a farm family at an acceptable standard of living, and in the Middle West, where the resulting uneconomic ownership units are exploited as segments of larger operating units.

Rights in a given parcel of land may be split between surface, subsurface, and above-surface. When rights in land are divided in this manner, those that may be classified as surface usually include enough area above the surface to permit operations on the surface and also enough of the area beneath the earth's crust to support the type of operation planned. That this was true in Colonial America is evidenced by the special concessions granted anyone who would establish a mining operation. Subsurface rights now usually are held for oil and mineral development and include sufficient rights to the surface and the area immediately above the surface to permit the planned type of mining operations.

The splitting of rights between surface and subsurface is quite frequent in some areas. It is not often, however, that above-surface rights are acquired separately. This happens in cities where skyscraper owners do not want other tall buildings too near. Also zoning against tall structures or acquisition of air easements are devices used to control the air space near airports. Ely and Wehrwein present several novel examples of a form of above-surface rights. The Daily News Building and the Merchandise Mart in Chicago, and the Grand Central, Pennsylvania, and Hudson terminals in New York are examples of the securing of the space above a certain point for building purposes and just enough of the surface for the pillars that support the buildings. (*Ely and Wehrwein. Land Economics, 79.*)

Another example of an above-surface right is the right to fly over the land of another. This right was not thought of at the time of the emergence of the national land system, although it was inherent in the basic tenure principles laid down by the founding fathers. This right is, of course, contrary to the early and commonly recognized dictum that he who owns the surface owns to the sky. The right of passage of the flyer in most cases is not of prime importance to the landowner or tenant, since it does not generally interfere with ground operation. It becomes exceedingly important at times, however, and may be either completely withheld or minutely regulated. Witness the restrictions on flying over military reservations or other important establishments, such as the Panama Canal, during war emergency conditions.

Rights in land may be held for varying lengths of time, or for an indeterminate period. An easement may last only so long as is required to pass over the land. Leases of agricultural land, on the other hand, usually run for one year but they may be drawn for a shorter or a longer period. In some states they must be in writing if the term is longer than one year. Frequently agricultural leases for a long period of time, from fourteen to twenty years, are specifically outlawed. But in some states a lease may run for as long as ninety-nine years. There is a general rule, however, against perpetual rights which was recognized by the end of the Colonial era. A person may control private rights in a piece of land not only for his lifetime through ownership but for a life or lives in being and twenty-one years through inheritance. Again, there is a general rule against entail — the transmission of an inalienable inheritance.

The latter term is indeterminate since the life or lives are indeterminate. Leases that continue automatically from year to year in the absence of a notice of termination are examples of rights covering indefinite periods. Indeterminate periods are not frowned upon in the law. Indeed, Iowa recently enacted a law which provides that all agricultural leases shall continue automatically from year to year in the absence of a notice of termination at least four months prior to the end of the lease year.

Tenure rights may be definite or indefinite. They are most definite when properly recorded and specified for a fixed period of time. They are most indefinite when unwritten and subject to termination under certain conditions.

Certain types of oral transfers or rights in land are so indefinite that neither party knows the type of relationship that is established. An outstanding example arises out of arrangements made for the cultivation of land in several of the southern states where the landowner and operator agree to share the produce of the land and certain expenses of production. If the two parties cannot agree whether a tenancy or a cropper relationship exists, and they take the matter to court, there is no assurance of the interpretation that the court will place upon the relationship.

A similar indefinite situation exists at the end of a tenancy if the tenant holds over and makes preparations for the planting of the next year's crops. The tenant may contend that there was a meeting of minds for continuation of the lease, while the landlord may hold the opposite. The court may have to decide the case on circumstantial evidence and may conclude that actions speak louder than words.

Convenants running with the land may be specified upon alienation. Reservations in leases, licenses, permits, and easements as to the manner in which the land is to be used are quite familiar. Less common, however, are covenants in the deed prohibiting certain types or kinds of uses. An example of a reasonable restriction is one prohibiting the use of the land for the sale of liquor. (*Tiffany. Treat. on Real Prop., 132.*) Another reservation that may be specified in the deed, and one that is becoming increasingly common, is concerned with a part or all of the minerals. The mineral reservation is becoming widely prevalent in transfers from quasi-public and private corporations to private individuals.

Flexibility and dissimilarity are characteristics of the system of land tenure. The land tenure system of this country probably is the most flexible in history. Considerable freedom may be exercised by the federal government in using and alienating any land that was ceded to it by the states or that it later acquired by treaty, purchase, or other methods. Similar powers are reserved by the states for using and alienating state owned land, and minor jurisdictions are relatively free in disposing of land under their control. Privately owned land is held under relatively free, but not absolute, tenures.

Growing out of the high degree of flexibility in the system of land tenure is a most heterogeneous mixture of tenures. Two factors, laissez faire and freedom of contract, have been influential in establishing this situation. The former appeared when feudalism was displaced; the latter was developed in legal theory to support the economic theory of universal free play of competition.

CHAPTER 2

Development of English Feudal Tenures

LITTLE KNOWLEDGE OF THE EARLY historical background of land tenure is available. Indeed, much of the information upon which the present concept of property in land is built is fragmentary and hypothetical. But a clear picture of developments during the Colonial period depends upon an understanding of available information on the English land tenure situation just before the settlement of America – and the evolution of the system to that time.

The sense of "belonging to" a particular family perhaps was the earliest germ of a property concept. Primitive, to be sure, but just as powerful as it was primitive. Geographic nearness and the need for leadership unified and strengthened the "belonging to" idea. This concept is directly opposite the present-day idea of "rights in." "Belonging to" is a sense of obligation – of responsibility – which grew out of self-dependency. The right to leave the family group was the germ out of which grew the idea of alienability, or transfer. Ideas regarding succession first appeared in the allocation of leadership within the family. Another early idea – this one close to modern forms of property – was the possessory idea regarding weapons, clothing, and handicraft tools; and later cattle and finally slaves. This possessory idea was in the nature of physical "attachment to." It sprang from the idea of "belonging to" the group. The articles that were almost physically "attached to," or held, by a person were "his" through the idea of possession. This was the first recognition of the possessory right. The idea of "rights in" seems to have developed out of possessory rights in armaments, cattle, and slaves, and not control over land. "Rights in" was concerned with use value long before the idea of exchange value was introduced.

Basic tenurial concepts developed among ancient civilizations many centuries before the time of Christ and long before the earliest English civilization. The Egyptians had highly developed ideas of ownership with appropriate instruments such as deeds, wills, and leases; a system of public recording of landownership had been developed; and rights in land became segmented to fit the requirements of economic life. Similar systems of inheritance were developed among the Mesopotamians and the Hebrews. The Greeks not only had a highly developed idea of ownership but were following the practice of leasing land under complex contractual arrangements. Later, the Romans developed tenure practices similar in many respects to the English, but their concepts followed allodial rather than feudal principles.

DEVELOPMENTS PRIOR TO THE NORMAN CONQUEST

In a sense, Anglican tenure concepts may be considered a combination of the customs and laws of numerous tribes and civilizations. Almost every conceivable type of ownership of, or control over, land has existed in England. Most of these have left a more or less conspicuous mark upon the composite structure of English tenure law. The uniqueness of English land law grew out of early and frequent legislative interferences with the natural development of tenure relations. It was nurtured by the slow evolutionary process as contrasted with the superimposition of a doctrinaire scheme of tenure relations upon an unsuspecting population.

It was about the sixth century before Christ when the Celts overran the island and subjugated the aboriginal tribes. They apparently developed some concepts of property in their endeavor to balance might and right. These warlike people all but worshiped might, and this feeling contributed to their concept of property in chattels. Students are not in complete agreement, however, as to whether property in land among the Anglicans developed by analogy to property in chattels. Numerous wars during the following centuries emphasized the meaning that "might makes right," forcing the weak to seek the protection of the strong and permitting the strong to assume leadership. As population increased men had to deal with the pressing problem of how to make sure they would be allowed to hold and control land. This was necessary before they could turn their attention to its cultivation and use. Out of this situation developed a political and military hierarchy from which the feudal system of land tenure was to come.

The Celts were replaced in England by the Romans following Julius Caesar's invasion in 55 B.C. How the Romans cultivated the English countryside, used the native population, and held land, is not known. Apparently they had little influence, if any, on the development of Anglican concepts of land tenure. The "Roman veneer" probably had all but disappeared by the sixth century, by which time the Roman legions had withdrawn and the Empire had fallen. Thus, any notable influences of Roman property law upon Anglican tenure concepts must be found in later developments.

After the fall of the Roman Empire, the Angles, the Jutes, and the Danes invaded England. They left little culture or law since the Saxon invasion followed so closely and was so much more thorough. The Saxons, of Germanic origin, brought with them a definite culture, which became an integral part of Anglican law.

Under the early Saxons all of the land belonged to all of the people and was called "folcland." Later, the land began to be parcelled out to individuals, and during this evolution political organization had become nationalized. One man, the king, spoke for the people. The king began the practice, for political and military reasons and otherwise, of granting certain parcels of the folcland to specified persons. To differentiate this new kind of land from the folcland, the term "bocland" was coined, meaning land granted by the book, that is, the instrument setting forth the grant. The ordinary peasant's land was folcland; the bocland was granted to selected persons and probably the grant represented office as much as it did property. (*Jenks. English Law, 12.*)

Bocland apparently did not exert an important influence upon the land system after the conquest. It is seldom mentioned after the appearance of William the Conqueror. Many of the holders of bocland were anxious to maintain Harold, whose coup d'etat had won the throne at the death of Edward the Confessor, and consequently they fought in vain against William. William the Conqueror's confiscations left little land under their control. The transition was made by replacing the English book with the Norman charter.

Along with the granting of bocland came the practice of inheritability. This characteristic distinguished it from the granting of annual tenancies and life tenancies. The term of the grant was important. As progress was made, the rights were granted for a year, then for life or lives, then in perpetuity. The earliest form of inheritance doubtless was developed with reference to personal property. At first, cattle – personal property – reverted to the common stock when the tribesman died. Later, it did so only if he died childless. (*Seebohm. Tribal Custom, 24–25.*) Finally, the Saxon could control his property by will. The early wills must have been precatory in nature; certainly the deceased could not disinherit his family. The laws after the second Danish invasion and the reign of Canute (1017–35) provided for equal inheritance among all of the children. Early civilized man seemed to have an innate concept of equality. Dalrymple has said it is impossible to determine when bocland became descendible, ". . .yet it is certain that the book-land went in general to the heirs of the immediate crown-vassals, among the Saxons, more early than in any other state in Europe." (*Dalrymple. Feudal Property, 201.*)

DEVELOPMENT OF FEUDALISM

The Saxons probably had a fairly well-developed feudal type of tenure when the Normans arrived. In at least one respect, Anglo-Saxon feudalism was superior, from the viewpoint of the overlord, to the feudal ideas that had developed on the Continent. In Normandy the obligations that were attached to military tenures ran only to the immediate lord. But in Anglo-Saxon England certain military obligations ran from every landholder to the king. William the Conqueror's advisers, therefore, built upon the already prevalent tenure practice that involved the idea of complete lineal dependency from the Crown to the lowest tenant.

The substitution of Norman lords for Saxon lords was easy. William merely asserted the right of conquest, which gave him title to all of Harold's land and also to that held by the great lords who fought on Harold's side. In regranting the land to his men, William could have given them the land under as free and easy tenures as were contained in the grants made to the New England colonies over half a millennium later. In fact, grants under easy tenures would more nearly have conformed to the Saxon land tenure system than grants under equally easy tenures would have conformed to prevailing ideas after feudalism had been fully developed. The settling of the rights and duties of all of the citizenry to each other and to their lord, and the relations of the lesser lords to the greater lords, and all their responsibilities to the king was not easy. This was the object of the Domesday investigation. Although many of the details are obscure, it apparently was significant in clarifying feudal tenure relations in Norman England.

Many of William's followers could not speak English, nor did they love the English soil. They wished to capitalize their "honor" and return to Normandy, and many of them did so by "renting" to others the land that had been granted to them for their military service.

The relations between the various parties in the feudal hierarchy were concerned with civil affairs as well as with land. Many of the feudal dues were in the nature of taxes paid for the support of civil government. In other words, feudalism was in this regard a system of government based upon the organization of society upon the land. In many regards the government aspects of feudalism were more important than the land phases. Or, at least, the two were interdependent, for political status was heavily contingent upon tenure status, and the two determined in large measure the economic and social status of the several parties. Nevertheless, attention must be directed to tenure status, and other aspects of feudalism will be considered only insofar as they are essential to an understanding of the tenure system.

Feudal Incidents

The government of feudal England placed various *burdens* upon the land in an effort to maintain control. These burdens usually are spoken of as "incidents," and they reveal many of the characteristics of feudalism. At the height of feudalism they were nine in number: fealty, homage, wardship, marriage, relief, primer seisin, aids, fines for alienation, and escheats.

Homage and *fealty* were the essence of feudalism and, although they ultimately came to be considered servile, they were once almost sacred to both parties. The first referred to proclaiming personal allegiance, and was generally restricted to land held directly of the king. The latter was the oath of fidelity, and was common to all tenure status.

The lord's right of *wardship* arose, after feudal rights became hereditary, when the tenant died leaving a minor child as heir. During the child's minority, he was the lord's ward, and the lord was entitled to the profits from the feud. The lord was not bound to account for the profits from the land. He was burdened only with maintenance of the heir, his ward. He could not, of course, commit waste. Dalrymple has pointed out that in that "boisterous age" giving the minor the lord's protection was a very material favor to the heir who would otherwise be driven from the land. (*Dalrymple. Feudal Property, 44–51.*) Wright said that wardship was eminently just because the lord who owned the land should be able to withhold it from a tenant who was too young to perform expected feudal services. (*Wright. Law of Tenures, 78–92.*) Probably both of these conditions were important in explaining the rise of wardship.

The incident called *marriage* arose because the tenure relation was personal as well as economic. Theoretically, a female child of the tenant might marry a sworn enemy of the lord and bring her husband onto the lord's land. To prevent this, the lord at first assumed the right to prevent a tenant's daughter from marrying an enemy. A breach of this understanding resulted in a forfeiture of the feud. However, as the personal element in the relation decreased in importance and as the kingdom became more unified, the drastic penalty of forfeiture was abandoned. For a breach of the duty to secure the lord's consent, the tenant paid "the value of the marriage." Of course, the lords soon learned to withhold their consent and "the value of the marriage" became payable in almost every case. Custom soon established the amount of the payment, however. The incident of marriage originally was inapplicable to male heirs. But by the thirteenth century, the lords desired to extend this incident to male heirs. Soon ". . . an unfortunate wording of a clause in the Great Charter" was made to accomplish this purpose. Thus, marriage is an example of feudal incident conceived in justice but later perverted. Wardship and marriage "continued, in theory at least, to disgrace the law, until they were abolished in 1660." (*Jenks. English Law, 34.*)

Another of the very old incidents was that called *relief* — a payment for admittance to the estate made by the heir on his father's death. It will be recalled that, at first, grants of land were "for life" and were not hereditary. When a life tenant died, of course, the land reverted to the grantor — the lord — who might or might not give it to the life tenant's natural heir. To assist the lord in deciding to whom he would give the feud, the heir often made a material offering. After feuds became hereditary the custom remained as a duty.

Another so-called incident was that of *primer seisin* — a prerogative right of the king to enter and take "seisin" (possession) of the land upon the death of a tenant-in-chief and to hold this "first seisin" until the heir had been determined and had paid his relief. The amount of the relief was usually the profits for a year. In substance, the right was merely a procedural method of enforcing the king's right to a relief.

Aids were among the earliest and most lucrative of the feudal incidents, and consisted generally of payments to the lord: (1) to ransom him when captured, (2) to pay the expenses involved in knighting his son, and (3) to provide a dowry for the lord's eldest daughter when she married. Numerous authorities point out that aids originally were voluntary contributions made in appreciation of the protection and other favors which the lord conferred upon the vassal. Thus, it is probable that aids originally were strictly military in nature, and later became blended with rent. As the personal nature of the feudal bond weakened, the voluntary nature of the contribution may have disappeared, but the custom remained. Aids soon became a fixed custom, and by the thirteenth and fourteenth centuries they were assessed by statute as a twentieth of the annual value of the holding. This applied only to the knighting of the son and the marriage of the daughter, for the practice of ransoming the lord had disappeared.

A *fine for alienation* apparently was the last feudal incident to be added. It was a payment made by a vassal when he transferred his land to another. In view of the personal nature of feudalism, the lord was distinctly interested in whom he should have as vassals. He would naturally object if an attempt were made to foist upon him an imbecile or anyone incapable of being a competent and trustworthy vassal. Thus, it was a natural prerogative of a lord to forbid unreasonable transfers. A lord's judgment, to some degree, was susceptible to control by the judicious use of money. It is not unreasonable to assume, particularly in view of the fact that the fine for alienation developed slowly, that this use of money was an invention of the vassal's genius. The gradual development of the practice into a custom followed. This fine, of course, had a marked effect on freedom of alienation.

The incident of *escheat* is well known in modern times. It is manifestly inherent in any system of tenure, and, therefore, may be called an inevitable consequence rather than an incident of feudal tenure. In feudal times it arose chiefly out of one of two circumstances: upon death of the tenant without leaving an heir, or upon corruption of the blood as a result of treason or felony. Today it arises only upon failure of an heir.

MAJOR TENURE TYPES IN FEUDAL ENGLAND

The absolute ownership of the land originally was, and is now, in the sovereign – whether called the Crown, the state, the public, or society. That is to say, the sovereign possesses the largest bundle of rights with respect to land. At no time – whether feudal or modern – could the sovereign, in making a grant to a subject, part with the whole bundle of sticks that made up absolute ownership. In feudal times the sovereign kept more of the rights in land and released those assigned others under more uncertain conditions than is done in modern times.

True feudal tenures in England at the height of their development were either *free* or *villein* tenures. The former included all tenures based on services considered proper for a "free" man to render to the lord, while the latter included those based on menial services of a low character involving the cultivation of the lord's land, or similar work, under particular and often oppressive conditions of servitude.

The free tenures were: (a) military tenures or tenure in chivalry, (b) socage tenure, or to use the more modern term, "free and common socage," (c) burgage tenure, (d) gavelkind tenure, and (e) tenure in frankalmoign. The free tenures were governed by the law of the land. The unfree tenures, that is, tenures in villeinage, were governed by local and customary usages. Because of the varying aspects of local custom, it is impossible to subclassify villein tenures. There were, in addition, several minor types of tenures that will be described briefly for a better understanding of the complex nature of feudal tenures in England.

Some of the land in feudal England was held "as of the Crown" and some of it "as of a manor." The distinction is of importance to us, for much of the land in the early American grants was held as of a particular manor named in the grant. The holding of land immediately of the king, or as of the Crown, was termed tenure *in capite.* That is to say, the king was the lord just above the tenant and the in capite holder was holding directly under the king, no one being beween the king and the tenant.

The typical in capite tenant held his land by knight service, or, if a church, the land was held by frankalmoign. Socage tenants usually held their land as of a manor. The copyhold tenant always held as of a manor. The socage tenant held land under conditions of tenure that lay between the tenant in capite and the copyhold tenant. The socage tenant was essentially a freeholder. His rights in land, however, were neither as extensive nor as certain as are present-day freeholders, that is, as owners in fee simple.

Military Tenures

The idea of rewarding a valiant soldier and of assuring his continued support by giving him a block of land and guaranteeing his rights to it was conceived at an early date. The consideration for this grant was usually both past and prospective military service. However, many types of valuable service came to be recognized. Thus, many types of military tenure developed, the chief one being "knight service," that is, to fight for the king. The other distinctive types were called escuage, grand serjeanty, and petit serjeanty.

Knight Service. For some purposes nothing but tenure by knight service should be regarded as military tenure but for present purposes the distinction which should be noted is that knight service tenure was always held as of the king, and involved a direct obligation to serve him militarily. In a tumultuous year, the king secured enormous services from this type of tenurial arrangement, but in a peaceful year his reward was almost nil. It is at least possible that this situation, aggravated by royal greed, aided in the development of the various incidents of feuds, which later became so burdensome. For all of the incidents mentioned in the preceding section were attached to tenure by knight service.

Escuage. Numerous attempts have been made to prove that this tenure was completely distinct from tenure by knight service, but many authorities believe it was merely a term used to denote a tenure by knight service where the "service" had been commuted into money. If the sum was fixed, the tenure was called escuage-certain. If the sum was dependent on the military situation, as was the service itself, it was called escuage-uncertain. The latter type obviously was subject to abuse. Therefore, the Magna Carta in 1215 provided that the king could not make any scutage without the consent of the common council, which was composed of the great lords. To change from personal service to a payment of money, however, did not change the character of the tenure in other respects. It was still military tenure, burdened with the incidents of military tenures.

Tenure by knight service, in a strict sense, was an innovation of the Normans, made late in the eleventh century. By early in the thirteenth century so many of the tenants had been transformed into escuage tenants that the lord's rights to escuage was one of the most important matters dealt with in the Magna Carta. Escuage is of interest to us as an example of how quickly "tenants by service" changed themselves into "rent-paying tenants."

Grand and petit serjeanty.[1] Grand serjeanty was to hold land directly of the king and to render an honorable service, such as to carry his sword or banner. Petit serjeanty was of the same nature and involved a more menial service, such as to cook for the king. As the personal nature of the feudal bond dissolved, the incidents became more unreasonable and, of course, unpopular. With the development of more social integration and the increase of population, knighthood declined and agriculture and industry advanced. The burdens of the incidents of the military tenures pressed heavily upon the common people.

Socage Tenure

After the abolition of military tenures the only free tenure of real significance was that called socage. Socage tenure, however, did not wait until the seventeenth century to become of importance. Indeed, long before the burial of military tenures, socage tenure was the principal type of holding.

In principle, socage tenure was about the same as tenure by escuage. Lord Coke defined it by saying: "To hold in Socage is to hold of any lord lands or tenements, yielding to him a certain rent by the year for all manner of services." (*Coke. Three Law Tracts, 310.*) The socage tenant of the American colonies called this rent quitrent. Noyes's comment on tenure in general is peculiarly applicable to our consideration of socage tenure. He said: "As landholding gradually developed into property the importance of status tended to disappear and the lower reaches of the system were converted from an organization of persons to an organization of property, from one of status to one of tenure." (*Noyes. Institution, 247.*) Estates held by socage tenures, while free, were devoid of honor and prestige. And, although they were feudal estates, they were not subjected to the incidents of wardship and marriage, the two incidents that came to be the most burdensome. The most important factor in socage tenure was the rent charge on the land. In its early development the rent could be in the form of services rendered on the lord's land, but this type was unimportant. The distinctive characteristic was that rent was fixed and certain in amount, whereas the obligations of military tenure were

---

[1] The word serjeanty involves the notion of servantship, according to Tiffany. Serjeanty and servant were probably the same word originally.

numerous and uncertain. The amount of the rent might be of considerable pecuniary value or nominal; or, apparently, it could be ignored entirely. However, in most cases it was distinctly real.

Socage was the least encumbered and burdened of the tenures. It was the new tenure that regarded landholding simply as a form of property, and did not mix civil rights and military duties with the holding of land. It was these characteristics, vague as they may be, that made such tenure desired by Englishmen even before America was discovered. It was because socage tenure was the freest and easiest of all English tenures that "free and common socage" was the tenure desired by those who requested charters to settle in the New World. When related to the liberal tenure custom of the manor of East Greenwich and the gavelkind tenure concepts developed in the County of Kent, free and common socage tenure was the most desirable form of all English tenures.

Burgage

Burgage tenure was the urban tenure of medieval England. It was probably founded upon Saxon customs, although Dalrymple referred to burgage tenure as ". . . a new, feudal, free tenure" brought into the law after the Conquest. (*Dalrymple. Feudal Property, 36.*) The Saxons encouraged commerce and therefore gave commercial towns unusual privileges, especially in relation to the charges upon the land of that day. The distinguishing characteristic was that the rent was certain. Other special privileges were recorded in the "borough costumal" and being in such concrete form successfully resisted any spread of other types of tenure into the boroughs.

Gavelkind

Gavelkind came from the Saxon term "gafol" meaning "rent paying." Thus, gavelkind tenure once meant rent-paying tenure. Soon most tenures were rent paying and gavelkind was restricted to apply to the principal tenure by which lands in Kent were held. Under this tenure the land did not escheat in case of execution for felony, and the tenant could devise the land even at common law. The most salient feature of gavelkind tenure, however, was equal inheritance of all children, as contrasted to primogeniture, and ultimately the term gavelkind came to be applied to any tenure where all children inherited equally.

Frankalmoign

In the long struggle between the church and the state the former was granted certain special privileges. One of these was a peculiar type of tenure under which the church could hold land. It was called "tenure in frankalmoign." Land held by ecclesiastical bodies or persons was accorded easy tenures on condition that they render service of a spiritual character. The ordinary incidents did not attach to land held by frankalmoign.

Villeinage

A *villein* – one holding land in *villeinage* – and a *bondman* are more difficult to describe than the higher forms of tenure. It is never easy, however, to draw the line between the free, the partially free, and the unfree tillers of the soil. The bondman was at the mercy of the lord in everything short of life and limb. Anything that his lord permitted him to hold was subject to withdrawal at the will of the lord. Many freemen became bondmen before the Conquest, and many freemen who did not take William's side were forced into that position after the Conquest. However, many stopped short of this degradation, and held their land on servile and precarious tenures. They never gave up either their personal freedom or their rights in movable goods. As the rights and responsibilities of one who held land in villeinage were being established by customary usage and court record, the more modern copyhold tenure was evolving.

A *copyholder* was a tenant of a manor who held his land under the lord according to the customs of the manor. Thus, the copyhold tenant's rights were really as certain as if he were an owner. His rights were evidenced by the records of the lord's court, and not by a deed in his own possession. He did not possess all of the rights of a fee simple owner. He could neither cut commercial timber nor open mines, and he had to pay a fine on alienation and a tribute of money or goods on succession. The fine and tribute, or heriot, doubtless at one time represented all the lord could get – all the traffic would bear. Later the fine became fixed in money and the tribute, which may have been the best animal or chattel, was infrequently demanded. The copyhold tenant also paid a rent to the lord, which varied up to the full annual rental value of the land.

The major disabilities of copyhold tenures arose out of the numerous ways the tenant could lose his estate through forfeiture to the lord. In addition, copyhold tenure varied from manor to manor. The intermixture of freehold and copyhold estates and the garbling of the court roll frequently made it advisable to convey the land under both tenures (without the lord's permission) to make sure that the title did not contain a defect. This was a big item, for fees payable at the lord's court were a heavy burden upon the land, even for a simple transaction.

But copyhold tenure was not all bad – some good features existed. First, neither the land nor the estate was liable for the debt of the copyholder either during his life or after his death. Also, the court rolls provided a ready means of registering the rights of the copyholder, which was of considerable value in those days. The copyholder's rights in land were more certain than those of our modern tenant. And the widow's right of dower formed no impediment to alienation of the copyhold. In spite of its numerous shortcomings and its few good qualities, copyhold tenure remained to complicate the English land system until the conversion of such tenure into fee simple estates by the Law of Property Act of 1922. (*12 & 13 George V, 1922, c. 16, sec. 128–37.*)

MINOR TYPES OF TENURE

As husbandry leases became common various types of leasehold interests were developed, all being, of course, mere variations of the term for years.

Tenancy at Will

In the thirteenth and fourteenth centuries the most important variation was called a tenancy at will, so-named because the legal relation of tenancy existed, but it could be terminated at the will of either party. Of course, the conventional actions to protect the tenant's "term" and to prevent waste had no application to this type of tenancy. For there was no term to be protected, and the lessor could stop any waste that might be committed by the tenant by terminating the tenancy.

This tenancy, however, forced the development, by judicial decision, of another type of protection – right of emblements, the right to crops growing on the farm at the time the lease is ended. Thus, if a tenant at will cultivated a crop and the lessor ended the tenancy just before harvest time, the tenant was allowed freedom to enter and to harvest and carry away the crop. Manifestly, this right was advantageous to the tenant, but still it did not afford adequate protection since the tenant might be forced to go several miles to find a place to live, thus making it difficult, and at times impossible, to use the right conferred. And so, once again, the courts stepped in, this time in the sixteenth century, and developed the tenancy from year to year, the so-called modified tenancy at will. This was done by the court presuming that whenever a tenant entered upon another's land with his permission and paid or agreed to pay some rent, the parties intended that the lease would not expire until the end of the crop year, thus creating a year-to-year tenancy.[2]

Tenancy at Sufferance

Tenancy at sufferance was of little importance in the Middle

[2] Another kind of tenancy at will developed within the manors, but it was essentially different from the tenancy now under consideration. It was the manorial "tenancy at will" that was transformed into a copyhold tenure.

Ages, although it was known. The most common case arose when a mortgagor remained in possession of the land without the consent of the mortgagee. Such a tenancy was really not a tenancy in anything but name, for a tenant at sufferance was legally in the same position as a "squatter," who occupied a stranger's land without his consent. He could be evicted at any time, but could not be subjected to a distress, for he was not liable for any rent. The "landlord" could, however, bring an action for the value of the use and occupation of the land. (*Holdsworth. English Law, VII, 243.*)

Dower

Under Roman law, the bride brought a "dower portion" to the altar, presumably to make herself more acceptable to the prospective husband. Under Teutonic custom, however, the husband gave a "dower" to the wife. The Saxons brought this Teutonic custom into England, where it became customary for the husband to transfer to the wife a portion of his worldly goods. At first, dower was an absolute gift consisting chiefly, if not exclusively, of chattels, but gradually it came to consist of land also. Originally, the gift was wholly voluntary and, of course, its amount varied. However, since the principal of the fund or estate usually was all the property belonging to the wife on the husband's death, the gift assumed public importance. Gradually a custom, determining the amount, attained the force of law. The amount varied in different localities from one-third to one-half of the husband's belongings. Since there was no "absolute and complete" property in land in feudal England, the tenure concept was applied to describe the widow's right in this land. It was called "tenure by dower," whereby the widow held one-third of her deceased husband's lands for her life. The Magna Carta shows the transition in the edition of 1217 with this provision: "And for her dower, shall be assigned to her the third part of all the lands of her husband, which were his during his life, except she were endowed of less at the church door."

Curtesy

Tenure by the curtesy of England was the correlative right of the husband in the deceased wife's land. Lord Coke has said, "To hold by the curtesy of *England* is where a man taketh a wife, inheritrix, and they have issue . . . and the wife dieth, whether the issue be dead or alive, the husband shall hold this land [all of the wife's land] for term of his life." (*Coke. Three Law Tracts, 307.*)

This tenure was unique to England. It is believed that it arose as a special right — as an exception to the rule — and was called tenure by curtesy because it actually was a holding by virtue of the courteous nature of English law. It should be noted further that the birth of issue was a prerequisite to this tenure right. This requirement has led some scholars to believe that the custom arose as a special exception to the lord's right to wardship.

Mortgage

Another more temporary type of tenure was that by "gage." Since this eventually grew into the presently popular "tenure of mortgage," it merits some consideration, although it was rather unimportant as a type of tenure in the Middle Ages.

"Gage" is the legal French term for "pledge." As pledges of chattels were known at an early time, we may assume that shortly after individual rights in land came to be recognized (that is, when bocland appeared) the pledge device was applicable to such rights. Probably we shall never know what theory the Saxons had – if they had one. As a practical matter, it seems that when *A* borrowed from *B* he let *B* hold his (*A's*) land until *A* repaid the loan. If *A* failed to repay the loan, exactly what would happen depended upon the agreement between the mortgagor and mortgagee, local customs, and above all, the provisions of the original grant of bocland. This being the case, no definite rule can be found. King Charles II may have been influenced, and William Penn may have been motivated, by this ancient arrangement when they met to discuss settlement of the money debt the King owed Penn. Although the loan was strictly personal, the King was merely following accepted practice in settling the debt by granting Penn a large body of land in America.

If under the classical mortgage the conditions were not performed, the mortgagee succeeded to all of the mortgagor's rights in the land forever. If the debt remained unpaid, the mortgagee could still sue and recover judgment. The obvious injustice of this led the equity courts to establish a rule that every mortgagor had an "equity of redemption" in the land, and that by paying the debt at any time he could acquire an equitable right to a reconveyance. This meant that a mortgagee's title would never be completely clear. Therefore, equity developed the doctrine of foreclosure whereby the mortgagee would come into court and, on due notice to the mortgagor, ask the court to set a future day after which the right of redemption would be ineffective.

Elegit

By the Statute of Westminster, the writ of elegit was established. This made it possible for a judgment creditor to obtain possession of one-half of the debtor's land and occupy it as a tenant by elegit until the rents and profits satisfied the debt. The Statute Merchant (*13 Edward I, 1285, Stat. 3, c.1.*) and Statute Staple (*27 Edward III, 1353, Stat. 2, c.1–23.*) gave similar rights to urban creditors for designated types of debts. However, under these statutes, the creditor took possession of all the debtor's land, holding it as a tenant until the rents and profits paid the debt.

These statutes and the development of the mortgage are interesting examples of the influence of urban economy. Commercial procedures were powerful in destroying feudal tenures, for every such act as those discussed constituted a direct attack on the personal nature of feudalism under which alienation was not allowed. The personal — the man-man or lord-man – relations of feudalism under these actions were giving away to the man-society-thing relation of modern economy.

THE ENGLISH MANOR

The troublesome days before the Conquest did much to establish firmly the manorial system. During the petty wars among the several minor kingdoms, and later the disorder of the Danish occupation, many small freemen sought the protection of prosperous gentry. Indeed, when conditions were worsened many freemen became not only dependents but bondmen. As differentiation proceeded apace and the king granted jurisdiction and finally revenues to leading landowners, there emerged the great landed estates with their manorial lord and system of courts. Intermixed with the manors, which were cultivated by free dependents and bondmen, were numerous free landholds and much land was still in communal use.

Large districts of land were held by individuals prior to the Conquest. Many of the grants, however, were designed to pass the king's dominion over them. Thus, the recipient of the grant received a personal status bearing a relation to land, rather than an estate in land. Digby has stated that probably there was no great addition to the number of manors after the Conquest primarily because the manorial court, which was the essence of a manor, owed its existence to long-established custom and ". . . the creation of a new [manorial] court was probably regarded as beyond the power even of the crown." *(Digby. Real Property, 44n.)* The authorities, especially Lord Coke, support this view, although, of course, the statement must be limited in application to England, for new manors were created in the American Colonies under authority granted by the Crown.

Thus, the framework of the manor was Saxon — based on a delegation of governmental authority over a given area. Every exaction of the authority served to confound "status" and "estate," and served to identify governmental status with proprietary status, which was virtually undistinguishable from estate. This confusion and the political disturbances of the eleventh century led to a gradual transition. The king's local representatives became proprietors of the land and from this political framework developed an economic organization called the manorial system. At first the manor probably consisted of a lord, his people, and a court. The first and third elements remained unchanged during the metamorphosis, but the second element subdivided itself into distinct classes – the bailiffs, the freeholders, and the villeins.

The *lord* was the possessor of that indefinable something which today would be called title to the land. His rights in the land were both political and economic. But they were qualified, at an early time, by a potent intangible called custom. The lord was a kind of small sovereign prince, possessed of his own courts, and doing justice according to his own procedure and custom. The law that the lord followed was, ". . . an unparalleled accumulation of layer upon layer of diverse materials." (*Pollock. Land Laws, 11.*)

The *bailiff,* as the agent of the lord, usually had almost as much authority as the lord himself. But, of course, all of his authority was strictly derivative and subject to the lord's desire.

The *freeholders* were a small class of farmers who occupied lands that were frequently located on the outskirts of the manor – lands so far from the manor house that it was impractical to assert day-to-day control over their occupants. They held their land under agreements with the lord. Usually, they held in socage tenure and usually in fee form, that is, they paid lump sums for the original grant and thereafter paid nominal annual charges to the lord. A comparison of the feudal manor with more modern plantations in this country would reveal the lord of the manor and the landlord of the plantation as occupying similar positions. The socage tenants, the copyholders, and the bondmen occupied the same relative position as present-day tenants, share-croppers, and wage hands.

By far the most important group and the most numerous folk in the manor were the *villeins.* Villein tenure was, from a classification standpoint, the illegitimate offspring of a tenure concept crossed with a master-servant relation. It corresponded somewhat to modern share-cropping. As Pollock and Maitland put it: ". . . 'villeinage' is a tenure, it is also a status." (*Pollock and Maitland. English Law, I, 358.*) In other words, it is called tenure for lack of another term but it is unique because it combines the idea of slavery with the idea of rights in land. The villein was a chattel, but a chattel with certain rights and thus distinguishable from a horse which, of course, was without rights. The villein was really a chattel only as to his lord, for to others he could, in most respects, act as a freeman. Contracts between villeins and freemen were frequent and could be enforced by the villein.

The status of the villein was low. When status and estate began to merge, the estate of the villein was worse than low – it was practically nil. However, the English villeins who survived when the Black Death swept the country, reducing the number of villeins by alarming proportions, were in a favorable position to bargain with their lords. The dearth of laborers forced wages up and even though a statute was passed setting maximum wages, they were so high that it was no longer profitable for the large landholder to hire farm laborers and he soon found it expedient to lease his lands to these erstwhile villeins. Many of them became, however, not socage tenants, but tenants for a term – our modern tenancy. At the same time, in another manner, villeins were becoming another type of tenants – copyholders on a manor.

TENURES OF KENT AND DURHAM

In addition to the free socage tenure discussed above, two particular types of tenure should be given special consideration, for they were mentioned specifically in the early American charters. They are the tenure of the manor of East Greenwich in the County of Kent, and the tenure of the Bishopric of Durham. The former type of tenure was mentioned specifically in the three Virginia charters and the charters under which most of the colonies were settled, while the latter system of holding land was contained in the charters for Maryland and Pennsylvania.

Free and Common Socage of Kent

Gavelkind tenure was one of the English free tenures. The term came to denote the kind of tenure under which land in the County of Kent was held, unless specifically provided otherwise. But why should Kent have a peculiar tenure situation? Why did it not conform to the conventional tenures throughout the kingdom? The county of Kent lay on the much-traveled route between England and the Continent. As a consequence, Kentishmen had three distinct advantages: (1) They were frequently exposed to new ideas and to the practices followed in other countries. (2) They were influenced by their contacts with men of commerce. (3) Money was introduced earlier and in larger quantities in Kent than elsewhere in the realm, and money was the great solvent of feudal control over those who operated the land.

The exact tenure situation that existed in Kent in feudal times is not known, but most authorities agree upon the general content of Kentish tenures, except for the situation on the manor of East Greenwich. Very little information seems to be available as to the tenure of East Greenwich during the first half of the seventeenth century.

The most distinguishing features of Kentish gavelkind or free and common socage tenures were: (1) The land was freely partible in equal shares among the male heirs since there was no primogeniture in the descent of property in Kent. (2) Kentishmen could freely sell or give their lands, and could sue for the same in the king's court, even against their lords. (3) There was no escheat for felony in Kent, nor was a felon's wife deprived of her customary dower. (4) The wife of the deceased received one-half of the land instead of one-third, and the husband's rights in his deceased wife's property were extensive. (5) An heir became of age at fifteen insofar as concerned alienation of land and marriage. (6) The guardian for an infant heir was appointed by the lord from among the relatives who would not inherit the property. (7) Court procedures were more direct and less cumbersome than elsewhere. (8) All Kentishmen were born free; villeinage was unknown in Kent. (*Holdsworth. English Law, III, 260-61.*)

In addition, the legal assumption was always in favor of gavelkind tenure in Kent. In other words, all land in Kent was presumed to be held in gavelkind until proved otherwise. Elsewhere in England the reverse was true; common law rules always were binding and any special exceptions had to be proved. Thus, William the Conqueror and his successors permitted Kent to retain its ancient Saxon liberties. Kent never was feudalized; the land remained free as before the Conquest.

If there was no villeinage in Kent, there were no villeins on the manor of East Greenwich. If there were no villeins there was no particular custom for only the existence of tenants in villeinage would create "custom" or customary tenures. Thus, East Greenwich would have been subject to the general customs of the county in which it was situated.

The records show conclusively that the best-known and most-sought-after "custom" was that of Kent. The distinct advantage of the occupier of the soil, as against the lord, put Kentish customs in a unique position among the various regional customs. Kentish custom was so fully recognized by the courts that it might be described as the common law of Kent. (*Neilson. Kent, 1–62.*)

The Palatinate of Durham

When William conquered England he found that the Highland Celts were too warlike and the land too poor to make subjugation profitable and advisable. On the other hand, the frequent and persistent difficulties between the Celtic clans and the English manors established by William made it expedient to establish a "buffer state," an eleventh century counterpart of twentieth century territorial expediency in Europe. William's inducement was to grant extraordinary feudal powers and exemptions to leaders who would establish and maintain a buffer against the wild Celts. In fact, the Bishop of Durham had almost sovereign power over the County of Durham – he was largely exempted from control by the king. The land was free of many of the burdensome incidents that later plagued the feudal lord throughout most of England.

The extensive powers granted the Bishop of Durham did not remain constant throughout the feudal era. During the Tudor regime one privilege after another was taken from the Bishop of Durham. In

1536, the judicial system of Durham was dependent immediately upon the king. A century later the palatinate was formally abolished. In 1649, it joined the northern circuit of courts, and five years later it became an ordinary county. But with the Restoration it assumed many of its original prerogatives.

Like the Bishopric of Durham, the settlement agencies that sponsored colonization in America were to be granted wide economic and political rights. The grants to the trading companies, proprietary groups, and individuals were designed merely to follow the same general pattern that had been used earlier in similar endeavors. They also were in harmony with grants for special developmental work in England proper. Also, wide governmental power and full control over land tenures were likewise granted the Scots who were encouraged to settle in Northern Ireland for the purpose of preventing that island from becoming a military base of the enemy.

CHAPTER 3

Adjustments in English Feudal Tenures

THE FEUDAL SYSTEM had not been fully developed when significant adjustments were introduced. Noteworthy changes started in 1215 with Magna Carta, the great cornerstone of English liberty, and reached their climax in 1660 with the Statute of Tenures, which outlawed the last important vestiges of the feudal land system. During this period ten major statutory adjustments were made in tenure relations, and two laws affecting the colonists were enacted following settlement in the New World. Some of these laws were in favor of the small landholder, and some in favor of the great lords. Some failed to accomplish their intended purposes.

MAGNA CARTA

When John I forced himself upon the throne in 1199 he immediately broke many of the obligations that bound the lord and vassal. Frequently, and to excess, he demanded scutage and aids. His flagrant abuse of the incidents of relief, wardship, and marriage was oppressive. He quarreled with the pope over the appointment of the Archbishop of Canterbury, and the pope excommunicated King John. A few years later Philip of France was commanded by the pope to deprive John of his kingdom. Fearing invasion, King John acceded to papal wishes, and the pope thereby increased his control over the kingdom. Later, in 1215, the new Archbishop of Canterbury, Stephen Langton, with the assistance of the oppressed lords, forced John I to sign the Magna Carta in the meadow at Runnymede. Magna Carta universally is thought of as the very foundation of modern representative and constitutional government. "It marks an epoch in the history of the English people." (*Driscoll. Charter of Liberties, 16.*)

Three features of lasting value in the Magna Carta dealt with the basic social agreement among men. These provided that justice should be neither sold nor bought, that no man regardless of status should be deprived of his liberty and property except upon the judgment of his equals or the law of the land, and that no taxes, except well-established, customary feudal dues, should be levied upon anyone without the consent of the national council. Four items that affected land tenure in particular dealt with aids, freedom of alienation, determination of possessory rights, and acquisition of land by religious bodies.

Prior to 1215, the feudal tenant never was quite certain as to his position in regard to aids, either as to their amount, frequency, or purpose. But the Magna Carta reduced aids to three purposes: ransom of the lord when he was held captive, knighting of the lord's eldest son, and marriage of the lord's eldest daughter. The tenant, of course, did not know how many times his lord might be captured, but he knew there could be only one eldest son and one eldest daughter. This stabilized greatly the purposes for which aids were demanded, and gave the tenant a fair idea as to when they would be levied. In 1275, the amount of the aid for the two last-mentioned events became relatively fixed, and by 1350 these amounts could not be changed by the Crown. (*3 Edward I, 1275, Stat. 1, c. 36; 25 Edward III, 1350, Stat. 5, c. 11, respectively.*)

Magna Carta made a feeble stab at the alienation problem arising out of subinfeudation. This endeavor, however, was the forerunner of *Quia Emptores,* enacted in 1290. The Great Charter provided that no freeman should transfer so much of his land that out of the remainder he could not do sufficiently the services due the lord of the fee. This did not prevent, however, a continuation of the various processes whereby the value of the land to the lord was seriously reduced.

Magna Carta also provided that the seat of the king's justice, as between two subjects, should be fixed at Westminster and that the people should have ready access to the courts through regular circuits of justices of assize. The name of these justices and their courts came from their commission to try actions for recovery of the possession of land. This was the major civil action regarding land, and was called assize. The superior county courts of assize represented a great step forward in regularizing the land laws.

A vague provision sought to prohibit ownership of land rights by religious bodies or persons "whereby such lands or tenements may any wise come into mortmain," or be held by a dead hand. The effective statute, however, was not enacted until two-thirds of a century had passed.

LAWS REGARDING WASTE

By the thirteenth century, rights in land had become so highly segmented that several persons could hold rights in the same piece of land. This gradual differentiation of interests in land gave rise to the law of waste. Obviously, the man who had only a temporary interest in a piece of land might make the most of his opportunity to the detriment of those whose rights were more permanent. The right of the successors to object to damaging or wasting the property apparently was unquestioned. The Magna Carta provided that the lord holding land by wardships should take nothing more than the customary produce and that he should maintain the building and estate in good condition.

This statute apparently applied only to knight service tenures at first, but was expanded to include socage tenures by the Statute of Marlborough in 1267. The Statute of Gloucester eleven years later included also tenants for life. Originally the law against waste was applied to persons who held rights in land for either long or short periods by virtue of the operation of feudal tenures. It was designed to protect parties who had no other way of protecting the land which eventually would fall into their possession. Later, and particularly in the United States, the same principle was applied to contractual relations between ordinary landlords and tenants. The concept of waste still is important in English tenure, and the early law has been copied almost verbatim in some American jurisdictions. (*Harris. Compensation, 76–80.*)

ALIENATION OF FREEHOLD ESTATES

The idea of one specified area of land belonging to an individual came with the transition from a nomadic to an agrarian society, and in the beginning the strength of the proposition lay in the inalienability of the land. The bar against alienation, or transfer, of land probably was absolute in the earliest days of Saxon law. By the ninth century, however, one could alienate land which he had acquired, although the bar remained as applied to land which had descended to him from his forebears. In all of this development, the interest of the heirs constantly was in mind, for the desired stability in the economic and social order was dependent upon the protection of rights. With the coming of feudalism and the development of the tenure concept, a new interest was introduced – the interest of the lord.

The earliest legislative recognition of a qualified right of the lord to restrict, but not prohibit absolutely, alienation of estates in land is found in the Magna Carta. This restriction on subinfeudation was concerned specifically with the rent aspect of the matter, and was not a complete statement of public policy on the subject of alienation. Indeed, it was not until the time of Henry III, in 1256, that the king effectively prevented the alienation of estates held immediately of him by tenants in capite. This was accomplished by an ordinance that forbade alienation without his license. The king, however, could not maintain this restriction for long, and in 1327, under Edward III, tenants in capite acquired the right to alienate freely on the payment of a fine. These fines were endured for over three centuries.

The effect of an alienation made without license was the subject of great controversy. By statute it was determined that the lord could levy a distress for the fine for alienation, but he could not declare a forfeiture and retake the land. (*1 Edward III, 1326, Stat. 1, c. 3.*) Thus, the theoretical bar against alienation was not absolute; the practical bar was even more lax. For example, that special type of tenure called serjeanty was, in theory, strictly personal and therefore theoretically inalienable. Yet, Pollock and Maitland have offered evidence that lands held by serjeanty, too, actually were alienated. (*Pollock and Maitland. English Law, I, 334.*)

Forms of Alienation

The principal forms of alienation were: (1) physical transfer of possession before witnesses, (2) symbolical delivery before witnesses, (3) symbolical delivery with a charter as the symbol, (4) substitution and subinfeudation, (5) levying a fine, (6) bargain and sale, (7) lease and release, and (8) conveyance by way of uses. The first three methods were employed by the Saxons and laid the foundation for modern conveyancing. The others developed during the feudal period. Most of them were the direct outgrowth of efforts to bypass burdensome feudal rules, or were developed to meet the peculiar conditions imposed by statutes enacted during the feudal era.

The concept of property was first applied to movables, and their transfer was simply and effectually made by a change of physical possession — a transfer from one hand to another. Land could not be handled in this way, so the obvious alternative was used — the individual transferred himself to the land. In other words, the recipient of the "gift" took actual possession of the land and the "giver" vacated. Because this ceremony was widely known and talked of, the neighboring people could easily arbitrate any later disputes.

The physical transfer of land was sometimes inconvenient, however, and soon symbolical deliveries were used. In these the grantor handed the grantee, in the presence of numerous witnesses, a piece of sod from the land, or the latch from the door, or some other appropriate symbol. This was as effective as the older method but both had one weakness – the witnesses would die and with them would die the proof of the transfer.

To correct this weakness, it soon became common also to put in writing what had been done. Sometimes the parties would not bother to actually deliver the piece of sod, but would merely execute the writing. Soon it was felt that the charter would be just as representative of the land as a piece of sod and so possession was completed by delivery of the charter serving both as a symbol and as permanent evidence of the transaction.

With the development of the tenure concept in the twelfth and thirteenth centuries, other methods of transferring rights in real property became popular. Chief among these were substitution and subinfeudation. The former involved the substitution of *A* for *B* as *C's* tenant; the latter involved a new feud so that *A* became a tenant of *B* who remained *C's* tenant. Substitution, though a very old device, was used little during early feudal times, for subinfeudation obviously was more lucrative to the first feudal tenant. The substitution of one tenant for another did not affect adversely the feudal setup so long as the new tenant was acceptable to the lord. The creating of a subfeud, however, greatly weakened the position of the overlord.

Another popular method of conveying land operated though the courts and was called levying a fine. One party sued another party who was a friend. When the case came up for trial, the parties received permission to compromise their "dispute." This compromise then was presented to the court, whereupon a fine was entered on the court records of the agreement. The agreement became binding within a specified period, usually a year and a day. The compromise, of course, involved an agreement by *A* to grant certain land to *B* who in turn agreed to pay a certain sum of money to *A*. This method of conveyancing had the advantage of furnishing indisputable evidence – a court record – of the transaction and of giving the grantee the protection of the court. It was used in Saxon England and retained its importance during the early feudal period. In 1360, a limiting statute (*34 Edward III, 1360, Stat. 3, c. 16.*) ruled that levying a fine did not affect the rights of strangers. The effect of this statute was bad, and levying a fine later was restored to much of its original value.

A modern method of conveyancing is through bargain and sale by use of a warranty deed, that is, by execution and delivery of a writing in which the seller conveys the land to the buyer and warrants his title to be good. This method was known in Saxon days and was used to a limited extent during the later feudal era, particularly after the Statutes of Uses and Enrollments. The idea, then as now, was that the seller would defend the validity of the right he conveyed – in olden times by force of arms, today by force of law.

All six methods of conveyancing required some form of transfer of possession — symbolic or actual. In feudal times this requirement was vital to all legal conveyances, although it often was bypassed in the fourteenth century. The original idea of a transfer of possession gave way to what was called livery of seisin (transfer of possession). Technically, the terms had a slightly different meaning from those imputed, but probably no one ever knew exactly what that meaning was. For present purposes merely note that corporeal things (tangible immovables) were said to "lie in livery" and that incorporeals (intangible rights in immovables) "lie in grant." In the former case livery of seisin was necessary for a conveyance, whereas in the latter a grant was sufficient.

By the end of the thirteenth century leases were in common use. The concept of a leasehold interest gave a qualified interest in land for a definite period of time but not forever. During this century the correlative concept of a release developed. Under this concept, a person who had some claim to certain land merely promised never to assert his claim. The modern quitclaim deed is a direct descendant, conceptually speaking.

The mechanics of the lease and release were simple: *A* leased Blackacre to *B* for ten years and thereafter, but before the ten years expired, *A* released his claim to Blackacre to *B*. There was, of course, no warranty involved, and there was no technical livery of seisin, as a lessee was not given seisin but merely possession (although there was no practical difference once the release was given). The release made the lessee's possession a seisin, and the legal actions dependent on seisin were available to him. Much of the popularity of the device was brought about by the Statute of Enrollments (1535) which required that all bargain and sale conveyances be enrolled. A heavy fee was charged for the enrolling. To avoid this fee, the lease and release type of conveyance was used — a lease was no sale and a release was just a promise not to assert any claim to the land. Requirements regarding enrollments did not cover these transactions. The Duke of York used the lease and release procedure in transferring his rights in New Jersey to Berkeley and Carteret in 1664. The lease was made on one day, and the release was entered into the next.

Conveyancing by way of use was another method of transferring land from one party to another. It was an equitable, as distinguished from a legal, conveyance. Originally it arose to circumvent the various statutes of mortmain, which sought to prohibit conveyances of land to religious institutions. The ecclesiastics were the best lawyers in England, and they soon found a way for their religious institutions to continue receiving land despite the statutes. *A* would convey land to *B*, using any of the recognized legal conveyances. The instrument would provide that *B* should hold the land for the use of *C*, a church. Thus, the church actually had the land, but, as far as the law was concerned, *B* had the land. As it was expressed at a later date, *B* had a naked legal title. This device worked out satisfactorily through the intervention of equity and the potent threat to excommunication.

Changes in Alienation

During the reign of Edward I (1272–1307) some of the most far-reaching tenure laws in history were enacted. Edward I was one of the ablest of all the kings of England. He often is referred to as the English Justinian. Being a student, he had a clear concept of many governmental problems when he came to the throne; as to the others, he studied them in detail before acting. Surrounding himself with capable advisers, his legislation was well timed and effective.

Mortmain. One matter to which Edward I gave early attention was the rapid loss to the Crown of feudal rights due the lord paramount under the original feudal system. The first situation undermining feudal tenures to which Edward I directed his attention was the enormous increase in land held in mortmain (by a church corporation or body). It is estimated that approximately one-third of the land of the kingdom was in the hands of ecclesiastical bodies during the twelfth and thirteenth centuries. Few feudal dues were attached to this land. First, the Crown never secured the lucrative incident of wardship, for the church, being a corporation, never was under age. Then there could be no marriageable daughters, so there was no opportunity for the Crown to receive income from the marriage incident. The church never died, and as a consequence no relief needed to be paid for the admittance of a new tenant. And lastly, the church could not commit treason, so the entire fee never escheated to the Crown. As a consequence, the king's revenues were seriously reduced. In addition, it was held that the church gradually was asserting and establishing the doctrine that its courts, and not the king's courts or the manorial courts, should decide litigation regarding land which had been given to God. If the church was not subject to civil courts, it could not be forced to pay any charges upon the land.

The Magna Carta sought to relieve this situation by preventing transfer of land to churches. But this provision was defeated by long leases on the land at a nominal or token rent, or by title in an ecclesiastical office occupied by only one person (Magna Carta referred to religious corporations), or by conveyancing by way of uses. To correct these loopholes and clarify the situation, the Statute of Mortmain was enacted in 1279, the real title of which was *De Viris Religiosis*.

The statute provided that no new grants of land were to be held in frankalmoign or to be held in any other tenure by a religious body except grants made by the king. In order to prevent the capable canon lawyers from going around the statute, as they had a similar proviso in the Magna Carta, one provision in the Statute of *Quia Emptores,* enacted in 1290, was that ". . . Lands or Tenements shall in no wise come into Mortmain, either in Part or in Whole, neither by Policy or Craft, contrary to the Form of the Statute made thereupon of late." Modern statutes have created some exceptions to the general law but prohibition has been maintained in England to this day. It is interesting to note that Maryland still has a statute mortmain.

Quia Emptores. A second great statute of the reign of Edward I related to the alienation of land by subinfeudation. To prevent alienations of this type the Statute of *Quia Emptores* was enacted. This statute made no changes in the alienability of land. However, it provided only that the land must be completely alienated so that the new holder held of the same lord and under the same services as the transferor. If only a portion of the land was alienated the services were apportioned. This was a sort of compromise. The great lords permitted legal recognition of the customary procedure of alienation and of substituting several tenants for one in return for the prohibition of subinfeudation with its disastrous effects.

Alienation by persons holding directly of the Crown was not covered by this statute. Furthermore, it referred to alienation of fee simple estates in land and not to the alienation of lesser estates, such as copyholds. Thus, subtenancies similar to our present-day tenancies were possible. This prevention of pyramiding of tenancies ultimately was to be the death of the feudal system, for the landowners' full recognition of substituting one feudal tenant for another fostered the development of full freedom of alienation of land.

De Donis. Thus far the presentation generally has been in terms of alienation of estates held in fee simple. However, slightly different principles applied to another type of tenure called fee simple conditional. This type of estate arose when *A* granted land to *B* under the condition that *B* have birth of issue. When a child was born, *B* immediately could alienate the land to a friend, repurchasing it in fee simple. *B* then could alienate the land at his own will in accordance with any of the recognized procedures. Prior to the birth of issue, however, he could not alienate the land. If he did not change his tenure from a conditional fee after the birth of issue, the land reverted to the original donor or his heir at any time the donee or his line failed in issue.

Defeating the conditional fee was common by the middle of the thirteenth century, but it was directly opposed to the growing sentiment in favor of primogeniture (the first born's exclusive right to inheritance) and entails (inheritances that are nontransferable by the heir and his descendants). In fact, opportunity for alienations of this kind arose chiefly when land was given to a man and his heirs-to-be in anticipation that it would be passed on from generation to generation. However, it was held that the land could be transferred in fee simple by the donee as soon as an heir was born, meeting the condition of the grant. It also was held that future heirs would be bound by the alienation. The fee simple estate could be forfeited for treason, while the fee conditional estate was not subjected to permanent forfeiture. In most cases the effect of granting a fee conditional estate was equivalent to receipt of a fee simple estate, for the conditional fee usually was changed into the more valuable fee simple upon the appearance of an heir.

The right of the donee to alienate the land to a stranger in fee simple upon the birth of a child was prejudicial, the great landowners contended, as it tended to prevent perpetuation of landed estates in their families. The desire and apparent need for perpetuation of the land in the same family was very realistic in those days. Considerable dignity and civil power were related to the holding of land, and because it was impossible to divide the dignity and the government among the heirs, it logically followed that it was impossible to divide the land. Therefore, the very favorable attitude toward primogeniture was not an unqualified idea of the landed gentry. Primogeniture was a practical necessity. In order to insure proper maintenance of the dignity and the landed estate, and to afford some protection of the "disinherited heirs" and future generations, entails were superimposed upon the practice of primogeniture.

Primogeniture rather than ultimogeniture was followed, for it was reasoned that the eldest son was more capable of performing military services than was the youngest son. In addition, particularly at first, the son who inherited the family estate was morally responsible for the younger sons. Another argument in favor of the practice of entails and primogeniture was the great need for the maintenace of a group of wealthy landowners who would see that land was fully and properly cultivated and that the cultivators were protected properly. The feudal lords also protested that the donor was deprived of the estate's return after the grant had ended when the donee alienated the land upon birth of an heir, but the heir predeceased the original donee. It should be explained that the reversionary interest was ". . . more valuable in the case of a fee restricted to such heirs than in the case of an absolute fee simple." (*Tiffany. Real Property, I, 48.*)

The Statute of *De Donis* (*13 Edward I, 1285, Stat. 1, c. 1.*) was enacted to eliminate these evils. This statute provided that the will of the donor should be observed. The donee could not alienate the land. It either passed to his heirs or reverted to the donor or his heirs. This prevented the donee from barring his issue or affecting the donor's right of reversion. The donee who earlier held a conditional fee which could become absolute upon the birth of issue now held an estate that descended according to the terms of the original grant. Fee tail estates, or estates in fee tail as they frequently were called, were thus firmly established. An estate in fee tail, after the death of the first owner, passed to his lawful heirs from generation to generation so long as there were heirs. The estate ended only upon the failure of such posterity.

Fee tails, being mere life estates, could not be forfeited to the Crown for crime and therefore they were popular with great landholders. It should be pointed out that almost any crime created a forfeiture of the estate, and in those turbulent times escheat was a matter of real importance. For exactly the same reason fee tails were unpopular with the king and with his courts. They were repealed during the reign of Henry VII (1485–1509) by a statute which provided that a fine was sufficient to bar estates in tail. (*Dalrymple. Feudal Property, 166.*) Blackstone in his *Commentaries* gives this version of *De Donis*:

> . . . Children grew disobedient when they knew they could not be set aside: farmers were ousted of their leases made by tenants in tail; . . . creditors were defrauded of their debts; . . . innumerable latent entails were produced to deprive purchasers of the lands they had fairly bought; . . . and treasons were encouraged; as estates-tail were not liable to forfeiture, longer than for the tenant's life. (*Blackstone Commentaries, I, 522.*)

ALIENATION OF COPYHOLD ESTATES

The alienation of copyhold tenures was a different matter, for the method of alienating copyhold lands varied in accordance with the customs of the manor. Copyholders could, in general, transfer their land, although the right was not absolute and the process was not simple.

The progress of copyhold tenants in securing full freedom of alienation was not marked by statutory action similar to *Quia Emptores* until they came under the jurisdiction of the king's courts in the sixteenth century. Alienation always was dependent on the lord's approval. A fine for alienation also was required frequently. This usually consisted of one year's rent. The method of conveyancing commonly used was for the "seller" to surrender his copyhold to the lord, who then would present it to the "buyer." In short, the lord or his steward always was the channel through which action was taken, and, in theory, he could refuse to be a conductor in any case. However, Lord Coke said that although in theory the lord could accept the surrender and refuse to make the presentment, actually he was bound to do so by custom – a custom so rigid that the lord could not change the terms of the grant in any way. The presentment was to be identical with the surrender. (*Coke. Three Law Tracts, 86–88.*)

INHERITANCE IN FEUDAL ENGLAND

The power of the feudal tenant to transfer all of his rights in land to another was important in feudal times, but it is doubtful if estates were transferred with such frequency as in the United States today. The transfers depended then as now entirely upon the will of man. That is to say, it was wholly within man's power to determine what restraints would be placed upon *inter vivos* alienation, and under what conditions the transfer would take place. There was and is involved no natural law, for *inter vivos* alienation could have been prohibited entirely. Only in the process of life and death must transfers of landed rights be provided for. When the holder of rights in land dies, these rights must reside somewhere. Two general possibilities are evident—either the deceased must provide by will for the transfer, or society must determine who will succeed to the estate of the deceased. Transfers because of death were much more frequent in feudal England than in contemporary United States for the life span in this country is more than double that of medieval England.

Succession

The feudal rules of descent, which began in Saxon times, were not complete until the time of Henry III (1216–72). These rules, as set forth by Sir Matthew Hale, writing in the eighteenth century, may be summarized as follows:

1. Males were preferred to females of equal degree.
2. The next of blood was preferred to the more remote, that is, a brother would exclude a half brother.
3. All descendants took by representation. For example, a female child of a dead son would exclude a younger son, the child representing the older son.
4. Primogeniture applied—the eldest took all.
5. Females of equal degree inherited equally.
6. As between collaterals—brothers, sisters, cousins, etc.—those of the blood of the first purchaser were preferred.
7. The "first purchaser" was the last ancestor actually in possession of the property. (*Hale. Common Law, II, ch. 11.*)

Preference of males was commonplace in ancient law, but is rare in modern law. This phenomenon originally was based upon the inability of women to perform the heavy duties of the primeval hunter and warrior. As society developed and the idea of hiring someone to do a task grew, the logic of this rule became weak. The "preference" rule represented a step in the evolution from complete exclusion to practical equality.

The so-called "rule of the whole blood" is one having only historical significance. In Bracton's day in the middle of the thirteenth century, the half blood deferred to the whole blood. If *A* died leaving no children but one brother and one half brother, the brother would inherit the entire estate. But if *A* died leaving only a half brother, he would inherit. A century later the law had completely excluded the half blood so *A's* half brother would not, under any circumstances, inherit from *A*. Sir Robert Chambers suggested the rule of whole blood was a rule of evidence, necessary because over an extended period the memory of the original feudal donation was lost and the only means of determining if it remained in proper hands was by forcing it to remain in those of the whole blood, ". . . for if any person was of the whole blood . . . then he must of necessity be of both bloods of that remote feudal marriage. . . . " (*Chambers. Estates and Tenures, 45.*)

The idea that a child represented his father, and therefore for purposes of succession was the father, developed slowly and was not accepted law until late in the twelfth century. In Saxon times even the Crown descended without regard to representation, a second son excluding the children of the deceased elder son. Gradually the idea became accepted that it was unfair to disinherit a grandson, who probably had been raised in idleness relying on his inheritance, merely because his father died before his grandfather. This principle was not discarded along with primogeniture, and today a grandchild whose parent is dead inherits along with the brothers and sisters of his parent.

Primogeniture – the eldest son takes all – was founded on economic factors. It was a positive move toward the common principle of equality to promote justice. Meanwhile, ultimogeniture developed in some urban areas. Under this rule, the youngest son took all. In many respects this custom did not vary from primogeniture. The identity of the particular heir was the only difference.

With primogeniture came the problem of what to do in case all the heirs were daughters. The eldest daughter, in the twelfth century, succeeded to the inheritance but she was supposed to evaluate it and pay her sisters their proportionate share. A similar duty existed in the case of males, but this was moral and not legal.

> . . . At one time it looks as if even among women there would be what we may call an external primogeniture, so that the eldest of the daughters would be the only representative of the fee in the eyes of the lord and of the feudal courts. Had this principle been consistently applied, the rights of the younger daughters might have become merely moral rights. But in the thirteenth century wardships and marriages were of greater importance than knight's service and scutage, and first the king and then the other lords perceived that they had most to gain by taking the homage of all the sisters. (*Pollock and Maitland. English Law, II, 278.*)

Before leaving the subject of descent, two special cases should be considered: the custom of gavelkind and the custom of copyhold.

Gavelkind land varied from other land in two important ways regarding the laws of descent. First, the inheritance was partible, each son taking an equal part, and second, the sons of a felon were allowed to inherit from their father.

Copyholds descended, if at all, according to the custom of the manor, which is similar to the early copyhold rule on alienation. In theory the transmission was always through the lord — when a copyholder died his land reverted to the lord, who thereupon admitted the heir. Determination of the heir depended upon custom. Copyholders often left precatory wills naming one person as heir and oftentimes the lord enforced the will. At times the supply of villeins did not exceed, or even meet, the demand, and thus manorial lords were happy to find and admit able-bodied tenant-laborers to farm their lands.

In feudal times the heir had no right until the ancestor died. In ancient Saxon law, and feudal law as it developed on the Continent, the expectant heir had a definite right, and therefore the landowner could not defeat the heir's expectancy by alienating the land without his consent. English law tended in the same direction, but commercial forces turned the tide in favor of complete freedom of alienation even though it defeated the entire inheritance.

Before turning to the discussion of wills, the descent of chattels should be mentioned. In Saxon days, if a man died intestate (without leaving a will) his chattels, or personal property, went to his wife and children. As the power of the church increased, however, the idea grew that the intestate's goods should be distributed by the wife and children for the good of the dead man's soul. By the twelfth century, the doctrine that a man who died intestate died unconfessed virtually was the law of the church. Of course, drastic action was taken to save the deceased's soul — such as giving all of his goods to the church to be used for charitable purposes. The right of the church to supervise the distribution of the intestate's goods was included in the Magna Carta of 1215 and, although the clause was omitted from the following charter and from all subsequent charters, it became the practice. In accordance with this procedure the church administered intestates' goods and "probated" wills covering chattels. In so doing, these ecclesiastical courts naturally applied canon law, which was a variation of Roman law. The obvious result was that one system of law applied to the descent of realty and an entirely different system applied to the distribution of personalty. Not only was the order of succession different, but also procedure and terminology were different. The person who succeeded to the deceased's realty was the "heir by descent," whereas the person who succeeded to his personalty (and who might well be the same person) was "the next of kin." He took by distribution rather than descent. And so today, many states have a statute of descent and a statute of distribution.

Wills

The long struggle of the English landholder for the right to dispose of his land by a written testament is one of the most interesting developments in the history of land tenure. To get the full sweep of this process it is necessary to go back to Saxon times. Saxon folcland could not be made the subject of a will, although it was possible that the occupant might express a desire that a particular person or persons occupy the land after his death and the "people" might respect his wishes. On the other hand, the possessor of bocland had whatever powers were transferred to him in the charter, and these occasionally might have included the power to devise by will. However, it seems to have been more common to withhold the right to name the successor. In such case, it it reasonable to assume that the landholder's wishes, which might be expressed in a written document, would influence the choice of his successor. But, again, the "will" in this situation was merely a humble petition, or precatory in nature.

In the eleventh and twelfth centuries the modern idea of a will began to develop and by the thirteenth century the true will was in common use. It did not embrace realty, however, which descended as the law of descent provided. The thirteenth century wills related only to chattels and just as the church gained control over the intestate's goods so it gained control over the wills of those who died testate.

By the close of the thirteenth century it was settled law that the succession of land was to be determined by the common law rules of descent without regard to a will and that the succession of chattels was determined by the canon law in the absence of a will. If there was a will the surviving wife took one-third and the children another one-third of the chattels, the remainder being subject to the will as administered by the church.

As early as 1383 equity enforced what may be called a "use will." Under this procedure, the holder of an estate in fee simple would alienate it to some trusted person who was instructed to hold the land for the uses indicated in the conveyance. The conveyee was bound in conscience to recognize the uses, which were enforceable by the ecclesiastical courts. (*Lawler. Real Property, 59–60.*) Thus, a grantor gained testamentary power regarding his land by an indirect procedure at an early date.

These conveyances by way of uses were similar to those employed to bypass the statutes of mortmain. The gaining of testamentary power, however, was the major cause for the popularity of uses.

Naturally, uses were unpopular with the Crown because of the circumvention of feudal relations. In addition, they could be established secretly and the king did not know who was supposed to pay rents and perform the numerous feudal incidents. They were unpopular with the common law legalists because they broke in upon the rules of their law.

In the fifteenth and early sixteenth centuries many kings wanted to abolish uses, but not until 1535 when the oft-married Henry VIII ruled was a king strong enough to get the Parliament to act. The revenues of the Crown had been seriously reduced by use conveyances, and Henry VIII sorely needed money in his treasury. He knew that a restoration of the conventional feudal dues would accomplish this purpose permanently. To this end he tried several measures, but was opposed by the large landowners and the lawyers. Eventually, as Maitland says, the Statute of Uses ". . . was forced upon an extremely unwilling Parliament by an extremely strong-willed king." This law was passed in 1535 and was designed to accomplish four objectives: (1) restore to the king revenues from the incidents of feudal tenures; (2) abolish the power of testamentary devise; (3) restore publicity to all conveyances; and (4) abolish the separation of legal and equitable ownerships.

The statute effectively accomplished the first two and the last purposes, but the restoration of publicity to all conveyances was not attained even in part until the Statute of Enrollments was enacted. The last purpose, that is, combining of legal and equitable ownerships, was accomplished by automatically conferring a legal estate upon the person in whose favor the use was held. The statute "executed" most uses, and the beneficiary, who automatically became the new freeholder, was subjected to all of the liabilities of legal ownership. But the legal power to devise lands was destroyed. The people objected violently and five years later, in 1540, Henry VIII sponsored an act called the Statute of Wills. This statute gave all socage tenants of fee simple estates the power to dispose of all of their land by will, and freehold tenants by knight service, the power to dispose of two-thirds of their land by will. It saved primer seisin, relief, and fines for alienation in case of land held by socage tenants, and one-third of the wardship of knight-service land.

The statute also was designed to compel that public attention be called to all transfers of titles in land. However, laws do not always have the effect intended. This statute in actual practice had the opposite effect, and transfers without any public act or ceremony were more frequent after the statute was in force than before. (*Pollock. Land Laws, 2.*) When tenure by knight service was abolished, all restrictions disappeared on the power of freemen to dispose of, by will, lands held in fee simple. The Statute of Frauds of 1676 and the

Statute of Wills of 1837 regulated the form of the will and clarified the procedure. The complete power conferred in 1540 remained unchanged.

LEASEHOLD INTERESTS

Conveyance of a feudal freehold estate was an act in which the public was interested, for it created a right in the feud against everyone. Conveyance of rights in land under a lease was a private agreement between two parties creating rights and duties between them – a mere contractual arrangement.

It will be recalled that a lease, as the instrument is known today, was used in ancient times. Early English leases seem to have been limited to forty years. Most of them were oral and dependent on "living memory" for proof of their existence. As writing became more common, the desire for longer-term leases became evident. By the fourteenth century one hundred-year leases were not startling to the legal profession and nine hundred ninety-nine-year leases soon appeared. Contractual arrangements for the renting of land were so varied in feudal England that no effort will be made to describe a typical lease agreement, but the essential features of the contract and the general laws relating to it will be reviewed.

Possession

One of the most important characteristics of real property, or rights in land, is possession. In early times a grant for a term of years was not considered an estate in land, and as a result the lessee merely had the right of action against the lessor and not against others who might eject him from his land. But early in the thirteenth century, in 1235, the English courts developed a new legal action which they called *quare ejecit infra terminum.* This gave the lessee an action to regain possession of the premises if he was ejected during the term by the lessor or by one to whom the lessor had sold the property. Bracton, writing shortly after this new action arose, was loud in its praise. He asserted that by its use a termor could regain possession of the property as against any ejector. The courts apparently were not as liberal as Bracton and the action was held not applicable to stranger-ejectors, that is, third parties. Later, however, this deficiency was cured by giving the lessee the right to recover the land against any ejector – against all the world, so to speak. The legal action was the writ of *ejectione firmae.* This action formalized the process by which the tenant's interests gradually became more than the mere rights resting on a covenant with the lessor. They became rights in property enforceable by a remedy analogous to that of freeholders. When this occurred the leaseholder, as distinguished from the freeholder, came into being.

Trespass

During this same era, the courts were developing one of the major legal relations of modern jurisprudence, trespass. The action, in its inception, was criminal in nature, a trespass being a breach of the peace, since it usually involved the use of force. Soon the action also was civil in nature, so that the injured party could sue the wrongdoer. This gave the freeholder, who had that magical thing called "seisin," a new action. At first the plaintiff recovered only damages, but by the end of the fifteenth century he could recover his possession of the land as well as damages. Thus, the leesee came to be protected against both trespass and ejectment.

Waste

Of course, so long as a lessor could eject his tenant at any time, there was no need for an action at law for waste. But by 1235 the tenant had protection against such ejection, and there was a need to protect the lessor against damages to his property. In 1278, less than half a century later, the Parliament enacted the Statute of Gloucester, which gave the landlord an action against, among others, a tenant for years. This is the same statute that protected the remainderman against damages by a life tenant. Under its terms, a tenant convicted of waste was punished by forfeiture of the thing wasted and was required to pay triple damages. The waste, of course, must have been the result of voluntary action of the tenant.

Because the statute was so severe, it soon became customary to insert a clause in every lease providing that the tenant should hold "without impeachment for waste." Thus the statute was avoided. This practice became so common that equity courts ultimately held it was inserted as a matter of form, and really meant nothing. This equitable construction generally is followed today. Its effect, of course, except in a few states, is not to make a tenant subject to the treble damage clause of the statute, but rather to make one liable to the extent of the damage caused. In actual practice, the damages must be of a most flagrant nature in order to be collectible.

Distress

The right of distress probably came from the Roman law designed to modify the rigor of the feudal rule. Under this rule a failure to do the feudal service or pay the feudal rent caused a forfeiture of the feud. Distress was not so drastic. It merely gave the lord power to enter upon the land to seize the tenant's goods and chattels, including crops, and to hold them until the rent was paid. The tenant could regain his goods by paying the rent or, if he contended there was no rent due, by posting a bond in the amount of the rent and bringing a legal action called replevin. In replevin, the tenant would state that he was the rightful owner of the goods held by the plaintiff and demand their return.

Originally, distress did not give the lord a right to sell the goods, but merely to hold them until the rent was paid. Thus, the articles were pledges and the lord had the duty of returning them, when the rent was paid, "in the same plight or condition as delivered." Of course, perishables such as milk, fruit, etc., would deteriorate and, therefore, could not be distrained. This made the right of distress a rather useless thing in many cases, and led to a statute which provided that if the tenant ". . . shall not within five Days next after such Distress [is] taken, and Notice thereof . . . " replevy them, the person distraining may cause the goods to be appraised and then may sell them to satisfy the rent, thus virtually bringing the law of distress into its modern form. (*2 William and Mary, 1690, Stat. 2, c. 5.*)

Rent. In connection with distress and the relations of landlord and tenant, the various types of rent should be noted. In the Middle Ages rents arising from leasehold interests were rare as compared to feudal rents. Thus, it was natural that the latter were the moving force in the development of the concept. Feuds usually were not created by contracts, but by gifts reserving to the grantor a rent or service. It was a basic feudal rule that rent issued out of land. Theoretically, therefore, the feudal tenant was under no personal obligation, for the *land* was subject to the charge, and had to pay the rent or the service. Of course, the land had to pay it through the tenant's hands and if he did not allow the land to make the payment, the punishment indirectly was upon the tenant. Rent was so "thinglike" it was treated almost as a tangible object. If a socage tenant failed to pay rent, the lord could not sue him, until a statute of 1709 allowed it. Rather he proceeded on the theory that the tenant had ejected the lord from his rent. The appropriate legal action usually was the *assize of novel disseisin* – the same action used to recover land. All of the "real actions," including the writ of entry and the writ of right, were available to the lord.

Finally, a personal obligation to pay the rent could be agreed to, if the parties wished. In such case, the lord could proceed by means of a real action, treating the rent as a thing, or he could bring a personal action, called "annuity," against the tenant. The right to hold a tenant personally liable is compatible with the idea of contract, and the right of distraint is in harmony with the idea of rent issuing out of land. The combination of these two ideas means that the landlord-tenant relation has a dual nature: there is a "privity of estate" and a "privity of contract," binding the parties together. The modern rule that when a tenant transfers or sublets the premises, both he and the subtenant are liable for the rent, logically follows. The landlord can sue the original tenant in debt, on the contract concept, and can distrain the new tenant, on the privity of estate idea.

Following the premise that rent issued out of land, rent was not due until the profits were taken from the land. This meant the end of the term unless a specific time was set for payment. In that case it was due at that exact time and not a minute sooner. In line with this principle, the practice seemed to be that if the lease ended before the time for payment no rent would be paid, for there would never be an apportionment in respect to part of the time. However, in the seventeenth century it became apparent that this rule often was unjust, and the courts began to modify it.

BONDMEN AND LABORERS

Even before the Conquest many freemen, for various reasons, sought the protection of the great lords. In turn they became what may be called bondmen. Their few rights in real and personal property were subject to the will of the lord. This situation was not greatly affected by the Norman invasion. It was almost three centuries later before the number and position of those on the lower rungs of the tenure ladder were disturbed greatly.

When the Black Death swept over Europe it took away thirty to fifty per cent of the total population in England, and probably even a much larger proportion of the peasants who were the main tillers of the soil. For several centuries the farm lands had been cultivated under the manorial system, but the sudden disappearance of so many of the peasants threw the system into disorder. In their efforts to get their manor land tilled, the lords tried to get in full the service due them by the villeins under strict feudal concepts. Wages were rising in England, and this rise meant a considerable loss to those landholders who had changed their villeins' service to money payments. Instead of accepting money they tried to make the villeins perform their labor service in full. They sought also to hire landless men for the old wages of two or three pence a day.

The landless, however, united to secure what they wanted and often asked and got twice as much as they had received in the past. The landholding class protested. The king, being an extensive landholder himself, sympathized with the lords. Parliament was not in session because of the epidemic, so in 1349, to meet the situation, the king's council proclaimed the Statute of Laborers, and it was confirmed the following year when Parliament met. This was the first of many statutes enacted during the next two hundred years.

It provided that all able-bodied men and women under sixty and without a definite means of support must, if requested, accept wages at no higher level than the rate of 1347. Punishment was threatened to both the workers who refused to work at these fixed wages and to the landholder who paid more — a feudal idea of a public control, not wholly unlike some more modern practices.

Even though the landlords frequently paid higher wages in the years that followed, sufficient labor to keep the ancient manorial system working was not available, for in addition to those lost in the Black Death epidemic many workers went to the towns to work. Gradually the landlords came to realize that the solution of the difficulty was to abandon the old custom of farming the entire estate with the labor of the peasants, and to divide the manor land into small farms, each of which was to be rented to a free tenant for cultivation at a stipulated sum. During the next half century these free tenant-farmers, chiefly known as copyholders, could be found everywhere. As a consequence the villeins — the peasant laborers on the lord's demesne — grew fewer in number. The struggle between the lords and their peasants extended into the fifteenth century, and Statutes of Laborers were re-enacted frequently in futile efforts to make the manorial system work. The struggle turned in favor of the laborers, and into existence came the sturdy and prosperous farming yeomanry — the copyholder, who gradually became more subject to public law and less subject to the custom of the manor.

LATER LEGISLATION

By the middle of the sixteenth century the old feudal system, foisted upon the people by William and his followers, had been both strengthened and weakened by a series of proclamations, ordinances, and parliamentary enactments. The burdensome feudal incidents were being attacked on every side and many of them were being weakened by default. The Black Death and mass migration to cities, as commerce and industry grew in importance, led to a depopulation of the countryside and a great relaxation of competition for land. Feudal tenants were in a favorable position.

Along with this came the great enclosure movement when wool became the important commercial agricultural product. The competitive situation shifted and arable land was in great demand. Also, just at the turn of the seventeenth century, colonization was started in America and a fanatical interest in exploration and trade was reaching its height. New ideas of the importance of thrift and economic activity were replacing the older idea of a slow-moving agrarian economy. Old concepts were being tested and found wanting. Principles of equity were rapidly taking the place of old feudal rules. The Reformation was exerting a powerful influence upon man's economic activities, including his feudal relationships. These disrupting events, first favoring one group and then another, led to the collapse of the feudal tenure structure.

But the old system would not die without a last struggle. The effort of the Stuart kings to revive the tottering structure cost Charles I his head. After the Restoration, Charles II gave his approval to an act of Parliament that, in effect, abolished nearly all of the dangerous and oppressive controls over land that had been reserved in early times to the feudal lords.

The third element in the original feudal system – military organization upon the land – had long since disappeared, but the old tenure forms had persisted in many regards. As excessive militarism subsided in the sixteenth century, free and common socage tenure came to be looked upon as equally honorable as tenure by knight service. With the change from military service to money rent and the rise of a mercenary army, and with the new attitude toward socage tenure, little justification of the outmoded military tenures was possible. So they finally were wiped out.

The Statute of Tenures (1660) converted all knight-service tenures into free and common socage. Scutage, homage, wardship, marriage, primer seisin, aids, and fines for alienation were abolished. The power to distribute all instead of only one-third of the knight-service estate was allowed.

The statute did not affect the minor incidents that were attached to socage and copyhold tenures. Escheat for felony and failure of issue remained. Money payments, or quitrent, generally were substituted for personal services. The right of relief on intestate succession still was reserved to the lord. The power of distress remained to enforce the few shadowy remnants of the old feudal incidents. In essence, land held by tenure in England was held under much the same conditions as that owned in the United States in later centuries. Free and common socage tenure was the dominant tenure, although copyholds were still numerous and were unaffected by the 1660 statute.

In the struggle to adjust tenures in England those close to the top of the feudal hierarchy found progress much easier than those on the lower rungs of the ladder. For example, tenants by knight service changed their uncertain services into certain payments at an early date. On the other hand, tenants in villeinage had to go through the long, slow, tedious process of the customs of the manor. They found it much easier to obtain security and certainty than to diminish or ease the burdensome charges upon the land. Again, as progress was being made, knight-service tenants obtained the very coveted permission to change their burdensome tenure into free and common socage as early as 1660. But copyholders had to wait until 1922 before they reached this objective. Adjustments have followed a similar pattern in the United States. Easy credit was made available through government action for owner operation over three decades ago, and improvements have been made from time to time. Meanwhile, many share-croppers still are saddled with interest charges of twenty or more per cent per annum. Again, federal and state moratoria and debt adjustment programs have tried to ease the impact of the recent economic dislocation upon owner operators, but tenant farmers, share-croppers, and wage laborers have been left to shift largely for themselves.

Social evolution lags in adapting the system under which land is held and used to the requirements of advancing agricultural techniques. Social processes seem to operate much slower than technical processes. Slow-to-change tenure arrangements often hold up technological progress. In the United States customary crop-share rentals have delayed needed adjustments in land use and farm organization, and the same arrangements are now making the introduction of livestock in the South both slow and costly.

A constant effort was made throughout feudal England to adapt tenure relations to contemporary requirements. But once an adjustment was made it tended to outlive its usefulness. The practices of primogeniture and entails remained in England, and even were brought to America, long after their need and justification had disappeared. The same can be said for many of the burdensome feudal incidents that remained until 1660.

CHAPTER 4

Conflicting Claims to the Land of the New World

EUROPEAN SOVEREIGNS CLAIMED OWNERSHIP RIGHTS to land in the New World chiefly by discovery and settlement. Relations among several European countries as to newly discovered territory were outlined partially in mutual understandings. These countries generally tried to follow their loose agreements by not encroaching upon territory claimed by other sovereigns. Discovery was the basis of claim to a new territory. But in the last analysis, land in the New World was held by the sword. As a consequence, actual settlement was most important, for it formed an effective basis for military might. The overlapping claims of various European sovereigns, therefore, resulted in armed conflict in more than one case.

On the other hand, the New World already was inhabited by numerous Indian tribes. These tribes claimed certain rights in the native plant and animal life upon which they depended for a living. The Indians based their rights upon occupancy, which was to them a more substantial claim than right of discovery.

Six European nations were involved in territorial claims to the New World by virtue of discovery. They were Portugal, Spain, France, Netherlands, Sweden, and England. The role played by the Portuguese was short-lived, and mainly was concerned with early disputes with Spain. Settlements were established by both Spain and France in the territory that is now the United States. Their relations to the English settlements were of some consequence, but owing to geographic location they were not crucial. The Dutch and Swedes, on the other hand, made substantial settlements along the Hudson and

Delaware rivers. Claims based upon these resulted in the most serious conflicts, because New Netherland and Delaware were located between the English colonies. Since the Spanish and French did not settle in the thirteen original colonies, the colonial land tenure system was not influenced directly by the systems of landholding in these countries. Although the English drove the Dutch and Swedish sovereigns from the eastern seaboard at an early date, their settlers remained and the Dutch land system left its imprint in New York.

CONFLICTING CLAIMS OF SOVEREIGNS

As flimsy as right of discovery may seem when looking back upon the situation, European sovereigns had to have some doctrine upon which to rest rights of ownership and possession. Perhaps right of discovery was as good a theory as could have been found at that early stage in the development of civilization.

Spain and Portugal tried to get their tenuous claims confirmed by proclamations from the pope. But a recognition of the various bulls of Pope Alexander and the other popes carried no conviction with sovereigns who did not submit to papal authority. Right of discovery, however, was merely an empty shell, for it could be maintained only by military might, which likely would fall to the countries that would plant permanent settlements in the New World.

Each European nation obtained by right of discovery a good and sufficient title. This doctrine was well established by the time of Columbus' first voyage. In case no other nation asserted a counterclaim, the doctrine of right of discovery seemed acceptable among various European sovereigns. As to uninhabited land, no one was involved except the sovereign or sovereigns who wanted to add the newly found territory to their realms.

In many of the later charters acquisition of territory by discovery was confined to lands uninhabited by a Christian prince and people. In short, un-Christian and unoccupied came to have the same meaning in this setting. It was reasoned that uncivilized heathens could have no superior right to occupy the Lord's holy earth, regardless of how long they had lived in a particular place. A Christian nation could move in at any time and occupy space needed by its own people. In addition, it was held that such occupancy was essential to the process of bringing heathens into the saving knowledge of the new religion, which was born out of the then teeming Reformation.

The arguments used in a brief report on this situation in Virginia within a few years after Jamestown was settled included both of these viewpoints. The report said, in part: ". . . it is not unlawfull, that wee possesse part of their land and dwell with them, and defend our selues from them. Partlie because there is no other, moderate, and mixt course, to bring them to conversion, but by dailie conversation, where they may see the life, and learne the language each of other."

It also was held that if, according to the book of David, ". . . it were a just cause to warre against the Ammonites, it is lawfull, in us, to secure our selues, against the infidels." Then the justification turned to secular matters. It was contended, ". . .there is roome sufficient in the land . . . for them, and us: the extent of an hundred miles, being scarce peopled with 2000 inhabitants;" and, in addition, the land either had been sold to the company for copper or given to its representatives by the Indian chief. These were the types of arguments used by early settlement agencies to convince themselves and possibly political leaders in the mother country that intruding on the Indians and ousting them from their ancient domain was justified economically, legally, and spiritually. (*Force. Tracts, III, No. 1, 5–7.*)

The Spanish claim was based upon a donation from the pope. An indication of how the pope had acquired the right to make the donation is entirely absent. It was assumed, by those sovereigns whom it suited, that the pope was an umpire among the nations of the so-called Christian world. The English claim at first was based upon the right of discovery, but later upon occupancy and acquisition of title from the Indians. The Swedes could not rest their case upon either donation or discovery, so they decided to contend that the Indians were the rightful owners of the land, which of course was true. Thus, the Swedes held that rights to the land of the New World could be acquired only by three methods – conquest, gift, or purchase. The Dutch, fifteen years earlier (1623), already had proceeded with the same idea in mind, knowing that sooner or later they would have disputes with the English or Spanish over landownership and sovereignty. Since the Swedes and Dutch were colonizing under similar circumstances and took the same point of view, they found it easy at first to recognize each other's rights – rights which were based upon deeds of transfer from the Indians and substantiated by grants from their respective Crowns.

The English argued that the right of discovery made the whole of North America an English protectorate, and that all rights in land were vested in the Crown. They held that rights in the land could be acquired only through grants from the Crown. Even the Indians could obtain rights in land only through British grants, and as a consequence the Indians could not give to anyone a title that would be recognized by the English Crown. In the last analysis this untenable position could be settled only by the sword. After compromising the matter through formal treaties, even as Henry Clay two hundred years later compromised the slavery issue, the Dutch drove out the Swedes in 1654 and ten years later the English subdued the Dutch.

Conflicting claims among European sovereigns will be considered in more detail when the rights and privileges contained in the various colonial charters are presented. But two situations should be dealt with briefly at this point: first, conflicts of the English with the French, who settled north of the thirteen colonies, and with the Spanish, who settled to the south; and second, conflicts of the English with the Dutch and Swedes, who occupied land lying within the area settled by the English. It appears that the conflicts among the French, Dutch, Swedes, and Spanish were inconsequential.

The ruthless way in which the Spanish treated the French Huguenots, who had settled in Florida, was important. The English felt keenly the need for protection against the Spanish colony in Florida as settlement moved down the seaboard from Virginia. They had much at stake in establishing a "buffer state" against the Spanish. This was so important that Georgia, established for frontier protection, was the only colony that used public funds to get established. Also, the Georgia settlers were given favorable tenures under their charter, and liberal adjustments in tenure relations were easily obtained as the colony grew. The desire of the British Crown for protection against the Spanish was influential in securing easy tenures for the Georgia colonists in spite of other forces pushing in the opposite direction.

During the early days the French and English did not have serious territorial difficulties. The French were interested chiefly in trade, and did not require much land for their trading posts. In addition, the French settled outside the area desired by the English. But the settlements of the two nations were destined to grow until difficulties arose. The French settlements on the St. Lawrence and Mississippi rivers needed to be related, economically and politically, for their mutual protection and growth. The Ohio River territory was the natural link between them in days when transportation by water was important. The English also desired the Ohio region, for it was in that direction that their colonies were growing. The English had followed for years the plan of protecting their western frontiers against the French by special grants to settlers who would move to strategic points. However, the French and Indian wars, ending with the Treaty of Paris in 1763, had to be fought to settle the overlapping claims. The peace gave the English complete freedom to the territory west of the mountains, and expansion in that direction was assured.

The chief impact of this situation upon tenures in the English colonies came through the special privilege granted to those who would equip themselves for military duty and occupy land on the frontier. This was a liberalizing influence of considerable importance. The relations among the French and English settlers were not concerned with land tenure and were so remote that the French did not affect English tenures. The conflict in America between the French and English governments, although concerned chiefly with territory, probably had little direct influence upon the evolving tenure system in the English colonies. Those who fought in the war must have felt that they had some claim upon the land west of the mountains and that it should be free to those who would settle it, particularly to those who fought for it. Coming as it did just before the Revolution, the French and Indian War doubtless had a unifying force upon the colonies.

Although the Dutch and Swedish sovereigns were driven out of America before settlement had progressed far, the grants that had been made, particularly by the Dutch, remained a part of the picture. The number of Swedes who settled along the Delaware was not great, and not all of them remained when the Dutch assumed sovereignty over their territory. Settlement under Dutch grants was more extensive, and some of the Dutch grants were made to Englishmen who were dissatisfied with conditions in the English colonies. The relation of settlements made under authority granted by the Dutch and the evolving tenure system was close and important. It grew out of the kinds of rights given the settlers rather than overlapping claims of the English and Dutch.

RIGHTS OF INDIAN TRIBES

Definite information regarding the land tenure concepts of the Indians is meager. Existing fragmentary information, however, plus the manner in which the early colonists dealt with the Indians, furnish some clues as to prevalent tenure practices among the Indians when white men first began to settle on the eastern seaboard.

The Indians in early times conceived the earth as "mother," and in this sacred role she supplied food for her children. They merely gathered the fruits, berries, grains, and herbs and killed the game. These things belonged to whoever would take them. This concept apparently existed as long as the Indians depended upon the spontaneous bounties of nature. As cultivation of crops became necessary, a gradual transition in land relations occurred.

The growth of a secular relation to the soil replaced the earlier religious or sacred sense with which the Indians regarded the earth. The earlier sacred concept was in keeping with their dependence upon the bounteousness of the earth. Their later concepts grew out of the necessity to cultivate the soil, to remain upon the land they cultivated, and to exclude others from it. Thus, they merely adjusted their concepts to the economics of their new method of gaining a livelihood.

During the hunting and fishing era, each individual within the clan or tribe had as good a right to the land as another. Even the various tribes generally assumed the right to hunt and fish where they pleased, although occasional conflicts broke out when a "foreign" people encroached upon the territory generally hunted by local tribes. Apparently the idea of right of ownership of, or title to, land did not exist, although there was a germ of pseudoright of occupancy. But even this was in tribal or communal sense, and was not individual or private occupancy as we think of it today.

The right of occupancy became well established only after cultivation made continued occupancy necessary. Among many of the tribes this right remained largely one pertaining to the entire group. In other tribes, when an individual cleared a piece of land and grew crops upon it, the right of occupancy and use was clearly recognized, even though the land was thought of as belonging to the clan or tribe.

It was during this period that other rights in land began to emerge. At the death of the individual, for example, the land could be taken over and cultivated by any member of the clan. Close relatives, however, were generally given preference. These relatives usually had to be of the same clan. Thus, the wife of the deceased was excluded from "inheriting" land, since she was usually of another clan. (*Hodge. Handbook of Amer. Indians, pt. I, 756–57.*) On the other hand, the wife or favorite child quite frequently "inherited" the wigwam and other personal property not buried with the deceased. The beginning of the concept of succession through inheritance was emerging, and a distinction between real and personal property was taking form.

Whether the Indians had fully matured concepts of landownership or title before their contacts with the colonists is a moot question. It appears that land was not commonly transferred through sale or gift, either between tribes or individuals. The right of occupancy, however, was strong and became stronger as expanding settlement by the whites began to drive the Indians out of the territory that they usually occupied. Some writers hold that during the time of colonization each tribe had absolute title to and sovereignty over the section of the country that it occupied and that such rights were recognized by other tribes. The various practices followed by settlement agencies and individual settlers indicate this was true. The Indians' concepts of rights in land were based chiefly upon principles related to occupancy. Because the right of occupancy is one of the fundamental rights of ownership, it may be argued that the Indians had an idea of ownership and a recognition of title. But this right of title was basically communal in many tribes. Many of the Indians held their territory as tenants in common. Paraphrasing a decision on the situation, tribal property was somewhat analogous to corporate property. Every member of the tribe was an "owner." His ownership, however, was not obtained as a purchaser, a patentee, or an heir. He had nothing he could sell, and if he left the tribal territory permanently he lost his rights. Yet he had a right in the land, a right that he could enjoy and one that his children after him could enjoy, not as heirs but as communal owners. (Adapted from *Cherokee Nation v. Journeycoke, 155 U. S. 196* [*1894*].)

Imposition of the death penalty for theft of maize, which was practiced among the Indians, is an indication of an ownership idea of things produced upon the soil. (*Spelman. Relation of Va., cx and cxi.*) In addition to the ownership of chattels, a concept of private occupancy rights in certain land seems to have developed. John Smith held that each family knew its own fields and gardens. It seems clear, however, that there was little concern over the taking up of outlying plots of land for cultivation. Unoccupied and uncultivated land was so extensive that no question of exclusion arose. (*Smith. Works, I, 66.*) MacLeod wrote that among the large agricultural tribes from the St. Lawrence River to the Chesapeake Bay, private ownership of land was known to exist. This was shown, he contended, by the severe rationing of hunting land, and the revocable reciprocity agreements among adjoining owners. These reciprocal agreements, under which use and occupancy shifted among persons, caused many early casual observers to conclude that land was held communally. The system of government and the organization of people upon the land were similar in many respects to the early feudal system in England. At the top of the Indian hierarchy were the civil chiefs, who held their rights hereditarily. Under them were bourgeois groups, who had acquired considerable wealth. Below these groups were the poor commoners, governed by the aristocrats and exploited by the bourgeois. In the lowest levels of society were the slaves. (*MacLeod. Amer. Ind., 18–19.*)

The chief, as ruler of the tribe, apparently acted as proprietor of the land. An annual tribute was paid to him in the form of maize, beasts, fish, fowl, hides, furs, copper, and beads. It is not at all clear, however, whether this tribute was paid to the chief as proprietor of the land as a tax or as rent, or whether it was paid to him as ruler of the tribe for personal services rendered in his capacity as chief. The weight of the evidence appears on the side of the latter.

Although private claims to allotted parcels of land were recognized, there is no indication that one Indian transferred land to another Indian in perpetuity through sale, or that land was transferred between tribes on a barter and sale basis. Transfers through gift were not observed. Neither were there indications of a system of tenancy, with the numerous rules regulating the landlord and tenant. Easements were unknown. The Indians probably never mortgaged their land, and thus were not forced to develop principles and rules governing the relationship between mortgagor and mortgagee. Furthermore, such items in our modern tenure system as trespass, squatter's rights, reversions, waste, ejectment, detainer action, bankruptcy, eminent domain, police power, and escheat (in the modern sense) were not parts of the Indians' economic, social, and political system.

CONFLICTING CLAIMS

When the English first came to America they found a vast continent occupied by uncivilized tribes of Indians, sometimes loosely associated together as nations or kingdoms. These tribes claimed exclusive possession and occupancy of the territory within their respective limits. They considered themselves sovereign proprietors of the land, whether cultivated or not, as they believed exclusive use gave them exclusive right to the soil. This claim was substantiated by generations of occupancy and the development of a few rather sophisticated practices of tribal and private ownership of land. Difficulties among individual Indians as to rights in land and produce from land were settled by the great lawgivers selected from among their own people. Intertribal problems were settled on an intertribal level, by war if necessary.

Then along came explorers, discoverers, adventurers, and finally settlers from civilized and Christianized England and Continental Europe. These people claimed rights in the land for themselves and their rulers by the well-recognized doctrine of discovery. Right of discovery, however, was maintained only by actual occupancy and settlement, and conflicting claims among various sovereigns were resolved by military force. Insofar as the original thirteen colonies were concerned, the English soon proved to be the best colonizers and held the superior military strength. So ultimately the perennial conflict in claims to land on the eastern seaboard was in essence between the English and the Indians.

Regardless of the doctrine of right of discovery, the settlers who were confronted with the practical problem of establishing themselves on a strange soil had to devise ways to quiet the Indians' claims to the land. Many of these practices indicate clearly that the settlers felt the land belonged to the Indians. Both the theory regarding right of discovery and the plans for missionary activities were of little consequence in actual practice. The great disregard of the civilizing and Christianizing mission of the English is a clue to their basic position. Apparently they never meant to carry out a religious and educational program among the Indians. Even if one would concede some sincerity of purpose, it appears that their pronouncements did not carry conviction. The doctrine of right of discovery also was disregarded by the English as soon as convenience showed an advantage. The doctrine was at fault in theory and a farce in practice.

When William the Conqueror invaded England he found the land occupied by a people with very definite principles and practices regarding land use and occupancy. William and his descendants proceeded to build upon the indigenous tenures, and within a century or more they established the feudal scheme of land and government.

The native population was used effectively in this process. In America the procedure was much different, although the Indians had relatively well-developed ideas of land tenure. The Indians were driven from their ancient seats by devious means, and their system of tenure went with them. It is improbable that any trace of Indian tenure, either in theory or practice, can be found among the adjustments made in English tenures during the Colonial era. It is improbable that any trace of Indian tenure can be found in the new principles outlined in the system of land tenure that emerged following the Revolution. It is improbable that Indian tenure per se had any influence upon the colonial mind in regard to tenure arrangements. This does not mean, however, that the quieting of the Indians' claims to the land did not influence the land tenure system and national land policy.

CHAPTER 5

Nature of Colonial Grants of Land and Government

RIGHTS IN THE LAND of the thirteen original colonies were granted by the English, Dutch, and Swedish sovereigns to numerous trade-monopoly and land-settlement agencies. These agencies usually received also, as a part of their chartered privileges, rights to govern the territory included in their grants. The control of land and powers of government outlined in these grants ranged from very limited to quite extensive rights and privileges. It is necessary, however, to study selected provisions of the several charters in order to understand the nature of these unusual rights and the differences that existed.

NATURE OF CHARTERS

The extensive privileges regarding land and government granted to the settlement agencies were based upon the experience of several centuries of charter-making for the promotion of trade and commerce. In fact, charters had been used by the Crown for many purposes, both in England and on the Continent, prior to the first Virginia charter under which settlement was established at Jamestown.

At first the term charter applied to the piece of parchment upon which it was written. It was introduced into England by church groups for the purpose of formalizing in writing grants of various privileges from the Crown and feudal lords. Later, the term gradually came to signify the instrument itself, and not the material upon which it was written. The Magna Carta and the Charter of Pardons, for example, referred to the granting or recognition on the part of the Crown of basic human rights that were guaranteed to the population as outlined in the written documents.

Another type of charter is represented by the privileges granted the Bishop of Durham. It gave him complete governmental jurisdiction over, and full rights in, the land of the bishopric. Charters issued to commercial and colonizing companies just prior to and immediately following the first settlement in America were chiefly for the purpose of regulating trade, usually through extensive grants of monopolistic power. These differed from the palatine charters chiefly by their regulations of commerce and internal organization. The landed rights and governmental jurisdictions granted to the Bishop of Durham were held by one individual, while the charters for the promotion of trade and colonization generally created two types of corporate organizations — the regulated company and the joint-stock company. The regulated company grew out of the earlier trade guilds, being formed chiefly to meet the larger problems of foreign trade. "Under it, each member paid a fee and traded on his own account and on his own liability; but, along with his fellow members, he enjoyed an exclusive right of trading in certain districts." (*Haney. Bus. Org., 102.*) This type of business organization was replaced, however, by the joint-stock company, which was closer akin to our present-day corporation. Under such organizations as the London and Plymouth Companies, the contributors formed a temporary joint-stock organization. Each company was operated as a unit and the members participated in proportion to the amount of their subscription. The transition from the regulated to the joint-stock system was gradual.

An intermediate joint-stock type of organization not frequently used should be mentioned, for it was the connecting link in this development. The joint-stock of the intermediate type was not permanent, but a separate stock was subscribed for each venture. During their early history, the Muscovy and East India Companies were of this type.

In addition, many settlement activities were undertaken by groups of people voluntarily associated together, but without a formal charter. Such were Weston and associates, who helped the Pilgrims to emigrate to America. Many of the New England towns were settled by voluntary associations such as the Dorchester Associates. Voluntary associations or companies also played a role in the settlement of the frontier, particularly the wild country in and beyond the mountains. Some of these associations had definite and full articles of agreement but the associates apparently preferred to take certain risks rather than pay the heavy fee for a charter or be officially incorporated.

PRESETTLEMENT CHARTERS

One of the earliest regulated companies was the celebrated Merchants of the Staple, which dated back to the thirteenth century. Some of the early joint-stock companies formed in England were the Muscovy Company, chartered in 1555 for Baltic trade, and the East

India Company, chartered in 1600. The first two were organized specifically for the extension and promotion of trade. The East India Company was established not only for trade but for discovery. (*Va. Co. Rec., I, 13.*)

An interesting change was proposed regarding the Muscovy Company in 1583 when a committee of the company drew up a set of resolutions that sought to modify its purpose to include colonization as well as trade among its powers. Explorations and attempts at colonization were to be made in America. The proposal was similar in many respects to the plan later set up in the Virginia charter of 1606. It provided for a joint-stock organization consisting of two groups, adventurers and enterprisers. The land was to be divided among the members of both groups while the trade belonged exclusively to the adventurers. According to the proposal the land would be held in socage tenure, as of the manor of East Greenwich in the County of Kent. The company proposed to send forth 100 men for one year; it provided £4,000 for this costly venture. (*Ibid., 13–14.*) This plan was never effectively put into practice, but its influence was felt when the Virginia charter was drawn up. Many of the foremost leaders in the Virginia enterprise already had been associated with trading companies that made exploratory and commercial expeditions during the late sixteenth century. These men lent their influence in outlining the principles upon which the London Company was to operate.

Each venture at colonization before 1606 had been the responsibility of one man who brought together a small group to assist him. Such ventures were those of the Cabots, Gilbert, Raleigh, and that of Sir John Popham, Chief Justice of the Court of King's Bench, who endeavored to establish a trading post at the mouth of the Kennebec River. The failure of these early settlement expeditions in the New World, however, showed that the task of colonization and the development of trade was beyond the resources of a single person or a small group of men.

The early grants to the colonial trading and colonizing companies were similar to those granted by the Crown for drainage and irrigation schemes in England. The promoters of such hazardous undertakings wanted to hold the reclaimed land on as free and easy tenurial terms as possible. Since they were increasing the king's depleted domains by these endeavors, they usually got what they wanted. The freer tenures granted the drainage and irrigation companies, unlike the more feudal tenures granted the Cabots, Raleigh, and Gilbert, were the immediate progenitors of the tenures granted those who eventually colonized the new continent.

POWER TO GOVERN AND RIGHTS IN LAND

In consideration of the influence of the original charters upon the land tenure system, it is necessary to consider two conditions: (1) the governmental structure, particularly insofar as it might impinge upon evolving tenure relations; and (2) certain characteristics of the settlement agencies and the nature of their rights in land. The first is important, for the tenure-related responsibilities of government are to interpret the law governing the tenure relationship, to adjust tenures from time to time as changing conditions make such adjustments advisable, and to put into effective operation such land tenure policies and programs as will expedite the attainment of specified objectives. The characteristics of the settlement agencies and their rights in land have distinct and direct influences upon how the land is conveyed to the first settlers.

Before exploring the power-to-govern and the rights-in-land aspects of the colonial charters, a third dimension of the total situation should be mentioned. It is this: All aspects of governmental jurisdiction and landed rights are related to space marked out upon the earth's surface, whether described definitively or vaguely. This is so simple that it is frequently either overlooked entirely or its importance is grossly underestimated. Territorial demarcation — the space concept — is the most distinctive feature of both rights in land and governmental control.

In Colonial United States the original grantees had the power to determine, within bounds, the type of tenure under which the first settlers would hold their land and the amount of land to which these rights would attach. To government was left the responsibility of making adjustments in the original kind of tenure under which the land was occupied, used, and transferred. This simple pattern was followed as settlement pushed across the mountains into the prairies and finally to the Pacific coast. The federal government, as the settlement agency, determined the kind of tenure and the quantity of land that would be granted to each type of settler, while the state governments made adjustments in original tenures from time to time. The same was partially true during the Colonial period; the settlement agencies made the decisions regarding the first grants of land, while the local assemblies made such adjustments in original tenure as they thought advisable, and as their powers permitted. The major divergence in the parallelism was the weak position of the early local assemblies as contrasted with the later state governments.

Colonial Governmental Jurisdiction

From the standpoint of governmental or political control over the immediate development of the land tenure system, the thirteen original colonies may be conveniently divided into three classes. These classes are based largely upon the type of control provided for in the basic charters and other fundamental documents. Owing to the sporadic and often spasmodic shifts in political control, each colony may be classified as to its situation at any time during the Colonial era or, as is frequently done, at the time when the Colonial Revolutionists declared themselves free and independent.

The three classes are: (a) royal, (b) proprietary, and (c) corporate. This classification follows the broad principles laid down by Blackstone (*Blackstone Commentaries, I, 96–97.*) wherever he speaks of provincial, proprietary, and chartered governmental establishments. However, Osgood (*Osgood. Col. Gov., 259–77.*) uses only two classes, provincial and corporate, holding correctly that for purposes of government the proprietors and the Crown occupied essentially the same relation to the colony, and that Blackstone's chartered colonies should be called corporate colonies, for all of the colonies were originally settled under some type of charter, and consequently the use of the term "chartered" is confusing.

The seven colonies under royal rule at the time of the Revolution were New Hampshire, New York, New Jersey, Virginia, North Carolina, South Carolina, and Georgia. The three colonies controlled by proprietors were Pennsylvania, Delaware, and Maryland, while Massachusetts, Rhode Island, and Connecticut were the three colonies whose government was corporate. This classification describes the situation in 1776 rather accurately, except for Massachusetts. However, the wide governmental powers granted to the inhabitants of the Bay State, and their long experience in self-government under their original charters, indicate that Massachusetts was much more like the corporate than the royal colonies following 1691.

The administration of the royal colonies, sometimes referred to as provincial colonies, was under the exclusive control of the king and entirely subject to his pleasure. In fact, the whole governmental structure was under his authority, for the royal colonies had no written constitutions under which they were governed, although many of them endeavored to go back to their original charters when questions of civil jurisdiction arose. The administration of governmental powers that influenced the evolving land tenure system depended entirely upon the orders, instructions, and commissions issued from time to time by the Crown to its official representatives in America, and the right of final veto regarding any enactments of the general assemblies.

In general, the governmental structure was similar for all royal colonies. The king appointed a governor to represent him and a council to assist the governor and serve as the upper house of the colonial assembly. Since the appointive power was vested in the king, both the governor and the council served at his pleasure. The governor usually had broad executive powers, including the right of veto upon all proceedings of the general assembly, the right to prorogue or dissolve it, and the right to appoint judges, magistrates, and other provincial officers. The freemen participated in the government through duly elected representatives, who composed the lower house of the general assembly. All local laws enacted by the assembly were not to be repugnant to the laws of England, "as near as might be convenient."

The proprietary governments were established under charters that granted powers of government from the Crown to one or more persons as proprietary or proprietaries. The proprietary possessed almost the same authority that the Crown maintained over the royal colonies. However, proprietors Baltimore and Penn had more rights in the establishment of tenures in their colonies than the king had regarding the land of England. The other exception was that the proprietary owed allegiance to the king as paramount sovereign, whereas the king as overlord owed allegiance to no one. The proprietary or proprietaries invariably provided for assemblies to be selected from the freemen of their colony, but maintained with few exceptions exclusive executive prerogatives, appointed judicial officers, and convened or dismissed the assemblies at will.

The corporate colonies were in reality great political corporations created by the Crown with full right to the soil and with extensive powers of government. Their charters provided for all branches of government, and safeguarded the inherent privileges and rights of a free people. The powers of each great department of government — legislative, executive, and judiciary — were defined in the charters, frequently in detail.

In all the colonies, whether royal, proprietary, or corporate, the common law of England was to govern, at least in theory, in the event no instruction or statutory enactment covered the situation. The inhabitants were to be subjects of the Crown and to enjoy all of the rights and privileges of Englishmen, which they always asserted to be their birthright and rightful inheritance.

The corporate colonies had practically the same freedoms and exemptions from arbitrary external power during the Colonial period as they did following the Revolution. In fact, Connecticut and Rhode Island continued to be governed under their Colonial charters until 1818 and 1842, respectively, when they adopted their first state constitutions. The proprietary colonies were subject to the will of the proprietors, except insofar as their liberties were safeguarded by the charters, which in the case of some colonies was very slight — Maryland for example. The royal colonies, likewise, were subject to the rule of one man — the king. These variations in the power to govern and to adjust tenures had an influence upon the evolving tenure system and the specific position in regard to land taken by the new states at the time of the emergence of the national system of land tenure.

Not one of the thirteen original colonies was settled by the Crown. As a consequence, all of their governments originally were either corporate or proprietary in nature. The three Puritan colonies were settled by chartered corporations, while the early governments of the other ten colonies were strictly proprietary, except perhaps for New York and Virginia. Three of the original proprietary colonies retained their proprietary control, except for brief periods, up to the Revolution. Royal control was substituted for proprietary rule in seven colonies.

From the viewpoint of political control and its possible influence upon tenure, the Virginia colony was unique throughout its entire history. Under the various charters of Virginia the chief governing body was a council established in England. Never once did the seat of governmental authority reside in America. During the life of the Virginia Company the colonists were permitted a local council and in later years a general assembly—the first representative assembly in America convened in Virginia in the summer of 1619. But actual control and final authority resided in a council of thirteen officed in England, originally appointed by the king.[1] After dissolution of the company in 1621, Virginia remained a royal colony until the Revolution. Thus, under the trading-company charters and later under the Crown, Virginia was essentially a royal colony. The governmental situation in New York was almost identical except for the two decades of proprietary rule after the English supplanted the Dutch trading company. New York automatically became a royal colony when the proprietor, the Duke of York, became king. New Jersey followed the New York pattern, with two exceptions. Proprietary rule was much longer, lasting essentially from 1664 to 1702, and the proprietary government was in the control of private parties, not the royal family.

New Hampshire was brought under royal rule in 1679, when the Mason family found that the venture could not be made financially successful. North Carolina came under royal rule in 1729, when the Crown bought the rights of seven of the eight proprietors, whereas royal rule in South Carolina began ten years earlier, when the colonists revolted and overthrew the proprietors' government. According to the original plan, the Georgia trustees would surrender their charter within twenty-one years. This they did, and Georgia became a royal colony approximately midway between the time of its establishment and the War of Independence.

All of the colonies, including even the corporate and proprietary groups, were subject to royal governors at one time or another before the Revolution. Even in Maryland, where the proprietary enjoyed the most extensive political rights of any American settlement agency, governmental powers were taken from Lord Baltimore in 1652, under

[1] Strictly speaking, the Crown controlled the government under the first Virginia charter, for the king appointed the council; while under the second and third charters the company had more effective control over the local government, for new members of the council were to be selected by the company.

the impact of the Puritan Revolution, but were restored five years later when Cromwell came to Cecil Calvert's aid. Again, in 1691, the Baltimores were deprived of their governmental powers. This time various excuses were given, the most important of which were the 1688 uprising in Maryland and the failure of Baltimore to send expeditiously his oath of allegiance and fidelity to the new king and queen of the House of Orange, William and Mary (1689–1702). Full proprietary rights were restored to the new Lord Baltimore in 1715, after he declared his allegiance to the Anglican church. William Penn lost political control over his vast domain, including both Pennsylvania and Delaware, in 1692, but his power to govern was restored two years later. Except for these interruptions, the Penns and Baltimores exercised governmental control over their colonies from their earliest charters to the Revolution.

The three corporate colonies – Massachusetts, Rhode Island, and Connecticut – were controlled ineffectively by royal rule during the infamous Andros regime from 1686 until 1689, when Andros finally was jailed. Connecticut and Rhode Island immediately reasserted their right to self-government and returned to the protection of their chartered privileges. Massachusetts did likewise but in 1691 finally submitted to a new charter, which provided for a modified form of royal rule. The latter colony's government remained under this charter until the Revolution. However, the governmental structure of the six corporate and proprietary colonies was little influenced under the temporary rule of provincial governors.

It would be inaccurate, however, to leave the impression that these experiences had no influence upon the colonial mind. Certainly the colonists in the corporate colonies were made to cherish more ardently the freedom that had been built up over a period of time and that came tumbling down with a stroke of the king's pen. Likewise, the proprietors must have been influenced to guard more jealously their political rights and to endeavor more earnestly to keep, insofar as reasonably possible, their colonists loyal to the proprietary.

SETTLEMENT AGENCIES' RIGHTS IN LAND

In general, rights in the soil followed the same pattern of classification as the power to govern. It should not be presumed, however, that ownership of land and governmental control always resided in the same hands in Colonial America, although such was usually the case.

In the royal colonies, ownership of the land and its distribution to occupying settlers was, in general, the responsibility of the Crown and proceeded according to royal instructions, concessions, and agreements sent to royal governors. In the colonies where ownership of the land resided in the proprietary, the proprietors sent instructions to their proprietary governors regarding land distribution. In the corporate colonies the people, through duly elected representatives, actually "owned" the land and controlled completely its distribution to the first settlers.

A shift in ownership from the colony was never conceded in any of the three corporate colonies, even during the royal rule of Andros; neither did Massachusetts relinquish its landed rights under the 1691 charter. Likewise, the three proprietary colonies maintained their rights in the soil down to the time of the Revolution, even during the brief periods when their governmental rights were cancelled. Thus, as to ownership rights in their land, six of the thirteen colonies are easily classified, and each remained in the same class throughout the Colonial era.

The situation in the other seven colonies, however, was not so clear-cut. In the early days of New York and Virginia rights in the land were divided between the Crown and the trading company. The Crown soon took over ownership of the territory of Virginia, and later the soil of Dutch New York came into the possession of the English proprietor, the Duke of York. In New Hampshire the ownership of the land shifted from the Crown, to proprietors Gorges and Mason, to Mason alone, to corporate Massachusetts Bay, and back to the Crown. The ownership of New Jersey was the same as New York, of which it was a part, until 1664 when it was transferred to two proprietors. It remained proprietary, although frequently transferred, until the Revolution. The North and South Carolina territory was originally owned by eight proprietors and later by the Crown, except Granville's part which remained proprietary until the Revolution. The land of Georgia remained in the hands of the Crown from the beginning, the Georgia trustees never acquiring ownership, although they could grant land to settlers.

LANDED RIGHTS AND GOVERNMENTAL CONTROL

Ownership of the land and final authority for determining how the land would be held privately resided in the people in the corporate classification; in the proprietors in the proprietary classification; and in the Crown in the royal classification. It should be noted that these classes are not separated distinctly by vast difference; rather they occasionally blend into one another in a twilight zone that makes identification difficult. The majority of the situations, however, fall into one class or another with sufficient clarity to make the classification useful for descriptive and analytical purposes.

The theoretical possibilities of this scheme of classifying two social phenomena would permit nine distinct classes. Actually the thirteen original colonies are classified in only four of the possible categories, as shown in Figure 5.1. The relationship between governmental control and landed rights is easy to comprehend in all of those situations where governmental authority and rights in land resided in the same entity — whether proprietors, people, or Crown. This was true, with the minor exceptions noted above, for eight of the thirteen original colonies.

Under the three corporate charters the *people* had full authority to dispose of the land under tenures consonant with their English heritage. And the *people* established the governmental processes under which these tenures could be adjusted from time to time. In the three proprietary colonies, rights to the land and to the formation

Rights in Landed Property	Type of Political Control		
	Corporate (people)	Proprietary (proprietor)	Royal (Crown)
Royal (Crown)	8. Royal-Corporate	9. Royal-Proprietary	3. Royal-Royal New York Virginia
Proprietary (proprietor)	6. Proprietary-Corporate	2. Proprietary-Proprietary Pennsylvania Delaware Maryland	7. Proprietary-Royal New Hampshire New Jersey North Carolina South Carolina Georgia
Corporate (people)	1. Corporate-Corporate Massachusetts Rhode Island Connecticut	4. Corporate-Proprietary	5. Corporate-Royal

Figure 5.1—Classification of the thirteen original colonies as to rights in landed property and type of political control.

and control of government were placed in the hands of the proprietors. The exercise of these extensive rights were circumscribed to a limited extent in the proprietary charters. In addition, of course, the proprietors did not operate in a vacuum; they were subject to a wide variety of stimuli and pressures, not the least of which were the desires of their respective colonists. For all intents and purposes, except for the short rule under the Dutch and English trading companies, the land and the government of New York and Virginia were in the hands of the Crown from the beginning. Possible autocratic control of the Crown was mellowed by distance, the generally weak position of the Crown, and the freedom-loving spirit of the colonists.

Eight of the thirteen original colonies are classified with regard to both land ownership and government control as royal, proprietary, or corporate. The other five colonies must be classified as *composite,* for either the land and government for long periods of time did not reside in the same entity, or they changed from one class to another during the period of their colonial existence.

The five composite colonies – New Hampshire, New Jersey, North Carolina, South Carolina, and Georgia – exhibit the following types of duality, among others, as regards control of government and ownership of land: (1) The land of New Hampshire at one time was "owned" by proprietor Mason while the government was lodged in corporate Massachusetts Bay. (2) In New Jersey, where proprietors Carteret and Berkeley held the land, the government was claimed by them, by the Duke of York, and later by the Crown. (3) North Carolina was first proprietary as to both land and government, but later one-half of the colony was a proprietary-royal combination and the other half was fully royal. (4) South Carolina was at first proprietary, then a proprietary-royal hybrid, and then later fully royal. (5) At first the land of Georgia was held in a trusteeship and the trustees had the powers of government, but later the Crown took over full powers of government and maintained complete ownership of land.

It is important to observe the effect of the various types of chartered rights upon the types of tenures under which the land was granted to bona fide settlers. Another question of importance is the relation between types of government, on the one hand, and types of settlement agencies, on the other, and the types of adjustments that were made in tenure during the Colonia era. Two other items must be given consideration: First, the influence that the type of settlement agency had upon the types of tenures under which the colonists received their land. Second, the influence that the type of government had upon adjustments that were later made in the tenures under which the colonists held their land.

CHAPTER 6

Two Royal Colonies

THE TWO COLONIES CLASSIFIED AS ROYAL are Virginia and New York. In many respects they were quite similar in the early days, even though Virginia was an English settlement while New Netherland was Dutch.

The original idea and motivating force behind each of these colonies was trade and the two trading companies – the London Company and the Dutch West India Company – were organized with this in mind. As a consequence, their chartered rights were designed to be effective in commercial development, and little or no thought was given to the establishment of agricultural communities. It was proposed to settle only enough people in New Netherland to man the trading posts, and possibly to mine gold and silver. The Virginia settlement also leaned heavily toward get-rich-quick trade ideas, although the advantages of the emigration of many people were recognized.

That reliance upon trade was a major mistake is attested to by immediate adjustments to facilitate the establishment of permanent agricultural settlements. In Virginia, the trading company was given three successive charters to cure this and other ills. And in desperation the Crown revoked the last charter before two decades had passed. Development was a little slower in New Netherland, but within less than a decade the rights under the charter were expanded and interpreted for the avowed purpose of encouraging agricultural settlement.

THE THREE VIRGINIA CHARTERS

Ownership of the land included in the Virginia charters was originally claimed by Spain, but the close of the war in 1604 left England free to plant colonies in most of the Western Hemisphere. In

July, 1605, many plans for the expansion of trade and some ideas on settlement were brought forward. Congestion on the home island was an added incentive to emigration. Particularly encouraging were reports on America that Gosnold made during the last year of the reign of Queen Elizabeth. The experience gained from the attempt of Sir Richard Grenville to establish a colony at Roanoke under the auspices of Raleigh was drawn upon. In addition, King James I was personally familiar by actual participation with settlement in the Highlands of Scotland. All of these items conspired to bring about an effective attempt at colonization.

In 1606, a large group of men from such cities as London, Bristol, Exeter, and Plymouth joined together in a petition to King James I for a charter to make settlements in America. As a result of this petition, a charter was granted, authorizing establishment of two trading companies, both with headquarters in England; the London Company was to establish colonies in Southern Virginia, the Plymouth Company in Northern Virginia. (*Lucas. Charters, 1.*)

The territory granted under the charter included the land along the coast of that part of America that lies between 34° and 45° north latitude, not actually in possession of any other Christian prince or people. The London Company was allocated the land between 34° and 41° and the Plymouth Company was assigned the territory from 38° to 45°. The area granted to both companies, that is, the land between 38° and 41°, could be utilized by either company so long as settlements of the two companies were not established within 100 miles of each other (Fig. 6.1.). This is the first of a long series of grants in which different settlement agencies laid claim to the same territory.

The grant included any islands adjacent to and within 100 miles out into the sea, but no indication was given as to the distance that the grant extended inland, for the "along-the-coast" proviso was very indefinite. The only clue to the proposed pattern of settlement, and one that is more indicative of a trading-post idea than of the establishment of an agricultural community, was a provision to the effect that the colony first settled by the London Company could claim rights in the territory along the coast 50 miles to the north and 50 miles to the south and 100 miles inland, as well as the islands 100 miles to sea. Essentially this meant a domain of 100 miles square, or 10,000 square miles.

According to the charter, all land, tenements, and hereditaments of the territory assigned to each company were held by that company under the king as of the manor of East Greenwich, in the County of Kent, in free and common socage only and not in capite. The only claim the sovereign reserved, except that the land was "to be holden of us," was one-fifth part of all the gold and silver and one-fifteenth part of all copper. The company, according to English custom, could keep for itself any of the baser metals. It had the right to exclude others from the territory and to prevent trespass.

Under this charter the company did not receive full ownership rights in the land. It was to be granted to private parties by the king's council. The company did not have power to create manors or new forms of tenure, as was permitted in some of the later charters. According to the last section, the estates granted to private parties were assured to the patentees regardless of the type of estate granted,

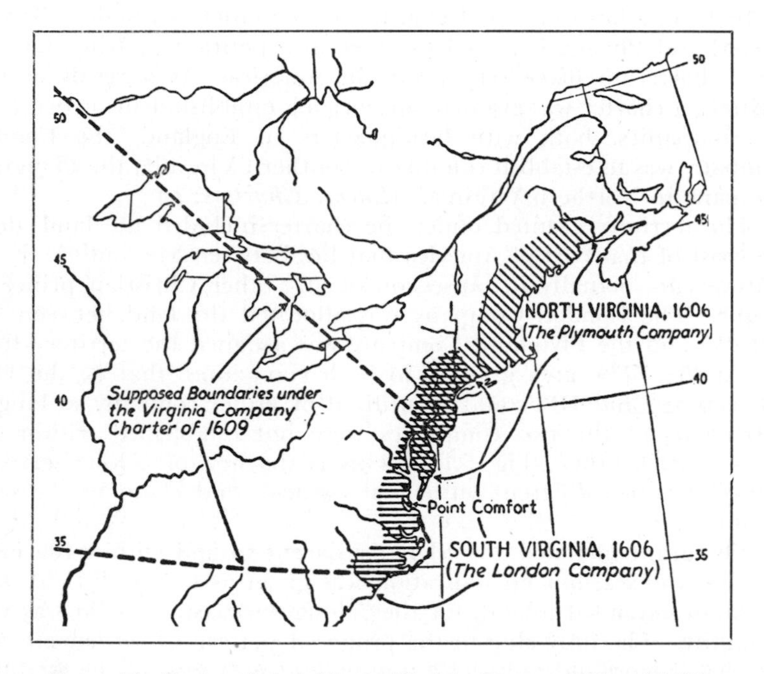

Figure 6.1—Territory included in the Virginia Charters, 1606 and 1609.

whether there was any mention or reservation as to the true yearly value of the premises, or any statute or provision to the contrary. Although this proviso was not specifically repeated in the second charter, it appears to be implied by virtue of the arrangement of the several sections in the charter and by repeated reference to the first charter.

The 1606 Virginia charter was strictly a royal charter; the government, as well as land distribution, was subject directly to royal control. The colony was to be governed by a local council, under the superior management of the Royal Council of Virginia, which resided in

England. It consisted of thirteen members appointed by the Crown to manage the affairs of the company. The local council of thirteen members governed the colony under instructions issued by the king. *(MacDonald. Charters, 5. Sections VII and VIII.)* The local council had the right to nominate the names of persons to whom lands were to be granted by the Crown. *(Va. Co. Rec., I, 19.)* It did not have the right to transfer land directly to private parties because that right resided in the king and his council.

All operational instructions also were to be issued and signed by the Crown. King James I issued his first "Instructions for the Government of the Colonies" on November 20, 1606. He outlined the form of political control over the colonists, and directed that the lands, tenements, and hereditaments were to be had, held, and inherited by English subjects according to the laws of England.

The responsibilities of raising funds, furnishing supplies, and sending out colonizing expeditions to settle in southern Virginia were left entirely to the London Company. For this purpose stock in the Company was sold. One writer says that as much as £200,000 was raised. *(Brown. Genesis, I, 51.)* The purchasers of the stock can be divided into two classes, those who remained in England and sent representatives to Virginia, and those who went in person to the New World. The first were known as adventurers and the latter as planters.

On December 20, 1606, three ships, under the command of Christopher Newport, set sail for America carrying 120 colonists and four months later, on April 26, 1607, entered Chesapeake Bay and sailed up the James River with 104 passengers who had survived the trip. Thereupon, the first permanent English settlement was made at Jamestown. Thus, the London Company based its claim to the land upon occupation and possession, under the charter granted to it by King James I of England.

The reports that the various governors sent back to England convinced the council that certain errors had been made in the charter, and that these had to be rectified. Actually, it was soon discovered that the requirements of a settlement agency were quite unlike those of a trading company. A trading company was interested in monopoly advantages in the realm of commerce; a colonizing company needed control over the land, and a simple and expeditious way of transferring it to occupying settlers. In addition, civil control in a temporary trading station, or a permanent one for that matter, was designed solely to maximize profits. On the other hand, the inhabitants of a permanent agricultural community were interested in civil rights, government under law, the political liberties of freeborn Englishmen, and free and easy land tenures.

An ordinance and constitution issued in March, 1607, alleviated the situation somewhat. The managers of the enterprise decided, however, to petition the king for a new charter with ample and enlarged privileges and powers to reform and correct errors already discovered and to prevent similar ones that might threaten in the future. *(Brown. Genesis, I, 206.)* As a result, a second charter was granted in March, 1609. This charter created a corporation called "The Treasurer and Company of Adventurers and Planters of the City of London for the first Colony in Virginia." The connection between the London and Plymouth Companies ceased, and the colony in southern Virginia became a separate body. The membership of the new corporate body was much larger than the first. It contained the names of about 650 people from about 56 cities. *(Lucas. Charters, 11.)*

The extent of land granted was considerably increased by the second charter. It included all of that central portion of the present United States which lies for 200 miles north and 200 miles south of Cape or Point Comfort, and extending from the Atlantic to the Pacific, as well as the islands lying within 100 miles of the coast of either ocean. This was roughly a million square miles as compared to ten thousand square miles in the first charter.

The tenure rights that the company held in the land were the same as in the first charter, except that the company had full power to grant land directly to settlers. This power was of tremendous importance in the establishment of agricultural communities. The tenure under which settlers were to hold their land, as implied but not specifically stated, was the same as under the first charter, any free tenure that was not contrary to English usage.

The power to govern was removed somewhat from the Crown, but the king's power was still felt, particularly in the general court of stockholders that resided in England. The officers who served in America were selected by the company and were composed of a governor and council with extensive local powers. The governors between 1610 and 1618 imposed harsh laws which were administered with iron discipline under an organization that was more military than civil, for the officers assumed military titles and the settlers were in many respects soldiers in a military outpost of the company. *(Nettels. Roots, 164.)* Four sections reduced considerably certain rights of the colonists. This was a definite abridgment of their chartered privileges, in complete disregard of the rights of those who had come to America under the earlier charter.

By a third charter, issued in 1612, the territorial bounds of the company were further increased to include all islands within 300 leagues of the continent between 30° and 41° north latitude. *(Lucas. Charters, 21.)* The company's governmental powers were extended, but tenure provisions remained relatively unchanged.

The chief reason for the company's desire for a third charter was to control the newly discovered Bermudas or Somers Islands,[1] which

[1] These islands are spelled Somers, unless in a quotation where the spelling varies.

were too far from the coast to be included in the 1609 charter. The company believed that these islands might become important to the Virginia colony as a source of food and might be used in defense against the Spanish. As funds were not sufficient to support two colonies, the company planned to form a smaller company within the larger one. So on November 25, 1612, it sold rights in the islands for £2,000 to a subsidiary joint-stock group of its own members, known as the Undertakers for the Plantation of the Sommers Islands. (*Va. Co. Rec., II, 47–48.*)

In 1614, this group surrendered the islands to the king as the preliminary step to the formation of their own joint-stock company. The Bermuda charter was issued June 29, 1615, incorporating the company under the title "The Governor and Company of the City of London for the Plantation of the Somers Islands." The territory included all the islands of the Bermuda or Somers Islands group. (*Andrews. Col. Period, I, 120.*)

As soon as the second Virginia charter had been granted, in order to encourage emigration to America, the company issued a call to all working people, male and female, who wished to go to Virginia to come to the house of Sir Thomas Smith, the treasurer of the Virginia Company, saying:

> . . . they will be entered as Adventurers in the present voyage to Virginia, where they will have houses to live in, vegetable-gardens and orchards, and also food and clothing at the expense of the Company and besides this, a share of all products and the profits that may result from their labor, each in proportion, and they will also secure a share in the division of the land for themselves and their heirs forever more. And all who would give (one hundred Philips) before the last of March will be admitted as Members of the Virginia Company and receive a proportionate share of the profits altho they do not go in person on this voyage. (*Brown. First Repub., 76–77.*)

This was the promise which later formed the basis for the granting of land in Virginia for shares in the company and for headrights.

All charges of seating and maintaining the plantation and of obtaining supplies were to be borne by the company until 1618 when the first division of land was to take place. Until then no goods were to be sold in private by either masters, mariners, or planters. The company was to supply all food, clothing, material for building houses, and fortifications. (*Force. Tracts, I, No. 6, 23–24.*) The colonists were forced to trade together in one stock, and bring not only all the fruits of their labors to the storehouses built for the purpose, but also to buy all the things they needed from the same places. (*Brown. Genesis, I, 71.*)

When it became evident that the full wealth of America lay in the productivity of its soil – that the future depended upon agricultural exploitation – the Virginia Company rapidly abandoned the trade idea. The common storehouse gave way to the individual larder, trade monopoly began to disappear, commerce was thrown open to all parties until later years when a monopoly in staples was fully operative, and individual enterprise supplanted the more communal activities of the settlers under the joint-stock trading company.

During the second decade many felons and vagabonds were sent to the Virginia colony. The level of living was exceedingly low. Discontent and indifference tended to thwart progress. Political unrest remained. So, in 1619, Sir George Yeardley reinstated full privileges of Englishmen to the colonists. The first representative assembly in America was established. Its records are not extant, but it is presumed that the action of this first assembly paved the way for the Ordinance for Virginia of 1621, which provided for the future form of government, and which was a model closely followed by later English colonies. Two councils were provided for, a council of state selected by the council in London, and a general assembly, later the House of Burgesses, selected by the inhabitants.

The assembly and plan of government survived the arbitrary dissolution of the company, which came five years later. This thread of control by the colonists over the development of their own institutions was frequently threatened by the Crown.

The charter was revoked because the Crown, among other things, desired to increase its revenues by receiving the customs on tobacco, which in 1617 were said to be as much as £4,450 annually. The mercantilistic theory of trade was dominant, and the Crown continued to press for larger gains from the tobacco trade. In the struggle the Crown assumed full control of the colony – its third charter was annulled by quo warranto proceedings only eighteen years after the first charter was granted. King James I assured the shareholders in the company that their interests in land would not be reduced in the slightest, for he intended only to change the form of government. Again, in 1625, he reassured them of his honorable intentions. The first charter was purely a royal charter, drafted by James I, and intended to keep the colony completely under royal domination. The second charter, the beginning of the popular charters, ". . . was the germ which gradually developed into a popular government (a free country) in America – the genesis of the United States." (*Brown. First Repub., 74.*) Besides granting land directly to the company, which could in turn grant the land to individuals without royal assent, the second charter left much of the governing of the colony up to the company and gave the colonists and their offspring ". . . all Liberties, Franchises, and Immunities of *free Denizens and natural subjects. . . .*" It was "To this chartered right – 'the inalienable rights of freeborn Englishmen' – our forefathers at the opening of our war for independence appealed when they again protested against the royal form of government in America." (*Ibid., 75.*)

When the charter was annulled all of the appointive powers were immediately transferred to the king. The Crown also assumed full powers to grant land to private parties, and to regulate all aspects of colonial life. It was not long until the Crown made another large grant, part of which remained of importance until the Revolution. Reference is made to the land between the Rappahannock and the Potomac rivers, which has been known as the Northern Neck since 1639. In that year, the Somers Islands Company, because of the small size of its colony, petitioned the king for that territory. (*Va. Mag. of Hist., XII, 396.*) No response appears to have been made to this petition. A few years later, however, Charles II, out of gratitude to the few who remained faithful to him during the dethroning and beheading of his father, issued letters-patent dated September 18, 1649/50 for this same piece of land. No copy of this patent could be found, but it is retold in an act of the Virginia assembly of 1736 which confirmed the land titles in the Northern Neck held under Thomas, Lord Fairfax. (*Hening. Stats., IV, 514–23.*)

Seven court favorites became the proprietors of the Northern Neck. They were to pay to the king £6 13*s.* 4*d.* as well as to reserve one-fifth of the gold and one-tenth of the silver. (*Ibid., 514–16.*) These proprietors had the right for a period of twenty-one years to divide the land into counties, hundreds, parishes, tithings, townships, hamlets, and boroughs. Also they had the right to sell or alienate the land to British subjects in any way they wished. This land was to be held by the settlers in free and common socage and not in fealty. The quitrent was to be what the proprietors thought fit. All land that escheated during this period could be regranted.

Sir Dudley Wyatt came to Virginia to look after the interests of the patentees but died in 1651 and, as the colony later was surrendered to the Parliament, no further action to take possession of it was made by the patentees at that time. (*Va. Mag. of Hist., XV, 393.*) When Charles II was restored to the throne in 1660 he renewed the grant, but the patentees were unable to establish authority in the Northern Neck because of the opposition of the Virginia government and the people who had settled there. (*W. and M. Quart., VI, 222.*)

As four of the original patentees were dead and one had sold his interest, the charter of 1649–50 was cancelled and a new one was issued. This new charter, issued on May 8, 1669, indicated that the land comprising the Northern Neck was to be held for payment of £6 13*s.* 4*d.* yearly and one-fifth of the gold and one-tenth of the silver; the land not granted, possessed, or inhabited within twenty-one years was to be returned to the Crown. (*Hening. Stats., IV, 516–19.*)

Before the settlement of title under the new charter could be put into effect, Charles II made a sweeping grant to Lords Arlington and Culpeper on February 25, 1673. This grant ignored previous grants and included not only the Northern Neck, but the whole of Virginia from the Maryland border to the Carolina border, westward to a line leading from the first spring of the Potomac River to the first spring of the Rappahannock and in a meridian to the Carolina border, together with the territory of Accomack. The king reserved one-fifth of all the gold and one-tenth of all the silver besides requiring a yearly payment of forty shillings of lawful English money. Arlington and Culpeper were given permission during a term of thirty-one years to give and grant in fee simple to any planter or planters, his or their heirs and assigns forever, any land not already granted or land that escheated or became forfeited during that term. The lords had a right to reserve for themselves a yearly rent of two shillings of lawful English money on every 100 acres of land granted. They also were given the power to confirm the grants that had already been made, as well as to divide and subdivide the region into civil units. Further, they were given permission to establish manors with proper courts, and to provide that all grants were to be registered. (*Ibid., II, 569–78.*)

In September, 1674, the general assembly of Virginia sent to King Charles II an address in which he was asked to revoke the patent he had granted to Arlington and Culpeper and to confirm the rights, privileges, liberties, immunities, and properties of the colony to its original settlers. (*Ibid., 311–14.*) The settlers feared that these lords would endeavor to make void their claims and thus cause to escheat their lands by imposing new rents, altering the form of tenure, and compelling new surveys.

Lords Arlington and Culpeper expressed their willingness to surrender the grant, when they found that the chief objection was not to the quitrent imposed by the new grantees but to the terms of the grant. (*Ibid., 519–20.*) One of the chief concessions asked by the settlers was that the quitrent be paid in tobacco at twelve shillings a hundred. (*Ibid., 520; Burk. Va., II, app. xlii.*) Later, under a new charter quitrents were to be paid in tobacco at three and one-half pence a pound, and a payment was to be made of £400 for each of the six shares of St. Albans and his associates. (*Hening. Stats., II, 521; Burk. Va., II, app. xlv.*) This was never carried out.

On September 10, 1681, Lord Arlington deeded to Lord Culpeper, for a competent sum of lawful English money, all his interest in the colony of Virginia, which had been granted to them jointly by Charles II. (*Hening. Stats., II, 578–83; W. and M. Quart., VI, 224.*) Three years later, Culpeper surrendered the whole territory included in the 1673 grant to the king for an annual pension of £600 for twenty years. (*Hening. Stats., II, 521–22; W. and M. Quart., VI, 224.*) So after eleven years had expired the whole territory of the colony of Virginia came again under the control of the Crown. This left outstanding only the Northern Neck grant.

The Northern Neck was purchased by Thomas, Lord Culpeper, from Lord St. Albans and his associates. Then on September 27, 1688, the Crown granted its third Northern Neck charter, which was issued as a royal confirmation of Lord Culpeper's purchase. It gave the land to Culpeper in fee simple, reserving one-fifth of the gold and one-tenth of the silver and an annual payment of £6 13*s.* 4*d.* to the Crown. (*Va. Mag. of Hist., XV, 392–99; Hening. Stats., IV, 519–23.*)

After Culpeper died in 1688, the land was supervised by agents who acted for the heirs. The practice of paying quitrent in the Northern Neck was continued until the Revolution. Denny Martin who inherited the title to the remaining land of the Northern Neck sold his interest to a syndicate which was financed by Robert Morris of Philadelphia for £20,000. The final deed was not made until 1796 by the last survivor of the Martin brothers. (*Harrison. Va. Land Grants, 119–20.*) By inserting in the charter of 1688 "first spring" as the definition of stream "heads," Culpeper pushed his western boundary across the Blue Ridge to the foot of the Alleghenies. Byrd reports that the holding then contained no less than 5,282,000 acres. In 1745 when the Rapidan River was declared the southern boundary and the head spring in the Conway River was fixed as the starting point, the estimated number of acres was six million. (*Va. Mag. of Hist., XIII, 115; XXVIII, 297–99; Harrison. Va. Land Grants, 77.*) In 1785, in accordance with the laws for confiscating the property of British aliens, quitrents were abolished in the Northern Neck. All lands unappropriated in 1785 were made subject to the same conditions as the other unappropriated lands in the commonwealth. (*Hening. Stats., XII, 113.*)

The early dissolution of the Virginia Company and the few grants made by the company to private parties would tend to minimize the importance of the provisions in these early charters, except for the fact that they set a pattern for future charters and that much land was granted, after 1624, for shares in the company and for headrights claimed under its operations. Also, the right of the colonists to participate through popular assemblies in the development of their own institutions was given considerable impetus by the general assembly of inhabitants provided for under the second and third charters.

It should be noted also that a significant shift was made in the second charter. Under the first Virginia charter, the king had final power in granting the land to settlers, for he reserved the right to approve land grants recommended by the council. Under the second charter and all subsequent charters, the settlement agency was given the power to make grants of land. Withdrawal by the Crown from control over who would receive grants in the land of America was a marked step forward in expediting settlement and in the development of free tenures in America.

NEW YORK UNDER DUTCH AND ENGLISH CONTROL

Like Virginia, the first permanent settlement in New York was made under the auspices of a typical seventeenth century trading company. Sovereignty over the land was claimed by the Dutch by virtue of Henry Hudson's explorations. The English also claimed ownership of the land, as is indicated in the Plymouth Company grant and subsequent grants that included it. But Dutch traders maintained a firm footing in the region, with headquarters on Manhattan Island and trading posts on the Hudson, Delaware, and Connecticut rivers, until the English assumed control over the entire area in 1664.

Dutch trading enterprise in the New World was sponsored by the United New Netherland Company, which was chartered in 1614 by the States General of Holland. The company, a "regulated company" in which each member traded individually using his own capital, was chartered for only three years. (*N. Y. Col. Hist., I, 11–12; Van Rensselaer. City of N. Y., I, 23.*) As a consequence of the restricted nature of anticipated activities, the company did not require, and did not receive, ownership rights in the land; its chartered rights merely permitted it to establish a series of trading posts in the area included in the grant. Granting of land from the company to private parties was not a part of the plan.

Trade developed slowly until 1621, when the great mercantile interests of the Netherlands secured from the States General a charter for a new trading corporation, known as the Dutch West India Company. The governing of this company was vested in five chambers or boards established in as many Dutch cities with a board of nineteen members to act as an executive committee. Again, the company was granted no landed rights, which became a source of trouble in later years. It was strictly a trading company, and as such was granted all of the powers needed in its trade activities. (*Thorpe. Charters, I, 59–67.*)

The founders of this organization hoped to promote national trade interests in the region of the western seas, as the Dutch East India Company was doing in the Indian Ocean and the Far East. The boundless territory in which the new company held trade monopoly included not only the Western Hemisphere but also the West African coast. Although extension of trade was the prime interest, it was this company that sent out the first permanent settlers, who founded New Netherland in 1623. (*Brodhead. N. Y., I, 150.*)

Continued lack of profit in trade in New Netherland, except the fur trade, led to the adoption in 1629 of the Charter of Privileges to Patroons, intended to encourage private individuals to establish settlements at various points on the Hudson and Delaware rivers. Even with this change in purpose the Board of Nineteen did not see fit to grant land to the company or outline a comprehensive plan for civil government. (*MacDonald. Charters, 43.*) The failure of the Dutch to give the corporation even nominal title to the land was a source of trouble to both the company and the States General in later years.

. . . in the subsequent difficulties with the large landowners were the latter able to twit the company upon its own insignificant ownership of land but in the disputes with the English this left a void in the Dutch claims to the province, so much so that early in 1664 the States General felt impelled to issue a declaration that this charter was not to be construed as directed only to trade, but that in the powers granted to the West India Company was implied the right to establish colonies and settlements on lands unoccupied by other nations. (*Nissenson. Patroon's Domain, 9–10.*)

The 1629 charter, issued by the Board of Nineteen, made it possible for any person of any status to plant settlements in New Netherland. This charter was a sort of grant within a grant to any person with sufficient means to establish a colony of fifty persons of fifteen years of age or older within four years of starting. It was not issued by the Crown, and as a consequence represents a different level of authority from most colonial charters. It was somewhat like the orders and instructions issued to supplement the first Virginia charter.

The charter allowed any patroon to choose his own land along the rivers, particularly the Hudson and Delaware. The land was to be held as the absolute property of the patroon. Quoting from section six of the charter, "They [the patroons] shall forever possess and enjoy all the lands . . . to the exclusion of all others, to be holden from the Company as a perpetual inheritance, without it ever devolving again to the Company. . . . " And the following sections give the patroons the ". . . liberty to dispose of their aforesaid heritage by testament." (*MacDonald. Charters, 45.*) In addition, the patroons were given the right to govern their individual colonies within the rules of government made by the Board of Nineteen.

The tenure provisions of this charter are instructive for three reasons. First, the rights in landed property assigned to the private owner conform more nearly to the ideas of fee simple ownership than other grants of that period, a result, in part, of the Dutch civil law influence. Second, the landowner (the patroon) was given extensive power of government, reminiscent of the feudal governmental prerogatives of the palatine fiefs. Third, no specific provision indicated how the land would be assigned to individual colonists, either as to the territorial size of their patents or the nature of the rights conveyed.

The combination of these three conditions made possible the development of large landed estates with subservient people to cultivate them. This is exactly what happened. Many of the old patroon estates remained undivided for two centuries. The heirs of the original patroons claimed some semifeudal privileges well into the nineteenth century. These patroonships did not attract particular attention in the early days of the Dutch; neither did the English worry about them when New Netherland became New York. In fact, the large manorial estates created by subsequent English grants were hardly distinguishable from their earlier cousins, the Dutch patroonships.

The many frictions and grievances between the patroons and the director of the company led finally to a new charter. The title of this charter was "Freedoms and Exemptions . . . to all Patroons, Masters, or Private persons who will plant Colonies in, or introduce cattle to New Netherland," and was issued on July 19, 1640. (*N. Y. Col. Hist., I, 119–23.*) The provisions of this charter, when considered as a whole, were calculated to increase greatly the number of persons who would come to New Netherland. First, the amount of land grantable to patroons was reduced to one Dutch mile along the shore of a bay or navigable stream instead of the original four miles. Second, the period of settlement was reduced from four to three years, and as many as one-third of the quota of fifty had to be sent each year. Third, a new type of landholder known as master or colonist was provided for. He would be granted 200 acres of land, along with hunting and fishing privileges, if he would bring to New Netherland five grown persons besides himself. Fourth, free passage was granted to those who came over "between decks." Fifth, patroonships would not occupy entirely any part of the region, for they could not be directly opposite each other along the rivers. It appears that family-sized freeholds were supposed to occupy the land not granted to patroons.

In case of the division of a patroonship the parts were to possess the same privileges as the whole and to pay the same fee, that is, one pair of iron gauntlets and twenty guilders. Inheritance of estates was to continue in the family with descent to females as well as to males. The charter also provided that the company would protect the settlers in case of war, but each colonist had to provide himself with a certain supply of arms and ammunition. Commercial privileges were extended, and the restriction on manufacturing was removed. (*Brodhead. N. Y., I, 311–12.*) Settlement on large patroonships was sponsored by the wealthy, but many settlers came on their own resources.

The famous Dutch villages or townships developed from the influx of independent freeholders. It was upon these small units of local government and the persistent demands of the freeholders that a popular government was established. The desire for political freedom in New Netherland was intense. The first three directors – Minuit, VanTwiller, and Kieft – were removed from office because of complaints of the settlers, who demanded the rights and privileges enjoyed by free citizens of Holland. This situation, of course, was not peculiar to New Netherland, for the colony of Virginia grew from a trading company's plantation to a royal province with its own assembly of freemen. Other colonies developed in the same direction toward representative government.

The fourth great charter under which settlements were established in New York was granted by Charles II to his brother, the Duke of York, in March, 1664. This grant was made in anticipation of the successful occupation of New Netherland, which was surrendered to the English in August of that year. The Dutch, however, retook New York in 1673 and proceeded to confiscate the property of the Duke of York. The Treaty of Westminster, in 1674, again restored New York to the English. The Duke of York secured a second charter in 1674 to remove any possible doubt that might arise, because of the temporary Dutch control, as to the validity of the 1664 grant and the grants made to settlers under its terms. The tenure provisions of both charters were essentially the same.

The territory that the Duke received not only was extensive but its location was awkward and unusually complex. In addition to the land along the Hudson and Delaware rivers, the Duke of York's patent took in half of the present state of Connecticut, the whole of New Jersey, an undefined stretch that included the present state of Delaware, and the major part of Maine. This vast empire soon was reduced by the loss of New Jersey, which was granted to Berkeley and Carteret; by the loss of Connecticut's western half, which Governor Nicolls gave back to that colony in 1667; and by the loss of lands along the western bank of the Delaware, which became the subject of a prolonged dispute with Lord Baltimore (Fig. 6.2).

The entire original territory was to be held by the Duke of York, his heirs and assigns, forever under the following tenure:

> . . . to be holden of us our heirs and successors as of our mannor of East Greenwich in our county of Kent in ffree and common soccage and not in capite nor by Knight service yielding and rendering and the said James Duke of Yorke doth for himself his heires and assignes covenant and promise to yield and render unto us our heires and successors of and for the same yearly and every yeare forty Beaver skins when they shall be demanded . . . (*Thorpe. Charters, III, 1638.*)

The Duke also was granted power to govern the colony.

Although these two charters were unusually short, they granted wide latitude for government organization and land distribution. The general conditions outlined in the grant indicate that it was strictly a proprietary charter. The Duke of York had full rights to grant the soil to private parties, presumably under any English tenures that he pleased, for the conditions of the grants to settlers were not mentioned. This, however, did not give the proprietary as much latitude as previous charters, because the Statute of Tenures enacted in England in 1660, did away with major aspects of basic feudal tenures, except copyhold estates.

When James, Duke of York, became James II, King of England, in 1685, New York automatically became a royal province. It was handled in a manner similar to other royal colonies of that time, for during the years that James II was king, he seemed to accord no more attention to New York than to any other royal colony.

During the Dutch rule of New Netherland constant pressure was exerted to secure enlarged freedom and liberties necessary to establish a thriving agricultural community. First, the charter of 1629 encouraged the patroons to plant settlements in the territory by offering them easy tenures and extensive powers of government. Second, the 1640 charter extended the right of independent settlement to small freeholders. Third, in 1641, when trouble with the

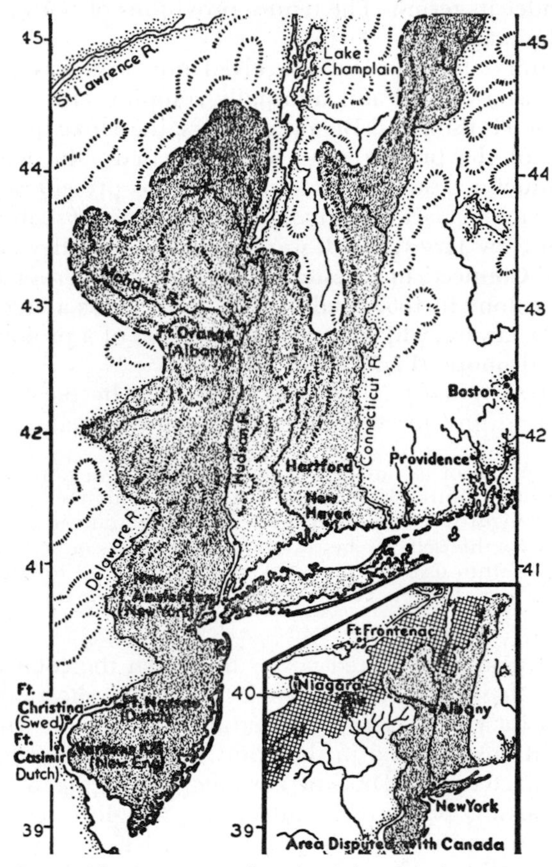

Figure 6.2—Area granted to the Duke of York in 1664.
(Due to vagueness of recorded data, boundaries can be considered only approximate.)

Indians became serious, the director appointed a committee of twelve to counsel with him and give advice when requested. This was the first participation of freemen in the government of New Netherland. In effect, its primacy corresponded to the 1619 assembly in Virginia. Again, in 1643, the director established a committee of eight to advise with him on steps to be taken for the welfare of the colony. But when the danger from the Indians had passed, Director Kieft disbanded these committees and threatened severe penalties for anyone who assembled in popular meetings. Fourth, the struggles for participation in government by the colonists between 1645 and 1652 resulted in establishment of a local government at New Amsterdam, liberalized somewhat the rights of the colonists, and restricted the arbitrary power of the directors. The battle line was drawn between the people and the director of the Dutch West India Company, with the States General taking the side of the people. Lastly, the English colonists who had settled in New Netherland finally undertook to secure personal freedom and participation in government by separation from the Dutch. This movement was spearheaded by Captain Underhill, who, on May 20, 1653, accused the director of unlawfully levying taxes, imprisoning citizens without the right of trial, imposing magistrates without elections, and generally issuing laws without assent of the home government. The people, however, would not revolt under Underhill's leadership, but the English practically separated themselves from the Dutch and those on the coast of Long Island became affiliated with the government of Connecticut.

Many of the large estates in New York were developed under Stuyvesant, but some were the creation of land distribution under early English rule, such as the manors of Livingston, Pelham, and Cortlandt. This strong feudal aristocracy left a marked impression upon the subsequent social and political life of the colony. Thus, in New York the chartered grants by the Dutch and the English permitted the establishment of Dutch patroonships, English manors, and numerous American family farms. It seems that the English manors would not have shown such vitality except for the influences exerted by the Dutch patroons, for the English manorial system had almost disappeared in England. On the other hand, the Dutch patroonships might have been undermined during the English regime much more easily, being of Dutch creation, if the English had not developed similar holdings during the time that they had the power to determine how the land would be held. That these large estates did not completely dominate the economic, social, and political life of provincial New York is traceable to the strong and numerous groups of small freeholders.

CHAPTER 7

Three Corporate Colonies

EARLY LAND TENURE and colonial government in Massachusetts, Rhode Island, and Connecticut were unlike the other colonies, except perhaps New Hampshire in a few particulars. The land system in these three colonies was distinctive from the beginning, and continued so until the Revolution. Differences were associated with the religious ideas of the first settlers, their extensive chartered privileges, their corporate form of organization, and the haphazard and uncontrolled pattern of colony location.

The influences of the land tenure provisions and the system of government established under the early charters, however, are more difficult to relate than are those of any other closely knit group that settled in Colonial America. The facts are complicated by overlapping and imperfect grants. The failure of the Plymouth Company to establish a settlement, and the unfortunate political complications that developed soon after the Council for New England was given a charter, finished attempts to settle New England under large trading and colonizing companies. These failures ushered in an entirely new idea of planting a colony. The individualism exhibited by religious groups intensified the confusion resulting from failure of the council and weaknesses of mother country leadership. Later, endeavors of the English government to divest these three colonies of all of their chartered privileges was another complicating factor.

The New England seaboard was fairly well known to the English seamen by the beginning of the seventeenth century. Tales of a bountiful supply of fish and fur stimulated trading interest in the region. It was upon the possibilities of developing trade and establishing the fishing industry that the Plymouth Company asked for and received a charter for the New England territory at the same time that the

London Company received its grant for the land lying to the south. The charter for the Plymouth Company carried the same guarantees and reservations as the London Company charter. (*Lucas. Charters, 1–8.*)

The first settlement attempt of the Plymouth Company was made at the mouth of the Kennebec River by Popham in 1607. (*Palfrey. N. Eng., I, 82–85.*) The experience was disheartening, and the following year, upon hearing of this failure, the Virginia Company sent a letter to the Plymouth Company describing the advantages of the southern part of the territory over the part assigned to the Plymouth Company. The subscribers to stock of the Plymouth corporation were asked to join the Virginia Company provided each member would subscribe twenty-five pounds. The answer of the Plymouth group is missing. (*Brown. Genesis, I, 238–40.*)

NEW ENGLAND COUNCIL

Members of the company showed no interest in attempting a second settlement in America until John Smith counteracted the sad experience on the Kennebec with a glowing description of the possibilities of the region. Under this influence Sir Ferdinando Gorges and some of the other men in the group at Plymouth determined to take advantage of this opportunity. Since the original charter had proved defective for the establishment of permanent settlement, Gorges and his associates petitioned for and received a new charter from the king. The charter, issued on November 3, 1620, incorporated them as the "Councile established at Plymouth, in the County of Devon for the planting, ruling, ordering, and governing of New-England, in America. . . ."

The charter covered the territory from 40° to 48° north latitude and from sea to sea. This grant was made without regard to the earlier grant to the Plymouth Company and it also overlapped the grant to the London and Bristol Company, set up to establish a colony in Newfoundland. But these conflicts did not prove of much consequence on either the northern or southern boundaries.

The Council for New England consisted of forty members who held the territory under conditions of tenure similar to those in the second Virginia charter. Land was held as of the manor of East Greenwich, in the County of Kent, in free and common socage, and not in capite nor by knight service, paying to the Crown of England only one-fifth of the gold and silver ore, the copper reservation being omitted. The council could grant land directly to adventurers and others, under its own seal, to be held of the council under the same tenures as indicated in the original grant. (*Thorpe. Charters, III, 1827–40.*) It had authority to grant trade permits, to make and enforce laws and ordinances for the governing of the colony, to deal with traders who fraudulently trafficked in goods, and to transport the people needed to settle the country, together with all things necessary for livelihood and defense. No customs or subsidies were to be paid for seven years, and no taxes or impositions for twenty-one years.

In the 1623-24 session of Parliament, the patent was denounced as a monopoly. This action was based in part upon the company's monopoly of the fishing industry. For the Virginia Company objected to the monopoly before the charter was granted, and suggested a compromise by which each colony would have limited fishing rights in the waters of the other. But Gorges was sufficiently powerful to force the patent through Parliament. He was not strong enough, however, to withstand the attack of the Virginia Company, representing the struggling colonists on the banks of the James River. For these colonists needed rights to fish in the waters off the coast as an assurance against the ever present possibility of food scarcity.

The practical importance and possibilities of the council came to an end without a significant contribution. Anticipating this outcome, the council, in July, 1623, divided the territory of New England by lot among the patentees. The members present drew on their own behalf, while the king drew for those absent. A new partition was made in February, 1634, in anticipation of final surrender of the patent. None of the grantees obtained royal charters covering their land except Gorges, whose grant was confirmed. The president and council formally surrendered the charter to Charles I in 1635, although the company continued some activities for a few years longer. The land covered by the unconfirmed patents reverted to the Crown. The grants to the Plymouth Company and the Council for New England were the only ones of importance, involving the territory later granted to the three corporate colonies of Puritan New England.

MAINE AND NEW HAMPSHIRE TERRITORY

Maine territory and New Hampshire were included with the corporate colonies in the early grants, and were closely related to developments in these colonies. Territory that now includes the states of Maine and New Hampshire was granted to Gorges and Mason by the Council for New England, on August 10, 1622. The grant covered all of the mainland of New England between the Merrimac and Kennebec rivers, extending inland toward their headwaters for a distance of threescore miles, together with the islands within five leagues of the coast.

The tenure provisions of the grant recited the conventional provision regarding East Greenwich, free and common socage, and the exclusion of tenure in capite and by knight service. Gorges and Mason were assured rights in the territory as extensive as those the Council for New England received in its charter. Thus, they owed no services to the council, which was simply conveying part of its territory to two of its members. Included also were the usual reservations of precious metals, but in addition to the one-fifth reserved for the Crown, the council was to receive a second one-fifth, and also as a token quitrent it was to receive ". . . yearly the sum of tenn shillings English money, if it be demanded." (*Thorpe. Charters, III, 1623.*) The grantees were given powers and responsibilities of government, the only restrictions being the right of the inhabitants to appeal to the council on grievances and conformity of the laws to those of England. In an unusual provision the grantees agreed to forfeit £100 if they did not succeed in establishing ten families on the land within three years.

Gorges and Mason divided their grant in 1629, Mason taking New Hampshire and Gorges retaining Maine. Mason's rights to the New Hampshire territory were confirmed in a new charter from the council in 1629 and again in 1635. The few settlements in New Hampshire in 1641 secured the protection of Massachusetts, which lasted until 1675. From 1675 to 1679, Robert Mason, a grandson of John Mason, established his own government under a royal decree. But he wearied of his endeavors to make the colony financially successful, and New Hampshire became a royal province in 1679, remaining so until the Revolution.

Before the New England council was dissolved it made several grants, and a second distribution of the land in 1635. Each of these actions was an endeavor to develop palatine fiefs in America. In 1622, the council granted to Robert Gorges, a son of Ferdinando Gorges, a tract of land along the New England coast extending ten miles inland. This he was to hold of the king by knight service tenure, and is not to be confused with the 1622 grant to Gorges and Mason. The military service required was four able men to attend upon the governor general whenever requested for any manner of service. This same type of tenure was included in the distribution, in 1635, of the land held by the New England council. Each of the eight patentees was ". . . to find four able men armed for war to attend upon the governor of New England for the public service within fourteen days after warning given." (*Calendar of State Papers, 1574–1660, 195, 204; Andrews. Col. Period, I, 417.*)

After the New England council was dissolved, Gorges received, in 1639, a royal charter affirming his rights to and enlarging the territory of Maine. He had claims to this area by virtue of the 1622 grant and the subsequent division with Mason, and also by the allotment made in 1635 by the New England council just prior to its dissolution. The territory received by Gorges has been interpreted to mean the land lying between the harbor at the mouth of the Merrimac River, which now flows through Massachusetts, and the mouth of the Kennebec River in Maine, extending from each of these points along the respective rivers for 120 miles inland, with these latter points joined by a straight line. This interpretation of the grant gave Gorges a thin slice off the northeast corner of Massachusetts, about one-half of New Hampshire, about one-eighth of Vermont, and something less than one-half of Maine.

Gorges' charter was similar to the one granted to Lord Baltimore seven years earlier. Gorges could create manors and establish necessary manorial courts. The freeholders were to participate in the enactment of laws, and all laws were to be subject to the rules of the Lords of Plantations, a special government agency resident in England and dealing with the English colonies.

Gorges established a government under this charter but it ceased to operate when he died in 1647. Two years later the settlements between Cape Porpoise and the Piscataqua River established a government of their own, which continued for four or five years, when they united with Massachusetts. In 1658, Massachusetts absorbed the remaining eastern settlements. Gorges' grandson revived the claim to Maine after the restoration of the Stuart kings in 1660, and a provisional government was set up in 1665, excluding Massachusetts from the territory. Three years later Massachusetts again asserted authority over the territory, owing to the impotence of the provisional government. In 1676, Gorges' title was again confirmed and Massachusetts was driven out, but two years later Gorges sold Maine for £1,250 to John Usher, a merchant of Boston, who in turn deeded the territory to the governor and company of Massachusetts Bay. Massachusetts maintained jurisdiction until Maine became a state in 1820.

Both rights in land and powers of government seem to have shifted with each of the changes mentioned. It is doubtful, however, if the tenure of individual occupiers was generally disrupted by these changes. Gorges evidently did not exercise effectively his right to establish manors, although he was an advocate of the feudal type of colony. Settlement was not extensive. The inhabitants were mostly freeholders, who held their land under free and common socage tenure. The hectic experience of the Maine colonists, in regard to both land and government, was similar to that in other sparsely settled territory. The influence of Gorges upon the final emergence of our land tenure system was insignificant. Of more importance were the infrequent contacts with Massachusetts up to 1678, and its political dominance during the following century and a half.

The Council for New England made several grants during its existence, and some settlements in New England were attempted without benefit of a formal grant. These may be summarized briefly as follows: (1) In 1622, Thomas Weston sent out a company of fifty or sixty men who settled at Weymouth without a charter, but who dispersed after a year, the attempt a failure. (2) Captain Wollaston attempted a settlement in Massachusetts in 1623 without a charter, but also failed. (3) Thomas Morton may have received a grant, but his venture came to the same end as those of Weston and Wollaston. (4) In 1622, Captain John Mason received the Marianna grant, covering Cape Ann. (5) In 1622, Gorges and Mason were granted the territory of Maine, which they divided in 1629. (6) In 1622, David Thomson received a 6,000-acre tract at the mouth of the Piscataqua, but the group left after three years. (7) In 1622, Robert Gorges received his grant. (8) In the following year Christopher Levett received a 6,000-acre grant from the council.

These early activities indicate that the New England council intended to distribute land to those who would sponsor settlements, but it had neither the inclination nor financial backing to undertake settlement on its own behalf. The grantees held their lands of the king and had extensive powers. In fact, it appears that the council desired the right to establish feudal estates, for in 1623, a new charter was drafted which would have eliminated the effect of *Quia Emptores* in preventing subinfeudation. It seems clear that those interested in settling America felt that they should have extensive powers of government and full freedom in the establishment of whatever tenure they desired. This trend was observable in the three Virginia charters and in the Dutch charters for New Netherland. It was also evident in the action of the New England council, but its full impact was not felt until the Maryland charter was granted.

MASSACHUSETTS AND PLYMOUTH

The Virginia charter of 1606 granted to the Plymouth Company the territory of New England, of which Massachusetts was a part, but both the right to grant land to settlers and the power to govern the colony remained in the hands of the Crown. These provisions continued in force until 1620, when the Council for New England was authorized by a royal charter. The land included in this charter lay between the fortieth and forty-eighth parallels and extended from sea to sea, including adjacent islands and fishing rights in the surrounding waters.

The 1620 charter conferred upon the council full power to dispose of the land and limited power to establish government. The inhabitants were to enjoy the same liberties as free citizens of England, which should not be thought of as a limitation, but rather as a guarantee of personal freedom in light of contemporary English practices. It was a restriction only when compared with the wide latitude of government possible under some charters, for example, the Maryland charter issued only twelve years later.

While these events were taking place a group of separatists in Holland obtained a grant from the Virginia Company to establish themselves in America. This group decided to settle at Plymouth, outside the influence of the Virginia Company, but in the territory held by the Council for New England. The Pilgrims took up land as mere squatters. Before they left the Mayflower, however, knowing that their charter did not pertain to the land on which they would settle, it became apparent that some type of social and political contract was needed. Some of the group had declared that they would use their own liberty when they landed; they made "discontented and mutinous" speeches declaring they would be under no established law as soon as they left the Mayflower. The famous Mayflower Compact was agreed upon forthwith. It combined the entire group into a body politic. All agreed that laws should be enacted from time to time, and all promised submission and obedience. This was the first free group compact originating in America, being born out of sheer necessity.

Since the Mayflower Compact was the first of three great voluntary social compacts, and since it is similar in content to the Exeter Agreement and the Piscataqua Combination, it is presented here in full.

In the name of God, Amen. We whose names are underwriten, the loyall subjects of our dread soveraigne Lord, King James, by the grace of God, of Great Britaine, Franc, & Ireland king, defender of the faith, &c., haveing undertaken, for the glorie of God, and advancemente of the Christian faith, and honour of our king & countrie, a voyage to plant the first colonie in the Northerne parts of Virginia, doe by these presents solemnly & mutualy in the presence of God, and one of another, covenant & combine ourselves togeather into a civill body politick, for our better ordering & preservation & furtherance of the ends aforesaid; and by vertue hearof to enacte, constitute, and frame such just & equall lawes, ordinances, acts, constitutions, & offices, from time to time, as shall be thought most meete & convenient for the generall good of the Colonie, unto which we promise all due submission and obedience. In witnes where of we have hereunder subscribed our names at Cap-Codd the 11. of November, in the year of the raigne of our soveraigne lord, King James, of England, France, & Ireland the eighteenth, and of Scotland the fiftie fourth. Anno: Dom. 1620. (*MacDonald. Charters, 33–34.*)

The Plymouth colony finally received a grant of land from the Council for New England in June 1621. A new grant was made to John Pierce for the Plymouth group the following year. These patents contained no mention of the exact territory to be included, nor were any definite restrictions entered as to the extent of the territory that would be occupied. The charter merely provided that the land was to be selected in an area not already settled. It indicated that 100 acres of land were to be allocated to the settlers and that 1,500 acres were to be set aside for public use.

A third grant later was made for the same colony from the council to William Bradford and associates (Fig. 7.1). After reciting the fact that the Pilgrims had lived in New England for nine years and had established a colony of 300 persons at their own expense, it describes the land over which the colony extended, assigning it to Bradford and his associates forever. The land included in this charter lay between the Cohasset River on the north and the Narragansett River on the south, as well as land for fifteen English miles on each side of the

Kennebec River. (*Maine Doc. Hist., VII, 108–16.*) A reservation of two-fifths of the gold and silver, similar to the one in Gorges' grant, was made. The council agreed to convey in writing to individual settlers so much land and under such terms as a competent lawyer should direct.

In March, 1641, Bradford, after reserving three tracts for himself, assigned this patent to the freemen of New Plymouth. Plymouth became a corporate colony in name and in fact, although none of these

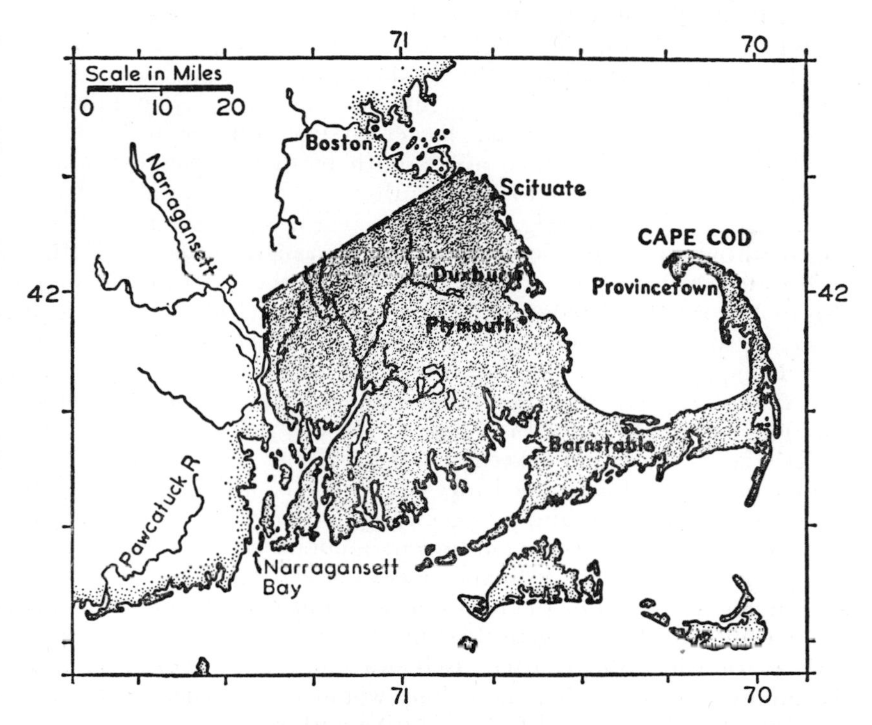

Figure 7.1—The Colony of Plymouth as outlined in the Bradford Patent of 1630. (Due to vagueness of recorded data, boundaries can be considered only approximate.)

grants received royal assent. For all intents and purposes it had been a corporate colony from the beginning, owing to the manner in which the group operated under the Mayflower Compact and the various grants. Plymouth never became fully provincial at any time, even for the short period under Andros. It finally was united with Massachusetts under the 1691 charter, and so remained until the Revolution. Thus, it never was incorporated legally into a body politic, but remained a voluntary municipal association subordinate to Massachusetts. Plymouth settlers maintained almost complete control, however, over their land system and government to the Revolution.

In March, 1628, the Council for New England made a grant to a land and trading company – the New England Company – which was concerned chiefly with the few fishing settlements that had been established in the region of Massachusetts Bay following the unsuccessful attempt to plant a colony at Cape Ann in 1623. The grant flowered into the first charter of Massachusetts Bay, which received royal approval in March, 1629. It supplanted the patent of the Council for New England, which was surrendered in 1635.

The Massachusetts Bay Company at first operated from headquarters in England, but it established a local government at Salem under John Endicott. A year later, both the charter and the government were transferred to America and the Endicott government was discontinued. This charter remained in full force until it was annulled in 1684. The land included in the charter lay from three miles north of the Merrimac River to three miles south of the Charles River and from the Atlantic Ocean to the South Seas, as well as the islands adjacent to both coasts (Fig. 7.2). This area was not extensive along the coast, but it was sufficient to deprive the assigns of Robert Gorges of land to which they were legally entitled by the patent of 1622. It also took from the Plymouth colony about half of its territory, which was restored by a later grant. In addition, it overlapped much of the New Hampshire and Maine lands of Gorges and Mason. (*Andrews. Col. Period, I, 359.*) But the major conflict lay in the duplication of land granted to the Council for New England by the charter of 1620.

The land tenure and governmental provisions of the charter were similar to those of the Council for New England, which it actually replaced for most intents and purposes. By and large, the requirements of the charter were not common to contemporary charters and English legislation. Not a single ordinance was imposed respecting the system of church government or the forms of ceremonies of religious worship. From a functional and practical point of view, the greatest divergence took place when the charter itself was moved to American soil. Essentially this meant that the colony would be governed, under the large municipal rights and full legislative authority of the charter, by the local people rather than by a "foreign" group resident in England. In addition, Massachusetts maintained full control over the land and distributed it to settlers under conditions also determined by the local people. None of the charters for the Virginia and New York colonies were ever transferred to America, and as a consequence top control of the government in these colonies remained away from American soil. It would be difficult to overstress the importance of the influence of local autonomy in Massachusetts upon later events.

The annulment in 1684 of the excellent 1629 charter, and the advent of Andros, was unfortunate for the colonists of Massachusetts. After several years of delay they sent Increase Mather to England to plead for the restoration of their 1629 charter. Numerous difficulties with Andros reached a climax, and he was finally deposed. But early in 1689 Mather learned that a letter was being sent to all the colonies confirming the existing governments until further notice. He succeeded in stopping those intended for New England and government under the 1629 charter was resumed. It soon became clear, however, that the old charter would not be recognized by William and Mary, the new king and queen. Thereupon Mather and associates

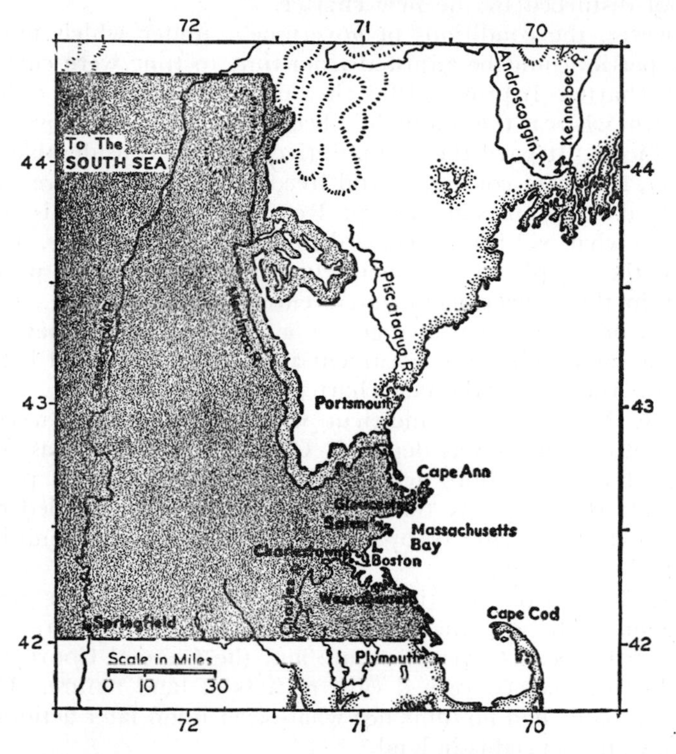

Figure 7.2—Territory assigned to Massachusetts under the Charter of 1629. (Due to vagueness of recorded data, boundaries can be considered only approximate.)

petitioned for a new charter on behalf of the colony. Mather's petition was favorably received, and the second charter of Massachusetts Bay was issued on October 7, 1691. The territory granted by this charter was redefined to include all the land included in the Massachusetts Bay charter, the Plymouth colony, the province of Maine, the territory called Acadia or Nova Scotia, and the land lying between the province of Maine and Nova Scotia.

All of this territory was granted to the colony as a corporate body. The land was held as of the manor of East Greenwich, in the County of Kent, by fealty only, in free and common socage. One-fifth part of the gold and silver and precious stones was reserved for the Crown, the precious stone reservation being quite unusual. All previous allocations of land to persons and corporate bodies were confirmed and continued under the same condition of tenure specified in the original transfers. It also was provided that the governor and general assembly could make grants of land in the same manner as they had been doing under the first charter of Massachusetts Bay. For all intents and purposes the rights under which the colony held its land of the king were not disturbed by the new charter.

However, the conditions of government under which tenures of private parties could be adjusted from time to time were changed by the new charter. It provided for the appointment of high officials by the Crown, whereas the colony had been electing its own governor and other officers. It gave these appointive officials considerable power. However, liberty of conscience and freedom of worship were expressly guaranteed to all persons, except Roman Catholics. This officially confirmed what had been presumed under the 1629 charter. In actual practice the people of Massachusetts Bay continued to participate actively in their government and eventually William and Mary permitted them to elect their own governor. As time passed they assumed about the same rights in government as they had exercised before the advent of Andros and the new charter.

Rhode Island and Connecticut were not forced to accept new charters after Andros was deposed. Of this concession Massachusetts was acutely aware. Along with the other colonies, the people of Massachusetts saw clearly that their rights were safeguarded only by their own vigilant dexterity, by successful intrigue, or by administrative blunders in England.

Massachusetts Bay continued under the 1691 charter until the Revolution. The explanatory charter of 1725, which grew out of differences between Governor Shute and the General Court (general assembly), was not concerned with matters of land tenure. The provisions probably had no influence whatsoever upon later actions of the General Court on rights in land.

It is clear in the charters of the London and Plymouth Companies, and in the first charter granted to the Massachusetts Bay colony, that the residence of these companies was to be in England and that all business was to be transacted there. But it was not clear at that time, either to the Crown or the companies, that settlements on the American seaboard could not be easily developed and adequately governed by companies whose official place of transacting business was in the mother country. It became clear, however, that the companies needed broad powers in organizing and governing their colonization endeavors; they were granted these powers. The most significant feature of Massachusetts Bay, apart from the unique conditions surrounding a corporate colony, was the early complete transfer to American soil of the government of the corporation (the corporate colony), and along with it the rights to distribute the land and to adjust land tenures.

The location of the governing body in the Massachusetts colony gave the colonists the rights to settle the country and develop free institutions, both economic and political. Thus, Massachusetts Bay enacted at an extremely early date, 1641, the famous Body of Liberties, which contained many liberal tenure provisions and which was followed from time to time by other farsighted legislation.

RHODE ISLAND AND PROVIDENCE PLANTATIONS

The soil of Rhode Island also was granted first in the Virginia charter of 1606, and regranted later to the Council for New England. No colonization, however, took place in Rhode Island under either of these grants, for the first settlement was made there after the council was dissolved in 1635.

The early settlers of Rhode Island were chiefly religious dissenters from Puritans at Plymouth and Massachusetts Bay. Roger Williams, who was forced out of Salem because of religious friction, established the first settlement. He took up land at Providence in 1636.

In settling at Providence, Williams did not have a charter from either the Crown or Massachusetts Bay. He believed his rights in the land were those which he derived from the Indians and the natural rights of man as recorded in the Scriptures. He felt that the Indians were the real owners of the land in America, and that title to the land should be secured from them and not from the English Crown.

The second Rhode Island settlement was made at Portsmouth in 1638 by William Coddington and other religious dissenters from the Puritan rule in Massachusetts Bay. Religious friction at Portsmouth soon sent Coddington into the wilderness again; he settled at Newport in 1639, but never relinquished his claim to the land at Portsmouth. He later returned and finally received from a parliamentary commission in England permission to occupy the land upon which he had settled.

None of the settlements in Rhode Island had been established under a royal grant, either for land or for government. People simply settled upon the land as squatters and their government was by the consent of those governed, being dominated chiefly by the person who represented religious leadership in the settlement. All of the settlers were religious dissenters who were more or less bound together by common religious beliefs. Nearby Massachusetts Bay tried to bring them under her jurisdiction, but these dissenters originally had left the Bay colony because they disliked Puritan rule. Therefore, they had no intention of submitting to the jurisdiction from which they had fled.

By 1640, the settlement at Providence felt the need of a formal social and political compact under which the colony would be governed. They established, therefore, the celebrated "Plantations Agreement at Providence." The agreement was largely concerned with political matters. The second section, however, placed land distribution in the hands of five men chosen by the inhabitants. Later sections provided for expeditious settlement of any differences arising over land and for the issuing of a deed for each landholding within the bounds of Providence Plantation, under which every man would hold his land forever. (*Thorpe. Charters, VI, 3205–7.*)

Pressure from Massachusetts caused Portsmouth and Newport to combine in 1640 under a common government. A year later at Portsmouth a document entitled "Government of Rhode Island" was drawn up which provided for, among other things, the determination of the property line between Portsmouth and Newport, the setting aside of land for the establishing of a road between the two towns, the prevention of fires in meadows, and the setting up of a system of recording land titles. (*Ibid., 3207–9.*)

This agreement did not seem sufficient to ward off persistent pressure for control by Massachusetts Bay. As a consequence, and driven by the impelling desire to have full and clear title to the land, Roger Williams went to England in 1643, where he obtained, from the Parliamentary Commission on Colonial Affairs, a charter uniting Providence, Newport, and Portsmouth under one government. This grant included the land that was bordered on the north and northeast by the Massachusetts patent, on the east and southeast by the Plymouth patent, on the south by the ocean, and on the west and northwest by the land occupied by the Narragansett Indians. These lands extended about twenty-five miles up the Pequot River and included miscellaneous bodies of land around Narragansett Bay.

The grant gave the settlements a free and absolute charter of incorporation under which they could establish their own laws and courts and select their own officials. No title to the vaguely defined land was specified in the charter. It was altogether possible that Williams did not request inclusion of a specific grant of title. First, he considered that the land belonged to the settlement since it had been purchased from its rightful owners, the Indians. Secondly, an item in the charter just prior to the provision for the granting of authority recites the fact that the settlers ". . . have also purchased, and are purchasing of and amongst the said Natives. . . ." (*Thorpe. Charters, VI, 3210.*) These two facts indicate that Williams was fully aware of the land title situation, and declined to give any indication of specific recognition of the so-called rights of the Crown to the land of the territory.

A government under the patent however, was not organized until 1647, when Warwick also was admitted. From this time until 1663, when Rhode Island and Providence Plantations received their great charter, each of the towns was independent of any overhead government for the colony. Each town had the right to propose measures to the General Court, or to refuse to accept rules enacted by it. The church and state were always completely separated in Rhode Island. Religious liberty to the settlers meant complete liberty of conscience with no coercion from a civil authority. During the first one-third of a century in Rhode Island, therefore, a striking illustration of total local autonomy is witnessed in several towns. The unifying force did not arise out of local need. It grew entirely out of the necessity of

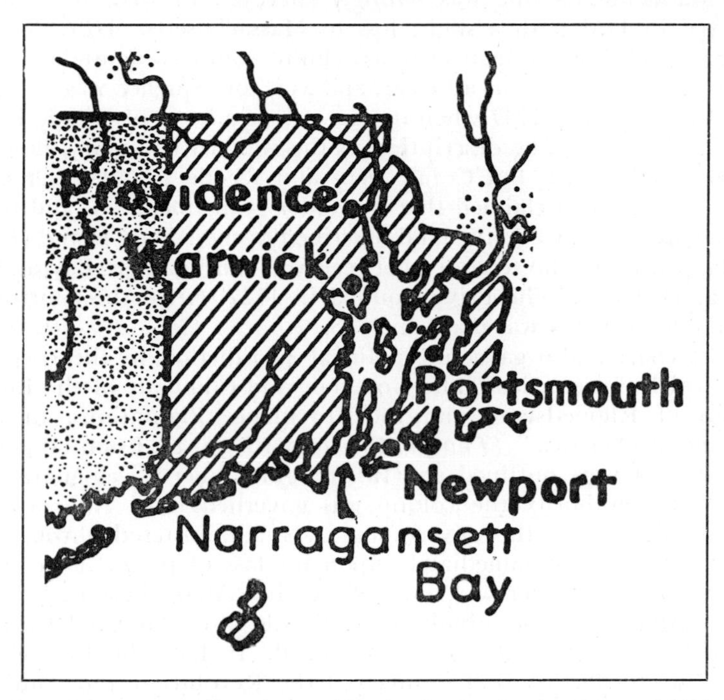

Figure 7.3—Territorial boundaries of Rhode Island under the Charter of 1663. (Due to vagueness of recorded data, boundaries can be considered only approximate.)

protecting the several settlements from the outside, particularly from the endeavors of Massachusetts to bring the towns under its jurisdiction. In 1661, John Clark, an agent of Rhode Island resident in England, petitioned for a royal charter for the colony. Rhode Island had promptly proclaimed King Charles II upon his ascension to the throne, and this, together with the fact that the new king wished to restrain the ambitions of Massachusetts, resulted in favorable action on the petition. The first draft of the charter included territory on Narragansett Bay which was in dispute between Massachusetts and Rhode Island. Arbitrators a year later gave this land to Rhode Island and the new charter was issued in July of 1663 (Fig. 7.3).

The territory granted by the Rhode Island charter was bounded on the west by the Pawcatuck River and a straight line drawn from the head of the river to the south border of the Massachusetts Bay grant; on the north by the Massachusetts colony; on the east beginning in the south at a point three English miles east of Narragansett Bay and running in a northerly direction to the south border of Massachusetts Bay; and on the south by the ocean. Of this ill-defined territory, only the northern and southern boundaries were clear from the description. The Massachusetts line was wrongly surveyed in 1642 but was resurveyed in 1751 with a slight loss to Massachusetts. (*R.I. Rec., V, 322–25.*) The ocean furnished a definite southern boundary. The eastern border was not at all clear, and as a consequence was an object of controversy until 1747 when it was settled in favor of Rhode Island. (*Ibid., 199–201.*) The description of the western boundary, however, was reasonably clear but Connecticut and Rhode Island never could agree. Connecticut claimed that her older grant included land to the Narragansett Bay, while the land described in the Rhode Island charter overlapped all of the territory between the Narragansett Bay and the Pawcatuck River. The Privy Council in 1727 settled the controversy and the final survey was made in 1738.

The charter also gave full political jurisdiction to the corporate body which was entitled "The Governor and Company of the English Colony of Rhode-Island and the Providence Plantations, in New-England, in America." (*Thorpe. Charters, VI, 3213.*) Essential governmental rules were outlined and full religious liberty was guaranteed. Under this authority the colony was governed until Andros came. During his regime the government was administered through the separate towns but immediately upon his loss of power, government under the 1663 charter was resumed. Unlike Massachusetts, however, Rhode Island did not submit to royal rule after Andros left, and a new charter consequently was not needed. In fact, the 1663 charter proved so satisfactory that it survived the Revolution and continued in force for half a century. It is significant to note that Providence and the other settlements in Rhode Island still maintain their individual identity, for the state constitution is concerned not only with the state of Rhode Island as is commonly supposed, but is entitled "The State of Rhode Island and Providence Plantations." (*Ibid., 3222.*)

The conditions under which the territory indicated in the 1663 charter should be held were clearly outlined. The corporation held the land in trust for the use and benefit of the freemen of the colony. The land was held as of the manor of East Greenwich, in the County of Kent, in free and common socage, and not in capite or by knight service. The only reservation from the Crown was for one-fifth of all ores of gold or silver. The charter specifically excluded any possibility of the Crown's imposing services, duties, fines, forfeitures or other types of claims upon the land. This charter was one of the first granted after the famous Statute of Tenures was enacted by Parliament in 1660.

CONNECTICUT AND NEW HAVEN

The territory that eventually became the state of Connecticut, like Rhode Island and the rest of New England, was included in the first grant to the London Company in 1606 and later to the New England council. Lack of settlement activities, both by the company and the council, led to sporadic settlement and conflicting grants in several localities in Connecticut. The situation there was further complicated by rival claims of Dutch traders and settlers from the Plymouth colony and from Massachusetts Bay, for the government of the latter harassed Connecticut as well as Rhode Island.

The first patent under which settlement was made in Connecticut was the one issued by the Council for New England to Lords Saye, Sele, Brook, and others, but this patent was not used until after the council was dissolved. In 1635, John Winthrop the Younger built a fort at Saybrook at the mouth of the Connecticut River. Prior to this, however, settlers from Plymouth had established a trading post at Windsor and the Dutch had already built a fort at Hartford. Settlers were pouring into Massachusetts at a rapid rate, and though little of the land had been taken up, a general feeling of congestion existed. This feeling was probably influenced by the strict Puritanical theocracy and the unyielding soil of Massachusetts. As a consequence, residents of Massachusetts who later settled at Dorchester, Watertown, Roxbury, and Cambridge (Newtown) secured from the General Court of Massachusetts, in 1635, permission to take up land and to establish a government wherever they might settle in the Connecticut valley. It was understood, however, that they still would be under the jurisdiction of Massachusetts Bay.

These emigrants from Massachusetts settled at Hartford, Windsor, and Wethersfield. Massachusetts immediately tried to establish jurisdiction over these three settlements by the issuance in 1636 of a specific commission to govern the Connecticut towns. They were, however, well removed from Massachusetts, and with the threat of Indian wars, the towns each elected three deputies to meet at Hartford in 1637 as a general council. Immediately they assumed full governmental powers. In 1639 they were fully united under the Fundamental Orders of Connecticut. These emigrants did not have a charter when they left Massachusetts, merely a commission from Massachusetts Bay under which they could establish a government.

New Haven and Springfield were established without charters. The settlement at New Haven was established in 1639 by emigrants under John Davenport, a minister, and Theophilus Eaton, a wealthy London merchant, who came to America with a desire to found an independent state on a scriptural model. The land at New Haven was acquired from the Indians by barter and sale and acknowledged by deeds; Saybrook, however, was established under a patent from the Council for New England. By the early 1660's settlements had been made at Farmington, Middletown, New London, Norwalk, Stratford, Fairfield, Norwich, Stonington, Killingworth, Haddam, and Simsbury. In 1643 New Haven, Guilford, Milford, Stamford, and Southhold united in the establishment of a representative government under which they were governed until 1662, when this group became a part of Connecticut under a royal charter. The settlers at New Haven had not received any type of grant to the land, but to them their title was perfectly clear, for they had purchased the land from the Indians. It appears that the same situation existed in other settlements in Connecticut.

It was not until 1662 that a grant for the territory of Connecticut was obtained from Charles II. During the interim, however, two great documents of human freedom issued from these towns – the Fundamental Orders of Connecticut and the Fundamental Articles of New Haven.

The former was strictly concerned with government, and was ". . . the first written constitution known to history that created a government." (*MacDonald. Charters, 60.*) It was the avowed purpose of the settlers to establish a civil government based upon the laws of God. The necessary machinery of government was provided for, including a governor, general court, and elected representatives.

The Fundamental Articles of New Haven was strictly an agreement among the group that settled there, and provided for the establishment of a constitutional government in harmony with the word of God. Like the Connecticut constitution, the New Haven articles were concerned almost entirely with the establishment of the machinery of government. The articles contained, in addition, a reference to the dividing of allotments by inheritance. This provision reads as follows, ". . . thatt as in matters thatt concerne . . . devideing allottments of inheritance . . . we would all of us be ordered by those rules which the scripture holds forth to us." (*Ibid., 68.*)

The General Court of Connecticut, early in 1661, appointed a committee to prepare a petition for a royal charter and included the territory around New Haven. New Haven resisted annexation, but hastened to submit when the English took over New Netherland in 1664 and the king granted the territory as far east as the Connecticut River to the Duke of York. New Haven preferred the jurisdiction of corporate Connecticut rather than that of proprietor Duke of York.

Under the 1662 charter the land of Connecticut was granted to the corporation to be held as of the manor of East Greenwich, in the County of Kent, in free and common socage, and not in capite or by knight service. The conventional reservation of one-fifth of the gold and silver ore was made. All other charges on the land were specifically excepted. The land tenure provisions of the Connecticut and Rhode Island charters were practically identical.

The land described in the charter was bounded on the north by the Massachusetts grant and on the south by the ocean, and it extended from Narragansett Bay on the east to the South Sea (Pacific) on the west, including the islands adjoining. The petition for the charter indicated that this land had been acquired by purchase and conquest. Of course, the territory included in what is now Connecticut was well known and many settlements already had been established there, but

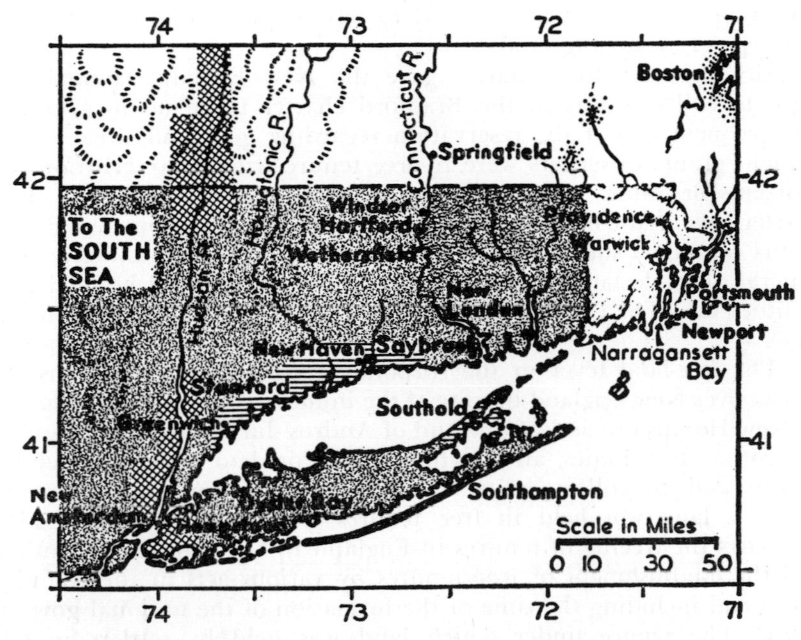

Figure 7.4—Land of Connecticut under the Charter of 1662.
(Due to vagueness of recorded data, boundaries can be considered only approximate.)

little was known of the vast territory to the west. It was upon this charter, however, that Connecticut based her claim to land in the west at the time of the controversy among the thirteen colonies as to how the western territory should be administered (Fig. 7.4).

The Connecticut charter was attacked in 1684 by quo warranto proceedings, but judgment was never entered. Andros unsuccessfully endeavored to seize it in 1687. When he was deposed in 1689 the government under the charter was resumed in Connecticut as it was in Rhode Island. The so-called state constitution of Connecticut in 1776 continued the 1662 charter in force, with a few minor changes. The original Connecticut charter remained the basic law of Connecticut until 1818. Thus, Connecticut and Rhode Island were the only two colonies that continued their old charters through the Revolution and well into the period of full statehood.

The three corporate colonies in actual practice were little theocracies in which the affairs of church and state were closely interwoven; most civil affairs were determined on an ecclesiastical basis. The colonists there seemed to sense the close relationship between the system of tenure under which land was held, the form of government, and freedom of religion. They seemed to know that religious and civil freedom and independence would be lost if they submitted to the power of an overlord and agreed to pay a quitrent to him for the privilege of occupying land.

Although the 1620 charter gave the New England council the right to collect quitrent, the Bradford charter made no mention of any payment except the reservation regarding gold and silver. Subsequent grants to settlers were in free tenure with no reservations of quitrents or other feudal dues. Likewise, the Massachusetts Bay charter gave that colony the power to reserve quitrents, but few if any grants contained such reservations. In the 1641 Body of Liberties the general court declared that all land in the colony should be held free of quitrents. The Connecticut general assembly did the same thing in 1650.

The free-land fever in the corporate colonies was contagious. It spread over New England in spite of the influence of Mason and Gorges in New Hampshire and Maine and of Andros during his brief reign in the corporate colonies, all of whom endeavored to reestablish feudal tenure and to collect quitrents. In the New England corporate colonies, land was held in free tenures from the beginning. This antedates the freeing of tenures in England by the Statute of Tenures and the establishment of free tenures by various acts in the colonies up to and including the time of the formation of the national government. The tenure under which land was held by settlers in the corporate colonies could be called allodial, and it was in most essentials very similar to present fee simple absolute tenures. This situation was recognized by the English Crown, and it exerted an important influence in the development of freer tenures throughout Colonial America than the English heritage otherwise would have encouraged.

CHAPTER 8

Three Proprietary Colonies

THE CONDITIONS UNDER WHICH THE LAND of Pennsylvania, Delaware, and Maryland was granted by the Crown to the agencies that actually settled the territory were vastly different from those just described for the three colonies of Puritan New England. In the corporate colonies, with the minor exceptions already noted, the colonists had complete control. In the proprietary colonies, on the other hand, the settlers were in a distinctly secondary position, being subject at every turn to the proprietary forms of holding land and of controlling the development of local institutions.

MARYLAND AND THE LORDS BALTIMORE

The territory that later became the province of Maryland was included in the early Virginia charters. The London Company, however, planted its settlements south and west of the Potomac River and left Maryland largely unoccupied. The revocation of the third Virginia charter in 1624 made this unsettled expanse subject to disposal at the pleasure of the Crown. This territory was granted to Cecil Calvert, the second Lord Baltimore, on June 20, 1632.

Cecil Calvert's father resolved to plant a colony in America, and purchased a tract of land in Newfoundland for that purpose. The Avalon charter of 1620 made him proprietor of the territory that he requested. Seven years later he visited his province but felt that the climate was so bleak and cold that it would discourage settlement. Later, he went to Virginia, but being a Catholic, refused to take the oaths of allegiance and supremacy and was forced to return to England. While in America, however, he explored some of the territory between the Potomac River and the Chesapeake Bay, and was much impressed with its soil, climate, and location.

George Calvert immediately petitioned Charles I for a grant to the territory of Maryland, but died a few months before the charter passed the seals. Since it was evident that the petition would have received royal approbation had not his father died, and since it was also presumed that the son "... was treading in the footsteps of his father ..." the charter was issued to Cecil Calvert as part of his inheritance.

The territory included in the Maryland charter lay between the ocean on the east and the Potomac River on the West (Fig. 8.1). It was bounded on the south by a line drawn from a cape of land called Watkin's Point to the ocean, and on the north by the fortieth degree

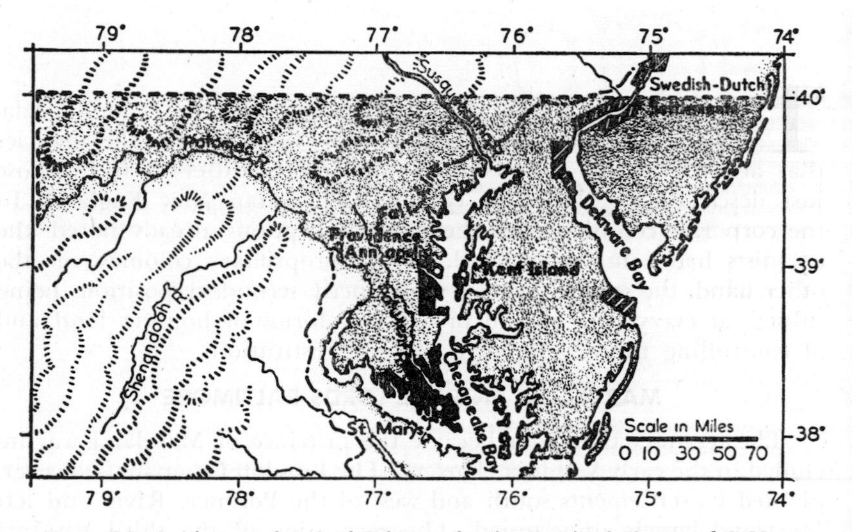

Figure 8.1—Land granted to Lord Baltimore by the Maryland Charter of 1632. (Due to vagueness of recorded data, boundaries can be considered only approximate.)

of north latitude. The northern boundary also extended westerly from the Delaware Bay to the headwaters of the Potomac River, and then southeasterly along the Potomac, and back to Watkin's Point. These 10 million to 12 million acres of land were described reasonably well, considering the crude development of mapping techniques at that time. This, however, did not prevent numerous and serious disputes over the exact boundary lines.

Unlike Virginia and Connecticut, Maryland had a fairly definite western boundary. This was of considerable importance in the history of the colonies at the time of the formation of the Northwest Territory. The northern boundary, however, was disputed with Penn, and several points of dispute were not settled for many decades. Territorial differences also existed with Virginia.

The first difficulty with Virginia was concerned with the southern line on the eastern shore, that is, the southern boundary on the peninsula between the Delaware and Chesapeake bays. In 1668, and again in 1671, a dividing line was run from Watkin's Point, which is now the southernmost point of Somerset County, across the peninsula to a creek that flows into the ocean. (*Hall. Narratives of Md., 102, n2.*) The exact line, however, was not determined until 1877, and it was ratified the following year. (*Andrews. Col. Period, II, 359–60.*) The other problem arose when Lord Baltimore claimed all of the Potomac River, that is, to the shore on the Virginia side, rather than the conventional to-the-middle-of-the-river claim. Baltimore's claim was based upon the following wording of his charter: ". . . unto the further Bank of the said River." (*MacDonald. Charters, 54.*) This boundary dispute was apparently never settled by English authorities. (*Md. Arch., V, 44–45.*)

The conflict between Baltimore and Penn over the boundaries was more pronounced than Maryland's difficulties with Virginia. Leading up to the difference were several items of importance. Between 1670 and 1682 Baltimore had laid out some forty-seven allotments of land to forty-five persons. This tract, consisting of about 19,000 acres, was to be erected into the county of Durham. (*Md. Mag., XXV, 157–67; Md. Arch., XXIV, 373–77.*) The region just north of this had been occupied after 1638 by the Swedes, and after 1655 by the Dutch, who made many grants along the west bank of the Delaware. (*N.Y. Col. Hist., XII, 177–83.*) After the fall of New Amsterdam, New York governors issued patents for lands this far south, claiming the land for the Duke of York as a part of the territory taken from the Dutch. In 1682 the Duke deeded the land of Delaware, or what was known then as the "Three Lower Counties," to William Penn. So the question of Baltimore's eastern boundary as well as the northern had to be settled. The question of the Delaware region was supposedly settled in 1685 by a report of the Lords of Trade, which then was confirmed by the Privy Council. This report recommended that the territory lying between the Delaware and the Chesapeake, above the latitude of Fenwick's Island (Old Cape Henlopen) should be divided into two equal parts, one to belong to the king and the other to Lord Baltimore. Thus, the original county of Durham that Baltimore had laid out became Sussex County of Delaware. (*Md. Arch., XXV, 399; Calendar of State Papers, 1685–88, sec. 456.*) The dispute continued until the northern boundary between Pennsylvania and Maryland was surveyed as the Mason-Dixon Line between 1763 and 1768.

Maryland, named after Queen Henrietta Maria, was to be a palatine fief with as extensive powers and privileges as those of any Bishop of Durham. Thus, Baltimore was given all the rights of government, full control over the land, and complete religious authority over the entire area. The land was to be held by Baltimore in free and common socage. (*Thorpe. Charters, III, 1679.*)

To make the various provisions on religion, government, and land explicit and extensive, the charter contains the following proviso:

> . . . We also, by these Presents, do give and grant License to the same Baron of Baltimore, and to his Heirs, to erect any Parcels of Land within the Province aforesaid, into Manors, and in every of those Manors, to have and to hold a Court-Baron, and all Things which to a Court Baron do belong; and to have and to Keep View of Frank-Pledge, for the Conservation of the Peace and better Government of those Parts, by themselves and their Stewards, or by the Lords, for the Time being to be deputed, of other of those Manors when they shall be constituted, and in the same to exercise all Things to the View of Frank Pledge belong. (*Ibid., 1685.*)

These provisions and the privileges accorded Baltimore in distributing land to settlers, although more extensive, are good examples of the powers and rights granted proprietors in the seven other colonies that were under proprietary control at one time or another. The extensive rights granted to Baltimore and the freedom with which he could legally operate under his chartered privileges made possible the establishment of any kind of land system conceivable so long as the land would be held of Lord Baltimore.

The Lords Baltimore were to be "... true and absolute Lords and Proprietaries ... saving always the Faith and Allegiance and Sovereign Dominion due ..." the English Crown. The token of that fidelity was to be "... Two Indian Arrows of these Parts ..." to be presented once each year on Tuesday in Easter week. The anticipated income to the Crown was to one-fifth of the precious metals found in the province. (*Ibid., 1679.*)

The Maryland grant was truly a remarkable document; it was as unique a proprietary charter as the Rhode Island and Connecticut charters were singular among the corporate grants. It was the first great American charter, under which one of the original colonies was settled, that conferred absolute proprietary power upon the grantee. These extensive powers were not unbridled, however, for the charter also secured to the freemen of the province greater rights than any other charter that had been issued up to 1632. (*Winsor. Narra. and Crit. Hist., III, 517–22.*)

Contrary to the trends in England, the soil of Maryland was exclusively the proprietor's. He could grant it in any kind of estates he saw fit, a power which the English king did not possess over his domain in England. For example, Lord Baltimore could establish feudal tenures, including manors with the usual manorial courts. He could also provide for subinfeudation, contrary to *Quia Emptores.* Upon his feudal tenants Baltimore could confer any title or dignity except those used in England.

The authority and power conferred upon Cecil Calvert was truly royal, while nothing of significance, except general sovereignty, was reserved to the king. Maryland was a feudal seigniory of the medieval vintage. The proprietary could make all laws, with the consent of the governed — the freemen — subject only to a general provision that they should be reasonable and not be repugnant to the laws of England. The proprietary had full executive power, including all those attached to the rapidly dying feudal setup. To complete the autonomy of Baltimore's colony, the colonists were exempted in perpetuity from all English tallages on goods and estates, which privilege in previous charters was granted for only a period of years. The laws enacted by the freemen and approved by Baltimore were not subject to review by the Crown, contrary to the practice followed in Pennsylvania and Delaware. Maryland was the first colony to be governed regularly by laws passed by a provincial legislature. (*Lucas. Charters, 87–97.*)

Former members of the Virginia Company objected to the grant of such extensive powers. They held that Baltimore could grant land in fee simple to aliens and enemies, and he could make war and peace, thus possibly embroiling all of the colonies. By the right to grant honors along with the land it was held that he might start a wave of immigration which would depopulate the other colonies. The item of Baltimore's religion was not overlooked. They also held that the charter was vague since no particular Bishop of Durham was named and that their rights had been changed from time to time. In addition, it was held that the territory was within the limits of the Virginia charter, and already occupied by settlers sent over by that company. In fact, the objectors levied all sorts of charges against both the charter and Lord Baltimore. (*Steiner. Md. Charter, 148–49.*) But all of this was to no avail. And with the exception of a period of twenty-five years, from 1691 to 1716, Maryland was completely under the control of the Baltimores. The 1632 charter was the basic law until a state constitution was adopted in 1776.

WILLIAM PENN AND PENNSYLVANIA

Prior to Penn's charter for Pennsylvania, which was dated March 14, 1681, the land had been granted several times under various conditions of tenure. The first charter of Virgina was the beginning; then in rapid succession came the other Virginia charters, the grant to the Council for New England, the Dutch grant to their West India Company, the charters of Maryland and Connecticut which encompassed territory in Pennsylvania, and the first and second grants to the Duke of York. However, the rights extended by these grants had not been fully proved by settlement and occupancy at the time that Penn applied for the territory. As a consequence, Pennsylvania, as late as 1681, was still available under customary usage to be granted in a block to one individual.

William Penn, a devout Quaker, inherited from his father, Admiral Penn, a claim on King Charles II to the extent of some £16,000. (*MacDonald. Charters, 183.*) The king requited this claim by granting extensive rights in land and governmental jurisdiction over a vast domain in America. From Penn's viewpoint the grant not only effected a financial settlement, but more important, it provided a religious refuge for his fellow Quakers who were severely persecuted in their native England. As soon as the charter cleared, Penn set himself to the task of settling the territory. He worked diligently, endeavoring in every way to provide for an effective and rapid occupancy of the colony. He issued vivid descriptions of the area, explained in considerable detail the liberal interpretations to be placed upon the content of the charter, and the great freedom which it guaranteed, and developed in cooperation with the settlers at least three great documents under which the colony was successively governed.

The land received by Penn was bounded on the east by the Delaware River and on the north by the forty-third degree of north latitude; it was to extend westward for five degrees of longitude. (*Lucas. Charters, 100–108.*) This is shown in Figure 8.2. These descriptions are reasonably definite, except for the southern boundary. This line was to be determined by a circle of twelve miles distance drawn westward and northward from New Castle, which line was to connect with the fortieth degree of north latitude, which was the northern boundary of Maryland described in its charter almost fifty years earlier. This description was inaccurate, for the twelve-mile circle around New Castle could not touch the fortieth parallel, which was much farther north. The land included within the twelve-mile radius from New Castle was, therefore, a part of the territory assigned to Baltimore, for his line followed the fortieth parallel from the Delaware River westward. This border difficulty was not eliminated until just before the Revolution.

Penn's rights in this territory were almost as extensive as those enjoyed by Lord Baltimore. Paraphrasing the charter, he was constituted true and absolute proprietor of the area, reserving to the Crown only faith, allegiance, and sovereignty and one-fifth of the gold and silver plus a token quitrent of two beaver skins yearly.

The land was to be held of the Crown in free and common socage, and not in capite or by knight service, as of the Castle of Windsor, in the County of Berks. Penn was given authority to erect manorial estates or to grant to others that privilege and to establish manorial governments suitable to conditions in America. The lord of the manor could regrant the land of the manor in fee simple or any other estate of inheritance to be held of said manor. It was further provided that subsequent alienation should be done in such a way that no further tenures would be created, but the land would be held of the same lord by the same rents and services as the grantor held. This was in contrast with the rights given Lord Baltimore, who could provide for subinfeudation without restriction. Penn could permit only one step of subinfeudation. Thus, Penn could establish manors himself or they could be established under a grant from Penn.

Conventional tenure transfers could be from the Crown to Penn,

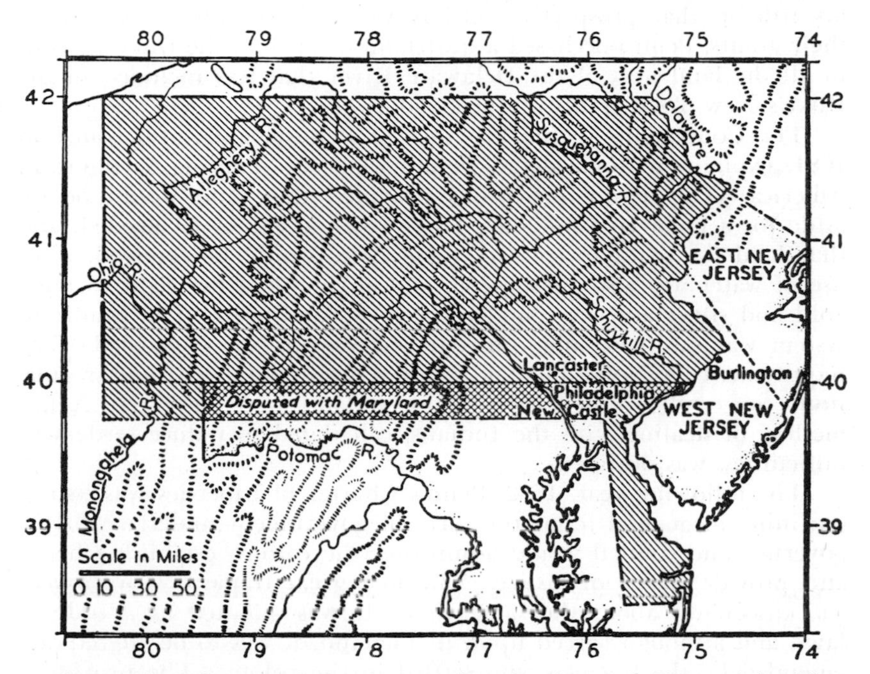

Figure 8.2—William Penn's domain granted in the Charter of 1681, and the "Three Lower Counties."

(Due to vagueness of recorded data, boundaries can be considered only approximate.)

to a manorial lord, then to an occupier or owner. Of course, the person holding an estate of inheritance could grant an estate for years, a lease, for example, but not an estate of inheritance, to be held of him. In addition to the establishment of manors, Penn could grant parcels of land directly to settlers to be held immediately of Penn and mediately of the Crown in fee simple, fee tail, for a term of life, lives, or years, as of the Seigniory of Windsor for such charges as Penn saw fit to impose, regardless of the Statute of *Quia Emptores*.

Since Penn could establish manorial courts and whatever other governmental organization that was deemed necessary, he had almost as extensive control over the government of Pennsylvania as Baltimore had over Maryland. In fact, Penn's charter was modeled after the one for Maryland. The major differences were three: (1) All laws had to be transmitted regularly to England for approbation or dissent. (2) An agent of the colony had to reside in England to reduce the customary interminable delays in securing information about the colony. (3) Parliament reserved the right of taxation.

Within a month after the charter was officially passed, the king issued a royal proclamation commanding all English subjects already residing in the area to yield such obedience to Penn as was provided for in the charter. (*Pa. Arch. 8th Ser., I, xl–xli.*) In order to perfect his title so that prospective settlers would have full confidence in their grants, Penn purchased a quitclaim deed from the Duke of York to all the land west of the Delaware River that was included in the Duke's New York grants of 1664 and 1674.

The Concessions to the Province of Pennsylvania, also issued in 1681, explains in some detail Penn's plan for planting a colony in America. The tenure provisions provided that land would be set aside for a great city and such lesser cities as might be needed, and that land for roads to connect these cities would be reserved. Free use of water was also guaranteed, and anyone had the right to mine gold and silver anywhere under specified conditions. The headright system was outlined, and quitrent reservations were specified. The requirements for planting and seating were indicated, and regulations concerning conservation of forest land were imposed. A fair method of dealing with the Indians, calculated to reduce settlement difficulties, was outlined.

The following year, 1682, Penn's Charter of Liberties was issued, outlining in general terms the form of government under which the governor and council would administer the colony, establish schools, and provide courts of justice. The first great frame of government was drawn up about the same time. It was adopted as a code of laws, and although agreed upon in England, it was to be altered and amended by the freemen who settled in the colony. The provincial council was organized in Pennsylvania the following year. Specific laws relating to land were concerned with taxation, mortgaging, wills, prescription, recording, indentured servants, escheat, and establishment of public schools. (*Ibid., xlvi–lxiv.*)

A new frame of government, confined largely to civil jurisdiction, was promulgated in 1683, at which time the Delaware settlements were brought into full union with the Pennsylvania colony. This new frame was issued for the purpose of remedying certain defects in the earlier frame.

Still another frame of government was issued in 1696, after the colony had been taken from Penn and subsequently restored to him when the charges against him were disproved. Only three provisions related specifically to land tenure. Almost immediately another movement was afoot to draw up a new frame or charter. A commission was agreed to in 1700 and its work was completed in haste in 1701, when it was rumored that the colony again would be taken from Penn. This charter of privileges continued in force until 1776 when the new state constitution replaced it. The privileges granted the settlers were extensive – so extensive that Penn's sons and legal advisers of the Crown held that this charter gave the assembly more power than was warranted by the original charter from the king. In 1701, Delaware, using a provision in the charter, established a separate assembly and continued as a separate colony until her formation as a state in 1776.

DELAWARE-PENNSYLVANIA RELATIONS

The early grants covering Delaware follow the same pattern as those in Pennsylvania, except for the intrusion of the Swedes. William Usselinx, who was interested in the Dutch West India Company but disagreed with its management, went to Sweden and interested the Crown in the establishment of a trading company. A trading company charter was issued by the Swedish Crown to the South Company in 1626 and renewed in 1637. Fort Christiana, the present site of Wilmington, was established in 1638, and the land around it was claimed in the name of Sweden. During the subsequent seventeen years a few hundred settlers – Swedes, Finns, and Dutch – came under Swedish protection to farm and trade in the area. The Dutch previously had established a trading post there, but it had been destroyed completely by the Indians.

The claim of the Swedes to the territory was based upon occupancy and purchase from the Indians. The Swedes maintained their control until 1655, when a Dutch army forced surrender and New Sweden, as it was known, became a part of New Netherland. During the seventeen years from 1638 to 1655, the Swedish settlers in Delaware were interested chiefly in fur trade; they farmed solely to support the company's employees who were resident there. Little is known of their system of land tenure. When the Dutch took over, the Swedes were permitted either to return to Sweden or to remain in America. Those who remained were allowed to retain their land.

"The Three Lower Counties," or "The Territories" as they were sometimes called, remained a part of New Netherland and New York until 1682 when the Duke of York conveyed them to William Penn. The boundaries of the "Three Lower Counties" are shown on Figure 8.2, page 123. This grant was for the land within a twelve-mile radius around the town of New Castle and the land south of this as far as Cape Henlopen, which gave Penn a clear outlet to the sea. Little concern was evidenced about overlapping with the Maryland grant, which included this territory and under which settlement there had already been made. (*Pa. Arch. 1st Ser., I, 52–53.*) The Delaware counties remained in Pennsylvania until 1701, when they were granted a separate charter by Penn. The 1701 charter was brief, and was concerned chiefly with government and freedom of conscience. This charter continued in force until 1776.

The contrast between the three corporate and the three proprietary colonies is sharp and clear. In the corporate colonies the inhabitants in general controlled land distribution and adjustment in tenure relations, while the settlers in the proprietary colonies were subject to the wishes of the proprietors. However, even in the corporate colonies the settlers were not completely free; the superior might of the mother country had to be reckoned with. In this regard, the corporate and proprietary colonies were alike, for the proprietary colonies also had to submit whenever the Crown found an opportunity and desired to exert its sovereignty. Regardless of this subservience, the corporate colonists were much freer than the inhabitants of the proprietary colonies.

It should be noted, however, that the Maryland charter guaranteed the settlers considerable participation in local affairs and that the colonists in Pennsylvania were likewise protected. One major difference was that enactments of the Maryland assembly had to be approved only by Baltimore, whereas those passed in Pennsylvania had to receive Penn's approval and also royal approbation before becoming law. But these differences did not plague the colonists as much as quitrents levied by the proprietors and the possibility of creating manors, which was attempted in Maryland.

The rights of the proprietors in land and government were subject to local influences, which were as potent in many regards in the proprietary colonies as in Puritan New England. But in major matters the proprietary colonists were not as free as the corporate colonists. The colonists who received corporate charters, for example, could have levied quitrents upon "new comers" if they so desired. But the collection of quitrents was not practical in Puritan New England. Thus, the essential difference in these colonies may well have been that the corporate colonists had the power to eliminate quitrents from the beginning, while the proprietary colonists had to wage a fight for their elimination.

CHAPTER 9

Five Composite Colonies

INSTITUTIONS IN THE FIVE COMPOSITE COLONIES – New Hampshire, New Jersey, North Carolina, South Carolina, and Georgia – were unlike those in the other eight colonies. The five were similar to the other colonies, at one time or another, in land tenure and government, except for certain corporate aspects of the three Puritan colonies. The land was held by proprietary groups or individuals and later returned to the Crown; government followed the same pattern. Control over land and government did not always reside in the same place. The confusion resulting from this was intensified by the splitting of the original proprietary grants among several proprietors, as in New Jersey, and between the Crown and a descendant of one of the original proprietors as in North Carolina.

NEW HAMPSHIRE

Since no permanent settlements were established in New Hampshire under the grant to the Plymouth Company, this charter is unimportant. The grant to the Council for New England is also of no importance, for under its subsequent regrant of New Hampshire, little was accomplished. When Gorges and Mason failed to plant settlers upon their 1622 grant, due to the wars involving England with France and Spain, they decided in 1629 to divide their territory, Mason receiving what is now called New Hampshire. His membership in the New England council after 1632 made it easy for the council to confirm his rights in the land, which was done in 1635, just before the council was dissolved.

The grants of 1622 and 1629 were of the same form and tenor, with the exception of the restricted boundaries of the latter. They contained the conventional free and common socage tenure provisions, with the precious metal reservation – one-fifth for the Crown and one-fifth for the council. The 1635 grant, unconfirmed by the Crown, gave Mason the territory under the same tenure enjoyed by the council.

Before this grant was made to Mason, several small grants of land, but not government, were made by the Plymouth Company, and some settlement had taken place. In 1637, a religious leader by the name of Wheelwright, who had been convicted of sedition by the Massachusetts General Court because of his teachings, journeyed north to Exeter and established a settlement there. Two years later, in the absence of a basic charter for a civil government, the Exeter inhabitants entered into an agreement similar to the Mayflower Compact for the purpose of better living together before God. They agreed to be loyal subjects of King Charles according to the liberties of the English colony of Massachusetts Bay, to submit to the laws of England, and to abide by the laws ". . . made and enacted among us [meaning the settlers] according to God that we may live quietly and peaceably together in all godliness and honesty." (*Thorpe. Charters, IV, 2445.*) In 1641, the settlers upon the Piscataqua River entered into a similar combination for the better ordering of civil government. Other settlements had been established at Dover and Portsmouth by Anglicans, and at Hampton by orthodox Puritans.

All of these settlements were annexed to Massachusetts between 1641 and 1643. This annexation is explainable in part by the dilatory action of Mason's heirs after his death in 1635. Massachusetts immediately took advantage of the situation and substantiated her action by an interpretation to the effect that her charter really included this area. (*Nettels. Roots, 209.*) These small settlements were so diverse religiously and otherwise that Massachusetts wisely permitted them a large measure of self-rule. They remained under the protection of Massachusetts Bay until 1677, when English judges declared them no longer a part of that colony. In 1679, New Hampshire became a royal colony, and remained so until the Revolution.

In 1635, John Wollaston received an interesting grant from the New England council. It was entitled a "Grant of the Province of New Hampshire" but actually was concerned with a tract of land in Maine. This grant and the regrant that subsequently was made to Mason were singular in that they provided for terms of 3,000 years, and were not grants in perpetuity. (*Thorpe. Charters, IV, 2438.*) These are the only grants that were made for a term of years. The reason for the unique time limitation is undetermined.

New Hampshire is an excellent example of the experience gained by colonists in running their own affairs. The colonists had to take matters into their own hands to form a government, owing to lack of positive action by the proprietors or the mother country. The New Hampshire towns had no over-all government until they came under the jurisdiction of Massachusetts Bay. Prior to that their separate governments were formed by voluntary agreements, which exercised both municipal and ecclesiastical jurisdiction. Their general operational procedures were similar to those of English towns from which the settlers came. They were not actually tied together governmentally under Massachusetts, for each town sent its own representatives to the General Court in Boston and ran its own affairs locally.

The colonists settled under the free and common socage tenures of the original charters. It seems clear that Mason purchased New Hampshire in the hope of setting up a hereditary fief, with himself as proprietor. But he could not reckon with, nor collect revenues from, the individualistic adventurers from England or the religious exiles and voluntary emigrants from Massachusetts Bay. When Mason's son wearied of the endeavor to make the venture financially successful the Crown took over. From that time to the Revolution, New Hampshire was a royal colony.

NEW JERSEY — EAST AND WEST

The territory that later became the state of New Jersey was included in the first Virginia charter (1606), the grant to the Council for New England (1620), the charter of Massachusetts Bay (1629), and the charter of Connecticut (1662), all of which were grants made by the English Crown. This land was also granted by the Dutch Crown to the Dutch West India Company (1621), and then attained the status of a Dutch province (1623). Later, the area was subject to the provisions of the Dutch Charter of Privileges to Patroons (1628), the Freedoms and Exemptions (1629), and the new Dutch charter of 1640.

It is probable that the Swedish colony in Delaware also had a claim to some of the territory, but the land included in that grant was not described accurately enough to merit a definitive decision. However, the Swedes had acquired by successive purchases from the Indians all of the land from Cape Henlopen to the great falls of the Delaware River, which may have included land on both sides of the river. In addition, it has been asserted that Charles I had ceded all of the territory of the Delaware Valley to Sweden, and if this is true, although the treaty has never been found, then the Swedes may have had at one time a good claim to the region. But these overlapping and contradictory rights represent only the beginning of the difficulty in New Jersey.

The patents under which most of New Jersey was settled were made subsequent to these grants. The first of these later charters was made by Charles II to the Duke of York on March 12, 1664. The Duke of York was to hold this territory under the following provision: ". . . to be holden of us our heirs and successors as of our mannor of East Greenwich . . . in ffree and common soccage and not in capite nor by knight service. . . ." A little over three months later,

June 23 and 24, 1664, the Duke of York conveyed by deeds of lease and release to Berkeley and Carteret the New Jersey portion of his original grant. The lease and release actions, as stated in the release, put Berkeley and Carteret "in actual possession of said tract" since the English statute for transferring uses into full estates was applicable. (*Ibid., III, 1638.*)

It should be noted here that the grant by Charles II to the Duke of York and his lease and release to Berkeley and Carteret were both made prior to actual possession by the English, for Stuyvesant did not surrender New Netherland to Nicolls until August 29 of the same year, almost six monthes after the grant to the Duke of York. In addition, the surrender was not formally acknowledged until 1667 when English occupation was confirmed by the Treaty of Breda. Although these grants preceded the acquisition of the territory from the Dutch, they never were questioned. Theoretically, the English did not recognize the Dutch claim to this territory, for it was English by right of discovery.

The land granted to Berkeley and Carteret lay west of Long Island and Manhattan Island, and was bounded on the east by the Hudson River and the Atlantic Ocean. It extended as far south as Cape May where the Atlantic Ocean and the Delaware Bay join; as far west as the Delaware Bay and Delaware River, and continued northerly to 41°40′, and thence in a straight line easterly to the Hudson River. (See Fig. 9.1.)

The land was transferred to Berkeley and Carteret ". . . in as full and ample Manner as the same is graunted to the sayd Duke of Yorke by the before recited Letters Pattents. . ." (*N.J. Arch., 1st. Ser., I, 12.*) No specific mention of the power to govern was made. The absence of a definite grant of government was the basis for later disputes between the proprietors and the colonists – the proprietors contended that they held all of the rights formerly granted to the Duke of York, while the colonists contended that the proprietors had no right to govern.

The proprietors found part of their land already occupied, chiefly by Dutch settlers and some dissenters from New England. But these settlements were scattered and the new proprietors felt the need of encouraging others to settle in their newly acquired territory. As a consequence, they issued their celebrated "Concessions and Agreements" on February 10, 1665, and named Sir Philip Carteret as governor. This document was similar in many respects to the one issued by William Penn almost two decades later. The land tenure provisions were numerous and extensive, and were issued chiefly to interest new settlers in coming to New Jersey rather than to protect the settlers already there.

Religious freedom was granted; the settlers were also to have considerable civil freedom, which would be exercised through a general assembly. The assembly was accorded the right of dividing the territory into hundreds, parishes, tribes, and such other divisions as they thought fit. The more specific tenure provisions related to collection of quitrent due the proprietors, to the recording of all land titles and deeds, and to leases for longer than one year, which were to be recorded. Forms for transferring land from one party to another were outlined, official surveying was provided for, and certain freedom of trespass on ungranted land was allowed. The system of settlement

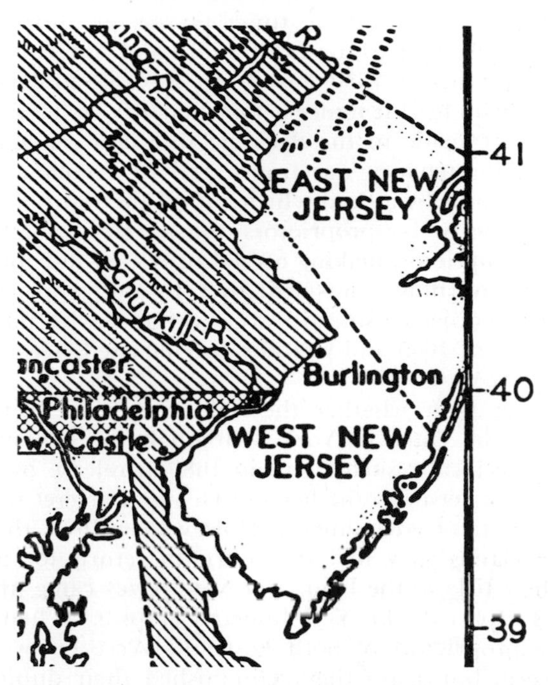

Figure 9.1—Land granted to Berkeley and Carteret under the New Jersey Patent of 1664. (Due to vagueness of recorded data, boundaries can be considered only approximate.)

by headrights and otherwise, including reservations for gold and silver, requirements for seating and planting, and allocations for such items as roads and streets, also were outlined.

The recapture of New York by the Dutch in the summer of 1673 had no appreciable effect upon the land tenure situation. The Dutch confiscation act of that year would have been important if the Dutch had not surrendered New Netherland again to the English in the fall of the year following.

In March, 1674, Berkeley sold his undivided part or share of New Jersey to Fenwick in trust for Byllynge, and two years later Carteret, who still held an undivided one-half, and Penn, Lawrie, Lucas (the three assignees of Byllynge), and Byllynge entered into the quintipartite deed, which divided the grant into East and West Jersey. The dividing line ran northwesterly from the mouth of Barnegat Creek, which evidently empties into the bay of the same name near the town of Thoms River, to a place in the Delaware River near Kenkokus Kill. The two provinces, East and West Jersey, were held in severalty in fee simple. Carteret took the eastern portion and Penn and associates took West Jersey. The new proprietors immediately issued a set of fundamental laws for West Jersey. Nine sections dealt with allotments of land, surveying, registration, quiet possession, quitrent, and taxation. They were similar to the Concessions and Agreements of 1665.

After Carteret died in 1680, East Jersey was sold to Penn and eleven other Quakers who held it under a joint tenancy in fee simple. Minor adjustments were made in the dividing line between East and West Jersey. The joint tenancy was transferred to a tenancy in common within a few months by a deed which cut off the right of survivorship. Later, each of the twelve proprietors transferred one-half of his holdings to a new proprietor, making a total of twenty-four proprietors. A new frame of government was sent over by the proprietors in 1683, but the assembly objected since it was at variance with the Concessions and Agreements of 1665 and was not duly enacted, according to their contentions.

It was never clear whether the right to govern New Jersey was transferred by the Duke of York. Although the original grant did not transfer specifically such right, in 1680, a release by the Duke of his claims to East Jersey to the heirs of George Carteret mentioned the transfer of powers of government. However, in 1688, the proprietors released any claims they had to govern in return for a full confirmation of their title to the land, and New Jersey came under the rule of Andros as a part of the New England empire. When Andros was deposed, the proprietors of both East and West Jersey assumed the right to govern, but again they relinquished their dubious rights to govern in 1702, when New Jersey was reunited as a royal province. During the last decade of proprietary rule difficulties over quitrents increased, and enforcement of the Navigation Acts became more difficult. Harried by internal strife, trade difficulties, pressure from the king, and small financial returns, the proprietors gave up their rights to government. New Jersey was ruled by a deputy governor from New York until 1738, and from then until the Revolution by its own governor.

The proprietors, however, retained their rights in the soil and continued to make grants to settlers. An endeavor was made by the proprietors to collect quitrents until New Jersey, along with the other colonies, declared herself free and independent.

THE TWO CAROLINAS – NORTH AND SOUTH

The charter to Sir Walter Raleigh, the three Virginia charters, and the patent to Sir Robert Heath each included the territory of the two Carolinas, but permanent settlement was not made under them. Heath's 1629 charter is of some interest because it antedated the one given to Lord Baltimore and like it contained the Bishop of Durham provision. Essentially it was not unlike the Maryland grant. Heath's patent was voided in 1663 because the purpose for which it was issued had not been fulfilled. Claims under it continued until as late as 1768, however, when the descendants of Daniel Coxe of New Jersey, to whom the patent had been transferred in 1696, received a grant of 100,000 acres from King George III in satisfaction of their claim. (*MacDonald. Charters, 120.*)

Failure to establish a settlement under the Heath charter left the territory free to be granted to whomever the king might desire. He granted the Carolina domain to eight proprietors in 1663. The territory extended from the northern end of Lucke Island, which was within the 36° north latitude, southward along the coast as far as the St. Matthias River, which was within the 31°, and extended from sea to sea.

The extensive powers of government and the right to create manors and new tenures were similar to, and in places identical with, those of the charter issued to Lord Baltimore. After the boundaries of the enormous holdings were laid out in the charter and the conditions under which the eight proprietors would hold their land were described, the proprietors were granted full powers to govern the colony so long as free assemblies were maintained and the enactments were consonant with the laws of England. They also could erect ports and carry on trade free of duties for seven years. They could confer titles of nobility, establish a militia, and declare martial law. Colonists already settled in the territory could be separated from any other jurisdiction. Full freedom of religion was possible, insofar as the proprietors saw fit.

A second charter was granted to the eight proprietors in 1665. It apparently had four purposes: (1) to quiet the title to the province, which might have been questioned because Heath's grant had been declared void by an order in council but had not been judicially annulled, (2) to enlarge the boundaries of the colony, (3) to protect interests in landed property established under prior grants, and (4) to reserve an additional quarter of the precious metals. In most other regards it was similar in content to the 1663 grant.

The boundary of the first Carolina charter was moved northward to about 36°30′ and two degrees southward to the twenty-ninth parallel. The latter line was almost one-third of the distance down the coast of the present state of Florida. Like the first charter, the territory extended from sea to sea, including islands adjacent to both coasts (Fig. 9.2).

The same year the proprietors issued a statement to indicate the general plan under which the colony would be governed and the land would be granted. The Concessions and Agreements provided for the recording of land transfers, the surveying of privately held land by an official surveyor, certain freedom of trespass upon ungranted land, and the levying of taxes only with the consent of the general assembly.

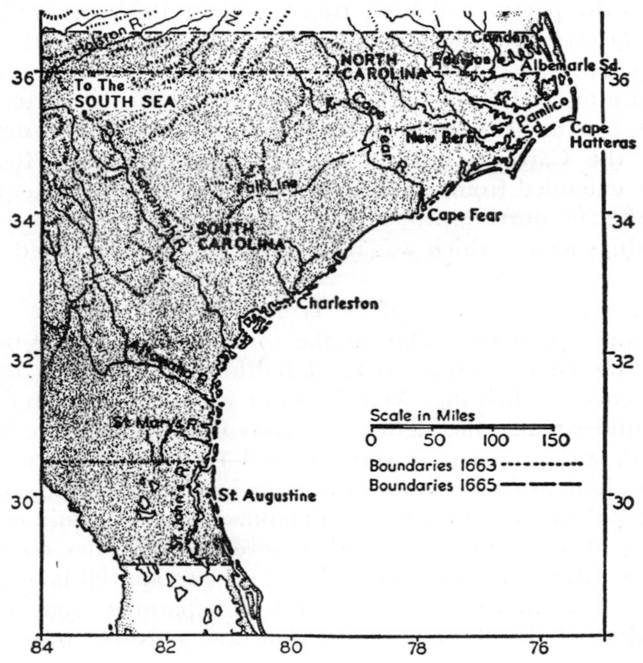

Figure 9.2—The Carolina Territory granted to the eight proprietors, 1665. (Due to vagueness of recorded data, boundaries can be considered only approximate.)

Religious freedom was guaranteed, and all inhabitants, old and new, were to swear allegiance to the king and faithfulness to the proprietors.

Utilizing the extensive privileges of their charter, the proprietors set up a rather democratic form of government. Great power was given to the popularly elected general assembly. The governor was chosen by indirect election, and to prevent him from usurping too much power the governorship was limited to one term of three years; as they agreed, he was ". . . to rule for three years, and then learn to obey."

(*Calendar of State Papers, 1675–76, 145.*) Within a few years, however, the proprietors completely reversed this position. By their own admission, they wished to avoid the erection of a "numerous democracy" and agreed upon the aristocratic scheme of land and government outlined in the Fundamental Constitutions.

Settlement proceeded slowly, and it was four years later, in 1669, before the first of the five drafts of the celebrated Fundamental Constitutions appeared. The second draft, the one usually quoted and discussed, appeared the next year. Two drafts were issued in 1682 and the last one was circulated in 1698.

The proprietors were to be the overlords of the proposed medieval feudalistic system. There would be manorial nobles, owners of large estates, small freeholders, and serfs. The territory was to be divided into two counties, each of which would be subdivided into eight seigniories – one for each of the proprietors. Each county was also to have eight baronies, and twenty-four colonies. It is usually surmised that the proprietors meant to hold about two-fifths of the land, either for themselves or in titled estates, and that three-fifths would be distributed to settlers. The free settlers would hold their land in free and common socage as of the manor of East Greenwich. The holders of the manorial estates could establish whatever type of tenure relations they desired.

The form of government was to be highly aristocratic, with both the judiciary and executive in the hands of the proprietors and nobles. The plan for a representative parliament was anything but democratic, for, *inter alia,* a person had to own 500 acres or more of land to qualify as a deputy of the freemen.

This scheme of landholding and governmental organization was not workable in an unpeopled territory. It was soon clear that feudal tenures were not adapted to the planting of a colony. The Fundamental Constitutions were never accepted by the freemen, yet were never formally abandoned by the proprietors. For half a century, until the revolution of 1719, the proprietors tried unsuccessfully to force them upon the settlers, and for fifty years they formed the basis for constant disputes between the colonists and the proprietors.

The first real endeavor to enforce the Constitutions was in the 1680's when the South Carolina colony was permanently established and consisted of over 2,500 persons. Small farmers and men of wealth opposed the imposition. They saw clearly that the proprietors would gain full control of the government for their own financial gain, that free land would be withdrawn from the reach of the settlers, and that serfdom would result. The wealthier traders would not submit to the proprietors' monopoly of the fur trade, nor would they cease to traffick in the lucrative Indian slave trade. Also, the endeavors of the proprietors to enforce the English Navigation Acts were obnoxious, and repeated violations continued. Finally, in 1685, members of the colonial parliament (assembly) were expelled because they would not submit to the Fundamental Constitutions, and differences between the governor and parliament became so acute in 1688 that the governor declared martial law and dissolved the parliament. Conflict did not end, but by the early 1690's it was becoming clear that the Fundamental Constitutions were dead.

The situation in North Carolina was similar. The original settlers who received their land grants from the Virgina colony were discontented for fear the proprietors might disallow these early land titles. Also, the 1673 Navigation Act placed an unbearable burden upon the tobacco industry. Riots and minor outbreaks followed each other until the disgruntled farmers finally succeeded in deposing the proprietors' governor.

The appointment of Ludwell as governor of both colonies in 1691 eased the situation. But South Carolina revolted in 1719 and became a royal province in government. Ten years later the proprietors gave up the struggle and North Carolina also became a royal colony. The Crown purchased the interest of seven of the proprietors, Granville retaining his undivided one-eighth interest.

It is difficult to imagine why the eight proprietors endeavored to harness a feudalistic regime upon their Carolina domain. The Statute of Tenures in 1660 had already converted all tenures, except copyholds, to free and common socage. Feudalism was dying in England. The struggle for representative government and a free land system was being rewarded by frequent and significant concessions. Yet eight English leaders set about deliberately to create a medieval feudal empire in America.

What men do is frequently determined by *who* they are. A look at each of the eight proprietors of the Carolinas as a possible explanation of the fact of the Fundamental Constitutions will be instructive.

1. The Duke of Albemarle, formerly General George Monck, was more responsible than any other man for the restoration of Charles II to the throne. After the Restoration in 1660 he was a popular idol, but he was also "an economic man," and as such was not averse to financial gain that might accrue from his influence with the new king.
2. Lord Ashley (Anthony Ashley Cooper), later Earl of Shaftesbury, once an owner of a large plantation in Barbados, was of the landed gentry. He became an expert on colonial affairs, and achieved fame as founder of the Whig party in England.
3. Lord Berkeley (John Berkeley) served well the Duke of York during the Duke's exile.
4. Sir William Berkeley, brother of John Berkeley, was governor of Virginia beginning in 1641, and contributed the prestige of his governorship and much factual information about the Carolina territory.

5. Sir George Carteret, reputedly "the richest man in all England," was governor of the Island of Jersey, off the coast of England, when Charles II sought refuge there in 1649 after the Commonwealth overthrew his father, Charles I.
6. Earl of Clarendon (Edward Hyde), father-in-law of the Duke of York and grandfather of Queens Mary and Anne, had opposed Cromwell, and returned with Charles II to be a powerful figure under the new king.
7. Sir John Colleton, as a Barbadian planter, had seen Barbados transformed from a land of small farmers into a domain of large sugar plantations manned by numerous Negro slaves.
8. The Earl of Craven was the least of the "big eight," but he too had plenty of money with which to speculate.

It is small wonder that the eight proprietors desired to establish and maintain on American soil the feudal system with its class distinction, superior-inferior relations among men, the nobility, the dependent small farmer, the tenants, and lower dependents. It is small wonder that they expected to increase their fabulous fortunes by land speculation in America. They would sell some of their vast domain to the highest bidder. The rest they would keep and develop into an enormous feudal estate. They would collect quitrents or other dues in perpetuity from all settlers. But such was not possible in frontier America.

In 1742, the Board of Trade recommended that the interest of Granville (descendant of George Carteret) be satisfied by assigning to him a portion of the land as a proprietary. Instructions issued in September of that year provided for the necessary survey. Accordingly a line was run separating the northern part of North Carolina from the rest of the colony. At first the line stopped at Bath. Then, in 1746, it was extended to the northeast branch of the Cape Fear River, where it remained for several years. For, as the commissioners reported, the region to the west was little settled, and the enormous difficulties made a more extended survey inexpedient at that time. Twenty years later the line was extended to the Rocky River in Rowan County and, in 1774, it was pushed on to the Blue Ridge Mountains. This extensive territory encompassed about one-half of the present state of North Carolina.

Granville held his domain until the Revolution, when it became an integral part of the state of North Carolina. It should be pointed out that this grant to Granville had at least one permanent effect. It resulted in the location of the line between North and South Carolina further south than would otherwise have been the case. For it was necessary to compensate the northern colony at least in part for the injury done her by this significant withdrawl of territory in favor of proprietor Granville.

In this vast territory Granville had the right to grant all unsettled land and to receive all rents and remainders due a territorial lord. He held no rights to government. His political position was similar to that of Lord Fairfax in Virginia. However, there was a vast difference between the development of the two proprietaries. Fairfax established his home within his holdings, while Granville never came to America. Granville's agents were in constant dispute with the settlers, many uncertainties as to titles existed, and innumerable controversies with the governor and council harassed the administrators. The result was widespread discontent throughout the entire area. Lord Fairfax had much less trouble in the Northern Neck. He had a better opportunity, by virtue of residence in the area, to succeed in the local administration of his estate.

OGLETHORPE'S GEORGIA

Territory included in the Georgia charter had been variously granted under the Virginia and Carolina charters. But it became subject to a final granting when the Carolina proprietors surrendered their charter to the Crown in 1729. Three years later a charter was granted to a corporation of twenty-one proprietors, headed by Oglethorpe, under the name of "The Trustees for establishing the colony of Georgia in America." (*Lucas. Charters, 110–23.*) The name Georgia was chosen in honor of George I, King of England at the time. The territory was intrusted to the trustees for a period of twenty-one years. Parliament donated £10,000 toward the project and the Bank of England was designated as financial agent and custodian of all moneys which might be contributed to aid the colony.

Three purposes for establishing a colony in Georgia were stated in the charter: (a) relief of poor subjects (not chronically poor only, but those of reputable families) who were reduced to great necessity and were not able to provide a maintenance for themselves and their families; (b) benefit of unfortunates, who by cultivating the lands which were lying waste and desolate, could gain a comfortable subsistence for themselves and their familes, and increase the trade, navigation, and wealth of the realm; and (c) establishment of a barrier for the defense of South Carolina and the provinces further north against the ravages of the Spanish and the Indians.

Members of the corporation were forbidden to hold offices for profit so long as they maintained membership. The services performed for the colony by these proprietors were to be entirely without a view of making a profit. (*Ibid., 115.*) This condition was precisely opposite that in other proprietorships. James Oglethorpe was appointed governor and retained that office until his resignation in 1752.

The land of the Georgia charter lay between the Savannah and the Altamaha rivers and from the headwaters of these rivers in straight lines from sea to sea, including the islands within twenty leagues of the coast. About one-half of the present state of Georgia is within the territory included in the original grant (Fig. 9.3).

The trustees were to hold the land as of the manor of Hampton Court, in the County of Middlesex, in free and common socage and not in capite. This is the only time that tenure as of the manor of Hampton Court in the County of Middlesex was used. This change from East Greenwich does not seem to have any particular significance.

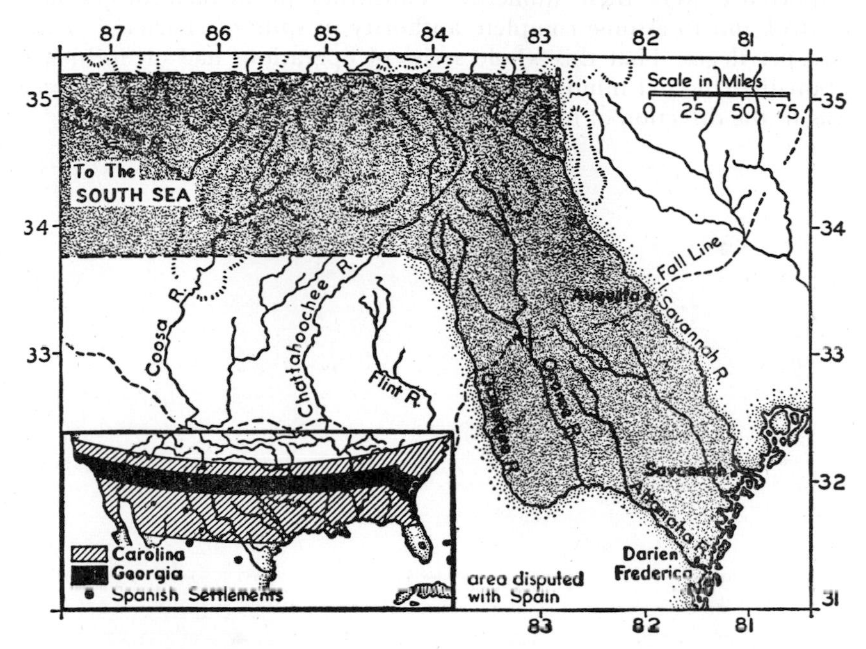

Figure 9.3—Land included in the Georgia grant of 1732.
(Due to vagueness of recorded data, boundaries can be considered only approximate.)

It should be noted that the Crown had not liquidated the claim of Granville to one-eighth of this territory since he did not surrender his right in the land included in the Carolina charters along with the other proprietors in 1729. As a consequence, he conveyed his one-eighth of Georgia to the trustees. The conventional royal plan of government was instituted with a governor, council, and assembly. The charter was surrendered on June 20, 1752, and Georgia became a royal colony earlier than required.

By way of summary, each of the five composite colonies exhibited characteristics similar to the proprietary or royal colonies, depending upon the location of control of the colony at a particular time. All of them started as proprietary colonies and ended as royal colonies. The influence upon the tenure system that developed in these colonies during the Colonial period and the effect of their tenure concepts upon the system of land tenure that emerged immediately following the Revolution are difficult to assess.

The fact that the Crown did not lend its influence to maintain the proprietors in control of their colonies is significant. But of more importance were their numerous endeavors to weaken proprietary control and to assume complete authority in spite of chartered rights and privileges. That this whole series of operations had an influence upon the colonial mind can scarcely be doubted. That this influence was in the direction of free and certain tenures seems axiomatic.

CHAPTER 10

Relation of Original Grants to Tenure System

DURING THE TWO CENTURIES OF THE COLONIAL ERA the governmental situation under which rights in land could be adjusted can be divided into four great periods. Roughly, most of the colonies were under the distinctive influences peculiar to each of these periods, although considerable variation existed in the colonies from time to time. The first period may be spoken of as the trading-company era, and lasted from the first Virginia charter to the time when the Massachusetts Bay charter was removed from England and brought to America. The second period was the power-granting era, and was marked by the placing of great powers of land distribution and government in the hands of settlement agencies and colonists. The planting of the Bay charter on American soil and the extensive governmental powers granted to Baltimore evidenced its beginning. It lasted for about fifty years, ending about the time Penn received his charter. The third era was the power-reducing period, and was characterized by many endeavors to return major and final responsibilities of government to the Crown. This period reached a turning point with the granting of the Georgia charter. The fourth period was very much like the third and may be termed the power-bargaining period. During it the Crown seemed to accept the general framework of colonial government and endeavored to make adjustments within the existing system.

POWER TO GOVERN

At the beginning of the trading-company experience the English, Dutch, and Swedes granted only those powers of government that were necessary to maintain civil order at the trading posts. The companies were more concerned with establishment of small posts and maintenance of monopoly of trade than with powers of government. This viewpoint was due to the purposes for which they were organized and to their heritage. The chartered corporate form of organization grew out of the early trade guilds that were organized into great regulated companies for purposes of foreign trade. Later the joint-stock trading company type of organization was developed with all of the monopoly advantages of the earlier regulated companies; the corporate form was developed later out of necessity and experience.

Slim indeed were the rights granted to the first planters and adventurers who came to America, for the primary powers to govern remained in England. At first local assemblies did not exist, and even land grants had to be approved in England. Those in charge of settling the new land soon learned from experience that they needed extensive powers to govern and to distribute land. Endeavors were made to adjust the situation within the framework of the trading company idea. But this was not possible, as experience proved, for trading companies were not adaptable to purposes of settlement. In moving away from the tight control of the trading companies, more and more powers of government were centered in the colonies, and land settlement agencies became freer of royal domination. It became quite evident that local assemblies had to be established, for Englishmen were accustomed to participation in governmental affairs. The first free assembly on the new soil was organized during this period.

Even at this early stage, it seemed clear that a colony could not be developed adequately so long as it was governed from a distance of 3,000 miles by persons unfamiliar with local needs. The centering of governmental power in the colony of Massachusetts Bay, which was one of the great turning points in colonial affairs, introduced the power-granting era. The Bay State inhabitants, after this action, assumed the right to grant land under conditions of tenure satisfactory to themselves so long as English law was not seriously violated. The centering of power to grant land in the hands of the people was one of the important events in the development of free tenures in America.

Another important influence that had its origin in this period was the free group compacts which were made among settlers who had no chartered rights of either government or land. The fact that the Crown recognized these free group compacts, and did not dispossess the members as squatters, indicates the general temper of this power-granting era. The influence of these associations of individuals was of major importance, considering their number. They developed unusual independence and freedom of action. When coupled with the fact that the Crown gave them very liberal charters after they were well established, the autonomy of these voluntary compacts greatly increased opportunity for development of free institutions.

The enormous power to govern that was granted to Lord Baltimore, when added to the right to establish manors, was an influence in exactly the opposite direction. One man, Baltimore, held in his hands the power to reproduce in the New World a thirteenth century feudal system of land and government, if the granting of unlimited authority could give one man so much power. All of the original charters from Baltimore to Penn gave the proprietors large powers in the establishment of government and in the determination of the kinds of adjustments that could be made in tenure arrangements.

Penn's chartered privileges, however, marked the beginning of a long period of conflict, uncertainty, and turmoil, the power-reducing era. During the following half century, the Crown made numerous endeavors to increase its control over colonial affairs. Basically, the Crown desired to convert the proprietary and corporate colonies into royal provinces. The notorious Andros fiasco was probably the outstanding incident. He usurped governmental power in over half of the colonies, from New Hampshire to Delaware and all colonies between. During this period Penn and Baltimore also were stripped of their chartered rights, and the eight Carolina proprietors were forced to relinquish their powers to govern. Finally, at the end of the period the Georgia charter provided that all rights conferred upon the trustees would be returned to the Crown within twenty-one years. This was in many ways a half-century of paradoxical action on the part of the Crown. In its endeavor to break the powers of the proprietaries, the Crown aided and abetted the settlers in many ways to become revolutionists, to overthrow the proprietors, and to acquire thereby more rights in government. On the other hand, the Crown was ruling with a hard hand those colonies where it had successfully asserted its power to govern.

Throughout the power-bargaining era, from the time of the Georgia charter to the War for Independence, the Crown generally ceased its direct attacks upon chartered rights, but much damage already had been accomplished. The Crown effectively had stabilized its control in Virginia and New York. Massachusetts had submitted to a modified and ineffective form of Crown rule, but Crown rule nevertheless. New Hampshire, New Jersey, North Carolina, South Carolina, and Georgia were brought under royal jurisdiction. Thus, the Crown had taken back power to govern in seven of the colonies and had compromised the sovereign position of the eighth colony, Massachusetts. Only the three proprietary colonies, Pennsylvania, Delaware, and Maryland, and two corporate colonies, Rhode Island and Connecticut, remained fully free of royal domination.

During the Colonial epoch, English legal influences were felt in other ways in all of the colonies. By the time settlement began in America the theory was well accepted that the laws of England were immediately in force when an uninhabited place was discovered and settled by English subjects. This was necessary in order that the settlers not be left in a state of insecurity and frustration for want of laws to govern them. The colonists generally held to this theory, which was well substantiated by specific provisions in several charters. They fought against the slightest implication that the Crown had the right to follow a second theory which held that when new countries were obtained by cession or conquest the Crown must abrogate existing laws and prescribe new ones, and until new laws were laid down the settlers were to be governed by existing indigenous law. It should be noted also that no endeavor was made by the English to force the Indians to accept the sovereignty of the Crown, as the Spanish exploiters did and as would have been conventional under early feudal lords. The colonists never recognized existing Indian law, and were never governed by it. In fact, it can be said that Indian law had no effect either upon the laws under which the colonists lived or upon adjustments in land tenure and government made during the Colonial period. The colonists looked to English law for basic principles but these were constantly brought under the refining influences of the Scriptures, particularly in the New England theocracies and the Quaker colonies.

Thus, in all colonies the theoretical basis for tenure law was the common law. Yet each colony was free, within bounds, to enact land laws consonant with its own institutions and best suited to its own situation. This universal heritage in the common law was one of the strong factors influencing the early land system in Colonial America. The common law understanding, either stated or implied in all the charters, tended toward homogeneity in the wild, lawless, and heterogeneous situation of early Colonial America. The common English heritage of most of the colonists, and the general understanding that the laws of England would govern in the absence of a specific statute and that new laws would conform to English patterns, were powerful unifying factors that did much to establish similar tenures throughout the colonies. That these tenures were free and easy seems unique. Wild and lawless times in the past had brought about a growing dependence of the smaller landowners upon the greater ones, as in early feudal England. For it was only the greater landowners who could afford to build a fortified dwelling strong enough to resist the robbers and lawbreakers of those turbulent times. This dependence expedited the rapid rise of feudalism under which the free allodial owners of land lost their free tenures and came to cultivate the soil in dependence upon the lords of the manors. The problems presented by wild and lawless times in an unsettled country five hundred years later were resolved by exactly the opposite process. Instead of giving up a relatively free landed status for protection, the colonial settlers agreed to face the hardships of the frontiers if they would be given a free tenure under which to hold the land.

Another liberalizing influence was the absence of penalities for nonfulfillment and nonutilization of chartered rights. In many charters no provision for enforcement was included. In others it was implied that the privileges would lapse if specific action for discovery or exploration or settlement was not taken, whereas in still others this requirement was stated explicitly. In only a few were any penalties provided. Gorges and Mason, for example, agreed to forfeit £100 if they did not plant ten families within three years upon their grant from the New England council. Most charters carried extensive rights but few responsibilities.

During the trading-company era the relation was slight between the power to govern and the rights of the settlers to make adjustments in tenure arrangements. In the first place, only a small quantity of land was distributed to settlers prior to the dissolution of the Virginia Company, and the colonists were accorded the privilege of meeting in a local assembly only five years before the Crown usurped fully the power to govern. However, the extensive powers placed in the hands of the inhabitants of the corporate colonies resulted in such liberal actions as those contained in the Massachusetts Body of Liberties and other similar actions. On the other hand, the extensive powers granted to Lord Baltimore and the eight Carolina proprietors worked in the opposite direction. The major influence, insofar as concerns all of the colonies, came at the time when the Crown was endeavoring to bring the colonies under strict royal control. Andros' endeavor to feudalize the New England and middle colonies, the unwarranted attacks upon Penn and Baltimore, and the strife fomented in the Carolinas no doubt made the typical colonist wary of those above him, whether Crown or proprietor. The constant bickering over governmental power, and the unstabilizing shifts back and forth, doubtless influenced the colonists to acquire as extensive powers to govern locally as possible, and thereby to minimize over-all changes in civil jurisdiction.

Frequent endeavors to prevent the normal development of local autonomy so that the rights of the citizens paralleled somewhat those accorded the inhabitants of England was another influence. In many ways the colonists were forced into the unsavory position of second-class citizens, and this was done contrary to the bright hopes of freedom and betterment held out to them as an inducement to migrate to the New World. The colonists found it difficult to understand why they were not as good as English subjects who remained at home, and felt that they should have all of the freedoms enjoyed by Englishmen anywhere. The necessity of guarding closely their rights, and of having to contend for freedoms that should have been accorded in the normal course of events, conditioned the colonial mind for the acquisition and permanent establishment of as many and as far-reaching rights as could be had.

It is generally agreed that the roots of the present system of land tenure are deeply grounded in the freedom of government granted in the "popular" charters, beginning with the second Virginia charter, and in the types of estates in land that were established under these charters. The experience of the Dutch with their less free grants in New Netherland, as it relates to trouble with the colonists and also to difficulties with the English, indicates the value of the free tenures of the early charters, at least from a colonizing point of view. As Brown indicated, when the second Virginia charter took the colony from royal control and domination, the germ of freedom began to develop, and this was "the genesis of the United States." This outcome was assured when the Massachusetts charter was transferred to American soil. To the extent that the form of government is related to the system of land tenure, the early charters were important, for the freedom granted in these charters was the basis for the colonists' protest against royal rule that precipitated the Revolution.

RIGHTS IN LAND

During the presettlement period, charters were more concerned with rights and privileges related to discovery, exploration, and trade monopoly than with the establishment of people upon the land. For example, the various bulls promulgated by the pope were concerned with the right of sovereignty as between nations. No mention was made either of the kinds of tenure by which the sovereign might convey the territory to settlement agencies or the conditions under which settlers might hold individual rights in the land. Essentially, the same situation existed in the chartered privileges accorded Columbus. Cabot's charter was similar in many regards to Columbus' patent. It was chiefly a license for adventure, discovery, and exploration. By the time of Gilbert and Raleigh the establishment of some type of trading settlement or outpost was visualized. Land was held of the Crown in free and common socage but not in capite. It could be granted to settlers in fee simple or otherwise according to the laws governing land tenures in England. They held their land by homage. The trading companies that followed them, however, could not do homage; therefore, they had to hold their land by some other method, whether token or substantial. Actually, the tenure burden, or charge upon the land, turned out to be a token payment, for the reservation of precious metals was largely unproductive.

From 1606 to 1732 the charters generally granted the land in free and common socage as of some manor. This was by no means a hard and fast rule. Exceptions are mentioned here chiefly to indicate that various types of tenure provisions were possible and that in actual practice several types were used. At least three charters were issued during the 1620's that provided for tenure *in capite per servitum militare,* that is to say, the land was to be held directly of the Crown by military tenure. These were the charters for Newfoundland to Lord Baltimore, and two charters granting land in the West Indies—Carolana and Montgomeria. The lands granted by the Bermuda charter and the charter granted to the New England council, including the grants made by the council, were to be held of the Crown and not of a manor.

However, all of the charters under which permanent settlements were established in the thirteen original colonies conveyed the soil to the settlement agencies in free and common socage as of a specified manor; holding of land in capite and by military tenures were specifically excluded. These charters were related directly to the colonial land tenure system. The earlier charters were only remotely related to the situation that existed after 1600.

In ten of the thirteen original colonies the land was granted to the settlement agencies in free and common socage, as of the manor of East Greenwich in the County of Kent, and not in capite or by knight service. The exact arrangement of the wording in these grants is not in every case identical but the meaning appears to be similar. The ten colonies are as follows: (1) New Hampshire, (2) Massachusetts, (3) Connecticut, (4) Rhode Island, (5) New York, (6) New Jersey, (7) Delaware, (8) Virginia, (9) North Carolina, and (10) South Carolina. The land of (11) Georgia, was granted to Oglethorpe and the other trustees "as of our manor of Hampton Court, in our County of Middlesex, in free and common socage, and not in capite." The land in (12) Pennsylvania and (13) Maryland was granted to proprietors Penn and Baltimore "as of our Castle of Windsor, in our County of Berks, in free and common socage, by fealty only, for all services, and not in capite."

Free and common socage appears to be the only tenure under which settlement agencies held their land. Although it was legally possible, there is little evidence to indicate that copyhold tenure was prevalent in any of the colonies, even in those where the greatest progress was made in the development of a manorial system. The reaction against feudal tenures was too great to permit the full development of manorial courts and the manor book, in which the rights and duties of the various types of tenants were recorded. With no copy roll there could be no copyholders. Likewise, it seems unlikely that burgage tenure was introduced in the colonies, and military tenures were generally specifically excluded. Although the churches held some property in the colonies, their holdings were never extensive, and tenure by frankalmoign, in a feudal sense, was never brought to America.

Socage tenure was the English tenure that seemed best adapted to the granting of land in America. It was the most common and most widely accepted tenure in England. In addition, from a practical viewpoint, socage tenure charges upon the land were those most easily collected from beyond the seas. On the other hand, it would have been difficult, if not impossible, to collect knight service charges. In addition, the English were greatly interested in encouraging emigration, and this could best be accomplished by granting the land under the easiest of English tenures. Socage tenure met this criterion. Advertisements, instructions, and regulations issued to the colonies subsequent to the charters indicate that no change was contemplated in the tenure under which the land was to be held.

TERRITORIAL OVERLAPPING OF GRANTS

The frequent duplication of territory included in many of the original grants was brought about by revocation of some grants, rearrangement of territory included in others, and in several cases faulty description. The resulting overlapping and conflicting claims furnished a basis for subsequent adjustments in land tenures. Any overlapping was of particular importance to the settlers, for they had to know to whom quitrents should be paid and where they would participate in local government.

The London and Plymouth Companies were granted most of the territory included in the original thirteen colonies. The Virginia colony part of the London Company's grant remained fairly intact, except for the mixup in grants to Lord Fairfax and others, and border disputes with Maryland and Carolina. The Carolina part of the territory was regranted to Heath, granted again to the eight proprietors, and part granted still again to the Georgia trustees. On the north, Maryland was carved out of territory that could be claimed by either the London or Plymouth Company. So was Pennsylvania and land lying to the north and east.

The grant to Penn also included land which was a part of the Maryland grant, and it overlapped some of the territory occupied by the Swedish West India Company under its commercial charter. New York and New Jersey were first included in the Plymouth Company charter, then the territory became Dutch by virtue of exploration and colonization, then English by conquest, later Dutch, and again English. The exact boundaries of these two colonies could not be determined under these various changes. Their history was further complicated by changes in jurisdictional control, being governed by a company, the king, an individual proprietor, groups of proprietors, and later by the Crown. New York and Connecticut never settled, during the Colonial era, their differences concerning land to the west claimed by Connecticut under her sea-to-sea grant. The territory in the four New England colonies was the subject of claims and counter claims up to the time of the Revolution. It was granted by the king to the Plymouth Company, settled upon by the Pilgrims without permission, usurped by the Massachusetts Bay Company, contested by Gorges and Mason, and remained up to the Revolution uncontrolled by anyone except the residents.

Many colonists were subjected to great uncertainty. They observed the recklessness with which the Crown granted rights in the same territory to several parties, and were familiar with the disputes among the several proprietors. The resulting bickering and confusion must have increased the watchfulness of the colonists, and must have added significantly to their distrust of the absentees who were trying to control the land tenure system from afar. Overlapping claims, uncertainty as to who had authority to collect such feudal dues as existed, and the heterogeneous conditions of tenure from colony to colony influenced the colonists to struggle for security and certainty of tenure. This could best be accomplished by giving the land occupier maximum rights in the land under his control.

POWER TO GRANT LAND

Land granted by the Crown to settlement agencies, regardless of duplication, overlapping, and border disputes, was held by them mediately of the king as of one of the English manors. The free and common socage tenure under which the land was held was the freest and easiest of all the English tenures. By and large, however, the land could be regranted to settlers in whatever tenures of common usage that these settlement agencies might select. Since it was possible for most of these agencies, if not all of them, to erect manors, it was theoretically possible to establish a feudal system in most of the colonies. This right was specifically mentioned in the charters of Penn and Baltimore, and the Fundamental Constitutions indicated that the right existed under the Carolina charter. The power doubtless existed in New Hampshire, and in New York, New Jersey, and Delaware under the Dutch and later under the Duke of York. The London Company reign was too brief to be of importance in Virgina, and the close control maintained by the Crown would have prevented the development of manors and the feudal system in that colony. Owing to the manner in which land was to be distributed in Georgia, it is clear that feudal tenures were not intended in that colony. The establishment of feudal tenures seems the avowed purpose of Gorges, Mason, the Dutch, Penn, Baltimore, and the eight Carolina proprietors.

The land of the three corporate colonies, on the other hand, was held in free and common socage mediately of the king as of a manor by the inhabitants of the colony, the inhabitants being the settlement agency. The citizens of these three colonies recognized the sovereignty of the king in much the same manner as present-day citizens recognize the sovereignty of government. The land was granted in free and common socage by the colonial governments to new settlers as they arrived. The development of a feudal system under these circumstances was impossible.

When the Crown usurped control in the various colonies, and

rights formerly vested in the settlement agency reverted automatically to the Crown, the ungranted land became Crown land. The land was to be transferred to landowners, who would hold it mediately of the king, for the king did not possess the power to create manors. By and large, this really meant that the land would be held in free and common socage, for by 1660 military tenures were eliminated and other feudal tenures were either inappropriate or not used by the time that settlement was under way in America.

Many of the charters under which the original thirteen colonies were settled would have permitted development of a feudal system of land tenure in most colonies, for at least part of the Colonial era. In the other colonies the tenure possibilities were largely confined to free and common socage. Feudalism was legally possible under many of the charters. Feudalism was desired by many of the leaders of colonization, and was actually tried in many places. It was an utter failure, however, well before the Revolution.

ORGANIZATIONAL DIFFICULTIES

Feudalism had not died out completely in England and northern Europe when English, French, and Dutch investors became intensely interested in making money from purely business endeavors outside of their native countries. In the change-over from a purely agricultural economy to heavy dependence upon industry and commerce, the businessman of that day was confronted with a problem of prime importance which took him the better part of two centuries to solve.

The early exploring and trading companies were not based upon a clear-cut corporate form of business enterprise that could be used for the planting of settlers in a strange new country. As a consequence, settlement was attempted under an outmoded feudal type of organization with which the government, the businessman, and the settlers were familiar. Practically all of the early chartered companies, forerunners of the modern corporation, were granted both governmental powers and the right to engage in business, whether trade or settlement.

The extensive feudal rights encompassing governmental organization (including military), business enterprise, and land ownership was the bane of operation of the sixteenth and seventeenth century businessman. Under these authorizations feudal estates were established in many parts of the New World. The seigniories of Canada and the patroons of New York were the respective contributions of the French and Dutch. The English even went beyond the setting up of mere manors, for in several places progress was made in the establishment of counties palatine.

Some of the early settlement groups were torn between establishment of a truly feudal manorial system built upon an agricultural economy and the development of industry and commerce based upon corporate enterprise. Their failure to fully resolve this dilemma doubtless resulted in the general lack of success, particularly in the early endeavors. Of considerable influence upon the land system in this period of indecision was the family farm freehold idea that was developing in many places. But progress was slow and was won only after painful experiments.

The frequent combination of commercial, governmental, and land settlement rights in the early American charters represented an almost unbelievable mixture of ancient feudalism and modern commercialism. The feudalistic principles were not adapted to the demands of the New World; the commercial ideas were. Gradual movement toward separation of governmental powers and the land system, and marked progress toward commercial and industrial specialization, were worked out in Colonial America under the various types of charters granted the early colonizing agencies.

The Crown was not in position effectively to carry on commerce and settlement; the businessman was not in position to perform governmental functions. At first both tasks were undertaken by the colonizing agencies, and many difficulties arose. Then the Crown took over, but it too could not do the whole job. Later, major responsibilities for settlement were assigned to private groups under special grants of privileges. But the American land system had to await the complete dissolution of the feudal system and the emergence of a system of democratic government and free business enterprise. Under the former the business of government was snarled up in the governing of business – the feudal lord was both a lawgiver and a businessman. As a lawgiver, he was executive, legislative, and judiciary, all in one. As a businessman he was president of the feudal corporation and directed the economic activities of all those below him in the feudal hierarchy. Under the latter, individuals were to be free to develop commerce, industry, and agriculture under associations fitting each peculiar need, with government laying down general rules.

From an organizational viewpoint, the attempts at settlement prior to Jamestown indicated that more resources were needed than could be assembled by one man. This experience gave rise to the large trading companies, but once settlements were established, and settlement techniques were generally understood, the trend was back toward grants to private parties or to small groups of political favorites and financially strong men. Finally, the last colony was settled, with the Crown helping to finance the endeavor. All the colonies except Georgia were financed completely by private funds. The Crown was quick, however, to recognize the financial value of the colonies once they were established and proceeded in many instances to develop a closer relationship to and more control over the various colonies than were provided for in the charter. That the Crown was successful in this endeavor in over half of the colonies indicates the power of the home government and the calculated advantage of getting the colonies under royal domination.

It seems unusual that the English Crown should have turned over the job of settlement to private enterprise. From the beginning of the national government the general policy has been one of alienating publicly held land directly to settlers, and in case some reclaiming of the land was necessary public funds have been used extensively. The over-all procedure followed in placing the land of the public domain in the hands of occupying farmers was not patterned after the plan used by the English government in getting settlers established in the New World. The former, particularly at the time the westward movement got in full swing, was direct and most settlers received the land under the same tenure. The latter, on the other hand, was indirect, being handled by various settlement agencies, each of which could give the settlers varying rights in the land upon which their new homes were built.

In both cases, however, some settlements were made without authority, and the colonial speculator, promoter, and developer was not unlike those who followed. Both took up unoccupied land, whether assigned or unassigned. No doubt the colonial squatter was influenced to a degree by the established process of settlement groups that settled upon land without authority or with very questionable rights. The groups that settled without authority generally endeavored to secure some type of grant within a reasonable time. It should be noted, however, that this was not always the case. In Rhode Island, the 1643 charter was concerned only with government and it was twenty years later before a land grant actually was secured. The pattern of operation and general attitude of these settlement agencies found expression not only in their action, but also the action of individual settlers.

KENTISH TENURE CLAUSE

The land of ten of the original thirteen colonies was held by the settlement agencies under free and common socage tenure as of the manor of East Greenwich in the County of Kent. Numerous other grants made during the early colonizing period carried the Kentish tenure provision, as did the grants to the Newfoundland, Bermuda, and Guiana Companies. Also, the forfeited estates of delinquent land in Ireland and the properties of abolished bishops and deans were vested in trustees who held them as of the manor of East Greenwich in free and common socage. By about 1550 East Greenwich was the usual form of grant. It was reported that about ten thousand tenants throughout England held land as of the manor of East Greenwich.

Many of the sales of Crown land were transferred under this type of tenure, and the lands restored to religious bodies by Queen Mary were to be held as of the manor of East Greenwich.

East Greenwich lies four miles down the Thames River from the London Bridge. It was a royal manor, which was occupied by over 250 free tenants holding land as of the manor. No copyhold tenures existed on the manor. These freeholders paid a small annual sum as quitrent, and were supposed to pay, by way of relief when the land changed hands by descent or sale, an amount equal to a year's rent, if demanded.

The land held as of a particular manor, and not as of the king, was not subject to interference by the Crown except insofar as manorial lords had let the king's judges encroach upon their civil jurisdiction. But East Greenwich was a royal manor, the king being lord of the manor. Legally the Crown and the lord of the manor were the same person. In actual practice, however, Crown manors were not greatly different from manors in the adjoining territory. The main points were: (1) that the land was not held as of the king, and as a consequence was subject to a minimum of exactions, much lighter than those to which the chief tenants of the crown were subject; and (2) that the charges were certain and fixed.

Not all colonial grants, however, provided that the land would be held as of East Greenwich. Calvert and later Penn received their grants as of the Castle of Windsor in free and common socage and not in capite with almost as complete lordship over the land as that of the king. They received power to erect manors and to subinfeudate at least one step. The land tenure provisions for the charters of Maryland and Pennsylvania were thus in sharp contrast with the tenure provisions of the charters for the other colonies. Penn and Baltimore owned the land included in their grants as fully as the king owned his castle or the land in the other colonies. They owed only fealty to the king, aside from the precious metal reservation. They had the right to establish the feudal system, and they could establish new manors, a power that the king did not have in England. Thus, they controlled not only the land tenure system but the entire governmental structure that supported and regulated it. The influence of the tenure provisions of these charters, however, was not great, for they were overshadowed by other factors.

It should be pointed out that the charters granted prior to 1660 included only Virginia, Massachusetts, and Maryland, and that Maryland's charter alone referred to Windsor and not East Greenwich. However, settlements were made in some of the other colonies under these charters, notably New Hampshire, Connecticut, and Rhode Island. Thus, the first grants for five of the thirteen original colonies — Virginia, Massachusetts, New Hampshire, Rhode Island, and Connecticut — were made prior to 1660 and under tenures as of East Greenwich. In fact, subsequent charters for the last three colonies included provision for the same tenures, and the English charters for four other colonies — New York, New Jersey, North Carolina, and South Carolina — were made so soon after 1660 that the law of that date could not have been expected to eliminate the influence of the Kentish tenure provision. Thus, nine of the thirteen colonies may be said to have to have been influenced directly by this provision, if it had any influence at all.

CHAPTER 11

Acquisition of Indians' Land

THE THEORY THAT ULTIMATE TITLE TO THE LAND was vested in European sovereigns did not exclude the idea, probably born out of necessity, that this title was subject to the Indians' right of occupancy. The Crown generally claimed the exclusive right to extinguish the titles of the Indians. In spite of this claim, the early charters and land grants almost invariably made no particular provision for extinguishing Indians' claims. Such was deemed unnecessary, for the Indians were not Christians and so could not rightfully and legally exclude Christian peoples from the soil. As a practical matter, however, the settlement agencies found it advisable to secure permission from the Indians to come upon and hold the land.

The processes by which the white man acquired the land of the Indians ranged all the way from outright seizure to free barter and sale. Most of the land was purchased, although many of the Indians probably never fully understood that they were alienating their possessions forever. Neither could they foresee that they would be pushed progressively from the Atlantic seaboard to the arid lands of the West. Some of the land was acquired by long-term leases. Few of these leases ever were renewed, for the Indians usualy drifted away before the lease expired. Or more than likely they had little comprehension of the difference between a lease and a deed or a patent.

GENERAL PROCESSES EMPLOYED

According to the agreement before he left Spain, and in harmony with the legal rights contained in his charter, Columbus took possession of the newly discovered lands in the name of the Crown of Spain. Following Columbus' voyages, Spanish explorers assumed that all land discovered by them in the New World became the legal possession of the Spanish sovereign.

Spanish and French Procedures

The official decrees and instructions from the Spanish government showed an interest in the well-being of the Indians, and indicated a desire to keep them satisfied. In actual practice, however, practically no consideration was accorded the rights of the inhabitants of any lands the Spanish desired. Although in many instances the Spanish compensated the Indians for the inconvenience caused by taking of their village sites and land actually in use, they never adopted the policy of purchasing title to the land from the Indians. Even responsibility of compensating them for taking land was often avoided by private parties and, wherever possible, was ignored by public officials.

The theory of the French regarding the land of the Indians was in a way different from the Spanish. When a tribe or nation of Indians agreed to come under French domination this agreement carried with it the right of the French government to full ownership and political control over the lands. (*Kinney. Lost Continent, 2–3.*) Also, the French immigrants to the New World fraternized and intermarried with the Indians. In addition, early French settlements in America were chiefly trading posts and fishing ports, but the English and Dutch came to live and establish homes in agricultural communities. The former use interfered only slightly, if at all, with Indian use and occupancy, while the latter interfered seriously in those areas where extensive settlements were established.

Dutch and Swedish Procedures

The Swedes did not make extensive settlements in America. They were concerned chiefly with the establishment of trading posts, and occupied only a small amount of land for agricultural purposes. However, the Swedish West India Company, as early as 1637, purchased from the Indians all of the land on the west banks of the Delaware River up to the falls. They seemed to have no disputes with the Indians regarding land.

The Dutch were probably more scrupulous than the English in quieting the claims of the Indians. The original charter required that title be acquired from the Indians and so did many subsequent grants. Direct and outright purchase was the procedure generally followed.

English Procedure

The early English attitude concerning the land of the American Indians is not stated specifically in public documents, for the charters, patents, and grants are silent on this subject. Apparently, however, the sovereign right of the Indians to the soil was not recognized by the English King. He granted territory on the pretext that it was his by right of discovery. (*Bruce. Econ. Hist. Va., I, 487.*) Ideas regarding the Indian's and the Englishman's rights in the land were expressed, in part, in some of the writings of the period. For example, the author of the tract entitled *Nova Britannia,* set forth the expectant policy of his country regarding the Indians as follows: "Wee purpose to proclaime and make it knowne to them all, by some publike interpretation that our comming thither is to plant our selues in their countrie: yet not to supplant and roote them out, but to bring them from their base condition to a farre better." (*Force. Tracts, I, No. 6, 13.*) The author of the paper, "Good Speed to Virginia," also stated that it was not the intention of the company to deprive the Indians of their rightful inheritance.

Even though the Crown generally failed to recognize the Indians' rights to the soil, some of those in whose hands the granting of it fell considered the peculiar position of the Indians. An outstanding example is that of Governor Yeardley who granted certain lands to Mr. Barkham in 1621 on the condition that the grant must meet the approval of Chief Opechancanough and be ratified by a quarter court. The company, however, condemned the part relating to the approval of Opechancanough, since this specification recognized the Indians' rights in the land. (*Va. Co. Rec., II, 94.*)

The English were not very meticulous in following the principle outlined in the statute of Elizabeth that discovery with occupation gave title to a new land. For example, they determined to seize New Netherland in 1664 on the grounds that the English were discoverers and that the Dutch were usurpers. The motivating force, however, was not the right of discovery, but the complaint of the farmers that the navigation acts of 1660 and 1663, providing for English commerce to be carried on English ships, could not be enforced as long as the Dutch held New Netherland.

Although England claimed the land by right of discovery, as did the other countries, she seemed to leave acquisition of title from the Indians to local authorities and grantees. That is to say, satisfying the Indians was the full responsibility of the settlement agencies. Therefore, several methods were used to obtain the rights of ownership and use. They were purchase by the white man, gifts from the Indians, treaty, abandonment by the Indians, acquisition by seizure, and occupancy under long-term leases.

RESTRAINTS PLACED UPON ALIENATION

Although the English sovereigns did not admit the rights of the Indians to the land and some of the officials of the companies failed to sense the attitudes of the Indians, many of the colonists and those in charge of local groups of settlers soon adopted the policy of satisfying the Indians before settling upon their land. In doing this the colonial governments in the colonies restricted, in one way or another, the colonist's right of acquisition and the Indian's right of alienation.

In New England

The Puritan colonies of New England were in a slightly different position in regard to quieting the Indians' claims to the land than were the other colonies. In the first place, most of New England was settled in the beginning without a charter from the Crown. Thus, the settlers did not have any pretense of a title from their king. Their rights in the land depended entirely upon a show of occupancy, purchase from native proprietors, or conquest. In order to have something upon which to base their occupancy, they naturally turned to the closest and easiest means, obtaining from the Indians deeds or other forms of permission for settlement. Later, they secured recognized authority from the English Crown. In addition, the Puritans, and possibly the Quakers, were more concerned with moral rights than the other colonists. Many of the New England religious leaders recognized the possibilities of various types of frauds if individuals were permitted to purchase promiscuously from the Indians. In 1658, by legislative action, Rhode Island provided that no person was to make further purchase of land from the Indians except when granted permission by the colony. The penalty was forfeiture of the land and a fine of twenty pounds. That the colony followed this act is attested to by the appointment of four men, one from each town, to purchase a tract of land known as Nyantecutt or Ninecroft. This appointment was made in May, 1659, and the purchase was later made. (*R. I. Rec., I, 403–4, 418.*)

Both Hartford and New Haven, Connecticut, as early as 1650, enacted laws prohibiting the purchase of land from the Indians by private persons without the consent of the General Court. (*Conn. Pub. Rec., I, 214, 364.*) In 1662, by an order of the court of the colony, it was provided that no person was to buy, hire, receive as a gift, or mortgage the land belonging to any Indian, except for the benefit of the colony and with permission of the court. (*Ibid., I, 402.*) In 1687 a fine of twenty pounds for every acre was imposed in addition to the purchase being declared null and void. (*Ibid., III, 422–23.*) In 1727, a penalty of £100 was placed on anyone purchasing land from the Indians without the consent of the colonial assembly. (*R. I. Laws, 148.*)

As late as 1717, Connecticut was still plagued with the problem of Indian land purchases by private parties. In that year the General Court affirmed that all of the land of the colony was held of the king of Great Britain as lord of the fee and that no person could obtain title by purchase from the Indians on pretense of their being the native proprietors. The order also provided that titles already so obtained could not be given as evidence of a person's title or be pleadable in court without special permission from the General Court. (*Conn. Pub. Rec., VI, 13.*) A fine of fifty pounds for making purchases in defiance of this order was imposed in 1722, and persons who suffered because of such transactions could recover treble damages from the wrongdoer. (*Ibid., 355–56.*)

In 1635, a Massachusetts law stated, ". . . that no person whosoever, shall henceforth buy land of any Indian without license, first had and obtained of the general court, and if any offend herein, such land so bought shall be forfeited to the country." (*Mass. Charters, 133.*) Plymouth enacted a similar law in 1643. (*Egleston. Land System, 8.*) On December 7, 1657, this was extended to cover the plantations given by the colony to the Indians, and by an act of 1747 it also covered all devises of real estate made by the last will and testament of any of the said Indians.

Many formal authorizations for purchase from the Indians indicate that these laws were rather well enforced. Many recorded cases of refusal to confirm purchases made outside of these laws also substantiate this conclusion. The New England colonies generally followed the practice of preventing private purchases from the Indians without specific authorization. In addition, settlers who took up land beyond the boundaries of the local government always secured titles from the Indians.

The Middle Colonies

Restraints upon purchase from the Indians in the middle colonies followed a pattern slightly different from those imposed in New England. The situation was complicated by the Dutch and Swedes and the mixture of royal and proprietary governments. Royal governors followed the pratice of buying large tracts of land from the Indians and regranting it in small tracts to settlers. Under this procedure, the need for settlers to purchase directly from the Indians was minimized. The problem was not entirely eliminated, however. It persisted in the proprietary colonies under the rule of the Penns and the Baltimores.

The Dutch in New Netherland were meticulous in their requirements that the rights of the Indians be properly extinguished before settlement. The 1621 charter, and secondary patents issued subsequently by the director general, conferred ultimate fee or right of dominion only after the Indians' claims were adequately satisfied. (*Rife. Land Ten. N. Neth., 48.*) In 1634, the patroons of New Netherland were bound to purchase from the Indians the land on which they proposed to plant their settlers. A similar requirement was outlined later. (*N.Y. Col. Hist., I, 99.*) According to these provisions, if anyone desired to settle on land not belonging to the company but belonging to the natives, he would be obliged to satisfy them before occupying the soil. Literature intended for settler consumption indicated that purchases could be made for a few trifles. (*Ibid., 401.*)

Transactions with the Indians came under closer public scrutiny and were made more formal in 1638 when an ordinance required that all legal instruments were invalid unless written by the provincial secretary. (*N. Neth. Laws, 17.*)

Land-hungry individuals, however, were not always content to await official action. They negotiated directly with the Indians, many times for their own profit. (*N. Y. Col. Hist., XIV, 1–5.*) As an outgrowth of these activities, Stuyvesant found it necessary, in 1652, to forbid the buying of land from the Indians or the conveying of lands so purchased to others without prior consent of the directors of the West India Company in New Netherland. (*N. Neth. Laws, 131–32.*)

Following English occupation of New York, the settlers still purchased lands from the Indians. To prevent this an act of 1684 provided that permission must be first obtained from the governor, signified by a warrant under his seal and recorded in the proper office of record. The transaction had to be acknowledged by the Indians from whom the purchase was made and the conveyance also had to be recorded. (*N. Y. Col. Laws, I, 149.*) New York continued to be troubled by purchases from the Indians even after she became a state. In 1788, an act provided for the punishment of any person who infringed upon that article in the state constitution which prohibited purchases of land from the Indians without consent of the legislature. The penalty was a fine of £100, which penalty was likewise applicable to settlement under color of title conferred by sale contracts made with the Indians after October 14, 1775. (*N. Y. State Laws, II, 366–67.*)

West Jersey, in 1683, ordered that no person should buy any tract of land from the Indians without special permission from the governor and commissioners. If purchases were made without such permission, the title was to be declared void and the purchaser would be subject to a fine not exceeding five shillings for every acre of land. (*N. J. Grants and Conc., 479.*) The proprietors of East Jersey instructed their governor the following year to do the purchasing of land from the Indians. (*Ibid., 196.*) The queen's instructions to Lord Cornbury, governor of New Jersey when it was under royal rule, provided that no person other than the proprietors or their agents were to be permitted to purchase any land whatsoever from the Indians. (*Ibid., 629.*)

In Pennsylvania before the turn of the eighteenth century, no lands were to be sold to any private persons by the Indians, nor were any purchases from the Indians valid except those made by Penn or his commissioners. Anyone who refused to submit to this ruling not only lost the land he bought, but was subject to a fine of ten shillings for every 100 acres purchased. (*Duke of York Rec., 9, 130.*) An act in 1700 provided that all purchases from the Indians should be void unless permission first was secured from the proprietor. (*Pa. Stats., II, 18.*)

Acts of the Maryland assembly in 1638-39 and in 1649 provided that no acquisition of land from the Indians would be valid except when the title was given by the proprietor. It provided that the proprietor could enter upon the land, seize it, and dispose of it, if it were not properly acquired through him. (*Md. Arch., I, 41–42, 248.*)

In the South

The southern colonies followed much the same processes in restraining settlers from purchasing land directly from the Indians as the middle colonies. The early stage at which Virginia became a royal colony, and the slowness with which many governors acted in granting land to small settlers, probably account in part for the widespread practice of settling upon the land without royal consent. Fraudulent purchases and encroachments led to dissatisfaction on the part of the Indians and culminated in open attacks by the natives. From 1637 to 1644 a series of raids and a constant state of warfare existed. But the whites finally triumphed, and the Indian empire was segmented by treaty. Transactions with the Indians were to be with the separate tribes, and they acknowledged the overlordship of the British Crown.

After considerable delay, the general assembly in July, 1653, passed a series of acts that finally described the lands to be inhabited by certain chiefs and their tribes. So closely safeguarded were the interests of the Indians in the land that an act of the House of Burgesses of Virginia was necessary to purchase any of it. For example, an act of November, 1654, empowered the commissioners of Northampton County to provide for the sale of the Indians' land in their county if a majority of the Indians desired to sell, if the terms were just, and if the proceedings were approved by the governor and council. As early as 1655, the Virginia assembly enacted a statute that made illegal the purchase of any land reserved for the Indians without the assent of the assembly. (*Hening. Stats., I, 380, 382, 391, 396.*)

Two years later, the assembly passed a law forbidding grants to Englishmen until the Indians first had been allotted fifty acres for each bowman. The Indians also were permitted by this statute to hunt on waste and unfenced land. It was also provided that if any land at Rappahannock or the adjacent parts belonging to the Indians was found to be patented, the patentees should either purchase the same of the Indians or relinquish their claim to it. (*Ibid., 456–57.*) Since this and former enactments of the assembly did not cure the ills growing out of encroachment upon the Indians by the whites, the next enactment was more far-reaching, in its pronouncements at least. The enactment provided that all Indians were to hold and keep the land that they had, and that no person was to plant upon such claims without full leave from the governor or council. It also provided that certain settlers who had been sent out should be recalled and granted land elsewhere. Furthermore, transfers of land contrary to the act were to be adjudged invalid. (*Ibid., 467–68.*)

Four years later the governor appointed a commission to inquire into claims made to any part of the Indian land, to confirm the just ones, and to remove the settlers occupying land under unjust claims to title. (*Ibid., II, 155–56.*) Apparently, as was the custom, the same assembly reaffirmed public policy by enacting another statute, which appears to be a digest of former laws relating to the Indians. This statute provided that it was unlawful to acquire land from the Indians without the consent of the government. (*Ibid., 138–43.*)

In 1660, upon petition from the Indians, a tract of land was set aside for the use of the Chickahominy tribe. The land was confirmed to the Indians by a patent which provided that no Englishman was to disturb them. (*Ibid., 34.*) In addition, the privilege to dispose of their land to the English was given by the general assembly to the Chickahominy tribe, provided each sale received the approval of a majority of their great men and each sale was announced in a quarter court or the assembly. The first sale took place on April 4, 1661 when Chief Harquip Mangoi sold to Philip Mallory 743 acres of land. (*Ibid., 39.*)

It was not until 1705 that the assembly provided that anyone making a conveyance with the Indians was to be fined. The penalty was ten shillings current money for every acre purchased, leased, or occupied, and would be imposed every year during the possession or occupancy of the land. (*Ibid., III, 464–69.*) About half a century later, however, restraints upon alienation were relaxed somewhat, at last in one case. In 1752, an act of the assembly empowered the Nottoway Indians to sell any part of a circular tract of land, six miles in diameter, situated on the north side of the Nottoway River. It was provided that no more than 400 acres could be sold to any one person, and that specific formalities in the transfer of land had to be met. (*Ibid., VI, 284–86.*) In 1756, the assembly granted the Nottoway Indians permission to sell 5,300 acres for the best price obtainable. The reason given was that the Indians needed money to supply themselves with the necessities of life. (*Ibid., VII, 44–46.*) Some years later, however, a more stringent restriction was placed upon alienation of land by the Indians. The assembly asserted its right to regulate these transactions to the extent of providing that only the commonwealth could purchase land from the Indians, and that all such purchases were to be for the benefit of the public. (*Ibid., X, 97–98.*)

In 1715, the North Carolina assembly provided that no white man should, for any consideration whatsoever, purchase any tract of land claimed by or in possession of any Indian without special liberty from the governor and council. A penalty of twenty pounds for every 100 acres was provided. (*N. C. Rec., XXIII, 88.*)

The South Carolina and Georgia legislatures followed the practice of enacting laws that made it unlawful to purchase land of the Indians. In 1739 a law provided for the forfeiture of any land purchased from the Indians. It also declared void any gifts, grants, contracts, or conveyances of any kind for Indian lands. (*S. C. Stats., III, 525–26.*)

Georgia provided, in 1758, that any type of conveyance of land from the Indians to settlers would be void and that the transferee would be fined £1,000. (*Ga. Col. Rec., XVIII, 248.*) This act was continued in force by acts of the assembly in 1759, 1765, and 1768. (*Ibid., XVIII, 359–61, 703–5; XIX, pt. 1, 69.*)

PURCHASE BY THE WHITE MAN

At first, throughout the colonies in general the right to purchase land from the Indians was accorded any individual, group of settlers, or company. The abuse of this right by many seeking possessions in America, the recognition of mistreatment of the Indians, and the religious beliefs and ideas of certain groups led to laws not only restricting the taking up of land but also acknowledging the moral and legal rights of the Indians. Purchase under governmental control was a well-recognized procedure for properly acquiring the rights of the Indians by those who admitted that the Indians possessed such rights, which soon came to be all of the colonies.

In New England

As early as 1629, two successive letters instructed Governor Endicott of the Massachusetts Bay Colony to pay particular attention to quieting the Indians' claims to land. (*MacLeod. Amer. Ind., 197.*) The advisability of formally quieting their claims eventually took firm root in New England, where Boston, Charleston, Salem, Dorchester, and other towns that had not purchased their sites from the Indians, located the descendants of the original native owners and obtained deeds to land. Boston peninsula was not bought until about 1670, and a deed was in time acquired even for the site of Plymouth, which had been given to the Pilgrims. In reporting on the situation before the outbreak of King Philip's War, Governor Winslow of Plymouth said, "I think I can clearly say that before these present troubles broke out the English did not possess one foot of land in this colony but what was fairly obtained by honest purchase of the Indian proprietors." (*Ibid., 200.*) The general situation indicates that Governor Winslow was reporting accurately, and that the Plymouth settlers were scrupulous in dealing with the Indians. Other evidence indicates that purchases were generally made by the Bay Colony. For example, on April 25, 1724, a deed was signed by twenty-one Indians for the transfer of a large tract of land lying on the Housatonic River, for which they received 3 barrels of cider, 30 quarts of rum, and £460. (*N. Eng. Reg., VIII, 215–16.*)

As early as 1633, Roger Williams believed that the king had no moral right to claim by right of discovery the land occupied by the

Indians. To Williams the patents of Massachusetts Bay, Plymouth, and the other colonies were of no value, for the king had granted something that he did not possess. As a true Christian, Williams felt he could not recognize these illegally granted rights. He proposed to purchase for a reasonable price the land of the Indians, deeming it the only proper means of acquiring the right to occupy the lands.

This struck at the heart of the early colonial governmental plan, which was based upon the same patents and rights as the rights to land. This was possibly as much the cause of Roger Williams' banishment from Plymouth as were his purely religious views. Carrying his conviction into practice when he started to settle at Rhode Island, Williams immediately purchased land from the Indians. On March 24, 1637, Canonicus and Miantonomo, the two chief sachems of the Narragansett, confirmed the grant made two years earlier to Williams. The grant was for land on the fresh water rivers called Mooshausick and Wanasqutcket. Ousamiquin, Chief of Paukanawket, granted to Williams and others the land lying between the Pawtuckqut and the Loqusquscit rivers. The former grant was for thirty pounds, while the latter was for ten fathoms of white wampum, four coats of English cloth, six of the best English hoes and English axes, and twelve great knives. The chief chose eight of the twelve knives and one of the six hoes, and promised to get the remainder the next morning, at which time he demanded four more coats and other things and otherwise raised the price of the land. (*R. I. Rec., I, 18–19, 31–32, 35–38.*) The Narragansett Indians deeded Acquedneck Island to William Coddington and others of Providence for forty fathoms of white beads. (*Ibid., 45–49.*)

These purchases from the Indians which antedated his grant from the English Crown gave Williams possession of a large domain in the vicinity of Providence. When he received the latter he became the undisputed owner of the territory included in the Providence Plantations. The charters of some of the colonies, where the settlers wanted authority from the Crown after they were fully established upon their lands, contain an admission of title in the colonists which already had been obtained from the natives. In the Rhode Island charter the admission reads, ". . . and [they] are seized and possessed, by purchase and consent of the said natives, to their ffull content, of such lands . . . as are verie convenient, both for plantationes. . . ." (*Thorpe. Charters, VI, 3212.*)

The colony of Connecticut was settled and its government was organized without a charter or grant from the Crown, but her leaders fully recognized the Indians' right of occupancy. The land was purchased from the Indians as the first Connecticut settlements had need of it. (*Conn. Pub. Rec., I, 569–70.*) However, the inhabitants did not always follow the plans laid down by their leaders. In 1699, for example, James Fitch was accused of purchasing land illegally from the Indians. (*Ibid., IV, 305.*) About three years later it was necessary for the General Court to order that all purchases made of the Indians were illegal except those made by the township to which the grants had been made. (*Ibid., IV, 397.*) And three years later, private purchases of thousands of acres on the west side of the Stratford River were declared illegal. (*Ibid., 526, 542.*)

The Middle Colonies

Although right of discovery was the legal basis of the Dutch to the land they claimed, the Indians' right of possession was recognized from the beginning. Apparently the Dutch king was the first European sovereign to assume the responsibility of purchasing land from the Indians. The original charter issued to the Dutch West India Company in 1621 alluded to this practice. It conferred ultimate fee upon the grantees only after Indian titles were extinguished. Subsequent grants and secondary patents issued by the director general provided for settlement of Indian claims. Manhattan Island was acquired in 1626 for goods valued at sixty guilders or about twenty-four dollars. (*N.Y. Col. Hist., I, 37.*) Staten Island was purchased by the English from the Indians in 1670, although the Dutch had purchased it fifteen years earlier. (*N.Y. Min. Exec. Coun., I, 337–44.*) "This was the initial transaction in the alienation of Staten Island from the New Jersey grantees and its attachment to New York." (*Chandler. Land Title, 199.*) By the Charter of Freedoms and Exemptions, the Dutch Government in 1629 gave its colonists permission to settle outside Manhattan Island only after they had satisfied the Indians for the land that they were going to occupy. (*N.Y. Hist. Soc. Coll., 2nd. Ser., I, 376.*)

When William Kieft acquired a part of the Connecticut Valley and Long Island, he paid the Indians one piece of duffels cloth twenty-seven ells long, six axes, twelve kettles, eighteen knives, one sword blade, one shawl, and some toys. (*O'Callaghan. N. Neth., I, 185.*) In 1638, he also purchased the western part of Long Island consisting of a tract of land two miles broad and four miles long extending from the East River to the swamps of Mespeachtes. (*Ibid., 185.*) Several years later he purchased land extending from Rockaway east to Sicktewkacky on the south and across to Martin Gerritsen's or Cow Bay on the north. (*Ibid., 210.*)

When the English drove the Dutch authorities from New York, they abolished forthwith all Dutch regulations concerning the acquisition of titles to land by settlers. They established the English procedure, by which the land was first purchased from the Indians by the colonial government and then granted to settlers. In the late seventeenth and early eighteenth centuries, Benjamine Fletcher and Governor Robert Hunter received instructions to purchase from the

Indians as much land as could be bought with small sums. (*N.Y. Col. Hist., III, 823–24; IV, 290; V, 140.*)

The colonial officers of New Netherland did not neglect the opportunity of advancing their personal interests, Jacob van Curler purchased from the Indians a flat of land on Long Island, Andreas Huddle purchased the meadows west of Curler's tract, and later Van Twiller purchased level land to the east. These purchases, which were estimated to contain nearly 15,000 acres, seem to have been negotiated without the knowledge of the Amsterdam Chamber. (*O'Callaghan. N. Neth., I, 172.*)

Governor Nicolls, the first representative of the Duke of York, granted a portion of New Jersey on Cull Bay to a group of men. This grant is known as the Elizabethtown grant. For this land the group gave the Indians a competent quantity of supplies. (*N.J. Arch., 1st. Ser., I, 15–17.*)

William Penn and the West Jersey partners required that presents be given to the Indians as payment for any lands they ceded to the colony. The first act of the legislature under the royal government was concerned with purchasing land from the Indians. (*Ibid., 1st. Ser., II, 517.*) It provided that after December 1, 1703, no person could purchase land from the Indians without first having obtained a license. Penalty for fradulent purchases was forty shillings per acre.

Penn was noted for the peaceful way in which he got along with the Indians. In 1683, he signed ten deeds with the Indians (*Pa. Arch., 1st. Ser., I, 62–67.*) and in 1684–85 he signed four more. (*Ibid., 88, 91–93.*) In all the patents or deeds a rather definitely described tract of land was granted by the Indians, but the amount of compensation was not always clear. In some of the deeds, for example, the amount of wampum, guns, shoes, stockings, blankets, and other goods which Penn was to give for the land was definitely stated, while in others the amount Penn wanted to give would be acceptable.

Several outstanding transfers of land took place in Pennsylvania between 1682 and 1736. In 1682, soon after Penn's arrival in America, he made his first treaty with the Indians. All of the land lying in the province of Pennsylvania between the Delaware River and Neshaminy Creek was transferred to Penn forever in exchange for clothing, weapons, and other usable goods. (*Ibid., 47–48.*) A year later all lands were disposed of that lay between certain creeks and a westward limit that could be reached by two days' journey with a horse. Penn was to reimburse the Indians for the land in wampum, guns, shoes, etc., in whatever quantity he wanted to give. One chief gave up his right to the land lying west of the Schuylkill River. Several chiefs sold all the region between the Schuylkill River and certain creeks west of it. Still others gave up their rights to territory between the Delaware and the Susquehanna rivers and extending southward to Chesapeake Bay. Not long afterwards several other Indian transfers included a large portion of land already sold, extending to Duck Creek in the lower counties, and westward as far as a horse could travel in two summer days. (*Ibid., 62–68.*) A similar deed for lands between Neshaminy and Pemopeck creeks was executed July 5, 1697. (*Ibid., 124–25.*)

In June 1692, land between certain creeks flowing into the Delaware, and stretching westward to the farthest bounds of the province, was purchased. (*Ibid., 116–17.*) Also executed in 1696 was a transaction known as Dongan's deed. Governor Dongan purchased from the Five Nations land on both sides of the Susquehanna River. (*Ibid., 74–76, 80, 121–22.*) In 1701, Dongan's deed, the original having been lost, was confirmed, and the Susquehanna, Shawnee, and Potomac Indians relinquished all titles of the Susquehanna tribes to lands on that river. (*Ibid., 133, 144–47.*)

In 1732 Penn purchased the land on the Schuylkill River and on all of its branches, as well as the swamps, marshes, fens, and meadows on the streams which flowed into or toward the river. For this land the Indians received numerous items. (*Ibid., 344–47.*)

The Indians of the Five Nations already had withdrawn from the region around the Susquehanna River and were living in what is now the present state of New York. The land they still claimed along the Susquehanna was bought by Penn in 1736 for many items of value. (*Ibid., 494–97.*) Again, in 1758, the general assembly appointed commissioners to purchase land from the Indians for occupancy by freeholders. The sum was not to exceed £1,600, and additional land was to be purchased from the Delaware Indians on the Raritan River at a price not to exceed £800.

In 1749, the proprietors purchased a large tract of land from the Six Nations for £500. (*Ibid., II, 33–37.*) Five years later, at Albany, the proprietors purchased for £2,000 all the land in Pennsylvania northwest of the Kittatinny Hills on the west branch of the Susquehanna River and extending to the southern boundary. (*Ibid., 147–58.*) At about the same time many of the same Indians sold much of the same land to the Susquehannah Company from Connecticut. This territory was claimed by both colonies, and had been the subject of some controversy prior to these transactions and prior to settlement by the Susquehannah Company. As the country became more thickly settled, the proprietors became more concerned with private purchases from the Indians. The seriousness of the situation is indicated by an act of 1767–68 which provided the death penalty, without benefit of clergy, for any person who continued to occupy land not purchased from the Indians by the proprietors. (*Pa. Stats., VII, 153–55.*) The following year a statute provided for the same offence a penalty of £500 and twelve months' imprisonment, together with security for good behavior for the following year. (*Ibid., 260–61.*)

Thus title to much of the vast holdings of William Penn was acquired by purchase from the Indians. Even though the land had been granted to him by the king of England, he regarded the Indians as the possessors, by right of occupancy, so he paid them for the land. Penn's practice of purchasing the Indians' land was carried over until after the Revolution. By the first and second treaties made at Fort Stanwix (1768 and 1784), between Pennsylvania and the Six Nations, all the remaining Indian lands in Pennsylvania were purchased. (*Agnew. Pa., 13–15.*)

The Swedes appeared to have lived on friendly terms with the Delawares; for example, they helped to protect them from the Iroquois in 1662. (*Scharf. Hist. of Del., I, 12.*) In 1637 the Swedish West India Company bought all of the land from the Indians from Cape Henlope, or Henlopen as it was sometimes called, to the falls of the Delaware River at Trenton. (*Conrad. Del., I, 17.*)

From the very first, Maryland paid the Indians for their land. Some of the early settlers selected the Indian town of Yao-Comoco as the place for their homes and gardens. This site, extending some thirty miles along the river, was purchased from the Indians with articles, ". . . suited to their state of life . . . ," which had been brought from England for that purpose. (*Kilty. Land. Ass't., 14.*) The articles included axes, hatchets, hoes, and cloth. (*Force. Tracts, IV, No. 12, 21.*)

Maryland declared that the acquisition of land from the Indians, whether by purchase or gift, without the consent of the proprietors was deemed illegal and void. (*Kilty. Land. Ass't., 15.*) However, in 1638, Clayborne purchased from the Indians the disputed Kent Island off Maryland shores. Other unauthorized purchases were known to have been made prior to 1649. (*MacLeod. Amer. Ind., 201.*) In 1744, Baltimore paid the Six Nations £300 for land on the Potomac and Susquehanna rivers. (*Md. Arch., XXVIII, 335.*) By 1768, all but a few of the Indians had gone from the south side of Sewalls Creek and these few desired to leave but wanted compensation to do so. A settlement was made for $666. (*Kilty. Land. Ass't., 354–55.*) Maryland continued the practice of paying the Indians for their land even after she became a state following the Revolution. In 1799, to the last of the Choptank Indians and their descendants, she made the following annuity provisions and land reservations: Mary Mulberry and her son Henry Mulberry, $160; Henry Sixpence, $100; Thomas Joshua, $160; and Esther Henry, $30. Land was to be reserved for each of these Indians in the amount of ten acres of cleared land and ten acres of woodland, ". . . to be held, used, and occupied by the said indians so long as they and their descendants should continue to inhabit the same and use it for their own cultivation and improvement." These payments were in return for approximately 4,000 acres of land known as the Choptank Indian lands which these Indians conveyed to the state of Maryland. Some payments were still being made to these Indians or their descendants in 1808. (*Ibid., 358.*)

In the South

Jefferson once remarked that a very important part of Tidewater Virginia was acquired not by conquest but by the process of lawful exchange. The records bear out this statement, for purchase was one of the chief methods by which legal title was acquired to a large amount of the land in Virginia.

The purchase of land on the James River in Virginia from Chief Paspehay for a quantity of copper was one of the earliest on record. This land was bought with the understanding that it was to be occupied and inheritable by the purchasers. (*Force. Tracts, III, No. 1, 6.*) In 1615, an unusual scarcity of provisions prevailed in some of the Indian towns, and in exchange for 400 or 500 bushels of corn the Indians traded a section of their holdings in Virginia as extensive as an English shire. (*Va. Hist. Reg., I, 106.*)

Occasionally, private transactions that had already taken place were confirmed by the assembly. Thus, the lands of the Wiccocomico Indians purchased by Governor Mathews would be confirmed if the Indians were tendered an additional payment. (*Hening. Stats., II, 14.*) A similar confirmation was acted upon in 1661 in regard to land purchased from the Wahanganoche Indians by Mr. Henry Mees. (*Ibid., 154.*) The same Indians acknowledged before the committee that they also sold a parcel of land to Mr. Peter Austin for which they received ten matchcoats; the assembly also confirmed Mr. Austin's claim. (*Ibid., 154.*)

Not only was Virginia faced with the problem of protecting the land of the Indians from contemporary and future unscrupulous purchasers, but it had to rectify some past wrongs. The Indians from whom Colonel Fantleroy had bought land were not satisfied, so the assembly of Virginia was called upon to adjust the claim. The colonel had improved the land and, since the Indians were unable to pay for the improvements, it could not be given back to them. The assembly decreed, therefore, that in addition to the recompense already given, Fantleroy was to give thirty matchcoats each containing two yards of material and one handsomely trimmed with copper lace to the king of the tribe. (*Ibid., 36.*)

The earliest purchases from the Indians in North Carolina took place before the colony was granted to the eight proprietors in 1661. Some of these purchasers held subgrants from the royal colony of Virginia. The first recorded grant from the Indians in North Carolina was made by the king of the Yeopim Indians on March 1, 1662, to George Durant for a tract of land on the Perquimans River and Roanoke Sound. A prior sale had been made to Samuel Pricklove, but was not recorded. (*N.C. Rec., I, 19.*) The early practice in North Carolina involved grants from the proprietors to the settlers, who in turn purchased the Indian rights. This policy was different from that followed in the royal colonies, where the colonial government purchased the Indian rights before granting the land to settlers. (*MacLeod. Amer. Ind., 202.*)

The preamble to a South Carolina Act of 1739, bluntly stated the situation that had developed in that colony as follows: "Such purchases being generally obtained from Indians by unfair representations, fraud, and circumvention, or by making them gifts or presents of little value by which practices great resentments and animosities have been created amongst the Indians towards the inhabitants of this Province." (*S.C. Stats., III, 525.*)

GIFTS FROM THE INDIANS

In many places the English found the Indians quite friendly and willing to give them land. So by gifts from the natives some of the first settlers secured title to the land they occupied in America. The basis or reasons for most of this generosity could not be determined. In a few instances the reasons were clear. For example, at Plymouth and again in New Hampshire, the Indians readily gave up their lands which had been desolated by a pestilence and were therefore uninhabited. The Indians often gave up land that they thought to be of no particular value. On the other hand, they frequently held fast to land plentifully supplied with game or otherwise well suited for their use.

On May 18, 1607, Werowance of Paspihe with 100 armed warriors came to the colonists and made signs which meant that he and his tribe would give the new arrivals as much land as they desired to take. (*Brown. Genesis, I, 162.*) How much was taken or whether any conditions were attached to it is not known, but this gave the Jamestown settlers their first foothold in America. Another overture of a gift was by Powhatan when he invited Captain Newport to leave Jamestown, as the place was unhealthful, and to take as a gift, ". . . an other whole kingdome." (*Force. Tracts, III, No. 1, 7.*)

One of the first permanent gifts recorded was at Wayanoke where a large body of land was presented to Sir George Yeardley by Opechancanough in 1617. (*Bruce. Econ. Hist. Va., I, 490.*) A gift which afterwards became controversial was that of the Wiccocomico Indians in 1658. They gave their lands in Northumberland County to Governor Mathews, and his claim was confirmed. (*Hening. Stats., I, 515.*)

TREATY AS A MEANS OF ACQUISITION

Land was also acquired from the Indians by means of treaty. Sometimes a small gift or token was tendered, but this neither approached nor was intended to equal a fair compensation for the land acquired.

The colony to profit most by the treaty method of acquiring land was Georgia. Soon after Oglethorpe arrived in America he met with the chiefs of the Mico, Lower Creeks, Upper Creeks, and Uchees. He explained that the English had not come to take away their lands but to live in friendship with them and hoped to obtain from them a portion of their land at Yamacraw Bluff and make a treaty of peace and commerce. (*Jones. Ga., I, 118–20; Estill. Oglethorpe, 51–52.*)

On May 21, 1733, a treaty was signed between Oglethorpe and the chiefs of the eight tribes of the Creek Nations. The Indians granted to the trustees all the land between the Savannah and Altamaha rivers, from the ocean to the head of the tidewater, and all the islands on the coast except Ossabaw, Sapelo, and St. Catherine, which they reserved for themselves for hunting, bathing, and fishing. A small tract of land lying above Yamacraw Bluff was also reserved by ten Indians as a place for encampment. (*Jones. Ga., I, 140–44.*) No definite price was paid by the trustees for the grant but they presented as token gifts to each representative chief a laced coat, a hat, and a shirt, and to each war captain a gun and ammunition, and to each of the warriors mantles of coarse cloth besides smaller presents to attendants. (*Ibid., 139–40.*)

About 1762 a treaty with the Upper Creeks and Cherokees gave the colony of Georgia about two and a half million acres. (*Mitchell. Ga., 40.*) Between 1763 and 1773 the area of Georgia was enlarged by 6,695,429 acres by treaties with the Indians. (*Ga. Hist. Soc. Coll., III, 160.*) Thus, through her successful treaties with the Indians, the Georgia colony secured most of her land.

In 1646, a treaty was made with Necotowance, king of the Indians, whereby the English would not encroach further upon his territory and in return he would give the English all of the land between the falls of the James and York rivers down toward Kequotan. The Indians were to hold their land under the king of England for twenty beaver skins yearly. (*Hening. Stats., I, 323–24.*) Two years later, however, the section of the treaty which reserved the land between the York and Rappahannock rivers for Necotowance was repealed and settlement there by the English was permitted. (*Ibid., 353–54.*)

A treaty with the Cherokees in 1755 gave the South Carolina colonists the territory included in about ten of the counties of South Carolina centering around Spartanburg. (*Gray. South. Agr., I, 121; Ramsay. Hist. of S. C., I, 94.*)

Although it could not be found, reference was made to a treaty between the North Carolina proprietors and the chief of the Tuscarora Nation, probably in 1748 or 1749, under which they would reside on the land lying in the county of Bertie. It also provided that they would not be disturbed in their occupancy. (*N. C. Rec., XXV, 239.*)

Two other important treaties gave the English large areas of unsettled land in the west. One of these treaties was with the Iroquois at

Ft. Stanwix, and the other was with the Cherokees at Hard Labor. Both were consummated in 1768. The Iroquois surrendered their rights to a small strip of land in central New York, a vast area of southwestern Pennsylvania, and the trans-Allegheny part of western Virginia. In addition, they relinquished their claims to the region between the Ohio and the Tennessee rivers. The treaty with the Cherokees strengthened the claim of the English to a part of this vast territory. (*N.Y. Col. Hist., VIII, 111–37; Chitwood. Col. Amer., 609.*)

An unusual type of acquisition by treaty was consummated by the Treaty of Utrecht under which France acknowledged that the Five Nations of New York were subjects of Great Britain. Title to their land seemed to follow their admission of European sovereignty. (*N. Y. Doc. Hist., I, 741.*)

ABANDONMENT BY THE INDIANS

From time to time each colony reserved by various means certain land for the Indians, who later deserted part of it. Virginia found it necessary, therefore, in 1676, to pass an act which provided that all lands which had been set aside for the use of the Indians and later deserted by them could be sold for the benefit of the public. (*Hening. Stats., II, 351–52.*) Gradually the Indian population diminished and great tracts of land became deserted. Certain Indian tribes to which the Blackwater River region had been assigned were extinct by 1685. In 1688, the kindred tribes in the Pamunkey Neck and on the south side of the Blackwater River sent a petition to the assembly in which they urged that all lands in their vicinity, which they were unable to use, be granted to English settlers. (*Bruce. Econ. Hist. Va., I, 499.*) Thus, by abandonment of land reserved for the Indians, Virginia came into possession of large areas.

Similarly, the Uchee Domains which stretched for 100 miles along the Savannah River came into possession of Georgia about 1746 as the Creeks, greatly reduced in number, had abandoned it. (*Ga. Col. Rec., VI, 147–48, 339, 349.*)

ACQUISITION BY SEIZURE

In some instances, however, the colonists seized the land without regard for the Indians' right to it. Two outstanding examples can be found in Virginia. In the summer of 1610, Lord Delaware decided to seize some of the Indian fields of grain. He partially fulfilled his intention after constructing Fort Henry and Fort Charles at the mouth of the James River. (*Smith. Works, II, 503.*) Another example was Dale's seizure of the Indian land near the confluence of the Appomattox and James rivers. He enclosed two large tracts. (*Ibid., 509–11.*) The Indians were so hostile to occupancy by the whites in Connecticut that a war with the Pequots was necessary to extinguish their claims to the soil.

Records of shady practices probably were not kept as scrupulously as were records of achievements by conventional means. Therefore, it is probable that seizure was practiced much more than the records show.

LEASES WITH THE INDIANS

Apparently acquisition of the land from the Indians by leasing was not prevalent in any of the colonies. There were, however, a few instances where land was thus acquired. For example, the Virginia legislature in 1772 granted permission to the Nottoway Indians to lease a part of their land on the south side of the Nottoway River. Any one lease was not to include more than 300 acres and was to run for twenty-one years at a rent acceptable to the trustees. (*Hening. Stats., VIII, 588–91.*)

On July 12, 1766, Robert Jone, Jr., William Williams, and Thomas Pugh leased from the Indians 8,000 acres of land for 150 years. The rental charge was £1,500. This lease was registered in the county of Bertie, North Carolina, and ratified by the assembly. The assembly also provided that this land held by and of these men should be subject to the same taxes and bear the same privileges as if the land were granted to these men directly by the assembly. (*N. C. Rec., XXV, 507–9.*) At the conclusion of the Indian Wars of 1676-77 in Maine, the peace treaty provided that the settlers would rent land from the Indians, the annual rental of which was one peck of corn for each family of Indians. (*MacLeod. Amer. Ind., 202.*)

A Maryland law of 1723 forbade Indians from letting out their lands for more than five years. Leases already made for years or life were to be void after seven years. All rents due the Indians on earlier leases were to be paid in full. (*Kilty. Land. Ass't., 353.*)

LAND RESERVED FOR THE INDIANS

Many acts were passed by the colonial assemblies to protect the Indians in their claims to land. An act in Virginia provided that no outlying ground should be conveyed to any white person until the aborigines had been allowed a portion of fifty acres for each bowman, and in case the land of any Indian or Indians was included in a patent which had been obtained by a white settler, the latter, if unable or unwilling to purchase the area encroached upon, was to be required to deliver it to its Indian owner. (*Hening. Stats., I, 456–57.*)

Bruce reports an incident which shows that the English dealt fairly with the Indians. When in 1660 the Accomack Indians complained of being deprived of their land and requested that a line or barrier be set up against further advances into their territory, the assembly was not satisfied to have the land laid off by a surveyor from the eastern shore where the land was situated, fearing that he might favor the whites. A surveyor from the western shore was obtained and was instructed to assign to the Indians sufficient territory for ample subsistence. In order to further protect them against the whites, it was provided that the Indians could not alienate their land. (*Bruce. Econ. Hist. Va., I, 495; Hening. Stats., II, 13–14.*) To protect the Indian reservations in general, the Virginia assembly in 1665 provided that such lands as were set aside by the Indians were not to be alienable by them to any man in the future. This law, it was held, would eliminate the necessity of continually allotting new lands for the use of the Indians.

The Indians in North Carolina were crowded westward without serious resistance as settlement progressed. Eventually, however, the Tuscarora War (1711-13) was precipitated. (*Rand. Indians, 25.*) Later the Tuscarora Indians occupied the north bank of the Roanoke River. (*Connor. N. C., I, 51.*) After 1675–76 the Chowanoc Indians were assigned a reservation along Bennett's Creek. (*N. C. Rec., II, 140.*) Their lands were gradually occupied until by 1775 only two men, five women, and some children remained there. (*Ibid., V, 162.*)

In 1786, the South Carolina assembly set aside a vast tract of land for the Cherokee Indians, and declared void any grants of any kind that had been made in the territory thus reserved. (*S.C. Stats., IV, 747–48.*)

A short-sighted policy in Georgia permitted the Indians to hold in reserve for hunting, bathing, and fishing certain islands adjacent to a large tract purchased from them. This reservation was a source of great danger and frequent annoyance. (*Arthur and Carpenter. Ga., 33.*)

In 1668, the Maryland assembly took up the matter of confirming the land allotted to certain Indian tribes, and provided that all persons were prohibited from settling on the land. (*Md. Arch., V, 34.*) The next year land was set aside for the Choptank Indians, in 1704 certain lands were reserved for the Nanticoke Indians, and in 1711 about 3,000 acres on Broad Creek in Somerset County were assigned to the Indians. (*Kilty. Land. Ass't., 352.*) In 1650, the proprietor directed that a tract of land of about 8,000 or 10,000 acres would be reserved for the Six Nations of Indians at Choptico at the head of Wiccocomico River and erected into a manor named Calverton. The land was to be distributed on a basis similar to the headright system, except the grants were not in perpetuity. The surveyor-general was directed to grant ". . . by Copy or Copies of Court Roll Copy hold Estates for one two or three Lives of any Part of the said Mannor except the Demesnes to any Indian or Indians that shall desire the same." No copyhold could exceed fifty acres to each Indian brave, except the chief, and a rent of one shilling was reserved. To what extent this system was followed is not known. Only one tribe, the Chopticons, however, was established on the manor. (*Md. Arch., I, 329–31.*)

Indian reservations disappeared one by one. The Indian habits of living did not change to meet the competition of the white man, who continued to come in ever increasing numbers. They rapidly dwindled to a few half-breeds and nondescripts, who by the end of the first 100 years occupied only a small fraction of the vast territory that once was ruled by their forefathers.

INTERPRETIVE SUMMARY

The views that the Indians took in regard to landownership may be illustrated by the remark of Blunt, an Indian chief, to Governor Spotswood to the effect that, as the country belonged to them before the English came, he thought that the Indians had a better title than the newcomers and should not be confined to such narrow limits for hunting. (*Jones. Va., 18.*) However, the seventeenth century settlement agency followed the practice of claiming full control over the whole territory of the original thirteen colonies, with little regard for the rights of natives. This practice was similar in many regards to the appropriation of equatorial Africa by European sovereigns of the nineteenth century. Many of the old practices still persist where noncommercial aborigines come in contact with money-minded Europeans.

Settlement-agency practice, on the other hand, was not completely effective, for rivalry between early colonial settlements influenced the formulation of on-the-spot policies for the quieting of Indian claims. Many of the decisions were never cleared with the Crown or settlement agency. The policies therefore varied widely from settlement to settlement and were never put together in a well-coordinated whole.

Mutual suspicion and distrust were frequently the basis of relations between the Indians and the whites. Percey's discourse on the situation in Virginia, in 1606, stated that the settlers thought the Indians were trying to be friendly merely to catch the colonists off guard and to murder them, but when the white man would not be fooled, the Indian chief indicated that the settlers could take as much land as was desired. (*Brown. Genesis, I, 161–62.*) Again, Powhatan's proposed gift of a whole kingdom, if settlement was made not at Jamestown but at a more healthful place, was said to be for the avowed purpose of eventually destroying the settlers. It was argued by the English that their ruthless methods were justified in light of such plotting on the part of the Indians.

On the other hand, many leaders felt that the Indians were not capable of negotiating on equal terms with the whites. In the notes of Sir William Johnson regarding the proceedings of commissioners from six provinces at a meeting at Albany in 1754, it was held that, since the Indians could not be entrusted at large with the sale of their own land, the laws requiring official permission to purchase from them seemed well founded. The meeting recommended that all future purchases from the Indians should be held void unless made with the consent of the various governments. It was also recommended that any complaints of the Indians should be thoroughly investigated. (*N. Y. Doc. Hist., II, 610–11.*)

From the viewpoint of good sound business, the colonists generally undertook to appease the Indians rather than act pugnaciously toward them. This attitude of an early Virginia assembly is revealed in a statute enacted in 1661. (*Hening. Stats., II, 39.*) Scrupulous care was displayed by the Virginia assembly in regard to a grant from the Indians to Colonel Fantleroy of Rappahannock. The evidence indicated that the purchase price was not reasonable and fair. Colonel Fantleroy was instructed by the assembly to make good the deficiency in an amount carefully prescribed. (*Ibid., 14, 36.*) In rendering this decision it was held that the Indians were in no way capable of compelling full payment for their land.

It seems clear that acquisition of land from the Indians cannot be studied as if the purchases were free barter and sale transactions between equal parties. The land buying relations between self-sufficing native tribes and a commercial minded settlement agency do not conform to an acceptable concept of a market-place transaction. It is doubtful whether the Indians clearly understood that they were alienating their ancient seats in perpetuity. It is doubtful whether they recognized the difference between conveying the right to occupy certain tracts of land for a time and the conveyance of a fee simple absolute title with full rights of sovereignty. It is doubtful whether they had any standards of value that were appropriate for use in transferring large tracts of land. For, although their concepts of rights in land as between various tribes and individual occupants were well developed, they had had little or no experience in buying and selling on so vast a scale.

Government action to prevent private parties from cheating the Indians indicates that fraudulent deals were not infrequent. Preventive action also indicates the superior position occupied by the whites and the inferior bargaining power of the Indians. The widespread practice of quieting the Indians' claims by outright purchase also indicates the awareness on the part of the whites that the Indians should be paid at least something for their land. On the other hand, the fact that much Indian property was actually seized indicates that all settlers did not have the same point of view. Land transactions with the Indians probably ranged all the way from purchase at as reasonable a price as could be determined to the most flagrant deception imaginable.

No clues appear as to why some land was leased rather than purchased. The practice probably was not widespread and was used only under unusual circumstances. The sheer necessity of keeping on good terms with the Indians doubtless had an ameliorating influence, and the practice of reserving certain lands for the exclusive use of the Indians was a step in that direction. It is doubtful if an evaluation of the reasonableness or fairness of the price paid to the Indians could be made with any degree of accuracy.

Purchase as a method of quieting the Indians' claims to the land during the Colonial period was a method adopted by the federal government after the establishment of the Union. Treaty making became more important after the national government was formed, and later Indian policy was marked by the reservation of much land for the Indian tribes as they were pushed westward. In short, the colonial forefathers used the various schemes for acquiring title from the Indians that were used following the Revolutionary War. Transactions with the Indians before 1776 were probably neither blacker nor whiter than those since.

Not one single attitude, principle, or concept as to the relations among men in regard to land was taken from Indian tenure. As the white man conquered the wilderness and the Indian, he also conquered Indian land tenure. As he drove the Indian westward, he drove Indian tenure westward.

This is not without significance, for it is in sharp contrast with the situation where aboriginal tenures and European tenures exist side by side. The English, the Dutch, and the French are still experiencing difficulties where the two conflicting tenurial concepts exist in the same area. This is true wherever colonial peoples have maintained customary practices in a region settled by commercially minded Europeans.[1] The harmonizing of completely divergent principles is no mean task if, indeed, it can be done at all. The Indians and their tenure were swept aside, and no adjustment in indigenous tenure was required. European tenures were given full freedom to develop in a new milieu. From this viewpoint, it can be said that the resulting system of land tenure would have been no different if the territory occupied by the thirteen original colonies had been completely uninhabited by human beings.

Even though nothing was borrowed from Indian tenures, the quieting of the claims of the Indians to the land had its effect. These influences can be stated as follows: (1) The unscrupulous processes followed by the settlement agencies in separating the Indian from his land made the colonists wary lest they be cheated out of their holdings once they were cleared and appreciated in value. (2) The cheapness and ease with which title to large tracts of land was acquired from the Indians made the settlers question the "right" of these large operators to their ill-gotten gain. (3) Fraudulent transactions with the Indians compounded and intensified the growing English principle of *caveat emptor* — let the buyer (or seller) beware. (4) The processes of quieting the claims of the Indians also intensified the growing attitude, fathered by English laissez faire and mothered by the economic principles of the Reformation, that it was all right to acquire for oneself as much of the world's surface as possible so long as the letter of the law was not infringed upon.

These categorical statements need expansion and clarification. In regard to the first, the settlers had a direct interest, along with the settlement agencies, in quieting the claims of the Indians to the land. In fact, they participated actively in many of the unscrupulous processes. Knowledge that fraudulent practices were common, whether through observation or participation, detracted from the confidence that the colonists placed in the settlement agencies. Particularly in the early days, when the settlers had not acquired much governmental power, the colonists had no assurance that they would not be treated similarly. The colonists accepted the old adage that there can be no honor among thieves. Shady dealings with the Indians made the colonists desirous of acquiring for themselves as many rights as possible and of stabilizing insofar as practicable their tenure relations to the settlement agencies, both of which would add security and stability to their landed property.

The colonists also observed that numerous tracts of land were acquired from the Indians in return for mere trifles, and that many of the original

---

[1] For recent conditions see: Liversage, V., Land Tenure in the Colonies; Pim, Sir Alan, Colonial Agricultural Production; Meek, C. K., Land Law and Customs in the Colonies; Pelzer, Karl J., Settlement in the Asiatic Tropics; and Maher, Colin, Looking Abroad, Looking Around, and Looking Ahead.

grants from the Crown were personal favors. In short, they observed that the settlement agencies frequently acquired their land for little or nothing. It is not surprising that they squatted upon unallocated land rather than pay the purchase price set by the settlement agencies, and that they revolted against burdensome quitrents. The colonial settler began to temper legal rights — the letter of the law — with concepts of equity. Equity, moral judgment, and fair dealings were slowly bringing about adjustments in customary legal practices and the rigidity of the common law.

A third, and quite contrary, working principle was crystallizing at the same time and out of the same situation. Sharp practices in dealing with the Indians and sharp practices of the Indians themselves in selling land to the whites gave impetus and concreteness to the idea that the buyer (or seller) should beware in conveying land. The placing of responsibility upon the buyer and relieving the seller of certain responsibilities, although quite the opposite of "let the Indian seller beware," nevertheless gained recognition under the impact of these transactions. It made little difference whether the stated principle was "let the buyer beware" or "let the seller beware," the practice was let the other fellow beware. This attitude still permeates bargain and sale transactions and land leasing in this country.

A fourth characteristic of our presnt land system that was obvious in transactions with the Indians was the lack of restraint on the quantity of land that could be acquired. The restrictions on direct purchases by settlers were concerned with who consummated the transaction and not how much was acquired, either at one time or by one person or agency. Enormous tracts were taken from the Indians under most of the procedures described. The attitude of many purchasers and the colonial squatter was similar. Those who purchased from the Indians, frequently purchased as much land as they could and then endeavored to wrest title from the English settlement agency by virtue of the Indian title. The squatter occupied as much land as possible and then tried to establish title by right of occupancy. Successful acquisition of land by squatters and purchasers tended to advance to the position where unrestrained acquisition was fully established.

CHAPTER 12

Transfers to Financial Supporters of the Trading Companies

THE LONDON COMPANY OF VIRGINIA was financed largely by two types of members: planters, who bought shares in the company and came to dwell in the new country; and adventurers, who also bought shares but did not come to America. (*Force. Tracts, I, No. 6, 23.*) In the London Company about one-third of those who bought shares emigrated to Virginia with the objective of becoming permanent settlers. This third of the shareholders played an important role in the development of the land tenure system.

TRANSFER OF LAND FOR SHARES

After the first Virginia charter was issued, money was invested by members of the company and by outsiders in sending settlement expeditions to Virginia. Records of these early money subscriptions are meager, and while it is not possible to determine definitely the value of each share, much of the evidence would indicate that a whole share was valued at £12 10*s*. One of the earliest records of subscriptions that we have is an extract from the *Fishmongers Record* entitled, "At a Court of Assistants at the Hall 24th April 1609." (*Brown. Genesis, I, 280–81.*) This extract gives the names of eleven members of the company, one of whom is credited with having adventured £12 10*s*., one £50, and the rest £62 10*s*.

Several additional groups contributed to the enterprise between the granting of the first and second charters. The Clothworkers'

Company on April 12, 1609, contributed one hundred marks; this was in addition to the personal contributions of two members of the Clothworkers' Company who contributed £12 10*s*. each. (*Ibid., 277–78.*) The Stationers' Records of April 28, 1609, showed that on that date the Stationers' Company ventured £125. (*Ibid., 292–93.*) The Merchant Taylors' Records of April 29, 1609, indicate that about £586 was subscribed by members of the Merchant Taylors. (*Ibid., 302–6.*)

Land Tenure Provisions

Land granted in the first Virginia charter was not subdivided and regranted to settlers during the time that the first charter was in force. According to the November 20, 1606, Instructions and Orders the land which eventually would be alienated to settlers was to be ". . . had and inherited and injoyed, according as in the like estates they be had and enjoyed by the lawes within this realme of England. . . ." (*Hening. Stats., I, 67–75.*) Since the kinds of estates in land were restricted in the first Virginia charter, this instruction provided that the English law governing such estates should be followed in America.

The second charter probably was drawn in January or early February of 1609. It granted the Virginia Company exclusive powers over the land for an unlimited term. Although the charter did not guarantee a monopoly, the company found it possible to maintain a position of monopoly through nondistribution of land, communal living, and taxation of other traders or companies. Since trading dominated the thinking within the company, it is probable that the trade monopoly was the major factor in delaying distribution of land until 1619.

Settler Inducements

The second charter was left open so the names of new adventurers and planters could be entered; therefore, it was not issued until May 23, 1609. (*Brown. Genesis, I, 206.*) In the meantime a pamphlet which contained important references to the distribution of land among the shareholders was circulated in England. This pamphlet, entitled *Nova Britannia,* explained the opportunities and advantages to be gained by settling in Virginia. (*Brown. First Repub., 78.*) It stated that £12 10*s*. was considered a share. At the end of seven years, at which time the joint-stock would cease to support the colony, a division was to be made of the land, and it was hoped that a minimum of 500 acres would be granted for each share. (*Force. Tracts, I, No. 6, 23–24.*) This was the first information given out as to the number of acres that might be claimed for each share. Although the estimate was far from correct, the pamphlet probably served its purpose, which was to encourage people to risk both their money and themselves for the establishment of the Virginia colony.

Provisions also were discussed for those whose contribution consisted of either transporting themselves or paying for the transportation of others to Virginia. These provisions formed the basis for the headright system of granting land.

Another settler-inducement document was a circular signed by ten well-known men. It bore no date, but its contents indicate that it was issued after the *Nova Britannia* tract. This circular was an attempt to encourage towns, societies, and groups of friends and neighbors, as units, to contribute money for stock in the company. For each share purchased, equal privileges among the members of the company were promised, not only in the land but in the goods and minerals which the land produced. (*Brown. First Repub., 100–104.*) Just what effect this offer had on the sale of shares cannot be determined, but it is evident that land and minerals, and not trade and commerce, were the inducements offered. Thus, Virginia was to be settled for agricultural purposes, insofar as the planters were concerned, but probably for quick profits from precious metals and from trade with the Indians and settlers, insofar as many of the adventurers were concerned.

Beginnings of Freeholds and Leaseholds

Later, Sir Thomas Dale promised twelve acres of fenced land, a four-room house, tools, livestock, and provisions for twelve months to every man with a family who would come to Virginia at his own expense. These items were to be provided on condition that the settler raise wheat, roots, and herbs, and that his family become self-sustaining after the first year. (*Hamor. Pres. Est. Va., 19.*) No record can be found of the number of persons who took advantage of this offer. Economic and social conditions in England encouraged people to take advantage of the opportunity to become a proprietor of twelve acres of cleared land. However, the poorer classes could not raise the amount required to pay for transportation to America. Although the exact cost cannot be determined, the amount must have been comparatively large, for seven years of indentured servitude were required if the company bore the expense. On the other hand, the offer was not particularly appealing to those who were financially able to pay their own passage. As a consequence, it is doubtful if many persons took advantage of Dale's offer.

In 1615, through the influence of Dale, the company granted fifty acres of land to every freeman in Virginia who had an absolute claim to land through his participation in the company. Charles Campbell, in his *History of Virginia,* interprets this as an important event. He said, "The year 1615 is remarkable in Virginia history for the first establishment of a fixed property in the soil." (*Campbell. Col. of Va., 116.*) Brown said that the first record which he found of land granted by the company was in the early spring of 1616, and that the patent was issued to Mr. Simon Codrington. (*Brown. First Repub., 233.*) The first grant took place about 1616 and was made by the Virginia Company. A petition sent later by the assembly in Virginia to the authorities in England forms the basis for this belief. It reads, ". . . they woulde vouchsafe also that groundes as heretofore had bene granted by patent to the antient Planters by former Governours that had from the Company received commission so to doe, might not nowe after so muche labour and coste and so many yeares habitation be taken from them." (*Va. Col. Rec., 15.*) Gray believed, however, that this referred to land held under tenancy agreements rather than land held under a freehold grant. (*Gray. South. Agr., I, 315.*)

Tenants could have been established under instructions to Governor Yeardley on November 18, 1618. To accomplish the avowed purposes of the company the governor was instructed to set aside three thousand acres of land for support of the governor, and to establish upon this land guards already in Virginia, persons accompanying the governor to Virginia, and others to be sent later at the governor's expense. The tenants were to occupy the land at one-half of the annual profits. They appear to have been persons transported to America largely by others, which would have made them in effect indentured servants. The fact that their "tenancy" was to run for seven years, which was a typical period of servitude, bears out the indentured servant interpretation.

Little information as to arrangements between the company and these land occupiers seems to exist. They worked the land on shares, half-and-half. They were closely supervised and "furnished" by company agents. They must have sold their produce through the company, accepting a company-determined price. Dwelling on company-held land, or land assigned to one of its representatives, they probably had few rights in the land they tilled, although each one probably was master of the dwelling place assigned to him. The furnish system may have been similar in effect to the present share-cropper furnish system, for part of a draft of a statement on the situation in Virginia in early 1619 alluded to the furnish system. It showed that the high prices at which the merchants sold corn and the restriction of the amount of tobacco that could be planted placed these tenants in a position where they must pay two years' labor for twelve months' bread, clothes, and tools. An essential difference between these colonial servant-tenants and modern share-croppers was that the former looked forward to landownership at the end of seven years. (*Va. Co. Rec., IV, 175.*)

The joint-stock system of holding land and organizing production in Virginia, as provided for in the charters of 1606 and 1609, was to exist until 1616. In addition to this planned distribution, Sir Thomas Dale allotted to every man in the colony three English acres of cleared corn ground, which were to be manured and tended. These allotments were on an individual rental basis, in sharp contrast with the communal system under which the colonists lived and worked the company's land for the first few years. In return for these acres each man was required to give two and one-half barrels of corn and no more than one month's service to the colony each year. These could be demanded neither at seeding time nor at harvest. (*Hamor. Pres. Est. Va., 17.*) In common parlance this was a standing rent agreement, the amount of rent being a fixed quantity of corn and labor.

Land Distribution

During the early existence of the company the right to convey land to anyone who had ventured a certain sum of money resided in the Crown. (*Lucas. Charters, 8.*) Under the charter of 1609 the authority resided in the treasurer, council, and general association of adventurers in England, but under a later regulation the authority could be delegated completely to those representing the company in America. (*Ibid., 12.*) Thus, the first granting of land in America was successively removed further from the Crown and England. This was an item of major importance, for the chances of development of free and easy tenures in America became much greater when the processes of granting land were centered here. Had the entire land granting process remained in England local pressures for free tenures could have been resisted much longer and probably staved off indefinitely.

The year 1616 ended the seven years after the granting of the second charter and marked the time when a division of land to all stockholders had been promised. (*Brown. First Repub., 232.*) A tract entitled "A Briefe Declaration of the present state of things in Virginia, and of a Division to be now made, of some part of those Lands in our actuall possession, as well to all such as have adventured their moneyes, as also to those that are Planters there" was issued by his majesty's council for Virginia about 1616. (*Brown. Genesis, II, 774–79.*)

The tract recommended that only the land lying along both sides of the King's River and near the new towns be divided first. Every man who had adventured himself or his money was to be given fifty acres for every share of £12 10*s.* in the first division of land. When the opportunity came to divide the rest it was hoped that 200 acres could be given for each share. This allotment of fifty acres was only one-tenth of the amount company officials had led prospective settlers to believe they would receive.

The company could have had good reasons for the making of such small allotments. There was the need of compact settlement as protection against the Indians, slow means of communication, and physical limitations on the amount of land that one family could bring under cultivation. This change in plans and promises was only the first in a long series of events that made the settlers wary of those holding control over the land and nurtured the growing desire of the occupier for complete control over the land he farmed.

A new governor was to be sent with commissioners and surveyors to make an impartial division. A book was provided in which the adventurers wishing to share in the first division were to record their names and the number of their shares. This recording was to be done before June 25, 1616, at Sir Thomas Smith's. An additional contribution of £12 10*s*. was assessed on each person wishing to share in the first division to cover the expense incurred; this assessment was payable within a month. Those who could not pay the full amount at once were allowed to pay one-half immediately and the rest in six months. Anyone wishing to pay more was to have land in proportion to the contribution made. The new assessment and the privilege of making additional contributions indicated the pressure of financial considerations and the lack of any idea of restricting the amount of land an individual could acquire.

The land allotted could be held either by the planter taking up residence on it or by his sending someone to manure and tend it for a specified yearly rent or for half the clear profit. The allotment was to be confirmed as a state of inheritance to him and his heirs forever ". . . to be holden of his Maiestie, as of his Manour of East Greenwich, in Socage Tenure, and not in Capite, according to his Maiesties gracious Letters Patents already granted to the Virginia Company in that behalfe." Although these conditions of tenure are stated in terms different from those outlined in the 1606 charter, they provide for essentially the same kinds of estates in land. On these terms a number of adventurers came forward and claimed their lots, and their grants were duly allocated. (*Brown. Genesis, II, 775–79.*)

On November 30, 1616, the Michaelmas Quarter-Court selected Admiral Samuel Argall as deputy-governor in Virginia, Captain Ralph Hamor as vice-admiral, Captain John Martin as master of ordinance, and John Rolfe as secretary and recorder. (*Brown. First Repub., 243.*) These men were sent to America to carry out the company's orders of 1616, ". . . for dividing and setting out the shares of land to the old planters in Virginia, locating new private plantations, or hundreds, for the adventurers in England, etc., and only to make a beginning toward settling the proposed new form of government." (*Ibid., 250.*) Under these orders the old and new adventurers were to share alike. The names of all who were to share in the first division and the number of shares held by each were to be given in writing to the commissioners, who were to bring back a map of the land allocated so every adventurer could see where his land lay.

It was not until 1619, however, that this division of land really took place. It was made according to the terms of the regulations entitled *Orders and Constitutions* and the *Instructions* given to Governor Yeardley. Although these two documents dealt principally with land for headrights, they contained some reference to the amount of land to be granted for shares held in the company. For every share of £12 10*s*., 100 acres were to be allotted to the shareholder to be held by him, his heirs, and assigns forever. This amount was to be granted on the first division, and a like number of acres was to be granted on the second division, which was to take place as soon as the land granted in the first division was sufficiently populated.

According to the usual procedure, the quarter-court would delegate to the governor and the council in the colony the right to lay out and describe the land to be included in each patent, but the court retained the authority to outline specifically the regulations under which it could be granted. Then the governor and council would lay out the land to those proving their right to it, carrying out the instructions and powers given to them by the company. The conveyances then would be forwarded to London, examined, and approved at a quarter-court before the grant was made final. (*Va. Co. Rec., III, 100–109.*)

How many persons subscribed to the shares of the company and were eligible for a portion of the land in Virginia under this distribution cannot be given exactly. The names of many appear in the charter, individuals as well as organizations. To the "Circular Letter" sent out on February 20, 1610, in an attempt to collect £30,000 in two years, was attached a list containing some 300 names of those who had already subscribed a total of £5,000. (*Brown. Genesis, I, 463–69.*) None of these subscribed less than £37 10*s*. while one subscribed as much as £175. Thirty-seven pounds and ten shillings was almost $1,000 in present-day money. The records of the Virginia Company give the names of the shareholders and the number of shares held by each from March 6, 1615, to June 9, 1623. (*Va. Co. Rec., III, 58–66.*) The number of persons contributing and the number of shares received by each are summarized in Table 1.

Another list of about 655 names appeared in the records of the Virginia Company, called "A Complete List of the Adventurers to Virginia with the Several Amounts of Their Holding." (*Ibid., 79–90.*)

Force has given other lists. (*Force. Tracts, III, No. 5, 19–44.*) Some of the names also appeared on the list given in the records of the Virginia Company, while each list contained names that did not appear in the other. Brown stated that about 150 persons joined the company between March, 1612, and July, 1616, but he gave no record of the amount each contributed. (*Brown. Genesis, II, 802.*) He also gave an additional list of 140 names of those who were members between 1606 and 1616. (*Ibid., 803–5.*)

With such duplicating and conflicting lists, it is impossible to determine how many adventurers and planters were eligible for a portion of land in Virginia and how many shares were issued. Those who bought shares in the company were entitled to a Bill of Adventure which was issued under the seal of the company. Although in 1609, the company issued a statement saying that no Bills of Adventure would be issued for amounts less than £12 10*s.* (*Ibid., I, 252*), an exception was made to this rule, for in 1622, the court finally allowed William Phetiplace, who had paid £10 to Thomas Smith in 1607, 100 acres of land, as he was considered an "ancient planter." (*Va. Co. Rec., II, 97.*) Information concerning grants made to individuals who had invested in the company was scattered throughout the records of the Virginia Company.

According to the third charter, the business for the company had to be done at one of the quarter-courts. Some of the shares had been

TABLE 1

DISTRIBUTION OF SHARES HELD IN THE VIRGINIA COMPANY

Number of persons	Number of shares	Total shares	Number of persons	Number of shares	Total shares
126	1	126	1	7	7
2	1½	3	3	8	24
60	2	120	4	10	40
1	2½	2½	1	11	11
33	3	99	2	14	28
1	3½	3½	2	15	30
18	4	72	1	16	16
19	5	95	3	20	60
1	5½	5½	1	25	25
2	6	12	1	35	35
263	....	538½	19	....	276

granted by the council and not at a quarter-court. These grants were at times questioned; most of them, however, were finally allowed. After 1616, requests for Bills of Adventure by the shareholders increased enormously, but in many cases the land was not granted until several years after the request was made.

The land-distribution process was slow and many shareholders had not received their land prior to the dissolution of the company in 1624. The Crown, however, recognized the legitimate rights of all shareholders and land grants for shares in the company continued to be made for several years. For example, Thomas Graies who had subscribed to the extent of £25 did not secure a patent until 1628 (*Nugent. Va. Land Patents, I, 13*), and it was not until 1636 that Captain John Hobson received his patent. (*Ibid., 54–55.*)

Bequeathing and Selling of Shares

Between 1616 and 1619, when the first real attempt at granting and setting out the land was begun, some developments took place that had a direct bearing on landholding in Virginia. Many shares were sold by their original owners, and the persons who bought them received grants of land. Large holdings were acquired by private parties and by societies that held large numbers of shares. Furthermore at the death of the original shareholder, his heir would request a grant of land for the shares held. In addition, many shares were assigned by the original owners to others as gifts.

As proof that the shares could be inherited, Thomas Buckly, in 1622, was granted land for the £25 that his father, Sir Richard Buckly, had adventured. (*Va. Co. Rec., I, 598.*) Furthermore, on July 10, 1621, land was set out for the widow of Captain Christopher Newporte; this was land for the thirty-two shares he held in the company at the time of his death. (*Ibid., 509.*) After settling debts due the company by Sir Edmund Harwell, his brother, Francis Harwell, was granted land for the remaining amount of his three shares. (*Ibid., 597.*) Richard Willaston received the land due his uncle who had died in Virginia. (*Ibid., II, 511.*) The largest number of shares was inherited by Captain Somers for £470 adventured by his uncle, Sir George Somers. (*Ibid., I, 434.*) Thus, land was granted to heirs for shares bequeathed to them, and promised estates in land acquired through inheritance were recognized.

Since shares in the company could be transferred through sale, some shares were sold and later land was granted to those who bought them. For example, in 1619, Elias Robert was granted 100 acres for a Bill of Adventure which he had bought from Mr. Threr (*Ibid., 289*), and Mr. Carter, in 1622, sold sixteen shares to Ed. Palmer. (*Ibid., II, 77.*)

Other shares were assigned by the owner without specifying whether they were gifts or sales. One such transfer, probably a gift, was made by Lady De Lawar and her son who assigned forty shares for land in Virginia to Mr. Carter for ". . . sundrie Adventurors of the Company." (*Ibid., I, 460.*) Sir Henry Maynwaringe assigned five shares of land to Sir Edward Sackvill in 1620 (*Ibid., 364*), Mr. Harper assigned a share to Mr. Whetcombe, and Sir Frauncis Parrington assigned a share to William Polland and another to Henry Hickford, and finally, Hickford assigned his share to John Martin. (*Ibid., 378.*)

When a share was subscribed the owner had a right to sell, will, or give it away. Therefore, much of the land granted for shares in Virginia was not granted to the original subscriber. The freedom with which shares in the Virginia Company were sold, traded, and bequeathed made it possible to increase further the concentration of landownership. The first important step in the development of large estates was the decision to sell to anyone as many shares in the company as he would subscribe; thus, several individuals acquired a large number of shares through direct purchase. Later, and even after the company was dissolved, these large holdings were added to and new ones were built up. This process involved the transfer of shares among private parties and groups of individuals by barter, sale, gift, and bequest. Nonrestriction of original purchases and freedom of disposal of shares held made possible concentration of land in large holdings in colonial Virginia.

TREASURY RIGHT GRANTS

When the Virginia Company began, in 1616, to grant land as dividends to the holders of shares in the company, some of the members, moved by impatience with the communistic planning that had been in vogue, struck out on their own to establish settlements in Virginia. They formed "societies" and sent groups of settlers to America. These groups were later granted land by the company in large tracts which were called plantations or hundreds. Impetus was added to this movement a year later when it was found that the company's treasury was exhausted. Many of those interested in the success of the company and in the possibilities of the New World decided to aid the company by subscribing large sums of money. For this money they did not receive shares in the company and did not become a part of the corporation; instead they received large tracts of land that they could settle as they saw fit and over which many of them had civil jurisdiction.

These associations were supposed to find people who were willing to come to America, to furnish them with supplies, and to provide for their transportation. Each of the large subcolonies established by these informal associations was supposed to establish people on the land under the same regulations. However, they were of different sizes and had diverse local regulations. The early records of Virginia show that between 1616 and 1624, seventy-two grants for such plantations had been made. (*Va. Mag. of Hist., VI, 372.*)

The intention was that all of these plantations or hundreds were to have individual municipal status and the right of self-government in local affairs. These particular plantations were to be "bodies corporate," similar to the four principal boroughs, Jamestown, Charles City, Henrico, and Kiccotan, laid out by the company. (*Va. Jour. of Burgesses. 1619–1668, 3.*) Regardless of plans, however, they did not follow the same political development. For example, some were permitted to send their representatives to the early assemblies while others were denied this privilege.

Sir Thomas Smith, treasurer of the Virginia Company, was the leading member of the first private plantation to be formed — Smith's Hundred. (*Brown. First Repub., 276.*) The name later was changed to Southampton Hundred. It was located on the north side of the James River. (*Brown. Genesis, II, 1063.*) At a meeting held in 1618 the committee for Smith's Hundred made plans for sending thirty-five men to the colony. (*Va. Co. Rec., I, 129.*) A report of May, 1625, said Southampton Hundred contained 100,000 acres. (*Ibid., IV, 555.*)

The largest of the treasury rights granted was Martin's Hundred. Captain Martin, an attorney for the company, had invested much money in the company (*Brown, Genesis, II, 943*), and in November, 1616, the company granted him a tract of land for ten shares which he held. The land was located on the James River. (*Va. Co. Rec., III, 58.*) He was ". . . to enjoy his landes in as lardge and ample manner, to all intentes and purposes, as any lord of any manours in England dothe holde his ground." (*Ibid., 163.*) Martin added further to his holdings by investing more money in the company; in 1618 he invested £95 (*Ibid., 86*), in 1620 he invested another £70 (*Ibid., 329*), and in 1622 he purchased two additional shares (*Ibid., 65*) when he received his patent. (*Ibid., 643.*)

The acreage of this hundred was extended by headright grants for persons that Martin brought to Virginia. It was further expanded through other means. For example, on January 30, 1621, 20,000 acres was added by a patent granted to Sir John Wolstenholme and a large number of associates. (*Ibid., 592–98.*) The land was located on the James River and joined the former grant to Martin. This grant, however, was more of the nature of a headright than a treasury right grant. Although the grant was made, in part, for some money that the group had paid into the treasury of the company, the major part was based upon more than 250 persons whom the association had transported to Virginia since 1618. The names of the ships on which these people were sent and in most instances the number of persons sent on each ship were recorded.

This land, with all the mines of gold and silver, woods, rivers, and all profitable commodities and hereditaments as well as the fishing, fowling, and hunting privileges, was granted to Sir John and the other adventurers and their heirs and assigns forever, in the manner granted to the treasurer and the company and their successors by the king under the great seal of England. It was to be held as of the manor of East Greenwich by fealty only and not in capite or by knight service. One-fifth of the gold and silver was to be reserved for the sovereign and another fifth for the company and their successors. An additional 1,500 acres was granted to the association to be used for the maintenance of schools and churches and defraying public charges. Martin's patent was revoked in 1622 and a new one offered, which he reluctantly accepted. It is estimated that Martin's Hundred contained about 800,000 acres at one time. (*Ibid., I, 585, 595; II, 78–79; IV, 556.*)

Another hundred, of which much of the land was acquired by shares or by headrights, was Berkeley's Hundred. It was formed in February, 1619, when the Hilary Quarter-Court issued a patent to five men who held a total of forty-five shares. These men were expected to build a town, including churches and schools, and to transport people to Virginia to settle on the plantation. For every share, the company agreed to allot 100 acres to the five men as a group and their heirs and assigns, and to the heirs and assigns of each of them individually, according to the number of their shares. In addition, 1,500 acres was assigned to help bear the expenses of the schools and churches which these adventurers agreed to build and maintain. Berkeley's Hundred extended its acreage by sending people to Virginia. A yearly rent of twelve pence was reserved. (*Ibid., III, 130–34.*) In May, 1620, Sir William Throckmorton assigned his interests to William Tracy. (*Brown. First Repub., 256, 364.*)

Several smaller associations which held land in Virginia were formed. At a meeting of the company in January, 1617, Bills of Adventure totalling sixteen shares were issued to Hamor and his six associated adventurers. Ralph Hamor came to Virginia and took up the claim. Where he settled cannot be determined. About this time, Bills of Adventure totalling twenty-four shares were granted to Argall and his associates. (*Va. Co. Rec., III, 58.*) This association settled at Argall's Town near the Chickahominy River on the north side of the James River. (*Brown. First Repub., 256.*) This grant was confirmed in the instructions given to Yeardley, November 18, 1618. (*Va. Co. Rec., III, 106–7.*)

The company expected that the adventurers in these private associations would transport themselves, servants, and tenants to Virginia and develop their holdings. This was done in some cases but the results were disappointing. After the dissolution of the company these private societies disintegrated. The lands belonging to some were transferred by patents with little regard to their original ownership. In order to confirm these patents, special instructions were issued which conferred upon the colonial authorities the power to assign to the associates in these endeavors a proportionate area of land elsewhere in case they laid claim to tracts already conveyed. (*Va. Mag. of Hist., II, 285.*)

The Crown endeavored after the dissolution of the company to satisfy claims for land based upon contributions to the treasury of the company. It appears that land was granted for all reasonable claims presented. The dissolution of the company prevented further creation of treasury rights, and the idea lay dormant for almost three-quarters of a century. Treasury rights never were revived in their old form, for there was no company and no company treasury. However, the Crown took the place of the company, and the operation of local government and expanded settlement activities were a drain upon the Crown's treasury. As a consequence, near the turn of the eighteenth century a new type of treasury right was brought into being. It provided that whosoever would pay the auditor five shillings for the king's use would be granted fifty acres of land. This method of acquiring land from the Crown did not replace the granting of headrights, which had been practiced both before and after dissolution of the company; it merely complemented the headright system.

DUTCH AND SWEDISH TRADING COMPANIES

Little specific evidence is found to indicate how the first Swedish and Dutch settlers acquired rights in their land. The companies were more interested in trade than in agricultural settlement, even more so than the London Company. The Swedes maintained this interest until their territory was taken from them by the Dutch. The Dutch, both in New York and Delaware, only reluctantly offered serious inducements for those who would establish farm homes upon the newly acquired land. When this decision was made, the system of granting land closely approximated the English headright method. It appears that neither the Dutch nor the Swedes followed either a treasury right or a "share right" system of granting land to those who contributed financially to the company. Even if a similar procedure had been inaugurated, such a limited number of grants could have been made that their effect upon our colonial land system would have been negligible.

INTERPRETIVE SUMMARY

The seventeenth century trading company type of organization was an experiment in corporate organization for planting colonies in distant lands. Earlier trading companies had solved many of the problems of trade that plagued the first endeavors in developing foreign commerce. The problems of settlement, however, were relatively new and quite different. They were monumental, for very little had been accomplished in the development of settlement techniques.

A major difficulty that plagued the trading company was the conflict involved in maintaining a trade monopoly and at the same time distributing land to individual settlers under sufficiently easy tenures to induce them to come to the New World. The basic purpose of the company was the maintenance of a trade monopoly. The fundamental desires of the settlers were large quantities of land to be held as their own, under free and easy tenures. The company saw clearly that it could not maintain a monopoly over trade with the Indians and with the mother country if it peopled the territory with numerous independent freeholders. Farmers who held fee simple titles in their land could not be forced for long to trade with company stores at company-controlled prices.

During the years immediately following the issuance of the second charter, the company was not forced to resolve this matter, for it was determined that no allocation of land would be made until the end of seven years. Distribution was held up three years longer by arbitrary action of the governor. Following the general distribution of land in 1619 the company tried to maintain a trade monopoly and a free land system side by side. The experiment was not permitted to run its natural course for the company was dissolved five years later. In fact, the trading company's fitness to plant colonies was never fully determined by experience, for the Crown decided to revoke the charter and appropriate for itself the revenues being derived from tobacco and other trade.

It is doubtful whether the Crown could have dissolved the company if its members had been satisfied with its operations, and if those who came to America had been contented. But members of the company, prospective subscribers, and other financial contributors were not satisfied. They formed separate organizations and obtained grants of expansive areas of land upon which they established many families. Also, the long delay in making private grants, and the inappropriateness of communal living and working, turned the colonists against the company.

Before the Virginia Company passed from the scene, however, it left its mark upon human institutions evolving on the new land. First, the endeavor of working in gangs upon another's land, of being supplied with all tools and detailed supervision, and of obtaining food from a common storehouse, proved disastrous. Englishmen were not accustomed to living and working together; they were freedom-loving and individualistic. Natural hazards and inexperience doomed whatever communal ideas anyone may have had. Although company servant-settlers cannot be thought of as participants in a purely communal endeavor, this experiment in pseudo-communal living, along with a similar experiment at Plymouth, was the end of large-scale communal landholding and living in Colonial America.

The methods of handling shares in the company and contributions to its depleted treasury permitted, and even fostered, land expansion. During the later life of the company landed estates grew to phenomenal proportions, approximating a million acres in at least one case. These plantations or hundreds were the colonial forerunners of the modern plantations in this country. The company contributed directly to this development by making large grants to company officials and by organizing company plantations on which settlers who were sent over by the company were to work during their period of servitude. The company added to land expansion by headrights and special-purpose grants.

The Virginia Company made the first grants of freehold land in America. Small freeholders, established under the auspices of this company, played an important role alongside the large plantation owners, that it also sponsored, in the development of the American system of land tenure. In addition, the company started the first renting of land in America under a system closely approximating the present system of share-cropping.

Transfer of land to refill a depleted treasury was instituted by the Virginia Company. This was the beginning of the system of selling public domain after the formation of the nation. Granting of land for the purpose of replenishing the treasury of the company, the Crown, the proprietors, or later the federal government, played an important role in establishing settlers on the new continent. Grants of land in Colonial America for shares and treasury rights were designed to yield financial returns without regard to the occupancy pattern established. A similar viewpoint was held in the sale of land after nationalization. Grants of these types had quite a different effect from that of headright and homestead grants, which were designed to allot a single farm to each family. The policy of granting land for the primary purpose of yielding the highest income to the grantor is in sharp contrast with a policy of establishing family farmers on homesteads of their own.

The Virginia Company made the first grants of land in the colonies for the support of educational and religious work. School and glebe land grants were quite substantial. The company also supplied servants to work on these lands. The later separation of church and state ended all direct public contributions to religious activities. As a consequence, this practice never became a fundamental part of national land policy. However, the Virginia Company's practice of granting land for educational purposes was a direct contribution to later land policy, for the colonial and federal governments set aside vast quantities of land for school purposes.

The settlement activities of the Virginia Company were not essentially dissimilar to the vast settlement schemes later concocted by the land merchandizing companies. However, though both groups' plans to make money by settling people upon the land were quite similar, the land merchandizing companies were less interested in trade monopoly than the early trading companies.

Under the eyes of the Virginia Company land speculators became interested in America. They became so thoroughly established and permanently entrenched that they became an integral part of the American land system. No attempt was made by the Virginia Company to eliminate or reduce the speculative influence.

A significant though intangible influence of the Virginia Company arose out of its procrastinating, haphazard way of doing business. Although original plans called for land distribution only after seven years had elapsed, it was clear to Dale and others that private rights should have been established in the land at a much earlier date. But what was worse, Argall arbitrarily delayed for an additional three years. It is natural that the colonists grew restive, suspicious, and individualistic under such circumstances. Errors in surveying, haphazard location of allotments, and overlapping grants only added to the discontent. Isolation from company headquarters and inability to present grievances directly to competent authorities helped to develop in the early colonists disrespect for absentee controllers of land.

On the other hand, when the land eventually was granted, the rights accorded the private landower were as large as the settler could have expected. In fact, if as liberal rights in government had been granted from the beginning as finally were given the Virginia settlers under the Crown's rule, these early Virginia settlers would have been as free as Englishmen anywhere.

CHAPTER 13

Headright System of Granting Land

THE PRINCIPAL BASIS FOR GRANTING LAND in most colonies, particularly in the early days, was the headright system, under which land grants were made to any person who would either pay his own way or pay for transporting one or more persons to America. With land as a reward, people of moderate means were induced to leave over-crowded Europe and come to America. Headright land also interested wealthy persons in providing funds for others to pay their way across the ocean.

Headrighting was the colonial antecedent of the system of homesteading used later. It was practiced principally in Virginia, New York, Maryland, Pennsylvania, Delaware, New Jersey, the Carolinas, Georgia, and to a much lesser extent in the four New England colonies where the township system was important.

Headrighting was admirably adapted to the exigencies of the situation in Europe and America. People were crowded upon the land in England and other European countries, and many had moved to cities only to become unemployed. Wealth was amassing in the hands of traders and merchants; pauperism was growing; and agricultural production was not meeting domestic demands, while a vast unsettled continent lay across the ocean. The problem was to combine unemployed human resources, surplus financial accumulations, and boundless landed resources into a productive agricultural unit. Those who furnished the money were granted land on the basis of the number of people who could be settled with the money; those who ventured their persons were promised land as an encouragement to come. Thus, people would be placed upon the land in productive sized units, and the problem would be solved.

The headright system during the Colonial era and later the homesteading system of encouraging people to settle the wilderness and prairie were similar in many respects, but in others the two systems were quite different. Similarities were: (1) Under both, land was granted in stated quantities upon the basis of the number of persons who would settle upon it. (2) All persons, with few minor exceptions, were treated alike regardless of race, creed, color, or previous conditions of servitude. (3) Surveying and recording were slow and cumbersome processes under both systems. (4) The impatient settler frequently was forced to become a squatter because of the slowness with which the settlement agency acted. (5) Little guidance was given by either system in peopling the country in an orderly manner. (6) Although requirements regarding seating and planting were different, the principle that the grantee must meet certain standards of performance was common to both systems. (7) Both were subject to numerous abuses.

Dissimilarities were: (1) Under the headright system the procedure was indirect while homesteading was direct; under the former the land was granted from the sovereign to the settlement agency who in turn granted it to the headrighter, while in homesteading the federal government made the grant directly to the homesteader. (2) The headright system was designed in general to yield financial returns to the settlement agency, while homesteading was a financial liability. (3) Under headrighting penniless families were placed upon the land, while under homesteading the settler had to have some capital of his own. (4) The homestead system was never in competition with itself, for all grants under it were made by a single agency, while headrighting competed with itself at every turn, for each colony acted independently and competitively. (5) Land granted for headrights was burdened with several feudal charges, chief among which was quitrent, while homestead land was not subject to such charges. (6) The headright system dominated only the colonial schemes of granting land, while the homestead scheme in later years practically excluded other methods except pre-emption.

Headrighting exhibited one anomaly that is difficult to evaluate. More land was granted per person when a wealthy man supplied funds for financing the sending of a destitute individual than was granted if the settler financed his own passage. The headright in each case was the same — 50 acres, 100 acres, or such quantity. The larger quantity of land per person arose out of the practice of making two grants — one for the headright and, when the period of servitude was ended, one to the destitute person, who came almost invariably as an indentured servant. It was reasoned that the supplier of funds should be paid off in land and that the servant had earned a right to land when he had served his term.

This scheme permitted, and even fostered, the development of large holdings operated with indentured servants. The process of giving land to landless people at the end of their servitude put the plantation operator under constant pressure in the maintenance of his labor force. The pressure was relieved only when planters began to substitute slaves for indentured servants. In order to meet requirements for seating and planting, large landowners turned to slaves, whose period of servitude would not end. Apparently the headrighting scheme of land setttlement had as much to do with the early growth of slavery in America as any other single factor.

The development of large holdings and plantations occurred in all colonies where headrighting was dominant. That these colonies were largely in the South, had nothing to do with geography, climate, crops, or soils. Pennsylvania and Delaware would have been subjected to the same influences if Penn had chosen headrighting in place of direct sales.

Other characteristics of the headright system were: the distinct tendency to offer the largest quantities of land to those who came first; permitting the first-settled land to be held under lower quitrents than land settled later; infrequent limitations on size of holdings; almost complete absence of restrictions on alienation; frequent reservation of a portion of the precious metals; and the invariable requirements of seating and planting.

The practice of favoring those who came early arose out of the need of some substantial inducement for "breaking the ice." An example of this practice was found in the Carolinas, where only half as much land was offered to those who came after 1666 as to those who came earlier. Another example was the practice in Virginia of granting twice as much land to those who came before Dale left Virginia as to those who came later. This practice also was pronounced in New Jersey under the proprietors. The trend, however, was not always toward less land per headright. Maryland followed a vacillating policy—she made little difference between the settlers who came during the first decade, later she reduced by more than one-half the amount of land that would be granted per headright, which quantity was later increased and again reduced.

Although the settlement agencies did not highlight favorable quitrents on headright land as an inducement to encourage settlers to start the trek to America, they charged the first settlers a lower rent than those who came later, and frequently they permitted occupancy of land for several years before quitrents became due. In the latter regard they followed the practice used later by many municipalities to encourage the coming of new industries by granting them a period of freedom from taxes. Also many landowners have permitted a person to occupy land rent free while it was being brought under cultivation. The colonial settlement agency recognized the fact that the settler could not pay rent until his farm had been developed. In regard to the former, the practice of increasing quitrents on land granted for headrights was not widespread and seemed to be a recognition on the part of the settlement agency that the land was worth more as the country became more thickly settled and as the number of persons demanding land increased.

With the exception of Georgia, limitation on the amount of land that one person could acquire through headrighting was unknown in the early days of each colony. This limitation was imposed in Georgia from the beginning, but later was relaxed. In most of the colonies no limitations ever existed, while in the others the maximum acreage was so large that it was relatively meaningless insofar as the family sized farm idea is concerned. In New York, for example, a limitation of 2,000 acres was imposed, but only after Governer Fletcher had made numerous excessively large grants. In general, limitation on size of grant seemed more of a curb on the power of the provincial governor than a land-policy measure. Indeed, the whole spirit of the colonial land policy, like the federal land policy of a later date, was to allow the settler as much land as his financial position or business ability would permit. Regardless of land enlargement under the headright procedure, a definite tendency existed to place land in the hands of occupying farmers in family sized units. Indeed, most headright holdings were of this size.

Georgia was unique in another regard. She was the only colony, where headrighting was important, that imposed serious restrictions on freedom of alienation. Maryland prevented alienation of large quantities of land to church bodies and also restricted for a while alienation of the demesne land of her manors, but these controls were of minor importance. In the beginning the land of Georgia could be neither divided or alienated, but was held in tail male. Later, it could be divided or alienated with special permission. These restrictions were to prevent persons unused to managing property from becoming landless. The problem was almost identical, and the solution was similar in some regards, to that proposed by the President's Committee on Farm Tenancy two centuries later. The results were similar; the demands for freedom of action by the financially and politically strong forced the adoption of a policy of laissez faire.

Invariably the Crown reserved a portion of the gold and silver ore and sometimes other minerals in the original grants to the settlement agencies. As a consequence, this reservation was implied in every grant to settlers for no one can grant a larger estate than he himself holds. An additional reservation of precious metals was frequently made on behalf of the settlement agency. This reservation was chiefly of speculative value only, for the value of the land was based largely upon agricultural production. The mineral reservation apparently had no effect upon the land tenure system, although similar reservations appeared occasionally as a part of national land policy. Also, mineral reservations have been incorporated infrequently in transactions among private parties. Nevertheless, such reservations have never been an essential characteristic of the land tenure system.

Early in the granting of headright land every colony was faced with the problem of bringing the land under cultivation. Quitrent could not be collected on land that had not been taken up, cleared, and cultivated. Neither could the colony be protected against the Indians, Spanish, and French if vast acreages were left idle and unoccupied. Specifications for seating and planting were laid down, sometimes in general terms and sometimes specifically. Frequently they were ineffective. The weak colonial governmental organization, the absentee landlord, and the unlimited quantity of land influenced the situation. Laxness of control in turn contributed to the settler's feeling of independence and his desire to hold his land under tenure conditions permitting complete freedom of action.

Under headright grants progress was made in the battle between the maintenance of feudal tenures and the establishment of fee simple ownership. A major feudal holdover, and one that was common to headright grants, was the quitrent. The problems of primogeniture and entails remained untouched. Two less common feudal practices were escheat for corruption of the blood and a fine for alienation. The former was practiced in Pennsylvania, the latter in Maryland. Pennsylvania and Maryland were two colonies in which the settlement agencies did not hold the land under Kentish socage tenures. It is doubtful if escheat for felony and treason could have been practiced in the colonies where the land was held in free and common socage as of the County of Kent. Neither were Kentish socage tenants subject to a fine upon alienation.

At an early date Virginia eliminated quitrents insofar as ancient planters were concerned. Since they did not have to pay the company, and later the Crown, any quitrent, their land was virtually free. This privilege in Virginia was definitely limited, for the number of ancient planters was small. In New Jersey, however, the twenty-four proprietors of East Jersey permitted anyone to buy off his yearly rent and become a freeholder. These two relaxations in the reservation of quitrent under headrights were comparable to the New England town system where quitrents were not required.

Headrighting on the eastern seaboard was subject to many abuses, as was homesteading in the westward march across the prairies. These abuses included land engrossment on a large scale, overgranting or duplicate granting, frequent infringement upon the requirement for seating and planting, and many false entries in the records. The experience gained in headrighting was used in homesteading, even with the intervening period when acquisition by purchase and sale was the dominant method of placing public lands in the hands of occupying farmers.

Study of the practices followed in the headright granting of land in Colonial America indicates: (1) Land ownership was not denied any person because of race, creed, or previous economic or social experience. (2) Everyone was free to accumulate as much land as his own circumstances would permit. (3) The conflict between family farms and large operational units was not sharp until after the land was taken up in a given location and the frontier had disappeared. (4) The settlers would strive to secure as free and easy conditions of tenure as possible. (5) Running a land distributing agency from 3,000 miles across the sea was at best precarious, generally ineffective, and frequently doomed to failure. (6) Competition among the several colonies for headrighters was sufficient to make untenable the more obnoxious provisions that many of the settlement agencies otherwise would have imposed. (7) Headrighting was exceptionally well adapted to the situation in the colonies and the mother country, regardless of its numerous shortcomings and abuses, in comparison with readily available alternatives.

THE HEADRIGHT SYSTEM IN VIRGINIA

This system was first used extensively in Virginia under proprietary and royal control, and records extant in Virginia give as complete a picture of headrighting as in any other colony. In addition, Virginia furnishes a picture of early royal experience with headright grants. This experience set the pattern for settlement operations in other royal colonies as the Crown assumed control over them.

Brief Period of Proprietary Control

The first charter of the London Company stated that the company could take to America ". . . such and so many of our subjects, as shall willingly accompany them." (*Lucas. Charters, 5.*) The company issued instructions to the effect that the acquisition of ownership of land was not confined to company shareholders. Everyone who emigrated to the colony, or who brought or sent over another person, was entitled to the same amount of land under the headright system. (*Force. Tracts, III, No. 6, 22.*)

The first specific inducement for many English people to settle in the New World, however, was a letter written to the lord mayor, aldermen, and companies of London by the Council and Company of Virginia. It outlined a plan whereby any person who should be called before the lord mayor and personally plead that he was in the streets because he had no place to go would be offered the privilege of settling on land of his own in America. Not only would he be transported to the New World, but meat, drink, clothing, house, orchard, and garden would be furnished him upon arrival, and later land, probably as much as 500 acres, would be given him, with a like sum for his wife and a portion for his child. (*Brown. Genesis, I, 250–53.*) Brown thinks this letter was written before March 20, 1609.

The headright system was more definitely outlined in the instructions given to Yeardley on November 18, 1618 (*Va. Co. Rec., III, 98–109*), instructions issued by the Virginia Company in 1620 (*Ibid., 307–16*), as well as those issued by His Majesty's Council for Virginia on June 22, 1620. (*Force. Tracts, III, No. 6, 21–23.*) These three documents provided that the ancient adventurers and planters who had paid for their own transportation and had remained as long as three years before the time Dale left Virginia, were to receive 100 acres for their personal adventure on the first division, and as many more acres on the second division, provided the land received on the first division was sufficiently peopled.[1]

Every man who became a tenant or a servant of the company before Dale left was allowed, at the expiration of the term for which he had bound himself, a patent to 100 acres of land. Those who had transported themselves to the New World since the time Dale left Virginia were allotted only fifty acres on the first division. The tenant or servant, by settling in Virginia and for a certain length of time devoting his physical powers to the cultivation of the lands of the company, was looked upon as having placed himself upon the same footing as the shareholder who had invested £12 10*s*. in its stock.

To the old and new adventurers, both for their personal adventure and for every person transported by them to Virginia between the midsummer of 1618 and 1625 and who continued there three years or died after the ship had left, were to be granted fifty acres on the first division and another fifty acres on the second division. No rent was to be paid to the company by these adventurers for the land obtained under either division. Thus, the adventurers held their land in fee simple, free of all feudal charges. Other persons who had transported themselves to Virginia at their own

[1] The company believed the difficulties and dangers of the colony in the greatest part overcome, and that to those who were there before Dale and who had paved the way for the others to come should go the greatest reward.

expense between the midsummers of 1618 and 1625 were to be granted fifty acres, rent-free for seven years with a yearly rent after that of 12*d.* for every fifty acres held, and were to receive as many more acres under the same condition on the second division.

The prospective grantees were required, from time to time, to make a certificate of the name, age, sex, trade, and condition of every person transported to the colony before the midsummer of 1625. (*Ibid., 21–22.*) All land claimed by grantees under these headrights was to be surveyed and the bounds were to be set out so the holdings could be distinguished. (*Va. Co. Rec., III, 108.*) All grants were to be examined and recommended by a committee selected for that purpose before they were issued. Final approval had to be given in a quarter-court before the seal could be stamped on the grant. (*Force. Tracts, III, No. 6, 20; Va. Co. Rec., III, 359.*)

The earliest headright patent of which there is a record was the one granted by Yeardley to William Fairefax on February 20, 1619.[2] Since Fairefax and his wife had resided in Virginia for eight years prior to 1619, they were considered ancient planters and Fairefax claimed and received 100 acres for himself and 100 acres for his wife. The grant was located at Archurshope. (*Nugent. Va. Land Patents, I, 109; Va. Co. Rec., IV, 556.*) Yeardley, on March 6, 1620, also made a grant of 200 acres to George Harrison who had defrayed his own expenses and had lived in Virginia three years. This grant was for transporting himself and three others to Virginia. (*Ibid., I, 146.*) This difference in quantity of land granted per headright indicates the preference accorded those who came early. The precedent set by Virginia in the amount of land that would be granted was frequently followed by other colonies to encourage settlers to come with the first wave of settlement.

The form of patents used by the first governors under the company showed the number of acres granted and set out the bounds for each tract. The bounds were usually a creek, a river, or the land held by another planter. Then the basis for the number of acres, the number allowed for the grantee and for those transported by him, was given. The land was granted to the patentee and his heirs and assigns forever with all rights and privileges of hunting, hawking, and fowling, and including all the minerals except those reserved by the Crown and the company. If a quitrent was to be paid the amount was stated. (*Ibid., III, 592–96.*)

In May, 1625, just before the Virginia Company relinquished

---

[2] Most writers give the grant made by Sir Francis Wyatt to Thomas Hathersall on January 26, 1621, as the first. The patents were recorded in Virginia as they were sent from England. The Hathersall grant appears first in the patent book; therefore it is regarded as the first patent issued. For some unknown reason the grant to Fairefax was delayed in being sent to Virginia, so its record appears a little later in the patent book.

its charter, Governor Wyatt sent to the company one of the best records available for any early period on the state of land titles and estates in Virginia. (*Ibid., IV, 551–59.*) Names of the holders of the patents and the number of acres each held were given. Individual holdings ranged in size from 12 acres, held by individual grantees in the Henrico Plantation, to 800,000 acres, the Martin Hundred. A statistical summary of this report is given in Table 2.

Under the above system of distribution the people knew their own property, and had the encouragement of working for their own advantage. Many became very industrious and began to vie with each other in planting, building, and making other improvements. (*Beverley. Va., Book I, 37–38.*)

The Royal Colony

Instructions to Governor Wyatt when the king dissolved the company gave no indication that the grants which had been made would be recognized and no provision was made for satisfying future claims. The only reference to the settling of people on the land was an imposition upon those already in America. It provided that all newcomers were to be well entertained and lodged by the old planters, and if the newcomers were not provided with land fit to manure they were to be permitted to occupy the company's land upon conditions expressed in the treasurer and council's letter of August, 1622.

Thus when James I took command of Virginia a feeling of uneasiness developed among the settlers regarding their titles to land. The colonists urged that existing holdings be confirmed by an act of Parliament. (*Bruce. Econ. Hist. Va., I, 514.*) Finally, royal approval was given on March 14, 1625, to the laws established by the company with reference to land granted under the headright system. (*Ibid., 515.*) The planters' rights were further assured on May 13 of the same year when Charles I, who had ascended to the throne since the previous approval, stated that it was his intention neither to take away nor impeach the particular interest of any private planters or adventurers nor to alter the same other than as should be necessary for the good of the public. (*Va. Mag. of Hist., VII, 132–34.*) He said nothing about future land grants or existing claims for which grants had not been issued.

West issued thirty-four patents and Pott made nine grants (*Nugent. Va. Land Patents, I, 9–14*) ranging from 12 to 1,000 acres. With the arrival of Harvey in 1630 the issuing of headrights in Virginia was greatly accelerated. The instructions given to him in 1628 when he was appointed governor contained a promise which was another step forward in making secure all headright grants. It read in part, "Wee do likewise promise hereby to renewe and confirme unto the said Collonies under our greate Seale of England there landes & priveledges formerlie graunted." (*Va. Mag. of Hist., VII, 267–68.*) Even with this, Governor Harvey was not authorized to grant new land, but like his predecessors he continued to do so. Harvey issued some seventy-three patents while he was governor the first time, few of which were for less than 100 acres. One was for 2,550 acres while another contained 2,000 acres. (*Nugent. Va. Land Patents, I, 14–21.*)

TABLE 2

SIZE AND NUMBER OF PATENTS AND ALLOTMENTS OF LAND OF THE VIRGINIA COMPANY IN VIRGINIA PRIOR TO DISSOLUTION IN 1625 *

Size of allotment	Number of allotments	Size of allotment	Number of allotments
Acres		*Acres*	
12	1	550	3
30	1	600	2
40	4	650	1
50	20	680	1
100	75	750	2
110	1	1,000	2
140	1	1,150	1
150	23	1,300	1
200	21	1,500‡	2
250	9	1,700	1
300	8	2,500	1
350	1	3,000§	4
400	2	3,700	1
450	1	10,000‖	1
		100,000¶	1
500	5†	800,000**	1

* Compiled from Va. Co. Rec., IV, 551–59.
† Includes one allotment to the Treasurer.
‡ Common land at Elizabeth City and Henrico.
§ Allotments kept by the London Company, at Henrico, James City, and Elizabeth City.
‖ University land at Henrico.
¶ Southampton Hundred.
** Martin Hundred.
Total allotments 198, with an average size of 4,891 acres; average size of allotment excluding those allotments which are footnoted is 222 acres; average size of footnoted allotments is 66,250 acres.

During this period, a movement was afoot to either reinstate the company or develop some other form of proprietary government for the colony. The Virginians feared, however, that in either case titles to land already granted, especially those issued since 1625, might not be recognized. On March 6, 1631, the council suggested that the Crown confirm all grants of land and dividends and that all who had arrived since June 24, 1625, likewise have tracts of twenty-five acres granted to each of them. (*Va. Jour. of Burgesses, 1619–59, 55.*) The Privy Council delayed, but finally in 1634 it sent assurance to Governor Harvey that it did not intend that land which men received from the company should be impeached, and that the governor was authorized to dispose of lands to all planters as he had power to do before 1625. (*Harrison. Va. Land Grants, 24–25; G. B. Acts of Privy Coun., Col. Ser., I, 203–4.*)

Thus, not until almost ten years after Virginia became a royal colony was a governor given the right to grant land. The number of patents issued for headrights increased rapidly, as did their size. West issued over 300 and Harvey issued about 640 during three years as governor. (*Nugent. Va. Land Patents, I, 21–118.*) Almost ten per cent of the grants ranged from 1,000 acres to 8,000 acres, while a much larger percentage ranged from 500 acres to 1,000 acres.

By 1646 much of the land granted in Virginia remained unsettled. However, in that year a law was passed which required all persons with title to land to make their claims within five years, and for orphans to make their claims within five years after they became of age. (*Hening. Stats., I, 331.*) In 1657 and 1661 this same law was re-enacted. This difficulty was accentuated by, if not based entirely upon, larger-than-family-sized grants. Throughout this period no limit seemed to be set on the number of acres an individual might have. Since those in charge were interested in settling people upon the land, the number of acres granted an individual was dependent upon the number of persons he was able to transport to the new country; thus some very large grants were made. (*Nugent. Va. Land Patents, I, 226–438.*) Most of the grants, however, were small; yet the amount of land included in the large grants was significant.

When Virginia surrendered to the Protectorate in 1651 she obtained a confirmation of the headright system as one of the conditions of submission. (*Hening. Stats., I, 364.*) Instructions issued after the Restoration again confirmed the headright claim of fifty acres for each individual. The privilege of receiving at least fifty acres for every person transported was confirmed repeatedly in the instructions given to subsequent governors. All large grants made previously to people who had not and never intended to plant and manure the land were to be revoked; this land was to be regranted and a quitrent was to be levied.

In all patents a provisional clause was inserted for planting and seating the land, which was to be done within three years. What was meant by sufficient planting and seating, however, was not explained until 1666. In that year the legislature declared that the building of a house and keeping stock upon the land for one year would be accounted seating, and that the clearing, tending, and planting of an acre of ground would be accounted planting. Either of these was considered a sufficient performance of the condition required by the patent. After the planting or seating of such land

and continued payment of the quitrent, no land could be adjudged to be abandoned or deserted. (*Ibid., II, 244.*) Later, seven years were allowed for the carrying out of provisions for seating and planting by those who had been molested by the Indians. All others were allowed only three years. (*Ibid., 397–98.*)

The Virginia legislature in 1675 decided that it was expedient to ask for another royal recognition of the headright grants. This request was granted in 1677.

Various land regulations for Virginia were brought together in one statute, entitled the Land Act of 1705. (*Ibid., III, 305–29.*) Up to this time no limit had been placed on the number of acres one person might acquire. To remedy this the act provided that not more than 500 acres could be claimed in one tract and the claimant had to be the owner of five servants or slaves; an additional 200 acres could be held for each slave above five. Also, no grant to any person was to exceed 4,000 acres on one patent, regardless of the number of slaves or servants, unless the headrights had already been duly entered with the surveyor.

Furthermore, all patents that had been granted in the colony were confirmed by the act. This had been done several times previously through instructions given to the several governors. Also, the question of surplus land was dealt with. If upon a new survey it was found that any person had a greater number of acres than his patent called for, a new patent was to be granted for the amount held and the grantee was not obliged to make new or additional seating or planting upon the land by reason of the new patent.[3]

This act, which is said by Light to be the basis of all subsequent land laws, was altered slightly by the Lords of Trade in 1707. (*Calender of State Papers, 1706–8, 406–7, 421.*) Hening has stated that, owing to an erroneous impression it usually is presumed that the entire Land Act of 1705 was actually repealed in 1710. All of the first part of the 1705 act, which related to the various modes of acquiring titles to lands and the forms of patents, was omitted from the Act of 1710. Therefore, Hening concluded that they were retained in force.

Penalty for failure to seat and plant the land was made more severe in the Act of 1710 than in previous ones. Any patentee failing to fulfil the requirements for seating and planting within three years, or failing to pay the full quitrent, not only lost the land not seated and planted but also lost all benefits and advantages he might otherwise have by virtue of these rights. (*Hening. Stats., III, 526.*)

The Virginia Legislature in 1713 passed still another land act. It provided that in every plot of land surveyed before October 31,

[3] For the first time, statutory provision was made in the Act of 1705 for those who could not claim by headrights the land that they needed. It was provided that such persons could obtain land by purchase.

1713, one-third of the tract was to be deemed as plantable and the remaining two-thirds was to be regarded as barren. For every fifty acres of plantable land the patentee, within three years, was to clear and work three acres of the most convenient and best land, or to clear and drain three acres of swamp, sunken or marsh land. Within the same length of time for every fifty acres of the part regarded as barren land, three cattle or six sheep or goats were to be put on the land. These were to be kept there until three acres of every fifty were cultivated. If no part of the land was fit for cultivation without manuring and improving the land, the patentee was obliged to build a dwelling and keep on the land three cattle or six sheep or goats for each fifty acres. If none of the land was fit for planting or pasture, within three years the patentee was to employ one able man for every 100 acres. This man was to be employed in the digging of a stone quarry or a coal or other mine. Proof of such seating and planting was to be made in the general court where the land lay. (*Ibid., IV, 37–42.*) These also were the provisions of the Land Act of 1748. (*Ibid., V, 409–31.*)

In 1720 conditions for seating and planting were further broadened. For every three acres of land cleared and fenced for the use of a pasture, and used as such for a period of three years, the patentee could retain fifty acres. Fifty acres were to be retained in case a patentee spent either £10 of money, or the value thereof in tobacco, in the building of houses, watermills, or other works, or in the planting of trees and hedges, or making other improvements not mentioned in the previous land acts. (*Ibid., IV, 81–82.*) In 1748 the amount of money spent was reduced to £5. (*Ibid., V, 425.*)

Spotswood, who became lieutenant-governor in 1710, brought home to the people the fact that it was Queen Anne's land they were taking up and not their own by substituting the name of the sovereign as grantor in place of that of the governor. He made more effective the conditions of seating, and introduced a provision for forfeiture in case of three years' default in payment of quitrents. However, he did nothing about limiting the size of holdings. (*Harrison. Va. Land Grants, 39.*)

Although by 1715 the headright system had ceased to be an important means of acquiring land, it continued until the middle of the eighteenth century. Statistics concerning the size of grants by years from 1626 to 1700 are summarized in Table 3.

In an endeavor to populate the colony, several large grants were issued between 1730 and 1736. They are tabulated in Table 4.

In 1779, the Commonwealth of Virginia passed an act to adjust the titles of claimants to unpatented lands. Headright claims for importation which had been duly proved and certified in any court of record before the passing of the act were to be filled, provided the claim did not exceed 400 acres. Any claims that had not been duly proved prior to the passage of the act were declared void. (*Hening. Stats., X, 35–50.*)

Abuses of the Headright System

Abuses of the headright system in Virginia were many and varied. In many cases several patents were obtained by the same person on the strength of the number of times he paid for his own passage across the ocean. (*Nugent. Va. Land Patents, I, 42, 44, 45.*) Another type of abuse arose when a shipmaster would swear before the proper

TABLE 3

SUMMARY OF HEADRIGHT GRANTS IN VIRGINIA, 1626–1700

Year or years	Largest patent	Average size of all patents
	Acres	*Acres*
1626–32	1,000	100 to 300
1632	350	....
1634	5,350	719
1635	2,000	380
1636	2,000	351
1637	5,350	445
1638	3,000	423
1640	1,300	405
1641	872	343
1642	3,000	559
1643	4,000	595
1644	670	370
1645	1,090	333
1646	1,200	360
1647	650	361
1648	800	412
1649	3,500	522
1650	5,350	677
1634–50	....	446
1650–55	10,000	592
1655–66	10,000	671
1666–79	20,000	890
1679–89	20,000	607
1685–95	10,000	601
1695–1700	14,400	688
1650–1700	....	674

(*Bruce. Econ. Hist. of Va., I, 527–32.*)

authority that he had on a stated occasion brought into the colony certain persons (in reality his seamen and passengers) for whose transportation he had never received the headright to which he was entitled. Although the seamen were attached to his vessel under articles of agreement and the passengers had paid their own expenses he would be granted the designated quantities of land. (*Hartwell. Pres. State of Va., 15–16.*) Furthermore, many grants for the importation of people to Virginia were made to seafaring men under questionable claims. A study of these grants revealed that the names of those imported were practically the same in each grant. (*Nugent. Va. Land Patents, I, 6, 35, 70, 100, 108, 110.*)

A further abuse of the headright system arose when different persons were granted land for the same headright. Many times the master of the ship secured fifty acres for transporting an individual on his ship, the merchant who purchased the period of service received fifty acres, and if a planter acquired an interest in the person brought in, he also received fifty acres. (*Spotswood Letters, II, 15.*) Many times two planters united in purchasing from the shipmaster the same individual and each was allowed fifty acres.

Another problem arose from ignorance and fraudulent actions

TABLE 4
LARGE GRANTS OF LAND ISSUED IN VIRGINIA, 1730–36

Name of person or group	Acres involved	Conditions specified
John Van Meter and Kercheval	30,000	20 families per 10,000 acres
Isaac Van Meter	10,000	10 families in 2 years
Alex Ross and Morgan Bryan	100,000	100 families in 2 years
Joseph Smith and Joseph Clapham	50,000	(none specified)
William Beverly	130,000	(none specified)
Smith, Chapman, Walkins, and Jefferies	20,000	20 families
Group of German Protestants	50,000	50 families in 2 years
Robert McKay and Joost Heyd	100,000	100 families

(Adapted from *Va. Mag. of Hist., XIII, 118-19, 120-23, 127-28, 130-34, 123-24, 356, and 360.*)

of surveyors. They often gave out drafts of surveys without going on the land. They gave descriptions by some natural bounds and nearly always allowed large measures so that the grantees received tracts of land larger than those for which they paid quitrent or were entitled to under the headright system.

HEADRIGHT GRANTS IN NEW YORK

In the field of land tenure the contribution of the Dutch was significant. Although not strikingly different in many respects from the English, Dutch tenure added sufficient variety to the land system of New York to make it more diverse than that of any other colony.

Since New Netherland was first settled for fur trade, agriculture did not appear until 1623. In that year the company erected a fort on Manhattan Island and another on the South River, and reconstructed the one at Fort Orange. Thirty families were sent over to occupy these places. (*Brodhead. N.Y., I, 150–51.*) Some of the families settled at the first two places, while eighteen families went up the river to Albany. These were not sent strictly as colonists to cultivate the land, but more as servants of the company to assist in trade.

(*N.Y. Doc. Hist., III, 32.*) Some of them returned home at the expiration of their term of service, and little was done toward advancing settlement and private landholding until 1628.

The directors of the company in New Netherland were divided into two factions. One favored colonization but the other was interested only in trade. One of the most ardent advocates of colonization was Kileaen Van Rensselaer, a merchant. With the help of others, he had persuaded the company to establish farms or bouweries on Manhattan Island with a view to supplying provisions to ships destined for the West Indies and Brazil. When these bouweries, through neglect, failed to prosper, the blame was placed upon Van Rensselaer and his associates. In order to prove the soundness of their policy, they offered to plant agricultural settlements at their expense, provided they were granted certain freedoms or privileges. Upon the basis of this promise, on March 10, 1628, a charter commonly referred to by the title of "Freedoms and Exemptions" was issued. However, no one actually took advantage of the terms of this charter to colonize in America. After serious deliberation a second charter, known as "Charter of Freedoms and Exemptions for Patroons in New Netherlands." was granted on June 7, 1629. (*O'Callaghan. N. Neth., I, 112–20.*) This second charter was drawn up to induce wealthy persons to come or send people to New Netherland to establish settlements there. It was chiefly concerned with two types of grants, lordly estates or patroonships of immense size and seignioral in character open to members of the company; and smaller grants available to private, less wealthy persons.

Headrights and the Early Patroons

The patroonships were open to members of the company who agreed to found, at their own expense, settlements of fifty persons over fifteen years of age within four years. Although this method of granting land has seldom been spoken of as the headright system, the same general principles were followed as those developed under the pure headright system in the other colonies.

Each holder of a patroonship had a right to dispose of his estate as he pleased and his heirs could inherit it. For ten years the colonists brought over by the patroon were to be entirely free from customs, taxes, excise, or any other contributions. None of them were allowed to leave the service of their patroon during the period for which they were bound except by written consent of the patroon. Each patroon was to establish a local government and maintain order on the land he held. This charter seemed to seek to establish a monopoly in land, as the previous one had in trade, and to put the valley of the Hudson largely in the hands of proprietors who were favorites of the company.

The patroon bore the expense of preparing the land for occupancy by setting off farms, stocking them with tools and cattle, erecting farm buildings, and bringing the farmer to his work unhampered for want of capital. In return for these outlays the old Dutch civil code gave the patroon many rights. He was entitled to the rent fixed and also to a portion of the increase of the stock and of the produce of the farm. The farmer was not at liberty to sell any of his produce elsewhere until it had been refused by the patroon. Each colonist could be required to grind all grain at the patroon's mill and to obtain license to fish or hunt within the domain. The lord of the patroonship was legal heir to all who died intestate within the colony.

Another type of grant was provided for in the Charter of Freedoms and Exemptions. These grants, made to private persons who would settle in the province, either on their own account or in the service of masters who remained in Holland, were to be made as outright grants for as much land as the grantee could properly improve. Owing to the strict policies of the company and the reluctance of the people to leave their fatherland, only a few settlers came. It was realized that more liberal terms and greater inducements had to be offered.

Liberal Settlement Schemes

In 1634,[4] a new scheme was issued for those wishing to move to the New World. Unoccupied and unreserved land was to be assigned to any patroon who within six years would undertake to plant a colony of forty-eight persons in New Netherland. The land was to be held in the propriety forever and ". . . all the land situate within the Patroons' limits . . . [was] to be holden as free, allodial and patrimonial property." (*N.Y. Col. Hist., I, 96–100.*) The patroons were not to impose on their colonists any custom, toll, excise, import, or other tax but would allow them to enjoy such freedom and exemptions as were granted or would be granted afterwards through a charter to the company. From reports of settlements made, it can be concluded that very few Hollanders took advantage of this offer.

In 1638, the States General demanded a still more vigorous and forceful policy of colonization (*Ibid., 106–7*) and the Chamber at Amsterdam made numerous concessions. The director and council issued an ordinance further liberalizing settlement regulation. It promised a patent and title to all holders of plantations after they had occupied and cultivated the land for ten years, provided they agreed to pay to the company a yearly rent of one-tenth of their crops and two capons for a house and lot. (*N. Neth. Laws, 16.*) These provisions were made more liberal in 1640. They provided that

[4] This was without date but both Brodhead and O'Callaghan set the date at 1634.

to either a master or a colonist, who would come to New Netherland and bring five persons over fifteen years of age, would be granted 100 morgens, or 200 acres, of land. The extent of a patroonship was reduced to one Dutch mile along the coast or the bank of a navigable stream and to two Dutch miles landward. The patroon's land was to remain allodial. This meant that the property of the patroon was free from burdensome incidents of feudal tenure such as knight service, quitrents, and similar disabilities. The jurisdiction, however, was to be ". . . as of a perpetual hereditary fief; devolvable by death as well to females as to males . . ."; in case of division, the parts were to remain of the same tenurial nature as the original fief. As an acknowledgment of the company's overlordship when the property passed to the heirs, fealty and homage were to be rendered to the company by the presentation of a pair of iron gauntlets. (*N.Y. Col. Hist., I, 119–23.*) Even though more concessions were made in this charter than in former ones, some evidence of feudal provisions persisted, the seigniorial aspect for example; however, the regulations of 1638 and 1640 attracted settlers to the colony.

A new draft of "Freedoms and Exemptions" was issued in 1650. It made a few changes in the holding and granting of land over the previous regulations. Anyone who wished to go to New Netherland and would pay his passage was permitted to go. Upon arrival he was allowed to choose, and to hold under quitrent or as a fief, such parcels of land as he would be able to cultivate for the production of fruit and crops. He was bound to commence settlement and cultivation within one year or be deprived of his land. A marked difference between the regulation of 1650 and previous ones was in the requirements placed on the grantee in return for holding land. Each person was exempt from giving the tenth of all the fruit and crops for a term of years, the number of which was not stated, plus one additional year for every legitimate child which he brought to America.

A patroonship would be granted to anyone on condition that he plant within four years 100 persons above fifteen years of age, provided as many as one-fourth be brought within the first year. The land was to be held by the same privileges as those stated in previous Freedoms and Exemptions. (*Ibid., 401–6.*) This was the last charter for settlement issued by the Dutch and remained in force until the end of the Dutch period of control about fourteen years later.

Headrights Under New Netherland's Towns

The early towns in New Netherland were located on Long Island. They were mostly of English rather than Dutch origin, although they were begun around 1644 to 1656, when the Dutch were in possession of the colony. Some outstanding ones were Hempstead, Flushing, and Gravesend. (*N.Neth. Laws, 42–46, 48–51, 53–57.*)

The charter or patent granted to Hempstead, although slightly more elaborate than the others, was typical. It was issued by Director-General Kieft with the consent of his council and by virtue of authority derived from the States General, the Prince of Orange, and the West India Company. The document granted to Robert Fordham and five others a large strip of land extending across Long Island from north to south. The patentees were perpetually to enjoy this extensive area in "large and ample manner as their own free Land of Inheritance," provided they procured 100 families to settle within five years. Thus, the New Netherland towns were granted on the headright principle.

From the very beginning a town-meeting type of local government, after the manner of the New England towns, was visualized by the inhabitants, with the customary powers of administering and granting lands. The grant was subject to the continued loyalty of the settlers to the Dutch government and to the payment after ten years of an annual quitrent of one-tenth of all revenue from the soil or pasturage. (*Ibid., 42–46.*)

Inasmuch as the town had been patented to the proprietors, these men, or the larger body of freemen in the town meeting, made what might be called tertiary grants. House lots, usually of small acreage, and some other lands were granted in severalty by the town but a check was retained upon transfers to other persons, especially outsiders, by the right of first purchase and by other means. "To lessen the evils of land speculation, it was sometimes provided that lots not built upon within a reasonable time should be subject to forfeiture. Some arable lands as well as meadow and pasture lands were held in common." (*Rife. Land Ten. in N.Neth., 56.*)

When the English took possession of New Netherland in 1664, there were three kinds of holdings in the colony: the patroonships, the small holdings, and the municipality or town holdings. The patroonships, however, did not gain as much prominence under the Dutch regime as is sometimes thought; one notable exception was that of Van Rensselaer. Why Dutch policy was unfavorable to patroons cannot be determined. The English in later days, however, succeeded in erecting an imposing manorial structure upon the crumbling Dutch patroonship idea. Small holdings, on the other hand, were granted in accordance with the regulations in the charters. These holdings were scattered throughout the colony. The municipality or township system was established largely by English settlers, chiefly from New England.

Headright Plans of the English

On August 27, 1664, the Dutch relinquished their claim to New Netherland to the English. (*N.Y. Col. Rec., 95–98.*) All the inhabitants of the newly acquired territory were to continue as free citizens and enjoy their lands, houses, goods, and ships, and were given the right to dispose of them as they pleased. The Dutch were to follow their own custom concerning inheritances. The English required all the landowners, whether individuals or towns, to have their grants confirmed. (*N.Y. Col. Laws, I, 18, 44.*) When Governor Nicolls discovered that the directors of the West India Company were resolved to disavow the articles of capitulation, he confiscated the company's property, thereby securing control of all the ungranted lands in the province. (*Brodhead. N.Y., II, 59.*) Van Rensselaer's holdings and rights, however, were recognized by Governor Nicolls, although an English patent was not issued to him for twenty years. The seigniorial system of Van Rensselaer was allowed to continue with little change, and it furnished a model for the manors established under English control. (*Rife. Land Ten. in N.Neth., 73.*)

Governor Nicolls was empowered to grant lands to anyone willing to settle and improve them. These grants, the amount of land the grantee was able to cultivate, usually were for 100, 200, or 300 acres. The land was granted to the planters as their freeholds forever, and they were to pay the customary rates and duties. The highest rent or acknowledgment was to be 1*d.* an acre for land granted by the king and 2*s.* 6*d.* for each 100 acres purchased directly from the Indians. (*N.Y. Doc. Hist., I, 59.*)

In 1665, under the direction of Governor Nicolls, the Duke of York's land laws were compiled from the statutes of other English colonies. Under these laws all lands and heritages were to be free from all fines and licenses upon alienation and from all heriots, wardships, liveries, escheats, and forfeitures upon the death of parents or ancestors. All former purchases were to be confirmed to the present possessor or rightful owner. All holders of patents were to return them and take out new ones, while holders of unplanted lands were to have them surveyed and the bounds indicated within one year. If such land was not seated, planted, or inhabited within three years, it was to be forfeited. Any person not having a legal claim to the land on which he lived and grew crops, but who had resided on the land for the four previous years, could receive title provided no legal claim was made by another person before September 1, 1665. (*N.Y. Col. Laws, I, 44.*)

For the next ten years the instructions were general regarding the granting of land and the terms upon which it was to be granted. Governor Dongan in 1686 was empowered to ". . . grant unto any person or persons for such term and under such moderat Quit-rents, services and acknowledgements to bee thereupon reserved unto us as you . . . shall think fitt." (*N.Y. Col. Hist., III, 381.*) Approximately the same instructions were given to Henry Sloughter in 1689, (*Ibid., 627*) and to Benjamine Fletcher in 1692. (*Ibid., 818–24.*)

Governor Fletcher was generous with the king's land, but this was not discovered until Governor Belmont succeeded him. He granted the land in parcels of 100,000 acres to a person, and to some favorites he granted four or five times that amount. Belmont reported that Fletcher granted away all land that was available when he found that he would no longer be governor. One grant was for a tract seventy miles long and eight miles wide. Others were for fifty miles and some for thirty miles. Belmont summarized the results of Fletcher's grants as follows: "But hath made it almost impossible to settle the Country with Inhabitants, there being no land but what must be purchased from his few Grantees, (who never can settle it themselves) . . . ." (*Ibid., IV, 334–35.*)

Not only was the land extravagantly granted but the quitrent reserved by Fletcher was small in comparison with conventional rentals. So on October 19, 1698, the Board of Trade ordered that no land be granted in the future for amounts less than 2*s.* 6*d.* for 100 acres. (*Ibid., IV, 392–93.*) On May 16, 1699, an act was passed for the vacating, breaking, and annulling of the extravagant grants made by Fletcher, (*Ibid., V, 21–26; N.Y. Col. Laws, I, 412–17*) but this was repealed in November, 1702. (*Ibid., 524.*)

The land system in New York in 1732 was summarized by Cadwallader Colden, at that time the surveryor general. He said that not only was the king deprived of most of his quitrent but the development of the province was hindered by these large uncertain grants. Young people left New York every year and purchased land in neighboring colonies. Landholders never were able to improve such large tracts. Other people would not become their vassals or tenants because they had left their native country to avoid dependence on landlords, and had come to the New World to enjoy lands in fee.

The proposal made to alleviate these evils was to abolish the variable quitrents by an act of the legislature and to establish a general quitrent of 2*s.* 6*d.* for every 100 acres with confirmation of all grants only upon payment of the quitrent. This would not only restore the quitrent but would destroy all grants that were actually so extravagant that the holders could not improve them in a reasonable time. (*N.Y. Doc. Hist., I, 249–55.*)

The instructions for granting land given to Governor Moore in 1767 (*N.Y. Col. Hist., VII, 900*), provided for a quitrent of 2*s.* 6*d.* for every 100 acres and included the specification that at least three acres for every fifty acres must be cultivated within three years or the grant would be forfeited. The land was to be located so that the patentee would receive both profitable and unprofitable land and so that the length of each patent would not extend along the banks of any river but into the mainland; this was done to give as many patentees as possible the advantage of the river.

These regulations seem to have prevailed until April 7, 1773, when an order was issued prohibiting all grants of land until otherwise instructed. This order was based upon a study of the conditions in the colony which revealed that the authority for granting land should be further regulated and restrained and that the grantee of such land should be subject to conditions other than those at that time prescribed. *(Ibid., VIII, 357–58.)* This seems to have brought to a close the headright granting of land in New York, since the new regulations provided only for sale of the land.

HEADRIGHTS UNDER THE LORDS BALTIMORE

Disposition of land in Maryland was authorized by the proprietor in England, in a proposal entitled "Conditions of Plantation," issued on November 15, 1633. These proposals gave all the subjects of England, except those explicitly forbidden, the right to transport themselves and their families to the colony to build houses, forts, and other places of strength at the appointment of Lord Baltimore. Land would be granted to those who came and to those who transported others. *(Calvert Papers, 131–40.)*

Conditions of Headright Grants

How much land each adventurer was to receive, and the conditions of tenure under which he was to hold it, are not known. Two obligations were mentioned: to pay a quitrent, and to take the oath of fidelity to Lord Baltimore. Later as a means of preventing too great diffusion of the people throughout the province, it was provided that each of the early settlers be assigned a house lot in the town of St. Mary's. *(Kilty. Land. Ass't., 32, 33.)*

In 1634 a second tract entitled "A Declaration of Lord Baltimore's Plantation in Maryland" was issued. It is thought to have been issued before a settlement was made and to have been written by a Jesuit, probably Father Andrew White. It promised 2,000 acres to anyone who would venture £100 for transporting five able-bodied men and sufficient food and arms for twelve months. Smaller or larger sums of money would warrant proportionate benefits. *(Force. Tracts, IV, No. 12, 4.)* The cost of outfitting and transporting a person to Maryland at that time was about £20. *(Osgood. 17th Cent., II, 20.)*

The first inclusive and specific conditions issued by Lord Baltimore for the granting of land by headrights were those of August 8, 1636, issued at Portsmouth, England. These instructions covered separately persons who came in 1633, those who came in 1634 and 1635, and those who came after 1635. Later, general instructions were issued in 1641, 1648, 1649, and 1651; these instructions dealt chiefly with quitrent and seating and planting. Specific information regarding the several instructions is summarized in Table 5. Baltimore favored large operators and doubtless visualized dotting his vast domain with numerous manorial estates. The early offers of land to those who would bring five or more additional persons were four times as large as to those who brought less than five. Later the differential was only two or two and a half times larger. A marked tendency also was exhibited to decrease the size of the headright grant as time passed. The justification given for the change was that so great an allowance of land, if long continued, would cause the people to settle too far apart. Baltimore, however, did not distinguish between large and small holders when he established quitrental rates.

Early conditions for taking up land did not require that the men be equipped with arms and ammunition. However, the 1641 Conditions which were issued on the eve of a local war with the Indians, provided that each man brought in had to be supplied with arms and ammunition consisting of one musket or balstard musket with a snaplock, ten pounds of powder, forty pounds of lead bullets, a pistol and goose shot for each, one sword and belt, and one bandoleer and flask. (*Kilty. Land. Ass't., 33–35.*)

Another important feature of the Conditions of 1641 was the clause forbidding the alienation of land to any corporation or ecclesiastical group without special license from the proprietor. The object of this restriction was to prevent the accumulation of large landed estates by the Jesuits. (*Johnson. Found. of Md., 64, 67.*) This ordinance was Maryland's statute Mortmain and its effect is still felt. Writing in 1884, Browne said that the general assembly had continued the position held by the proprietor and in Maryland no real property could be devised to a religious corporation without a special act of the assembly. (*Browne. Md., 57.*) Even today, land in Maryland cannot be devised to religious bodies without an action of the assembly, except five acres for a churchyard. (*Md. Const., Art. XXXVIII, see Thorpe. Charters.*)

The specifications of June 20, 1648, contained two liberal features: One, headrights were to be given also to the French, Dutch, and Italians who were already in the colony, or to anyone who transported them. They had been excluded under the previous conditions as this privilege had been extended only to the British and Irish. The other, every manservant who had served at least three years and whose servitude had expired was to have land granted to him and his heirs on the same terms and conditions as if he had transported himself into the province at his own cost. (*Kilty. Land. Ass't., 36–43.*) This was the first mention of granting land to servants in Maryland.

Quitrents and Seating

Baltimore encountered two insoluble problems in peopling his colony: the collection of quitrent, and the lack of immediate seating and planting of land granted. The 1642 assembly passed an act which provided that the rent on any land taken up under the headright system should begin the following Christmas. To effectuate this policy it also provided that in case the surveyor delayed in laying out

TABLE 5

ACRES GRANTED PER HEADRIGHT FOR VARIOUS CLASSES OF PERSONS AND MISCELLANEOUS CONDITIONS OF HEADRIGHT GRANTS IN PROPRIETARY MARYLAND

Class of person or condition of grant	Conditions of 1634	Conditions issued in 1636 for:			Conditions outlined in later years			
		1633	1634–1635	after 1635	1641	1648	1649	1651
For transporting several persons:								
Number of persons	5	5	10	5	20	20	30	....
Number of acres	2,000	2,000	2,000	1,000	2,000	2,000	3,000	....
Average acres per person	400	400	200	200	100	100	100	....
Quitrent per 100 acres:								
Kind of payment	....	wheat	wheat	s.	s.	s.	s.	s.
Amount of payment	....	20 lb.	30 lb.	2s.	2s.	2s.	*	2s.
For transporting few persons:								
Mature settlers:								
Man	....	100	100	100	40	40	100	50
Woman	....	100	100	100	40	40	100	50
Mature servants:								
Man	....	100	100	100	40	40	100	50
Maid	....	100	100	50	40	40	100	50
Children—Settler or servant	....	50	50	50	25	40	100	50
Servant after servitude	....	....	....	....	....	40	....	....
Quitrent per 100 acres:								
Kind of payment	....	wheat	wheat	d.	d.	....	s.	s.
Amount of payment	....	20 lb.	20 lb.	24d.	24d.	....	2s.	2s.

*The rent for the first 7 years was 2*s.*; for the next 14 years it was two bushels of wheat or 6*s.* at the choice of the proprietor; and after 21 years, rent was to be one-twentieth of the annual yield or 10*s.*

the plot, or the secretary delayed in granting the patent after the survey had been made, the one responsible for the delay would be liable for the rent. (*Md. Arch., I, 159–60.*)

Prior to 1659 an annual rent of 1*s.* for each fifty acres had been levied. However, after June 20, 1659, the annual rent was increased to 2*s.* for every fifty acres. An exception was made for the land on the seaboard side of the eastern shore and on Delaware Bay; here the rent was 1*s.* a year for fifty acres. This provision was re-enacted ten years later, and again in 1670. A proviso was ordered put into every grant that no tenant could alienate any part of the land granted unless he had lived on it at least a month. (*Kilty. Land. Ass't., 57, 60.*)

In 1683, quitrent was increased so the annual rental for every fifty acres would be 100 pounds of tobacco in cask and 2*s.* sterling, except on the seaboard side, where fifty pounds of tobacco in cask and 1*s.* for every fifty acres were required. (*Md. Arch., V, 394–95.*) In 1684, quitrent was again increased to 120 pounds of tobacco and 2*s.* yearly for every fifty acres, except on the eastern shore where sixty pounds of tobacco and 1*s.* for every fifty acres were required. At this time no person could hold more than 500 acres. In the section at the head of the bay called New Ireland, however, any quantity of land could be taken up for 120 pounds of tobacco and 1*s.* rent for each fifty acres. (*Ibid., XVII, 239–40.*)

As early as 1638 Lord Baltimore had trouble getting people to take up their claims. The delay was due at times to the uncertainty of the party claiming the land as to the location that was desired and at other times to the desire of the claimant to sell his rights. (*Kilty. Land. Ass't., 68–70.*) To remedy the situation the assembly of 1638–39 enacted a law which provided that all who had not complied, within the space of three years, with the provisions regarding the number of able persons to be settled on the grant would lose land in proportion to their failure to comply. The proprietor maintained the right to regrant or lease to any other person for life or for years any part or parts of the land unoccupied, and to receive the fine and the first year's rent. (*Md. Arch., I, 63.*) In his instructions to the council of 1642 Baltimore requested that all claims be taken up within twelve months or the claim be refused. (*Ibid., III, 129–30.*) Similar instructions were given in 1649, 1650, 1653, and 1678, with the time limit of six months in which to take up the claims in each act, but at the end of each time limit an extension was made. (*Ibid., III, 229–30, 242–43, 253–54, 298–99; XV, 177–78.*)

The 1650 bill provided that for land either granted or claimed, regardless of whether it had been seated and later deserted or had never been taken up, if the claimant was over sixteen years of age, the title either had to be requested before March 25, 1651, and all rents had to be paid or the land was to be declared deserted. If this was done the land could be regranted. In addition, all land on which rent had not been paid for three years could be declared deserted and then regranted. (*Ibid., I, 288–89.*) Another attempt was made to relieve this situation in 1653 when Governor William Stone issued a proclamation on the situation. He stated that many persons in the province had neither taken up their patents nor taken the oath of fidelity to the proprietor. All of these would hold their land by virtue of the Conditions of 1649, provided that within three months they take the oath, sue out their patents, and pay their rent arrears. (*Kilty. Land. Ass't., 53–54.*)

In 1663, the assembly passed an act which required that all persons having land in Baltimore County should seat the same before December 25, 1664. If this condition was not met, the land was to be granted to others. New grantees were to seat the land with three able hands within two months or the land would revert to the original owner. If the original owner failed to seat the land within two months after it reverted to him, the land again could be regranted to anyone who would seat it within two months. (*Md. Arch., I, 499–500.*)

In the proceedings of the assembly of 1663 it was asserted that only a small part of the territory remained unpatented. (*Ibid., 487–88.*) Within a single generation nearly the whole province had been subdivided among the settlers, in sharp contrast with the slower progress made in other colonies. Like the other proprietors, Baltimore made large grants, and it is possible that he granted a greater proportion of his land in tracts the size of manors than any other proprietor. Exceedingly large estates, however, except those reserved by the proprietor, were not common in Maryland. Prior to 1676, about sixty manors were erected, containing an average of about 3,000 acres. (*Mereness. Md. as Prop. Prov., 52.*)

The headright system continued to be the principal basis on which land was granted until 1683 when by proclamation of the proprietor it was abolished. After this, the land could be procured only by payment of the purchase price or caution money which consisted partly of tobacco and partly of specie. (*Md. Arch., V, 394–95.*)

Under the headright system three types of holdings were established in Maryland; the so-called freeholds, held by paying to the proprietor a certain annual rent; the proprietor's large manors; and the smaller private manors which were composed of land lying contiguously and controlled by one man who was both the landholder and the political head of the people who lived on the manor land.

Manors in Maryland

The common people were attracted to Maryland by pamphlets issued by the proprietor on the fruitful soil, the mild climate, and the abundance of fish and game. The tenantry of England, on the other hand, was reached by the offer of large tracts of land and great local power and authority over the territory which would be theirs if they would settle in America. (*Wilhelm. Inst. of Md., 317.*) By erecting manors, Lord Baltimore sought to keep the land as a source of income to himself and yet not be plagued with detailed administration of local affairs of government.

In the Conditions of 1636, Baltimore directed that every plot of 1,000 acres or more granted to one person was to be made into a manor. (*Md. Arch., III, 48.*) In 1648 the size of a manor was enlarged from 1,000 to 2,000 acres. One-sixth part of every manor became demesne land. This part of the manor could not be granted to another person, except by inheritance. The rest of the manor, however, could be granted to any person of British or Irish descent either in fee simple or fee tail, for life or for years. (*Kilty. Land. Ass't., 38–39.*)

In 1665, Baltimore ordered that two manors in every county be reserved for the proprietor. Each of these manors was to contain no less than 6,000 acres. (*Ibid., 95–98.*) About ninety years later the proprietor inquired about the possibility of having another manor in each county set out for his use. Baltimore instructed Governor Sharp to investigate this possibility. Sharp, in his reply in 1754, stated that the land office had informed him that not enough land remained in a single tract sufficient to constitute a manor unless it was in the lower part of the eastern shore where the land was barren and in Frederick County near the frontier where he had two manors reserved already. Baltimore instructed Sharp to have the counties surveyed and if any surplus land lay next to the proprietor's to join it to the manors which already were formed. (*Md. Arch., VI, 128–29.*)

There was a tendency toward making the large landholders high officials in the government, and many of these, especially after 1660, were relatives of the proprietor. (*Osgood. 17th Cent., II, 71.*) The introduction of slavery, however, led to the gradual decline of the manors and the expansion of the plantation system. The government phase of the manorial scheme was not a part of plantation organization.

HEADRIGHTS IN PENNSYLVANIA-DELAWARE

From the beginning the principal method of conveying land to settlers in Pennsylvania and Delaware was by sale. The Swedish trading company evidently did not introduce headrighting into Delaware. In fact, very little can be found in regard to headrights in that state. Presumably the land of Delaware was conveyed to settlers by much the same procedures as those used in Pennsylvania. The headright scheme therefore never gained a very prominent place in the land tenure system of the Quaker colonies.

In 1681 Penn promised to grant fifty acres for each person who would transport either himself or servants to the colony, reserving a quitrent of 1*d*. an acre; twice the rent reserved in Carolina. (*Pa. Col. Rec., I, 26–29.*) Six months later, in a letter to James Harrison, Penn explained that he had to be paid for the land by either purchase or rent. (*Hazard. Annals of Pa.,* 522–23.) Those who could not buy would be permitted to take up land. The head of the family was allowed as many as 200 acres at 1*d.* an acre, which was four times as much as he would have received under the earlier instructions. Fifty acres for each servant at the same quitrent would be granted. To encourage poor servants to emigrate he promised them fifty acres at 4*s.* an acre when their term of servitude was over.

An unusual condition for seating and planting which was attached to the land granted in Pennsylvania concerned the maintenance of forests. One acre of trees was to be left for every five acres of land cleared for cultivation. Special care was to be taken to preserve oak and mulberry trees to aid in the construction of ships and the production of silk. These conditions continued throughout the Colonial period but were fulfilled on only a small scale. Pennsylvania was the only colony in which forest conservation was introduced during the Colonial period.

After Penn's first visit to America he published in 1685 a paper entitled *A Further Account of the Province of Pennsylvania.* In this pamphlet he stated the provisions under which land might be taken up by persons who transported themselves but who had nothing with which to begin farming, and those who were transported by others and consequently had no funds or supplies with which to start operations. For the first group he proposed to set aside 5,000 acres and settle ten families on it. He would build each a house and a barn for the cattle and furnish each family with four cows, two sows, two mares, a horse, a bull, a boar, and a yoke of oxen, as well as tools and seed for the first year's planting. Each family so provided was to live on the land seven years. A garden and orchard (the trees were to be paid for by Penn) were to be laid out and at least twenty acres of land were to be fenced and made ready for either grass or corn. At the end of the seven years, if the man chose to remain on the land, he was to pay Penn £2,400 for land, stock, and improvements; he then would be free to leave the land or dispose of it in any way he saw fit. (*Myers. Narratives of Pa.,* 274.) If the family chose to leave the farm, the house was to be left in good repair.

For those who were not able to pay for their transportation, 5,000 acres would be set aside and 100 acres would be given to each family with the same stock and improvements as promised to those who were able only to transport themselves. At the end of four years each family was to pay £5 yearly as a "Fee farm rent," with the privilege of purchasing later. (*Ibid.,* 275.) The extent to which these offers were accepted cannot be determined. It appears, however, that little land was granted under the headright system in Pennsylvania.

Headright grantees of soil of Pennsylvania held it immediately of Penn by socage tenure. Most estates were subject to quitrents, and to forfeiture for lack of heirs or because of corruption of the blood. Pennsylvania may be viewed as a seigniory divested of the heaviest burdens imposed by feudal law and endowed with such powers of territorial control as distance from the realm of the lord paramount required. (*Shepherd. Prop. Gov. in Pa., 16–17.*)

HEADRIGHT GRANTS IN NEW JERSEY

The 1664 grant to the Duke of York included the present state of New Jersey, which was transferred to John Lord Berkeley and Sir George Carteret that same year. (*N.J. Grants and Conc., 3–11.*) Some of the land included in this transfer already was occupied by Dutch settlers. In the Articles of Surrender these landholders were to have their estates confirmed. This promise was kept by Berkeley and Carteret, and the original Dutch settlers received liberal treatment at the hands of these proprietors. The only conditions required of them were that they take the oath of allegiance to the king and of fidelity to the proprietors, and to fulfil the requirements laid down in the patenting of their lands. (*Brodhead. N.Y., I, App., 762.*)

Headrights Under Berkeley and Carteret

Conditions for settlement issued by Berkeley and Carteret on February 10, 1665, were known as *Concessions and Agreements.* (*N.J. Grants and Conc., 12–26; N.J. Arch., 1st Ser., I, 21–23.*) According to these, the amount of land granted per headright would decrease after January 1, 1666, until it was less than one-half of the number of acres given before that date. But quitrents per acre were to be the same for all sizes of grants. Selected data regarding the size of headrights are presented in Table 6.

The patent form to be used also was specified. It stated that the land granted would be held in free and common socage but subject to a yearly quitrent of one-half penny per acre to the proprietors; the rent would not begin until March 25, 1670. The patentee could enjoy all the benefits and profits of the grant except one-half of the mines of gold and silver, and the rents assessed. These regulations continued in force until 1674 when the western part of New Jersey changed hands. Even under these conditions there was a great influx of settlers, partly from the old country but largely from New England. The New Englanders, however, found the system too feudalistic, for they were used to settling not individually but by compact groups, and the burden of the quitrents was something to which they were not accustomed. (*Tanner. Prov. of N.J., 36.*)

Headright land in New Jersey was to be held upon condition that one able man servant or two weaker servants would be maintained for a space of thirteen years on every 100 acres of land a master or mistress possessed. In case of failure to comply with this provision, three years were given to attain the required number or for the sale or distribution of such part of the land as was not peopled. All lands were to be taken up by warrants confirmed by the governor and council, who also would divide the land into seven parts, one of which would be reserved for the proprietors and their heirs and assigns.

Elizabethtown and Monmouth Purchases

The status of two large tracts of land which embraced some of the most valuable territory in New Jersey should be clarified. These tracts usually are referred to as the Elizabethtown and Monmouth Purchases. Both were purchased from the Indians with the permission of Colonel Nicolls, then governor of all of the Duke's territory (*N.J. Arch., 1st. Ser., I, 15–19, 43–46*), and were occupied in part by settlers from Long Island before the transfer of the New Jersey territory to Berkeley and Carteret was made known in America. (*Ibid., 183–84.*) Baker, Ogden, Bailey, and Watson and their associates had the Elizabethtown Purchase completed on December 1, 1664. The Monmouth Purchase, by William Goulding and associates, was completed on April 8, 1665. The principal points of question were whether Berkeley and Carteret acquired legal title to these tracts which already had been conveyed by the Duke's governor in America, and whether the charge of quitrent or any other payment required by the proprietors was valid within these tracts. (*Ibid., II, 124–29.*)

The Monmouth Purchase included the lands between the Raritan River and Sandy Point and extended into the country. (*Ibid., I, 43–46.*) The settlers recognized in no way the control of the proprietors over the land within their bounds, and no effort was made to comply with the Concessions. In two towns settled under this patent, Newark and Middletown, the lands were allocated by lot in town meetings as in New England. (*N.J. Hist. Soc. Coll., VI, 5, 7, 9, 27.*) Only a few of the Monmouth Purchase patentees took the oath of allegiance to the king and the oath of fidelity to Berkeley and Carteret. (*N.J. Arch., 1st. Ser., I, 51.*) They refused to recognize the proprietors' governmental powers over their patents. (*Whitehead. East Jersey, I, 53.*) When the day arrived upon which the first quitrent payments fell due, March 25, 1670, there was a general refusal among the holders of the Monmouth Purchase to pay the rent. After more than two years of controversy, an agreement was reached by which the grantees received a confirmation of the land included in the Monmouth Purchase and were allowed to dispose of it as they saw fit. The land was to be conveyed by individual grants subject to the terms of the Concessions. (*N.J. Arch., 1st. Ser., I, 88–89.*) The original patentees in this area were granted 500 acres apiece. (*Ibid., 171.*) Of the thirty-five patents issued to the inhabitants of Middletown in 1664 and 1677 one was for less than 100 acres, with only seven above 300, and the largest for 500. (*Ibid., XXI, 1–28.*)

The Elizabethtown Purchase was made by six settlers of Jamaica,

TABLE 6

ACRES GRANTED PER HEADRIGHT FOR VARIOUS CLASSES OF PERSONS AND MISCELLANEOUS CONDITIONS OF HEADRIGHT GRANTS IN EAST AND WEST JERSEY

Class of person or condition of grant	Persons arriving before Jan. 1, 1666, who:		Persons arriving:		Persons arriving in East Jersey before Jan. 1, 1684	Persons arriving in West Jersey before:		
	met governor at port	did not meet governor	before Jan. 1, 1667	after Jan. 1, 1667		April 1, 1677	April 1, 1678	April 1, 1679
	Acres	*Acres*	*Acres*	*Acres*	*Acres*	*Acres*	*Acres*	*Acres*
Mature settler								
Man	150	120	90	60	25	70	50	40
Woman	....	....	....	....	25	....	....	....
Mature servant								
Man	150	120	90	60	25	70	30	40
Maid	75	60	45	30	25	50	30	20
Children—settler or servant	75	60	....	....	25	50	30	20
Servant after servitude	75	....	45	30	....	50	30	....
Quitrent per 100 acres								
Kind of payment	*pence*	*pence*	*pence*	*pence*	*pence*	*pence*	*farthings*	*pence*
Amount of payment	50	50	50	50	200	50	300	100

Long Island, on October 28, 1664, after Nicolls' consent had been obtained. Ownership of the tract by Captain John Bailey and Luke Watson and their associates was confirmed by Nicolls. They were to hold the land with a yearly quitrent to be paid to the Duke of York or his assigns, the rate of which was to be the customary rate of the country for new plantations. (*Ibid., I, 15–19.*) The purchase contained approximately 400,000 acres. (*Elizabethtown Bill, 23.*) A few settlements were made before Governor Carteret took over the control of the province for Carteret and Berkeley (*N.J. Arch., 1st. Ser., I, 183–84*) and obtained a share in the grant by purchasing the interest of Captain Bailey. (*Elizabethtown Bill, 29.*)

The next year, sixty-five male inhabitants of Elizabethtown took the oath of fidelity to Carteret and Berkeley. (*N.J. Arch., 1st. Ser., I, 49–50.*) The principal settlements thus were made under the terms of the Concessions. In May, 1666, Carteret, Ogden, and Watson sold to Daniel Pierce and associates a large share of the tract for the settlement of Woodbridge and Piscataway. (*Elizabethtown Bill, 29.*) The first demand for quitrents, however, changed the entire situation. There was a general refusal by the associates of Elizabethtown either to pay the rent or to take out new patents. A long struggle ensued, and at one time the controversy was carried to King Charles II, who sided with the proprietors. (*N.J. Arch., 1st. Ser., I, 107, 272–74.*) With the regrant to Carteret, the grant made by Nicolls was declared null and void, and the original eighty Elizabethtown associates and their heirs, excepting Benjamin Homan, took out patents for their land. (*Elizabethtown Bill, 43, App. Sched. VIII.*)

Headrights in East Jersey

After the territory of New Jersey was divided into East and West Jersey the headright system was continued. Land was granted, as provided for in the Concessions, for the importation of relatives and servants. Most of the persons imported were members of the families of settlers, usually wives, sons, and daughters. Only a few headrights were issued for the importation of Negroes; Captain John Berry probably brought in the largest number, thirty-two. (*N.J. Arch., 1st. Ser., XXI, 46.*)

After the death of Carteret the province of East Jersey was sold on February 1, 1681, to twelve Friends for £3,400. (*Ibid., I, 366–69.*) They took in twelve others, increasing the number to twenty-four. (*Ibid., 383–94.*) The twenty-four new proprietors continued the Concessions with some modifications. Their new terms were made known in the tract entitled, *Brief Account.* (*Smith. Hist. of N.J., App., 539–46.*) The inducements they offered to the settlers, as shown in Table 6, provided that all persons who transported themselves and their families into the province by December 25, 1684, were to receive twenty-five acres of land for each person included. This land was to be taken up in one of the townships already settled and laid out. Anyone wishing more than twenty-five acres could purchase additional land up to 100 acres at the rate of £10 for 100 acres. Quitrent, of 2*d.* an acre, which had already caused so much trouble, could be bought off, for it was provided that, ". . . whosoever is willing to buy off his yearly rent and become a freeholder may so do, paying after the rate of twelve years purchase, which comes to fifty shillings for a lot of twenty-five acres and so paying for the same rate, for a greater or lesser quantity." (*Ibid., 545–46.*) The headright grants to colonists later were continued until January 13, 1685 or 1686 and then were discontinued until the proprietors had their first division of the land. (*Elizabethtown Bill, 16.*)

Headrights in West Jersey

The regulations issued by the West Jersey proprietors provided for a division of the land and a disposition of it by sale, which was rapidly becoming the principal method of distributing land, but the Concessions also made provisions for persons, not proprietors, adventuring to West Jersey with the consent of one or more of the proprietors. The terms are shown in Table 6; they grew less liberal the longer the settlers delayed.

Under the West Jersey proprietors two able-bodied male servants or three weaker ones were to be maintained on the land for each 100 acres, not including the grant for the importation of the master himself. If such conditions were not fulfilled within three years from the time of notification, loss of land not so peopled would result, unless the general assembly judged the requirement impossible of fulfillment because of poverty or other reasons. (*N.J. Arch., 1st. Ser., I, 241–70.*)

When the period of proprietary government came to an end in West Jersey the Council of Proprietors that had managed the granting and sale of land continued under royal rule. All claims for land were submitted to this body, and the headright system of granting land in Jersey was similar to that in other royal colonies.

HEADRIGHT SYSTEM IN THE CAROLINAS

Throughout the two distinct periods – proprietary and royal – in the history of the Carolina colony little difference appears in the laws and regulations relating to the headright system of granting land. Headright laws established during the proprietary period were confirmed in most part by the king. However, a few special rules relating to South Carolina after the colony was divided are important.

The Proprietary Period

During the entire proprietary period the right to grant land was delegated by the eight proprietors to the governor and council, who issued warrants that were entered with the surveyor-general. The surveyor ran out the bounds, made a plat of each tract, and certified it to the secretary. The certificate was recorded by the secretary in a special book kept for that purpose. After final approval of the council was obtained and the secretary affixed the seal, the land grant was made by the governor. (*N.C. Rec., I, 50–52.*)

Soon after the first charter of Carolina was issued to the eight proprietors, negotiations were opened by two groups of would-be colonists. One was a group of New Englanders who wished to establish a colony near Cape Fear, on the southern coast of what is now North Carolina. This group, besides asking for land on which to make a settlement, requested the right to choose its own governor, make and confirm laws, and to be exempt from all proprietary taxes. (*Ibid., 36–39.*) The other group, from the Island of Barbados, asked for 1,000 square miles. They wanted the land forever, to be held in as full, free, and ample manner as the proprietors had received in the original grant. These two requests for so many liberties and privileges influenced the proprietors to issue liberal instructions as to the tenure under which early settlers of Carolina could hold their land. (*Ibid. 39–42.*)

Several sets of instructions were issued to the various governors and established by order from the governor and council. The first of these instructions, entitled *Declaration and Proposal,* was issued on August 25, 1663, five months after the charter was granted. Two years later special instructions were issued to cover the settlement of a second group of people from Barbados. Then separate instructions were issued for the settlement of the three counties – Albemarle, Clarendon, and Craven – into which the colony was to be divided, and in 1667 additional instructions were prepared for the planting of Albemarle County. These were supplanted by new instructions three years later. At frequent intervals between 1670 and 1754 minor adjustments were made in specific items, but major changes were made at the later date. Selected information regarding these instructions is shown in Table 7.

Table 7 shows an endeavor to entice settlers to come to America at the earliest possible time by offering more land if they came before 1665 than if they came during that year, and still less land if they waited until later to come. The tendency also was to offer a larger number of acres for settlers than for servants and more for men than for women and children. However, these are only tendencies for notable exceptions exist. It also should be noted that the bringing of servants was especially encouraged by offering land to the person who brought them and by offering the servants grants of land at the end of their period of servitude. This double granting of land was nothing new, for it had been done ever since the Virginia Company made grants for shares in the company.

Reservation of quitrent usually was mentioned, and if not, was implied. As a general rule, the instructions indicated that the settlers

TABLE 7

ACRES GRANTED PER HEADRIGHT FOR VARIOUS CLASSES OF PERSONS AND MISCELLANEOUS CONDITIONS OF HEADRIGHT GRANTS IN COLONIAL CAROLINA

Class of person or condition of grant	First general instructions		Instructions for specific areas												
			Clarendon County			Albemarle County					Third County (Craven)				
	1663	1665	1665	1666	Later	1665	1666	1667	Gov.	1670	Early	1665	1666	1667	1670
	Acres	*Acres*	*Acres*	*Acres*	*Acres*	*Acres*	*Acres*	*Acres*	*Acres*	*Acres*	*Acres*	*Acres*	*Acres*	*Acres*	*Acres*
Mature settler															
Man........	100	150	100	75	50	80	60	40	60	60	150	120	90	60	100
Woman......	......	......	100	75	50	80	60	40	60	60	......	......	......	......	......
Mature servant															
Man........	50	150	100	70	50	80	60	40	60	50	150	120	90	60	50
Maid........	30	......	50	40	25	40	30	20	50	......	75	120	45	60	50
Children—settler or servant......	......	......	50	40	25	40	30	20	50	......	75	120	45	60	50
Servant after servitude.......	10	......	50	40	25	40	30	20	50	50	75	60	45	30	......
Armed man for acres shown....	50	150	100	100	100	100	100	100	......	......	100	100	100	100	......
Quitrent reserved..	*yes*	*yes*	*yes*	*yes*	*yes*	*yes*	*yes*	*yes*	......	......	*yes*	*yes*	*yes*	*yes*	......

would hold their land under free and common socage, but this was not always mentioned. Quitrents were frequently deferred, usually at the discretion of the governor, for as many as five years, if the parties were not in position to begin paying immediately. This rent-free period was necessary while the land was being brought under cultivation. The practice was followed later by individual land-owners in clearing land as settlement moved across the continent. However, the records do not indicate that the colonial forefathers used sale contracts in bringing their land under cultivation as was practiced at a later date and as is still used in some sections of the country.

One requirement stressed in the Carolina instructions was the maintenance on each 100 acres of land of an armed man, who was to be armed with a good firelock or matchlock rifle and ten or twenty pounds of powder with an equal amount of bullets. The grantee usually was given as much as three years to fill a vacancy in the number of armed men required. Protection was stressed, for failure to maintain an armed guard would mean forfeiture of the grant.

Under this system land was to be laid out for sixty-six feet, or one chain, along the river and extending for 100 chains back from the river. The remainder of the grant to any person was to be no nearer to the river than 200 chains. This procedure would have placed 200 armed men along the river within each one and one-quarter miles. Ten acres, the amount included in these portions, was considered all that one man could plant and keep clean after reserving enough for convenient home pasturage. The remainder of the grant was to be laid out where the governor and the council thought best. (*N.C. Rec., I, 50–51.*)

Although the proprietors apparently were willing to do all they could to settle the province quickly, they offered less land for headrights in Albemarle than in Clarendon County. As Albemarle was nearer to Virginia than Clarendon, some settlers already had been attracted from Virginia. Albemarle also was farther from the Spanish settlements and thus not so vulnerable to attack. But since the number of acres granted to adventurers was greater in Virginia and the restrictions on land were less, opposition arose in Albemarle. The dissatisfaction had been growing when in June, 1665, Thomas Woodward, surveyor-general for Albemarle, wrote to the proprietors and pointed out that the heavy restrictions were hurting the colony. He alluded to the situation in Maryland as a compromise and said that the conditions in Albemarle would have to be lightened if the population was to increase. (*Ibid., 99–101*).

After some delay the petition was granted, for in 1668 the proprietors, in a letter of instructions to Samuel Stephen, the governor of Albemarle County, said that they would ". . . consent and do grant that the inhabitants of the said County do hold their lands of us the Lords Proprietors upon the same terms and conditions that the Inhabitants of Virginia hold theirs." (*Ibid., 175–76.*) This compromising and liberalizing action of the proprietors was referred to in the Carolinas as the "Great Deed of Grants."

The people of Carolina cherished these instructions as the basis for holding land and paying quitrent, but apparently the proprietors soon disregarded them, for in 1670 they issued new instructions to the governor of Albemarle that were different from those sent to Governor Stephen in 1668. Later, in 1679 and 1686, other instructions infringed upon the "Great Deed of Grants." The disregard of conditions outlined in these instructions was the basis for much controversy as long as the proprietors had charge of the development of the Carolinas. For example, in 1694 Governor Archdale was instructed to inquire into the grants said to have been made by Colonel Ludwell for a farthing an acre. If Ludwell had made the grants they were to be approved, but he was to signify to the inhabitants of Carolina that this applied only to Albemarle County which joined Virginia on the north and was bounded on the south by Albemarle Sound. The amount of rent on the rest was left to the discretion of the governor but was not to be less than one-half penny an acre. (*Ibid., 391.*)

The Royal Colony

When seven of the proprietors relinquished to the Crown their claims to the Carolinas in 1729, the headright system was not upset, for as a Crown colony the practice continued. Burlington, the first royal governor, was empowered to negotiate with the inhabitants of the province concerning land grants. The land was to be granted on such terms and under such quitrents as he thought fit. (*Ibid., III, 72.*) In his administration of the colonies, Burlington attempted to remedy some of the bad practices that had developed. For example, in the early granting of land, blank warrants signed and sealed by the governor had been placed in the hands of the secretary, who could fill in the name of the grantee and the amount of land to be granted. In addition, quite frequently the surveyors did not take the trouble to survey the plots and rather often failed to set definite bounds. As a result many people held more land than called for in their grants. Burlington required that the warrants be filled in before they received his signature, (*Ibid., 337*) and a little later, in 1735, the king ordered that the land of all persons holding over and above what their patent called for was to be resurveyed. (*Ibid., IV, 53.*)

As late as 1736 there was so much granted land which had not been planted that the king directed every possessor of land, within three years after the passage of the act, to enclose and clear three acres of land for every 100 acres or build one habitable house on it, and to put at least five head of cattle on every 500 acres, and so in proportion for a greater or lesser quantity of land. Those failing to comply were to have their grants declared null and void. (*Ibid., 185.*) Later the number was raised to five acres for every 100 acres held. In 1754, however, there was a complaint from Governor Dobbs that five acres was too much (*Ibid., V, 156*), and the number was lowered to three. (*Ibid., 1133.*)

In Carolina, as in the rest of the colonies where headrights were granted, many abuses arose. Men claimed a headright for each entrance to the colony, as was the case of James Minge who claimed six rights for himself, three for Ruth Minge, and four for his Negro, Robin. Richard Turner claimed three for himself and two for his wife. (*Ibid., I, 653–54.*) Finally, in 1712, a law was passed which allowed a claim of only one headright for any one person. (*Bassett. Landholding in N.C., 160.*)

In addition, surveys were not always accurate. A plot of land would be granted with the boundaries set without any kind of a survey. As a result, many grantees had much larger plots than their deeds called for. An illustration is the case of Maurice Moore, who in 1729 received a tract for which the survey called for 1,000 acres. (*N.C. Rec., IV, 1047–48.*) Twenty years later a resurvey found that it contained 3,834 acres.

Regulations in South Carolina

Regulations governing the distribution of land under the headright system in South Carolina were not numerous and relatively little land was transferred on that basis, as distribution by sale was the chief method used for transferring land. About 1693 the proprietors issued instructions entitled *Rules and Instructions for Granting Land.* The surveyor-general was directed to set out two counties on Ashby River. The county to the north was to be called Craven County, the one to the south, Colleton County. Each county was to be divided into squares of 12,000 acres each, and the land was to be distributed in a manner somewhat similar to the plan outlined in the *Fundamental Constitutions.*

Those who desired to become inhabitants of South Carolina and did not have the money to purchase land could have land granted to them provided they were over sixteen years of age. No more than fifty acres of land could be granted to an individual as his headright and fifty acres could be granted for each servant imported provided the importation was reported within fourteen days after the boat arrived. Less than the maximum fifty acres could be granted if the governor thought best. As much land as the governor thought just was to be granted to each servant who had served his or her time, provided the grant did not exceed fifty acres. One penny quitrent an acre each year, starting after two years, was to be paid. (*Com. and Ins. to S.C., 50–56.*)

Headright claims to land were not numerous in South Carolina. The reduced number of acres of land, heavy quitrent charges, and rigid requirements for obtaining a headright indicate why this system was not popular in South Carolina after the 1693 instructions were issued. In 1712 a law was passed which declared that all claims to land by residents of the province were to be taken up within five years, while persons living outside the province were allowed seven years. Minors were to take up their claims within two years after coming of age. (*S.C. Stats., II, 583–84.*)

The proprietors closed the land office in South Carolina in 1719, and it remained closed until 1731. In the meantime, the colony had become more populous and the land, particularly near the coast, had become more valuable. Many of the early headright claims were not asserted until the Carolinas were fairly well settled and the land had increased in price. (*Gray. South. Agr., I, 376.*) It is estimated that while the land office was closed and new grants could not be made, nearly 800,000 acres were taken up under old patents. (*Smith. S.C. as Royal Prov., 35–36.*) The assembly attempted to restrict this process by requiring each claimant to fulfil his obligation to establish 100 settlers on each 12,000 acres before asserting a claim to another area of land. Later a vigorous but unsuccessful attempt was made by the surveyor-general to prevent confirmation of these claims. (*Ibid., 38.*)

On August 20, 1731, a bill passed by the assembly, and later approved by the king against the recommendations of his agents, provided that patents or grants, except those for town lots, would be forfeited unless registered in the auditor-general's office within eighteen months. The assembly, however, under pressure of land speculators, included in the bill provisions which guaranteed the validity of all patents issued by the proprietors, regardless of irregularities in the description of the land, provided that at least a part of the grant had been surveyed by a sworn surveyor. (*S.C. Stats., III, 289–304.*) Therefore, practically all of the claims to land during the period from 1719 to 1731 were confirmed, since a large part of the best land was surveyed for speculative holders of old patents. (*Smith. S.C. as Royal Prov., 34–38.*)

Evidence shows conclusively that some large holdings or plantations were developed in South Carolina under the headright system. For example, in 1673 a tract was set aside for Thomas Lane who agreed to settle twenty persons. In 1690 Seth Sothell was granted a manor of 12,000 acres on condition that within five years he would build a town of not less than thirty houses and settle at least 120 people. Also 12,000 acres were granted to Jacob Waite. (*S.C. Hist. Soc. Coll., V, 410, 464, 469.*) In 1680 two manors of 5,000 acres each were granted on condition that the grantee would settle more than forty able persons on each manor within three years. One grant of 12,000 acres was made to the Earl of Shaftesbury, while Sir Peter Colleton received several large grants (*Salley. S.C. Land Warrants, I, 3–5, 16, 17, 104, 144, 155, 164, 170, 203, 209*), and Simon Berringer received two grants of

3,000 acres each. (*Ibid., 86.*) In spite of those numerous large grants, most headright allotments of land were for less than 300 acres.

Much overlapping in boundaries was due to failure of the surveyors to properly mark the boundaries, to the disturbance of boundary marks, and to the failure of patentees to take up their claims. Additional difficulties arose when the land had been granted but had not been occupied by the patentees. The legislature, however, recognized the legitimacy of the claims of squatters and provided that all titles to, or possession of, land existing for seven years without interruption were good against any other claims.

OGLETHORPE AND HEADRIGHTS

Settlers receiving headright grants in Georgia can be divided into two classes; those granted land for transporting themselves, or others to Georgia, and those who had suffered misfortune and were transported to the colony by the trustees and given land and subsistence for a year after their arrival. Provision for the latter group was necessary, for the founding of Georgia was "for the relief of poor subjects who, through misfortune and want of employment, were reduced to great necessity."

Headrights Under the Trustees

With relief of the poor in mind, the trustees set up the early land tenure system in Georgia, holding that "It was desired to establish upon this territory not a landed aristocracy, but a self-supporting landowning citizenry." (*Banks. Land Ten. in Ga., 11.*) This ideal was in sharp contrast with the objective of the eight proprietors of the Carolinas in the *Fundamental Constitutions*, where they were definitely against the establishment of a "numerous democracy" and in favor of a self-perpetuating landed gentry.

Rules surrounding the granting of headrights in Georgia were contained in the 1732 charter, agreements among the trustees in 1733 and 1750, and later instructions by the Crown. The Board of Common Council was given the power under the charter to assign land only in tail male. No person was to have more than 500 acres of land, and one headright was to command only fifty acres. These grants were to be made on the terms provided in the charter. By 1750 this number had been increased to 500 acres for ten men servants, six times as much land as in the 1733 agreement. The land was still to be held in tail male, but the yearly quitrent was increased to 20*s*. for every 100 acres, the payment of which was not to commence until ten years after the grant. (*Ga. Col. Rec., III, 376, 412–13.*) Servants were to receive twenty acres each at the expiration of their service. (*Ibid., 413.*)

Unique Features

The land system of Georgia under the trustees had some features that were not practiced in the other colonies. They were: (1) The land could be held only in tail male. (2) The right of alienation was at first denied to all holders of land. (3) The holdings of any one person were limited by law to 500 acres. (4) Holdings reverted in whole and not in part for failure to meet specifications for seating and planting and otherwise.

The revival of the antiquated rule of descent, that the land could be held only in tail male, was the most peculiar feature of the land system of Georgia and the one which provoked most criticism. (*Ibid., 373–74.*) Even though this rule of descent was designed to prevent either the parcellation of family sized holdings or the concentration of numerous acres, it was a source of controversy as long as it was followed.

Regarding freedom of alienation, Osgood has pointed out that as a class those going to Georgia had not been financially successful in England; therefore, it was reasoned that they could not be expected to manage property very thriftily. (*Osgood. 18th Cent., III, 47.*) Since the trustees considered fifty acres a family sized farm sufficient for the support of a planter and his family, it was not thought advisable to place more than fifty acres in the hands of anyone whom the trustees had to transport to Georgia. On the same basis that it was reasoned that fifty acres of land was enough for one person, it was thought that a smaller portion was inadequate for the proper support of a planter and his family; therefore, the grant could not be alienated in part. On the other hand, to permit disposal of the whole might lead to the concentration of land in the hands of the few, thereby reducing a number of the colonists to their original state of landlessness and decreasing the number of men capable of rendering military protection to the colony. Also, people opposed to the Protestant religion might get into the colony if the grantees could dispose of their land. For these reasons, according to original plans, the grant could not be alienated in its entirety.

After two years, however, in 1735, a grantee was permitted to alienate his land, either as a whole or in part, with special license. (*Ga. Col. Rec., III, 375.*) The restrictions on alienation were relaxed still further when in 1741 the holders of the land were permitted to make leases of any part of their lots for a term not exceeding twenty-one years. The lease could be made to any person or persons who would reside on the land and cultivate it. (*Ibid., I, 381.*) In 1755 the principle of absolute ownership of land in fee simple was recognized in the colony. (*Jones. Ga., I, 487.*) Thus, alienation became relatively free within a few years.

The rule of not granting more than 500 acres of land to any one person was intended to help prevent concentration of land in the hands of a few. This restriction, however, was frequently evaded. One method of evasion was to grant to a man the maximum acreage allowed and then lease to him an additional amount on terms that practically would make the lease a free grant. Another type of evasion was to grant to a man's brother or nephew or friend a tract of land that by private arrangement between them could be held for the benefit of one to whom the trustees could not legally grant any more land. (*Ga. Col. Rec., V, 289, 705–6.*) Still another way was to make allotments of 500 acres of land in the name of each of a person's children, even though some were mere infants. (*Flippin. Royal Gov. in Ga., 5.*)

Unlike many of the other colonies where the part of the land remaining uncultivated at the end of a certain specified time would revert to the grantors, Georgia required that the whole grant revert to the trustees if specified conditions were not met. This was a serious restriction. By 1741, however, the requirements covering clearing and cultivation were relaxed. At first, within a term of ten years, five acres in every fifty were to be cultivated and on every ten acres cleared 100 mulberry trees were to be planted. If these conditions were not fulfilled the whole grant was forfeited. The requirements for cultivation were reduced to five acres a year for every 100 acres and instead of taking over all of the grant, the trustees reserved only the right to re-enter and take the part that remained uncultivated. (*Ga. Col. Rec., III, 375–76.*) When it became evident that Spanish oppression, successive droughts, and other accidents had prevented the colonists from cultivating or fencing the required number of acres in the specified time, the trustees resolved to cancel all forfeitures. (*Jones. Ga., I, 108.*)

From 1732 to 1741 the total number of persons sent on charity was 1,521, three-fifths of whom were British and two-fifths, foreign. A total of only 41,600 acres had been granted to those coming at their own expense, and 1,400 acres had been granted for the support of churches and schools. (*Ga. Col. Rec., III, 383–89.*) Some of the persons who were granted land for settling at their own expense never went to the colony; others were gentlemen of Carolina who neglected to take up their lands, while still others quit their holdings and went to reside in Savannah as shopkeepers. (*Ibid., 396–97.*) It is surprising that so little land had been granted for settlement when Georgia became a royal colony in June, 1752.

Headrights Under Royal Rule

By command of the king the same rules and regulations that had governed the colony during the trustees' supervision held good for the first two years of royal control. In January, 1755, however, a committee composed of representatives of both houses sent to the king a remonstrance concerning land tenure conditions in Georgia. They held impractical the requirement that all grantees of land either clear and cultivate at the rate of five acres a year for every 100 acres held or have the proportionate part of the grant declared void. It was believed that the requirement would prevent future settlement of the colony, and in addition, it made necessary the cutting of valuable timber. At least one-half of the land which had been granted was not fit for any manner of cultivation. It also was pointed out that within twenty years under these restrictions, if the conditions were complied with, such lands would nevertheless become forfeited as the proprietors would then have no more land to clear. The king was asked, therefore, to alter this unfair requirement. (*Ibid., XVI, 21, 22.*) This request was complied with on November 14, 1755, in instructions which relaxed greatly the seating and planting requirements. (*Ibid., VII, 295–98.*)

During the period that Georgia was a royal province small grants were made by the council, while the approval of the British government was required on large grants. The amount of land transferred to settlers under headright grants varied from rather small acreages to large plantations — from 50 to 5,000 acres in size. (*Ibid., VII, VIII.*) It was not until after 1754, however, that grants were made for over 500 acres, except by evasion. The grants from March, 1755, to March, 1756, which might be considered as a year typical of the early part of royal rule, are summarized in Table 8. (*Ibid., VII, 135–334.*)

TABLE 8

Size and Number of Headright Grants in Georgia, 1755–56.

Number of acres	Number of grants	Number of acres	Number of grants
50	2	640	1
60	1	700	8
100	25	750	1
150	15	800	2
200	14	900	1
250	8	1,000	7
300	18	1,200	1
350	7	1,300	1
400	3	1,400	1
500	34	1,500	1
550	1	1,800	1
600	1	2,000	1

The population of Georgia grew slowly; in 1773 an estimate by Governor Wright showed 33,000 people; 18,000 were whites and 15,000 Negroes. They were utilizing 120,000 acres of improved land. (*Flippin. Royal Gov. in Ga., 16.*) Of course, a large number of acres which had been granted were still uncultivated. It was estimated in 1759 that although 304,884 acres had been granted, taxes were collected on only 197,817 acres. (*Ga. Col. Rec., XIII, 349.*) By 1761 as much as 394,944 acres had been granted. (*Ibid., 522.*) After 1783 the quantity of land granted and sold to one person could exceed 1,000 acres. (*Ibid., XIX, pt. 2, 201.*)

CHAPTER 14

Disposition of Land by Sale

ALTHOUGH MUCH LAND WAS SOLD to settlers in most of the colonies, sale as a procedure for getting the land into the hands of farm owners was of more importance in some colonies than in others. Also, it was started early in some colonies but late in others, and the prices varied from colony to colony and from time to time. With a few important exceptions the settler held land acquired from the settlement agency by purchase under the conventional socage tenure at a specified quitrent.

PENN'S SYSTEM OF SELLING LAND

When William Penn left England for America he was the largest private landowner in the world. His vast domain of 47,000,000 acres (*Ferree. Pa., 191*) included both Pennsylvania and Delaware, and an interest in New Jersey. It was settled only in a few localities, chiefly in New Jersey and Delaware. Since the Pennsylvania territory was acquired in satisfaction of a debt, Penn no doubt proposed to make his colonial empire a financial success. In attaining this objective his first problem was to induce people to come to America and settle in his colony. Penn approached this task with vigor. He was relatively free in this undertaking, for his ownership of the land was almost as complete as could be granted to an English subject. The kind of units into which the land was to be divided for administration and settlement, the manner in which it was to be distributed to settlers, and the terms on which it was to be granted were all left to the proprietor. The principal way chosen by Penn for disposing of the land was by sale. Pennsylvania was the only colony to employ this method from the first, and was one of the few colonies that disposed of most of its land by sale.

Penn's first instructions outlined the conditions under which the land of Pennsylvania would be distributed. (*Hazard. Annals of Pa., 505–13.*) The conditions were listed under three heads, one of which was by sale.[1] Those who wanted to buy land were permitted to purchase a 5,000-acre share free from Indian encumbrances. The price of each share of £100. According to this plan, 47,000,000 acres would have made 9,400 shares, which at £100 each would have grossed Penn £940,000, a sixtyfold increase of the £16,000 debt that the original grant cancelled. In addition, a quitrent of 1*s*. English money annually was reserved on each 100 acres. If quitrent was paid on all of the land, the annual rental would have exceeded the purchase price by fifty per cent. This quitrent, theoretically at least, would have yielded an income to Penn and his heirs forever.

Before Penn left England for America he sold large tracts of unlocated and unsurveyed land in Pennsylvania to persons who became known as "first purchasers." On July 11, 1681, certain conditions or concessions agreed upon between him and these purchasers were issued. (*Ibid., 516–20.*) These agreements laid down the rules of settlement and provided that a city would be laid out in the most convenient place. In this city every purchaser would have a parcel of land, chosen by lot, in proportion to the amount of land that he had bought. The ratio was fifty to one; that is, for every fifty acres bought in the colony the purchaser was entitled to one acre in town, if the space would bear it. The portions sold were mostly 5,000-acre plots, thus entitling the purchaser to 100 acres in the city. The idea behind the scheme of reserving a large area of land in the city for each large purchaser is not clear. Protection against the Indians would have been a possible explanation, for experience of over half a century in some colonies indicated the seriousness of the problem. But this seems unlikely, for Penn proposed to purchase outright the lands of the Indians, and he did a creditable job of this. Living in London may have influenced him toward city life, or he may have wanted to appeal especially to certain religious groups on the continent who were accustomed to city living.

When purchases of large estates were made Penn advised that the owner send an overseer with the settlers, and that plans for division of the land be made. Men skilled in laying out plantations were to do the dividing, and land in town was to be set aside for every purchaser. (*Ibid., 517.*) To effectuate this policy, on June 6, 1681, Penn appointed James Harrison as his agent to sell land in Pennsylvania. (*Ibid., 524.*)

No purchaser was to have more than 1,000 acres of land in the colony in any one place, unless he planted a family on each 1,000 acres. Within three years after his land had been surveyed every man

[1] The other two conditions were headrights and leasing.

had to settle it, or another purchaser, who complained to the proprietor that the rules of settlement had not been obeyed, would be permitted to purchase the land. On receipt of the purchase money, Penn was to convey to the purchaser a certain number of unlocated acres by a lease for a year and a release in fee dated the next day after the lease, which provided that the number of acres were to be surveyed under the direction of the surveyor-general. After the land had been located and described the patent was to be granted. (*Ibid., 117.*)

In a letter to Harrison dated September 4, 1681, Penn explained his view with regard to land for servants who would be transported to America to work on the large grants of land. When servants had served their time, Penn proposed that they would be permitted to buy 250 acres for £5, the same rate charged large proprietors. On January 29, 1682, Penn gave what was perhaps his first view on the value of land in Pennsylvania. He estimated that 5,000 acres should be worth £500 (*Ibid., 523, 538*), which was five times the selling price.

Captain Markham, Penn's cousin, was appointed deputy-governor and was given instructions to settle boundaries with neighboring proprietors and to sell land according to instructions of April 8, 1681. (*Ibid., 503–4.*) Eight days later Penn appointed three commissioners (*Ibid., 527–31*) and instructed them to lay out a town with 10,000 acres of grantable land contiguous to it. If the land had already been taken up on the Delaware by the English, Dutch, or Swedes in larger proportions than were consistent with the town plots and if 100 acres for each purchase of 5,000 acres could not be given, the commissioners were to try to persuade the settlers to part with as much of their land as they would. After the commissioners had secured all the land obtainable, lots were to be assigned proportionately, even if it meant giving fifty acres in the town instead of the 100 acres promised for each 5,000 acres purchased. (*Ibid., 527–31.*)

In the next year Penn issued the method to be followed by the Friends in taking up land. For a whole share of 5,000 acres £100 would be paid and a yearly quitrent of £2 10*s.* or 1*s.* per 100 acres would be reserved. Anyone who would settle six families could have his allotment all in one place. Those who desired to pay no rent were to pay £120 instead of £100 as the purchase price. (*Ibid., 539.*) Permission to buy land upon which no quitrent was reserved was tantamount to holding it in fee simple absolute, except for a few minor feudal incidents retained by Penn.

Thomas Holmes was appointed surveyor-general in March, 1682, and was ordered to set out the bounds for a list of purchasers containing the names of 460 individuals and two societies. These grants, ranging from 100 acres to 10,000 acres and totaling about 521,500 acres, averaged over 1,100 acres each. All of these sales were made in England to people who had little knowledge of what they were buying. (*Pa. Arch., 1st. Ser., I, 39–46; Hazard. Annals of Pa., 576,* gives 565,500 acres.)

Penn had trouble getting those who had acquired title to land by purchase to settle and improve it. As an example, a large tract of land containing 40,000 acres was sold to a group of people from Wales and was known as the Welsh Tract. Just when the purchase was made is not known, but in 1690 a notice was served on David Powell and the other purchasers to show cause why the land had not been seated and improved according to regulations. The response was that inconvenience, boundary disputes, and trouble had prevented settlers from coming. They expressed their willingness to pay quitrent in the future but not the past. (*Pa. Arch., 1st. Ser., I, 108–10.*) This was regarded as an insufficient answer, so the grant was declared void.

The Free Society of Traders in Pennsylvania, a joint-stock company, was formed in London in 1681. Over 200 persons in Britain became subscribers to the stock of this society and by June, 1682, £10,000 had been subscribed. To the nine persons acting for the society, Penn sold 20,000 acres in trust for the society, reserving 1*s.* yearly per 100 acres as quitrent. This first manor sold by Penn was known as the Manor of Frank. The society was privileged to hold the conventional manorial courts and to alienate to any person any part of the land. (*Hazard. Annals of Pa., 541–50, 557.*)

Large single tracts were granted in addition to the grant to the Free Society of Traders and the large grant known as the Welsh Tract. For example, on August 21, 1682, Dr. Nicholas More was granted a 10,000-acre plot known as Moreland. In 1699, Penn sold to four Londoners 60,000 acres. Out of this three manors containing 5,000 acres each were to be laid out in the beginning. These manors were known as Highland, Gilbert, and Rockland. In 1701, the proprietor sold 10,000 acres of land for the Growdon's manor. Among the larger tracts granted for manors was the one granted to Joseph Pike of Ireland for 25,000 acres. This tract was kept by him and his heirs through the Colonial period. (*Keith. Chron. of Pa., I, 74–77.*) In 1701, the proprietor directed the commissioners of property to erect manors whenever possible, to promote the sale of land. (*Pa. Laws, II, 142.*)

Buell believed that if Penn's land system had been carried out on its original lines it would have resulted in a landed gentry. The establishment of manors and the sale of large sections of 5,000 acres to individuals would have placed large quantities of land in the hands of the few. (*Buell. William Penn, 122.*) On the other hand, Osgood says that although a considerable number of estates in Pennsylvania were organized as manors, none of them ever possessed manorial courts. A few of the larger grants, a good example of which was the manor of the Free Society of Traders, were even known locally as manors, but they were really no more than large estates on which rent-paying tenants lived. (*Osgood. 17th Cent., I, 29.*)

The price of land varied from time to time in Pennsylvania. According to Penn's earliest plan, land was to be sold at £2 per 100 acres, with a quitrent reservation of 1*s*. In 1713, land sold for £5 for 100 acres, and the quitrent remained the same. Later the price was raised to £10 for 100 acres with 2*s*. reserved as quitrent. For a number of years after 1732, when the proprietor's strained financial condition forced him to resort to the scheme of selling land by lottery, land sold for £15 10*s*. in currency for 100 acres with a quitrent of a half-penny sterling an acre. Many tickets were sold but lots were never drawn, and the 100,000 acres which had been set aside for the venture was long held apart from the other land. The price was reduced in 1765 to about £5 for 100 acres with quitrent at 1*d*. sterling an acre. Except for the last change, after much of the good farm land had already been taken up, both the sale price and the quitrent generally increased as settlement of the colony progressed. Improved land repossessed by the proprietor when an excess number of acres was discovered by a resurvey sold at a considerably higher price. (*Ferree. Pa., 191.*)

The rapidity with which Penn secured settlers and the comparative smoothness with which the colony operated speaks well for his system of disposing of the land and for the management of government. In his will Penn left his holdings in America to his wife and children. (*Pa. Hist. Soc. Mem., I, 212–15.*) Following the Revolution the land held by the Penn family was turned over to the Commonwealth of Pennsylvania, for which the family was paid £130,000.

SALE OF LAND IN NEW JERSEY

When New Jersey was divided into East and West Jersey the new proprietors eliminated almost completely the practice of conveying land by headright and instituted distribution by sale. As the procedure of disposing of land by sale was different in the two parts, each will be discussed separately.

Sales in West Jersey

The West Jersey proprietors issued in March, 1676, instructions entitled, *The Concessions and Agreements of the Proprietors, Freeholders, and Inhabitants of the Province of West Jersey in America,* which provided for a division of the land and its disposal by sale. The province of West Jersey was to be divided into 100 equal parts, and these were to be grouped together in ten larger divisions known as "tenths." If the entire province was divided into exactly equal parts each tenth would have contained around 300,000 acres. Three tenths were disposed of immediately – one to Elbridge and Warner, another to five Friends of Yorkshire for £3,500, and the third to a group of Quakers from London.

It seems clear that these groups, like others in Jersey, contemplated disposing of the land for a profit, and did not visualize the establishment of a large landed proprietary. As a consequence, they immediately started selling tracts of land out of their tenths. For example, in 1676, William Peachy and Thomas Budd each bought a proprietary, and began at once to sell fractional shares of their holdings. These purchasers likewise sold fractional shares; so each proprietary became smaller and smaller, frequently as small as a sixty-fourth of the original. Translated into acres, most of the purchases were for 200 and 300 acres, with 500 not being uncommon; the number purchasing 100 acres was comparatively small. (*N.J. Arch., 1st. Ser., XXI, 394–541.*) Thus, West Jersey was rapidly becoming a land of relatively small landowners, at least theoretically, for these were paper transactions not involving actual occupancy and use. This was in sharp contrast to the original feudalistic ideas of Berkeley and Carteret. (*Tanner. Prov. of N.J., 15–17.*)

When the 1682 orders for surveyor Daniel Leeds to divide the entire river front into ten equal parts were not executed, the idea of dividing the colony into tenths was dropped. This brought to an end the attempt to lay off the province mathematically, and a few years later the council permitted the proprietors to take up their shares when and where they pleased. (*Ibid., 103–5.*)

When the period of proprietary government came to an end, the council of proprietors which had managed the granting and sale of land continued under royal rule. It had the responsibility of purchasing land from the Indians and distributing it to the proprietors who had not received all the land accorded them in the division of tenths. By June, 1703, about 150,000 acres had been purchased above the falls on the Delaware River for an estimated cost of £700. (*Ibid., 670.*) All of the proprietors who were eligible to receive land and who would share in the cost were to receive a part of the land. This was the first of five divisions which took place between 1702 and 1737. In the second division thirty-three plots ranging in size from 100 to 500 acres were laid out and were allocated by lot to those who paid their share of the purchase price. (*Ibid., 682.*) In the fourth purchase 205,374 acres were divided into 1,250 plots and distributed on the same basis as the second. (*Ibid., 686.*) In one division Penn claimed twelve proprietaries; Colonel David Cox, who was elected president of the council, received from 4,170 to 20,000 acres in each division. (*Ibid., 677, 678, 681, 682, 685.*)

Sales in East Jersey

After the death of Carteret the province of East Jersey was sold for £3,400 on February 1, 1682, to twelve Friends, of whom William

Penn was one. (*N.J. Arch., 1st. Ser., I, 366–69.*) This price was considerably less than the £9,800 paid for one-fifth of the land of West Jersey, and the £3,500 paid for one of the tenths. To make their purchase entirely legal, the proprietors secured a new grant from the Duke of York for East Jersey. (*Ibid., 383–94.*)

One of the first plans of the new proprietors was to lay out the capitol city. Fifteen hundred acres were divided into 150 equal lots, of which 100 lots were to be sold and fifty lots were to be reserved for those proprietors who would reside in the province. The lots were to be sold for £15 up to December 25, 1682, and for £20 to December, 1683. (*Smith. Hist. of N.J., 543.*) The proprietors next turned their attention to the subdivisions of the unoccupied land of the province. Ten thousand acres were set aside for each of the twenty-four proprietors. Convenient tracts were ordered surveyed and divided among the proprietors, each of whom could dispose of his land as he saw fit. (*N.J. Grants and Conc., 182–84.*)

An agreement about taking up the land, issued by the proprietors, provided that about 10,000 acres were to be surveyed and laid out. Anyone who had purchased a part of a proprietary or share, and who went himself or sent servants to settle upon it, was to have his lot surveyed. Anyone who had purchased a full proprietary could have as much as 500 acres laid out for himself in one location. (*Ibid., 186–87.*) No land was to be sold for less than £10 for each 100 acres with the reservation of a quitrent of 6*d.* English money yearly for every 100 acres.

Land began to be taken up on a large scale by the proprietors and their assigns. (*N. J. Arch., 1st. Ser., XXI, 48–91.*) Tanner says that thousands of acres of the most desirable land, especially along the bay, the Kills, the Hudson, and the lower courses of the rivers, had already been assigned. The proprietors were forced to take the land lying farther back. As was usual in such cases, these surveys followed chiefly the valleys of the principal streams. (*Tanner. Prov. of N. J., 50.*)

Not many of the original twenty-four proprietors contemplated keeping their undivided shares. A subdivision of their estates was planned to make possible the purchase of farms by bona fide farmers. This was the subject of lengthy instruction to the officers in East Jersey. In 1684, it was agreed that small purchasers should receive at once their shares of land. The small purchaser was to have no more land in the later divisions than his own share came to, unless he already had improved his. (*N.J. Arch., 1st. Ser., I, 470–74.*)

Although much was said about making the land available for small purchases, tracts of land bought under the twenty-four proprietors greatly exceeded in average size those headrights patented under Berkeley and Carteret, when grants as large as 500 acres were rare. The period of comparatively large surveys began in 1683. (*Ibid., XXI,*

1–130.) Within the disputed Elizabethtown tract, thirty-eight surveys were recorded from 1683 to 1703 for tracts of land over 500 acres. About twenty-three exceeded 1,000 acres, and eight were for over 2,000 acres. Campbell and Blackwood obtained two tracts, one for 7,600 acres and the other for 3,900 acres. Peter Sonmans received 2,800 acres, while George Willocks and Dr. John Johnstone each acquired 3,150 acres. (*Elizabethtown Bill, App. Sched. III, 88–89.*)

Sale Under Royal Rule

On April 17, 1702, the period of proprietary government came to an end. By Queen Anne's acceptance of the proprietors' surrender of the power of government, the government of the province passed into the hands of representatives of the Crown, but the management of the unallocated land remained in the hands of the proprietors of each division. (*N. J. Arch., 1st. Ser., II, 462.*)

Lord Cornbury was made captain-general and governor-in-chief of New Jersey, and the instructions given to him concerning the land may be paraphrased as follows: For better quieting the minds of our good subjects and for settling the properties and possessions of all persons concerned therein, either as general proprietors of the soil under the original grant made by King Charles to the Duke of York or as particular purchasers of any parcels of land from the general proprietors, you shall propose to the general assembly of the province, the passing of acts under which the right and property of the general proprietors to the soil of our province, may be confirmed to them, according to their respective rights and titles, together with all such quitrents as have been reserved, or may become due to the said general proprietors, from the inhabitants of our said province. You are further to take care, that by these acts the particular titles and estates of all the inhabitants of the province, and other purchasers claiming under the said general proprietors, will be confirmed and settled under such obligations as shall tend to the best and speediest improvements or cultivation of the same. Provided always that you do not consent to any act that lays any tax upon unprofitable lands. (*Ibid., 517.*)

In West Jersey the management of the land was placed in the hands of the council of proprietors, composed of nine members. (*Ibid., III, 220–23.*) From June, 1703, to October, 1714, about 550,000 acres of land were purchased from the Indians and distributed among the proprietors. Each proprietor was privileged to sell any or all of the land allotted to him. (*Tanner. Prov. of N. J., 668–87.*)

In 1704 Peter Sonmans arrived in East Jersey to act as agent for several of the English proprietors who held claims. (*Ibid., 615–16.*) He was to sell their lands at the highest possible prices, to sign warrants of survey, and with certain other persons to grant patents. Also, he had the right to appoint or suspend a surveyor-general, to collect quitrent, and to prosecute those who refused to pay. He disposed of some of the land of Peter Fauconnier, and to seven men he sold 42,500 acres at Rampo in Bergen County (*Roome. Early Days and Early Surveys, 31*), and in Essex County a large tract known as New Brittain was sold to a group of five men. (*Tanner. Prov. of N.J., 619.*)

TRANSFERS BY SALE IN VIRGINIA

Disposing of land by sale did not gain prominence in Virginia until late in the seventeenth century. Land in the outlying sections under the headright system, particularly after the seaboard was settled, was costing the settlers more than its value; the value of the land on the frontiers was not sufficient to induce adventurers to send planters to the colonies to settle this land. Likewise, small unappropriated parcels adjoining land owned by bona fide settlers would cost more under the headright system than their value. So the granting of land upon the payment of a fee came into being. By 1699, disposal of the land by sale had proved so advantageous that the Virginia legislature provided that the granting of land for importing settlers should cease insofar as convenient and that as much of the land as possible should be disposed of by sale. (*W. & M. Quart., 2nd. Ser., III, 138–39.*) The right of purchasing public lands with coin, or its equivalent — tobacco — was at last given legal recognition. Thus, a person either not having a right to any land for importation or wishing additional land could secure it by paying 5*s.* for every fifty acres. (*Hening. Stats., III, 305; W. & M. Quart., 2nd. Ser., III, 138–39.*) This price was fixed by law in 1705. Anyone wishing to purchase land would have a certificate issued. It would be turned over to a surveyor who then laid out the land and made a report to the office of the secretary, where the patent was issued and the money paid. (*Hening. Stats., III, 305–6.*)

Although the act of 1705 which contained the provision permitting the sale of land was vetoed by the Crown, the practice was continued. Lieutenant-Governor Spotswood testified to this in his annual report for 1717. (*Spotswood Letters, II, 269.*) Evidence that the practice was continued is further substantiated when William Robertson, on October 21, 1716, received from Lieutenant-Governor Spotswood a tract of land containing 3,229 acres lying twenty miles above the falls of the Rappahannock River in what was then Essex County. For this amount he paid £16 5*s.* "of good and lawful money." (*Harrison. Va. Land Grants, 50–51.*) Bruce believed that early disposition of land by sale, ". . . did not have the countenance of law, but popular convenience suggested and sustained it. Its liability to gross abuse could not discredit the substantial reasons in which it had its origin." (*Bruce. Econ. Hist. Va., I, 525.*)

In 1755, an act was passed which empowered the secretary of the colony to sell certain lands. (*Hening. Stats., VI, 510–13.*) In 1779, another Virginia act permitted those who held certificates for head-rights, treasury rights, or proclamation warrants for military service not in excess of 400 acres to add to this amount up to 1,000 acres by buying land and paying to the treasurer the same price required from other purchasers. (*Ibid., X, 39–40.*)

As late as 1780 an act was passed providing that £160 for 100 acres would be the purchase price of treasury warrants. (*Ibid., 245.*) In 1781, an enactment for the relief of the poor on the western frontier provided that the surveyors were to lay out any vacant tract of land for destitute residents in specified areas, and that within two and one-half years a payment of 20*s.* for 100 acres would be made. No more than 400 acres was to be assigned each family. (*Ibid., 431–32.*)

LAND SALES IN THE CAROLINAS

Sale of land in the Carolinas started within a decade after the eight proprietors received their charter, and later became an important procedure for transferring rights in land. The purchasers held their land in free and common socage subject to a quitrent, the rate of which depended upon when the land was purchased and its location. Land occupiers were not completely free in their holding of land; all land laws of the general assembly were subject to veto by the proprietors, and appeals to the courts of England were allowed.

North Carolina

Although the right to dispose of land by sale was contained in the instructions given to Governor Samuel Stephen in 1667, selling as a means of distributing land was given very little consideration until about twenty years later when it was clear that a number of persons in the colony who were unwilling to pay the quitrent had expressed a definite desire to buy their lands outright. (*N. C. Rec., I, 163.*) In 1691, Governor Phillip Ludwell was given the right to sell land in Albemarle County and 6,000 acres were set aside to be sold to the colonists. (*Ibid., 383.*) Three years later, a similar power was given to Governor Archdale. He was instructed to sell the land for at least £10 for 1,000 acres and reserve a quitrent of 5*s.* for each 1,000 acres. (*Ibid., 392.*) Early in 1700, the proprietors limited all sales to individuals to 640 acres in one tract without special permission from the proprietors. (*Ibid., 706.*) In 1702 the price of land near a settlement was to be not under £20 for 1,000 acres and the price of land 200 miles distant was to be £10 for 1,000 acres with a quitrent of 1*d.* for each 100 acres bought. (*Ibid., 556.*) Soon afterwards the proprietors agreed to a sale to Able Ketelby of 5,000 acres for which he paid £100, and agreed to pay a quitrent of 10*s.* on each 1,000 acres. (*Ibid., 705.*)

An exceptionally large purchase of land was contracted for in the colony of North Carolina in 1709 when Mr. Mitchell, in the name of the Swiss canton of Berne, bought 10,000 acres of land between Cape Neuse and Cape Fear for which the proprietors were paid £10 for each 1,000 acres with a yearly quitrent of 5*s*. on each 1,000 acres. An additional 100,000 acres were to be reserved for twelve years, and could be purchased at the above rate for seven years, and after that according to the price of land in the province at that time. On this land, the promoters, one of whom was Christopher de Graffenreid, a Swiss nobleman, were to plant families (*Ibid., 707, 718*), with 250 acres set out for each family.

Arising from the sale of the land were many abuses which prompted the proprietors in 1712 to prohibit all sales and grants of land except those sanctioned by the board of proprietors. Willing to give encouragement to planters who would come to settle, the board agreed for the next seven years to sell land not in excess of 640 acres in one tract to anyone who would pay at the rate of £20 for 1,000 acres and 12*d*. yearly quitrent for every 100 acres. (*Ibid., 832, 846.*) This induced a large number of people to come to the colony. (*Ibid., 847.*) Another deal that had the same effect took place between 1724 and 1729 under the direction of Governor Edwards. Some 400,000 acres at £20 for every 1,000 acres was sold to raise money to defray the expense of running the boundary between North Carolina and Virginia. (*Ibid., V, 95.*)

After the Crown took over seven-eighths of North Carolina, the king issued a statement that all legal purchases would be recognized by the Crown and the money would be returned for those that were not legally consummated. (*Ibid., III, 273.*) One such recognition for a valid sale was that of Martin Frank who held 10,175 acres for which he had paid at the rate of over £20. (*Ibid., IV, 61.*)

As late as 1777 an act provided for the sale of land at £2 10*s*. for 100 acres plus the usual fees. It also provided that if the claimer should ask for a greater quantity than 640 acres for himself and 100 acres for his wife and each child, the price was to be increased to £5 per 100 acres. (*Ibid., XXIV, 43–44.*)

South Carolina

The distribution of land in South Carolina was subject mainly to a law passed March 16, 1694. (*S. C. Stats., II, 96–102.*) This act continued to regulate the sale of land until its repeal in 1731. According to this regulation, land could be sold at £20 current money for 1,000 acres with 12*d*. quitrent for each 100 acres. Any land bought could be held by the purchaser, his heirs or assigns, forever in free and common socage.

In 1693, the proprietors provided that anyone who purchased a square which contained 12,000 acres had the privilege of choosing the location of his land from among the unoccupied squares. Before the choice was confirmed, however, he was required to subscribe allegiance to the English sovereigns. (*Com. and Ins. to S.C., 52–53.*)

In 1703, Governor Nathaniel Johnson was instructed to dispose of the land by sale, and was requested to reserve a quitrent of 12*d.* a year on each 100 acres. The price of land was to be not more than £20 for 1,000 acres within 200 miles of the settlement. Beyond 200 miles the price was to be £10 for each 1,000 acres. (*Ibid., 167, 169.*)

Because of injustices that had been caused by many transactions, the proprietors in 1713 declared that no more land could be sold in the colony except that directed by special warrants signed by the proprietors' board in London. A short time later an exception was made; under it grants could be made from the secretary's office for purchases not exceeding 500 acres. (*Ibid., 254–55.*) In 1718, land still could be bought according to the provisions of the 1694 law and paid for in money, rice, tar, or pitch. The price established in 1694 remained the official price until the Revolution, although some land was sold for £3 for 100 acres. (*S. C. Stats., III, 44–46.*)

In 1730, instructions sent to the colony under royal authority provided for the sale of land at £20 for 1,000 acres. The greater part of the land of the province, however, was already in private hands. Just before the Revolution, the governor was induced to break up the Crown's land into lots of not more than 1,000 acres and to sell them at public auction. After the Revolution, commissioners were appointed to sell at public sale all the land on which forts and fortifications had been erected as well as Pollawahna Island. (*Ibid., IV, 648–49.*) A year later authorization also was made to sell the land on which Fort Lyttleton on Port Royal Island was located and the land adjoining the town of Beaufort. (*Ibid., 701–2.*) The standard price of land in South Carolina in 1785 was £10 for 100 acres. (*Ibid., 706–10.*)

DISPOSAL BY SALE IN MARYLAND

For the first forty years, approximately, land was granted in Maryland by headright. In 1673, however, Lord Baltimore authorized his son to sell as much of the escheated land as was necessary to raise £200 (*Kilty. Land. Ass't., 179*), but no record is found of the price received. In 1687, the proprietor directed that all land escheated to him after that date was to be sold for ready money. (*Ibid., 179.*)

After 1683, anyone desiring land in Maryland could obtain it by paying a definite amount which was known as "caution money." The price varied from time to time but the first price was fifty pounds of tobacco for fifty acres of land along the seaboard and 100 pounds of tobacco for fifty acres in the interior. The usual amount of quitrent was reserved. (*Md. Arch., V, 394–95.*) In this same year Baltimore likewise made a change in the land granted to servants who had finished their term of service. In the past, the rights of servants to land had been purchased by merchants, transporters of servants, and others who sold the rights to poor inhabitants at excessive rates, about 400 weight of tobacco being average for fifty acres. Baltimore declared that he would accept 100 weight of tobacco for every fifty acres. (*Ibid., 390–91.*)

In 1766, the proprietor appointed a commissioner to sell his manors and reserve land to any good tenants who would undertake to cultivate it. This land was to be sold at such price and under such terms and conditions as were deemed best. (*Ibid., XXXII, 134–35.*) Within seven years 50,000 acres were sold.

The value of land continued to increase; in 1722 the price was 40*s.* for 100 acres. (*Ibid., XXXVIII, 431.*) After a study of the deed books, Gould said that between 1720 and 1730 land was sold at about 5*s.* an acre. The sale price according to the various deeds recorded in Annapolis during the years from 1724 to 1730 varied between 9*d.* and £1 an acre. The average of sixty-two deeds was 4*s.* 8*d.* an acre; about the same number of deeds recorded between 1763 and 1765 ranged between 4*d.* and £3 an acre with an average of 12*s.* an acre. (*Gould. Land System Md., 60.*) The normal value of the medium land was about £1 an acre, with forest and undesirable lands somewhat lower, and the more desirable lands running as high as £2 or £3. Another writer has stated that the price of land up to 1738 was £2 an acre and after that it was £5 an acre, at which price it remained until the Revolution. (*Mayer. Ground Rent in Md., 19.*) In 1789, the price of land for which no warrants had been issued was set at 3*s.* 9 *d.* current money an acre. (*Md. Laws, 1785–92, n.p.*)

SALE OF LAND IN NEW YORK

The first request for acquiring land in New York through purchase was made in 1658 when the city fathers asked the Amsterdam Chamber for the sale of ungranted lands within their jurisdiction. This request was granted later. (*N. Y. Col. Hist., XIV, 433.*) The distribution of land by sale in New York, however, never gained much prominence.

In 1774, instructions sent to Governor Tryon provided that with the advice of the lieutenant general, the receiver general, and the surveyor general, he was to have surveys made of such parts of the province as had not already been granted or disposed of. The lots were to contain not less than 100 acres or more than 1,000 acres. A minimum price of 6*d.* per acre was set. Four months' notice would be given of the sale and then the lots would be offered to the highest bidder above the fixed price. All land sold was to be subject to an annual quitrent of one-half penny sterling an acre. The purchaser was entitled to hold the land in fee simple subject only to the payment of the annual quitrent and with all mines of gold, silver, and precious stones being reserved for the Crown. (*Ibid., VIII, 410–13.*)

After the Revolution, 4,000 acres of land in Ontario County were sold to James Parker for 2*s.* an acre and also a tract containing 8,000 acres in the same county for 1*s.* an acre. (*N. Y. Doc. Hist., III, 649.*) On the east side of the Genesee River the best unimproved land sold for from $2.00 to $4.00 an acre after the Revolution, while on the west side the price was from $1.50 to $2.50 per acre. (*Ibid., II, 687.*) In addition, a tract supposed to contain 8,000 acres, also in Ontario County, sold for 1*s.* 6*d.* an acre. (*Ibid., III, 649.*) A tract on the Chenango River containing 6,000 acres was sold for 4*s.* 1*d.* an acre. (*Ibid., 650.*) Four tracts of land containing 10,908, 43,377, 150,000, and 120,000 acres, respectively, sold for 3*s.* 3*d.* an acre. (*Ibid., 651.*)

In 1786, the state of New York passed an act for the rapid sale of the unappropriated lands. The lands would be laid out in townships of 64,000 acres each and as nearly square as possible. Each township would be divided into lots of 640 acres each. No land would sell for less than 1*s.* an acre. In case a person without a grant had settled on any of the unappropriated land prior to July 25, 1782, and had made improvements on such land, he would have the privilege of purchasing the land. The tract was not to exceed 200 acres and would include all improvements made by the squatter. The price was set at 1*s.* an acre. (*N. Y. State Laws, I, 328–31.*) All land was exempt from taxes for seven years. (*Ibid., 336.*)

SALE OF LAND IN GEORGIA

In colonial Georgia distribution of land by sale was used very little. It is probable that land was sold infrequently, if at all, by the trustees. This judgment is based upon the policies and plans of land disposal in Georgia under the trustees and on the lack of records of sale. However, the practice soon was common after Georgia became a royal province. Doubtless local pressure for the acquisition of land by purchase caused agents of the Crown to dispose of some land by sale. In 1757, an act confirmed sales of land by attorneys and agents (*Ga. Col. Rec., XVIII, 161*), and in 1759, special wording was to be inserted in all grants obtained by purchase, which would show that the land was acquired by purchase and the amount of the purchase price. Not until June 11, 1768, was any provision made for widespread sale of land in the province. On that date, Governor Wright issued a proclamation that 2,100,000 acres recently acquired from the Cherokee Indians would be parceled out in tracts varying in size from 100 acres to 1,000 acres and sold at moderate terms. In conformity with the king's instructions 100 acres were to be sold to the master or head of a family and fifty additional acres for his wife and each child. The same number of acres could be bought for each slave brought in, and the same number could be bought for each able-bodied white man servant and twenty-five acres for every woman servant between the ages of fifteen and forty. Just how extensively this offer was used cannot be determined. After 1783, any one who took up 200 acres as a headright was permitted to purchase land at a rate of fifty acres for each headright in his family at 1*s*. an acre for the first hundred acres, 1*s*. 6*d*. for the second hundred, 2*s*. an acre for the third hundred, and so on in that ratio until as much as 1,000 acres was purchased. (*Ibid., XIX, pt. 2, 201–15.*)

INTERPRETIVE SUMMARY

With the exception of the four New England colonies, which followed a unique land disposal system, all of the colonies alienated much of their land by bargain and sale. Many aspects of the sale procedure differed from colony to colony and from time to time within the same colony. However, two procedures were common to all colonies: (1) Land was sold directly to individual settlers for immediate occupancy and use in family-sized farm units and in larger units which were developed into plantations; (2) Land was sold in excessively large blocks to land dealers and speculators, the sole purpose of both being to make a profit by resale to occupying farmers or smaller land merchants. The direct sales to family farmers and to plantation operators furnished a partial basis for the land pattern that is observed today in many areas where plantations dominate, where family farms are prevalent, and where the two sizes of holdings exist side by side. The sale of land in large blocks to speculative purchasers was the immediate forerunner of large land merchandising companies.

All of the land disposed of by sale was to be held in free socage tenure. A quitrent usually was reserved, but not always. By and large, socage tenure varied little, except in details, throughout the colonies. The reservation of quitrent varied. Occasionally it was more in the nature of a token rent rather than representing the true rental value of the land, but usually the quitrent followed the old feudal principle of levying "all the traffic would bear." Competition between colonies for settlers had an influence in keeping quitrents from being too burdensome.

In spite of these circumstances the proprietors and the Crown experienced great difficulty in collecting quitrents. Repressive measures were frequently taken, but the colonists in many instances resented this charge upon the land and openly defied the rent collectors. The problem of quitrents was so acute that at least two colonies, Pennsylvania and Carolina, sold land to settlers at a slightly higher price if they desired to hold it rent free. Some land was alienated to holders of headrights without reserving quitrent. Thus, from the very beginning some settlers held their land under what was essentially a fee simple absolute tenure.

Purchase and sale as a means of placing land in the hands of settlers did not have a common origin. In Pennsylvania, for example, this procedure was followed from the beginning, and was doubtless based upon a relatively arbitrary decision of the proprietor. On the other hand, sale was first introduced in Virginia by the agents of the Crown as an inducement to encourage settlers to take up the backland and to round out their holdings with land that had been missed in the original surveys. The pressure for this procedure came from the settlers in Virginia, whereas in Pennsylvania it came from Penn. The experience with sales of backlands in Virginia was so successful that the assembly later provided for general disposal of land by sale. However, the Crown vetoed the process forthwith, but the practice continued without royal sanction. The civil weakness of the mother country and the handicap of endeavoring to make crucial decisions without ample information were evident. The colonists took advantage of this situation, and even the agents of the Crown, who were practical men, faced the facts of day-to-day transactions. The veto by the Crown could not stop sales of land. That sale gained in popularity up to the time of the Revolution is evidence of the changing demands of the situation and the attitude of the colonists in favor of freedom to deal in land.

In regard to the price paid for the land, only a few general statements can be made. A distinct long-term rise in the price of raw land was observed. With the vast quantity of unpeopled land to the west, it might be reasoned that the price of unimproved land should have remained relatively constant as settlement moved westward. But settlers, except for some squatters, had little desire to push beyond the frontier; they preferred to stay close to civilization even if the cost of land was greater than on the frontier. Throughout the Colonial period improved land that escheated or otherwise fell into the hands of the proprietors was sold at a higher price. In Georgia, the price of land per 100 acres increased at one time with an increase in the quantity of land that was purchased by one individual. But this was an unusual procedure and was not followed generally. Also, after most of the level fertile land along the streams was taken up, an attempt was made to maintain a different price for good and poor land. This same tendency was observed under headrights where the quantity of land was greater per headright in some areas than in others. This was only a rough differentiation of value based upon quality or location of land.

The land settlement agencies of Colonial America made little attempt to control size of holdings. An occasional restriction on sale endeavored to prevent one person from holding more than 640, 1,000 or 2,000 acres in one place, but no effort was made in most colonies to control the amount of land sold to any one person. In fact, the financial resources of the individual, as is true now, was the only limitation, and many large holdings were sold. Proportionately, it appears that more large tracts were disposed of by sale than under the headright system.

A greater flexibility of sale as compared with headrighting added to its attractiveness. Although headrights passed from hand to hand in Colonial America almost with the ease of money, the only way to establish a headright was by transporting someone to America; also a headright was customarily granted in America, rather than in England. These were distinct handicaps as compared with the ease with which sales of land were handled. East Jersey will suffice to illustrate. Penn and eleven Friends bought the province of East Jersey and took in twelve other Friends. Each sharer or proprietor could sell all or any part of his share in the various parts of the province before the shares were laid out. This they did freely, frequently selling fractional shares that called for large holdings. The purchasers from the proprietors in turn sold fractional shares to others, who in turn resold parts of their shares, and fractionization continued. These operations were not confined to America, for all of this took place in England, even before any decision was made as to the part of the province in which the land might be located.

The practice of selling fractional shares in an unlocated piece of land, the consummation of many sales in England, and the great flexibility of the procedure made land sales subject to many abuses. But little evidence was found to show that disposing of land was abused any more under sales than under the headright system. In fact, surveying and recording abuses were common to both. Requirements for planting and seating were more pronounced in the headright system than under sales, and as a consequence more difficulties were encountered in holding headrighters to their agreements than was true of purchasers.

The practice of transferring rights in land from settlement agencies to land speculators and occupying farmers by sale, had at least five observable influences upon the evolving land system. First, the infrequent and unusual selling of land at a higher price to some settlers who did not want to pay quitrents gave these purchasers a freer tenure than those whose purchase agreement provided for the payment of a perpetual quitrent. The omission of the quitrent reservation, whether under headrights or sales and whether for a short period or permanently, was instrumental in removing this substantial feudal incident. Quitrents were always obnoxious to the settler who had carved a farm and home out of the forest. As a consequence, any weakening of the quitrent structure which would lead to its final doom was significant.

Secondly, the selling of land directly to settlers by colonial settlement agencies set the stage for the system of land disposal endorsed by Hamilton after nationalization. In addition, the experience gained in transferring land to settlers by sale in Colonial America was usable later by the federal government. Without the precedent and the experience it is highly improbable that the advocates of sale would have won the controversy over the process of disposal of the public domain. Indeed, if colonial land settlement agencies had followed the headright procedure almost exclusively, it is probable that pre-emption and homesteading would have been in use from the beginning rather than coming to the front only after about half a century had elapsed.

Thirdly, the system of selling land to occupying settlers also set the stage for wholesale land engrossment in Colonial times and later. Some aggregation of land was possible under the headright system of land disposal, but it was small compared with what took place under sales. In addition to what happened in actual practice, the potentialities of the two procedures were significantly different. Land engrossment under the former depended largely upon the assembling in America of a large number of people, while under the latter all that was necessary was the accumulation of a large amount of money in England. The fact that land was sold in both large and small tracts made it possible for family farms and plantations to exist side by side. The attempt, as in Georgia, to control size of holdings by charging a higher price per acre for large holdings than for small holdings had no appreciable effect. It is significant chiefly as an indication that the colonial powers were not averse to graduating costs on the basis of size of holding.

Fourthly, probably the most significant and most characteristically American aspect of land tenure that flowed directly from the disposal of land by sale was speculation. The motivation of many men who sponsored the early trading companies was speculation, but this fever largely subsided after the first wave of failures and the dissolution of the companies. Speculation on a grandiose scale began with the introduction of selling land as the chief method of disposal. All of the procedures, except those used in Georgia, actually encouraged speculation. The proprietors let it be known that the land could be resold for more than they were charging; the selling of land in England even before it had been surveyed added to speculation; and sale in unlimited quantities made speculation and not settlement the moving force.

Fifthly, the land selling schemes of the proprietors, who had accumulated political power and financial wealth in England, developed into the land merchandising companies of America, that had their beginning when men in America had likewise accumulated political power and excessive wealth. The large land selling companies appeared on the scene about the middle of the eighteenth century, and were financed largely by fortunes that had been accumulated in Colonial America.

CHAPTER 15

Special-Purpose Grants to Settlers

NUMEROUS SPECIAL-PURPOSE GRANTS were made by the various settlement agencies to colonists and groups of settlers during the Colonial era. The basic motivation on the part of the settlement agencies for liberal offers of land was to supply as rapidly as possible the various economic activities and social facilities that a normal community needed. Also of importance in making land bounties available was the simple fact that settlement agencies had plenty of land and little money. The practice of offering land in return for frontier protection is a time-honored one and was used as justification of a grant in Virginia as early as 1630. At an earlier date special considerations were given to the Bishop of Durham for protection against the wild Scottish clans. Land bounties for soldiers were likewise a common practice. For example, William the Conqueror gave land to the men who had fought in the Battle of Hastings.

Another motivation for these special-purpose grants, and one that was common to practically all grants, was the desire to entice settlers to occupy uncultivated land. This was an important consideration in the grants for frontier protection, for the frontier line was moving ever westward. The same was true of grants for schools and churches and grants made to disbanded soldiers. The process of pushing settlement into the wilderness was just as important as the protection of settlements already established, and special-purpose grants were made with this in mind.

Those who received land for military service in feudal England and elsewhere frequently were given special tenures, but in Colonial

America military bounty land usually was granted under free socage tenure with reservations of quitrent, which was the same tenure under which most other settlers held their land. Customarily the grantee was not required to pay quitrent for a period of time ranging from three years in Maryland to fifteen years in Pennsylvania. The large size of many of the grants for military service was in the nature of a special concession. In addition, at least during the Revolution, an endeavor was made to protect the military grantee; the warrants could not be transferred until the end of the war. Generally, however, the grantee held under the same tenure and had to meet

TABLE 9

SIZE OF PROPOSED LAND GRANTS FOR MILITARY SERVICE IN SPECIFIED COLONIES FOR SELECTED YEARS

Rank of grantee	Acres granted by colony and year					
	New York		Pennsylvania	Virginia		
	1699	1781	1755	1754	1779	1780
Major general	....	....	....	....	....	15,000
Brigadier general	....	....	....	....	....	10,000
Field officer	....	....	....	5,000	....	....
Colonel	....	....	1,000	....	5,000	*
Lieutenant colonel	....	2,000	750	....	4,500	*
Major	....	2,000	....	....	4,000	*
Captain	400	1,500	500	3,000	3,000	*
Lieutenant or ensign	200	1,000	400	....	....	....
Staff officer	....	....	....	2,000	2,000	*
Noncommissioned officer	60	500	....	200	200	*
Private	40	....	200	50	....	....

* One-third more than in the grant for 1779.

about the same specifications for seating and planting as other settlers.

The number of acres included in special-purpose grants varied considerably. Georgia offered as little as twenty acres for soldiers who had served seven years, while William and Mary College received 20,000 acres. A good example of differentiation in size of grants on the basis of both location and time is shown in Table 9 regarding grants for service in the militia. Three tendencies generally held for almost all grants. The most obvious feature is the wide variation from colony to colony. The amount of land which a captain would have received in New York (1781), Pennsylvania (1755), and Virginia (1780), ranged from 500 to 4,000 acres. A second observation relates to the magnitude of the differences between officers of various ranks; in Pennsylvania a captain received only two and one-half times as much land as a private, while in Virginia (1754) the difference was sixtyfold. There also was a slight tendency to increase the size of grants. In Virginia, the 1780 grants were one-third larger than those provided for in 1779. Again, in New York, the grants to Revolutionary officers and men were much larger than those offered almost a century earlier.

The practice of granting land on the frontiers primarily as protection against the Indians began soon after the colony of Virginia was established. It took on particular significance when difficulties with the French and Spanish became frequent. Frontier military grants grew in importance in the northern colonies about the time of the French and Indian War, and expanded in the middle colonies at about the same time. This type of protection was so important as a barrier against the Spanish that it was one of the chief purposes for the establishment of the colony of Georgia.

Settlers on frontier-protection grants had to be adequately equipped for fighting, and their grants were customarily exempted from rents and other charges for a period of years, depending apparently upon the length of time required to get established upon the frontier and the length of time the particular settlement would serve as frontier protection. Grants for frontier protection were generally effective, although few settlers were thus encouraged to venture far into the wilderness. Pennsylvania made the mistake of granting excessively large tracts which did not foster compact settlement, a requirement on the frontier. Also, large grants encouraged speculation. On the other hand, the frontier grants in Georgia were exceedingly small.

Grants for militia service were generally of a later date than grants for frontier protection. Major emphasis on grants for military service came after the French and Indian War and following the Revolution. The Continental Congress, the state legislatures, and the federal government sincerely desired to reward, at least partially, the Revolutionary soldier. Administration of these grants was difficult, and their objective was not fully reached; however, their generous size was a partial recompense. The states claiming vast areas of land to the west were in a better position to grant extensive holdings to their soldiers than the states with definitely restricted boundaries.

Meritorious-service grants covered a wide range of items and included grants for establishing printing, bringing about harmonious relations with the Indians, encouraging workmen with desired skills to come in, helping to quell a rebellion, supplementing low salaries for public officials, and assisting in the political campaign against the would-be state of Vermont. Although grants for these and similar purposes frequently were made after the service had been performed, they also were made to encourage the rendering of the service.

Glebe land grants were provided for as early as 1619 in Virginia, and seemed to characterize community development throughout the

Colonial period. Free land was granted upon which to locate the church building and the cemetery, and frequently additional land was granted for support of the minister and other church expenses. In some cases the parishioners were required to give a certain amount of free labor on the glebe land. Free glebe land had an influence in the religious development of the colonies.

Probably the most spectacular special-purpose grants in the Colonial period were for institutions of higher education. Harvard, William and Mary, Transylvania, Hampden-Sydney, Franklin, and others were financed in part by early land grants. In New York at one time two lots out of each township were granted for education; one for schools and one for literature. Grants for the encouragement of industry included the establishment of ironworks, glass and bead factories, sawmills, flour-mills, ferries, potash- and powder-works, and town lots for tradesmen.

Since the special-purpose grants almost invariably provided for free and common socage tenure with a conventional reservation of quitrent, their impact upon the evolving tenure system was not particularly unique. The brief period during which settlers were exempt from the payment of quitrent influenced them to resent the rents when they became payable, and rendered collection more difficult. This contributed to the ultimate decay and final disappearance of quitrents. The large quantities of land included in some of the special-purpose grants added to land engrossment during the Colonial period, but this practice was not extensive and the influence was not widely felt.

On the other hand, the settlement agencies perpetuated the idea of using settlements on the frontier as military protection. Over the centuries this idea has persisted although it has taken on various forms, depending upon contemporary military requirements. In feudal England, sovereign rights over the land, including feudal tenure rights and powers of government, were given in exchange for frontier protection. In Colonial America, only "ownership" of the land was given in return for military protection – the grants usually contained no prerogatives of government and the grantor retained control over tenure.

Land-grant practices for special purposes in Colonial America set the stage for at least three policies adopted after nationalization. First, the numerous and widespread grants to soldiers who served in the Revolution and subsequent wars followed the same pattern as that established in the colonies. Differentiation as to the amount of land granted on the basis of the rank of the soldier decreased in importance and finally disappeared, indicating a shifting of emphasis from appreciation to need. The money bonus idea supplanted the land bounty idea only after free land disappeared.

Secondly, land grants for educational purposes were carried over and considerably improved upon. The reservations of sections 16 and 36 in every township for secondary schools and the establishment of land-grant colleges under liberal allotments from the public domain are the two outstanding examples.

Thirdly, land to encourage the development of industry also continued as a national policy after the Revolution. The enormous grants for the development of railroads are the outstanding example. After free land ceased to be available for similar grants local taxing units abated real property taxes for a specified period of time to encourage needed industry.

GRANTS FOR MILITARY PURPOSES

The kinds of military service for which grants were made may be divided into two classes: first, grants for settling on the frontier to protect the colonies against opposition from the outside, particularly against the Indians in the early days, but later against the French and Spanish; secondly, grants for specific services rendered in the more formal military campaigns. Much land was granted in the middle and southern colonies for frontier settlement. These grants served not only as military outposts, but helped to push the frontier westward. Large and numerous grants were promised and later confirmed to those who served in the armies prior to the Revolution, and officers and soldiers of the Continental Army also received grants for their services.

Grants for Frontier Protection

Virginia. As early as 1630, Virginia began the practice of granting land to those who would establish military posts. Although this practice was unusual, its justification was outlined in the introduction to an order which gave the governor and council the right to grant land for military outposts. The justification was based upon the usual policy and custom of all nations, especially England, to safeguard and provide security for the frontier part of the country. Therefore, an order of the court at James City, bearing the date of October 8, 1630, provided that for the securing and taking up of a tract of land bordering upon the chief resident of the Pamunkey King, the most dangerous head of the Indian enemy, several portions of land would be set aside for each commander and fifteen acres for all other persons who would establish themselves in the territory. (*Va. Mag. of Hist., V, 341–42.*) Another offer of land was made in 1632 to each person who would settle between the heads of Archer's Hope Creek and Queene's Creek. A grant of fifty acres would be made, and this land would be free of all general taxes until the area became more densely settled and was no longer a military outpost. (*Hening.*

Stats., I, 199, 208.) Among those who took advantage of this method of acquiring land was John Chew, who in 1636 obtained a patent to 500 acres for himself and nine companions. (*Nugent. Va. Land Patents, I, 44.*)

Several years later, following the peace with the Necotowance tribe, the assembly decided to dispense with the public maintenance of some of the forts, for the cost was too much of a burden to the inhabitants. To this end the assembly passed an act in 1646 which provided that the forts with a competent quantity of land would be granted to adventurers who would maintain a sufficient number of people there for frontier protection. On June 9, 1653, Captain Abraham Wood, whose service had been employed at Fort Henry, was granted 600 acres of land at the Fort, which was located at the falls of the Appomattox River. A patent also was issued to Roger Marshall for 600 acres for the establishment of Fort Royal at Pamunkey, provided he kept ten men at the place for three years, during which time he would be exempt from all taxes. Thomas Rolfe also was granted 400 acres of land for Fort James on the Chickahominy Ridge, together with all the houses and edifices which belonged to the fort, as well as all of the boats and ammunition. This land was exempt from all public taxes for three years, provided six men were kept on the place for that length of time. (*Hening. Stats., I, 326–27; Nugent. Va. Land Patents, I, 187, 234, 255.*) In July, 1653, the assembly acted favorably upon the petition of Roger Green, on behalf of himself and others, that 10,000 acres of land be granted to 100 persons who would first settle on the Roanoke River, provided that such settlers were sufficiently furnished with ammunition and strength for military protection. (*Hening. Stats., I, 380–81.*)

In 1679, Major Lawrence Smith was granted a piece of land a mile long and a quarter of a mile inland, which was later extended to five miles long and one-half mile inland, on the Rappahannock River. This land was to be used for the erection of a fort and was to be settled within fifteen months with fifty armed men, which number was eventually to be increased to 250. (*Ibid., II, 448–54.*) Major Byrd was made a grant on the James River for the same amount of land, which was to be settled on the same conditions as the grant made to Major Smith. (*Ibid., 453–54.*) It was further provided that other land on the frontier could be seated on the same terms as the two grants mentioned above. (*Ibid., 454.*)

On September 29, 1701, an act entitled *Land for Defense* was passed by the Virginia assembly. It provided that any group who would enter into a society, and agree to undertake habitation, would be granted a quantity of land, not under 10,000 acres and not exceeding 30,000 acres, upon any of the frontiers where land had not been taken up. This land was to be held by such societies or companies of men in common — as tenants in common — and undivided to each of them. The responsibility and authority for managing, planting, and seating remained, however, in the society. The act further provided that there was to be maintained for every 500 acres of land at least one Christian man between sixteen and sixty years of age, able and fit, and properly equipped for military service. Each person undertaking habitation was to be granted a right to 200 acres, which he could hold as long as he remained a part of the group. All who remained on the land were to be exempt from public taxes for the first twenty years. (*Ibid., III, 205–8.*)

One of the few grants made under the provisions of this act was the allotment of 10,000 acres of Manakintown above the falls of the James River made to the French Huguenot refugees who were then coming into Virginia. In 1709, a grant was made on the upper Potomac to Christopher de Graffenreid. (*Va. Mag. of Hist., XXIX, 14–17.*) In 1730, the Van Meter land on the Shenandoah River was granted under the Spotsylvania and Brunswick Acts of 1720. (*Ibid., XIII, 115–17; Hening. Stats., IV, 77.*) As early as 1725, however, in Virginia's expansion westward, land was granted without cost and free of quitrent for seven years, to those who would settle on the frontier in Brunswick and Spotsylvania counties. Because this territory was popular with the Indians, settlement there was slow, particularly in Brunswick County. (*Va. Mag. of Hist., XIII, 4–5.*) No explanation can be found why the exemption from taxes was for seven years rather than twenty years, as provided in the act of 1701. It is possible that settlement had gained such momentum that the assembly anticipated that this grant would lose its frontier military significance within seven years.

Pennsylvania. Pennsylvania apparently did not grant land to encourage the formation of a colonial militia until late. Governor Morris was permitted by the proprietors in 1755 to make an offer to grant land west of the Alleghenies free of purchase money and with exemption from quitrent for fifteen years. This land was known as "campaign land" and the offer was extended to all persons, in Pennsylvania and the neighboring provinces, who would join an expedition for the expulsion of the French. According to the announcement, the people were under strict regulations to settle on the land and not dispose of it to speculators. A colonel was to receive 1,000 acres, a lieutenant colonel or a major 750 acres, a captain 500 acres, a lieutenant or an ensign 400 acres, and a common soldier 200 acres. (*Pa. Arch., 4th Ser., II, 439.*)

This offer was defective in at least one respect. The granting of land in such large quantities did not result in the formation of a compact settlement that would render military protection to the colony. Speculators crept in, despite the proviso. These evils led to the issuing of new regulations ten years later which provided that no person could receive, without special order from the proprietor, more than 300 acres of land.

Maryland. In 1661, Maryland offered land to encourage soldiers to settle on the frontier. (*Md. Arch., I, 408.*) Again, in 1732, the policy was announced that permitted persons to settle the backland and receive 200 acres in fee without the payment of £2 caution money per 100 acres and without being subject to quitrent for three years after settlement. (*Ibid., XXVIII, 25–26.*) It is not completely clear, however, whether these easy terms were offered to encourage settlers to serve as protection against the Indians or as a strategy in the controversy with Penn regarding the boundary line between the two colonies.

These seem to have been Maryland's only offers to those who would help defend the colony. Of course, Maryland's restricted boundaries did not create as great a frontier problem as did the extensive westward boundaries of Virginia and Pennsylvania. Apparently, the frontier offer was not accepted extensively for no record was found of land taken up as a result of such offer.

Georgia. One of the major motivations for the settlement of Georgia was for protection against the Spanish and Indians. From this viewpoint it could be said that Georgia was a vast military frontier, and that all of the land during the trusteeship was granted with military protection in mind. Thus, each inhabitant actually was regarded as both a planter and a soldier; as the latter he had to be provided with arms and ammunition for defense. The tenure established there was the type judged to be most favorable for military protection. The land was to be held in small acreages in tail male. (*Ga. Col. Rec., III, 373.*) This plan was in sharp contrast with the large grants made by Pennsylvania, and was much more effective from a military viewpoint.

New York. In 1756, New York saw the necessity of increasing protection on the western frontier. Three stations within 100 miles of each other were to be established. The soldiers who went to these stations and remained there until hostilities ceased were to be given 200 acres in the western part of the province, free of quitrent for ten years. (*N. Y. Col. Hist., VII, 75.*)

Grants for Militia Service

In addition to the military grants of land for frontier protection, land was granted to individuals for having rendered military service, and promises of grants were made to individuals as an inducement to enter military campaigns.

Virginia. An early grant for the encouragement of soldiers was made in 1676 when 200 acres of land were set aside on which soldiers were to plant grain. (*Va. Jour. of Burgesses, 1659–1693, 72.*) Two shares in the Virginia Company were granted to Captain Martin Prim of the ship *Royal James* in acknowledgment of the important assistance which he and his crew had given to the Virginia colony. (*Neill. Va. Co., 314.*) Much later, upon the advice of Governor Dinwiddie, the Virginia assembly in 1754 granted funds to wage war on the French "...for the encouragement and protection of settlers on the waters of the Mississippi." (*Hening. Stats., VI, 417–20.*) This legislation authorized a loan of £100,000. Dinwiddie made 200,000 acres of land available to those who would enlist in the military campaign and settle in the Ohio territory when the war was over. Thus, he accomplished a double purpose – encouraged men to join the military expedition in sufficient numbers to drive the French and Indians from the territory, and enabled them to take up land on the frontier so it could be held against any future encroachment. After the campaign George Washington attempted to secure land for himself and his officers. Finally, in 1772, numerous patents were issued by Lord Dunmore to Washington's men.

One of the greatest of the pre-Revolutionary steps taken to reward soldiers for their military services was through King George III's proclamation of October 7, 1763, which contained provisions for military grants of land. It commanded the governor of Virginia and all other governors in North America to grant, without fee or reward, to such officers as had been disbanded in America and were actually residing there the following quantities of lands, subject at the expiration of ten years to the same quitrent as other lands in the province within which they were granted: to every field officer, 5,000 acres; captain, 3,000 acres; subaltern or staff officer, 2,000 acres; noncommissioned officer, 200 acres; and private, 50 acres. (*Ibid., VII, 666.*)

Under this provision several grants of Virginia lands were made. William Byrd III, who had served as colonel of the Virginia regiment, made a claim for 5,000 acres in his own behalf in 1764, followed by another claim in December, 1768 on behalf of his officers, seeking patents within the bounds of the "land lately purchased of the Six Nations" under the Treaty of Fort Stanwix. (*Va. Mag. of Hist., V, 242.*) As a means of expediting the taking up of military claims arising out of the king's proclamation of 1763 and also to prevent those in sympathy with the British from acquiring land under this proclamation, an enactment of October, 1779, provided that these claims had to be presented within eight months and that certificates would be granted only to those who had taken the oath of fidelity to the commonwealth. (*Hening. Stats., X, 177–80.*)

Several laws were passed in Virginia during the Revolution to make land available for soldiers who had served in the war.

The year 1779, however, was one of great activity in behalf of Virginia's soldiers. In May of that year, a general enactment provided that officers and soldiers would be entitled to waste or unappropriated land reserved for them upon the presentation of a certificate from the proper superior officer. (*Ibid., X, 50–65.*) In October, an act provided that the claim to the land had to be presented within twelve months after the officer or soldier was released from duty. (*Ibid., 132.*) An enactment of the same month gave land to chaplains, surgeons, and surgeon's mates who had served for as long as three years. Each was to have as much land as was allowed to commissioned officers receiving the same pay. (*Ibid., 141.*) Again, during October, all the land lying largely in Kentucky between the Green and the Tennessee rivers from the Allegheny Mountains to the Ohio River, except the tract granted to Richard Henderson and Company, was declared reserved for soldiers and sailors.

Every colonel had a right to 5,000 acres; a lieutenant colonel, 4,500 acres; a major, 4,000 acres; a captain, 3,000 acres; a subaltern, 2,000 acres; a noncommissioned officer who served until the end of the war, 400 acres; noncommissioned officers who enlisted for three years and served out that time, 200 acres; while the heirs or legal representatives of those who had been killed in the service were to receive the quantity of land due the officers or soldiers that they represented. (*Ibid., 159–62.*) In October of the following year the assembly provided for an enlargement of the grants to officers and soldiers. Under this enactment a major general was to receive 15,000 acres and a brigadier general, 10,000 acres, while others were to get one-third more land than was provided for in the earlier acts. (*Ibid., 375.*)

Maryland. In an attempt to encourage enlistment, Maryland in 1777 passed an act which provided a bounty of fifty acres for each recruit who served three years in the army and 100 acres to every recruiting officer who enlisted twenty soldiers. (*Md. Laws, 1785–99, n.p.*) There was considerable difference in size of grants for military service in Virginia, a royal colony, and in Maryland, a proprietary. Of course, Virginia's boundless domain in her sea-to-sea grant also had an influence, whereas most of Maryland's restricted territory already had been granted.

Provision for laying-out the necessary land was made in an act of 1781. (*Ibid.*) Also all land not settled west of Fort Cumberland in Washington County was reserved for Maryland soldiers who served with the Continental Army. Six years later the governor authorized that the land be laid out in tracts of fifty acres each. Before the autumn of 1785 some 4,165 lots of fifty acres each had been surveyed. Any officer or soldier who took up military bounty land was to cultivate, within eighteen months, three acres in every 100 acres. That same year an act was passed by the assembly which provided that the military lots were to be allocated by lottery. (*Kilty. Land. Ass't., 343–45.*)

New York. The Empire State started early to reward her soldiers by granting them land for their services. In 1670, lots of ten acres were laid out on Staten Island for soldiers. (*N.Y. Min. Exec. Coun., II, 488.*) In April, 1699, the Earl of Belmont asked the Board of Trade that an order be made for the distribution of the remote lands among the officers and soldiers. (*N.Y. Col. Hist., IV, 504.*) This request was granted, and land was to be distributed among officers and soldiers who had served as long as seven years. A quitrent of one-half crown for every 100 acres was reserved. Land granted under this request, however, could not be sold. (*Ibid., 553.*) Queen Anne made a special grant of land to Major Lancaster Symes of the English Army, rewarding him for the services he rendered in helping the English retain Staten Island. (*Mershon. Staten Island, 23, 26–27, 41, 52–54.*) The land on both sides of Lake Champlain and extending many miles to the south was granted chiefly to reduced officers and to disbanded soldiers who had served in America in obedience to the king's proclamation in 1763. These lands were exempt from quitrent for ten years. (*N.Y. Col. Hist., VIII, 139–40, 705.*)

Even as Cornwallis' surrender at Yorktown drew near, New York needed to raise two new regiments for the defense of the state and the confederation. Provision was made by an act of the assembly for grants of land to all who served three years or until dismissed or discharged. This land was to be granted without a reservation for quitrent, which was another break in the chain that bound feudal tenures to America. Any land that was taken up and not improved within three years after the war was over could be declared forfeited. (*N.Y. State Laws, I, 62–65.*)

A few months later the length of service was reduced from three years to two years. Also, any person who engaged an able-bodied man to serve for three years or during the war was promised 600 acres, and if he was engaged to serve for only two years 350 acres were promised. (*Ibid., 74–76.*) To satisfy these claims, and for other purposes, the commissioners of the land office purchased a large tract of land from the Onondaga and Cayuga Indians. In 1789, the assembly directed that this land be laid out in as many townships of 60,000 acres as necessary to satisfy the claims. Each township was to be divided into 100 lots and all claims were to be made before January 1, 1791. (*Ibid., II, 459–64.*)

New Hampshire. A royal proclamation on October 7, 1763, gave the governor power to grant land without fee or reward to ex-officers and soldiers. These grants ranged from 580 acres to 5,060 acres, but the majority were between 2,000 and 3,000 acres. (*N.H. Doc. and Rec., XXIV, 431–33; XXV, 533–35.*)

Other Colonies. Grants to officers and soldiers probably were not uncommon in the other colonies; however, the information is meager and the situation is not clear. In Connecticut, for example, land was granted to those who assisted in the Pequot War. (*Conn. Pub. Rec., I, 70, 208.*) That land was granted to soldiers in Massachusetts was attested to by the enactment of 1773, which provided that the governor was prohibited from issuing warrants or making grants except to officers and soldiers who were entitled to land under the king's proclamation of October 7, 1763. (*Mass. Hist. Soc. Coll., 4th Ser., X, 696–98.*)

As an encouragement for entering the militia, a five-acre tract was offered to each soldier of the Georgia colony to cultivate for his own use and to hold for the time he was in the king's service. At the end of seven years if he desired to quit the service he would be given twenty acres if he remained in the colony. (*Ga. Col. Rec., III, 391.*) Georgia also promised land to her men who fought in the Revolutionary War. She sought to fulfil these promises in 1783 when it was provided that a soldier holding a warrant for land was to have his warrant fulfilled. (*Ibid., XIX, pt. 2, 202.*)

In North Carolina 100 acres of land were granted as a bounty to soldiers as a reward for service. This land was to be located on western waters. (*N.C. Rec., XXV, 4–6.*) In 1782, each soldier was to receive 640 acres and each officer was to receive land in proportion to his annual pay. (*Ibid., XXIV, 420.*) The land between the Cumberland and Tennessee rivers, today a part of Tennessee, was reserved by North Carolina for the officers and soldiers who had served in the Revolution. (*Ibid., 483.*)

South Carolina set apart land between the Togolo and Keowee rivers for officers and soldiers who served in the Continental Army. (*S.C. Stats., IV, 647.*)

Pennsylvania, by an act of the assembly of March 12, 1783, set aside a tract of land for officers and soldiers, and the widows and children of those who had died in service. Major generals, brigadier generals, and colonels were accorded 500 acres. Two-thirds of this amount was to go to lieutenant colonels. Surgeons, captains, majors, and ensigns were to receive 300 acres, while sergeants were to have 250 acres and all the others 200 acres. (*Pa. Stats., XI, 494–502.*)

In Delaware, the English granted to William Tom about 500 acres of land for commanding the forces that helped to get the land from the Dutch. (*Duke of York Rec., 26.*) The estate of Gerrett Van Swerring was confiscated and given to Captain John Carr for his work in aiding the English in their conquest against the Dutch. (*Ibid., 25.*)

Continental Congress. Immediately following the Declaration of Independence, the Continental Congress began offering land, although it did not possess any, to soldiers of the British Army who would desert and a special bonus was offered to officers who would influence their soldiers to desert with them. On September 15, 1776, and again in 1780, special grants of land were made to the officers and soldiers of the Continental Army. The soldiers were protected in their grants by a later enactment which provided that warrants were not assignable during the war. (*Hibbard. Land Policies, 32, 117.*)

During the land controversy between the several states and the Confederation following the Revolutionary War, military grants to soldiers were an important topic. Virginia reserved specifically, in her deed of cession, land for all of her citizens who served in the militia and in the Continental Army; North Carolina did likewise. Some of the other states attained the same objectives indirectly by requiring that the titles to all of the land of their citizens be confirmed by the government upon accepting the ceded territory. (*Ibid., 10–14.*)

GRANTS FOR MERITORIOUS SERVICE

Another basis upon which land was granted in Colonial America was for meritorious service. The first authority for making such grants was issued soon after Lord Delaware was made governor of Virginia in 1610. He was given the right to give bills of adventure for land to all persons whom he believed to be entitled to some special recognition. (*Brown. Genesis, I, 380–81.*) No record has been found whether Lord Delaware used this privilege. Later governors, however, used this authority, for in recognition of his service to the Virginia Company a bill of adventure was given in 1619 to Captain Newport. This bill was for thirty-six shares, and after his death his widow was given an additional thirty-five shares. (*Ibid., II, 958.*) These shares entitled the Newport family to land in Virginia on the same basis as the original shareholders in the company. At 100 acres per share, Newport's services to the company brought a bounty of over 7,000 acres.

Sir Thomas Dale, in return for his especially noteworthy service in advancing the welfare of the colony of Virginia, was allowed land in proportion to £700. (*Ibid., I, 453–54.*) If Dale was classed as an ancient planter for this purpose, as was doubtless the case, he was awarded 5,600 acres. Fifteen shares of stock in the Company were given to both Christopher and Walter Earle; fourteen shares were awarded to Thomas Gates; two shares were given to Edmond Hackett; and one share each to Elias Foxton, Edward Lawley, and Edward Clark. (*Va. Co. Rec., I, 341.*) These shares could be converted into land at the usual rate. The company, however, restricted the sale or transfer of the land granted for meritorious service unless the committee appointed to examine the circumstances gave consent. (*Va. Co. Abs., I, 121.*) This practice of granting land for special services was continued after the company was dissolved. For example, in 1638 Wyatt was given instructions to grant land to every person who was entitled to it. (*Va. Mag. of Hist., XI, 54–57.*) Also, in 1653 it was provided by the assembly that Roger Green should have 1,000 acres as a reward for his expenses, hazard, and trouble in encouraging settlers to seat in the southern part of Virginia. (*Hening. Stats., I, 380.*)

Kilty has said that the proprietors of Maryland frequently made grants of land as a special favor or in return for meritorious service. For example, land was granted to those who brought over a large number of needed workmen, or who rendered service during the time of Ingle's rebellion. (*Kilty. Land. Ass't., 79–80.*) New Jersey likewise recognized the service of certain people with gifts of land. One large gift was that of 1,000 acres to Dockwra. (*N.J. Arch., 1st. Ser., I, 486–87.*)

The New England colonies also made grants to those who had rendered outstanding service. Massachusetts granted 500 acres of land to Mr. Eaton, a teacher, on condition that "he continue his employment with us for life." (*Mass. Bay Rec., I, 262.*) Stephen Day was rewarded with land for "being the first to set up printing," (*Ibid., 344*) and a year later (1642) Goodman Stow was granted land for writing the laws of Massachusetts. (*Ibid., II, 14.*) Large grants of land were made to those who assisted in arranging peaceful relations with the Indians.

Also, a number of grants of land from 300 to 500 acres in size were given for ordinary civil services. (*Ibid., III, 339.*) For example, in some instances the salaries of the governors were nonexistent or were so low that land was granted to help compensate them for their services. A good example of this was the granting of land, not to exceed 2,200 acres, to Governor Yeardley ". . . in consideration of the long good and faithful Service" and the two shares he held in the company. This land was to be held by him and his heirs forever. (*Va. Co. Rec., III, 102–3.*) In 1674, a tract of 1,090 acres was granted to Sir William Berkeley for the services he had rendered to the colony. (*Hening. Stats., II, 319–20.*) East Jersey at one time set aside 600 acres for one of her governors whom the proprietors felt had not received just compensation. (*N.J. Grants and Conc., 471.*)

Land was also granted to an Indian named Hobbamock who had acted as an interpreter. (*Elliott. N. Eng. Hist., I, 85.*) Furthermore, land was granted to Major Lyman Willard and Captain Daniel Goodkin of Massachusetts in recognition of public service rendered; each received 500 acres. (*Mass. Bay Rec., IV, pt. 1, 304.*) Captain William Hathorne of New Hampshire received 400 acres for public service. (*N.H. Doc. and Rec., I, 197.*) Richard Russell was allowed 500 acres for his service as treasurer of Massachusetts. (*Mass. Bay Rec., IV, pt. 1, 304.*)

New York in 1786 set apart 16,000 acres to Major General Baron Von Steuben. (*N.Y. State Laws, I, 336.*) At the same time a tract of land eight miles square was ordered laid out for Colonel Timothy Church, Major William Shattuck, Major Henry Evans, and others who had helped in the opposition to the governor of the pretended state of Vermont. (*Ibid., 332.*) In New Jersey, Governor Philip Carteret was given 2,000 acres in 1774 because no provision had been made for his maintenance and support. (*N.J. Grants and Conc., 54–55.*)

GLEBE LAND GRANTS

According to instructions given to Governor Yeardley in 1619 concerning the distribution of land in Virginia, four cities or boroughs were to be set up. The Virginia Company ordered that in each of these boroughs 100 acres of land be set aside as glebe land. The income from this land was to be used toward the maintenance of the ministers of each borough. (*Va. Co. Rec., III, 102.*) These instructions further ordered that an additional 100 acres of glebe land be set out ". . . for the Minister of every________." (*Ibid., 106.*) Whether the blank was intended to mean every parish is not known.

The instructions received by Berkeley in 1642 provided that 200 acres of glebe land be given to every congregation that had an able minister. On this land every parishioner was supposed to give some labor over a period of three years. (*Va. Mag. of Hist., II, 281.*) Several years later, in 1661, glebe land was ordered to be set aside in every parish in Virginia and a convenient house was to be built for the minister. (*Hening. Stats., II, 45.*) The number of acres to be laid out in each parish was not given but evidence was found that the land was surveyed and definite allocations were made. In the eighteenth century, for example, the assembly gave many of the parishes the right to sell the original grant and re-invest in other land. In 1730, special permission was granted to the Westover Parish to sell the land then in possession of the church of that parish and to secure other more suitable land. (*Ibid., IV, 306.*) In 1744, similar permission was given to the Stratton Parish of King County and Hungars Parish in Northampton County. (*Ibid., V, 251–52, 390–91.*) In 1753, a like right was given to the South Farnham Parish in Essex County. (*Ibid., VI, 388.*) Four years later the vestry of the St. George Parish in Spotsylvania County was given permission to sell its glebe land. (*Ibid., VII, 142–43.*) As late as 1761, the glebe land of St. Anne's Parish was permitted to be sold. (*Ibid., 422.*)

The colonists had hardly arrived in Georgia before the trustees ordered that a document be drawn and presented to the corporation requesting that sites be chosen and set out for churches and glebes sufficient for the ministers. (*Ga. Col. Rec., I, 87.*) The amount of land allowed for a church seemed to be two acres, (*Ibid., VI, 255*) while fifty acres were allocated to the minister. (*Ibid., III, 379.*)

Delaware donated land for a church and graveyard in New Castle in 1772, (*Del. Acts, 268–69*) and in 1787 New York gave twenty acres at Butlersburg to the Dutch church there. (*N.Y. State Laws, II, 137.*)

Under the concessions granted by Berkeley and Carteret each parish in New Jersey was to have 200 acres for the support of a minister, (*N.J. Grants and Conc., 20–23*) and later, in 1702, instructions sent to Governor Cornbury provided that appropriate churches were to be built, that competent maintenance be assigned to each minister, and that a sufficient portion of glebe land be set aside. (*Ibid., 638.*) Pennsylvania in 1791 made a grant of 5,000 acres to the Society of the United Brethren for propagating the gospel among the heathen. (*Pa. Stats., XIV, 71–73.*)

SCHOOL LANDS

Beverley indicates that in many parts of the country large tracts of land were granted for free schools for the education of children. (*Beverley. Va., Book IV, 40.*) The major step toward providing education in Virginia was made by the company when it authorized Yeardley to set out 10,000 acres of land in the borough of Henrico for endowing a university. (*Va. Co. Rec., III, 102.*) In 1621, 1,000 acres were set aside for the building of the East India School (*Ibid., 537–40.*), and builders were sent to Virginia in 1622 to erect the building. (*Ibid., IV, 15.*) In 1692, King William and Queen Mary gave 20,000 acres toward the endowment of a college which later was established and named William and Mary College. (*Hening. Stats., III, 122.*) In that part of Virginia which is now Kentucky, an act of 1780 provided for a donation from the commonwealth of 8,000 acres of escheated land for public schools to be erected as soon as circumstances would permit. (*Ibid., X, 287–88.*) Three years later, an enactment provided that escheated land, which formerly was vested in trustees for a public school, was to be transferred to the trustees of Transylvania Seminary, later Transylvania College, the oldest school of higher education west of the Alleghenies. (*Ibid., XI, 282–84.*) In the same year, it was provided that title to certain land of Spiers and Company which escheated to the commonwealth should be vested in Hampden-Sydney College. (*Ibid., 272–75.*)

In 1652 and again in 1658, Massachusetts granted land to Harvard College; 800 acres were included in the first grant, while the latter was for 2,000 acres. (*Mass. Bay Rec., IV, pt. 1, 114, 344.*)

Following the Revolution, Pennsylvania made numerous grants of unappropriated land for colleges. In 1786, a grant of 10,000 acres was made to Dickenson College. (*Pa. Stats., XII, 222.*) The next year a grant of 10,000 acres was made to Franklin College (*Ibid., 397*) and another for 5,000 acres went to Pittsburgh Academy. (*Ibid., 489–90.*) Reading Academy received 5,000 acres in 1788. (*Ibid., XIII, 40.*) The German Lutheran Congregation near Philadelphia was allowed 5,000 acres for the endowing of a free school for the poor of the congregation. (*Ibid., 182–84.*)

In 1786, when New York laid out the unappropriated lands in the state into townships of 64,000 acres, each township was to be divided into 640 acres with two lots – one for churches and schools and the other for promoting literature – to be set aside. (*N. Y. State Laws, I, 330.*)

GRANTS TO ENCOURAGE INDUSTRY

To encourage the establishment of certain industries which were needed in the early development of the colonies, land was given to those who were willing to begin the undertakings. For example, the Virginia Company early recognized the need of saltworks in Virginia. The assembly enacted two laws providing land for those who would develop saltworks. The first was not very specific, but the second provided that the governor and council were to choose twenty persons whom they thought capable of establishing saltworks on Smith Island and to grant fifty acres of land to each of them. For five years, one-half of the profit realized from the works was to go to the company, and the other half to the grantees. (*Va. Co. Rec., III, 279–80.*)

The company made a bargain with Captain Norton to set up a factory to make glassware and beads, but the venture proved too expensive and Norton discontinued operations. In order that the factory would not be wasted, the company outlined certain conditions to encourage other adventurers to take up the industry. Under these conditions anyone who wished to engage in glassmaking would be given a patent to the glass furnace for seven years, and fifty acres of land were promised for each person taken there to work. A suggestion was made that this be limited to eleven, but the number was not definitely set. The company was to have one-fourth of the profits, with the rest going to the adventurers. (*Ibid., I, 513.*)

Virginia, North Carolina, and Maryland offered land to those who would establish ironworks. The Virginia offer came during the Revolution and provided that any person in company with a justice of the peace could open up such a works on any unimproved land within the commonwealth, paying damages to the proprietors of such land in an amount to be determined by a jury. This offer gave all persons interested in developing ironworks a quasi-right of eminent domain in any unimproved land in the colony, regardless of who owned it. (*Hening. Stats., IX, 304.*) The North Carolina offer differed somewhat. It provided that anyone who would establish ironworks would be granted 3,000 acres of vacant land that was unfit for cultivation. The works had to be erected within three years and the deed would pass when it was proved that 5,000 weights of iron had been produced. The land was to be exempt from taxation for ten years. (*N. C. Rec., XXIV, 978–79.*) As early as 1719, Maryland offered uncultivated land to any person desiring to set up ironworks. (*Md. Arch., XXXIII, 467–69.*)

Virginia went so far in encouraging industry as to provide tradesmen a place to live. A house and four acres of land were to be given to every tradesman; he was to practice his trade, and could hold the land as long as he continued in business. The land was to be held in fee simple for paying a free rent of 4*d.* a year (*Va. Co. Rec., III, 103*) and was to be devolvable to the heirs of the deceased.

The proprietors of New Jersey permitted 1,000 acres in one place to be granted to William Hampton for the better accommodation of a sawmill (*N.J. Grants and Conc., 448*), and the Trustees of Georgia granted to John Salmon and Charles Harrison 1,200 acres of land in trust for twelve persons who desired to engage in potash production. (*Ga. Col. Rec., II, 12.*)

To offset dependence on northern mills for its flour, Georgia granted 500 acres to Michael Bourghalter, provided he would build a flour-mill. (*Ibid., VI, 4.*) North Carolina likewise sought to encourage the building of mills by offering anyone who would build a mill two acres for a water-mill and one-half acre for a windmill. The mill had to be built within two years after the land was granted. (*N. C. Rec., XXIII, 48–49.*) Maryland, in 1694, passed a law for the encouragement of the building of water-mills. Land on a stream would be granted to anyone who wished to set up a mill, presumably for milling flour. (*Md. Arch., XXXVIII, 31.*) In 1720, Maryland made a grant for the encouragement of another type of mill. Edward Smith was granted 120 feet of ground in Annapolis to be used as a sawyer's yard in connection with his sawmill trade. (*Loc. cit.*)

South Carolina sought to promote the establishment of ferries as a public service, so to this end 1,000 acres were promised to anyone who would establish and maintain one. (*Com. and Ins. to S.C., 52.*)

New England also lent encouragement to those interested in establishing an industry by granting them land. Massachusetts granted land to E. Rawson on condition that "he go in the powder business." (*Mass. Bay Rec., I, 263.*) In 1645, a large grant was made to a group for the promotion of an iron industry that had already been established. (*Ibid., II, 126.*) J. Winthrop, Jr., in 1644, was given land on condition that he establish ironworks on the Massachusetts Bay. (*Ibid., 71.*) The setting up of copper-works was encouraged by a grant of land to Governor Endicott in 1651. (*Ibid., III, 256.*)

CHAPTER 16

The New England Land System

THE LAND OF NEW ENGLAND generally was granted to families acceptable to the corporate groups that composed local government units. Although any free distribution that places land in the hands of occupying farmers is similar in some regards to the headright system, very little land was granted in New England under a procedure that approximated closely the headright system. Nor was much land granted for shares in the Plymouth Company, and the company never developed treasury rights. The Massachusetts Bay Company, however, did grant some land for shares in the company. New England was similar to the other colonies in that some land was sold and some special-purpose grants were made. However, these never characterized the New England land system, for they played only a minor role throughout the Colonial period. The unique distribution system of the New England towns furnished one of the most instructive features of the entire colonial land system, and one that had important influences in the formation of the national system of land tenure.

THE COUNCIL AND THE COMPANY

The New England council was unhampered in selecting a land-distribution system, for it had the full right to grant unoccupied land to settlers and others. In 1622, it issued a paper which described the proposed land system under which two-thirds of the province was to be assigned to the members of the council to be settled by themselves and their friends, and the remaining one-third was to be reserved as a source of revenue to the council. (*Osgood. 17th Cent., I, 103–4.*)

The council granted land in large tracts to the men who became the proprietors of the New England towns, and to private parties or groups who also were known as proprietors. Two additional methods were used by the New England town proprietors in acquiring title to the land, right of occupancy and purchase from the Indians. The last two methods were in practice before the Council for New England received its charter, and lasted for many years in spite of the superior rights of the council. Title to land claimed under these two methods was generally recognized by the council, particularly when the title holder was also an occupier.

Right of Occupancy

When the Pilgrims landed on Plymouth Rock without a patent for the land upon which they settled, Pierce, the leader of the group, succeeded in securing a patent from the New England council. The grant resembled the headright system; it provided 100 acres of land for every person and 1,500 acres extra as the leaders saw fit. A yearly rent of 2*s.* for every 100 acres was reserved but was not to begin until after seven years. (*Mass. Hist. Soc. Coll., 4th Ser., II, 156–63.*)

By the spring of 1623, the settlers desired to abandon the system of common labor and to receive separate allotments of land. After some discussion agreement was reached that each colonist should work for himself. The plan proved a success, and a system of barter was established. The next year an acre of land near the town was granted to every person. (*Bradford. Plymouth, 134–35, 167.*) Thus, inroads upon the communal land system were made without delay, but this was not fully satisfying for the private grants were still held under the New England council, and were subject to annual quitrent. To remedy this shortcoming, eight of the planters, on behalf of the settlers at Plymouth, bought from the council in 1627 all of its claims to the land and other property of Plymouth for £1,800; no quitrent was reserved by the council.

By lot, the tillable land near the town was divided among the heads of families and all able young men, each receiving twenty acres of land, five acres wide on the banks of a stream and four acres in depth. This allotment was a sharp increase over the one-acre grant to each man in 1624. (*Elliott. N. Eng. Hist., I, 84.*) The poorer land and the meadow land, remote from the town, was held in common until 1633. (*N. Plymouth Rec., XII, 13–14.*) In this way New Plymouth developed into a community of small farms, and the unique New England town system had its beginning. The development of individual holding among the Pilgrims was not a mark of undue individualism, lack of cooperativeness, or an antisocial point of view. Subsequent action shows their cooperativeness, and the fact that they continued to carry on the trade of the colony until 1642 in order to pay off the £1,800 debt attests to the singleness of purpose of the entire colony. New Plymouth became a closely knit, unified, well-integrated community of small freeholders.

A year after the grant to Pierce, a Mr. Thompson and three merchants of Plymouth, England, secured a patent from the New England council for 6,000 acres. Settlement on the land was to have begun within five years and the allotments to those who would inhabit the towns were to be in parcels of 600 acres. (*N.H. Doc. and Rec., XXV, 663–73.*) Whether this grant was ever used cannot be determined, yet it is instructive for in sharp contrast with the Plymouth grants it provided for much larger than customary grants to individuals. Later, a grant was made to William Bradford and his associates for the territory that was called the Kennebec Purchase. (*Maine Doc. Hist., VII, 108–16.*) This grant was surrendered in 1640 to the freemen of the New Plymouth colony (*Ibid., 256–59*), who in 1661 sold the patent for £400. (*Ibid., 296–300.*) Nothing was heard about this patent for almost 100 years. (*Akagi. Town Prop. of N. Eng., 242.*)

Grants From the Bay Company

Before another settlement was made, the New England council sold rights to the territory to Sir Henry Roswell and others, who formed the Massachusetts Bay Company. (*Sullivan. Land Titles in Mass., 48.*) This transfer was given royal confirmation in 1629 (*Mass. Bay Rec., I, 3–20*), and a plan for the division of the land was adopted immediately. It provided that the company's governor and council in New England would have power to allot the land. The first two methods of distributing land were similar in many regards to those followed by the Virginia Company in Virginia, where the land was allocated on the bases of shares and headrights. Each share of £50 in common stock was to be worth 200 acres of land with lesser or greater amounts in the same proportion. Adventurers who went or sent others at their expense were to have fifty acres for each person transported. Persons with families other than adventurers going at their own expense were to have fifty acres for the head of the family and such further portion for the other members as the governor and council might determine. For each servant transported fifty acres was to be given to the master, who could dispose of it at his discretion. (*Ibid., 42–44, 363.*) If a settler did not like the land allotted to him he could, at any time before the general distribution was made, select another parcel. (*Ibid., 387–88.*)

Grants under these provisions did not form great estates for few members either subscribed to many shares or brought over many servants. The court, representing the company, on December 1, 1631, issued a set of regulations for the granting of land. Private holders were to occupy their land under such tenure as the court should order, including the demand not to alienate it without permission, and to settle upon the grant a certain number of people within five years. The grants were generally for fee simple estates without a major reservation. But in a few cases grants were made for life, or lives, or for some other term, and a specified quitrent was reserved.

Grants to Private Parties

The first grant to a private person appearing in the records of Massachusetts Bay was to Governor Winthrop in 1631 for 600 acres. (*Ibid., 91.*) It was the only entry for that year. In 1632, grants averaged 148 acres; in 1633, one grant of fifty acres was made; and in 1634, the number rose to nine grants with an average of 383 acres, one of which was to Haynes for 1,000 acres. In 1635, a large grant was made to former Governor Cradock and two other grants for 500 acres each were made; in 1636, a grant for 1,000 acres and several small grants were issued; in 1638, the number was fourteen, with one grant for 1,500 acres, while the average for the year was 372 acres; and, in 1639, twenty-three grants averaged 360 acres. (*Egleston. Land System, 24.*)

At this time a committee was appointed to report on all applications for land and the number of grants decreased. During the period of the next twenty-five years only about 100 grants were made. Many of these grants, although large compared with the other New England holdings, were small in comparision to those of the middle and southern colonies. The executors of Isaac Johnson, for example, were granted 3,200 acres in consideration of his large adventure in stock. Lieutenant-Governor Saltonstall was granted 3,200 acres, and a 2,000-acre grant to Nowell was ordered laid out in two or three farms, while 3,000 acres went to John Winthrop. "It will be noticed that these grants were made to the men most prominent in the history of the company and of the colony—many of them magistrates and clergymen." (*Ibid., 24, 25.*) Few of the other grants were for more than 500 acres; most of them were for not more than 250 acres.

In 1632, the court of the Massachusetts Bay Company granted a patent to Thomas Purchase and George Way for land at Pejepscot on both sides of the Androscoggin River. (*Maine Doc. Hist., VII, 177–79.*) Other partners were admitted, and land also was purchased from the Indians. Richard Wharton in 1683 purchased the titles from the partners for £208. (*Ibid., XXIV, 200–211.*) After Wharton's death eight merchants bought the land in 1714 and the Massachusetts General Court confirmed the purchase in 1715. (*Ibid., 218–25, 241.*) Land was sold and proprietors were added until, in 1737, there were nineteen proprietors. (*Ibid., 245–318.*)

Large Grants

A large tract of land between the Muscongus and Penobscot rivers and extending ten leagues inland was granted to John Beauchamp and Thomas Leverett by the court in 1629. (*Ibid., VII, 125–28.*) Leverett came into possession of the whole patent on the death of Beauchamp in 1650. The unimproved territory in 1719 fell into the hands of President John Leverett of Harvard College who divided it into ten shares and with other direct and lineal descendants formed a land company known as "The Lincolnshire Company and Ten Associates" and later the same year twenty associates were added. (*Mass. Hist. Soc. Coll., 4th Ser., II, 226–29.*) Samuel Waldo, for services rendered to the company, was given one-half of the whole patent, and in 1734 he secured an additional 100,000 acres. The other 200,000 acres remained in possession of the associates of John Leverett. (*Loc. cit.*) Parts of Waldo's interest were sold but the rest remained in possession of his heirs until the company was dissolved in 1804. (*Maine Hist. Soc. Coll., 1st. Ser., IX, 227–34.*) The associates of the Lincolnshire Company proceeded to lay out and settle their lands and gave the name of Camden to the first township. The proprietors proceeded from year to year to encourage and place settlers upon their lands until interrupted by the Revolution. In 1785 settlement was resumed and the town of Hope was founded. (*Mass. Hist. Soc. Coll., 4th Ser., II, 226–29.*)

One of the early large grants of land was made to R. Aldworth and G. Elbridge in 1632, for the Pemaquid tract of 12,000 acres and an additional 100 acres for every person transported within seven years. (*Sullivan. Land Titles in Mass., 44; Maine Doc. Hist., VII, 165–72.*) Some of the land was sold, but Nicholas Davidson, between 1653 and 1657, brought together all the land and became the owner of the whole patent. (*Ibid., 207–14.*) Little is known about this tract until 1743 when the heirs of Davidson revived their claim and twenty-one of them organized themselves as the Pemaquid Proprietors. By 1744 the greater portion of the territory was divided among the proprietors. (*Akagi. Town Prop. of N. Eng., 251–53.*) Some of the larger grants included the Waldo Patent, the Lygonia Patent, the Black Point Grant, Richmond's Island and adjacent land, and patents to Richard Bradshaw, David Thomson, and Edward Hilton.

Large grants did not exert a significant influence upon the New England system, for they were not numerous and many of them were never, or were only partially, occupied. The desire for freeholds dominated, and the type of agriculture except in a few cases was not conducive to large scale operations. The smaller grants from the council or the company to private individuals likewise were not numerous, and few families were established upon the land under these grants. In general, the land was held by the actual occupants in free socage tenure. The tendency to forego the reserving of quitrent gave many settlers a taste of holding land relatively free of feudal charges.

THE NEW ENGLAND TOWN SYSTEM

Under the New England town system, land was acquired by settlers in a group, the members of which were generally known as proprietors. This group laid out the town and the land around it, controlled settlement and development of the land, laid down regulations governing its occupancy, and admitted others to share the land with them. Variables in this land system included the number of proprietors in the several towns, the way in which the land was acquired by the proprietors, the amount of land received by each settler, and the regulations governing the land. Acquisition of land by the town proprietors followed conventional procedures — some of the proprietors took possession of the land as squatters, others bought it from the Indians, and many had it granted to them, at first by the New England council and later by the colony in which the town was located. Some of the new towns were settled by colonists as they arrived in America, while religious and political conflicts and the desire for better farming lands and more favorable locations for trade led to the development of others.

Salem, for example, was acquired through appropriation and settlement by squatters. It was founded as a fishing station on Cape Ann, but in 1623 the town was moved to its present location without authority from either the New England council or the Indians. (*Akagi. Town Prop. of N. Eng., 16.*) Another example is that of Winthrop and his followers who settled chiefly at Boston, Watertown, Roxbury, and Dorchester. It was six years after they were settled before their rights were confirmed by the council. (*Mass. Bay Rec., I, 172–73.*)

The most widely used method of acquiring land for the New England towns, both from the length of time followed and the area covered, was by grants from the council and company. The group desiring land would petition the general court for a grant. If the petition was approved the town was laid out, and if this plan was approved by the court the grant was made. (*Osgood. 17th Cent., I, 429.*) Such towns as Dedham, Suffield, and Hadley in Massachusetts, and Hartford, Wethersfield, and Windsor in Connecticut were granted land by the general court. North Hampton, New Hampshire, was granted six miles square by the council (*N.H. Doc. and Rec., XXIX, 411*), as were Dover and Portsmouth in the same colony. (*Ibid., I, 301.*)

Establishing Towns

The land under the town system fell roughly into four classes: The town plot, which included the home lots, the streets, and the commons; the adjacent arable land for planting; the meadow lands that lay around the town plot, generally used for pasture and hay; and the woodlands that furnished the wood and sometimes were used for pasture for hogs, sheep, and cattle.

The towns differed somewhat in the details employed in the laying out of the land and in the occupancy pattern that resulted. The general procedure, however, was as follows: The first step in the settlement of a town was laying out the central plot with the necessary streets and assigning home lots. After reserving a portion of the area for the town common, home lots surrounding the common usually were assigned by lot. This was followed immediately by laying out the arable land, and sometimes individual allotments of this land were made at once, but frequently the land was held in common for a while. Then adjacent lands — meadows and woodland — were divided from time to time into large fields, in tiers, or in rectangular plots and allotted to the proprietors or sometimes to nonproprietors who had been admitted to the town.

The number of original proprietors varied from town to town. The land for Hadley, Massachusetts, was granted to fifty-nine men in 1659 (*Judd. Hadley, 19–20*), while in 1636, Dedham, Massachusetts, had only nineteen proprietors. At Providence, Rhode Island, Roger Williams and twelve of his followers formed the first "town fellowship," and others later were admitted and known as "Second Comers," but were granted the same privileges as the first members. (*Dorr. R.I. Props., III, 203–4.*) At Milford, the number of proprietors was twenty-one when the town was started in 1667. (*Ballou. Milford, 10.*) Groton had eight proprietors. (*Mass. Bay Rec., III, 388.*)

Sometimes the new proprietors were given equal rights in the land distribution while at other times they were given only partial rights. In Connecticut, Colchester added twenty-four names (*Mead. Conn. as Corp. Col., 69*) and Waterbury conferred the proprietary rights on ". . . yong men that desire to settle in ye town." (*Waterbury Rec., I, 44.*) Ipswich, Massachusetts, also admitted new proprietors. (*Felt. Ipswich, 9–14.*) Another group in many of the towns was known as nonproprietors or noncommoners. These inhabitants came to live in the town after the original settlement had been made. They usually were excluded from all ownership in common undivided lands belonging to the town as a whole and from all ownership in common fields used by all of the inhabitants.

The land granted for a town was usually six to eight miles square. (*Egleston. Land System, 33.*) Dedham, Massachusetts, however, received only five miles square (*Mass. Bay Rec., I, 179–80*), while Newbury was eight miles square. (*Ibid., IV, pt. 1, 402.*) Groton received eight miles square (*Ibid., III, 388*), while Springfield was six miles square. (*Ibid., IV, pt. 2, 469.*) The court offered ten miles square to Captain Hawthorne to found a settlement west of Springfield. A tract of land eight miles square, located west of Woodstock and north of

Mansfield, Connecticut, was granted to John Hooker and six others. (*Conn. Pub. Rec., V, 160–61.*) Newport, Rhode Island, was allowed five miles square. (*R.I. Rec., I, 88.*)

The boundaries of the towns were fixed by order of the general court, it settled boundary disputes. In 1647 an act was passed which required that all boundaries be "perambulated" once every three years. This was done in May by men appointed for that purpose. Any marks by which the land had been laid out, such as heaps of stones, and ditches, that had been destroyed were restored. (*Mass. Bay Rec., II, 210.*)

Freedom of Granting

The manner in which the land was to be divided among the settlers in some towns was specified by the court, while in others it was left to the town. At Ridgefield, Connecticut, the council ordered that each proprietor was to have equal and even shares of the land (*Conn. Pub. Rec., V, 121*), and it ordered that Bantam, in the same state, was to be divided into sixty lots, three of which were to be reserved for pious purposes. (*Ibid., VI, 127.*)

Other towns were given the right to dispose of their land as they saw fit. Such was the case at Hartford, Windsor, and Wethersfield, after 1639. (*Ibid., I, 36.*) In fact, after 1635 the distributing and granting of land generally was left to the individual towns. The Massachusetts Bay Company in that year declared that the towns had many things which concerned only themselves, so the freemen of each town or the major part of them were given the power to dispose of the land, which meant generally that it could be allotted to whomever the towns selected and upon whatever terms met with their approval. (*Mass. Bay Rec., I, 172.*)

Size of Home Lots

The size of the home lots differed markedly, varying from one-quarter of an acre to twenty-two acres. Physical surroundings many times restricted the size of the lots. Cambridge, a compact settlement on the north bank of the Charles River, allotted from one-fourth to about an acre for home lots. (*Cambridge Prop. Rec., 7.*) Several towns allowed as little as one-half an acre each, and Charlestown had one-half an acre by estimate. (*Osgood. 17th Cent., I, 439.*) Other towns had no definite number; for example, Roxbury had two to five acres with some as large as nine and one-half acres; Hartford laid out one-half to two acres (*Porter. Hartford, 18*), and Haverhill provided that twenty-two acres would be the maximum. (*Chase. Haverhill, 56.*) Groton had ten to twenty acres, and four acres was the minimum at Newbury. Springfield had one home lot of thirty acres granted to William Pynchon (*Burt. Springfield, I, 158*), while home lots in Northampton were from four acres up. (*Trumbull. Northampton, I, 20.*) In Salem the town lots consisted of two acres until 1635, and after that of only one. (*Salem Rec., IX, 9, 28.*) In some towns a definite number was given, such as five acres at Providence (*R.I. Tracts, No. 15, 17*), while Dedham allotted twelve acres to married men and eight acres for unmarried men. (*Dedham Rec., III, 4.*) Marblehead, which was a part of Salem at first, granted two acres, and at Hadley original lots consisted of eight acres. (*Judd. Hadley, 31.*) In New Hampshire all but three of the charters, Barrington, Epsom, and Kingswood, were granted to towns before she became a separate colony with a governor, and provided that the lands within the town would be divided among those to whom the land was granted. (*Fry. N. H., 283.*) Dorchester and Watertown allowed four acres, and Waterbury three acres for home lots. (*Waterbury, Rec. I, 4.*) Lots at Guilford, Connecticut, varied from one to ten acres (*Steiner. Guilford, 50–55*), and Wallingford and Enfield in the same state had from eight to twelve acres (*Davis. Wallingford, 81*), while Portsmouth, Rhode Island, set out a little over six acres for nine of its first eleven proprietors and two received five acres each. (*R.I. Rec., I, 53–54.*)

Other towns had their own bases upon which they determined the size of the home lots. At Guilford every proprietor paid his share toward all the charges and expenses for carrying on the necessary public affairs of the town and all divisions of land were to be made in exact proportion to the sums each had advanced. (*Steiner. Guilford, 166.*) In New Haven it was ordered ". . . that every planter give in the names or number of the heads or persons in his famylye, . . . with an estimate of his estate, according to which he will both pay his proportion in all rates & publique chardges . . . & expect lands in all devissions which shalbe generally made to the planters. . . ." In the first division the rate was five acres for every £100 and two and one-half acres for each person. (*New Haven Rec., 192.*) The husbandmen of Dedham who had the financial ability or manpower to improve the land more than others were given special consideration in the allotting of arable land. (*Dedham Rec., III, 82.*)

In a division made at Ipswich in 1665 lands were divided according to rates in proportion of four, six, and eight, giving the poorest one-half as much as the richest. (*Felt. Ipswich, 16–17.*) At Wallingford, Connecticut, a similar plan was followed. Here the whole population was divided into three ranks. Persons in the first rank paid double the amount of taxes of those in the lowest rank and one-third more than those of the middle rank. Land was then divided among the ranks in the proportion of four, six, and eight. (*Davis. Wallingford, 81.*) In Guilford on the fourth division of land the rule was that one acre was given for every pound of property owned and eighteen acres for each male child and ten acres for each woman or female child. (*Steiner. Guilford, 173.*)

The land at Haverhill was proportioned according to the amount of taxes paid. The tax list was made up showing the amount paid by each person toward the public expense. In 1643, anyone who was worth £200 was to have twenty acres for his house lot with planting land and meadows accordingly. Those having less than £200 were to share proportionally. (*Chase. Haverhill, 56.*) In Springfield, the planting ground went chiefly to those who would use it, while the meadow land went to those most likely to use it. Each person with a home lot was to have not less than three acres of planting ground. (*Holland. West. Mass., I, 25–26.*) In Northampton allotments were made to families according to "name, estate, and qualifications." (*Ibid., 47.*)

Arable and Meadow Land

The next item of importance was the division of arable and meadow lands. The size of these allotments also varied from town to town and as to individuals within the same town. Large fields of several hundred acres each were roughly surveyed and then divided into strips which were numbered and distributed among the settlers by lot. In many of the towns one person had his meadow and sometimes his planting land in noncontiguous lots, as was the practice in Northampton and Hadley, Massachusetts. These differences were due to the methods of distribution. One principle followed was to distribute the land evenly, giving each allottee a share of good land and some of the marsh and rough land as well, thus the holdings of one man would lie in several parcels. Another reason for this situation was that all the land was not divided at one time.

In some towns the fields were tended in common at first while in others both the arable and meadow lands were allotted individually at an early date. Toward the latter part of the period holding in common was followed in only a small number of towns, if at all. At Cambridge some of the planting ground was divided in 1634 and a considerable number of individual planting lots were established the next year. In 1635, it was ordered that all the undivided meadow ground belonging to the town should be divided. (*Cambridge Prop. Rec., 7–16.*) At Hingham the planting ground was allotted at about the same time as the home lots. (*Osgood. 17th Cent., I, 442.*)

In 1636, sixteen lots of from fourteen to fifty-four acres each were laid out in Weymouth. (*Nash. Weymouth, 280.*) Dedham ordered that every twelve-acre lot of upland was to have four acres of swamp and as many acres of meadow as of upland. (*Dedham Rec., III, 4, 5, 30.*) In three divisions, those of 1652, 1656, and 1659, a plot of 3,000 acres was divided according to the estates held by the grantees. (*Ibid., 142, 211; IV, 6–7.*) Ipswich, which was laid out on the banks of a stream, made two divisions, with lots of six acres each the dividend. At Springfield, in granting the pasture land, a minimum of three acres was granted with one acre added for each cow, steer, or yearling and four acres for each horse. (*Holland. West. Mass., I, 26.*) At Northampton, the holders of home lots were granted upland and meadow land varying in size from eight to fifty acres. The rule that was followed in the assignment of the meadows was that twenty acres should be bestowed for every £100 of estate, fifteen acres for the head of each family, and three acres for each son. (*Trumbull. Northampton, I, 22.*) Salem gave ten acres of arable and meadow lands as the minimum to the smallest families and other families got land according to their number. (*Salem Rec., 10.*) Sometimes lots were granted irrespective of sex. For example, Tom Moore's widow received ten acres and Mistress Fellow and son twenty acres (*MacLear. N. Eng. Towns, 83*), and at Barnstable four acres were voted to every widow. (*Freeman. Cape Cod, II, 379.*)

In some of the towns planting and meadow lands adjacent to the home lots were laid out on the first division; this was the practice in New Haven. Every settler in Dorchester was given in addition to his home a "great lot" of from sixteen to twenty acres. (*Dorchester Rec., 14.*) In Waterbury the plow lands at Beaverbrook Plain, which lay next to the town lots, were granted to the 106 freemen. About 697 acres were included, and the lots varied in size from one to forty acres. (*MacLear. N. Eng. Towns, 85.*)

The inhabitants of Watertown shared in four divisions in 1636. In the first division thirty-one shared in lots ranging from twenty to seventy acres; in the second, thirty shared and each received about thirty-five acres; in the third, thirty shared in lots of twenty to 100 acres; and in the fourth, twenty-nine shared with lots ranging from twenty to sixty acres. (*Ibid., 84.*) In the second division at New Plymouth twenty acres were given to those deserving a share. (*N. Plymouth Rec., XI, 4.*)

Common Fields

A unique system of common fields had its place in the early history of the New England towns. From the beginning, common fields, though owned by the especially designated proprietors, were supervised and controlled by the town, acting usually through the selectmen. The common fields were not allowed to pass beyond the town's control. Fencing regulations were made and enforced by the town. The common fields included not only arable land but also pasture and woodland. As common fields the arable land was the first to disappear. The "cow pasture" probably remained longer than any of the rest. Salem, in 1640, decreed that none of the land within the cattle range would be granted to any man for his individual use. (*Felt. Salem, I, 199.*) The fields held in common had to be fenced by the proprietors holding that particular field. The height of the fence was specified in many towns while in others it had to be of sufficient height to safeguard the crops. As the towns increased in population and more home lots were assigned, the common land largely disappeared.

The common fields caused disputes between the participating commoners. In 1643 an act, indicating the nature of some of the difficulties, was passed giving the town officers the right to settle disputes in Massachusetts. (*Mass. Bay Rec., II, 49.*)

The early lists of estates in the New England towns reveal that often an individual's land was in tracts widely separated from each other. Later there was a tendency toward consolidation of estates. This was effected by exchange of land and purchase and sale, with intermarriage and inheritance also sharing in the consolidations.

Right to Alienate

Many of the New England towns were practically closed organizations. The land was granted to a group of men who became the owners of the land by division of it at various times depending on the town and its needs. Connecticut apparently was the only New England colony to have a general regulation regarding alienation. In 1660, a law was passed which declared that ". . . noe Inhabitant shall haue power to make sale of his accommodation of house and lands until he haue first propounded the sale thereof to ye Towne, where it is situate, and they refused to accept of ye sale tendred." (*Conn. Pub. Rec., I, 351.*) Elsewhere the subject was left to the individual towns. In many towns the original proprietors were forbidden to dispose of their lands without the permission of the other inhabitants. Such was the case in Boston. (*Osgood. 18th Cent., I, 463.*) Watertown, in 1635, passed the following regulation, ". . . no Foreigner coming into the Towne, or any Family arising among our selves shall have any benefitt either of Commonage, or Land undivided but what they shall purchase, except that they buy a man's right wholly in the Towne." (*Watertown Rec., I, 2.*) Hadley had a similar regulation. No proprietor could sell his share until he had lived there three years and then he could sell to no one who did not meet the approval of the other proprietors. (*Judd. Hadley, 35.*) The Sowams proprietors in 1660 ruled that, ". . .none of us shall at anytime Let or sell any of the said Lands to any stranger that is not allready a proprietor without the Joynt Consent of us all . . . ." (*Bicknell. Sowams, 40.*) Enfield required a person to occupy his land for seven years to obtain the consent of the town before selling.

Portsmouth, Rhode Island, prohibited a proprietor from selling his share until after he had offered it to the other proprietors or obtained permission to sell it. (*R. I. Rec., I, 71.*) Newport, in the same state, had a similar restriction. No person of Newport was to sell his lands to a person of another jurisdiction without the permission of the proprietors. Should a sale contrary to the above regulation be made the land involved in the sale was to revert to the town. (*Ibid., 126.*) These restrictions on alienation met with some opposition. For example, the court of the Massachusetts Bay Company in 1637 questioned whether a town had the right to restrain an inhabitant from the sale of his land. (*Mass. Bay Rec., I, 201.*)

The proprietors at Springfield granted land only in small holdings and forbade the sale of land by any grantees ". . . soe noe person may ingross more then One share of the land there." (*Burt. Springfield, I, 318–19.*) Hartford required that anyone desiring to sell his land within four years first offer the lot to the town which would either give the worth of the labor done upon it or grant permission to sell it to any other person that the town would approve. (*Conn. Hist. Soc. Coll., VI, 1.*) In 1641, the Massachusetts colony endeavored to regulate the alienation of land in all its towns by providing that the land could not be sold to anyone except a free inhabitant of the same town unless the town gave its consent or refused to give a reasonable price for the land. (*Mass. Hist. Soc. Coll., V, 178–80.*)

In Salem the inhabitants who had purchased home lots and the poor who had obtained permission to build houses on undivided land became so numerous and powerful that they demanded a right to the same privileges as the commoners. This question was the basis of a bitter fight in Salem from about 1660 until 1702 when an act finally was passed which provided that all who had dwelling-houses were to have the privilege of commonage. Those who came later finally shared in the division of over 4,000 acres in 1722. (*Adams. Salem, 161–79.*)

Other towns did not have strenuous regulations but still guarded their rights. No one was permitted to plant in Marblehead without permission. (*Mass. Bay Rec., I, 147.*) At Dorchester the original inhabitants and admitted inhabitants alone could claim the right to deal with the town lands. At Cambridge in 1689 the "cow common" pasture was divided. In this allotment those inhabitants who had ". . . no rights in the land but who had settled there were to have a share amounting to twelve acres more or less apiece." (*MacLear. N. Eng. Towns, 86.*) Dorchester ordered that all who had home lots granted to them before 1635 would be considered commoners. (*Dorchester Rec., 14.*)

INTERPRETIVE SUMMARY

The New England land system is an outstanding example of looseness of control from the viewpoint of the colonizing agency and strictness of control by the local proprietors, although from town to town the procedure was quite variable. To begin with, the Plymouth Company, recipient of the original charter, took only feeble and ineffective steps to colonize the area under its control. As a consequence, it slowly disintegrated and was superseded by the New England council, which was little better and which soon gave way to the Massachusetts Bay Company. Although this company did not acquire complete control over all of New England, it had an influence on the land system.

Many of the grants made by the Massachusetts Bay Company were for large areas of land, and normally they carried the same rights and reservations as grants in the other colonies. The New England council and influential proprietors such as Gorges desired to develop a feudal land system, and many grants of the Massachusetts Bay Company were for large tracts. But inserted into the situation were closely knit religious groups that imposed upon New England an entirely new method of getting land into the hands of the settlers. By and large, New England was a land of small proprietorships and family farms; nowhere were found numerous manors and plantations similar to those in the middle and southern colonies. This was due largely to the enormous difference in settlement procedure that contrasted New England with the other colonies. Why these religious groups selected the town system cannot be determined.

Regardless of its origin, the New England town was the most distinctive characteristic of the land system of the northern colonies. Under it, the land was granted to, or pre-empted by, relatively homogeneous groups. The area in each town generally covered from six to eight miles square, which was granted to, or occupied by, the group jointly. The land was laid out into home plots, arable land, grazing and meadow land, and woodland. The home plots usually were small and located close together, the arable and meadow and pasture land lay as close as conveniently possible, and the woodland was the rough or more remote land. At first the land was held in common. Later, small home plots were granted to private parties and later still, the arable land was divided among smaller groups and finally among individuals. Eventually, the town was held largely in individual parcels, but this transition was slow. As it was in progress, the tracts held by an individual were seldom contiguous; later, however, through marriage, barter, and purchase, many of the separate parcels were brought together into one contiguous ownership unit.

Home lots ranged in size from one-half an acre or less to over twenty acres. The factors taken into consideration in determining the size of home lots varied from town to town. In some towns an arbitrary number of acres was agreed upon, and everyone received the same size lot. In other towns, physical surroundings were influential. Other considerations of importance included the extent of participation in the cost of getting the town organized and developed, the valuation of the grantee's estate, the size of the family, their ability to use and improve the land, the amount of their contribution to local taxes, and combinations of these factors. In one place, where the value of a man's estate and the size of his family were both used, one person equaled as much as a £50 estate. This is in sharp contrast with the headright system where one headright could be acquired for much less than that amount.

In many places the same general principles were followed in allotting the arable land and the meadows. Sometimes the arable and meadow lands were adjoining, while in other towns they were in different locations. Usually these allocations were much larger than the home plots because the over-all surveys were rough and many individual allotments were estimated. Sometimes a minimum allotment was made and additional land was added for each horse, cow, sheep, or hog owned by the allottee. Frequently the arable land was tended in common and the hay was harvested together for the first few years. However, individual property soon was established in most places and each farmer cultivated his own acres.

Proof is not conclusive, but judging from meager evidence it would appear that as the towns become more densely populated the inhabitants in some places divided into small groups and farmed together. That this plan was followed at Salem at one time is shown conclusively by a regulation providing that proprietors holding particular fields must fence them. The breaking up of common fields was rapid as a rule but in some places they remained until the middle of the eighteenth century. Of course, the town commons around which the individual home lots were located still remain characteristic of many New England towns.

With the exception of the few large grants, New England granting was characterized by small grants to actual settlers. Many of the grantees receiving large acreages doubtless would have gladly subdivided their holdings into small farms but the scarcity of settlers, due in part to the cold climate and the confusion surrounding land titles, prevented disposal to bona fide settlers. Large estates, however, probably had no effect upon the land system other than to retard settlement. In most of the New England territory large landed estates were carefully avoided. The land generally was administered for the good of the whole community.

Probably the most distinctive feature of this unique method of granting land was the restraint placed upon alienation. Some specific condition formed the basis upon which most New England towns were organized. Because of this unifying force it was desirable that caution be maintained in bringing in new members. The inhabitants were very conscious of the damage that could be wrought by someone who did not share the common unifying viewpoint. For the purpose of preventing strangers from upsetting and disorganizing their towns, most groups placed some restraint upon alienation. This restraint was similar to that imposed upon free landholders in ancient England. The purposes were very similar. On the other hand, the "fine for alienation," which formed a part of the feudal system, was different in principle and in purpose. It did not prevent alienation or even effectively control who the new feudal tenant would be; its purpose was revenue and not control, at least during the last few centuries of feudalism.

Another reason for restraint upon sale was to prevent land engrossment by a few wealthy inhabitants. The Springfield restriction to the effect that no person could have more than one share of land is typical. This restriction, as well as the attitude surrounding the limitation of size of holdings, was an important influence in behalf of small independent family farmers in New England. In actual practice, it is a good example of the conflict between what is judged to be the general welfare and freedom of action. The towns felt that the public interest would be served best if there was little or no land engrossment. The legalists in the Massachusetts Bay court questioned the right of the town to restrain alienation under English land laws. That full alienability was established indicates the strength of the idea of freedom of action. That much land engrossment took place when freedom of alienation was fully permitted indicates the wise judgment of the inhabitants of early New England towns.

The infrequent reservations of quitrent in New England towns was a second distinctive feature of the New England land system. Indeed, both restraint upon alienation and absence of quitrent were integral parts of the system. In the other colonies quitrent was almost universally reserved. With a few minor exceptions, the absence of quitrent meant that the land was held by the individual in essentially fee simple absolute tenures, since quitrent was the chief feudal appendage of consequence that generally followed English tenures to America. Freedom of alienation is often thought of as an essential of fee simple property, but to most New England settlers a reasonable restraint upon alienation, imposed by the group, was much more acceptable than a quitrent imposed by an absentee landlord.

With the exception of frequent restraint upon alienation and the almost universal absence of quitrent, the New England colonists held their land under free socage tenure of the same general characteristics as other colonists. Their pattern of laying out the land, of course, was significantly different. The early communal organization at Plymouth was similar in many regards to the communal living at Jamestown under the London Company. The experience at Plymouth was similar to Jamestown but was more readily remedied, for the colonists and not a company were in authority. The common lands, whether arable, meadow, or woodland, were a second type of experiment in communal activity. The colonists, however, favored individual living and economic activity. That private property should reach its highest degree of privacy under these conditions is not surprising.

The evolution of the land tenure system in New England was not at all easy. Quitrent had to be completely broken; restraint upon alienation had to be eliminated; the scattered field system had to be done away with; the separate individualistic town plans had to be harmonized into a system for a whole colony; and new settlers had to be accepted on equal terms. All of these adjustments required patience and persistence. That these adjustments could be made was due largely to the forms of government and land holding under which the changes took place. The corporate forms of government and settlement agency were crucial in the evolution of free land tenures of New England. No conflict existed between the holder of the power to govern and the holder of rights in land, and no conflict existed between either or both of these and the majority of the private landowners. This was possible because those powers, rights, and interests all resided in the same place — the people. In no other colonies were these conditions duplicated.

In colonial New England the last land to become private property under the full force of freedom, individualism, and commercialization was the pasture and woodland. Years later, after the energy of this revolution had spent itself, and some of the liabilities of this newly found property system had been observed, the people stopped alienating into private hands forest land and certain grazing land of the public domain and later instituted a positive purchase program of bringing these lands back into common ownership. In some areas where these processes were too slow to cure the ills of unrestricted private ownership, private owners formed cooperative grazing associations under various types of collective tenure arrangements. (*Craig. Collective Tenure.*)

CHAPTER 17

Land Companies

THE EARLY LAND COMPANIES of Colonial America were not numerous, and they were so heterogeneous as to form of organization and plan of operation that few generalized statements can be made regarding them. The pre-Revolutionary companies more nearly conformed to an accepted pattern so that some generalizations can be made. The post-Revolutionary land merchandising companies are of little importance to the problem under consideration.

The major differences between tenure-related activities of the early companies and those that appeared just before the Revolution are traceable largely to differences in the purposes for which they were organized and changes that had occurred in the tenure situation throughout the colonies over the century and a half. The earliest companies were organized chiefly for purposes of trade and were concerned with the establishment of agricultural settlement mainly as it related to the carrying on of trade and commerce. The later companies were strictly land merchandising companies, interested largely in making money from selling land to settlers, or to others who would establish bona fide farmers upon it.

In light of these differences the early companies were concerned over the power to govern the area granted to them, while the later land merchandising companies were little concerned with possessing powers of government. In fact, the government of the area was mentioned only in the Vandalia scheme, and it appears that the responsibilities of the company for the establishment of civil government were due largely to the fact that it was visualized that the territory would be made into the fourteenth colony.

Furthermore, the early companies showed little concern over the soundness of their title to the land, while the later companies looked upon a clear title as the prime requisite. They generally would not proceed without first being as certain as possible of a reasonably clear title. The early companies were very careless in their endeavor to extinguish the claims of the Indians, whereas the pre-Revolutionary companies were meticulous in quieting the Indians' claims before proceeding. Likewise, the early companies did not bother much about whether their claims to the land would stand up against all comers, but the later companies generally would not proceed until their grant had received royal approbation or the sanction of a responsible local assembly. The early companies were free to establish a wide variety of tenure when they alienated the land to private parties. On the other hand, most of the later companies were confined largely to the then prevalent and well-accepted free ownership, save for the questionable reservation of a quitrent that customarily was not collected.

The basic policy that the British government pursued throughout the Colonial era, and one that it never lost sight of in spite of frequent vacillation as to ways and means, was one of increasing British trade. Therefore, little endeavor was made at any time to derive revenue for the Crown from the sale of its colonial lands. This was reflected in the basic policy throughout the Colonial era, the few minor exceptions being of little consequence. The lack of interest of the British authorities in direct royal revenue from the land of the colonies is attested to by the consistent lack of concern over the collection of quitrents. However, it appears that the inner circle in London was becoming conscious of the fact that the western territory was a potential source of royal revenue. One bit of evidence is the proposal of the Crown to reserve for later sale the western part of the territory that was to have become the fourteenth colony under the Vandalia scheme.

In pursuing the basic policy, the Crown sanctioned plans, particularly after the first century, that would make the land available to actual settlers who bought goods from, and sold raw products to, British merchants. The later land companies understood this point of view and usually agreed to establish settlers upon the land within a short time. The Crown generally did not require conditions, either in the operations of the company or in the tenure under which the settler would receive the land, that would retard settlement of the country. The policy observed after 1700, of favoring royal against proprietary colonies, was due largely to the slowness with which the proprietary system settled the country. This slowness grew out of the interest of the proprietors in deriving income from the sale of land and of receiving an annual income from quitrents, and their lack of interest in expanding commerce and trade.

To accomplish the objective of making money from land merchandising, all the later companies followed about the same pattern of operation. After the association was formed and the general scope of the undertaking agreed upon, the company either petitioned for a grant of land from the colonial or royal government or secured an extinguishment of the Indian title. Frequently the trade with the Indians was negotiated first, for it was usable as evidence in pleading for official approval of the activity. Then, if successful, the company proceeded to sell land to bona fide settlers or to dispose of it to smaller speculators.

Although the years of vacillation in the British ministry wiped out the majority of the land companies, except those receiving some compensation from the Virginia legislature or the Congress, the pre-Revolutionary land companies set the pattern for the form of organization and type of operation of the post-Revolutionary land speculation companies. The experience of the former proved to the land speculator that he needed the right to buy and sell land freely in whatever quantities appeared desirable. He desired to evade various colonial restrictions, and this he did very successfully. He needed to be freed from the necessity of dummy sales and other questionable means of sidestepping colonial law. However, the ideas regarding land in Colonial America were sufficiently flexible to permit the colonial speculator to operate without too much handicap. For example, Andrew Craig was a dummy owner who immediately reassigned his part of the Burlington Company venture to Cooper. Also, Washington's share in the Dismal Swamp venture was sold to a dummy owner at auction in Alexandria. He immediately reconveyed it to Bushrod Washington, one of the executors.

The scandalous plans and operations of the various land companies prior to the Revolution, as much as anything else, forced the federal government to take charge of settling the western public domain. The conflicting claims to the territory among the several states was another major force acting upon the situation.

EARLY COLONIAL LAND COMPANIES

Even while the Virginia Company was struggling with its youthful colony at Jamestown it sold its rights in the Somers Islands for £2,000 to a joint-stock company, which was the first company that had land merchandising as its chief aim — the London and Plymouth Companies and the Dutch and Swedish Companies were organized chiefly as trading companies with land settlement as a distinctly subsidiary activity. Within two years the Somers Island Company surrendered its rights to the king as the first step in getting a direct charter grant from the Crown for the same territory. Thus this company, which existed for only two years, made no contribution to tenure development.

One of the earliest land companies to originate in the colonies was the Atherton Company, which operated in the Narragansett territory around 1660. This company was organized by a group of early colonial land speculators. In contravention to Rhode Island law, it made an unauthorized purchase from the Indians of a large tract of the best land in the Narragansett area. A second tract was acquired through foreclosure of a questionable mortgage that the Narragansett Indian chiefs had given to the Atherton Company for the payment of a fine which had been forced upon them by the United Colonies. These two transactions gave the company dubious title to nearly all of the Narragansett country. (*N. Plymouth Rec., X, 227, 248; Field. R.I. Hist., I, 99.*)

Governmental jurisdiction over the area was disputed between Connecticut and Rhode Island because of conflicts in their charters. The company supported the claims of Connecticut and sold some of the land to settlers. This dispute was finally settled in 1727 when the Board of Trade awarded jurisdiction over the territory to Rhode Island, which left the company's heirs no tenable claim to the land. (*Dict. of Amer. Hist., I, 134.*)

The land was divided into what was called the North Tract and the South Tract. The former was set aside for settlement, and was to be divided into sixty shares which were to be given out to persons that the original group approved. It appears that the settlers were to pay 12*d.* per acre for the land so allocated. The purchasers, their heirs and successors, were required to contribute forever to the maintenance of an "able and goodly" orthodox minister. The South Tract was divided into farms for the eight members of the company. (*Arnold. Fones Rec., I, 5.*)

The Free Society of Traders was organized by Penn in 1681 to settle a large number of people in his new colony. This company, in sharp contrast to many of the later land companies, was composed of ordinary people who proposed not only to stimulate population of the country but to encourage establishment of essential industries. Although Penn issued the original charter to the company, the 1683 session of the Pennsylvania assembly failed to ratify it. No reason could be found why it was not ratified, although possibly the assembly resented the extensive manorial rights granted to the society. These rights included membership on the council, power to levy taxes, privilege of holding the various manorial courts, claim to part of the minerals, and the right to establish fairs and markets.

In an endeavor to make the society effective, Penn donated 100 acres of land in Philadelphia and 20,000 acres in the country. The commercial activities of the company were successful, but bickering among the officials, misunderstandings with Penn, trouble with the Pennsylvania assembly, suits against the officials of the company, and failure to secure approval of the charter caused the endeavor to fail. The society finally was dissolved by order of the assembly in 1721. It too left no significant imprint upon the tenure system of Colonial America.

At about the same time that the Free Society of Traders was organized, the Frankfort Company was organized in Germany. The original group, composed of twelve members, largely teachers and ministers associated with Spener's College of Pietists, did not intend to migrate to America, but hoped to sell the land in small parcels to others in Frankfort who would go to America.

The idea was held that ownership of the land involved should be maintained in the hands of persons of the same religious faith. To this end, it was agreed that the shares of any member dying intestate should revert to the company, according to the rule of joint tenancy. This plan remained in common use until about the middle of the eighteenth century, and no resale of allotted land could be made without the consent of, and prior decline to purchase by, the company. In an effort to speed up operations, the business of the company was placed in the hands of three joint agents in about 1700. One of these men turned out to be dishonest and dissipated the land holdings of the company through fraudulent sales to various accomplices. (*Pennypacker. Germantown, 21–50.*)

The West Jersey Society of 1691 was a land speculating company designed to make profit from the sale of land. Its extensive holdings, equal to about one-fifth of West Jersey, were placed in the hands of agents for sale to settlers. The land, however, was not well situated, sales were slow, and the company finally failed.

Perhaps the most grandiose land speculative venture of the Colonial era was John Law's Mississippi Company (1717–19). It is of interest although it was non-English and it was not concerned with land immediately related to any of the thirteen original colonies. Law's fantastic scheme to exploit French Louisiana ended in utter failure and broke financially many of the subscribers to its stock. This speculative scheme was known to all Europeans and colonial leaders who were eager to make a fortune through land speculation. Its sobering influence upon those who resided in England was one of the reasons why pre-Revolutionary speculation was carried on largely by colonists who were familiar with problems of settlement in the unconquered territory west of the mountains.

The early colonial land companies did not have an important influence upon the evolving land tenure system. The four companies – the Atherton Company, the Free Society of Traders, the Frankfort Company, and the West Jersey Society – were forced to operate within the framework of colonial land tenures as laid down in the original charters. The restrictions on sale of the Frankfort Company, however, would have had an influence if similar restrictions had become widespread, but they were not. However, even a few minor restrictions when imposed in a milieu of unrestrained freedom, stood out clearly, and perhaps when added together had some weight in favor of the more popular free land tenure ideas. The requirements of the Atherton Company that the purchasers would maintain *forever* a minister ceased to be a charge upon the land under the impact of the forces that eventually brought about complete religious freedom and separation of church and state.

PRE-REVOLUTIONARY LAND COMPANIES

Many private parties participated in land speculation as the land of the eastern seaboard was placed in the hands of occupying farmers. Speculation and concentration were involved in the headright and treasury right systems and in distribution by sale. Only allotments for special purposes and disposal under the New England town system were relatively free from widespread speculation. However, as the plantation system of farming in the middle and southern colonies and the commercial endeavors of the Philadelphia traders began to yield larger profits, the big commercial and financial operators sought ways of utilizing their surplus funds in the hope of creating additional profits.

At first many of them acquired large land holdings and brought them into production through the use of indentured servants, slaves, hired laborers, and tenant farmers. Soon economic forces began to affect adversely these endeavors. The holdings became too large to oversee properly; tobacco growing depleted the land; and settlers were pressing for land of their own. As a consequence, many of the large land owners began to invest their funds in western land which they hoped to sell to occupying settlers at a profit. It is probable that land was the chief, if not the only, item that offered good speculative opportunities at that time. General economic forces were operating toward the same end. The large planters wanted to restrict crop production to fit market demands; they desired a less costly marketing system; and they endeavored to curtail the importation of slaves. Since the British financial interests had the support of the home government in opposing these changes in commercial policy, it was necessary for the successful plantation and commercial operators to seek their fortunes outside of active farming. Investment in the western land was an obvious and logical alternative.

Speculation in western lands was confined largely to the middle and southern colonies. The absence of colonial New Yorkers from early western land-grabbing schemes was due more to the geographical location of the colony and other considerations than to freedom from the mania that affected other colonies. Geographically, New York was wedged in between New England and the contested land westward; in addition, strong Indian tribes were located in western New York and her colonial governors were reluctant to make grants in the west. (*Sakolski. Land Bubble,* 25.) The nonspeculative Yankee of the New England colonies might have acted quite differently if he had had surplus funds to invest and had had vast quantities of land lying just to the west rather than being hedged in on the south and east by water, on the north by cold, and on the west by other colonies.

Another item of significance in motivating land speculation was the fact that some colonies claimed land to the west and considered it a right, if not a responsibility, to develop this land. Of the six landed colonies — Massachusetts, Connecticut, Virginia, the Carolinas, and Georgia — Connecticut and Massachusetts participated in the scheme to place settlers on the banks of the Susquehanna. Virginia and North Carolina furnished most of the power behind the pre-Revolutionary land companies. South Carolina was neither financially strong nor well situated, and Georgia was too young to participate widely in settling the West. Of the other seven colonies, Pennsylvania was the only one that furnished any real impetus to speculation in the western lands. This can be explained chiefly by the speculative activities in settling parts of Pennsylvania and the accumulation of surplus funds in the commercial endeavors of the Philadelphia merchants.

Another specific item that lent encouragement to the colonial land speculator was the famous Camden-Yorke opinion that purchase directly from the Indians would give a sound title to western land. Students of this period emphasize the tremendous influence of the circulation of this opinion among several land-minded groups and the land lobbyists in London. In spite of this garbled version of the opinion, it was used as a general sanction for all purchases from the Indians, and its influence was considerable. Furthermore, in an endeavor to expedite settlement, a strong policy was maintained throughout this period of requiring fair treatment of the Indians in the acquisition of titles to their land. At first the motivating idea was that they would be material assistance against the French. Later it was held that the Indians must be "conciliated and reconciled" before western expansion should be pushed. Finally, the Camden-Yorke opinion encouraged the purchase of Indian lands.

Prior to the middle of the eighteenth century the landed colonies were not handicapped in making grants and encouraging settlements to the west; in fact, the home government actually encouraged this activity.

By 1761, however, the controversy between the landed and the landless colonies was of concern to the mother country. When Lord Halifax resigned in favor of Lord Egremont the latter felt that pushing settlement westward was too dangerous, in spite of the conventional precautions taken, until the Indian problem had been settled. As a consequence, on December 2, 1761, instructions were issued to the royal governors to cease making land grants within or adjacent to lands still held by the Indians. (*Alvord. Miss. Valley. I, 123–26.*) The immediate effect of these instructions was the cessation of operations of the Virginia land companies — the 1748 Ohio Company, the Loyal

Company, and others. In addition, the soldiers who were promised bounty land in the western territory were prohibited from taking up their claims.

To remedy the latter situation, to protect the fur trade, to assure the natives that their landed rights would be respected, and to bolster the restrictions on settlement across the mountains, the Proclamation of 1763 was issued. Under its provisions the colonial governors were empowered to begin again the making of military grants, and the proclamation set forth in definite terms the amount of land to be given to each rank. On the other hand, the proclamation prohibited for the time being the granting of land west of a line running through the sources of the rivers flowing into the Atlantic. The governors were also to refrain from issuing patents for any land anywhere to which the Indian title had not been properly extinguished. Presumably, these restrictions were to last only until a definite policy regarding the western lands could be developed. Besides withdrawing the western lands from the control of the governors, the proclamation forced the land companies to appeal directly to the Crown for the desired land. This set a precedent that was instructive to the confederation when the western lands problem reappeared after the Revolution.

From 1763 to 1774 the British policy toward the western land was one of absolute restriction on the part of the land companies as well as the governors. The final blow was struck in 1774 by the issuance of the Quebec Act and a new set of instructions to the colonial governors. The Quebec Act extended the Province of Quebec to include all of the territory west of the mountains that lay north of the Ohio River and east of the Mississippi. This included much of the land claimed by the landed colonies. This act ended the hope for expansion westward, or the establishment of new colonies by those who would yet come from the mother country.

New instructions to the governors promulgated stringent regulations covering the settling of any ungranted land in New Hampshire, New York, Virginia, the Carolinas, and Georgia. The new policy provided that the haphazard system of laying out grants was to cease, that all future grants were to be laid out and surveyed in regular lots, that quitrents were to be raised from 2*s.* to 4*s.* 2*d.* per 100 acres, that free gifts of land were to cease, and that all tracts were to be sold at auction to the highest bidder at a price of not less than 6*d.* per acre. Jefferson enumerated the grievances which grew out of these instructions in the Declaration of Independence, which objected to the new regulations on the ground that they ". . . endeavoured to prevent the population of these States; for that purpose obstructing the Laws for Naturalization of Foreigners; refusing to pass others to encourage their migration hither, and raising the conditions of new Appropriation of Lands."

The Susquehannah Company

One of the more important of the pre-Revolutionary land companies was the Susquehannah Company, which was organized at Windham, Connecticut, on July 18, 1753. In the articles of agreement the purposes set forth were ". . . to enlarge the English settlements, to spread Christianity, and to promote their own temporal interests." (*Livermore. Land Companies, 85.*) The Company and colony were interested also in preventing encroachment from the north and west by the French, and in expanding their Indian trade. The territory desired by the Susquehannah Company was claimed by both Connecticut and Pennsylvania under grants from the Crown. Up to this time the land had been reserved as a hunting ground for the Indians. Since Pennsylvania had not purchased it from them, and since Connecticut's grant antedated the grant to William Penn, the Susquehannah leaders held that the Pennsylvania claim was not valid, or at least that their own claim was superior.

The leaders of the Susquehannah Company, therefore, engaged John Lydius to purchase from the Indians for £2,000, New York currency, land along the Susquehanna River between the 41st and 42nd parallels. The purchase was made from the Six Nations at the Albany Congress in 1754 by Lydius who presumably used questionable methods in securing the deed. The Indians by this time were rapidly acquiring the ways of the white man, for at the same Congress and in the same year, they sold the same land to the Pennsylvania authorities. These two deeds strengthened the claims of both Pennsylvania and Connecticut to the territory along the Susquehanna.

The Susquehannah Company pushed its plan for settlement. As early as 1755, a group went out to settle in the rich Wyoming Valley, a territory along the Susquehanna River about twenty miles long and three to four miles wide. This endeavor was not pursued when the French and Indian War broke out and made settlement inadvisable until 1762. The new endeavor of 1762 resulted in a massacre of all of the settlers by the Indians. In 1769, a new group of settlers established themselves at Wilkes-Barre, but this settlement was interrupted by the first Yankee-Pennamite War. In 1772, permanent settlement began and was given a great impetus two years later when Pennsylvania gave up her effort to oust the Connecticut settlers and they were formally given the protection of Connecticut laws. By the time of the Revolution the territory was inhabited by 2,000 taxable persons. But armed conflict broke out again in 1778 when the Loyalists and Tories defeated the settlers in the Wyoming massacre. This did not deter the persistent Yankees, for settlers began again to pour into the valley within the year.

When the territory was awarded to Pennsylvania by the Trenton Commission, appointed by Congress in 1782, the second Yankee-

Pennamite War broke out and most of the Connecticut settlers were dispossessed. The determined Connecticut Yankees again were not completely dismayed, for under the leadership of John Franklin, in 1786, another abortive attempt was made to settle in the northern part of the valley. In 1787, the Philadelphia land speculators, tired of the conflict, induced the legislature to confirm titles under the Susquehannah Company in seventeen townships which were settled prior to 1782. In 1790, the Confirming Act was repealed, but the Connecticut settlers were not disturbed in their occupancy. Finally, their Connecticut titles were exchanged for Pennsylvania titles in 1803.

The Susquehannah methods of settlement proved superior to the Pennsylvania process. Superior settlement procedures made it possible for the Connecticut settlers to cross two rivers and establish a settlement against the wishes of the Pennsylvania proprietors and in spite of the Indians. The Connecticut Yankees already had almost a hundred years' experience with group settlement, which made the Susquehannah leaders think in terms of making free land available to actual settlers under fee simple ownership rather than in terms of holding control over the land by small groups of wealthy and carefully chosen insiders. The allodial land system was in sharp contrast with the semifeudal system that prevailed in Pennsylvania where quitrents were collected by the agents of the proprietors. Under the New England system, land was vested with a public interest and was defended by all inhabitants. Under the Pennsylvania system the land was the interest of the proprietors and each citizen was ready to fight only for his own land, expecting the proprietors to protect the general or public interest. In addition, the fairly modern democratic procedures of government in Connecticut exerted among the settlers a stronger cohesive force than the semi-autocratic proprietary governmental structure in Pennsylvania. Furthermore, the Connecticut scheme provided for immediate establishment of schools and churches, an advantage to any group isolated in the wilderness. In short, a significantly different atmosphere prevailed where land was distributed free to the occupiers for their own benefit than where important rights remained in the hands of the proprietors for the benefit of a favored few.

The Connecticut Yankees were frequently aided by native Pennsylvanians who appreciated the enormous advantages of their allodial land system and their distinctive institutions. Some Pennsylvanians were impressed by the fact that settlers from Connecticut owned their land completely free of any rent or service, which was quite in opposition to their own system, characterized by absentee ownership by landed proprietors, manors, and quitrents. Some Pennsylvanians were also impressed by the importation intact of the New England town organization, with free public schools, churches, and town officials elected from among the inhabitants.

The settlement endeavors of the Susquehannah Company in Pennsylvania are a good example of the intermixing of ideas, ideals, and institutions among the several colonies. The New England corporate town system had an influence upon the proprietary system of Pennsylvania, and vice versa. The blending of ideas of land tenure and government made possible the establishment of a "more perfect Union" following the Revolution.[1]

The Ohio Company

The Ohio Company, which was formally organized in 1748, was the first of the large land companies to focus attention on the land west of the mountains. Although it was not important as a land merchandising agency, it took the lead in bringing before the colonists and the mother country the importance of the western lands. Following the activities of the Ohio Company the significance of the land over the mountains never waned, and this land became a hotbed of controversy among the several colonies at the end of the Revolution.

The Ohio Company, although composed of men of affluence and influence, was originally unable to obtain a grant from the Virginia authorities. Lieutenant-Governor Gooch at first deferred the petition because other Virginians, as prominent as the Ohio group, also were interested in the western lands. Among these men was John Robinson, founder of the Greenbrier Company that had obtained a grant in 1745 of 100,000 acres along the Greenbrier River. The Ohio Company then went direct to the king with its petition and received a favorable reception. For unlike many of the land companies the Ohio Company had paved the way by including among its members a London merchant influential in court circles. When Robinson saw that the Crown was likely to act favorably upon the Ohio Company's request, he and a group of prominent Virginians formed the Loyal Company and requested a grant larger than that petitioned for by the Ohio Company. Thus, the landed gentry of Virginia were actively competing among themselves for land that lay beyond the mountains.

The Ohio Company's petition to the Crown was for a grant of 500,000 acres, of which 200,000 was to be granted at once. In March, 1749, the Board of Trade ordered Lieutenant-Governor Sir William Gooch to make a grant of 200,000 acres to the company, and to grant it another 300,000 acres if within seven years a fort had been built and 100 families had been established within the territory. On July 13, 1749, Sir William Gooch reluctantly made the grant to the com-

[1] For an excellent study of the Susquehannah Company, see *Boyd. The Susquehannah Company*.

pany as he was instructed (*Bailey. Ohio Co., 30, 31*), but the second grant never was formally confirmed by the governor of Virginia. The desired land lay in the vicinity of the forks of the Ohio and extended a considerable distance north, south, and west.

Between 1749 and 1761, the company made several unmethodical efforts to explore the territory and to locate a body of land that would be attractive to settlers. The activities of the company were completely interrupted from about 1754 to 1758 by the French and Indian War, which it had helped to precipitate. In 1761, the instructions to the governors, promulgated on the basis of Lord Egremont's policy, "put a full stop to the operations of the Ohio Company and compelled the governor and council of Virginia to refuse to renew the cession of land to the Loyal Company." (*Alvord. Miss. Valley, I, 126.*) After the Proclamation of 1763, the activities of the company were confronted with a new road block, and only intermittent efforts were made to secure the grant. But the Revolutionary War shifted the scene from England to Virginia and in 1778 the Virginia assembly was petitioned to grant land individually to each member of the company for his proportionate share of the 200,000 acres. Owing at least in part to the influence of George Mason in the Virginia assembly the petition was acted upon favorably and the land was divided among the members of the company.

As early as 1753 sentiment against large grants to individuals and companies was taking shape in Virginia. An address by Governor Gooch to the assembly, later sent to the Crown, as reported:

> . . . stressed the desirability of granting His Majesty's land beyond the mountains in small quantities free from the payment of rights and quitrents for a term of ten years. . . . It then refers to large tracts of land granted with an indulgence of several years for completing the surveys of the same and making settlements thereon whereby "the poorer people are deterred from settling themselves on any of the Lands between the said Mountains and River Mississippi for fear they should be taken in these Grants." (*Gipson. Brit. Empire, IV, 261–62.*)

A year later, July 18, 1754, the authorities in London provided for a remission of ten years of quitrent on land west of the mountains as well as a remission of 5*s*. upon each fifty acres for ten years to come, with an added provision to prevent any person from taking more than 1,000 acres in his own or any other name in trust for him.

The closely knit nature of the company and its restricted membership, about twenty members, together with its reluctance to venture money on developing Indian trade is similar to the purely proprietary companies of the previous century. It is probable that the land system which the company would have developed, if the various obstacles already mentioned had not interfered, would have resembled that of the proprietors of a century earlier.

The Transylvania Company

The Transylvania Company was sponsored by Richard Henderson of the lawyer-officeholding Hendersons of North Carolina. Like his father, Henderson held the lucrative office of sheriff and built up a large fortune.

As early as 1764, Henderson and a few associates sent Daniel Boone on an exploration trip to the western country that lay within the chartered limits of North Carolina and Virginia. They did not press toward the establishment of settlement, owing to some uncertainty as to the effect of the British Proclamation of 1763. However, by 1769 many colonists were openly flaunting the proclamation and Henderson sent Boone and Finley on their famous exploration expedition into the Kentucky wilderness. It was not until the spring of 1771 that Boone returned and reported in glowing terms on the immense possibilities of the region.

The Indians who occupied the Kentucky-Tennessee territory were hostile to anyone who appeared to be establishing a settlement on their favorite hunting ground. For a while Henderson bought them off with gifts, but the end of Lord Dunmore's War in 1774 secured peace, at least temporarily. This cessation of Indian hostilities opened the region to the land-seekers. Seemingly in anticipation of peace, Henderson assembled his group for their first recorded meeting and organized what was called the Louisa Company, which was reorganized into the Transylvania Company within a few months, on January 6, 1775. Before two months had passed, the company negotiated a treaty with the Cherokee Indians for the purchase of 20,000,000 acres of land. The conveyance was absolute, although the company had earlier discussed the advisability of securing a long-term lease from the Indians. The territory included most of the present state of Kentucky and part of northern Tennessee, and the purchase price was £10,000, or two to three cents per acre. Included in the territory were the Watauga, Brown, and Holston settlements and several miscellaneous parcels in which various private parties were interested. The Transylvania Company was apparently honest in dealing with the Indians, for some historians hold that this was one of the fairest and best-conducted Indian negotiations during the Colonial era.

In spite of this the company was denounced by Governor Martin of North Carolina as an "infamous band of land pirates" and by Lord Dunmore of Virginia. It was attacked by the whole group of Virginia land speculators whose settlement schemes were threatened by this new purchase in a territory a part of which was claimed by Virginia.

Under the influence of those in Virginia who were interested in the financial possibilities of the western land and the reaction against

Henderson's proposed form of government and land system, the Virginia House of Delegates began a series of hearings that lasted for two years and resulted, in June, 1779, in declaring void the purchase of the Transylvania Company insofar as it lay in the chartered limits of Virginia. Virginia compensated the company, however, with 200,000 acres of land lying between the Green and Cumberland rivers in the vicinity of what is now Henderson, Kentucky. This land was later sold in small parcels to actual settlers.

Following this action, Henderson moved his activities south of the Virginia line, but there he had the same experience. In 1783, North Carolina likewise declared the Transylvania purchase void insofar as it lay within the area claimed by that state. North Carolina consoled the company with another 200,000 acres, making a total of 400,000 acres of frontier land. This was ". . . a return far less than the expenditure of money which had probably been incurred." (*Livermore. Land Companies, 97.*)

The articles of agreement of the Transylvania Company indicate that the members visualized the formation of a distinctly proprietary form of government and a semifeudal land system. The settlement at Boonesborough was organized on this basis. Title to the land remained in the proprietors, quitrents were reserved, and the acts of the elected assembly were subject to proprietary veto.

The settlers resented the power reserved by the proprietors to veto legislative acts and the reservation of quitrents. They also claimed that the company was asking an exorbitant price for the land. Also, the title was none too secure in light of the North Carolina and Virginia claims, the weakness of the Cherokee claim, and the Treaty of Fort Stanwix with the Iroquois Confederation. The relation seems far from coincidental between the proposed form of government and the land tenure system and the experience of the Henderson family with the government and land system of Granville District in the northern part of North Carolina. The system of proprietary control that had succeeded a century earlier in Maryland and Pennsylvania gave way before the free land and free government fever that swept the country during the Revolution. The abortive attempt to form a government at Boonesborough in May, 1775, duplicated the same type of experiment with the same result at Watauga three years earlier. Quitrents were deferred in 1776 until 1780. Proprietary government and quitrents were not in keeping with the revolutionary spirit. The controversy over these two items would have broken the company even if it had not experienced the devastating action of Virginia and North Carolina legislatures and refusal of the Continental Congress to recognize the Transylvania government as the fourteenth colony.

The Military Adventurers

The policy of granting land to officers and soldiers who served in military campaigns already was well established long before the advent of land merchandising companies around the middle of the eighteenth century. It was not singular that the men of Connecticut who served under Generals Lyman and Putnam in the Havana Campaign of 1762 sought to increase their reward for military service by requesting land in adddition to the cash that was offered them when they enlisted. Also, it was natural for these men to choose Lyman, one of their officers, to act as spokesman for the group, and for them to make the request for land as a group rather than as individuals.

The group had ample opportunity on their return trip to discuss the matter, but their first formal meeting was not held until the middle of June, 1763. Lyman was instructed to go to London to present the request and plead for the grant. This decision was made, and he left for London, before news reached the colonies of the Proclamation of October, 1763, in which bounty land was to be offered to soldiers who served in the war that had just been successfully concluded.

Lyman continued without success over a period of about a decade his endeavor to obtain the grant. During these years there was nothing for the members of the company to do but to wait. Finally, Lyman addressed his request directly to the king, and so encouraging was the reply that he returned home confident of final confirmation. As a consequence, on November 18, 1772, a third meeting of the group was held, at which time plans were made for exploring the territory around the Yazoo junction of the Mississippi River where the land grant would be situated. The endeavor took on new life and was prosecuted with unusual vigor. The land was to be explored in detail, and a campaign waged for recruiting new members. Plans were developed for granting the land to private parties, and the system of government for the new settlement was worked out.

After favorable reports had been made by the exploring parties, and in spite of the absence of a grant from the Crown, four groups of settlers were sent to establish homes near the mouth of the Yazoo River. The problems of establishing a settlement on the banks of the Mississippi were quite different from those that these settlers had experienced in New England. Many of them, including General Lyman, died within a year or two. Interest in the endeavor subsided rapidly, and the advent of the Revolutionary War brought the activity to an abrupt end.

A quarter of a century later some of the heirs of the leaders of the company endeavored to revive their claims, but since no official record of a grant could be found in London the matter was dropped. The settlers who remained in the original settlement got titles to their land from Congress after 1800. Those who contributed financially to the company apparently received nothing. Lyman and the Company of Military Adventurers were not speculating in land for purely private gain. The membership of the company included several hundred men of ordinary means and the contribution of each person was just sufficient to obtain the grant and defray the expenses of surveying the land. This was in sharp contrast with the wealthy speculators who formed most of the other land companies.

The Mississippi Company

Another pre-Revolution land speculation company that met with failure was the Mississippi Company. It was organized on September 26, 1763. According to plans, the company was limited to fifty members, although it apparently never included more than forty names, and each member contributed equally to the expenses of securing the grant from the Crown. Each member was to receive 50,000 acres, which was to be granted to him in fee simple, and not in joint tenancy, as was the customary practice. No quitrents were to be assessed for twelve years, and the settlement was to be protected from the savages by royal troops. Although membership was large for a company from the Virginia colony, it was selective, and voting was rigidly controlled. No share could be sold without notice being given at an annual meeting and a prior offer to sell to the company.

The first petition for a grant at the junction of the Ohio and Mississippi rivers was prepared in 1763, but the request was not granted. Public policy in London was against the development of the newly acquired territory by private companies, especially companies made up of members from only one colony. Later, in December, 1768, a second petition, this time for 2,500,000 acres, was presented. The requested territory overlapped the Walpole-Wharton petition and the Ohio Company claim. Failure to receive favorable action ended the endeavor, whose leaders were losing rather than gaining influence with the Whig ministry that was in power in London and whose plans were overshadowed by the energetic Vandalia project.

The Illinois Company

The Illinois Company was formally organized under articles of agreement dated March 29, 1766. According to this agreement the shares were to be ten in number, one for each of the ten partners. The petition for a grant of land was to be for 1,200,000 acres. Each partner was to have full title to his individual share. The petition proposed that the Crown purchase the land between the Ohio and Illinois rivers from the Indians according to the long-accepted policy of quieting the Indians' claim to the land. The Crown also was to establish the proper civil government in the area. The company would undertake to colonize the area, for which effort it would receive an outright grant of 100,000 acres. Allotments to private settlers would be made in the conventional manner, with proper reservations for the clergy.

The only land that the company ever claimed was a small amount which was purchased in 1768 by Governor Wilkins from the Indians and deeded to the company. However, General Gage never confirmed this transaction. The Illinois project subsided when the Fort Stanwix agreement with the Indians was made known, and when the leaders of the endeavor became engaged in the larger Indiana and Vandalia schemes.

The Illinois-Wabash Companies

This project was the result of the consolidation of two purchases of land from the Indians. The first purchase was made at Kaskaski in the summer of 1773 by William Murray. The deed from the Indians was made in the names of the individual members of the company and in the name of the Illinois Company, which Murray represented. The second purchase was made by the Wabash Company which was organized for the purpose, among others, of securing confirmation of the first purchase.

The sequence of events was about as follows: Even before the 1773 purchase, the leaders in the English cabinet did not subscribe to the doctrine that direct purchases from the Indians made the title legal. The next year the Boston Tea Party and other colonial breaks with the mother country made matters worse. The Quebec Act followed. This stymied confirmation of the Illinois purchase, so Murray turned to Virginia for title clearance. In order to interest the Virginia authorities in a Pennsylvania transaction the Wabash Company was organized with Governor Dunmore as a leading member.

This scheme was stopped abruptly when news reached Philadelphia that fighting had broken out in New England. However, the leaders again were active within a year in their endeavor to secure confirmation of their title from an independent Virginia. The Revolution occupied first place in the minds of the Virginians and no action was taken until it was too late, when the Articles of Confederation called for the cession of all western lands claimed by the various colonies. Then the leaders turned to the Continental Congress and used the same device, adding influential names to its roster of shareholders, to secure favorable action. Various petitions were presented without success over the next decade, and as late as 1811 Congress turned down a petition from survivors of the group for some sort of compensation.

The Indiana Company

During the Indian outbreaks of 1754 a group of Pennsylvania merchants suffered large losses of goods. The *Sufferers of 1754*, as they were called, petitioned the colonial government as well as the mother country for redress in either money or land. During a similar outbreak in 1763 additional losses were sustained. The two groups of *Sufferers* were largely the same individuals. They joined together and secured a promise of a grant of land from the Indians in 1765. This agreement was carried out at Fort Stanwix in 1768 before the treaty was formally signed. The land cession involved 1,800,000 acres between the Little Kanawah and Ohio rivers.

After this land cession was consummated with the Indians, an endeavor was made to get it confirmed by the Crown. But soon after the representatives arrived in London they were easily persuaded to combine their claim with the more important Vandalia project, under which their claim would be confirmed automatically if and when the Vandalia scheme went through. It is probable that the group was not formally organized at that time. However, within a few years, by 1774, it was clear that the Vandalia project was hopeless, and it was decided to reorganize the group into the Indiana Company. This took place at Fort Pitt, September 21, 1776. The new company made plans to get their Indian deed recorded and to begin settling their land, which was offered for sale to the public.

These activities aroused Virginia to renew her efforts to protect her boundaries. The claims of the Indiana Company were denied, first by the Virginia assembly and later by the Continental Congress. Since no compensation ever was secured, the company shared the same fate as the Illinois-Wabash group. "Had the Indiana plan succeeded, a large tract of land would have accrued to the sole benefit of the profit-seeking promoters. As it was, the land was sold for the public welfare." (*Lewis. Indiana Co., 293.*)

The Vandalia Company

When the agents of the Indiana Company went to London in 1769 to present their petition for a grant of 1,800,000 acres they found it necessary to use devious means to gain favorable action from the court oligarchy. Before much progress was made they became involved in the largest land development scheme of the pre-Revolutionary era. When the modest petition of the Indiana Company was presented to Lord Hillsborough at the Board of Trade in June, 1769, he suggested the establishment of an entirely new colony west of the mountains. This would have represented a gigantic undertaking, involving millions of acres of land and requiring considerable financial backing. It was clear that various interests would have to be merged, two of the most important being the Ohio and the Indiana companies. The Vandalia Company arose out of this situation.

The proposed new colony was to include 20,000,000 acres of land and the cost of government would be borne by the promoters. The latter would involve a heavy expense since no quitrent was to be payable for twenty years. If settlement under this scheme eventually had become the fourteenth colony it would have had a royal government superimposed upon a proprietary land system.

The conditions to be laid down in the grant would have protected prior claims to the land within the area granted, and they set aside specifically 200,000 acres that had been promised the officers of Virginia by Lieutenant-Governor Robert Dinwiddie in 1754. As was customary in the original grants, all mines of gold, silver or precious stones were to be reserved to the king. (*Lewis. Indiana Co., 127–28.*) "This land was planned to be sold to settlers and speculators at £10 per hundred acres, about 50¢ per acre, with a perpetual annual land rent of a half-penny per acre in addition." (*Chandler. Land Title, 439.*) The grant specified that as much as 300 acres would be set aside in each parish for support of the Church of England.

Before these plans had time to materialize, the colony of Virginia through its House of Delegates presented a formal petition asking that Virginia's jurisdiction officially be extended over the territory under consideration. During the years that followed, Virginia continued to press her claim for jurisdiction over the territory, and it was this opposition by Virginia that brought about the delay which finally killed the project. Contributing to the difficulties developed in 1771 was the opposition of Lord Hillsborough to the scheme that he had proposed two years earlier. Also, the failure of the British law firm to issue immediately a final patent as ordered had an adverse effect. The law firm objected to the patent in that the land asked for and the area to be governed were not the same. The lawyers also objected to the joint tenancy form of the grant to the holders of the seventy-two shares. They proposed to substitute tenancy in common so that subgrants could be made without legal difficulty.

The delays held up the issuance of the patent until the Battle of Lexington turned the attention of financial and political leaders to another matter. The Vandalia project, largest of the pre-Revolution land-grabbing schemes was so completely out of the question by 1775 that the company thereafter never pressed its claim. (*Sakolski. Land Bubble, 17.*)

The Dismal Swamp Adventurers

In sharp contrast to the various schemes to acquire land in the territory that lay beyond the mountains was a project to drain and develop the Dismal Swamp region in southeastern Virginia, an area covering about 750 square miles. In 1764, the Virginia legislature granted a group of twelve men the necessary authority to proceed with operations by empowering them to trespass upon adjoining land without being liable for damages. Immediately money and slaves were made available, and within five years two drainage canals were built to connect with the main rivers. Additional land was purchased and by the time war broke out considerable progress had been made in the development of the area.

After the war, the Virginia legislature granted 40,000 acres to the group, and reclamation of the area continued to progress. Individual members disposed of their shares, but it was not until 1814 that the group was formally incorporated as a company. The activity was a financial success due to the valuable timber production, although no large part of the area ever was well enough drained to be arable.

Small Land Companies

Several smaller companies, as well as other land speculation activities existed in the quarter of a century preceding the Revolution.

Organized similarly to the Ohio Company was the Loyal Company, made up of prominent Virginians. It received a grant of 800,000 acres from the Council of Virginia on July 12, 1748; the land was located on the southwestern Virginia frontier in what is now eastern Kentucky. Unlike the Ohio Company, the Loyal Company was not required to settle any families in the territory, but was required to complete the survey within four years. By 1754, however, land had been sold to about 200 families. The French and Indian War caused the settlement activities of the company to be held up temporarily. Indian hostilities and the Proclamation of 1763 were additional handicaps.

Another of the smaller land speculating companies was the Onion River Company formed in 1773 by Ethan Allen, three brothers, and a cousin. They purchased outright about 77,000 acres of land lying in the vicinity of what is now Burlington, Vermont, from claimants who held under New Hampshire titles that were contested by New York. The venture was purely speculative – the Allens hoped for financial gain by selling it to settlers, and were aware of the dispute over the title. Within two years, about 16,000 acres had been sold, largely to settlers. Apparently the partners benefited little from the project, but the endeavors of the Allens to break the New York claim and to make good their New Hampshire titles had an important influence in the early history and the struggle for independence of the present state of Vermont.

The Burlington Company was concerned with land speculation and development only indirectly. The Burlington group was composed of eight investors, acting largely as bankers to hold various mortgages of George Croghan when he encountered financial reverses in the late 1760's. Previously he had purchased the Otsego tract, about 100,000 acres on the west side of the Susquehanna River, embracing the present city of Cooperstown, New York. After beginning to improve the land Croghan ran short of money and, unable to sell the land to actual settlers, mortgaged it. Finally, through various transactions and a sheriff's sale proceeding under a judgment of 1773, the land passed into the hands of William Cooper and Andrew Craig, the latter only a nominal owner. Cooper began developing it at once, and made a fortune from sales to settlers who came largely from New England.

Another speculative land merchandising scheme involved the Great Bend of the Tennessee River near Muscle Shoals, which at that time was claimed by Georgia and the Carolinas. The territory was purchased from the Cherokee Indians, and the Georgia legislature established Houston County as the basis of civil government in the area. By 1785, a land office was opened and warrants were issued. But settlement did not proceed rapidly, for the Indians continued to resist the encroachment of the white man, and Georgia did not maintain a stable policy regarding her western lands. In addition, the strong national land policy in that area after the passage of the Southwest Ordinance, together with the above factors, made the project fail financially. (*Driver. John Sevier, 70–73.*)

POST-REVOLUTIONARY LAND COMPANIES

The Boston Tea Party and subsequent events halted most speculative activities in the land west of the Alleghenies. Land speculators became interested in the conflict, and many of the pre-Revolutionary land companies never became active after the war. However, in the decade following the issuance of the Ordinances of 1785 and 1787 numerous land speculating companies sprang into existence. The varied activities of the pre-Revolutionary companies furnished considerable experience upon which to base post-Revolutionary operations. The controversies between the colonies over their western land claims were greatly reduced by the various agreements and cessions that resulted from the activities of bringing the colonies together in a federated union. However, settlement of Indian claims still plagued those who sponsored settlement west of the mountains, and Indian hostilities still hampered the settlers in their endeavor to build farms, to develop commerce, and to establish comunity life in the untamed wilderness.

The system of land tenure under which the post-Revolutionary land companies had to purchase land and the tenure under which it had to be distributed to actual settlers were fairly well defined before these companies began their operations. Not only were they organized too late — usually after 1787 — but they operated within the established system of tenure and did not influence the genesis of the land tenure system of the United States.

CHAPTER 18

Emergence of the National Land System

THE VARIOUS AGENCIES THAT COLONIZED AMERICA parceled out their land under a wide variety of tenures, ranging from the small fee simple holdings of New England to the large feudal estates of the middle and southern colonies. During the period of colonization adjustments in the land tenure system were being made both in England and in America. Those in England during the seventeenth century were either formalized in specific statutes or accepted as a part of the common law. Those in America during the first century of the Colonial period were either contained in the original grants to settlers or agreed upon in the separate assemblies for the several colonies. They were concerned largely with expediting settlement by persuading people to leave Europe and establish homes in America. During the next three-quarters of a century, with the settlement of the country progressing rapidly, attention was attracted by the emergence of the larger land problems that would demand solution at the time of the Revolution. Quitrents were being questioned and in many places delinquencies continued unabated; land taxes were emerging as a local problem; primogeniture and entails were losing ground rapidly; surveying and recording procedures were being improved; alienation was becoming easier as restrictions were lessened; and land was being looked upon more as a commodity to be sold for a profit and less as a family estate to be kept for posterity. Adjustments in some of these matters were accepted in common practice while others awaited specific action at the time of the War for Freedom.

COLONIAL LAND TENURE SYSTEM CHARACTERISTICS

The right of the government to levy charges upon privately occupied land for the support of public activities was well established long before the first settlers came to America. Indeed, some method of defraying the expenses of government arose at the same time that people began to function together in an organized manner, and land taxes were fairly well developed by the end of the Colonial period.

The Right to Tax

Generally the right to levy a tax on land granted to the colonists was not reserved by the king. His chief reservation was a portion of the precious metals. Taxation of land was usually in the hands of the colonial governments, chiefly a prerogative of the governing body in each colony. At first many of the local governments tried to meet the expenses of government without levying a land tax. The poll tax was the chief source of revenue with general applicability, and it was supplemented by various excise taxes. Although the people realized that the poll tax fell heavily upon those least able to pay, they were reluctant to dispense with it and substitute for it a general land tax. This was shown in the 1663 session of the Virginia assembly; the proposal was made that the poll tax should be repealed and a tax on land should be levied in its place. It was rejected. Whether this was due to ancient prejudices or apprehension over the right of suffrage is not clear, for Virginia had levied a tax on land prior to this controversy. In 1645, for example, the assembly provided that all public and county levies would be raised by equal portions on all visible estates of the colony and specified that the rate on each 100 acres of land was to be four pounds of tobacco. Rates also were levied on personal property — livestock — and the poll tax was continued.

Special levies on land were imposed from time to time as necessity demanded. In 1755 Virginia levied a special tax to meet the cost of the French War and for the protection of the settlers on the frontiers. The town of Edenton, North Carolina, levied a special tax to build and maintain the town fences, bridges, musket-house, and schoolhouse. North Carolina had a special levy for running the line between that colony and Virginia, and a tax to help provide for the poor. She also had a tax levied for the purpose of granting bounties to persons who would kill wildcats, bears, panthers, crows, and squirrels. Numerous references to other special taxes were found. Although the taxes apparently were reasonable, the people were scrupulous in removing the tax when the specific need no longer existed.

Apparently a land tax could be levied on persons who did not have title in the land. For example, in 1753, New Jersey provided that people seated on land and having no property therein were to pay taxes on as much as they pretended to hold. (*N.J. Acts, 1703–61, II, 1–18.*) On the other hand, certain lands were exempt from taxation. The levy of 1757 in Georgia specifically exempted churches and other property for divine worship or for charitable use. (*Ga. Col. Rec., XVIII, 164.*)

One of the more serious tax problems arose in Pennsylvania when the settlers insisted that the proprietary estates should bear their share of the taxes. The proprietors argued that the land was unoccupied and held only for sale, while the assembly contended that the defense of this land was necessary and costly. Finally, the colonists won out, as they usually did in such controversies. (*Ferree. Pa., 79.*)

Another characteristic was the heavier rate, usually double the normal rate, placed on the land of certain classes of individuals. In South Carolina, in 1778, a double rate was assessed against absentee landowners, with exceptions for persons under twenty-one years of age and those in the army and navy, including any who had been captured or taken prisoner. (*S.C. Stats., IV, 413–22.*) After reciting the necessity that all persons bear arms in time of war and that those who had refused to do so for conscientious motives should bear a heavier tax, North Carolina provided in 1783 that such persons refusing to take the oath of allegiance to North Carolina within six months should be taxed the double rate. (*N.C. Rec., XXIV, 492.*)

Generally the land tax system, except as a war-time measure, provided for equal assessments and levies, for appeals by the landowner if he thought his assessment too high, and for forfeiture in case of failure to pay the tax levied. Land taxes were common throughout the colonies and were levied at a very early date. The right of taxing was unquestioned, the rate could be changed from time to time, special rates could be levied for special purposes, and certain land could be exempted from taxation while other land could be taxed at double the normal rate.

The Right of Eminent Domain

The right of the government to take private property for public or quasi-public use was recognized in Colonial America. Apparently, however, few general enactments were made on the subject; each time private property had to be taken a special act of the local governing body outlined the procedure.

Most of the cases were for the taking of land for public buildings, towns, forts, water-mills, and ferry sites. An early instance of one that had general application was for storehouses in Virginia. The assembly, in 1680, provided that where it was necessary to take land for storehouses the reimbursement was to be at the rate of 10,000 pounds of tobacco for fifty acres, and that the owner would have to accept the sum and give a proper deed. (*Hening. Stats., II, 472–73.*) At a later date when land was needed upon which to erect a naval storehouse, the Virginia assembly provided that a jury should decide the value of the acre that was required. (*Ibid., IX, 235–36.*) When

Virginia became a state one of the early enactments was to provide that land needed for the purpose of building houses for the state government was to be taken and the owners were to be properly reimbursed. (*Ibid., X, 85–89.*)

Maryland by statutory enactment in 1790 provided that in case any of the proprietors within a specified district refused to sell and accept reasonable compensation for land for the use of the federal government, a commission would be appointed to set the value of the land and to conduct the transfer but could take no more than 130 acres. (*Md. Laws, 1785–92, n.p.*)

In numerous instances land was condemned for use in establishing courthouses and necessary auxiliary buildings. In Maryland, the assembly, in 1692, empowered the county commissioners to purchase land for courthouses. If the owners refused to sell, the commissioners were to have the sheriff impanel a jury to decide the value of the land and to assess such damages as they thought fit. Since this act was to expire in 1696, it was necessary that a similar provision be made for Kent County because at that time that county had not secured the land for its courthouse. (*Md. Arch., XIX, 376–77.*) North Carolina enacted a similar law in 1722, but provided that the value of the land was to be set by three persons rather than a jury. (*N.C. Rec., XXIII, 101.*) In four separate enactments, in 1705–6, 1729, 1780, and 1785, Pennsylvania made provisions for courthouses in the counties of Bucks, Lancaster, Chester, and Westmoreland, respectively. (*Pa. Stats., II, 278–79; IV, 131–34; X, 142–44; XII, 52–53.*)

The taking of privately held land upon which would be erected towns, ports, and wharves also was practiced. A general act for Virginia provided that, if landowners refused to sell, twelve men should set the value of the land and that they should take into consideration the inconvenience which might be caused the owner. (*Hening. Stats., III, 55–60.*) A Pennsylvania act provided for the establishment of public landings in southwest Philadelphia County. (*Pa. Stats., X, 512–19.*) A South Carolina enactment provided that commissioners could take a piece of land two miles square for a town and that they should value the land, allowing a generous price for it in its present state without reference to its future or increasing value. (*S.C. Stats., IV, 751–52.*) The assembly of Delaware provided that the value of the land over which the streets of Wilmington were to be laid should be determined by three impartial freeholders. (*Del. Laws, 1829, 684.*)

The North Carolina assembly, in securing additional land for a fort, provided that each and every patent or deed previously made, so far as it related to the specified 300 acres, was declared null and void and of no force or effect whatsoever, but that the absolute right and fee simple would be and remain in His Majesty forever. The value of the land, however, was to be decided by a jury of twelve men in order that those who held under color of title might be adequately reimbursed. (*N.C. Rec., XXIII, 757–58.*)

Virginia provided a procedure whereby private land could be taken by private parties for private use. If a person owned land on one side of a river and desired to build a water-mill and the owner of the land on the other side refused to sell the necessary land, then the first party could appeal to the county court to have the land valued and condemned for his use. (*Hening. Stats., II, 260–61; III, 401–2.*) In the place of an outright condemnation and conveyance by deed, Pennsylvania provided that in case any landowner on or near a proposed ferry site refused to build and to maintain a ferry, it would be lawful for any other person to have one acre of unimproved land, paying yearly to the owner as much as the county court would adjudge reasonable. (*Pa. Stats., II, 76–77.*)

The Police Power

The very vagueness of the police power makes it a difficult and technical subject. Regulations regarding fences and livestock and rules on hunting and fishing were the chief items of legislation in Colonial America that involved the exercise of this power in the field of land tenure.

Requirements Regarding Fences

At least ten of the original colonies provided by law certain regulations regarding fences.[1] In general, these laws encompassed the requirement that privately held land be fenced, specifications for a good and sufficient fence, an outline of damages to be paid to the landowner and livestock owner when the other party was responsible, restrictions against killing livestock that might break through fences, and requirements that unruly animals be confined. Some colonies, however, had special provisions that permitted local people to make their own regulations regarding fences, and a few colonies had laws indicating the responsibility of neighbors as to dividing line fences, and a few special prohibitions against burning fences.

In general, as the colonies grew older there were more statutory requirements that the landowner supply a good fence, more statutory specifications as to what constituted a good fence, and more stringent provisions whereby the damages recoverable from the owner of livestock became larger.

Requirements for a Sufficient Fence. The specifications for a "good and sufficient" fence varied widely from colony to colony and from

[1] The data were secured from the statutes and colonial records of the several colonies. They came from the following sources: For Virginia, Hening, Stats.; N.C. Rec.; S.C. Stats.; Ga. Col. Rec.; Md. Arch.; Pa. Stats.; Del. Laws; N.J. Acts; N.J. Grants and Conc.; N.Y. Col. Laws; Conn. Pub. Rec.

time to time. The specifications regarding the height of fences in the several colonies are summarized in Table 10.

Another important regulation was concerned with partition or division line fences. The general rule was to the effect that the cost of partition fences was to be borne equally by each party. In Connecticut it was provided that if one party would not build his part of the fence, three persons were to be selected to divide and set out each party's share of the fence and that this division, which would be recorded, would be final and binding on both parties.

Damages Recoverable. In case farm animals should break through a fence the owner of the animals was to pay for the damage done. Generally, the law of the several colonies provided that the actual amount of the damage, and no more, would be the sum due. Only four laws provided a different means of arriving at the amount of the damage. They were as follows: The damage would be decided by two men; it would be equal to 200 pounds of tobacco; it would be three

TABLE 10
Legal Specifications Regarding the Height of Fences

Colony	Year	Height	Colony	Year	Height
New Jersey	1730	4′6″	Virginia	1705	4′6″
Pennsylvania	1700	12′	North Carolina	1715	5′
Pennsylvania	1782	4′6″	North Carolina	1771	5′
Delaware	1700	5′	North Carolina	1777	5′
Maryland	1654	4′6″	South Carolina	1694	5′
Maryland	1699	5′	Georgia	1755	5′
Virginia	1646	4′6″	Georgia	1759	6′
Virginia	1661	4′6″			

times the value estimated; and the livestock could be impounded and sold if their owner did not show up and make a proper reimbursement.

Several states made special provision for unruly or roguish animals, particularly horses. An enactment of the Virginia assembly of 1661–62 provided that the fence law was not applicable to unruly horses, and that such horses had to be confined between July 20 and October 31. The New Jersey law provided that unruly animals had to be confined within sufficient fences or by fetters, yokes, or rings, or the owner had to pay all damages, losses of grain or fruit, damages to fence, and expense for catching, impounding, or driving home such animals.

Regulations — Hunting and Fishing

Grants by the sovereigns to those who wanted to establish colonies in America included hunting, fishing, and fowling. The colonizers transferred these rights to the settlers, generally without reservation.

Hunting on Another's Land. The first law in Virginia against hunting on another's land was enacted in 1639. It imposed a penalty of 40*s.* for hunting on land that was seated, bounded, and marked.

(Hening. Stats., I, 228.) Three years later a law provided for a penalty of 400 pounds of tobacco for hunting without permission after having been warned. One-half of the tobacco was to go to the owner and one-half to the public. *(Ibid., 248.)* Similar laws were enacted in 1657, and in 1661. *(Ibid., 437; II, 96–97.)* In 1705 a more stringent law provided for a fine of 500 pounds of tobacco, and upon the third offense the party was to be jailed in the absence of a bond of £10 for good behavior for one year. *(Ibid., III, 328.)* A similar law was enacted in 1710, and in 1738, the fine was changed to 20*s*. while a similar law was re-enacted ten years later. *(Ibid., 534–35; V, 62–63, 430.)*

North Carolina's restriction on hunting on another person's land was slightly different; that state provided a penalty of £5 for hunting without permission on any person's land except neighbors whose lands were adjacent. *(N.C. Rec., XXIII, 113.)*

A general rule apparently existed that a person could hunt on vacant land without restraint or penalty. This was permissible although the bounds might have been laid out and marked. The Virginia legislature of 1657 made this rule explicit by statutory action. *(Hening. Stats., I, 437.)*

The laws against hunting were relaxed to the extent that a person could pursue deer shot on his own land, regardless of where the wounded animal ran. Virginia enacted statutes to this effect in 1639, in 1657, and in 1661. *(Ibid., 228, 437; II, 96–97.)* A Virginia statute of 1705, however, provided that such permission would be granted only to a person with as many as six slaves. *(Ibid., III, 328.)*

Hunting on the Sabbath. As early as 1642 the Virginia legislature enacted a statute which provided that any freeman found shooting on the Sabbath would be fined 20 pounds of tobacco, unless such shooting was necessary to protect the land or as defense against the Indians. It also provided that the master was to punish his servant for such an offense or forfeit 20 pounds of tobacco. *(Ibid., I, 261.)*

The Right Of Escheat

According to English law, escheat generally was possible under two situations, failure of heirs and attainder of blood. Of course, if land was left vacant and not claimed by anyone, it reverted to the Crown. In Colonial America, however, escheat also included failure to conform to the conditions of the grant and forfeiture by suicide. *(Gould. Land System Md., 28.)* The important conditions in the grants included failure to plant and seat, to permit the land to be vacated, and nonpayment of either quitrent or the purchase price.

Colonial laws and custom regarding escheat were even more vague than those on most other subjects, and their administration was more difficult because of the vagueness of the law and the drastic nature of the action. Regardless of the looseness of the regulations and administration, escheats must have returned a relatively large revenue, judging from the numerous regrants of escheated land shown in the warrant books at the land offices.

Planting and Seating

One of the most important reasons that land escheated in Colonial days was the failure to meet the specifications for seating and planting as outlined in the patent obtained by the settler. Although specific instructions regarding the use of the land were issued occasionally, it is doubtful if much land was forfeited to the government for failure to use it in the manner outlined. Colonial land records, however, are full of instances of forfeiture for nonseating. The necessity of escheat for not taking up the grant seemed obvious, both as it might refer to grants to colonizing agencies, and to patents to planters and settlers. Escheat for nonseating was much more prevalent in the middle and southern colonies than in New England. Georgia was a possible exception, particularly in the early days, owing to the fairly strict adherence to the family farm pattern and to the less obvious opportunity for speculation.

Vacated Land

Closely related to escheat for failure to seat and plant was forfeiture where the owner or heirs could not be found and the land lay vacant. In the case of failure to plant, the owner quite frequently was resident, either on the land or nearby, and even if he were an absentee, usually he could be located. Frequently, however, it was impossible to locate the rightful owner of the land; he might have moved off and left the land vacant, disclaiming any rights in it, or have died intestate and his heirs could not be located. This happened frequently owing to poor methods of communication and faulty colonial records.

Aliens

A general rule providing that land held by aliens would escheat to the colony was in force in at least one place, Virginia. As early as 1660 an act of the legislature established this rule. (*Va. State Papers, I, 3.*) That aliens could hold land only under certain conditions is obvious from the content of the numerous confiscation acts.

Quitrent and Taxes

After forfeiture for failure properly to plant and seat, the next most important reason that land escheated to the colonies was for failure to meet certain fixed levies — quitrent and taxes. The problem of collecting quitrents was insoluble, although numerous regulations were imposed and various collection devices were tried with the ever-present threat of forfeiture for failure to conform. As participation of local people in government became more influential the importance of quitrent declined, and as utilization of taxes became more prevalent delinquency became more common for quitrent than for taxes. Probably a major contributing cause was the fact that the quitrent was levied on the land by the colonizing agency with the settler frequently getting little or no return. On the other hand, land taxes were usually levied by the people acting through their duly elected representatives, and they were levied for specific purposes that would benefit local inhabitants.

A somewhat unimportant reason for escheat was failure to pay the purchase price for land that was acquired under special warrants and certificates. In Maryland, for example, purchasers were given two years to pay the debt thus acquired. (*Md. Arch., XXVIII, 341.*)

THE RIGHT TO ALIENATE BY SALE

Certain restrictions on the sale of land by the grantees were imposed in several of the colonies, but generally the conditions of the grant did not substantially reduce complete freedom of alienation. Probably the colonies in New England had more numerous and more stringent regulations against sale than those in other areas. The colony other than New England with the most rigid rules against alienation was Georgia. The rule against alienation, however, was relaxed in Georgia within a few years, and within about two decades it was completely lifted. Other colonies had minor rules that either restricted alienation for a few years, as in Pennsylvania, or placed a penalty upon alienation, as in Maryland.

Probably the first instances of the sale of rights in the lands of America was the selling of shares in the Virginia Company. Shares in this company were transferred freely from one private party to another, both in England and in America. The earliest record in America, and only by implication, was in 1626 when the Virginia Company required that all transfers be brought before the court and properly recognized and recorded. (*Tyler's Quart., III, 253–55.*)

North Carolina enacted in 1715 two restrictive laws on alienation. The first one provided that no one should sell or alienate his right to land unless he had paid the purchase price and had obtained a patent and grant. (*N.C. Rec., XXIII, 42–44.*) The other law was enacted for the purpose of prohibiting alienation by sale until the grantee had been an inhabitant of the province for at least two years. (*Ibid., 1.*)

The most frequently mentioned item regarding alienation was concerned with debt. Numerous acts were concerned chiefly with making it easier for the land to be utilized in satisfying encumbrances, whether they were mortgage debts or personal obligations. A typical example of the former was an enactment by the 1705–6 session of the Pennsylvania assembly, which provided that in case of default the mortgagor could be summoned to appear before the magistrates of the county to show whether there was any reason why the mortgaged premises should not be sold for payment of the debt. If he made satisfactory explanation the land would not be sold; otherwise, it would be subject to seizure and taken in execution for payment. (*Pa. Stats., II, 244–49.*) A typical example of the latter was an enactment of the North Carolina assembly of 1764, which provided that the land of any person who had contracted debts, and who did not have sufficient personal effects to satisfy the debts, would be sold to the highest bidder after having been advertised. The act also provided that the sheriff could convey the property to the purchaser. (*N.C. Rec., XXIII, 636–39.*)

Regulations concerned with the sale of land by minors, married women, executors, administrators, corporate bodies, and persons holding less than fee simple absolute estates also were numerous. Frequently, special acts of the assemblies were passed to cover particular cases. For example, in 1744, the Virginia legislature gave John Belfield special permission to sell certain lands specified in the statute in spite of his infancy. (*Hening. Stats., V, 285.*)

Apparently certain bodies could not dispose of property except by special permission. For example, as late as 1789, the South Carolina assembly passed an act to empower the vestry and church wardens of the Episcopal Church of Claremont in the Parish of St. Marks to dispose of 150 acres of land and purchase more convenient property. (*S.C. Acts, 12.*) The colonial laws are replete with similar illustrations.

INHERITANCE IN COLONIAL AMERICA

The rules governing the disposition of an estate of one who died without a will are vague and sketchy. Although many of the colonies followed the general rules of the common law, some important exceptions existed in Connecticut. For example, not only was primogeniture nullified by custom, for the colonists disapproved of it, but in a 1639 law the general court provided that intestate estates should be divided between the wife, children, and kindred as in equity it would be deemed just. Later, in 1699, a statute gave children equal shares, except that a double portion was given the eldest son. The king and council declared the statute null and void in the Winthrop case, but the colonists disregarded the decision. Later, in 1745, after some discussion, Parliament sustained the 1699 law, since it was within regulations laid down in the Connecticut charter.

The Connecticut colonists felt that if common law descent were followed in the colony and the eldest son took all, the uncultivated land would remain unsubdued, for the younger sons would go to some other colony or turn to some other way of life. (*Conn. Hist. Soc. Coll., IV, 187–90; Davis. N. Eng. States, I, 448–49.*)

The influence of religion must have been powerful in the Massachusetts pronouncement of 1641. The statute may be paraphrased as follows: Inheritances are to descend naturally to the next of kin, according to the law of nature, delivered by God. Observe, however, if a man have more than one son, then a double portion would be assigned to the eldest son unless his own demerits deprived him of the dignity of his birthright. (*Mass. Hist. Soc. Coll., 1st. Ser., V, 178–80.*)

Succession

The major rules of intestate descent commonly accepted in England may be briefly summarized as follows: inheritances lineally descended but never ascended, males were preferred to females, the eldest son was preferred to younger sons, whole blood was preferred to half blood, grandchildren could inherit by representation, females inherited equally, and collateral heirs of the first purchaser were preferred.

Lineal Descent. Although most American states have discarded the old feudal rule that inheritances descend and never ascend, colonial statutes apparently did not deal with this adjustment until late in the period. For example, it was not until 1786 that New York provided by statute that if a person should die without lawful issue leaving a father, then the inheritance would go to the father of the deceased in fee simple unless the inheritance came to the person from his mother, in which case it would descend as if the person had survived the father. (*N.Y. State Laws, I, 245–47.*)

Equal Devolution. The process of attaining equal inheritance for all children is concerned with two rules of descent – the preference of males over females and of the eldest son over younger sons. Both of these vestiges of feudal descent were wiped away, in some jurisdictions, before the Constitution. For example, in 1786 New York provided that property descended in direct line of lineal descent equally to all of equal degree of consanguinity. (*Ibid., 245–47.*) Earlier, however, she had provided that sons should have a double portion, and in the same statute had taken another step toward equal devolution by providing that if any ancestor should have given any part of his real estate to any of his issue and its value equalled that claimable under the law of descent, then said issue should have no more; if, however, it should have been less valuable, then he should be given enough more to make up his legal share. As early as 1700 Pennsylvania provided for devolution to all the children, except if the first born should be a son he would receive a double portion. (*Pa. Stats., II, 31–34.*) It appears that there was a tendency to dethrone male heirs, first, by providing that they would receive only two portions to one portion for females; and second, by providing that the eldest son should have only a double portion.

Whole Blood Preference to Half Blood. The colonies also made inroads on the rule of the whole blood, and generally provided equal devolution. For example, New York in 1786 provided that the half blood should share equally with the whole blood unless the inheritance came from an ancestor in which case those not of the blood of such ancestor would be excluded from the inheritance. (*N.Y. State Laws, I, 245–47.*) In 1785, Georgia provided that half blood and whole blood should inherit alike. (*Ga. Col. Rec., XIX, pt. 2, 455–58.*)

Representation. The idea that a child represented the father in regard to succession was so completely accepted that apparently few of the colonies saw fit to cover this aspect by legislative action. At least two states, South Carolina and New York, thought it necessary to mention the matter. By statute both of these states provided that if a child died in the lifetime of the father or mother and left issue, the issue would share as the child would have shared had he survived his parents. (*S.C. Acts, 20–26; N.Y. State Laws, II, 71–76.*) The innumerable instances of wills under which the children were to share equally furnished a good background for the equal sharing of the estate by all the children.

Dower. New York provided that a widow would have a dower, and that she could remain in the chief house for forty days during which time her dower would be assigned, and that it would be one-third of the estate of her husband during coverture, unless she was endowed with less before marriage. (*N.Y. Col. Laws, I, 111–16; N.Y. State Laws, II, 4–6.*) If there were no children, the widow was to receive one-half instead of one-third. (*N.Y. State Laws, loc. cit.*) This was true in Virginia (*Hening. Stats., III, 372*), except that later it was provided that a widow should have at least a child's part which might be less than one-third in the case of large families. (*Ibid., V, 444–48.*) Dower interests, however, were barred in Virginia in case a woman left her husband; (*Ibid., XII, 162–65*) this rule probably was followed in most of the colonies. South Carolina gave the widow one-third of the property (*S.C. Stats., IV, 742–43*); the same was true in Maryland (*Md. Arch., I, 60–61, 157*), and in New England. (*N. Plymouth Rec., XI, 188; N.H. Doc. and Rec., III, 196–97.*) Maryland later provided that the widow should have one-third after all debts were paid. (*Md. Arch., XIII, 430–37.*) Although the enactments do not consistently include references to the debtors of the deceased having first claim on the estate, it appears that this practice was followed.

In South Carolina if a wife had made jointure with her husband, that is, made a settlement to take place of her dower interest, then she would not be allowed to claim a dower. (*S.C. Stats., III, 302–3.*) A law on the same subject in Virginia provided that if the jointure were made before marriage and during the infancy of the wife or if it were made after marriage, then in either case the widow could elect to waive such jointure and demand her dower. (*Hening. Stats., XII, 162–65.*) A similar rule was in force in New York. (*N.Y. State Laws, II, 4–6.*)

On the other hand, it was provided that a husband could not

defeat the dower of his wife through any type of alienation during coverture, except with her permission. To this end, in 1664, New Jersey provided that no estate of a feme covert could be conveyed except that she be secretly examined to determine that she freely desired to convey such estate. (*N.Y. Col. Laws, I, 111–16.*) A similar law was in effect in North Carolina (*N.C. Rec., XXIII, 35*), in South Carolina (*James. Laws of S.C., 80*), in Georgia (*Ga. Col. Rec., XVIII, 417–20*), in Delaware (*Del. Laws, I, 397–98*), in New Jersey (*N.J. Grants and Conc., 371*), in Virginia (*Hening. Stats., II, 317*), and presumably in the other colonies.

Pennsylvania, however, did not follow consistently this widely accepted rule, for it was provided at one time in that state that the dower of a wife was not recoverable in any lands sold by her husband during coverture regardless of the wife's relation to the alienation. (*Pa. Arch., 1st. Ser., I, 155.*)

In at least one instance it was realized that the law of descent which provided that the wife of an intestate was to receive one-third of the estate was unjust at times, for in 1780 an act of the North Carolina assembly granted all of the property of the intestate to his widow, it being found that the property was acquired through marriage with his widow. (*N.C. Rec., XXIV, 332–33.*)

Although the common law concept of dower has undergone some change nearly everywhere in the United States, it appears that the colonies generally followed the old law and that no significant adjustments were made.

Wills. Wills as a means of conveying land were apparently in common use from the beginning in all the colonies except Georgia. That wills were used frequently at an early date was attested to by their recordation in the courthouse and other files maintained in the colonies and by the many statutes enacted by the colonial assemblies governing their execution. Nearly fifty such statutes had been passed before the time of the Revolution.

An oral will was not valid in South Carolina if for more than £10 unless proved by three witnesses requested to do so by the testator. (*S.C. Stats., III, 341–42.*) A similar rule was in force in Pennsylvania (*Pa. Stats., II, 48–49, 194–98*), in Delaware (*Del. Laws, II, 18*), in New York (£30) (*N.Y. State Laws, II, 93–98*), and in other states.

In South Carolina, if a will contained no provision for a child born after the testator's death, the child was to share equally with other children. (*James. Laws of S.C., 444.*) Furthermore, if a person made a will and later married and died leaving a child, the will was to have no effect. Similar rules were in force in other colonies.

A will in writing was revocable in New York only by some later will or codicil in writing or by the testator destroying the same himself. (*N.Y. State Laws, II, 93–98.*) The same was true in other states.

It was generally provided throughout the colonies that married women, persons under twenty-one years of age, idiots, and persons of unsound mind should not be deemed capable of making wills, and that wills made by them should be declared null and void. Such an enactment was passed in South Carolina in 1712, (*S.C. Stats., II, 551*) and re-enacted in 1731. (*Ibid., III, 341–43.*) This was true in Pennsylvania of oral wills (*Pa. Stats., II, 48–49*), while in New York there was a provision similar to the one for South Carolina. (*N.Y. State Laws, II, 93–98.*)

In 1744, Virginia provided that where a will devised away land that would have descended to the heir or heirs by law, then such heir or heirs could come into court and contest the validity of the will. (*Hening. Stats., V, 231–32.*) The same rule was followed in other colonies. Pennsylvania provided that a will or deed made by any person who purchased land within the province and who died without becoming naturalized would be valid. (*Pa. Stats., V, 443–45.*) New York and other states had general provisions to the same effect. (*N.Y. Col. Laws, I, 858–63.*)

The Barring of Entails

An instructive aspect of land tenure development of Colonial America was the constant drive against the influence of large landholders to maintain estates in the same families through entail. One example of the process by which this was done can be found in Georgia, although she was not a colony of large landowners. The trustees of Georgia were to distribute the land in small units to be held in tail male. The colonists hardly had arrived in America before it was recommended that the tenure should be changed to permit the husband of a daughter, for example, in the absence of male issue, to inherit the land if he would go on it and establish a home. The avowed objective of granting estates in tail male would not be adversely affected if such were done, it was reasoned. (*Ga. Col. Rec., I, 164.*) A few years later the recommendation was made that tail male be dispensed with entirely, but that those who inherited should be under obligation either to occupy and cultivate the land or to forfeit it. (*Ibid., XXI, pt. 2, 75.*)

One scheme for practically nullifying estates in tail male was to permit the possessor to name a male successor who would hold in tail male with the privilege of naming a male successor in failure of male issue. Since the male successor could be a son-in-law, at least one daughter could inherit indirectly. (*Ibid., I, 345–46.*)

The controversy continued, for in December, 1738, a petition was signed by 121 male inhabitants asking that the land be held in fee simple instead of fee tail. In the petition it was argued that such a change would cause a great number of new settlers to come to Georgia, and would likewise encourage those who remained to make further improvements to their property. (*Ibid., III, 422–26.*) Even the trustees were not free of the desire to dispense with tail male estates. They desired that daughters as well as sons might inherit and that the widow's dower might be restored. Thus, they resolved that this would be the policy. (*Ibid., 378–79.*)

In September, 1739, less than a decade after the charter was granted, they had indicated that on failure of male issue the grantee's daughters would inherit, and in case of no issue the land could be devised by the grantee or it would descend to the heirs-at-law. There was a proviso that prevented the recipient from holding more than 500 acres. It was further provided that the widow could occupy the dwelling house and garden and have one part of the estate. (*Ibid., 397.*) In 1740 the trustees reiterated their position by providing that the daughter of a grantee or any other person by devise or inheritance could enjoy any quantity of land not to exceed 2,000 acres. At the same time they made it possible for grantees to lease their land. Thus, within a decade estates in tail male became estates in fee simple and the rule against alienation by leasing was removed. (*Ibid., 400.*)

Georgia was not the only colony that struggled with the problem of entails. As early as 1705, Virginia provided that no person should bar an estate in fee tail by fine and recovery or by any method whatsoever except by an act of the assembly, despite all laws, customs, and usages to the contrary. (*Hening. Stats., III, 320.*) This law probably was designed to prevent the establishment in Virginia of the fine and recovery procedure for barring entails, and little thought was given to its effect on fee simple conditional estates. It probably was reasoned that the assembly could pass upon all essential cases without their becoming a burden. That this procedure was followed is attested to by many acts of the assembly that converted estates in fee tail to estates in fee simple. But Virginia soon found this procedure too expensive for holders of small parcels of land. So, in 1734, that colony provided that any parcel of land held in fee tail and of less value than £200 could be transferred in fee simple and that all interests of the grantor in remainder or reversion would be barred. (*Ibid., IV, 400.*)

North Carolina went through the same steps as Virginia by providing first that estates in fee tail could be barred by acts of the assembly and later by permitting small estates in fee tail to be barred by action of the possessor and the local court. (*N. C. Rec., XXIII, 315–16.*) New York permitted the barring of estates in fee tail under special circumstances by legislative action, for example, the selling of such an estate to pay a debt of over £4,000. (*N. Y. Col. Laws, IV, 97–100.*) As early as 1731, South Carolina enacted a law which provided that all wills creating estates in fee tail were invalid. (*S.C. Stats., III, 341–42.*)

RESERVATIONS OF QUITRENT

In all of the colonies except those in New England, and there in certain cases, a quitrent was reserved by the settlement agencies. The rents varied from colony to colony and in some colonies from time to time.

The First Quitrent

When the London Company granted land in Virginia in 1618, a quitrent of 12*d.* was reserved on each fifty acres granted. (*Va. Mag. of Hist., II, 161, 165.*) Prior to 1635, Lord Baltimore reserved a quitrent of ten pounds of wheat on each 100 acres. (*Md. Arch., III, 47, 48.*) At first the rate in the Carolinas was 2*s.* for 100 acres (*N.C. Rec., I, 51, 60–61*), while Georgia at a much later date reserved 4*s.* on each 100 acres. (*Ga. Col. Rec., I, 18–19.*) Soon after Berkeley and Carteret received their grant for the territory included in the present state of New Jersey, they reserved a quitrent of a penny or a halfpenny an acre, according to the value of the land. (*N.J. Arch., 1st. Ser., I, 41.*) When the Duke of York took over New York he waived the feudal dues on the land settled under the Dutch regime and required that quitrent be levied at 2*s.* 6*d.* on each 100 acres. (*N.Y. Col. Laws, I, 81.*) In Pennsylvania the first grants reserved 1*d.* an acre on rented land and 1*s.* on 100 acres of land that was purchased. These terms were not strictly adhered to, for many patents were for one-half penny an acre. (*Pa. Arch., 2nd. Ser., XIX, 47, 192.*)

Changes in Rate

Quitrent rates were changed frequently and significantly throughout the Colonial era. For example, after 1635 the rate in Maryland changed from ten pounds of wheat to 1*s.* for 50 acres, and this rate was reaffirmed in 1641. (*Md. Arch., III, 47–48, 99.*) In 1658 the rate was increased twofold to 4*s.* for 100 acres, while in 1669 to encourage settlement on the Eastern Shore 1*s.* for 50 acres was offered. (*Ibid., 458–59; V, 63–64.*) From 1717 to 1733 quitrent in Maryland was suspended. When quitrents were renewed in 1733 the rate on new grants was placed at 10*s.* on each 100 acres (*Ibid., XXVIII, 45–46.*), but five years later the rate of 4*s.* on 100 acres was restored, and remained until the Revolution. (*Gould. Land System Md., 56–57.*) In an unusual provision Maryland provided that papists were to pay double what the other settlers paid. (*Md. Arch., III, 507–8.*)

Efforts were made many times by the king to increase the original quitrent in North Carolina from 2*s.* for 100 acres to 4*s.* (*N. C. Rec., III, 78.*), and many grants were issued at this rate although the assembly never accepted the higher rate. The settlers along the Virginia border were permitted by the *Grand Deed of Albemarle* to hold their land for the same quitrent as the settlers in nearby Virginia. (*Ibid., I, 175–76.*) In 1735 Governor Johnson revoked this deed and levied a rate of a penny and a half an acre. (*Ibid., IV, 42–43, 110–14.*) In 1718 the South Carolina assembly declared that for the next fifteen years the quitrent on new grants was to be 12*d.* for 100 acres. (*S. C. Stats., III,*

44–49.) After 1731 the assembly finally passed a quitrent act which permitted distraint if rents were not paid promptly. (*Ibid., 289–304.*)

In order to provide for the support of the colonial administration the trustees of Georgia increased the original rate of 4*s.* to 20*s.* on each 100 acres. (*Ga. Col. Rec., III, 412.*) Occasionally on large estates the quitrent was reduced to 10*s.* on 100 acres. (*Bond. Quit-Rent System, 127.*) This high quitrent was one of the economic causes that interfered with the rapid development of the colony. Finally in 1742 the trustees, with the consent of the board of trade, reduced the quitrent to 2*s.* on 100 acres. (*Ga. Col. Rec., I, 406–7.*) No record appears to indicate that this act was either confirmed by the Crown or put into effect. As no particular effort was made by the trustees to collect the quitrent in Georgia, no trouble or disturbance resulted in that colony. The Crown in 1755 set the rate at 2*s.* on 100 acres. (*Jones. Ga., I, 487.*)

When New Jersey was divided, the Quakers, who controlled West Jersey, made quitrent optional with each proprietary. In most deeds there was a nominal quitrent or token of fealty, such as two capons or the like. (*N.J. Arch., 1st. Ser., XXI, 447–541.*) This situation finally brought about the virtual abandonment of the whole system in that division. After Carteret became the sole proprietor of East Jersey, he reserved a quitrent of a halfpenny an acre. (*N.J. Grants and Conc., 59.*) The twenty-four proprietors who purchased East Jersey in 1682 offered grants with quitrent at 2*d.* an acre, or, if a purchase price had been paid, 6*d.* for 100 acres. (*N.J. Arch., 1st. Ser., I, 493.*)

Although the Duke of York, in New York and New Jersey, reserved 2*s.* 6*d.* on each 100 acres, in most grants the quitrent clause was indefinite. Instructions to the governor directed that he, with the aid of the council, was to determine the quitrent in each case. (*N.Y. Col. Laws, I, 81; N.Y. Col. Hist., III, 216–17, 331–34.*) At the beginning of the royal period the first rate was one bushel of wheat for each 100 acres, and when specie became more plentiful the usual quitrent was 4*s.* of current money, equivalent to 2*s.* 6*d.* in sterling. (*Bond. Quit-Rent System, 255.*) This remained the rate in New York until 1774 when the rate for new grants was fixed at a halfpenny an acre. (*N.Y. Col. Hist., VIII, 412.*)

In 1719 quitrent was raised in Pennsylvania on purchased land from 1*s.* to 2*s.* for 100 acres, in 1732 it was increased to a halfpenny an acre, and in 1765 to 1*d.* an acre. (*Shepherd. Prop. Gov. in Pa., 34, 35.*)

In addition to the quitrent reserved by various settlement agencies, many individual proprietors with large holdings in the various colonies reserved quitrent on the land they leased or granted. Such individual proprietors as Sir Ferdinando Gorges in Maine and John Mason in New Hampshire included quitrent in their grants. Gorges proposed a quitrent of 6*d.* an acre as a feature for settlement in his holdings in Maine (*Williamson. Me., I, 282*), and in 1637 he actually made a lease for 2,000 years, reserving a quitrent of 2*s.* on 100 acres. The quitrent system of Gorges vanished with the collapse of his government. The sale of Gorges' claim in Maine to the Massachusetts colony in 1678 ended quitrent in that region. (*Bond. Quit-Rent System, 52.*)

Although Mason announced that he would reserve a quitrent upon his lands, he seems not to have carried out that policy. Robert Mason, his son, in 1679 placed a quitrent of 6*d.* on the yearly value of all improvements and cultivated lands and for vacant lands the rate varied. (*Thorpe. Charters, IV, 2450–51.*) He was unsuccessful in collecting the levy, and this ended quitrent in New Hampshire.

The inhabitants of Carteret's part of North Carolina claimed their land under the *Grand Deed of Albemarle* which provided for the same rate of quitrent that Virginia used. (*N.C. Rec., I, 175–76.*) Carteret, however, authorized his agents to reserve either 3*s.* sterling or 4*s.* proclamation money on each 100 acres. (*Coulter. Granville Dist., 40.*) It was impossible to collect this rate, for, among other things, many inhabitants claimed and held land for which they had no patent.

Periods Free from Quitrent

The time that the quitrent was to begin varied from colony to colony. In Virginia the payment was not to begin until seven years after the grant, which for the first division of the land would have been in 1625. (*Va. Co. Rec., III, 108.*) This was still in practice in 1643. (*Hening. Stats., I, 280.*) Quitrent in Maryland started as soon as the grant was made, (*Kilty. Land. Ass't., 29–31*) whereas in the Carolinas time for the beginning of the payment was indefinite. If the grantee was able to pay the rent immediately, it was to begin at that time; if he was unable, the time could be extended for three, four, or even five years. (*N.C. Rec., I, 51.*) Such indefiniteness existed throughout the Colonial period and was responsible to a marked degree for the unsuccessful quitrent system.

Georgia reserved quitrent but permitted what was apparently the maximum period before it was to start; the colonists were allowed ten years before they had to make their first payment. (*Ga. Col. Rec., I, 19.*) This was done to enable those seeking a new start to attain it before having to pay for the use of land.

In New Jersey the quitrent payments were to start March 1, 1670. (*N.J. Arch., 1st. Ser., I, 41.*) This was five years after the Concessions, under which land was to be taken up, were issued by Berkeley and Carteret.

Quitrent in New York was payable from the time the patent was granted with only a few exceptions. In 1760 quitrent was waived for ten years for the settlers on the land around Lake Champlain and on the land of the soldiers who fought in the French and Indian War. (*G.B. Acts of Privy Coun., Col. Ser., IV, 459.*)

Payment in Kind

When the first division of land was made in Virginia the payments for the quitrent were to be made in valuable agricultural articles. (*Va. Col. Rec., 16.*) By 1645 the valuable agricultural article was tobacco. (*Hening. Stats., I, 316.*) When the planting of tobacco was prohibited in 1660, other agricultural products were added to the list. (*Ibid., II, 233.*) When the growing of tobacco was resumed, it again became the principal product for payment. Current money or tobacco was accepted in 1720 (*Ibid., IV, 79*), but in 1755 the officials for the Crown were obliged to accept paper money. (*Va. Mag. of Hist., XI, 348.*) Wheat first was used in Maryland in the paying of quitrent and then "the commodities of the country" were used. (*Md. Arch., III, 47–48.*)

Several mediums of payment were used in North Carolina. At first the quitrent was paid in "lawful English Money." (*N.C. Rec., I, 237–38, 335–36.*) The assembly in 1715 permitted payments to be made in commodities. The list of acceptable articles was similar to those of Virginia and Maryland. Time after time, however, demands were made that the payments be in sterling, proclamation money, or specie instead of commodities. (*Ibid., IV, 110, 237.*)

In both New Jersey and New York a peppercorn, a lamb, a barrel of fish, or a capon was reserved as the payment of the quitrent instead of money. (*Bond. Quit-Rent System, 111.*) Penn at first requested that quitrent be paid in silver (*Ibid., 136*), but in 1705 wheat was accepted. (*Pa. Stats., II, 223–28.*)

Penalties for Nonpayment

A penalty for the nonpayment of quitrent was common to all the colonies. The Virginia assembly in 1647 declared that delinquents were to have their lands entered by the treasurer's receivers, and if they still refused to pay, they were to have their cases heard either at the county court or before the governor and council. (*Hening. Stats., I, 351.*)

Maryland enacted a still more drastic law. It provided that all owners of large tracts who had not paid their quitrents would have to forfeit their lands unless the arrears were paid within a year and in the future land would be forfeited if the quitrent was left unpaid for three years. (*Md. Arch., III, 95.*)

Before the end of the seventeenth century North Carolina passed a law which declared that if land had been held for six years or more without the payment of quitrent and the patentee refused to pay the collectors, distress would be levied. (*N.C. Hist. and Gen. Reg., III, 78, 144.*) This act was renewed in 1735 and again in 1749 and remained the basis for collection throughout the Colonial period. (*N.C. Rec., XXIII, 333; XXV, 215–19.*)

As early as 1695 the proprietors declared that, in the section of Carolina which later became South Carolina, distress on goods and chattels could be made on the owners of land on which quitrent was due. If there was not personal property sufficient to satisfy the claim then the land could be sold in proportion sufficient to cover the amount due. (*S.C. Stats., II, 96–102.*) About 1731 and again in 1744 South Carolina passed quitrent acts; they provided that land on which quitrent was due and remained unpaid for five years would revert to the Crown. (*Ibid., III, 295, 633–37.*)

In Georgia land was forfeited if the quitrent remained unpaid for six months. (*Ga. Col. Rec., III, 412.*) During the time the twenty-four proprietors had control of East Jersey, distress was ordered on all grants where quitrent was not paid within ten days after it became due. Apparently this was not rigidly enforced as many settlers were in arrears when the Crown took over the government of the colony. In 1742, 1762, and 1768 New York passed laws which permitted the sheriffs to sell the land of patentees who refused to pay their quitrent. (*N.Y. Col. Laws, III, 209–22; IV, 589–90, 1036–38.*) A law passed in 1705 provided that if the quitrents were not paid the collectors were empowered to levy distress after six months' notice. In case there was not sufficient personal property to pay the rent, land could be sold. (*Pa. Stats., II, 223–28; IV, 322–26.*)

Effectiveness of Quitrent

It is estimated that income from quitrent in Virginia should have been around £950 in 1665 (*Va. Mag. of Hist., III, 42–47*), but no indication was found that this amount was collected. In 1684 Auditor-General William Blathwayt came to America and helped to convert Virginia's quitrent system from one under which very little income had been derived to a system which became an important source of revenue by establishing an effective means of collection. (*Bond. Quit-Rent System, 224.*) Governor Spotswood reported that for each of the years 1714 and 1715 the amount of quitrent collected was over £3,000. (*Spotswood Letters, II, 181.*) The net returns from 1720 to 1730 varied from £3,500 to £4,000 annually. By 1739 the amount totaled £4,749 and by 1771 the collection had almost doubled – the amount was £7,839. The amount collected in Virginia was enough to pay the Crown's expenses in that colony after 1720 and to add large sums to the royal exchequer in London.

Bond has stated that between 1731 and 1745 about £22,500 was sent from Virginia to London, and in 1775 as much as £7,420 was sent. (*Ibid.*, *248–49*.)

The complete rent rolls kept in Maryland aided greatly in the collection of the quitrent. In 1745 the net returns from quitrent were about £4,500, while ten years later the net returns approximated £5,100, and the year before Maryland became a state they were £8,500.

The lack of an adequate rent roll in North Carolina hindered the collection of quitrent in that colony. In 1735 only £1,200 was collected, and this was spoken of by the colonial authorities as an excellent return. (*N.C. Rec.*, *IV, 8–9, 15, 24–25*.) By 1761 hardly a sixth of the rent roll was collected. (*Ibid.*, *VI, 618–19*.) South Carolina in 1740 collected about £1,500, only about half of what was due. From July, 1729, to March, 1732, the amount collected was a little over £389, while from March, 1739, to March, 1740, the amount collected was £1,584. By 1770 approximately three-fourths of the quitrent due was being collected. (*Bond. Quit-Rent System, 330, 346*.) Apparently no attempt was made by either the trustees or the Crown to collect quitrent in Georgia. Bond has stated that in 1767 the unpaid quitrent in Georgia was equal to £2,081. (*Ibid.*, *350, 353*.)

Under both the proprietors and the Crown the quitrent system in New Jersey was ineffective. During the early years of New York little attention was paid to the collection of quitrent, and such was the case when the Crown took over the colony in 1684. (*N.Y. Col. Hist.*, *IV, 419*.) Prior to the coming of Governor Hunter in 1710 it was found that some people had not paid their rent for many years. Under his direction the collection was pushed vigorously and large sums of arrearages were paid as the patentees feared court action. (*Ibid.*, *V, 357–58, 368–71, 499*.) This improvement was only temporary. The Crown's attorney-general in 1713 decided that the grants with customary quitrent should be paid in full but arrearages could not be collected for the lack of a definite rate. (*Ibid.*, *179–80*.) In 1762 a law was passed which allowed the sheriff to sell the land of those who refused to pay their rent. This law lasted throughout the remainder of the Colonial period. (*N.Y. Col. Laws, III, 1107–21; IV, 589–90*.) From 1700 to 1720 the annual collection was between £75 and £300. In 1761 it was about £800 and by 1767 the estimated rent roll had increased to £1,806, and the arrears were estimated over £18,888. (*Bond. Quit-Rent System, 278*.) Thus, the quitrent system in New York was virtually a failure.

By 1776 it was reported that the annual value of quitrent in Pennsylvania was over £10,200, but only about one-third of the amount due was collected. It was estimated that from 1700 to 1779 the value of quitrent in that colony was about £182,248, but only about £63,679 was collected (*Ibid., 161*). The quitrent system in Pennsylvania could scarcely be considered a success.

After Independence

An act passed in 1776 by the assembly transferred from the Crown, without its consent, to the Commonwealth of Virginia the right to reserve quitrents (*Hening. Stats., IX, 127–28*), and in 1779 the quitrent charges on land were abolished. (*Ibid., X, 64–65.*) The payment of quitrent in Maryland ceased with the outbreak of the Revolution, and in 1780 an act of the legislature presumably abolished the payment of quitrent in that state. (*Md. Laws Since 1763, n.p.*) The assembly of Pennsylvania abolished its quitrents in 1779. (*Pa. Laws, II, 481.*) After the outbreak of the Revolution, North Carolina asserted in her Declaration of Rights, and later incorporated in her state constitution, the principle that the property in the soil belonged to the people and all suits for quitrent were dismissed; this brought quitrent in North Carolina to an end. (*N.C. Rec., XXIII, 977–79.*)

With the outbreak of the Revolution, quitrent in South Carolina, Georgia, New Jersey, and New York was allowed to lapse. The resolutions and constitutions passed after independence did not mention quitrent. (*Bond. Quit-Rent System, 107, 284, 349, 353.*) So these states seemed to have allowed quitrent to die instead of abolishing it. The unimportance of quitrent in these colonies probably was the cause of their attitude. They did not regard quitrent sufficiently important to require an act abolishing it.

RECORDING TRANSFERS OF LAND RIGHTS

Each colony had its own system of granting patents, recording deeds, mortgages, and wills, and surveying the land. In certain colonies the keeping of these records was started early, while in others many years elapsed before an attempt was made to keep records of conveyances in land and then it was hard to get an accurate record of the early transactions. In some colonies where the records were started early, they were rather complete while in others the records were fragmentary.

Requirement for Recordation

From an early date, Virginia maintained a register of patents. The Virginia Company kept a complete record, beginning with the division of land in 1619, and following the transition of Virginia into a royal province the grants were confirmed in England and sent to the colony where they were entered in patent books as they were received.[2]

[2] These books are now in the Land Office at Richmond, Virginia.

The instructions given to Governor Yeardley were that all the grants were to be registered. The Orders and Constitutions of 1620 provided that the names of all the adventurers who received land were to be placed in one book. In case any of these shares were transferred from one person to another, this transfer was to be recorded in another book.[3] At first, all deeds were to be recorded in James City within a year and a day after they were made; later, however, provision was made for recordings to be entered at Charles City and Elizabeth City. In 1634 the counties were formed, and later transfers were recorded in the county where the land was located. (*Tyler's Quart., III, 253–55; Va. Mag. of Hist., XXVI, 242.*)

Although in the early days all patents for land in Virginia had to be confirmed by the Crown, this had been changed by 1705 and grants were made by the governor and council. (*Hening. Stats., I, 552.*) Trouble had been experienced in getting such patents recorded. The land act of that year directed that all such patents were to be entered on the records of the secretary's office. (*Ibid., III, 307–8.*) This same act further stated that title to land could not pass from one person to another unless it was made in writing, indented, sealed, and recorded in the records of the general court of the colony or in the records of the county court of the county in which the land was situated. At the time the instrument transferring the land was recorded, the livery of seisen, in like manner, had to be acknowledged and proved. The recording was to take place within eight months if the party lived in the colony, and within two years if he resided in another colony or country. (*Ibid., 321–22.*) These provisions were repeated in the act of 1710 for settling titles and bounds (*Ibid., 517–21*), in a similar act in 1734 (*Ibid., IV, 397–402*), and again in 1748. (*Ibid., V, 408–12.*)

During the Revolutionary War many records were destroyed. The Virginia assembly in 1781 decreed that where deeds, wills, judgments, or court orders had been destroyed by the enemy they could again be issued and recorded. (*Ibid., X, 453–54.*) After Virginia became a state, a law was passed which stated that all conveyances were to be made in writing and recorded within eight months in the county where the property in question was located. If the party was out of the state, the acknowledgment could be made in the town or county where the person resided and delivered to the proper county court within eighteen months. (*Ibid., XII, 154, 155.*)

As early as 1665 the Carolinas required that all deeds for land were to be registered in the office of the registrar, whose duty it was to record grants from the proprietors to the grantees as well as those from one private party to another. (*N.C. Rec., I, 791.*) In 1715 North Carolina provided that no bills of sale and deeds for land were good and valid

[3] This regulation was not always carried out as the transfer from individual to individual was sometimes recorded in the book which contained the record of the original grants.

in law unless registered within twelve months after the date of the deed, by the public registrar of the precinct where the land lay. Deeds made by persons living out of the colony were valid if they were acknowledged before the chief justice, or in a precinct court, and recorded in the precinct in the colony where the land was situated. (*Ibid., XXIII, 49–52.*) This was a part of the instructions sent to Governor Johnson in 1740 by the Crown. North Carolina, like Virginia, provided that any deed, grant, or patent lost during the war was to be recorded again upon order of such from the governor and council. (*Ibid., XXIV, 966–67.*)

South Carolina, in 1694, passed an act for "... the better and more certain keeping and preserving of the old Registers and Publique Writings ..." but the contents of the act are not available. (*S.C. Stats., II, 78.*) Four years later a law was passed which provided that the sale or mortgage on a piece of land that was registered first would be adjudged the first or prior sale or mortgage. (*Ibid., 137–38.*) In 1731 another law was passed which provided that all grants and deeds, after being duly proved before the justice of the peace, were to be recorded in the registrar's office. (*Ibid., III, 303.*) All deeds had to be made in writing, signed, sealed, and recorded in the office of the registrar of the district where the land lay. All deeds had to be registered within six months if the party was a resident of the colony and within twenty-four months if he lived out of the province. (*Ibid., 290–92.*) After South Carolina became a state, a law was passed which allowed only three months for a deed to be registered if the person lived in the state, and twelve months for those living out of the state. A person neglecting or refusing to register his deed would have it declared fraudulent. (*Ibid., IV, 656–57.*)

The recording of grants, conveyances, liens, and settlements was provided for in the charter granted to the trustees of Georgia. (*Lucas. Charters, 120.*) The office of registrar was established in 1735 (*Ga. Col. Rec., VII, 414*), and it served the colony during the time that Georgia was under the supervision of the trustees. After Georgia became a royal province in 1755, an act was passed which provided that all conveyances, mortgages of land and Negroes, and wills made before the passing of the act had to be registered within three months, except those executed in England which had to be registered within a year and a day. (*Ibid., XVIII, 77–80.*) A year later another act was passed which stated that all petitioners for grants had to take them out within seven months and register them within another six months. (*Ibid., VII, 337.*) In 1768 a law required that deeds made by persons residing in the province were to be registered within six months, by those residing in another colony within nine months, and by those residing in England within twelve months. (*Ibid., XIX, pt. 1, 96–99.*) This continued throughout the Colonial period and was confirmed by the legislature of the state of Georgia in 1785. (*Ibid., pt. 2, 459–64.*)

Maryland, in the first few years of settlement, had no legally established system of transferring land. It was usually done by writing the transfer either on the back of the patent, or on a separate sheet of paper which was given to the buyer, or by placing him in possession of the land by livery of seisin. (*Kilty. Land. Ass't., 36.*) But this procedure did not meet the Maryland requirements and in 1638 the assembly passed an act which provided that the registrar of every court keep a book of records in which all grants, conveyances, titles, and successions to land would be entered by those desiring that such entries be made. (*Md. Arch., I, 61–62.*) This act placed the recording of all conveyances of land on a voluntary basis, and was in effect until 1663.

The 1663 act provided that anyone who, by either purchase or inheritance, had held, possessed, or occupied land in fee simple without disturbance was to hold the same thereafter. In the future no estate was to pass from one person to another except by deed. The deed had to be written, indented, sealed, and enrolled in the court of the province in the county or counties in which the land was situated. (*Ibid., 487–88.*) This act did not prove effective, so in 1671 another act provided that, after September 29, 1671, no manor, land, tenement, or hereditament could pass from one person to another except the deed be made in writing, indented, and sealed and acknowledged in the provincial court of the county, or before the justices of the peace in the same county where the land lay. (*Ibid., II, 305–8.*) In 1785 Maryland declared valid all deeds which had been enrolled, and provided that all new deeds should be registered in the future. (*Md. Laws, 1785–92, n.p.*) Maryland's records have been preserved well and can be seen at Annapolis.

In order to prevent frauds and suits within the province, Pennsylvania provided on May 5, 1682, that all charters, gifts, grants, deeds, and conveyances of land (except leases for a year or under) were to be enrolled or registered within six months or else the transfer would be void. (*Pa. Arch., 4th Ser., I, 40.*) In 1700, however, it was provided that no deed or other writing would be declared void because it was not recorded. (*Pa. Stats., II, 21.*) Five years later an act provided that all deeds were to be recorded within six months after they were made. All old deeds not acknowledged and recorded within five years would be declared void. Any deed made out of the colony was to be recorded within six months after the arrival of the person or ship bringing it to the colony. (*Ibid., 206–12.*) This same law was re-enacted in 1710 (*Ibid., 349–55*), and again in 1713. (*Pa. Arch., 1st Ser., I, 158.*) A similar act, involving most of the principles of the last-named act, was passed in 1774. (*Pa. Stats., VIII, 412–16.*) In 1782 it was provided that any deed made between 1776 and 1778 and recorded before the end of six months would be valid. (*Ibid., XI, 166–68.*)

By an ordinance of 1638 all legal instruments in New Netherland were declared invalid unless written by the provincial secretary. The secretary kept a general register in which he recorded, usually in chronological order, the legal instruments presented to him. These included deeds, leases, other agreements, and mortgages. Patents were issued by the director-general in his name and that of the council and were signed by the director and the provincial secretary. (*N.Y. Hist. Soc. Coll., XLIV, 68–69.*) By 1683 a change eased this requirement somewhat. It provided that all grants, deeds, mortgages, and other conveyances would be valid if recorded within six months in the register of the county where the land lay. (*N. Y. Col. Laws, III, 141–42.*) [4]

In the concessions and agreements, sent to New Jersey in 1665 by Berkeley and Carteret, a provision was made for recording conveyances. The books in which the records were to be entered would be kept by the chief secretary of the colony. Grants for land from the proprietors to the planters and all deeds and leases made from planter to planter were to be recorded in this book. (*N. J. Grants and Conc., 12–13.*) After the division of New Jersey into two colonies, East Jersey provided in 1698 that all records were to be kept at Perth Amboy; all grants, patents, and deeds were to be kept by the registrar and were to be recorded within six months after being made. (*Ibid., 369–70.*) West Jersey, as early as 1683, required all persons holding grants, patents, and deeds to clear their rights to the land they held and have such recorded or their titles were to be void. (*Ibid., 478.*) In 1695 West Jersey provided that deeds or other conveyances for land were to be recorded with the clerk of the county where the land lay. The recording was to be done within six months if the person lived in the colony and within two years if he lived beyond the area. A fine of 20*s*. was imposed on each deed not recorded. (*Ibid., 541–42.*) After New Jersey became a royal province the assembly passed an act which provided that all deeds and conveyances were to be recorded in the county in which the land lay. (*N.J. Acts, 235–39.*) In 1782 New Jersey provided that any person who had lost his deed could, with proper proof, have another deed issued to him. (*N.J. Laws, 54–56.*)

In the New England colonies the keeping of records at first was left to each town. The settlers of Plymouth in 1620 were given a plat of the land, but there were no actual recordings until 1627. (*Tyler's Quart., III, 253–55.*) It was not until seven years later that Massachusetts passed her first act requiring general registration of deeds and grants. (*Mass. Bay Rec., I, 116.*) In 1650 a second Massachusetts law provided that any deed made and recorded by the recorder of the town was sufficient security and guaranty to the purchaser.

[4] The patent and deed books for New York have been preserved and are in Albany, N.Y.

(*Ibid., IV, pt. 1, 22.*) New Hampshire had a general law regarding recordation. No bargain, sale, grant, or conveyance made for any land or house was to be valid unless the same had been acknowledged before a court and recorded within a month. (*N. H. Doc. and Rec., I, 584.*) The records in New Hampshire, like those in Massachusetts, were kept by the towns.

The General Court of New England authorized the first three towns in Connecticut (Hartford, Windsor, and Wethersfield) to keep a record of their disposals. (*Conn. Pub. Rec., I, 36–37.*) Connecticut soon realized that the great defects found in the records of conveyances of rights in land and houses were due to the lack of a specific law regulating such. So, in 1667, a law was passed which required the possessors of lands and houses, within a space of twelve months, to enter their property on the record books of the town where the land and house lay. (*Ibid., II, 67.*) Rhode Island, like the other New England colonies, left the recording to the individual towns. (*R. I. Rec., I, 28, 177.*)

All colonies experienced some difficulty in getting the livery of seisin and deeds recorded within the time specified. Numerous acts were passed to improve the situation and gradual improvement was observed as the country became settled. The enactments generally were concerned with specifying the place where land records would be kept, how soon after the transfer the instrument had to be recorded, and making it possible to attest to a transfer in a jurisdiction aside from the one in which the land was situated.[5]

Signatures of Married Women

In Colonial America all transfers of titles to land generally were made by both husband and wife. Usually the wife was first examined privately by a responsible official to determine that the transfer was completely voluntary on her part.[6]

Recordation of Mortgages

Mortgages as well as deeds had to be recorded. In 1639 Virginia provided that a mortgage made without delivery of possession was adjudged fraudulent unless it was entered in some court. (*Hening. Stats., I, 227.*) Then, in 1642, an act provided that mortgages made after January, 1639, had to be registered in the quarterly or monthly

---

[5] Hening. Stats., III, 519, 523, 524; *Ibid.,* IV, 397; *Ibid.,* V, 409; *Ibid.,* VIII, 199–200; N. C. Rec., XXIII, 185–86; *Ibid.,* 432–34; Ga. Col. Rec., VII, 762; *Ibid.,* IX, 90; *Ibid.,* XIX, pt. 2, 459–64; Md. Arch., XXVI, 262–66; N.J. Grants and Conc., 246–47.

[6] Hening. Stats., III, 518; *Ibid.,* IV, 401–2; *Ibid.,* V, 410–11; N. C. Rec., XXIII, 358–60; S. C. Stats., II, 583–88; *Ibid.,* III, 302–3; Ga. Col. Rec., XVIII, 417–20; *Ibid.,* XIX, pt. 2, 459–64; Md. Arch., II, 307–8; *Ibid.,* 391; *Ibid.,* XIII, 473–75; Pa. Stats., II, 210; Del. Laws, 1827, 295–96; N.Y. State Laws, I, xi–xii; *Ibid.,* II, 266; N.J. Acts, 235.

courts in order to be valid. (*Ibid., 248–49.*) In 1657 another act required that mortgages had to be registered within six months and such conveyances, together with acknowledgments, would not be valid until four months after acknowledgment. (*Ibid., 472–73.*) Georgia likewise required that mortgages be registered (*Ga. Col. Rec., XVIII, 533–36; XIX, pt. 1, 96–99*), and so did North and South Carolina. (*S. C. Acts, 36.*) Any mortgage on real or personal property in Pennsylvania had to be recorded. (*Pa. Stats., II, 210, 353.*)

Director-General Kieft of New Netherland required that mortgages be registered in that colony. In 1753 a law was passed which required that all mortgages made after June 1, 1754, had to be registered. In case there were two mortgages, the first mortgage registered would be deemed the prior one. (*N.Y. State Laws, I, App., vi–vii.*) This law was re-enacted in 1774 (*Ibid., App., ix–xi*), and also in 1788 after New York became a state. (*Ibid., II, 266–69.*) New Jersey had a law regulating the recording of mortgages similar to the one New York passed in 1753. (*N.J. Acts, 1765, 270–72.*) Mortgages had to be registered to be valid in the New England colonies, but like the recording of deeds, registering was left to the individual towns.

Recordation of Wills

Provision was made for the recording of wills in Virginia in 1626. It required that, as soon as possible after the death of the owner, an inventory would be taken of his estate and goods, and the will and testament would be proved as soon as possible, but the proving could not be deferred beyond the meeting of the next quarter-court. (*Tyler's Quart., III, 253–55.*) The act stated that failure to have the will proved had many times in the past been of great inconvenience. Thus, it was concluded that the proving of wills had been used in the past but not with sufficient regularity. So this act required, as in England, that the proof of the wills be accompanied by recordation. (*Hening. Stats., III, 318–19.*)

North Carolina laws of 1762 and 1773 provided that all wills should remain in the clerk's office among the records of the respective counties. (*N. C. Rec., VI, 701; XXIII, 886–87.*) A similar law in New York provided that the original will should remain as a record in the probate office (*N.Y. State Laws, I, 152–54*), and Rhode Island provided that wills should be kept among the records of the recorder. (*R. I. Rec., I, 188–90.*) Pennsylvania likewise provided that all wills were to be recorded. (*Pa. Stats., IX, 259–65.*)

SURVEY INACCURACIES AND DIFFICULTIES

In each colony the land was laid out by the surveyor and his deputies. His principal duties were to survey the land for which warrants were issued, to draw up plats of land for granting, to keep a record of the surveys, and to mark the bounds of each patent surveyed.[7]

The warrants when issued to the patentees usually were for a definite number of acres, and in some instances the number was followed by the phrase "more or less." The surveyors, however, were supposed to lay out the number of acres called for in the warrant. The surveyors, especially the early ones, did not always survey to the patentee the correct number of acres. Many plats were drawn without the use of surveying instruments, and frequently the surveyors did not even go on the land. They gave the description by some natural bounds and were sure to allow a sufficient quantity of land so their measurements would not be questioned by the settlers and so the person for whom they surveyed might enjoy a larger tract of land than for which he was to pay quitrent. (*Hartwell. Pres. State of Va., 15.*) In 1705 Virginia provided that if it appeared that a person possessed more land than his patent called for, and if a new survey revealed that to be true, it was lawful for the proprietor to sue for a new patent for this land under the regulations used in getting the first patent. (*Hening. Stats., III, 313.*) In North Carolina when a survey was made and surplus land was found in the patent the owner had a right to take the land on a new patent or to leave out the surplus in such parts or places as he pleased. (*N.C. Rec., XXIII, 35–36.*)

It was not until 1733 that the proprietor of Maryland took a definite step to get control of the surplus land. In that year he instructed the judge of the land office to have the attorney-general make void any patent containing more than ten per cent over the number of acres called for in the patent. A new patent was to be issued, in the place of the annulled one, for the correct number of acres and the surplusage was to be granted to anyone applying for it. (*Kilty. Land. Ass't., 233.*) This order apparently did not prove successful.

New Jersey provided that in case of a surplus of land in a grant, the possessor had the liberty to purchase the same at the current rate. If the possessor did not wish to make the purchase, four men were appointed to make an inventory of the improvements and adjudge the value of the surplus or set aside the surplus where it would do the least injury to the possessor. (*N. J. Grants and Conc., 521.*)

Penn found that there were discrepancies in the surveys made in Pennsylvania, and to remedy the situation a law provided that the proprietor's surveyors might, within two years after a grant had been made, resurvey any person's land. After allowing four acres in every 100, over or under, for the difference of surveys and six acres in every 100 for roads, barrens, uneven ground and such, if there should be found more land than the amount for which the tract had been originally laid out, the proprietor was to have all such surplus land if the

---

[7] Brown. Genesis, II, 778–79; Ga. Col. Rec., IX, 270–72, 273–76; Kilty. Land. Ass't., 64–66, 248; Md. Arch., V, 94–96, 477; N. J. Grants and Conc., 53, 389, 629; Pa. Col. Rec., I, 26.

possessor refused to buy it. The proprietor had to make good any deficiencies found in the resurvey. No surveyor was allowed, under heavy penalty, to enter upon any person's land to make a resurvey without due notice to the owner. Should a surveyor willfully or negligently survey in favor of the owner he was to pay the proprietor double the compensation for the damage done. (*Keith. Chron. of Pa., I, 84–85; Pa. Stats., II, 118–23.*)

The bounds laid out for early Virginia patentees were often incorrect and caused later disputes. As early as 1623-24, Virginia was forced to enact a law which provided that when a difference of opinion as to boundaries existed between neighbors the disputed parts were to be submitted to a more perfect survey and if the results were unsatisfactory the final decision was to be left to the governor and council. (*Hening. Stats., I, 125, 173.*) Conditions were so bad that Virginia required the people in every neighborhood, once every four years, to assemble at a designated spot and from that point march in a body to examine and if necessary renew the terminal marks of every plantation boundary in that precinct. (*Ibid., II, 101–2; III, 325, 530.*) In case of dispute two surveyors were to be appointed to run the line. (*Ibid., II, 102.*)

The North Carolina council, at a meeting held in 1718, declared that the surveyors of the province had laid out land which was sometimes prejudicial to the people or to the proprietors. (*N. C. Rec., II, 323–24.*) A few years later it was ordered that all bounds were to be processioned every three years, and if any person's land had been processioned twice with the bounds found to be in accordance with the original grant, that person was adjudged the sole owner of the patent. (*Ibid., XXIII, 103, 105.*)

In 1718 Maryland claimed that when the colony was first settled the Indians were so numerous and barbarous that the surveyors were deterred from making a strict scrutiny of the rivers, creeks, and bays and thus were prevented from setting out true and exact bounds in the patents issued. Therefore, nine persons in each county who were best skilled in the art of surveying were to set the bounds of the land of all who made application for such to be done. (*Md. Arch., XXXVI, 517–24.*)

LEASING IN COLONIAL AMERICA

That there has been tenancy in America since the beginning of Colonial times is attested to by numerous records. In early Virginia, for example, the Virginia Company reserved certain land for itself and some for schools and churches. This land was to be cultivated by "tenants" who were to be assisted by laborers. An examination of the record of the company for 1619 reveals that 100 boys were sent to be apprentices or laborers for these tenants. In the same year 611 persons were sent as planters to establish farms of their own. Thus, it would appear that freeholders were coming or being sent in larger numbers than "tenants." (*Va. Co. Rec., III, 115–16.*)

Although Gray (*Gray. South. Agr., I, 314–15*) and others deal with these tenant-settlers as if they were tenants as the term is used today, the evidence does not seem to support such a conclusion. The relation existing in the early Virginia situation was clearly not one of landlord and tenant, and was hardly one of employer and employee. It was somewhat of a hybrid. Tenant-settlers were more like share-croppers than tenants of the present time. In the first place they were "furnished," or transported to America at the company's expense, and they were supplied food and clothing and tools and livestock, very much in the same manner as is customary under present share-cropper arrangements. Secondly, they were supervised in their daily work, as is the present practice. When the year's work was over the crops were sold through or to the company, and the furnish and supervision continued for the new year. It is incidental that the present share-cropper theoretically receives a share of the crop, for this is frequently nullified in the marketing and accounting process.

There were other examples of share-cropping in Colonial days. For example, "In the Virginia back country, settled largely by Irish and Germans, there were many white hirelings employed as croppers. They furnished nothing but their labor, eating with their employers and receiving a share of the crop." (*Ibid., 406; Va. Mag. of Hist., II, 274.*)

Evidence exists to show that leasing was introduced early and increased rapidly as the colonies became more closely settled. Although by the time of the Revolution leasing was quite common in many areas, it was not prevalent in some areas owing to the abundance of relatively free land. For example, as late as 1785 it was said that there were no tenants in Caroline County, Virginia, even though landowners wanted tenants to operate their farms; in 1726 there was practically no tenancy in North Carolina (*N. C. Rec., II, 633*), and leasing was prohibited in Georgia in the early days without special license from the trustees.

Leasing arrangements were most heterogeneous, being designed to fit the economic conditions existing at the paticular time and place. For example, Washington leased 240 acres and furnished slaves and livestock, together with money for the construction of certain buildings and for the purchase of tools and clothing for the slaves and for incidental charges. The tenant agreed to buy half interest in the slaves and livestock and to pay half the cost of the buildings and incidental operating expenses. At the end of ten years there was to be an equal division of slaves, stock, and equipment. The practice of leasing slaves with the land was quite common in the areas where the use of slaves was prevalent. Both cash and share rentals were common.

The conditions that made leasing both possible and advisable in Colonial America may be summarized as follows: Those wishing to establish patroonships, manors, and large plantations were willing to lease on reasonable terms and were forced to lease in order to get their land brought into cultivation. Many settlers came to America without money with which to buy land and as a consequence were forced to rent. Others wanted to locate near friends or blood-relations. Compact settlement was advisable as a protection against the Indians, and many settlers rented parts of large tracts owned by absentees. Many landowners held more land than they could cultivate without the help of tenants. Some holders of entailed estates could not divide them into family-sized units, but could rent parts of them out to tenants. The policy of immigration employed during the later years of the Virginia Company was an important influence in establishing the relation of landowner and share-cropper. Land engrossment had an influence, particularly in South Carolina. The desire to get good cleared land to cultivate made renting, even with its disabilities, preferable to carving a farm in fee simple absolute out of the virgin wilderness.

Although some leasing doubtless existed in each of the colonies, it was most prevalent in those areas where the proprietors tried to establish large manorial estates. Maryland, with numerous large manors reserved for Lord Baltimore, and New York, with its patroon system, particularly in the Hudson River valley, are good examples. In recording impressions of the country and people the Reverend Mr. Taylor makes the following comments regarding the tenure situation at the settlement of Western, New York, where he stopped on August 11, 1791:

> It is incredible how thick this part of the world is settled . . . . The land in the farms is more excellent . . . crops are rich. The same evil operates here, however, as in many parts of the country — the lands are most of them leased. This must necessarily operate to debase the minds and destroy the enterprise of the settlers — although rent is small — only 19 an acre; yet if men do not possess the right of soil, they never will nor can feel independent. And what is as great an evil, they will always be under the influence of their landlords.

In a letter over a month later, September 17, he commented on the tenancy situation around Lyden in about the same words. (*N.Y. Doc. Hist., III, 1136–48.*)

Term

Leases in the Colonial period were frequently quite different in length of term from those generally used today in the United States. The better tenants, those who approached the status of overseers, usually held informally under oral agreements for short periods, frequently from year to year; the less substantial tenants held under contracts for longer periods. The most prevalent leases were for five, seven, fourteen, and twenty-one years, and usually were written. Leases for twenty-one years probably were most common. On some of the larger estates, leases for a life or lives were used frequently, the most common term being for three lives. (*Kilty. Land. Ass't., 221.*)

There were two reasons for long-term leases. The lessor who often dealt with many tenants did not want to be troubled with changing them frequently, and the lessee, who often had to develop the land, desired a term sufficiently long to obtain recompense for improvements put upon another's land. (*Gould. Land System Md., 68.*)

Leases for ninety-nine years were not unknown. For example, instructions to Baltimore's overseers permitted them to lease all of the land on the Susquehanna River for terms as long as ninety-nine years. (*Md. Arch., XLII, 648.*) In Georgia, instructions to the trustees indicated a preference for short-term leases. Permission was granted in 1740 for all persons in possession of land in the colony to make leases for any part of their lots for a term not to exceed three years. (*Ga. Col. Rec., III, 400.*) North Carolina probably influenced the settlers to use annual leases by providing that a lease for a term longer than one year was to be registered. (*N. C. Rec., I, 79.*)

Possession

At least two states – South Carolina and New York – enacted statutes to govern the then prevalent practice of holding-over. These statutes are unique and their wording indicates that the situation during Colonial times was not unlike present conditions. Both provided that if tenants should hold-over after they were notified to vacate, they should pay double rent. (*S. C. Stats., II, 572–80; N. Y. State Laws, II, 233–41.*)

Improvements

No statute or reference to a legislative enactment can be found that mentions the subject of repairs and improvements on rented farms, except those which required that estates of orphans should be properly maintained. Leasing arrangements in the colonies included such items, but generally they were more concerned with adding improvements to the rented property than with the distribution of rights and responsibilities regarding improvements between landlords and tenants.

Waste

Practically every colony, in its regulations governing the handling of orphans' estates, provided that if the premises were leased there should be a provision preventing waste of the property of orphans and that special attention would be accorded the cutting of any timber except that used on the land. To prevent the wasting of orphans' estates it was a practice to have the land viewed to fix a valuation of rent expected of the guardian, and to limit the amount of land that might be cleared for cultivation. Quite frequently provisions were made that only timber needed to maintain the farm could be cut. In addition to provisions of this type in leases, some colonies had rules against waste. For example, New York provided that if a tenant removed or destroyed any timber that might be used for ship building or fencing, other than what was necessary in clearing, he would be assessed a fine equal to the value of the timber plus £3. (*N.Y. Col. Laws, II, 206–14.*)

Another type of waste of which tenants were guilty was excessive cropping, especially in tobacco growing. The first few crops of tobacco were the heaviest and afterward the land was worthless until it had been fallow for a few years. Also, during the last few years of their lease, tenants would plant so much tobacco that the land was left impoverished. To prevent this Governor Sharpe proposed that a clause be put in each lease limiting the number of acres that might be planted to tobacco during the last three years of the lease. (*Gould. Land System Md., 70.*) As early as 1754 Secretary Calvert complained that impoverishment of the soil and waste of timber by farm tenants were the chief causes for lands of the proprietor to go untenanted.

Rental

It is difficult, if not impossible, to assess the level of rent during Colonial days. The records are scarce and many give little or no indication of the total area of the farms, the amount of improved land, or its general state of cultivation. It appears, however, that the existence of a vast unsettled territory, the persistent campaign to get settlers on the land, and the sparse population must have operated to keep rent within reasonable bounds.

Records of renting parcels of land on Long Island for 200, 350, and 500 guilders are found but no data were given as to extent of the area. (*N. Y. Col. Hist., XIV, 164, 242, 294.*) Information for Maryland indicates a gradual increase in rentals from 10*s.*, to 20*s.*, to £3, and then to £5 per 100 acres. (*Md. Arch., VI, 71, 294.*)

Making improvements in lieu of rent must have been followed extensively since much of the land in certain areas was rented from the very beginning and the settler was in the best position to erect the buildings.

Distress

Judging from regulations concerning the collection of rent, colonial landlords must have experienced as much trouble in collecting the sums due them as the colonial proprietors experienced in collecting their quitrent. Statutes on the subject could not be found in all of the colonies, but New York, Virginia, and South Carolina gave the landlord a ready statutory remedy in his collection problems.

As early as 1709 South Carolina enacted a statute (*S. C. Stats., II, 547–48*) which provided that after May 1, 1710, no tenant could remove goods from the land unless all sums due the landlord for rent had been paid, provided the amount was equal to no more than one year's rent. If the lessee should remove such goods, it was provided that the lessor within five days could seize and sell whatever could be found, but apparently he could not follow the goods and take them from third parties. These regulations covered leases for life or lives in addition to the conventional lease for a term.

Since holding-over was commonly practiced and since the lessor previously could not distrain for rent due after the termination of the tenancy, it was provided that, in such cases of holding-over, the landlord could distrain for rent in the same manner as if the lease had not ended. The distress had to be made, however, within six months after the end of the lease and during the landlord's title and the tenant's possession.

This act apparently did not solve the landlord's rent collecting problem, for in 1738 a far more stringent law was passed. It was along the general plan of the earlier law but permitted the landlord to seize the goods at any time within thirty days instead of five days. He could also follow the goods into the hands of third parties. If the tenant should fraudulently remove such goods or if any person knowingly should aid in such fraudulent conveyance, the landlord could collect double the amount of the rent due. In addition, he could break in and seize the goods if they were locked up. If the tenant were leasing for an indeterminate period and the landlord died before the end of the lease year, his executors could recover rent for the part of the year that the lessor lived. (*Ibid.*, *572–80.*)

In New York a similar statute was enacted in 1788. The New York statute, however, was not as stringent. It merely provided for ordinary distress and in addition specified that if a landlord had reason to believe that his tenant was going to remove goods without paying rent, then the landlord could secure an attachment against the goods and chattels of the tenant and proceed to sell them and return to the tenant any surplus. The statute applied to tenants for life and lives as well as to tenants for a fixed term. (*N. Y. State Laws, II, 233–41.*)

CHAPTER 19

Some Forces That Influenced the Evolving Land System

ONE OF THE MOST POWERFUL PHILOSOPHICAL yet practical ideas that developed during the Colonial era was the concept of equality. It had a pronounced influence upon the land system that emerged about the time of the formation of the Union.

When making adjustment in the tenure system and when laying out the democratic form of government, a majority of the founding fathers did not bother to think through and work out a finely spun theory about equality. They knew that the word represented an understandable cause. The 1776 reforming revolutionists needed a banner, a catch word or phrase, to help rally the unorganized nation behind a cause. The men of affairs knew from practical experience that a whole line of reasoning, a complete philosophical conclusion, must be presented to the masses in a single word or phrase. The word *equality* expressed a whole group of practical ideas, meaning different things to different persons. It was a cause around which fighters could rally and a thought-idea with which men of letters could toy.

As an idea around which revolutionary military force might be rallied, the term *equality* was used by many to mean that the Americans were equal to the British – that they were not second-class citizens and, as a consequence, would not tolerate a second-class position, politically, economically, or otherwise. Since they could not attain civil equality within the framework of the mother government, the implication was that they would seek it outside of the commonwealth. In addition, the word meant to the colonial revolutionist (1) that all men ought to be equal before the law, (2) that all men ought to have equal access to the ballot, and (3) that all men ought to have equal opportunity in the world. The first meaning took on concrete form in these words in the fourteenth amendment to the Constitution: ". . . nor deny to any persons within its [any state] jurisdiction the equal protection of the laws." The second meaning has not been attained for all citizens in all states, and is a subject before the present Congress of the United States. The latter is an ideal upon which slow progress has been made over the years.

Equality seemed to be a rather flexible term in the Revolutionary period and during the formation of the various state governments. The idea was not a fixed thing – its meaning was varied, and the concept changed with time and place. In the Declaration of Independence: ". . . all men are created equal. . . ." In New Hampshire's 1784 constitution: "All men are born equally free and independent. . . ." In the Connecticut and first Kentucky constitutions: ". . . all men, when they form a social compact, are equal. . . ." And when necessity seemed to demand it, Alabama, Arkansas, Florida, and the 1799 Kentucky constitutions stretched the idea to accommodate both human slavery and human equality: ". . . all free men, when they form a social compact, are equal. . . ."

The Aristotelian concept of equality was that God made all men free and nature has made no man a slave. The Revolutionary idea followed natural law reasoning and the accepted idea of the Reformation that all men are equal before God. A century later the Lincolnian idea was that the fact of inequality existed and consequently equality was an objective to strive for. Equality of opportunity has been added by the present-day concept. The Revolutionary concept of equality, however, needs further analysis.

Although the social contract or social compact theory of the state was not full-blown by the time of the Revolution, it was basic in the existing concept of equality. The reasoning is summarized by Smith, and may be boiled down to four simple propositions: (1) Man as an individual antedated man as a citizen. (2) In this native state men were free and equal. (3) Men entered into compacts, that is, formed government for purely prudential reasons. (4) This origin of government casts light upon the conditions that must surround the continuation of the contract – the originally free and equal men must remain free and equal. (*Smith. Equality, 19–20.*)

The Revolutionists found support for these propositions in the religious concepts that they brought with them to America and that gained widespread acceptance in the new receptive environment. The political philosophy that denied the divine-right-of-kings idea supported the all-men-are-equal idea. The particular kind of people who ventured to the New World made possible the shaking-off of old shackles. The conditions in Colonial America did not present the binding force of custom and tradition, for the frontier was peopled with those who would not tolerate exploitation by the rich seaboard or tidewater landowner — and the seaboard reformer was not only critical of the economic and social conditions of the day but was openly against the political relationship with the mother country. All these ingredients helped to make up and to sustain the equality idea.

By the time of the Revolution, the concept of equality accommodated wide differences of national origin, creed, and social background; in spite of these, it held that all men are equal in ultimate worth. There was neither a desire nor an endeavor to reduce all men to a dead level of sameness. To the contrary, the Revolutionist sought to attain justice through equal private rights, among which were private property and private enterprise.

Equality was not without meaning in regard to the evolving land tenure system. Jefferson saw clearly many of the problems of the acquisition and accumulation of property, and he weighed well on the scales of equality his idea of land reform. He led the fight against entails because the maintenance of large estates in the same family did not meet his standards of equality. He uprooted the practice of primogeniture, or even the Hebrew idea of a double portion for the eldest son, in favor of equal devolution. Then he helped formulate the plans for distributing the public domain, which provided for placing the land in the hands of many persons in units suitable to the typical farm family. But he went beyond these in his study of the equal treatment of all citizens.

In a letter to the Reverend James Madison, written from France in the fall of 1795, Jefferson actually suggested, as a means of decreasing inequality of property holding, what was in effect both homestead tax exemptions and graduated land taxes. In introducing the matter, he recounted in some detail a conversation with a French peasant woman and related the unequal distribution of property to the widespread wretchedness that he had observed in France and also all over Europe. The latter part of this excellent letter read:

> The property of this country is absolutely concentrated in a very few hands, having revenues of from half a million of guineas a year downwards. These employ the flower of the country as servants, some of them having as many as 200 domestics, not labouring. They employ also a great number of manufacturers, & tradesmen, & lastly the class of labouring husbandmen. But after all there comes the most numerous of all the classes, that is, the poor who cannot find work. I ask myself what could be the reason that so many should be permitted to beg who are willing to work, in a country where there is a very considerable proportion of uncultivated lands? These lands are undisturbed only for the sake of game. It should seem then that it must be because of the enormous wealth of the proprietors which places them above attention to the encrease of their revenues by per-

mitting these lands to be labourd. I am conscious that an equal division of property is impracticable. But the consequences of this enormous inequality producing so much misery to the bulk of mankind, legislators cannot invent too many devices for subdividing property, only taking care to let their subdivisions go hand in hand with the natural effections of the human mind. The descent of property of every kind therefore to all the children, or to all the brothers & sisters, or other relations in equal degree is a politic measure, and a practicable one. Another means of silently lessening the inequality of property is to exempt all from taxation below a certain point, & to tax the higher portions of property in geometrical progression as they rise . . . . It is too soon yet in our country to say that every man who cannot find employment but who can find uncultivated land shall be at liberty to cultivate it, paying a moderate rent. But it is not too soon to provide by every possible means that as few as possible shall be without a little portion of land. The small land holders are the most precious part of a state. (*Jefferson. Writings,* [*Ford*] *VII, 33–36.*)

The vast quantity of unappropriated land distributed under liberal terms of sale and later under the Pre-emption and Homestead Acts made unnecessary action to prevent concentration of landed wealth at that time. However, with the recent upsurge of Jeffersonian ideas more than a dozen states have endeavored to foster home ownership for the common man by exempting small homesteads from a variety of taxes. Intense interest is found in at least one state and among liberal thinkers as to the advisability of following Jefferson's second suggestion by increasing real estate taxes on large landholdings, probably in geometrical progression, as they become larger.

The impression should not be left that the land tenure system provided as much equality as might be implied from above, for it was far from perfect. The most obvious inequality was the difference between heirs. Some states still followed the Hebrew principle of a double portion for the eldest son, and in some states the daughters were excluded if a son survived. Also, the wife's interest in the husband's property was not as substantial as the husband's interest in the wife's property. According to the Scriptures and the common law, husband and wife become one; but in regard to property relationships *he* was considered the *one.*

IMPRINT OF RELIGION

For the first three centuries of the Christian Era, the church and state in western civilization were entirely separated. The church had no legal status whatsoever. But by the reign of Emperor Galerius, Roman law placed the Christian religion on the same legal basis as the worship of the Roman gods. Thereafter the church gained privileges under the state, beginning particularly with the reign of the first Christian Emperor, Constantine.

During the Middle Ages that followed, the people of all countries in western Europe were members of one church and one faith — Roman Catholic. Dissent from that faith was rigidly forbidden, and was put down by both church and state wherever it appeared. However, by the early sixteenth century the religious revolt had grown to such proportions under the Protestant Reformation that serious difficulties were being encountered. Great pressure from church and state suppressed religious uprisings in Italy, Spain, and southern Germany. In France the reformists – the Protestant Huguenots, followers of John Calvin – were granted limited religious toleration. In Holland, Scandinavia, and parts of Germany, independent Protestant churches were established by various rulers, and revolt against the pope became strong. Across the channel in England, the rule of the pope was broken and the state church was established by an act of Parliament. The people were required to become members of the Church of England under threat of fine or physical punishment. Freed of one type of religious intolerance and saddled with another, the people protested immediately against this new religious regimentation. The Puritans wanted to "purify" the state church, while the Quakers, Baptists, and Presbyterians wanted to worship God according to the dictates of their own conscience.

Thus, when settlers began pouring onto the eastern seaboard, little religious tolerance existed in the Old World. People were neither privileged to join any or no church nor to express opinions freely in regard to religion. In the Catholic countries, Protestants were outlawed and persecuted. In the Protestant countries, Catholics were likewise maltreated. In England the Catholics and all Protestants except those who adhered to the Church of England became liable to punishment ranging from a fine to death. Civil strife in England added to the religious quarrels and revolts. The common man clamored for a right to vote for his own rulers, and he held that man was endowed with certain "natural rights" which government could not abolish.

It was not until the 1688 Revolution that limited religious toleration was granted the Protestant dissenters and at the same time the common man gained the English Bill of Rights and the supremacy of Parliament. This mild form of religious toleration, however, did not enfranchise either Catholics or Jews, and while Quakers could vote in eighteenth century England, they could not hold office. The difficulties in England not only sent more dissenters to America but heartened those who were fighting for the "cause" on this side of the Atlantic.

During the first century after Jamestown, conditions in this country became more important than conditions in England or on the Continent. The corporate theocracies in New England were far from a homogeneous group. Rhode Island, for example, was a stronghold of religious freedom, as were Penn's colonies in the middle group. Rhode Island's advanced position was due largely to Roger Williams. His colony, for the first time in colonial history, provided for full liberty of conscience and complete separation of church and state. The convictions regarding religious freedom in Rhode Island were so great that Williams, although he disliked the Catholics and made many attacks upon their religious beliefs, demanded for them the same freedom of religion that he claimed for himself. Thus, from earliest time Rhode Island had no religious establishments and for all practical purposes had complete religious freedom, for the charter of 1663 declared that no person should be "molested, punished, disquieted, or called in question for any difference in opinione in matters of religion," provided of course that in exercising this freedom he did not disturb the civil peace.

On the other hand, Catholics were discriminated against in New Hampshire and Massachusetts. According to seventeenth century custom, Catholics could not vote, and in Massachusetts, Quakers also could not vote. In early Massachusetts only freemen could vote, and all freemen were required to be members of the chuch of jurisdiction. By 1662 the English government ordered that any church member in Massachusetts should be permitted to vote, and this was approved by the general court. When Massachusetts became a royal province, she was forced to tolerate Episcopalians and other dissenters, but the inhabitants still had to support the Congregational ministers. The Episcopalians, Baptists, and Quakers protested violently against this requirement, but without success. Similar requirements prevailed in New Hampshire.

The middle colonies were similar to the New England colonies, being both liberal and conservative. The colonies under the influence of Penn were similar to Rhode Island, while New York and part of New Jersey were plagued with religious requirements. In the early days of New Netherland, the patroons were obliged to support a minister, and several clergymen of the Dutch Reformed Church were sent out under the Presbytery of Amsterdam. But other faiths crept in and were tolerated. Although at times they were persecuted, the Lutherans, Congregationalists, Quakers, Baptists, and English Puritans became much more numerous than the small group that represented the Church of England, which was given a preferred position by a 1693 law that provided for state support of a Protestant clergy. Religious toleration extended to the Jews, who had a regular place of worship in New York City. But neither the Catholics nor the Jews could vote — the former being excluded by law, the latter by court decision. Both New York and New Jersey had liberty of conscience clauses in their basic laws, the former in its charter and the latter in the Concessions of 1665.

Penn and his Quaker followers, next to the Rhode Island liberals, came the nearest of any colony to following closely the principle of religious freedom. He planned his colony, including Delaware and West Jersey, as a refuge for all persecuted people regardless of faith and religious beliefs. Freedom of worship was granted to all law-abiding persons who "acknowledged one Almighty and Eternal God to be Creator, Upholder, and Ruler of the World," which meant freedom of religion for Jews and Catholics as well as Protestants. Although he was finally forced by the Crown to enact laws against the Roman Catholics, they doubtlessly enjoyed as much or more freedom in Pennsylvania than in any other colony. As a partial consequence of liberal views in regard to religious liberty, coupled with a relatively liberal land policy and government, Penn had less difficulty in securing settlers than did Baltimore and some of the other proprietors. In addition, the Quakers, unlike the Catholics, belonged to the economic class that was inclined to emigrate. Penn's policies appealed particularly to the dissenters and disadvantaged groups in the lower Rhine, the source of many German immigrants.

Some of the religious conflicts of the era were exemplified in the conditions surrounding the Maryland Charter of 1632. Cecil Calvert was a Roman Catholic. He may have been expected to establish a Catholic empire in America, if left completely free to do so. As a consequence, a provision in the charter granted him the right to erect churches, chapels and places of worship, ". . . dedicated and consecrated according to the Ecclesiastical Laws of our Kingdom of England. . . ." which was Anglican at that time. It should be noted that this was a right granted. Calvert was not in any way instructed or compelled to establish places of worship. He was merely given the right to do so. No penalty was added if he did not exercise this right, and none was implied if he saw fit to erect Catholic places of worship. It appears that this clause was copied from the Newfoundland charter and was meant to protect the king's position. It is evident that Charles I, who granted the charter, could not have favored Baltimore's venture, as he most certainly did, and at the same time through a proviso in the charter have compelled a Catholic to use exclusively the English Church. It is surmised that Cecil and Charles had a secret understanding that the Crown would tolerate the Catholic Church in Maryland. The vague wording of the charter gives an impression of rendering lip service to the Anglican Church and at the same time denying the specific means of forcing conformity to established ecclesiastical forms.

However, Baltimore clarified the situation when he sponsored Maryland's Toleration Act of 1649, the first "liberty of conscience" legislative event in America. Although this was a negative sort of toleration act, it represented the first real step toward personal freedom and individual equality.

In the southern colonies the Church of England was entitled to public support, and was firmly established, particularly in Virginia. However, it lost ground everywhere, and by 1776, when British support was cancelled by the Revolution, the situation was ripe for separation of church and state. The first toleration act was passed in Virginia in 1699, when only a few Quakers and Presbyterians were involved. Other dissenters, including the Lutherans, poured into the Valley of Virginia and soon formed the majority, but Virginia was glad to have her frontier secured even by sects whose religious ideas were considered a little unorthodox. It was in the Piedmont region that the Anglicans from the Tidewater and the Protestant dissenters from the Valley came into conflict. The difficulty arose out of a law which required that ministers and places of worship be licensed by civil authority, and under which dissenters from this rule were fined. An appeal from this law to the home government received a favorable decision and a simple toleration act cleared the road for complete separation of church and state following the Revolution.

The Carolina charter definitely authorized the proprietors to tolerate dissenters if they saw fit, which they did. They wished to attract settlers who could not be induced to come to Carolina if strict ecclesiastical controls were in vogue. This chartered proviso was unique and remarkable, for some of the proprietors, who were members of the home government, were making life difficult for dissenters in England. The proprietors, of course, made proper provision for the services of the Anglican church. But churches were soon established by Congregationalists, Huguenots, and Scotch Presbyterians, for the Church of England enjoyed only a preferred position in the Carolina colonies.

The Revolution did not do away completely with the state church in those colonies where the practice was followed. For example, Massachusetts continued to require public support of Protestant teaching. Virginia did not withdraw public support completely until 1785, when Jefferson's bill provided for complete religious freedom. The constitutions of New York (1777), Georgia (1777), and South Carolina (1778) granted religious freedom and equal privileges to Christians of all sects. Religious tests for office holding, however, were almost universal. Delaware alone prohibited such a requirement. North Carolina's religious test for holding office ". . . forbade the holding of office by anyone who denied the being of God, the truth of the Protestant religion, the divine authority of the Bible, or 'held religious principles incompatible with the freedom or safety of the state.'" Civil freedom and religious freedom were thus related. Although in some states ministers were disqualified from holding office and freedom of worship was an accepted fact, some still required compulsory support of religion. (*Bond. Polit. Ideals, 302–3.*)

Between the signing of the peace and the establishment of the Constitution the various Protestant churches began to establish separate administrative organizations in the New World, which severed many ties with English church establishments. Progress was being made toward a free church in a free state. It was during these years that the ordinances covering the land to the west recognized religious liberty, although church establishments were not definitely and specifically forbidden. Full religious tolerance had not been achieved. For example, the Catholics were relieved very slowly of civil disabilities. (*Condon. Constitutional Freedom, 145.*)

Throughout this discussion reference has been made to the dissenters — first, those who dissented from the Catholic religion, the Protestants; then, those who dissented from the requirements of particular Protestant groups, who become "established" at one place or another; and finally, the dissenters from the dissenters. It was the last group, the unchurched liberals, as Sweet calls them, whose mark upon the evolving religious situation at the time of the Revolution was most indelible. By the end of the Colonial period, more unchurched people were in the colonies than anywhere else in Christendom, for church membership was not required as in those countries where state churches were firmly established. Many of the revolutionary leaders were liberal in their religious views. Washington probably never considered himself a full-fledged member of the church, which was the typical attitude of most Virginians of his class, for there was no Anglican bishop in the colony. Madison, Jefferson, and Franklin, although they accepted the ministrations of the Episcopal church, were never communicants. By religious experience and temperament such men were ripe for the liberal religious ideas that were floating around the colonies during the Revolutionary days. (For an excellent discussion see *Sweet. Religion, 334–39.*)

It should be remembered, however, that religious liberty did not originate among those religious groups in control or representing the majority religion at any place. Separation of church and state and the granting of full religious freedom were advocated as a matter of principle by some groups. Others who were not members of the established church advocated liberal religion as a matter of expediency — they did not disfavor a state church but felt that religious freedom was preferable in event theirs could not be the privileged church.

Similarly, those in control seldom recommended a change. The feudal lord whether in England or America generally desired to maintain his preferred position. Usually it was the common man, the left-wing group, the nonconformist who forced the adjustment. The American system of free enterprise, the free land tenure system, and the other freedoms for which the founding fathers stood — freedom of conscience, separation of church and state, individual rights, self-government, free speech, and free press — all had their roots deep in the principles of the left-wing religious bodies that fled European oppression and came to America.

No endeavor has been made to prove the thesis that the land tenure system could only have arisen as a result of the religious reformation as it developed in Colonial America. The fact that similar, and in some respects perhaps more advanced, forms of tenure arose under quite different circumstances is sufficient to refute such a claim. Religious freedom, however, contributed to its qualitative development and to its quantitative spread throughout the colonies and later to the new public domain.

Of fundamental importance is the close connection between Protestant spiritual teachings of honestry, sobriety, hard work, thrift, saving, abstinence, moderation, faithfulness, and piety and the emerging land system. These qualities made for economic success, for the accumulation of wealth, and for the acquisition of a large quantity of land. It is small wonder that the "problem of size of holding" was left largely unsolved by the founding fathers, and that many colonial leaders and believers in democracy were large landholders.

The idea of the Protestant Reformation that man might commune with God without the medium of a priest and the idea of individualism inherent in the growing capitalism were closely parallel as to basic principles. Freedom of the individual to worship God according to the dictates of his conscience and to participate in the making of laws and in the administration of justice were incompatible with a rigidly controlled and dependent land system, so the land system was liberalized. Those who were against state churches and their centralized control were against, and forcefully resisted, the absolute power of government and its hierarchial control over the land system as practiced in feudal England.

COMMON LAW INFLUENCE

The full impact of the concepts of equality and religious freedom cannot be interpreted until their relation to the legal system is studied. The most widely accepted legal theory is that English common law was brought to America by all English settlers, and claimed by them, at least in most places, as the birthright of all free Englishmen. It is held that the colonists looked upon the common law as a system of positive law and subsidiary law, which was in effect without need of legislative sanction and which applied where not specifically replaced by chartered privileges, concessions, agreements, and colonial legislative enactments. This theory, of course, was developed after legal procedures became fairly well formalized and after many enabling legislative enactments were on the statute books. In addition, it conformed rather well to the Mayflower Compact, the original charters, and many of the special agreements between the settlers and the proprietors.

In spite of all this, it appears that English common law was not accepted in all of the colonies, at least in equal degree; that many of the colonies, the corporate colonies in particular, openly disavowed allegiance to common law principles; that the common law as it relates to property rights and arrangements was accepted less widely than that which was related to human rights and liberties; that the common law was less accepted during the seventeenth century than during the eighteenth century; and that the theory of acceptance of the common law more nearly fits the situation after the Revolutionary War than at any time during the two centuries of the Colonial era.

In Massachusetts, for example, religion had a direct influence upon the development of the system of land tenure. It appears that this influence was greater in regard to the land laws than in many other aspects in the life of that colony. This closer relation to land laws seems reasonable since the great outstanding principles of English law of that day, which were far in advance of the time, referred to personal liberty. On the other hand, the most backward of English laws were those regarding land. Thus, when the Massachusetts Puritan was forging a social and economic order it was easy for him to rely in part upon English common law for personal liberties, and it was necessary that he ignore, at least partially, the English feudal system when considering the law of property. Thus, he turned easily to natural law and to the law as laid down in the Scriptures.

His concepts of natural law were crude and slow to mature, not taking form until the second century of the Colonial era. On the other hand, the concepts of Scriptural law were well developed and firmly intrenched from earliest times in the mind of the Puritan dissenter. For example, as early as 1636 (*Mass. Bay Rec., I, 174*) the government of Massachusetts was given the task of drafting laws ". . . agreeable to the word of God . . ." to be the fundamental charter of liberties for the commonwealth. It was clearly understood that during the interim all causes were to be decided ". . . as near the law of God as they can be." Even after the adoption of the basic constitution in 1641, the law of God, and not the English common law, was used as the guide in deciding issues not covered in the Body of Liberties. The Massachusetts Bay charter of 1629 provided only authority for the making of laws and ordinances ". . . not contrarie or repugnant to the Lawes and Statuts of this our Realme of England." (*Thorpe. Charters, III, 1853.*) The colonists, conscious of the charter, were somewhat reluctant to put their laws into writing. They felt that the growth of law by custom, though the law might be radically opposed to English principles, was no infringement upon the charter, for it referred only to formal legislative enactments and, in addition, English common law was subject to gradual evolution. What the Puritan magistrate held was that the law of Massachusetts should grow out of the nature and disposition of the people and the new situation in which they found themselves. But the people desired a formalized statement of their rights, privileges, and immunities, and the celebrated Body of Liberties appeared as their fundamental constitution in 1641. This statement of principles again provided that in the absence of law the case would be decided according to the Bible. It said in the first article that no person's freedom should be infringed upon except by virtue of some expressed law or ". . . in case of the defect of a law in any partecular case by the word of god." The relation between the excellent work of ecclesiastical bodies on usury and the section in the Body of Liberties on interest rate seems peculiarly close. After establishing "eight pounds in the hundred for one year" as the legal limit, Section 23 provides that "neither shall this be a coulour or countenance to allow any usurie amongst us contrarie to the law of god."

Again, the law of inheritance was taken from the Scriptures rather than the common law. But an even greater departure from the laws of England was the section that specifically outlawed the burdensome feudal incidents.

The Puritan theory was that law was the command of God, which was the medieval conception unadulterated by seventeenth century views of sovereignty. As John Cotton remarked about a body of law that he submitted to the general court, we should not ". . . call them laws because God alone has the power to make law, but conventions between men." The Body of Liberties were never enacted into law, but the general court did ". . . with one consent fully authorize and earnestly entreat all that are and shall be in authority to consider them as laws." (*Reinsch. Common Law, 14, 12.*)

The law of God and not English common law was the subsidiary law in Connecticut. The first section of the Fundamental Orders of 1638-39, after giving the duly elected magistrates the responsibility of administering justice according to the rules therein established, provided that in the absence of a law covering the case it should be decided ". . . according to the rule of the word of God." The Connecticut and New Haven colonies departed even further from English common law than Massachusetts, particularly in New Haven where is found ". . . the clear and unequivocal assertion of the binding force of divine law as a common law in all temporal matters, as a guiding rule in civil and criminal jurisdiction." (*Ibid., 26.*)

New Hampshire was settled chiefly by dissenters from the Puritan colonies. They did not possess, therefore, the binding force of a homogeneous religion. Thus, they tended to cite English common law rather than the Scriptures. They recognized their chartered responsibility to follow civil procedure consonant to the laws of England, but this they qualified according to conditions in the colony. But the common law could not have been administered in New Hampshire for ". . . no real jurist, no man acknowledging a regular development of the law by precedents and finding an authoritative guidance in the adjudications of the common law judges, held judicial power in New Hampshire during the entire 18th century." Chief Justice

Livermore as late as 1782 refused to be bound by precedents, holding "... that every tub should stand on its own bottom." (*Ibid., 28, 27.*)

Rhode Island rendered lip service to the common law, but was far more democratic. Also, the land system was not restricted to accepted English principles of land tenure law. For example, it was provided at an early date that all conveyances of land must be in writing. This proviso antedates the English Statute of Frauds by a third of a century. In the Plantation agreement at Providence in 1640 it was agreed that every man shall have "... a deed of all of his lands lying within the bounds of the Plantations, to hould it by for after ages." (*Thorpe. Charters, VI, 3207.*) And by a meeting of the general court at Portsmouth in 1641 it was provided that each town should keep a record of land granted and should give a copy of the record to each grantee as evidence of ownership.

The common law could not have had an important influence in Rhode Island, either in legislation or administration, until late, if at all, for the general assembly as late as 1729 forbade persons trained in law to be deputies. (*Arnold. Hist. of R.I., II, 98.*)

The common law fared better in New York than in other colonies. The population was unusually heterogeneous, without the unifying force found in the New England colonies. The common law influence was felt, as in all colonies under royal rule, almost from the day when the English took New Netherland from the Dutch. But at no time, especially before 1761, did the common law form a complete subsidiary system. It seems clear, however, that many American ideas of needed reforms of the law of real property were carried to completion and given permanent status in New York. No doubt this work was expedited by the experience of her jurists in endeavoring to follow a regular system of jurisprudence. New York developed a special court, a court of adjudicature, to hear land cases.

New Jersey had a system of popular courts and followed more closely the Scriptures than the common law until the close of the seventeenth century. In 1698, the privileges of English common law were assured to everyone. In the Grants and Concessions of New Jersey it was enacted that persons guilty of murder or treason "... shall be sentenced by the general assembly, as they in the Wisdom of the *Lord* shall judge meet and expedient." (*N.J. Grants and Conc., 404.*) In East Jersey the laws of trespass and injuries by cattle were in agreement with the laws of Exodus.

Penn's concessions, charter of liberties, and first frames of government were not looked upon as bodies of law, binding between the proprietor and the people, although they were developed under the extensive privileges granted in the charter. In 1687, Penn appointed five commissioners to represent him in the colony, but they accomplished little in systematizing the law. He then appointed a Puritan governor, who accomplished little. Finally, in 1699, Penn came to the colony himself to straighten out the laws under which the colonists were governed. The 1701 Charter of Privileges was the result. This charter was "the most memorable organic law of the colonial epoch." (*Channing. William Penn, 197.*) It was a mixture of common law, Quaker religious principles, and local custom. The numerous difficulties with law in Pennsylvania also attest to the wide departure of that colony from the established common law of England.

In Maryland, Lord Baltimore was given full and complete powers of government by his charter. The people in assembly and the proprietor had difficulty in developing a system of government; frequently they mutually objected to and rejected the laws of each other. In general, the colonists strove for the use of English common law and later English statute law. After 100 years of struggle the proprietor acceded to the wishes of the people, but even then neither English common nor statute law was brought to Maryland intact. English law was used only as it was suitable to American conditions, and largely for illustration, but not as subsidiary law. English common law was given a peculiar Maryland flavor by the injection of equity and good conscience.

In Virginia, under the trading company, laws suitable to the conditions of the colony were promulgated. The land laws were concerned chiefly with descent. The first code, harsh and strict, was printed in London in 1612. Eight years later an unsuccessful endeavor was made to liberalize it. In 1619 the first general assembly passed laws but made no claim as to their relation to the common law. Since the jurists were not educated at law, they were doubtless motivated by equity and conscience, much as in Maryland and in the Puritan colonies, but without much evidence of the same strength of the Scriptural influence. At the time of the Restoration, Virginia seemed to want to please the new king by showing her loyalty to England. The preamble to the laws of 1661–62 stated that the legislature had endeavored to follow the "excellent and refined laws of England to which we profess to acknowledge all due obedience and reverence." (*Hening. Stats., II, 43.*)

In the Carolinas the proprietors endeavored unsuccessfully to establish, by the extreme reactionary Fundamental Constitutions, the feudal system of land and government. The Constitutions were so obnoxious to local concepts of equity and the Carolina colonial mind that the colonists never acknowledged them. The proprietors evidently accepted the general applicability of rules of the common law, but an act of 1712 put in force English statutes except those relating to military tenures and ecclesiastical matters. In 1715, the common law was specifically enacted, as were other English statutes including the Statute of Frauds promulgated in England over thirty years earlier. Court procedure was very informal, being conducted by judges generally unfamiliar with the law.

In summary, in all colonies except Maryland a strong tendency was found to establish at an early date a basic body of law. The degree of refinement varied from the extensive endeavors of Penn to the simple social compact of the Plymouth Puritans. Written law seemed essential in the American wilderness where facilities for the study of English law were scant and where the vast output of statute books, legal reports, and technical documents were not available to those who found it necessary to administer simple justice.

All early codes, except those of Pennsylvania and perhaps Massachusetts, were relatively brief, simple, and covered only major items. Matters not covered were largely left up to the sense of justice and fair play of the popularly elected magistrates and appointed judges. In the southern colonies the common law was supposed to be subsidiary, while in Massachusetts, Connecticut, and Rhode Island, and to a lesser extent in New Jersey, the Scriptures were supposed to be the guide in the absence of a statute.

The first century of the Colonial era was the century of the common man. A large proportion of the freemen participated in the assemblies and the town meetings; the average citizen participated in the administration of justice; court procedure was so simple and democratic it was presumed that a man of ordinary intelligence could plead his own case; trained jurists were absent until the eighteenth century; and the Scripture and the popular sense of right were the bases for many judicial decisions.

In the seventeenth and early eighteenth centuries the common man was forging a new land system inhibited only slightly by tenure institutions of the past. Failure to transport bodily to the new country English statute law, and expressed ignorance of the common law, particularly in regard to matters of use and occupancy of land, if not in regard to personal liberties, indicate that the colonists had considerable freedom to establish whatever system of land tenure seemed to meet their new conditions. They did not fail to avail themselves of this opportunity.

The colonists brought with them the great charters under which the country was settled. They also brought with them general ideas of equity, justice, and right developed in their mother countries over the centuries. They brought with them very little statutory and common law. Common law ideas were adhered to in Maryland from the beginning but they found their way into the other colonies very slowly, generally beginning about the first quarter of the eighteenth century, and even then the influence of English jurisprudence seems to have been one of assisting in the regularization of "American common law." Thus, the laws of land tenure came from three sources: (1) the creative genius of the colonists in the development of simple rules to meet their peculiar conditions, (2) the principles either laid down or derived from the Scriptures, and (3) the older English law — common and statutory — where it did not conflict with the first two. The strength of the tenure system lay in the skillful blending of the three and the modifying effect of the latter two upon the former.

In the heat of the revolutionary development the colonists claimed by assertion that they were not bound by the laws of England. This departure from the drift of the preceding three-quarters of a century appears to have been used purposefully in the defense of asserting political and economic freedom from the mother country. It also indicates how strongly the early view of colonial law appealed to the colonial sense of justice and its ability of survival. John Adams, in his statement in the Novanglus, said:

> How, then, do we New Englandmen derive our laws? I say, not from parliament, not from common law, but from the law of nature, and the compact made with the king in our charters. Our ancestors were entitled to the common law of England when they emigrated, that is, to just so much of it as they pleased to adopt, and no more. They were not bound or obliged to submit to it, unless they chose it. (*Adams. Works, IV, 122.*)

Jefferson took a somewhat similar point of view in presenting the case of the right of the colonists to declare themselves free and independent of the mother country. He held that our ancestors before emigration to America were free to leave the country in which chance and not choice had placed them, and to establish a new society in a new land under such laws and regulations as seemed most likely to promote their happiness. This principle of expatriation Jefferson held to be in accord with English history under which the Saxons left northern Europe and established themselves on Britain and developed a system of law peculiarly their own. He held that expatriation was a natural right, acted on as such by all nations in all ages. In a letter to Peter Carr on June 22, 1792, Jefferson's reasoning in regard to the rules of waste indicated that he felt perfectly free to make whatever adjustment in common law appeared advisable but that by no means was he a reformer just for the sake of making a change. After reviewing the reasons for the rules in regard to waste in England, he raised a question as to whether conditions in the country were sufficiently different to require a difference in the laws. The evidence seemed to indicate that it was safer to follow the old rule, and he concluded, "Consequently there is no reason for adopting different rules of waste here from those established in England." (*Jefferson. Writings,* [*Ford*] *VI, 91–92.*) Thus, the colonists from earliest time had and used the right to adopt as much of English common law as suited their conditions and to develop such new law as would promote their individual and collective welfare.

Common law did not hold full sway in the colonies because those trained in the legal profession played no part in the formation of law in the colonies. By an act of the Rhode Island general assembly, as late as 1729, lawyers were forbidden to be deputies, because of the ill consequences of their presence in the chambers of the lawmakers. Also, the early judges and chief justices of New Hampshire were all businessmen, farmers, or seamen. It was as late as 1726, over a hundred years after the Pilgrims had landed on Plymouth Rock, before a man of liberal education appeared on the bench. He was Judge Jaffray, a graduate of Harvard in 1702, and it was not until 1754 that a lawyer, Theodore Atkinson, also a graduate of Harvard, became chief justice. The magistrates of Massachusetts were chiefly laymen, and the colony was almost a century old before a professional lawyer became chief justice.

The same practice was followed in most of the other colonies. In New York a professional English lawyer by the name of Attwood became chief justice in 1700. His avowed purpose was to introduce common law and English court procedure into New York, but his methods were unpopular and he accomplished little. In reporting to Hillsborough, Governor Colden said that lawyers were unpopular in early New York. "The general cry of the People both in Town and Country was, 'No Lawyer in the Assembly.' " (*N. Y. Col. Hist., VIII, 61.*) No professionally trained judge held office in Delaware before the Revolution. (*Grubb. Judiciary of Del., 9.*) The first lawyer to become chief justice in Pennsylvania was Guest, in 1701. (*Penn and Logan Correspondence, I, 19, 48.*) In Virginia an act of 1645 was passed expelling the mercenary attorneys (*Hening. Stats., I, 482*), and two years later it was enacted that none should plead for recompense. (*Reinsch. Common Law, 48.*)

The absence of legal information and trained legalists in early Colonial America, coupled with the laxness of requirements for formal training in law and the open disdain for legalists, made it easy, if not necessary, for the land laws of the Colonial era to depart from the common law of England. In fact, the rough and ready summary processes followed in the administration of justice gave ample opportunity for the full play of peculiarly American concepts of equity, of conscience, and of natural law.

The upsurge of the common law idea came after the formation of the federal and state constitutions and after the legal profession was well developed in the several states. In fact, by constitutional provision and otherwise, the theory that the common and statute law of England was in force unless specifically altered by the legislature was accepted in practice throughout the new states. This was a necessary expediency, rather than a cleaving to the common law. The provision in the Delaware Constitution of 1776 was specific in this regard. It provided:

> The common law of England, as well as so much of the statute law as has been heretofore adopted in practice in this State, shall remain in force, unless they shall be altered by a future law of the legislature; such parts only excepted as are repugnant to the rights and privileges contained in this constitution, and the declaration of rights, &c., agreed to by this convention. (*Thorpe. Charters, I, 566–67.*)

ECONOMIC AND POLITICAL CONSIDERATIONS

The chief items in the day-to-day economic life and political experience of individuals and the colonies and those that may have influenced the land system were the ever present conditions of a frontier economy, the unusually high degree of isolation from central governmental authority and from established social contacts, the abundance of free land, and the peculiarly democratic spirit of the colonial mind.

Ever Present Frontier

Settlement of America afforded a unique opportunity to speed up the advancement of civilization, particularly those aspects concerned with relations among men as to the institution of property. People coming to America were dissatisfied with the land system from which they came. More important, settlement was being undertaken in a new territory completely free of all vestiges of the past, insofar as the white man was concerned. Here was in effect a vast new laboratory in which experimentation with new tenure relations was unhampered by established patterns of occupancy and rigid controls of relations. The colonial charters represented broad grants of powers and wide latitude for discretionary action, both in government and land tenure. On the other hand, aboriginal tenure exerted no influence that hampered the development of new tenure concepts. Indeed, the methods followed by the colonists in obtaining the consent of the Indians to occupy the territory actually expedited change in the ideas that the colonists brought with them.

The characteristics or requirements of the frontier economy of Colonial America were the necessity, first, for protection against harassing disturbances by outsiders, whether they be Indians, Spanish, or French; secondly, for permission to subdue new territory, unhampered by restrictive rules and regulations; thirdly, for an adequate supply of finances, at least in the early stages of settlement; and fourthly, for an impelling force driving the individual in his struggle to establish a home in the frontier.

Some of the measures taken to meet the first demand were the actions of individual settlers and colonizers to keep the Indians satisfied and cooperative, including most of the factors outlined under the procedures followed in the relinquishment of claims by the Indians; the development of frontier-military settlements, as exemplified by the grants on easy terms for military purposes, including the whole colony of Georgia; and the military campaign to drive the hostile Indians and French from the area.

Permission to subdue new territory without restrictive regulations was the essence of the colonial settlement scheme. The claims of the Indians were rather easily and expeditiously satisfied. Record keeping was very lax and nonconformers were not penalized severely, if at all. The requirement for surveying was speedy and liberal; even in New England, where the most meticulous care was exercised, it was not a retarding influence. Squatters were looked upon unfavorably only when they rebelled against the quitrent charge. The general spirit of the movement was to get settled on good land and then take the time necessary to work on the formalities of deeds and records.

Most of the colonists needed some financial backing in getting to this country, in establishing homes, and in producing the first crop. To this end the first trading companies were organized and large sums were subscribed. To keep a steady stream of settlers flowing into the wilderness, great effort was exerted in interesting men of wealth in the possibilities of the New World, and as a further inducement they were given the territory included in their grants on most liberal terms. In some instances, as in Georgia for example, the government advanced funds for settlement purposes. Gifts of land, low purchase price, deferred payment of principal, and freedom from quitrent were other devices used.

The settlers had to have a reason for leaving their native land to brave the hardships of the new country. To inherent characteristics of man and to economic, social, and religious motives must be added the advantage of adequate size holdings, the value of relatively low charges upon land, and the necessity for a future assured of better things than those of the past.

These characteristic requirements of the American frontier economy had important influences on the development of a free tenure system.

The factors that influenced the king to grant the land to the colonizing agencies on liberal terms were important, for the settlers knew of the liberal tenure terms in the original grants. The abundance of free land that made large grants possible, and the reasonable future expectancy of an estate in land, spurred the settlers in their struggle to obtain as free and as large estates as possible. The frontier economy apparently was an important influence in liberalizing the tenure structure during Colonial times, and in the maintenance and further liberalization of those principles when decisions had to be made at the time of the emergence of our land tenure system. (For more detail see *Turner, Frontier,* and other writings; also, the later work of his students.)

Isolation

Without overemphasizing the frontier aspect too much, its corollary — isolation — should be presented. Early American institutions were distinctly indigenous and in part grew out of isolation. The most important characteristics of isolation were self-confidence, equality, and distrust of the absentee. The colonists could not well escape the feeling of loneliness and self-dependence, and these made for newness and resourcefulness and lessened the restrictions of earlier associations. The few who failed milled about, or went back to England, or perished. The young, self-made, self-confident leader remained as the maker of the new land system and the new form of government.

The feeling of equality and self-dependence, coupled with the weakness and slowness of ruling from a distance, formed the basis for distrust of the absentee, whether in administration of government or control of land. The agents of the proprietors were not the solution to this problem, for they were of no more influence psychologically than the absentees whom they represented. Self-confidence and equality did not go hand in hand with paying tribute — quitrent for example — to an absentee who rendered little service and who occupied his position largely because of circumstances with which he had little or nothing to do.

Free Land

Another reason that the English system of land tenure was not transplanted to America intact was the vast difference between the position of land in the two economies. In England, land was relatively scarce; the population was pressing hard upon the land resources. Under these conditions land could be and had been monopolized and vested interests could be maintained for a relatively long period of time. In America, land was plentiful; the population was not pressing hard upon the land even on the seaboard, and there remained the vast expanse of free land to the west.

Even though manors of a weak type existed for a while in the valleys of the Hudson and the Potomac rivers and in the Carolinas, they could not be maintained. Anyone dissatisfied with conditions in an area that had been developed could move on westward. Concepts of tenure and government had to be adjusted to the exigencies of the demand for settlers in a country where good land lay awaiting exploitation by anyone who would venture beyond the established community.

Democratic Spirit

Another powerful influence on the system of land tenure evolving in Colonial America was the political system envisaged by the colonists. It was reasoned that political democracy could not be maintained in the absence of economic and social democracy. The feudal system, as it had developed in England, was geared to the maintenance of a rigid caste system, both socially and economically. American political democracy could be neither attained nor maintained without a wide distribution of land in the hands of the many. No one felt this more strongly than Jefferson, for he had observed the influence of the great landowning families in Virginia. One of the important measures which he advocated and fought for was a law abolishing entails, which he calculated would bring about wider distribution of landed property and a more stable political democracy.

The relation between democracy in government and democracy in the land system was not a one-way relationship, for it operated in both directions – political considerations influenced tenure and the land system influenced government. This relation was well understood by the founding fathers as is shown by the celebrated Plymouth oration of Daniel Webster when he said that the political situation of New England was determined by the fundamental laws respecting property. (*Webster. Works, II, 203–16.*) Robbins takes a similar position when he holds "Colonial experience attested to the fact that the nature of society was to a very great extent determined by land policy." (*Robbins. Our Landed Heritage, 7.*)

The struggle for free tenure took place in a frontier economy, rather isolated from outside influences. On the frontier was an abundance of unsettled land and a democratic spirit, based upon the equality and self-confidence of a frontier, and sustained, if not compounded, by the economic, social, and political forces that caused people to leave their native land. It was in this setting that the colonizing agencies obtained the land from European sovereigns and proceeded to dispossess the Indians. And it was within this framework that the land was granted to the settlers and that they worked out their day-to-day land tenure relations.

The free tenure system handed down by the founding fathers was conditioned largely by the spirit of freedom and self-confidence prevalent throughout frontier America. The revolutionary spirit growing out of hatred for the absentee and resentment against feudal charges upon the landholder without commensurate services had its influence. The lax enforcement of rules laid down by the colonizing agencies, the weakness of local governments, and the outlets readily available to those not satisfied with local conditions, as exemplified in the vast unclaimed domain and competition among the colonies for settlers, were also important. The desire to establish and maintain freer institutions than those from which many of the colonists fled was important.

It was under these influences that equal devolution was made a basic tenure principle, that the right of alienation attained its highest freedom, that principles of primogeniture and entails were generally outlawed, that the possibility of escheat was reduced to a minimum, that the man-man relation of lord and vassal completely (at least theoretically) gave way to the more stable man-society relation of fee simple absolute tenure, and that the holder of the fee was given permission to parcel out his rights in land in a wide variety of heterogeneous tenures.

CHAPTER 20

Adjustments During the Revolutionary Period

FOR A PERIOD OF OVER 150 years the British government allowed the various colonies considerable freedom to develop their own land system. However, by the middle of the eighteenth century it was becoming clear that expansion to the west was no longer a matter of colonial determination but rather an imperial problem of prime importance. The Proclamation of 1763 was the first significant official action that severely restricted the colonists in their westward movement. The various orders in council leading up to the Quebec Act of 1774 made the 1763 restrictions more effective. The Quebec Act is usually considered an act of war as well as a land policy measure.

The Declaration of Independence, which soon followed, transferred land ownership and control over land settlement and occupancy to the colonies by the same token that the colonies assumed the prerogative of a sovereign government. The successful prosecution of the war and the conclusion of the Treaty of Peace gave official sanction to the transfer of powers of government and rights in land thus asserted.

Soon after the Declaration of Independence, the states in their basic constitutions and by legislation and judicial action confiscated the landed rights of those who did not support the Revolution, confirmed many existing private rights in land, and adjusted others to meet the fundamental principles of the revolutionary forefathers. The Articles of Confederation and various actions of the Continental Congress strengthened the acts of the newly formed states and advanced toward the goal of an acceptable federal government. The matter of the western lands did not hold up the Declaration of Independence but delayed action on the Articles of Confederation until the other colonies had indicated their intention of meeting Maryland's demands in regard to the lands west of the mountains. Also, the major cessions of the western land and the ordinances that outlined the land policy and system of government for the western territory had to be completed before the new federal Constitution could become an instrument for holding together the newly formed union.

TREASON AND CONFISCATION

The most wholesale and widespread confiscation of property in land at any time during American history took place soon after the Declaration of Independence. The procedure of confiscating land, however, was in practice long before the Revolution. For example, land was supposed to revert to the grantor if the grantee failed to meet the requirements for seating and planting. The estates, both real and personal, of three men who took part in the Rebellion of Nathaniel Bacon were confiscated by an act of the Virginia assembly. (*Hening. Stats., II, 376–77.*)

The ink was scarcely dry on the Declaration of Independence before the Continental Congress recommended to the states the confiscation of the estates of all men who did not support the Revolution. The newly self-constituted sovereigns confiscated estates belonging to all British subjects who remained loyal to the English Crown, and by early 1782 every state had followed the advice of Congress. During the first year, New Hampshire confiscated the property of twenty-nine persons. New York seized immediately the lands of fifty-five Loyalists, among which were large patroonships that had resulted from early Dutch land grants. (An extensive list of confiscated New York estates can be found in *Flick. Loyalism in N.Y. Appendix.*)

The outstanding examples of the confiscation of large estates, however, were those of the Penns of Pennsylvania, the Baltimores of Maryland, Lord Fairfax of Virginia's Northern Neck, and Lord Granville of North Carolina. The Pennsylvania assembly, however, later made a token payment to the Penn family of £130,000, for a vast domain reputedly worth more than £1,000,000, "in remembrance of the enterprising spirit of the founder and of the expectations and dependence of his descendants." In consideration of the loss not covered by the reimbursement of the Pennsylvania assembly, the British government paid to the representatives of the proprietors an annuity of £4,000 for over 100 years and then commuted it to a principal sum. (*Keith. Chron. of Pa., I, 88.*) Likewise, the Maryland assembly granted the Baltimores £10,000 for their estate when it was confiscated in 1780. This sum was so inadequate that the

British government felt compelled to supplement the grant by an additional sum of £90,000. The Fairfax estate of 5,000,000 acres was not confiscated until 1781, after the death of Lord Fairfax, for he was never proved to be a Loyalist during the war. It seems that loyalism could not have been the cause of the confiscation, a better reason being the opposition of the revolutionary Virginians to the feudal characteristics of the Fairfax estate. (*Nettels. Roots, 678.*)

Under the acts of confiscation the definition of those who were to be considered enemy aliens was of paramount importance. By and large, all of the states followed approximately the same concept. A good picture can be gained from one of the more complete definitions. In the second Virginia pronouncement on the subject the following categories of persons were specified: All British subjects not resident in the United States on April 19, 1775, or who had not since that time either entered into public employment of the states or joined them and by overt acts adhered to them; all inhabitants of the states who were away on the same day and who had since by some overt act adhered to the enemies of the states; and all inhabitants of the states who joined the British of their own free will after that day and before the commencement of the act of the assembly defining what was to be considered as treason or who by any county court were declared to be British subjects under the resolution of December 19, 1776.

Procedurally confiscation was more or less the same in the several states and seemed to follow customary practice. First, the assemblies "attainted" all such persons, that is, they extinguished all their civil rights; their property was sequestered in many of the states and held in protective custody until final acts of confiscation were passed, while in some of the states the confiscation was direct and immediate. Next, as soon as local authorities could accomplish the task, the property was regranted through sale to persons who swore allegiance to the several states. During this procedure, however, it was found that many persons would be treated unjustly if the letter of the law were followed. Consequently, the assemblies passed numerous laws making less stringent their original confiscation enactments. (*Ga. Col. Rec., XIX, pt. 2, 100–3; S.C. Stats., IV, 639–40, 756–58; N.C. Rec., XXIV, 123–24, 398; Hening. Stats., IX, 377–80; X, 66–71; XI, 35–36; Md. Laws, 1785–99, n.p.; Pa. Stats., IX, 201–15, 328–32; N.Y. State Laws, I, 39–51, 159–79; N. Eng. Reg., XII, 71–72.*)

Most of these enactments of confiscation were retroactive to July 4, 1776. Virginia and New Jersey, however, went back to April 19, 1775, while New York gave the enemy aliens a five-day respite by making the law effective as of July 9, 1776.

Two major forces probably motivated these enactments: one, to bring as many persons as possible into the new confederation in the struggle for freedom by solidifying public reaction in favor of the Revolution; and, secondly, to tap a ready source of revenue. The latter force, however, did not operate immediately, for the process of confiscation was slow. Confiscated property later became a good source of state revenue; it is estimated that Maryland received £450,000 and New York $3,085,000 from the sale of land that they confiscated. (*Nettels. Roots, 683.*)

This wholesale confiscation of Loyalist property put the new states in the real estate business on a large scale. It presented many new problems, for the sale of estates already settled, or partially settled, was quite a different undertaking from the disposition of unappropriated lands. Although the alienation of confiscated property did not result in the establishment of family farms in every instance, the trend was definitely in that direction and most of the larger estates were broken up into small units. The family farm principle was put into practice in several ways. First, land bounties were given to soldiers, predominantly in small units; then, New York discouraged sales in excess of 500 acres, and divided much of its land in 100-acre units; also North Carolina sold land at a price which the small farmer could afford to pay; in addition, squatter rights were generally recognized. As two examples of the breaking up of large estates, in New York James DeLancey's land went to about 275 persons, and Morris' estate of 50,000 acres in Putnam County went to nearly 250 persons.

In all parts of the country men without social rank came into positions of importance. This was true not only in the southern and middle colonies but also in New England where many Tory sympathizers lost their property and were forced from their social position. (*Nevins. Amer. States, 441–45.*) Along with the barring of entails, the virtual elimination of primogeniture, and the ending of quitrents, the confiscation acts broke up many semifeudal characteristics of the large estates of the old English squirearchy and deposed many of those who believed in a feudal land system, thereby eliminating their influence and opening the way for far-reaching land reforms. (*Nettels. Roots, 677.*) Shrewd operators, however, amassed huge speculative holdings through dummy sales and otherwise.

The right of the various state assemblies to confiscate the property of persons who did not aid in the Revolution was established by precedent. Confiscation for treason, and for lesser offenses against society, had been well-recognized for many centuries. In at least one instance, the Crown lent its sanction to the process by taking a similar action. This happened during the Revolution when Governor Wright returned and established a royal government in part of Georgia. One bill passed by his legislature was an act to attaint of high treason the several persons therein named, who were either absent from the province, or in that part of it which was still in rebellion against his Majesty, and to vest their real and personal estate in his Majesty. (*Revolutionary Rec., I, 364.*)

The various official acts of the several legislatures which called for confiscation, and also subsequent events, had a disquieting influence. To make property holders feel more secure in their rights to property, several states provided in their constitutions or otherwise, and the federal Constitution also provided, that no attainder should work corruption of the blood, nor cause forfeiture of estate to the commonwealth, except perhaps in some cases during the life of the offender. (*McElreath. Const. of Ga., 80–81.*) The wording of the Pennsylvania Constitution of 1790 was as follows: "That no attainder shall work corruption of blood, nor, except during the life of the offender, forfeiture of estate to the commonwealth." (*Thorpe. Charters, V, 3101.*) Thus was outlawed the old feudal practice of depriving a person or his family of his estate because of his commission of treason or felony.

The confiscation of Tory property put the new states in the unique business of selling land that had been brought into cultivation. This experience was valuable as a guide in the formulation of the land policy for the new public domain. The confiscated estates were a ready source of revenue for the financially embarrassed state governments, even as sale of the public domain helped to put money into the national treasury. In neither case, however, was the income as large as anticipated or sufficient to meet the urgent needs of the government for revenue. The general confusion and disquieting effects of the various confiscation acts were of considerable effect locally and on a short-time basis. But the first reactions soon died down with the successful prosecution of the war. One of the lasting effects was to cause the new states to enact laws reducing to a minimum the conditions that might lead to confiscation in the future. Since many large estates were subdivided and the political power of their owners was broken, the confiscation acts made for a more democratic government and a land system made up of family-sized farms.

PROPERTY ACQUISITION — PURSUIT OF HAPPINESS

The British Crown was little concerned with the land system in the colonies during the early Colonial period. The land question became important, however, as the country became more fully settled and as tension mounted between the mother country and her colonies. The Proclamation of 1763 and the Quebec Act of 1774, if carried out, would have tightened up the colonial land settlement policy of the home government. Various orders to governors during the years just prior to the Revolution had the same objective in view. Even so, the several colonies continued to control, by and large, the local rules and interpretations in regard to land already alienated.

Among the grievances presented in the Declaration of Independence against King George III was one in regard to the appropriation of new land and the further settlement of the colonies. The Virginia assembly had already appointed a committee to inquire into the right of the king to advance the terms of granting land in that colony and recommended that all persons forbear either purchasing or accepting grants of land on the conditions laid down in recent instructions. The exact language of the grievance in the Declaration is, "He [the king] has endeavored to prevent the population of these States; for that purpose obstructing the Laws for Naturalization of Foreigners; refusing to pass others to encourage their migration hither, and raising the conditions of new Appropriation of Lands." Difficulties with the Crown no doubt influenced the situation in at least two particulars: It stressed the importance of a free system of land tenure, based in part at least on human rights, as an encouragement and inducement to settlers to take up new land; and it emphasized the need of a well-defined system of settlement for the land beyond the 1763 proclamation line.

One of the most interesting aspects of the ideas that were developing at that time in regard to property was the distinction in the Declaration of Independence between property rights and human rights. The distinction was clear to Jefferson, who drafted the Declaration, but probably meant little to many of his contemporaries. The rights that Jefferson held to be inalienable were human rights and those only, while others mixed human and property rights as if there were no difference, as shown by the language of the Declaration of Independence in comparison with similar pronouncements of several state constitutions of the same era.

The Declaration of Independence says, "We hold these truths to be self-evident, that all men are created equal, that they are endowed by their Creator with certain inalienable Rights, that among these are Life, Liberty, and the pursuit of Happiness. . . ." Whereas in the Pennsylvania Constitution of 1776 the corresponding provision reads as follows: "That all men are born equally free and independent, and have certain natural, inherent and inalienable rights, amongst which are the enjoying and defending of life and liberty, acquiring, possessing and protecting property, and pursuing and obtaining happiness and safety." The Massachusetts Constitution of 1780 and the New Hampshire Constitution of 1784 contained provisions almost identical in thought to the Pennsylvania provision. In the preamble to the Georgia Constitution of 1776 "life, liberty and property" were mentioned twice and the first South Carolina Constitution also specified property and not happiness. In addition, the Declaration on the Violation of Rights, adopted by the First Continental Congress, and the Virginia Bill of Rights specified that one of the inherent rights was the acquiring and possessing of property.

In his study of Jefferson, Chinard holds that the omission of property in the Declaration of Independence was not unintentional, "for when Lafayette submitted to Jefferson his 'Déclaration des droits de l'homme,' Jefferson put in brackets the words 'droit à la propriété,' thus suggesting their elimination from the list of natural rights." He adds that Jefferson had come to the conclusion that the right of acquiring and possessing property had to be protected by society in order to be enjoyed securely, and that property rights had to be abridged in the protection process, for it was necessary to levy taxes or to take property in the interest of the community. (*Chinard. Jefferson, 83–84.*)

It seems that Jefferson was separating human rights, which are inherent and inalienable, from property rights which are neither necessarily inherent, natural, nor inalienable. Although society has long followed the practice of taking human life and restricting personal liberty when in the interest of the community, as it has taken property and restricted its use and transfer for the public good, it seems clear that the human rights of life, liberty, and happiness are essential in any social compact — in any economic and political system — while the acquisition and possession of property — the ownership of real property — is not essential, as for example in a purely socialistic state. This must have been clearly understood by Jefferson, although he was in no way trying to introduce a different economic system — he was neither a communist nor a socialist. He recognized, however, the need for making significant adjustment in the property system — in abridging existing property rights — and within a few months Jefferson began his effective legislative endeavor to take from the individual property holder the right to entail landed estate, and later he helped outlaw primogeniture in intestate succession.

BARRING ENTAILS AND OUTLAWING PRIMOGENITURE

The reaction against various sorts of restrictions on freedom of alienation had been developing since the earliest days of feudalism, and the major restriction that survived the centuries of change was the one designed to perpetuate large landed estates through entails. By the time of the Revolution, although much land throughout Colonial America was still held in fee tail estates, the practice of holding land in fee simple estates was widespread. Great strides had been made in barring fee tail estates by provisions in original grants to private parties, by private action in the making of wills, and by special acts of the colonial assemblies on behalf of individual cases. However, there still remained the job of outlawing summarily the principle, and of settling once and for all the policy, of entailing estates.

Soon after the colonists declared their freedom from British sovereignty, the colonial assemblies, one after another, passed the legislation necessary to make impossible the perpetuation of estates in the same family through entails. It was not until after the federal Constitution had been adopted, however, that the job was completed. Since many entailed estates were in existence and in keeping with the ideal regarding freedom of action, many of the acts simply provided that the holder of an entailed estate could alienate it in fee simple, while other acts provided that estates should not be entailed. The effect of either action was to kill the principle of entails, regardless of the purpose for which rights in land were so encumbered.

The practice of primogeniture likewise was dying rapidly before the Revolution. But it was not so summarily dismissed. Many of the colonial assemblies during this period left it possible for the eldest son to receive a double portion, and some colonies continued to discriminate against daughters by giving them only a half-portion, while at least one colony prevented daughters from inheriting if any sons survived. Of course, the landholder continued to have the freedom, as he does today, to devise his land by will to whomsoever he desired, subject only to dower and curtesy.

The arguments for and against entails and primogeniture were many and varied. Since Virginia was one of the first states to abolish entails and since Jefferson led the fight not only in Virginia but nationally, it is instructive to examine the arguments against entails that were inserted in the preamble to the statute of 1776, which he drafted. The preamble may be paraphrased as follows: Whereas the perpetuation of property in certain families by means of gifts in fee tail is contrary to good policy, tends to deceive fair traders who give credit on visible possessions, discourages the holder from taking care of and improving the same, and sometimes does injury to the morals of youth by rendering them independent of, and disobedient to, their parents, and whereas the barring of such large estates by the legislature is time-consuming and the barring of small estates is costly, it is deemed advisable to enact a law to remedy the situation.

North Carolina held that entailing property gave wealthy families an undue influence in a republic, that it was a source of great private injustice, and that perpetuities and monopolies were contrary to the idea of a free state and should not be allowed. It also was argued that a continuation of primogeniture and entail would be in effect subscribing to the idea that honesty could be bought with money and that wisdom was hereditary. Most of the discussion ran in terms of equal distribution of real estate among the heirs. However, the 1790 constitution of South Carolina instructed the legislature to pass laws for the abolition of primogeniture and for giving an *equitable* distribution of the real estate of intestates. (*Thorpe. Charters, VI, 3265.*) It appears that *equitable* meant *equal* to most people, and it was generally so interpreted throughout Colonial America and the new republic. This interpretation has remained relatively unchanged.

Jefferson relates that after entails were outlawed in Virginia he proposed the abolition of primogeniture when working with conservative aristocrats of the Old Dominion under legislative authorization to revise the laws of the state. The landed gentry, however, wished to maintain the status quo, but when they saw that this was out of the question, the Hebrew principle that the eldest son have a double share was suggested. Jefferson's answer was that this could not be, unless the eldest son could eat a double portion of food and do a double allowance of work. The strength of the Biblical precedence, however, was effective in seven of the northern and middle colonies, but it did not prevail in Virginia and other southern colonies. In a recent study Haskins recognizes the influence of Jefferson and alludes to the importance of the Mosaic law. He also mentions economic and social conditions in the colonies and the early procedures in Massachusetts. (*Haskins. Inheritance, 1281, 1297.*)

Many of the wealthy landed families not only practiced primogeniture and entails but contended earnestly for continuation of that privilege. The reformers and the small farmers, artisans, and merchants turned the tide. The common man was already dividing equally his family estate, for he held that the labor of all the children contributed to the estate and that equal inheritance was a strong incentive to work during childhood. The equal division of estates among the children of merchants induced intermarriage within the class, which multiplied business contacts, reduced competition, and broadened possible financial resources in time of need. These arguments were not applicable to large landed estates, for they were worked by slaves, laborers, and tenants, and the children of the owner did not contribute to the estate through work. Likewise, large landholders were not concerned with business contacts and financial security other than that provided by the estate.

The unpopularity of primogeniture and entails also grew out of the fact that hereditary estates in land and concentration of economic power were closely associated with hereditary positions in government and the concentration and perpetuation of political power. As a consequence, when hereditary governmental offices were abolished it followed that entails and other types of perpetuities should be outlawed. Following the same general theory, it was argued that one generation had no right to bind succeeding generations — that the gain of the land belonged to the living and not to the dead.

In addition, economic and social development in the colonies had not progressed to the same degree as in England, and younger sons could not be made economically secure in positions of dignity in the professions, the military services, the government, the church, or commercial activities. Furthermore, many fathers and mothers in Colonial America had been disinherited under primogeniture and entails in England. They were literally driven from the family by the unequal system of devolution. It is reasonable to assume that many of them provided in their wills for an equal division of their property among their children, male and female alike, and that they proposed to kill, at the first opportunity, such an inequitable phase of the land tenure system. This idea had been handed down from father to son since early Colonial times, and many were opposed to primogeniture and entails by the time of the Revolution.

The point of view has been expressed that the English practice of primogeniture and entails has many beneficial effects to commend it. It was argued that the rule of primogeniture created a class of landless younger sons educated to the idea that they had to shift for themselves. They were reared as aristocrats in positions of culture and social prestige, and if they desired to live as aristocrats, as many of them did, they would have to succeed in endeavors quite unrelated to the ancestral family estate. This forced the younger sons into the law or the church; into the army, the navy or other public service; into commerce or colonization; and even into piracy, which was both colorful and lucrative in those days. Through the operation of the policy of primogeniture and entails, English aristocracy created a class of ambitious and energetic younger sons who carried the traditions of the English aristocracy into other walks of life and into all parts of the known world, so the argument ran. (*Nettels. Roots, 95.*) However, the Revolution ended primogeniture and entails and eliminated the adverse effects and antisocial results of these complementary land tenure devices.

TAXES AND QUITRENT

Primogeniture and entails were not the only feudal practices that passed out with the Revolution; the colonial quitrents also largely disappeared. Originally, quitrents and reservations of precious metals were not designed to yield much net revenue to the Crown and proprietors. Precious metals failed to enrich the British exchequer, and the collection of quitrents became more difficult as time passed. By the time of the Revolution their collection had become so difficult that in many places only half-hearted endeavors to collect were made. During the first century, and up to the years just before the Revolution, the mother country was content to use the colonies largely as a source of raw materials and a market for manufactured products rather than as a source of direct royal revenue through taxation either on land or by levying various import and excise taxes.

The reasons for this policy are deeply rooted in the original purposes for the development of the colonies, none of which were to derive revenue from land in addition to the nominal quitrents which were reserved largely for purposes of defraying current expenses. This was true, although it was clear that certain individual proprietors looked upon quitrents as a basic source of personal income. Then, as the colonies assumed more and more the responsibilities for government and levied taxes to meet necessary local expenses, arguments for the payment of quitrents became less cogent. Finally, the colonists generally recognized them as a sort of tribute to the landed proprietors rather than reimbursement for services already rendered or to be rendered in the future.

The various colonies recognized the need for levying taxes and taking property for the public good. These practices were well established, but some of the founding fathers felt the need of inserting provisions in the various constitutions that would prevent any abuse of these powers. To this end the federal Constitution provided that no person shall "... be deprived of life, liberty, or property, without due process of law; nor shall private property be taken for public use, without just compensation." It further provided that no state should ". . . deprive any person of life, liberty, or property, without due process of law." Several state constitutions – those of New Hampshire, Massachusetts, Pennsylvania, Maryland, Virginia, North Carolina, and South Carolina – contained provisions in regard to the protection of property rights of the individual. Although none of the provisions were worded exactly alike, they contained essentially the same protection. They provided that no man's property should be taken from him or applied to public use without his consent, or by the law of the land and then only upon payment of just compensation. Some of the provisions also indicated that since every member expected of the community certain protection he had to share in the expenses of such protection – in other words, his property was justly subject to taxes levied for the public good.

That the subject of land taxation was before the British authorities, even at an early date, is shown by a communication in 1716 to the Board of Trade from Archibald Cumings, one of the custom-house officials at Boston. After proposing the imposition of an import duty on rum, sugar, and molasses, Cumings suggested the following year that colonial revenues could be increased by stamp duties, additional import duties, and excise taxes on rum distilled in the colonies and by a direct tax on unimproved land. These and similar proposals were not accepted, and "... the colonists insensibly drifted into the idea that Parliament could not legally tax them." The tax on unimproved land anticipated some modern thinkers, for it was to be levied on such land because "... great tracts of land are ingrossed, in the hand of Rich Men, and growing in value daily, tho' unimproved, but never taxed." (*Beer. Colonial Policy, 38, 40 n.*)

Years later, when revenue was sorely needed in the prosecution of the French and Indian War, Governor Dinwiddie proposed to raise some of the funds locally by the imposition of parliamentary taxes, and he added frankly that such taxes as he proposed would arouse opposition in the colonies. He suggested a poll tax for two years to raise the funds necessary to build the forts and a permanent land tax modeled after the Virginia quitrents for their support. (*B.T. Va. 25 W 208, Feb. 23, 1756,* quoted in *Beer. Colonial Policy, 45 n.*) However, the tax on land was never imposed and the feeling continued to grow that the people were against all forms of taxes imposed by the highest governmental authority — the mother country.

Colonial practices and the attitude of the people that had been developing slowly over the years set the stage for the policy that was finally adopted whereby the federal government did not levy a land tax; land taxes were levied chiefly for local purposes, and the states and local units of government did not levy a tax on federally owned land. The strong colonial attitude against the payment of quitrents and the denial of British dominion over the land, together with the several acts of confiscation which included the large landed estates that collected quitrent, rendered inappropriate the assumption of the right to collect quitrent by the several states. In the New England states no action was necessary, for quitrents were practically never collected there, while in other colonies specific legislative acts stopped their collection, and in others they were ended by the disappearance of the quitrent collectors along with the landed proprietors.

MINOR ADJUSTMENTS

At the height of English feudal tenure every opportunity was seized to cause rights in land held by the feudal tenant to revert to the lord. Thus, if a person took his own life, was killed accidentally or by casualty, his property passed automatically into the hands of the feudal lord. In early America under some such occasions rights in land went back to the granting authority. By the time of the Revolution such practices were rapidly disappearing, and following the war several states specifically outlawed these types of forfeitures, although they were not outlawed in England until 1846. The New Hampshire constitution of 1784 provided:

> The estates of such persons as may destroy their own lives, shall not for that offence be forfeited, but descent or ascent in the same manner, as if such persons had died in a natural way. Nor shall any article which shall accidently occasion the death of any person, be henceforth deemed a deodand, or in any wise forfeited on account of such misfortune. (*Thorpe. Charters, IV, 2469.*)

These acts contributed to the freeing of landed property of feudal burdens and added greatly to the security with which private owners held rights in land.

The problem of quieting Indian titles also plagued the Revolutionary assemblies as it previously had the colonies. To remedy the situation the states during and after the Revolution followed the colonial practice of safeguarding the rights of Indians in their land by requiring that no purchases from the Indians should be valid unless made under the authority, and with the consent, of the legislature of the state. Two states, New York and North Carolina, went so far as to place this provision in their state constitution during the early years of the Confederation. The brief North Carolina proviso said ". . . no purchase of lands shall be made of the Indian natives, but on behalf of the public, by authority of the General Assembly." (*Thorpe. Charters, V, 2794*. The longer New York provision is on page 2636.) Thus, Revolutionary states bridged the gap between the colonial practices in regard to acquisition of the Indians' land and the policies followed after the establishment of the national government.

Several states felt it sufficiently important to mention in their constitutions other safeguards of private property rights. For example, New Hampshire provided that every citizen had the right to be secure from unreasonable seizure and searches; Maryland provided that trial of facts is one of the greatest securities of the lives, liberties, and estates of the people; and Maryland, and New York also, guaranteed to the people that all properly acquired colonial titles to land would be fully recognized by the new states.

In the colonial struggle to free the individual from the bondages of feudalism, one step of progress was the early relaxation and final outlawing of the practice of holding a person in prison when his property was not sufficient to pay his debts. Early in the history of his colony Penn decreed that debtors could not be imprisoned when they did not possess property enough to pay their debts. Parenthetically, Penn spent eight months in the Tower of London because of his religious activities and was imprisoned a second time for the same offense. Although the practice was fast disappearing by the time of the Revolution, North Carolina and Pennsylvania provided through constitutional provisions that a debtor, where there was not a strong presumption of fraud, should not be continued in prison after delivering up his estate for the benefit of his creditors.

STATE LAND OFFICES

The newly formed states were confronted with the matter of unappropriated and confiscated lands within their own boundaries. The unappropriated lands in the thirteen states, whether owned by individuals, large proprietors, or the royal government, fell into the hands of the colonies, theoretically at the Declaration of Independence and actually with the signing of the peace. The states thus became the possessors of vast quantities of "public lands" that lay within their final boundaries. The question arose immediately as to how this land was to be administered. Rules and regulations covering the disposition of these lands had to be established.

Following the Declaration of Independence, yet preceding the passage of the ordinances in regard to the Northwest Territory, several states established land offices to have charge of alienating state-owned land to private settlers, including frequently the distribution of military bounty lands to soldiers. They usually specified in some detail the quantity of land to be allocated to each settler, its price, conditions of credit, the type of conveyance, and the system of surveying and recording. The conditions generally were similar to those followed by the governors during the preceding half century, except for the elimination of the quitrent provision. The newly established land offices were designed to tighten up and regularize the procedures and to make the grants in a more orderly manner.

Like the federal government, the states needed cash with which to pay the expenses of the war and land with which to reimburse their soldiers. Sale of land for cash had been common practice for some time, particularly the last half century before the Revolution. With the precedent readily at hand and the need for cash so urgent, the states turned to sale as a means of disposing of their public land. The granting of land for service in the Continental Army also was well grounded in colonial precedent. The military grants generally tended to establish family-sized farms. The same was true of the land that was sold, for much of it was disposed of in small tracts, while much of that which was sold in large tracts to speculators was soon resold in small farms to settlers. The family-farm idea was thus advanced another step and given substance in actual practice.

CESSIONS TO THE FEDERAL GOVERNMENT

In addition to the unappropriated and confiscated land within their own bounds, seven of the original thirteen states laid claim to land west of the mountains. These states were: Massachusetts, Connecticut, New York, Virginia, North Carolina, South Carolina, and Georgia. All except New York claimed sea-to-sea grants under terms of their original charters from the English Crown. New York claimed territory to the west by virtue of suzerainty over the Iroquois Indians. The other six states made no claims to the western land. Their boundaries were definitely established prior to 1780, except for a few minor border disputes.

The problem of the western lands was twofold: (1) it was concerned with who should have charge of the settlement of the area and the conditions under which the land should be held, and (2) who should have sovereign power over the western country and the form of government it should have. Experience during the preceding century and a half in those colonies in which sovereignty and land control were separated had shown some of the colonists that it was always difficult, usually artificial, and invariably ineffective to separate completely sovereignty over a people and control over the basic tenure system of the country. It took much effort and time before all of the states could see the utter necessity of joining, under proper safeguards, government of the territory and control over the land.

Maryland sponsored the idea a full month before the Articles of Confederation were proposed to the states for ratification. She proposed ". . . that the United States in Congress assembled, shall have the sole and exclusive right and power to ascertain and fix the western boundary of such states as claim to the Mississippi River or South Sea, and lay out the land beyond the boundary, so ascertained, into separate and independent states, from time to time, as the number and circumstances of the people may require." (*Jour. of Congress. II, 290.*) This idea was so revolutionary at the time that the Ninth Article of Confederation was forthwith amended to include a proviso that no state should be deprived of territory for the benefit of the United States. Yet soon after declaring independence, and again within a little over four years, the Continental Congress was requesting that the states make such cessions, and New York and Connecticut were taking the lead by appropriate legislative action. (For a more complete discussion see, *Adams. Maryland's Influence; Robbins. Our Landed Heritage, chap.* I; *Abernethy. Western Lands, chap.* XIII.)

It seems singular that nowhere in the literature was found a single suggestion which would indicate that the possibility of making a colonial possession out of the northwest country was ever considered. Yet this was a distinct possibility, at least theoretically. It is to the credit of the founding fathers that such a possibility was not discussed and that they readily recognized the advantages, in fact the absolute necessity, of bringing this territory into the union on an equal basis with that part of the country already settled.

The six states that did not claim territory beyond the mountains contended that the unsettled territory should be used for the common purpose, since it was won by common effort and since the landed states would have too much power if they maintained control over the vast westward territory. But it was Maryland that made the decided stand which was necessary for ultimate solution of these problems. Whereas the other five states agreed to a plan permitting the landed states to maintain sovereignty over the territory if they would transfer title to the federal government, Maryland maintained that both title and sovereignty must be transferred, and she would not sign the Articles of Confederation until these stipulations had been met. Maryland's position during the controversy was based upon six factors, in some of which Maryland was chiefly involved while others were of concern to all of the colonies.

First, provincial Marylanders had never lived too harmoniously with their aristocratic Virginia neighbors. In addition to the cultural and ideological difference, the Maryland grant of 1632 was carved out of the territory granted to Virginia and this had never suited the Virginians. Furthermore, the grant did not follow the usual channel of the river demarcation but extended to the southern bank of the Potomac, and this too did not make for amicability between the two colonies. Thus, Maryland and Virginia were wary of each other insofar as their original grants of land had an influence.

Secondly, the western boundary called for in the Maryland grant was a line drawn due north from the first fountain of the Potomac River. Lord Fairfax, the proprietary owner of the Northern Neck, claimed that the source of the river was farther east than Maryland claimed, and again the two colonies were at odds over land ownership and governmental jurisdiction.

Thirdly, in a boundary dispute Maryland had previously lost the territory which is now Delaware, and in another border misunderstanding she had lost, in a fight with Pennsylvania, a narrow strip of land on her northern boundary. The Virginia, the Delaware, and the Pennsylvania border conflicts made Maryland unusually conscious of territorial claims and counter claims.

A fourth factor was the conflict between "the haves and the have-nots." The revolutionary break with the mother country did not involve land except on a national basis. It was not until the relative political and financial strength of the colonies was up for review during the establishment of the central government that the unsettled territory from sea to sea became important. Throughout this discussion Virginia was one of the "haves" while Maryland was one of the "have-nots" — Virginia had a claim to the western land, Maryland did not.

Fifthly, the boundaries of the various claims of the seven states were not at all clear. They overlapped in many places, and the evidence was not conclusive as to which state held the best claim. As a consequence, it was argued that the matter could never be untangled in a satisfactory manner by negotiation among the states and hence the most expeditious resolution of the problem was the cession of all of the lands by each of the states to the central government.

A sixth factor presented a unique need of the federal government for control over at least some of the western territory. Following the precedent already fully established of granting land as a bounty to those who would serve in the militia, the Continental Congress offered land to soldiers within two months after the Declaration of Independence was signed. Unlike the earlier offers by the colonies, the national government had no land with which to back up this commitment. Nevertheless in August, 1776, it offered land to deserters of the British army with an especially large grant for officers who would induce their soldiers to desert with them. The following month land was offered to American soldiers and officers, ranging from 100 acres to soldiers and noncommissioned officers to 500 acres to a colonel. In 1780 larger grants were offered to higher ranking officers. (*Jour. of Congress, V, 707, 763; XVII, 726–27.*) These offers of land as bounties to soldiers anticipated either that the western territory would be administered by the federal government or that the government would otherwise acquire land with which to fulfil its obligations.

Although Maryland stood firm in her refusal to ratify the Articles of Confederation until the territorial problem was solved, she was not alone in the fight. The other five states without landed claims supported her in the demand for cession of the unsettled territory. In addition, some of the smaller states later supported her fight as a basis for some equality of political strength among the several states. The states without surplus land did not see the justice of permitting those with vast territorial claims, based upon royal grants, to acquire the power that would be theirs when the vast domain was populated. The acts of the English Crown were repudiated by the Declaration of Independence, and the unsettled portions of the country did not contribute to the gaining of independence.

The claims of the several colonies to land was based upon the charters issued by the English Crown between 1606 and 1732, the dates of the first Virginia charter and the Georgia grant. During the century and a quarter between the first and last grants many proclamations and orders further complicated the already overlapping and conflicting grants. The British Crown's complete jurisdiction over the colonies was well recognized under English law, and consequently such adjustments in land grants as were deemed necessary could be made. The king reserved and exercised the right to alter boundaries and the current grant always was the one in effect. The only exception was afforded by grants from the proprietors. The Proclamation of 1763 and the Quebec Act of 1774 did not affect basically the claims of the several colonies since the former was only a deferment imposed in regranting land to individuals and the latter was considered as an act of war rather than a change in the original grants. (*Paxson. Amer. Frontier, 51.*)

The contest among the seven states over their territorial claims was a matter of major concern. It was so acute that North Carolina dealt with the difficulties in her constitution of 1776. After indicating the importance of precise territorial delimitations, North Carolina's constitution set forth the boundaries between North and South Carolina on the southern boundary and Virginia on the northern side. (*Thorpe. Charters, V, 2788–89.*) Also, Virginia's constitution of the same year contained a statement in regard to the boundaries with North Carolina, Maryland, and Pennsylvania. In addition it specifically reserved for Virginia the northwest region.

The landed colonies gave up their favorable position only after much discussion and thorough consideration, and then very reluctantly. At least five times the Continental Congress pleaded with these colonies to relinquish their claims to the western land. The first request came soon after the signing of the Declaration of Independence. The second request for western land cession was on September 6, 1780, after New York had laid her cession before the Congress. The third request was discussed after the Connecticut legislature had acted and after the Congress had accepted the New York cession; this was on April 18, 1783, but it failed to pass after involved debate. The fourth and fifth requests came in 1785, and were concerned chiefly with the North Carolina, South Carolina, and Georgia cessions.

Following the second request, the Congress on October 10, 1780, the same day that the Connecticut legislature acted favorably upon its cession, indicated the conditions that would bind the federal government as to the handling of the western lands. Although the resolution failed to pass, it showed the items of major concern at that time. They were (1) how the new states would enter the union, (2) the suggested size of the new states, with the range of 100 to 150 miles square being suggested, (3) the reimbursement of states for Revolutionary War expenses, (4) rules and regulations covering the settlers to be made by the central government, and (5) the ratification of all Indian land purchases.

New York led the larger states in accepting the conditions laid down by Maryland and the smaller states by offering to cede the disputed territory on February 19, 1780. In the deed New York indicated that her cession was granted ". . . to facilitate the completion of the Articles of Confederation." Based upon this cession and the promise of similar action by the other six landed states, Maryland broke the deadlock. Connecticut followed on October 10, but withheld cession until she received a grant of land 120 miles long along Lake Erie and considered equal to the Wyoming Valley land that had been settled by the Susquehannah Company. This territory was known as the Western Reserve, and of it half a million acres were set aside to compensate Connecticut families for losses that they incurred in British and Indian raids. Connecticut sold the land that remained to the post-Revolutionary Connecticut Land Company in 1795 for $1,200,000, thereby establishing her educational fund. In 1800, to insure clear land titles, Connecticut formally relinquished governmental jurisdiction over the territory to the federal government, and the region was made Trumbull County, Northwest Territory. Virginia showed her good intentions on the following January 2, the final agreement being reached on March 1, 1784. Maryland accepted these actions upon their face value, with good faith, and signed the Articles of Confederation on March 1, 1781. Final cession was completed in 1802 when Georgia ceded her western land; thus, over two decades elapsed from the time New York made the first cession to the completion of the last cession by Georgia. Important steps in the ceding process in chronological order were:

Year	Month	Day	Event
1780,	Feb.	19,	Act of New York Legislature.
	March	7,	New York cession laid before Congress.
	Sept.	6,	Congress again requests cessions.
	Oct.	10,	Congress indicates conditions binding Federal Government.
	Oct.	10,	Act of Connecticut Legislature.
1781,	Jan.	2,	Act of Virginia Legislature.
	March	1,	New York deed of cession executed in Congress.
1782,	Oct.	29,	New York cession accepted by Congress.
1783,	April	18,	Previous cession requests again discussed.
	Sept.	13,	Virginia cession rejected.
	Oct.	20,	Second Virginia act of cession.
1784,	March	1,	Virginia cession completed.
	June	2,	Act of North Carolina Legislature.
	Nov.	13,	Act of Massachusetts Legislature.
	Nov.	20,	Act of North Carolina Legislature repealed.
1785,	March	31,	Congress again petitions states to cede western land.
	April	19,	Massachusetts cession completed.
	Sept.	20,	Congress puts more pressure on states to cede western lands.
1786,	May	11,	Second Act of Connecticut Legislature.
	May	26,	Connecticut cession completed.
1787,	March	8,	Act of South Carolina Legislature.
	August	9,	South Carolina cession completed.
1788,	Feb.	1,	First Act of Georgia Legislature.
	July	15,	Georgia offer rejected.
1789,	Dec.	22,	Act of North Carolina Legislature.
1790,	Feb.	25,	North Carolina cession completed.
1802,	April	24,	Articles of Agreement and Cession entered into between the Commissioners of the United States and of Georgia.
	June	16,	Ratified by Georgia Legislature.

(Adapted largely from *Treat. Land System, 14.*)

As a document for establishing a central government the Articles were totally inadequate, but were sufficient to hold the union together until the more adequate Constitution could be adopted. One of the strong holding forces was the common trusteeship in the newly created public domain. This common interest in the vast territory to the west not only helped to hold the confederation of states together, but also was a major factor in facilitating perfection of the national government. The common ownership of this domain, its disposition and settlement, the prospective revenue with which to pay the common debt, and the matters relating to the government of the area emphasized the necessity of acting together for the common good. This common interest helped to harmonize widely divergent economic views, to minimize the differences between various social institutions and customs, and to reconcile varying political practices and ideals.

The relation between the states and the federal government in regard to the land question was not a one-way affair by which the states bowed to the central authority. Substantial reservations were made in behalf of the states in some of the cessions, but on the other hand the United States transferred to Pennsylvania in 1791 a tract of land lying between Lake Erie and the northern boundary of that commonwealth. The authorization of the Pennsylvania assembly gave the governor wide latitude in completing this purchase, but the act provided that the conveyance should be in fee simple. This was in complete harmony with the concepts of rights in land that were becoming firmly established at that time.

Of the seven state cessions, four contain reservations and conditions that proved of considerable importance in the distribution and administration of the western land. The federal government lived up to the spirit of the conditions outlined in the cessions and cooperated fully with the states concerned, Connecticut, Virginia, North Carolina, and Georgia.

The Western Reserve was administered by Connecticut until it was disposed of and the establishment of a government was necessary. Since that colony did not care to provide the local government machinery, she turned jurisdiction of the area over to the United States. The Virginia Military Reserve called for as much territory in Ohio between the Scioto and Little Miami rivers as was necessary to complete her military bounties after the lands reserved in Kentucky were exhausted. Additional reservations were made for Clark and his men, and for the claims of French settlers already in the area. The central government fulfilled the latter two conditions, and all of the Virginia bounties, covering more than 6,000,000 acres, were recognized. The North Carolina cession covering areas in Tennessee proved of little financial value and much trouble to the federal government, and was finally turned over to Tennessee for administration. The Yazoo land claims involved in the Georgia cession occasioned more difficulties than any other cession reservation, but these conditions were finally fulfilled in 1830 after much controversy, speculation, and fraud in the ceded territory. (For a more complete discussion of these reservations see *Hibbard. Land Policies, chap.* II.)

TERRITORIAL ORDINANCES

Before the signing of the Constitution, and even before the first deeds ceding land to the federal government were executed, population movement made necessary the adoption of a policy for the distribution and administration of the yet unborn public domain. Three possibilities were readily evident — (*a*) the loose, individualistic, indiscriminate location plan used generally in the South, (*b*) the more rigid township planting system of the North, or (*c*) a doctrinaire system laid down without reference to local practices. Since many of the leaders were practical landowners, theoretical concepts apparently were disregarded in favor of the best arrangement in common use. Since neither the southern nor the northern procedure was perfect, the public policy adopted the good features of both.

In the South the common practice was for the colonist to select the tract of land which he desired and to describe its boundaries as best he could; then, after securing title, to record his deed in the county office. Settlement was spotted and uncorrelated, and many overlapping claims resulted. There were also many small areas to which no one laid a claim.

In the North the practice was quite different. The land usually was granted in large tracts to groups of individuals and regranted by the group to individual members. These groups made up the famed New England towns, and this practice was the foundation of the township system. Settlement was made only after prior survey and then on a somewhat diagrammatic basis. Each tract was easily bounded, and disputed borders were infrequent. The frontier advanced by relatively compact settlement as new territory was needed. Reservations for educational and religious purposes were frequent and specifications regarding improvement of the land were often inserted in the grant.

Whereas the southern system was more in accord with the individualistic frontier spirit, the New England town system made for more orderly settlement and record keeping. The southern system was adapted to large plantations and slaves, a mild climate, and infrequent difficulties with the Indians, while the northern system was more suited to a free population, severe winters, and hostile savages. The two systems were discussed both on their merits and with prejudices, since the Congress was made up of representatives from both sections.

Probably the first plan for the distribution of the public domain was presented by Pelatiah Webster early in 1781, even before the New York cession was executed in Congress on March 1. He dismissed summarily the earlier proposal that the vast domain be sold or mortgaged to a foreign nation and suggested (*a*) that the land be surveyed and laid out in townships, (*b*) that settlement follow rather than precede surveying, (*c*) that the land be sold to the highest bidders with a minimum price, (*d*) that the purchaser settle and improve the land within two or three years, and (*e*) that each township be settled completely before another one was opened up. (*Treat. Land System, 16–17.*)

During the interim between the presentation of this plan and the report of Jefferson's land committee in 1784, several other proposals were made. In the first Connecticut Act of Cession that state insisted that the ceded land be laid out in surveyed townships. In the spring of 1783 two plans were proposed. One, the "Army Plan," called for the satisfaction of the bounties offered soldiers on the public land, and, after that was completed, the turning over of the remaining land to be the common property of the individual state for the common good, to support roads, schools, public expenditures, and for other public uses. The other, the "Financier's Plan," was similar, except that the unappropriated land was to remain forever the common property of the United States, unless disposed of by the Congress, and the land granted to the soldiers was to be free of taxes and quitrents for seven years. No action was taken on the latter plan, but the former was presented to the Congress with Washington's approval on June 17. Four months later the Congress pleaded that appropriation of land was impossible, because the cessions were incomplete. (For a more complete discussion see *Treat. Land System, chap.* II.)

The Report of 1784

Positive congressional action was not taken until 1784, when the Virginia cession was completed. A congressional committee, probably appointed before November 4, 1783, with Jefferson as chairman, was instructed to draw up plans for distributing the public domain. Previously, on January 16 of that year, in writing to Governor Harrison, Jefferson enumerated six important items before the Congress. The fourth item was in regard to disposing of the western territory, while the fifth was concerned with treaties of peace and land purchases from the Indians. His committee's report was read on April 30, 1784, and assigned on the calendar for the first official reading on May 7 and the second reading on May 14, and called up for vote on May 28, at which time Congress voted not to consider the report at that time. (*Jour. of Congress, XXVI, 356; XXVII, 446–53.*)

The plan outlined in the report was similar to the New England township system, with surveyors and registers appointed by Congress. Surveys should precede sales, and receipts should be applied to a sinking fund. There were no provisions for land for religious or educational institutions, and no land was to be granted to individual states for public use. The transfer of title was to be by warrants and certificates, which had to be held by the register several months after final selections in order that conflicting claims could be settled by arbitration. The latter provision was practiced in Virginia.

The report also called for a qualified bonded surveyor, and for the carrying out of resolutions of September 15, 1776, and August 12, 1780, in regard to land for soldiers. More significant was the provision that the grant should provide that the grantee and his heirs were to have and to hold the land forever. It further provided that ". . . the lands therein shall pass, in descent and dower according to the customs known in the common law by the name of gavelkind; and shall be transferable by deed or will proved by two witnesses, but so soon as a temporary government shall be so established they shall become subject to the laws of the State, & shall never after, in any case, revert to the United States."

In regard to the 1784 report Ford says, "Next to the Declaration of Independence (if indeed standing second to that), this document ranks in historical importance of all those drawn by Jefferson; and, but for its being superseded by the 'Ordinance of 1787,' would rank among all American state papers immediately after the National Constitution." (*Jefferson. Writings, [Ford] III, 430.*) He adds that Jefferson's idea of banning slavery in all of the western territory was unpopular in the South as slavery became more and more profitable. After about 1790 Jefferson carefully avoided public statements on slavery, and omitted reference to the report in his later writings, presumably because of mounting tension over the slavery question.

The Land Ordinance of 1785

The report was not before the Congress again for about a year after the May 28, 1784, vote not to consider it at that time. When it was brought to the attention of Congress in the spring of 1785, it was first presented on March 4, and read a second time on March 16. After revising the report, it was presented for Congressional action on April 14, 1785.

It was referred, after some debate, to a committee which considered it for a month and presented a more carefully worked out report than the original, although it contained many of the same features. In addition, it provided for reserves to be set aside for schools, for religious uses, and for future disposition by the United States, and sales were to be made by auction instead of warrants.

Grayson was representing Virginia since Jefferson had sailed for Europe. In a letter forwarding a copy of the report to Washington his arguments favoring the report were as follows: (1) prior rectangular surveys would preclude overlapping titles and would be more economical, (2) auction sales would give equal opportunity to all, (3) sales by townships would make for orderly settlement and the poorer classes could unite to purchase a township, (4) the market would not be flooded and prices would be maintained, (5) transfers would be simplified since the deed was to be both the first and the last instrument, and (6) the plan could be easily altered as experience pointed the way.

He likewise presented the ideas which formed the basis of the differences during the preparation of the report. They were concerned with (1) the fact that it was a revenue measure only, (2) that the money should be gotten without depreciating land values in the states and without their losing part of their population (labor force) by the westward movement, and (3) that the present balance would be upset as new states came into the confederation.

Such an important report could not be adopted without controversy and compromise. The rectangular system was accepted by the southern members, but the "township planting" system was amended to permit settlers to purchase smaller amounts of land, retaining the compact settlement aspect of the original scheme. The range, the six miles square township, and the 640-acre section were included, and the reservation of sections for educational purposes was retained. The provision setting aside a section in each township for the support of religion, however, was deleted. Prior survey and deeds to specific tracts were kept in preference to either the indiscriminate location system of the southern colonies or the future selection scheme proposed earlier by Jefferson. Congress reserved four sections in each township for future distribution and a third part of certain minerals.

The main provisions of the Ordinance of 1785 may be briefly summarized as follows:

1. Congress would appoint surveyors, and the surveying of the land would be under the direction of the geographer of the United States, who would supervise the surveying and make appropriate reports to Congress.
2. After the land was purchased from the Indians, the country would be laid out in townships six miles square and sections of 640 acres, each numbered in an orderly manner and appropriately described and plainly marked.
3. Tracts would be drawn by lot for the military bounties promised the Continental Army, according to commitments made in earlier legislation.
4. The remaining tracts would be drawn and allotted to the several states for sale within the states by whole townships and by smaller lots.
5. The minimum price would be one dollar per acre with an additional charge of thirty-two dollars per township for surveying.
6. Reservation of section 16 for educational purposes, four sections for later distribution, and one-third of certain minerals — gold, silver, lead, and copper — was called for, and the Virginia reservation between the Scioto and Little Miami rivers was accepted.
7. Deeds would evidence the transfer, and would be recorded in the land office in the state.
8. The land would be held under fee simple tenure according to a provision which reads, "To have to the said (*insert name of grantee*)

his heirs and assigns forever, or if more than one as tenants in common."

The controversy about the Ordinance of 1785 was largely over rigid rectangular surveys, compact settlement, and discriminate location versus a modified southern system of rectangular surveys, scattered settlement, and individual location. Of considerable importance was the difference between the sale of whole townships and sale in smaller units to individual settlers. Discussion also centered on land reservations for schools and charitable purposes, and the granting processes, including the extension of loans to purchasers. The reservation of land for religious purposes was discussed. Probably the basic consideration that influenced various provisions was the desire to use the western land to pay off the public debt.

Apparently all parties relinquished some provisions and the ordinance was a compromise of conflicting local practices and preconceived ideas. It finally passed on May 20, 1785, and formed the tangible plan from which the land system has been developed and which it has followed in many particulars. It proved of very little immediate usefulness, however, since it was not put into effective operation forthwith; it was later supplemented and amplified in important particulars by the Ordinance of 1787. However, the Ordinance of 1785 was the foundation upon which the whole public domain disposition policy was built. Its basic principles continue to affect the land system.

The Northwest Ordinance of 1787

When the Continental Congress met in 1787 it had lost much of its earlier importance and it was difficult to get a quorum, for the Constitutional Convention which was to meet in Philadelphia in May overshadowed it. It appears that only considerations regarding the public lands kept the Congress alive. Two major items were under discussion – the Ohio Associates' proposition to buy land and Monroe's report on the Northwest. Both matters met with favorable action soon after a quorum was assembled in July.

The former was a speculative scheme involving a million dollars worth of land in which certain public leaders were financially interested. The conduct of public affairs for private gain was not uncommon in those days. In fact, it may be concluded that considerable stability was added to government during this period by the questionable acts of public officials to enrich themselves.

The Northwest report was a document of the highest type, and tends to clear some of the clouds cast by the former action. Contemporary and modern writers are loud in its praises. Daniel Webster said, "I doubt whether one single law of any lawgiver, ancient or modern, has produced effects of more distinct, marked, and lasting character than the Ordinance of 1787." (*Webster. Works, III, 263.*)

Mr. Justice Story said of it, "American legislation has never achieved anything more admirable as an internal government than this comprehensive scheme."

The land-tenure phases of the ordinance began with an outline covering inheritance and wills and the transfer of property, and contained many items concerned with property rights, although the ordinance basically was concerned with government. The land-tenure aspects may be briefly summarized as follows:

1. Estates of persons dying intestate would descend to the children, the descendants of a deceased child sharing their parent's share in equal parts. If no children, the next kin of equal degrees would share equally. Distinction between whole and half blood would not exist. The widow would receive a third part of the real estate for life and a third of the personal estate.
2. Estates could be bequeathed by wills in writing, signed and sealed and witnessed by three parties.
3. Real estate would be conveyed by lease and release, or by bargain and sale, signed and sealed and witnessed by three parties.
4. Wills and deeds would be duly proved and recorded within a year.
5. Personal property could be transferred by delivery.
6. Laws and customs in force among certain French and Canadian settlers would not be disrupted.
7. Residents and nonresidents would be taxed alike on their real estate, and no tax would be imposed on land belonging to the federal government.
8. No man would be deprived of property except that public exigencies made it necessary and then only upon full compensation for the same.

Although the Ordinances of 1785 and 1787 laid out a comprehensive plan for the distribution and administration of the public domain, and were based upon complete discussion and considerable experience by the colonies, some defects still remained. The first amendment relaxed the provision that all lines be run by the true meridian and the variations of the magnetic needle be certified on each plot. The ordinance was almost two years old before this action was taken, but it was the practice at the time when the first surveying under it was started. It was taken purely to expedite the surveying and recording process.

The second change occurred in the ordinance when four ranges were surveyed and Congress decided to begin selling rather than wait for the completion of seven ranges as provided. A third change involved locating the place of sale at the seat of Congress (New York) rather than in the thirteen states, according to the original plan. The fourth change, relating to the selling process, was the beginning of the credit arrangements which were fastened on the land system and which later proved troublesome. In place of complete payment at the time of sale, the amendment provided that one-third of the purchase money was to be paid immediately and the balance within three months.

Reservation of a part of the mineral resources by the sovereign was an invariable practice under all grants to the colonizing agencies. Almost universal also was the practice of reserving minerals in grants to settlers, as well as giving instructions regarding the preservation of timber, particularly in Pennsylvania, and the development of quarries and mines as one of the colonial conditions in the seating requirement in some of the colonies. With this colonial background it is not surprising to find proposals that similar reservations should be made in parcelling out the new federal land. The mineral reservation had no lasting effect for it was soon dropped. It is interesting to note that in the struggle for freer tenure, reservations of this type were laid aside only to be revived in a different form within the century when we entered the conservation phase of our national existence.

The Southwest Ordinance of 1790

The territory south of the Ohio River, not including Kentucky which was to be admitted as a state under provisions in the Virginia deed of cession, consisted of the future state of Tennessee and the twelve-mile strip which South Carolina had ceded, and the western lands of Georgia, which were ceded in 1802. The rest of the Southwest Territory, not included in the states already organized, was Spanish land claimed as a part of the Florida colony.

The Southwest Ordinance of May 26, 1790, provided for a government to be established under the same principles as those outlined in the Northwest Ordinance, except for minor adjustments requested in the 1789 cession of North Carolina. The ordinance also provided for the merging of the office of Superintendent of Indian Affairs and the territorial government. When Tennessee became a state in 1796 the territorial government fell in abeyance, but took on life again in 1798 when the Mississippi Territory was organized.

The Southwest Ordinance added nothing significant to the land tenure principles and the land policy provisions of the earlier ordinances, but it extended the same land system and plan of government to the southwest. However, the development of land tenure in the southwest later encountered the French influence in Louisiana and the Spanish grants in Texas and other southwestern states. No such obstacles were in the path of the development in the northwest.

The effect of the three ordinances for the territory to the west upon the land tenure system and the pattern of land occupancy was significant. They not only laid out an excellent scheme of settlement and plan of government but their liberal provisions influenced the disposition of the land held by the thirteen colonies and the legislative enactments and judicial interpretations of the period following the Revolutionary War.

CHAPTER 21

Some Antecedents of Public Land Policies and the Tenure System

MANY OF THE POLICIES adopted in the land ordinances to encourage population of the vast public domain that lay over the mountains had been tried during the Colonial period. Practically all the principles that form the tenure system were well accepted by the time of the Revolution or were agreed upon before the formation of the national government. The land system that emerged in 1787 was quite different from the one brought to America by the early settlers, and it was in sharp contrast with the feudal tenures forced upon rural England by William the Conqueror. The land system today is essentially the same as outlined in the 1785 and 1787 ordinances, although the plan of government adopted two years later has been amended significantly.[1]

CONTRIBUTIONS TO GENERAL LAND POLICY

The experiences of the colonists from the landing at Jamestown to the final establishment of a national government proved valuable in the formation of basic land policies and programs. Some of the connections are close and clear, others are more remote and cloudy. Nevertheless, these antecedents indicate the reasons why, as a nation, the United States has followed certain land policies. The policies can

[1] For a fuller discussion of the contrast see the article by the author in *Harris and Ackerman. Agrarian Reform, 78.*

be divided into three major categories: (1) those followed by the thirteen original states, (2) those that had various influences by indicating what should not be done, and (3) those involving the federal government and the public domain.

Land Policy in the Original States

Whereas the settlement agencies had an excellent opportunity to establish occupants upon the eastern seaboard unprejudiced by prior occupation, and the same opportunity existed in regard to the new public domain after the Revolution, the newly formed states had to live with the pattern of occupancy developed during the Colonial period.

First, much of the land in the new states had already been placed in the hands of private parties under the old metes and bounds survey system. A major operation would have been required to undo this pattern and to lay out the farms under the symmetrical rectangular system. So the Colonial era fastened upon much of the eastern area the distinctive irregular pattern of farm boundaries. Secondly, the unique New England towns were of colonial origin. Thirdly, although family-sized farms were prevalent, the large grants to plantation owners and the land engrossment that had otherwise taken place was an established fact at the time of the Revolution. On the other hand, the founding fathers were unhampered, in this way, in dealing with size of holdings on the public domain. Fourthly, the peculiar tenure system under which many acres of the old Dutch patroonships were held remained until adjustment of the situation following the New York rent wars in the 1840's.

Fifthly, although quitrents were generally done away with soon after the Revolution, they still exist in a few places. A release of the Associated Press under the dateline of March 15, 1948, Sharpsburg, Maryland, stated:

> One of the country's last vestiges of the feudal land system will disappear if Mrs. Graham Allen carries out her plan to sell her quit rents.
>
> Mrs. Allen is a direct descendant of Joseph Chapeline, who received a large land grant here in 1749 with the privilege of collecting quit rents.
>
> Not construed as a lease under the law, the quit rents are direct tributes such as those levied by Feudal lords on property owners dependent on them for protection.
>
> When Chapeline laid out this town, he subdivided the property into 82-by-200-foot lots and sold each lot for a small sum. Each sale carried the proviso the owner should pay the sum of 3 shillings, 6 pence annually to Chapeline and his heirs 'in perpetuity.'
>
> Mrs. Allen now collects about 78 cents a year from each of the lots. Her total income from quitrents is about $200 annually.
>
> She has authorized Samuel C. Strite, Hagerstown attorney, to sell the quit rents to the present property owners — including the city itself. The community building and town hall stand on part of the original Chapeline grant.

Mr. Strite said Mrs. Allen — sixth owner of the quits — decided to sell them because present owners can never have a clear title to their property as long as they are in force. They constitute a first lien on the property.

Quit rents differ from the system of ground rents prevalent in Baltimore, which are voided if 20 years elapse without payment.

At present, quit rents are held only here and in certain limited areas of New Jersey.

A sixth holdover of the colonial experience is the ground-rent scheme followed in a few cases in two states. The ground-rent practice arose because Penn and Baltimore were both given the right to create manors. The wording of Baltimore's grant indicates that this power could not be extended to persons to whom he granted land. In other words, the right to erect manors was expressly given only to Baltimore and his heirs. In Pennsylvania, on the other hand, this power was given not only to Penn but also to every person to whom Penn or his heirs granted a similar estate of inheritance.

As a result of these provisions, Pennsylvania and Maryland, particularly the metropolitan areas of Philadelphia and Baltimore, have had from pre-Revolutionary times a unique feature in their system of land tenure, the collection of ground rent. Under it, semiannual interest is paid on a mortgage of a specified sum, the principal of which never matures so long as the interest is paid. This result is accomplished in Pennsylvania by both the owner of the rent and the owner of the property object holding separate estates in fee in the land. In Maryland, the owner of the rent is the owner in fee, but the owner of the property object has only a leasehold estate. The rent in Pennsylvania is created by a deed in fee simple reserving the stipulated amount of rent, while in Maryland the rent arises from a lease for ninety-nine years renewable forever.

Since Penn's charter permitted subinfeudation by his grantees, and since the Supreme Court of the State held that *Quia Emptores* had never been in force either in the province or in the state (*Ingersoll v. Sargeant, I. Whart. 337 Pa. 1836*), it was legally possible to arrange for ground rent as described above. On the other hand, the Statute of *Quia Emptores* operated in Maryland prior to the Revolution to prevent the erection of English type manors by Baltimore's grantees, and it was out of this situation that the unique method of establishing ground rents in Maryland originated. The ground-rent lease form of conveyance was developed in Maryland, for *Quia Emptores* did not apply to leases or to other grants less than fee simple. Thus, the legal mind found a way to circumvent the disability in Baltimore's original charter and to attain the same purpose as was attainable directly under Penn's charter. (*Chestnut. Ground Rents, 137–52.*)

Difficulties were caused by gross inaccuracies in surveys throughout the colonies, and some of these inaccuracies still plague landowners in the original states. In New Jersey the heirs of the proprietors still maintain a land office which, among other things, claims ownership of tracts of unappropriated land wherever they may be found.

One of the requirements of the proprietor in Pennsylvania was the preservation of a specified amount of forest land for each grant to a private party; this was required only in Pennsylvania.

Cautionary Contributions

Some of the contributions of the Colonial era to general land policies were negative in type; they indicated what should not have been done. Two such contributions were concerned with organizational matters in regard to land settlement and experiments with communistic tenures.

Coordination of Land Settlement Activities. The British government followed haphazard, heterogeneous, planless procedures of settling the New World. Land was granted to large trading companies, proprietary individuals, proprietary groups, and private parties, who were supposed to develop their own schemes of placing settlers upon their land. The conditions of the grants varied widely. Settlement agencies used various procedures to get the land populated, maintained various relations with their colonists, and granted the land under numerous conditions. Direct transfers were made to financial supporters; headright grants placed land in the hands of bona fide settlers and those who would finance settlers; disposition was by direct sale; grants were made as military bounties for actual service and for frontier protection; grants for meritorious service, for schools, for churches, and for the encouragement of industry were not infrequent; and grants were made direct to members of the New England corporate theocracies. Some settlement agencies collected quitrents, others did not; some required that the settlers meet fairly rigid requirements for seating and planting, others were very lax; some permitted wide latitude in local self-government, others maintained rigid political control; some permitted a high degree of religious freedom, others demanded conformity to the established church; and some sponsored education, while others left up to the individual settlers the mental development of the younger generation. Some of the grants were in fee simple absolute, and others ranged on down the tenure scale to outright leasing, while others tried to populate their land with indentured servants and slaves.

Thus, the colonial land settlement scheme showed little uniformity and no coordination. That this should not be continued to the western territory was obvious to the framers of the Northwest Ordinances. On the other hand, in some colonies land distribution and governmental control were not under the same authority. That this was also a major mistake seems self-evident. Furthermore, the colonial scheme provided for the settlement agency to act as an intermediary between the sovereign government and the actual settler. While this was not completely missing in the national settlement scheme, by and large the government dealt directly with the settler, the exception being the transfer of large tracts to men of means who later sold the land to occupying settlers.

One other difference between the colonial land distribution scheme and the plan later adopted by the federal government should be mentioned. From earliest time to the Revolution, land was granted for the establishment and maintenance of churches. This policy was included in the early draft of the Land Ordinance, but it was stricken out of the final draft. The complete separation of church and state was rapidly becoming an accomplished fact.

Communistic Tenures. A second precautionary contribution is concerned with the merits of holding land under a common or semicommunal type of tenure. The two experiences were at Jamestown and Plymouth. They were quite different, however, owing to their origin. The communal aspects of the Jamestown experiment began while the settlers worked the land in common and ate out of the common storehouse during their indenture period. The practice attained its maximum development when the company endeavored to maintain the system rather than to allot land to each person when his period of servitude was ended. The fact that the early settlers were employees of the company for awhile was overshadowed by the fact that their very existence depended upon the common effort of all. The communal feature of holding land at early Plymouth, on the other hand, dates from the Mayflower Compact signed before the voyagers landed upon Plymouth Rock.

The early experience of the Jamestown settlement makes it difficult to assess the forces behind the reasons given for the breakdown of communal living. If accepted upon face value it would appear that the influence was concerned solely with the private ownership of land. So much internal strife existed, however, that political and administrative instability may have been important. The position of the Pilgrims, contrariwise, appears to present a clear-cut case of the breakdown of a pseudo-communistic landholding idea in spite of complete loyalty on the part of the members. That the Pilgrims were loyal to the group is attested to by many factors, not the least of which was their long and harmonious association in paying off debt while holding the land in common. They were unanimous, as were the settlers at Jamestown, in their desire for free tenure in individual ownership units.

It would appear that the early colonists were certain that their best individual interests and the general welfare also would be most adequately served if the driving force of individual initiative and private enterprise was a fundamental part of the system of land holding. The experience at Jamestown and Plymouth seemed to warn the settlers to beware of communistic ideas and experiments, and to continue the struggle for private ownership of land, free of all feudal encumbrances.[2]

Federal Land Policies

Chief among the federal land policies derived from colonial experience were those relating to the rectangular system of land surveys, the granting of land bounties, the sale policy, the pre-emption plan, and the homesteading system.

Rectangular Survey. The system of rectangular surveys that became a fundamental part of the Northwest Land Ordinance was derived from colonial experience. By the time of the Revolution an orderly system of rectangular surveys was an accepted theory in all of the colonies. It was in widespread practice in all colonies except in the south, and there endeavors to put it into practice met with some success. The idea was so well accepted that its adoption was relatively easy as a part of the plan for settling the Northwest Territory.

Along with the practice of rectangular surveys came the township system.

> The township system had developed through three stages: first, that of a single township laid out here and there as need arose; second, a group or tier of townships laid out in advance of settlement, in order to secure and defend by occupation a certain territory; third, that of laying out a whole region in parallel and contiguous tiers of townships, as a prerequisite for opening up land to settlement. (*Ford. Colonial Precedents, 38–39.*)

The latter practice was adopted in the Land Ordinance.

The third feature of the rectangular survey procedure was the orderly division of townships into smaller squares of 640 acres each, the well-known "section of land," which was eventually agreed upon after some experimentation on the frontier. To these specific features Jefferson added the idea of running the lines north and south and east and west, and these ideas found their way into the Land Ordinance.

Land Bounties. Land was granted freely during the Colonial period to those who would settle on the frontier and help in the protection of the colonies. It also was promised to soldiers to encourage enlistment, and later land was given to them as a bonus to supplement low pay. Land was also granted for schools, including institutions of higher learning, and churches in order to expedite their establishment and expand their services. The development of needed industries was

[2] The allusion here and at other places to the communistic system is not meant to imply that the settlers either at Jamestown or Plymouth were communists or that a pure communistic system existed. Indeed, a pure communistic system would be hard to find anywhere in the world, at the present or in times past. The Pilgrims held all of their land in common until the 1624 division, and part of it in common for some years thereafter, actual ownership being ascribed to the group as a whole. The group controlled the means of production and the distribution and consumption of the products produced by common effort.

encouraged by land grants, and special grants were made to persons who rendered particularly meritorious services.

The colonial practice of granting land free to those who served in the armed services was continued after the Revolution and followed the same general pattern. The matter was so important by the time of the Civil War that it was combined with the general demand for free land into the homesteading scheme, which might never have been established except for the demand for bounty land for soldiers. Grants for schools were an important feature of the Northwest Land Ordinance, and the colonial grants to higher educational institutions were followed by liberal allotments to the land-grant colleges. Grants for religious purposes, on the other hand, were discontinued with the separation of church and state. The colonial policy of granting land to encourage industry was followed after the United States became a nation, with grants to railroads the most spectacular.

Sale Policy. Although the headright system dominated the land disposal scheme for the early part of the Colonial period, disposal by sale soon became important. Sale to settlers was prevalent in all but the four New England colonies, and just prior to the Revolution the British Crown instructed the various colonies that all Crown land was to be sold at a substantial price in place of the nominal fee then being charged. Later, the states sold the unappropriated land and Tory land which was confiscated.

Land was sold in family-sized units to settlers and in larger tracts to plantation operators and land speculators. The conditions of tenure under which private parties held this land were generally similar to those under which other grants were held. The practice of selling land in large blocks led to land engrossment and speculation, and this foreshadowed the land merchandising companies that grew up just before and after the Revolution. In some cases the owner had more rights in the land than he held after the Revolution, when entails were eliminated and when primogeniture fell into disrepute. Where land was sold without a reservation of quitrent, the practice hastened the end of this charge upon any land.

The experience with land sales during the Colonial period was tailor-made as a basis for the practice, supported by Hamilton, of selling the public domain. It is not surprising that Congress accepted the practice and formalized the procedure in 1796, a method followed almost exclusively for about half a century. The colonial experience with land sales was probably more satisfactory than the later endeavors of the federal government. The sale price was not too high for the settler, it supplied some income to the settlement agencies, and it did not lead to much speculation, comparatively speaking. The widespread use of the system during the Colonial era proved its popularity. The practice was readily adopted after the war, and the experience kept the federal government out of many pitfalls as it proceeded to sell the vast public domain that lay to the northwest and the southwest.

Squatters and Pre-emptors. Although squatters were outside the law and the formal settlement plans of the Colonial era, they were numerous and therefore contributed to the settlement of the country. Frequently they exhibited more radical characteristics than those who followed established procedure. The squatters of an early date, of whom the Pilgrims were probably the first, settled themselves upon the land and established possessory rights by the construction of houses, barns, fences, and other improvements upon the land and by clearing and cultivating it. In Colonial times these possessory rights usually became ownership, generally without significant cost to the squatter. The absentee colonial colonizer generally did not object seriously, for this speeded up settlement of his land, and even if he had objected, he usually was unable to prevent this procedure of obtaining rights in land. The frontier spirit of equality and justice sustained the squatter-settler, and his position was reinforced by the vast quantity of unappropriated land. During the Confederation the practice continued for the same reasons. The practice of taking up a home site on the public domain continued until it was duly recognized in the Pre-emption Act of 1841, and the occupant became a pre-emptor rather than a squatter. Significant changes brought about by the 1841 Act were the full legalization of the practice and the switch in names. Prior to 1841 the Congress had enacted legislation that automatically confirmed the rights of large numbers of squatters, a practice not unknown during the Colonial era.

There were two significant differences. Whereas the colonial squatter usually received his land free of charge, his counterpart after the Constitution had to pay a "small cash price." Also, the squatters on the public domain found it expedient to form protective associations to look after their interests. These associations were not observed in Colonial times, although apparently the community of interest of colonial squatters was sufficiently strong to give rise to informal mutual aids of one kind or another. On the other hand, the local colonial land agent apparently was able occasionally to extract from the squatter a nominal payment, particularly after sale to settlers became prevalent.

Headrights and Homesteads. In his study of public land policies, Hibbard shows that free grants of land by the government to settlers antedated the Constitution. He traces the homestead system back to the headrights and gifts of Colonial America. Although the two systems differed procedurally, essentially they were the same. They both involved the free presentation of unappropriated land to anyone who would settle upon it, subdue it, and establish a home upon it. They were designed chiefly to expedite the peopling of the unoccupied domain.

In general the amount of land granted to each settler was the amount calculated to meet his family needs as a permanent occupant. The rights reserved by the colonial settlement agency were generally more substantial than those reserved by the national government, but in both instances they conformed generally to customary usage in settled areas. The rights in land granted to the homesteader were substantially greater than those granted to the colonial headrighter, both those outlined in the instrument of conveyance and in the laws under which the land was held and occupied.

CONTRIBUTIONS TO THE SYSTEM

The land tenure system was not evolved out of the reforming doctrinaire mind of colonial revolutionists; rather it was an outgrowth of centuries of trial and error, of adjustment and change. This process is in sharp contrast with the newness and freshness of the revolutionary political system, of the young democratic principles upon which the government was based.[3]

The feudal land system did not exist in full vigor when the colonists came to America, for many changes had already been made. However, some feudal practices possessed vitality and were changed only slightly, even under conditions in Colonial America. Still others either were changed radically or disappeared entirely.

Summary Characteristics of English Feudal Tenure

Burdensome and restrictive incidents were attached to the land tenure system by William the Conqueror when his army took over England. In assuming political control the king decreed that all land of the realm should be held of or with reference to him, and he proceeded to parcel it out to his loyal men. They in turn permitted occupancy of the land by tenants who would pledge personal subjection and fidelity to them, and through them to the king.

In those days apparently nothing was particularly wrong with the idea that all land of the realm should be held of the king, as lord paramount. If this was granted, it followed that a few favored lieutenants should hold princely estates of the king, with numerous under tenants who held their land by relation to these overlords, and that these under tenants should be relatively free to grant rights in land to other tenants to be held in a similar manner. But onto this idea the early Norman kings added many onerous charges in their

[3] For a fuller discussion of this contrast see the article by the author in the *Journal of Farm Economics*, XXIII, No. 1, February, 1941, 173.

endeavor to derive a large income from their domain. However, the personal services and incidents which were thus attached to the feudal system of landholding were not acceptable to the common man as he became more socialized and as society became more highly integrated.

Feudal Incidents. The most familiar incidents attached to pure feudal tenure were homage, fealty, wardship, marriage, relief, primer seisin, aids, escheats, and fines. Feudal tenure with its numerous incidents, however, did not remain pure for long. A gradual transition was manifested both in legislative action and judicial decison, from the incidents that restricted freedom of action, in the absence of heavy payments for such freedom, to the much freer tenure system that existed when many of the colonists came to America.

Significant Adjustments. The first major turning point was Magna Carta. It contained at least three items that had an important influence upon the tenure system: First, it provided that aids could be demanded only upon three occasions. Secondly, it made a feeble and unsuccessful attempt to prevent subinfeudation, but paved the way for *Quia Emptores,* the effective statute that followed. Thirdly, it prevented the giving of land to religious bodies and again this provision had to be made effective by several statutes that came later, particularly Mortmain and those that outlawed uses. These statutes, *Quia Emptores,* Mortmain, and the statutes regarding uses, should not be overshadowed by Magna Carta since each was an important milestone.

Another statute of significance was *De Donis,* enacted almost three-quarters of a century after Magna Carta. It had no liberalizing effect, but instead laid down a tenure principle that was a handicap to American colonists. It provided that estates in fee tail should be observed so that the donee could not bar the inheritance by alienating it upon the birth of an heir and so the estate would revert to the donor or his heirs upon failure of issue at any time in the future. The principle of entails was generally outlawed late in the Colonial era.

The Statute of Enrollments, passed in 1535, was another turning point, since it set the pattern by which the public could be kept informed about conveyances of estates in land. It paved the way for the requirement that conveyances of estates of inheritance should be in writing, indented, and recorded in one of the courts of record. Out of the condition created by this statute arose the necessity for the next important enactment, the Statute of Wills. This statute, enacted in 1540, was of major significance. It gave the feudal tenant the right to dispose of his entire estate by will if he were a socage tenant, while if he were a tenant by knight service he could dispose of two-thirds of his land by will.

The crowning event of the English struggle for freer tenures was the Statute of Tenures, enacted in 1660. It converted all military tenures—tenure by knight service—into tenure by free and common socage and abolished the burdensome feudal incidents.

English Tenures of 1660. The tenure situation in England after the Statute of Tenures was passed was as follows:

1. The doctrine of tenure was well established; all land was held of the king by great lords, lessor lords, termors, tenants, copyholders, and villeins and so on up and down the hierarchy from the highest to the lowest tenant in whatever sequence was deemed advantageous.
2. Substitution was possible, but not subinfeudation.
3. All military tenures, along with the burdensome incidents, were abolished.
4. Land was held chiefly under four types of tenure:
   a. Free and common socage, in fee simple absolute.
   b. Free and common socage, in fee simple conditional.
   c. Copyholds, that eventually became freeholds.
   d. Leaseholds, our present tenancy.
5. Estates in fee simple absolute were freely alienable under relatively straightforward rules.
6. Estates in fee simple conditional could not be barred.
7. Copyhold estates for all practical purposes were freely alienable.
8. Leasehold interests were alienable only with permission of the landlord.
9. Estates could be devised by testamentary evidence.
10. Dower interest was recognized, as was tenure by curtesy.
11. Intestate succession was governed by well-established rules as follows:
    a. Males were preferred to females.
    b. Whole blood was preferred to half blood.
    c. Descendants took by representation.
    d. Primogeniture applied.
    e. Females inherited equally.
    f. Collateral heirs of the blood of the first purchaser were preferred.
12. Escheat was confined largely to failure of issue and to treason.
13. Transfers of all estates except leaseholds were to be in writing and recorded.
14. Waste of fee simple conditional estates was prohibited by law, at least theoretically.
15. Mortgages were commonly used.
16. Leasehold interests were held under rules as follows:
    a. Possession was in the tenant.
    b. Rent was reserved by the landlord.
    c. Distress was provided as a rent collection procedure.

d. Waste by the tenant was prohibited.
e. The term could be by will, sufferance, year to year, a term of years, or for life or lives.

Although the Statute of Tenures virtually did away with feudal tenures in England, it was not necessarily applicable to tenures in the United States, particularly those established under charters granted before 1660. Thus, the problems of adjusting feudal tenures to suit American conditions fell directly upon the colonists.

Feudal Practices Changed Only Slightly

Although significant changes in the land tenure system took place during the Colonial period, the colonists failed to contribute much with reference to certain practices fairly well established in feudal England. Chief among these were the requirements concerning writing and recording conveyances, the lack of control over size of holdings, and the nature of leasing arrangements between landlord and tenant.

Recording of Conveyances. The practice of using written instruments and the maintenance of public records of all conveyances of significant interests in land was established in England prior to first settlement in America. This practice was introduced in the colonies at an early date, but the records were frequently poorly kept and occasionally destroyed. Nothing was added by the colonists in the way of systematizing the recording of deeds, wills, mortgages, and leases, except that the process of simplification was continued. The significant contributions of Colonial America were concerned more with the substance of tenure than with legal procedure.

Size of Holdings. Enormous holdings were granted to the capitalistic associations and the wealthy proprietors who assumed the task of settling the country. The colonial land policies of the mother country created conditions favorable for the plantation system. The disintegration of many of the large holdings indicates that other forces were in operation. The laxity of the colonizing agencies in administering regulations governing the acquisition of large estates was important. The headright system, with its indentured servants, and later introduction of slaves, was influential. An inexhaustible supply of cheap land and the favorable position of American staples made large farming operations effective. On the other hand, favorable to the establishment of small family-sized farms were the fairly successful restrictions on size of holdings particularly in New England, the granting of land under the headright system to individual occupiers in small units, difficulties in bringing the land into cultivation, and the necessity of competent daily supervision in some colonial farming enterprises.

Thus, colonial settling actually fostered both large plantations and family farms. In addition, colonial tenure law permitted large holdings to become small through partition and inheritance, while the lack of restrictive measures permitted land engrossment limited only by the financial resources of the individual. Thus, in Colonial America the spirit of equality and the struggle to become free of feudal restrictions did not permit a direct frontal attack upon the still troublesome problem of size of holding, whether as a freehold estate or as a leasehold interest. The ideological conflict between equality and freedom has continued to the present to plague public and private land policy. (For some additional notes on this subject see, *Ackerman and Harris. Family Farm Policy, chap.* 2.)

Leasehold Interests. The review of copyhold tenure in England indicated how the villein tenant over a period of years was changed into a copyholder, how the regular termor was protected by law, and that both had much the same relation to the land that some American tenants have today. It was possible, then as now and in Colonial America as in England, to have tenancies at will, by sufferance, for a term of years, for life or lives, or from year to year. Rent was much the same as it is today except that it has taken on more of a contractual type of obligation, whereas in the earlier times it was reasoned that rent arose out of land. The latter idea apparently was unchanged during the Colonial period. Distress was available in the colonies, as in feudal England. The tenant supposedly was responsible for waste and the situation regarding improvements had not generally changed, except that the American tenant frequently constructed improvements in lieu of rent. The requirements regarding written leases did not undergo significant adjustments, as the Statute of Frauds in most jurisdictions required a written lease if the term was longer than one, two, or three years.

The leetmen mentioned in the Fundamental Constitutions of North Carolina were to be tied to the soil very much as the villein of ancient England and the position of slaves and indentured servants was not unlike that of some of the earlier servile tenants. The colonial sharecropping arrangement was a kind of hybrid, occupying a position not recognized independently at law but somewhere between the landlord-tenant and master-servant relation.

Adjustments in Feudal Principles

Since the colonizing agencies and the colonists were relatively free in establishing any type of tenure that appeared advisable, as provided in the early charters, the colonists soon began to make inroads on the undesirable features of feudal tenure. During the Colonial period feudal incidents either disappeared or were changed significantly. The colonists were in an experimental mood and were not constrained by law. They discarded or retained feudal principles or other tenure features, depending upon their usefulness. Many of the minor tenures found in feudal England were either eliminated completely or were not permitted to take root. But the process did not turn away completely from the tenure concepts developed in feudal

England, for many of them flourished. Others, however, were changed significantly.

Alterations Affecting Estates in Land. The colonists did not experiment with all types of feudal tenures. In the first place, military tenures, particularly tenure in capite and by knight service, were specifically excepted in the grants to most groups in charge of colonizing America. These tenures were the backbone of the feudal edifice in England. Although they began to deteriorate within a century after they were established by William, it took almost five centuries before they disappeared. By the time settlement began in America, they had been completely destroyed. Even the Fundamental Constitutions of North Carolina did not provide for strictly military tenure.

It might seem peculiar that military tenures never existed in this country, for one of the major objectives for colonizing Georgia was the establishment of a military barrier against the Spanish and Indians. Also, many grants were made to those who would establish military settlements on the frontiers in other colonies, and much land was awarded soldiers who had served in the Colonial Militia or in the Continental Army. Yet, in no instance was present the slightest reference to the making of these grants under military tenures; all of this land was to be held in free and common socage. As a consequence, military tenures never were significant in the land system of America.

Another type of feudal tenure which was not established in this country was tenure by frankalmoign. Frankalmoign, the special tenure accorded religious bodies, could not be created in England after the Statute of Mortmain, in 1279, restricted such tenure and *Quia Emptores,* in 1290, prevented religious bodies from acquiring land under any tenure except that permitted directly by the king. This would not have prevented tenure by frankalmoign in the United States, however, for the broad privileges in some of the charters — Maryland, for example — made it possible to ignore the tenure laws of England.

In fact, land was set aside for religious purposes and was free from quitrent and other charges, as was tenure by frankalmoign in England. The colonists, however, did not favor granting much land to religious bodies and did not reserve land for religious purposes in the Ordinances of 1785 and 1787. Since such a reservation was made for schools, the colonists evidently felt strongly in this matter. Their final decision must have been based upon the conflict between the church and the state, as experienced by the colonists before coming to America, and upon a desire on the part of the colonists to maintain freedom of religion in this country.

Tenures by dower and curtesy were maintained throughout the Colonial period, and in one form or another the principle exists in the land system today.

Burgage and gavelkind, along with socage tenure, were the immediate forerunners of the tenure called fee simple ownership. Tenures by mortgage and elegit were closely akin to the mortgage-foreclosure-redemption procedure of the present day. Data accumulated on the mortgage procedures in Colonial America are not sufficient to shed much light on the mortgage practices of those days. Delaware possibly still maintains the writ of elegit, but the procedure has been changed in the other states. (*Tiffany. Treat. on Real Prop., 824–25.*)

The processes followed by the colonists seemed to have been: To hold fast to principles of feudal tenure that were adapted to American conditions, even if they found it advisable to change their names; and to dispense with characteristics that were restrictive and burdensome.

Persistence of the Concept of Tenure. Strictly speaking, the principle of tenure does not exist now in the United States; land is not held of another under the concept of tenure. But this statement needs interpretation. The term *tenure* is still used in referring to the manner in, and the period for, which land is held. It would have been possible to establish the concept of tenure in the United States; in fact, legalists are not certain that Pennsylvania and South Carolina have outlawed the holding of land of or with reference to another. Many of the states, however, were specific in their action and ruled against the feudal concept of tenure, either by statutory enactment or by constitutional provision. But the matter must be explored in more detail, not only on the basis of legal theory, but also in the light of its economic and social implications.

Two major principles are involved in the holding of land under another, the possibility of escheat and the privilege of partial alienation by subinfeudation. Under the basic theory of feudal tenure, upon failure of issue the land reverted to the original donor or his heirs, regardless of the remoteness of that early transaction. If this principle of tenure were entirely eliminated and if an owner of land in fee simple died intestate and without heirs, then the land would be free to anyone who would take it, for no one could show either a better right to the land or a right to put out the possessor. But such is not the situation — the land reverts to the state; whether it wants the land is immaterial, for it must take the land. Following this line of reasoning the land in this country is held of the state, for the state is the overlord and recipient of the land when the owner dies intestate and heirless. This is of significance from another point of view. In an agricultural economy this may be a lucrative source of revenue, although its position as an income-producing incident is quite different from the one it occupied in feudal England. Thus, in outlawing tenure in this country the objective must have been apart from the effect on escheat as between the state and the individual.

With reference to partial alienation, if the doctrine of tenure still prevailed and if *Quia Emptores* was not in force, it would be possible to subinfeudate. But this is not the situation in this country, and it has been impossible to subinfeudate in England since the thirteenth century. This has not always been true in the United States, however, for the grant of Penn, as an example, permitted him to establish any type of tenure that he saw fit, despite the laws of England. Baltimore and some of the patroons also were given wide latitude in establishing tenures, and pseudo-manorial estates were established. So it was legally possible to duplicate English feudal estates in the United States.

The abolition of feudal tenures in the United States, or of any of the major principles involved, must be considered with caution. Chief Justice Tilghman said, "The principles of the feudal system are so interwoven with our jurisprudence that there is no removing them without destroying the whole texture." And Chief Justice Gibson said, "Though our property is allodial yet feudal tenures may be said to exist among us in their consequences and the qualities which they originally imparted to estates. . . ." (*Tiffany. Real Property, I, 16.*) Gray, in a dissertation on perpetuities said, ". . . it does not seem that so fundamental an alteration in the theory of property as the abolition of tenure would be worked by a change of political sovereignty. Tenure still obtains between a tenant for life or years and the reversioner; and so in like manner, it is conceived, a tenant in fee simple holds of the chief lord, that is, of the State." (*Gray. Perpetuities, sec. 22.*)

Thus the term *tenure* is sanctioned not only by common usage, but also by the fact that land is still held in the United States under a superior. The relations, however, are quite different from those established in feudal England, and no aspect of the tenure system exemplifies these differences more than inheritance.

Inheritance in the Colonies. Estates in land were devolvable under rather formalized and restrictive rules from an early date, but the struggle to gain free testamentary power was long and hard. Inheritance in regard to chattels was first liberalized and probably was the opening wedge for more liberal rules. The abolition of fictitious uses, in 1535, marked the second great step in the process, for then control over land after death was completely lost. Thereafter, the clamor for the right to control the descent of land by wills could not be denied. The freedom granted at that time was substantial, and marked the beginning of the next stage in the evolution of testamentary devise.

The feudal laws on intestate succession and their influence on wills underwent major adjustments during the Colonial period. The rule of the great landholders that the eldest son should take all and the widespread preference of males over females as heirs was largely dispensed with. Primogeniture grew out of the need for military service and the desire for the maintenance of large landed estates, but this practice was not consonant with colonial thinking. For the same reason, with emphasis on equality, all heirs of the same degree were to inherit equally.

The other major adjustment was with reference to estates in fee tail. From the beginning the creation of estates in fee tail in Colonial America was possible. Such estates were necessary under the original land-tenure scheme laid out for Georgia, and the struggle to eliminate this necessity was not easy. Throughout the Colonial period it was felt that estates in fee tail were not in the spirit of the time, and many of the same factors that operated against primogeniture also were effective in changing the situation in regard to entails. The practice was largely eliminated before the formation of the nation.

Changes in Feudal Incidents. The important incidents that were attached to military tenures in England, except wardship and marriage, were attached also to the free and common socage tenure. Since socage tenure was provided for in the original charters, what happened to the incidents during the Colonial period is important.

Homage was not common in the colonies, although fealty was almost universal. Many people did not like to take an oath of personal subjugation; the oath of fidelity and allegiance was considered more suited to "free" men. Homage had largely disappeared in England except in military tenures, and when military tenures were conquered in 1660, homage, too, was eliminated. Fealty — the oath of allegiance — still is the mark of citizenship, whether assumed because of being born in a country or "taken" in the naturalization ceremony.

Wardship and marriage in their feudal form were not recognized in socage tenure. From the standpoint of characteristics of rights in land, however, control of the state over minors is very similar to wardships from the power viewpoint. It is dissimilar from both wardship and marriage since it does not recognize the privilege of the overlord to make profits from the minor's estate.

Relief and primer seisin probably were practiced to a limited extent in some of the colonies. Their twentieth century counterpart is inheritance taxes, but they would hardly be recognized in the modern tax regalia. Taxes are just as real, however, and when they appear in a rapidly graduated form they outdo the feudalists.

The aids of Colonial America were the quitrents. The aids of today — real property taxes — are commonplace. The increasing prevalence of homestead tax exemptions, the decreasing part that real property taxes play in present revenue-raising schemes, and the proposals for graduated land taxes would serve as a basis for commentaries on this whole line of development.

Fines upon alienation were practiced in some colonies. They were too feudalistic for the colonists, however, and since they were not widely used in England and were abolished in 1660, they must have been of only minor importance. They may be likened somewhat to present stamp taxes and recording and registration fees.

Escheat is still in use; it has not even changed its name. The theory is somewhat different, and it has completely lost the "attainder of the blood" since land no longer escheats for a felony.

Eminent domain was practiced in Colonial America, and is still a characteristic of the system of land tenure. It is, however, more an essential prerogative of organized society than an incident. Distress, as it applied to copyhold tenures, has carried over to modern tenancy. As a power incident, although it may still exist in Pennsylvania, it has changed its form to meet the requirements of the tax collection procedure.

That the revolutionists wanted to assure themselves freedom from the feudal incidents was shown by the positive actions taken by most of the states and the attainment of the same objective by Delaware, North Carolina, and Georgia without statutory action. Of course, the two most burdensome incidents did not follow socage tenure to America and in many instances others were lost or changed their form during the Colonial period. In fact, fealty, escheat, and quitrent, and its corollary distress, were the significant incidents in Colonial America. The first two were really inconsequential. Quitrent was so obnoxious to the free men of New England that they would not pay it, and where it was levied it had begun to disappear before the Revolution. From New York southward it was a source of dissension from the earliest time. It does not appear, however, that the colonists resented paying for the support of government, for they levied taxes upon themselves for many purposes. The colonists seemed incapable, however, of rationalizing payments made for the personal comfort and pleasure of colonial lords.

Bibliography

(*Abernethy. Western Lands.*)
Abernethy, Thomas P. *Western Lands and the American Revolution.* New York: Appleton-Century, 1937.

(*Ackerman and Harris. Family Farm.*)
Ackerman, Joseph, and Harris, Marshall (eds.). *Family Farm Policy.* Chicago: University of Chicago Press, 1947.

(*Adams. Maryland's Influence.*)
Adams, Herbert B. . . . *Maryland's Influence Upon Land Cessions in the United States.* ("Johns Hopkins University Studies in Historical and Political Science," 3rd Ser., Vol. I.) Baltimore: N. Murray, Publication Agent, Johns Hopkins University, 1885.

(*Adams. Salem.*)
Adams, Herbert B. *The Great Pastures of Salem.* ("Historical Collections of the Essex Institute," Vol. XIX–XX, 1882–83.) Salem, Mass.: Essex Institute, 1859–19–.

(*Adams. Works.*)
Adams, Charles F. *The Works of John Adams, Second President of the United States.* 4 vols. Boston: Little, 1851.

(*Agnew. Pa.*)
Agnew, Daniel. *A History of the Region of Pennsylvania North of the Ohio and West of the Allegheny River.* Philadelphia: Kay and Brother, 1887.

(*Akagi. Town Prop. of N. Eng.*)
Akagi, Roy H. *The Town Proprietors of the New England Colonies.* Philadelphia: Press of the University of Pennsylvania, 1924.

(*Alvord. Miss. Valley.*)
Alvord, Clarence W. *The Mississippi Valley in British Politics.* . . . 2 vols. Cleveland, Ohio: Clark, 1917.

(*Amer. Law Inst. Restatement.*)
American Law Institute. *Restatement of the Law of Property.* . . . St. Paul: American Law Institute, 1936–.

(*Andrews. Col. Period.*)
Andrews, Charles M. *The Colonial Period of American History.* 4 vols. New Haven, Conn.: Yale University Press, 1934–37.

(*Arnold. Fones Rec.*)
Arnold, James N. (ed.). *The Records of the Proprietors of the Narragansett Country.* [Otherwise called the *Fones Records.*] Providence, R. I.: Narragansett Pub., 1894.

(*Arnold. Hist. of R. I.*)
Arnold, Samuel G. *History of the State of Rhode Island and Providence Plantations.* 2 vols. New York: Appleton, 1878.

(*Arthur and Carpenter. Ga.*)
Arthur, T. S., and Carpenter, W. H. *The History of Georgia From Its Earliest Settlement to the Present Time.* Philadelphia: Lippincott, 1852.

(*Associated Press.*)
Evening Star (Washington). March 15, 1948, Sec. A, 7.

(*Bailey. Ohio Co.*)
Bailey, Kenneth P. *The Ohio Company of Virginia and the Westward Movement, 1784–1792.* . . . Glendale, Calif.: Clark, 1939.

(*Ballou. Milford.*)
Ballou, Adin. *History of the Town of Milford.* Boston: Rand, Avery and Co., 1882.

(*Banks. Land Ten. in Ga.*)
Banks, Enoch M. *The Economics of Land Tenure in Georgia.* ("Columbia University Studies in History, Economics, and Public Law," Vol. XXIII.) New York: Columbia University Press, 1905.

(*Bassett. Landholding in N.C.*)
Bassett, J. Spencer. "Landholding in Colonial North Carolina," *Law Quarterly Review* (Boston and London), XI (April, 1895), 154–66.

(*Beer. Colonial Policy.*)
Beer, George L. *British Colonial Policy, 1754–1756.* New York: Macmillan, 1907.

(*Beverley. Va.*)
Beverley, Robert. *History and Present State of Virginia, in Four Parts.* London: Printed for R. Parker, 1705.

(*Bicknell. Sowams.*)
Bicknell, Thomas W. *Sowams; With Ancient Records of Sowams and Parts Adjacent.* New Haven, Conn.: Associated Publishers of American Records, 1908.

(*Blackstone. Commentaries.*)
Cooley, Thomas M. (ed.). *Commentaries on the Laws of England by Sir William Blackstone.* 2 vols. 4th ed. by James DeWitt Andrews. Chicago: Callaghan, 1899.

(*Bond. Polit. Ideals.*)
Bond, Beverley W., Jr. *Some Political Ideals of the Colonial Period as They Were Realized in the Old Northwest.* ("Essays in Colonial History Presented to Charles McLean Andrews by His Students.") New Haven, Conn.: Yale University Press, 1931.

(*Bond. Quit-Rent System.*)
Bond, Beverley W., Jr. *Quit-Rent System in the American Colonies.* New Haven, Conn.: Yale University Press, 1919.

(*Boyd. Susquehannah Co.*)
Boyd, Julian P. (ed.). *The Susquehannah Company Papers [1750–1772].* 4 vols. Wyoming Hist. and Geological Soc. (Sheldon Reynolds memorial publications.) Wilkes-Barre, Pa., 1930.

(*Bradford. Plymouth.*)
Bradford, William. *History of Plymouth Plantation,* ed. Charles Deane. Boston: Little, 1856.

(*Brodhead. N.Y.*)
Brodhead, John R. *History of the State of New York.* 2 vols. New York: Harper, 1853.

(*Brown. First Repub.*)
Brown, Alexander. *The First Republic in America. . . .* New York: Houghton, 1898.

(*Brown. Genesis.*)
Brown, Alexander (ed.). *The Genesis of the United States. . . .* 2 vols. Boston and New York: Houghton, 1890.

(*Browne. Md.*)
Browne, William H. *Maryland — The History of a Palatinate.* Boston and New York: Houghton, 1884.

(*Bruce. Econ. Hist. Va.*)
Bruce, Phillip A. *Economic History of Virginia in the Seventeenth Century. . . .* 2 vols. New York and London: Macmillan, 1895.

(*Buell. William Penn.*)
Buell, Augustus C. *William Penn as the Founder of Two Commonwealths.* New York: Appleton, 1904.

(*Burk. Va.*)
Burk, John. *History of Virginia From Its First Settlement to the Present Day.* 4 vols. Petersburg, Va., 1804–16.

(*Burt. Springfield.*)
Burt, Henry M. *The First Century of the History of Springfield.* 2 vols. Springfield, Mass., 1898–99.

(*Calendar of State Papers.*)
Calendar of British State Papers, Colonial Series, 1574–1715. 28 vols. (Preserved in Public Records Office.) London, 1860–1928.

(*Calvert Papers.*)
. . . *The Calvert Papers.* ([Md. Hist. Soc.] Fund Publication No. 28.) Baltimore: Murphy & Co., 1889–99.

(*Cambridge Prop. Rec.*)
The Register Book of the Lands and Houses. . . . [Generally called "The Proprietors' Records."] Cambridge, Mass.: J. Wilson & Son, 1896.

(*Campbell. Col. of Va.*)
Campbell, Charles. *History of the Colony and Ancient Dominion of Virginia.* Philadelphia: Lippincott, 1860.

(*Chambers. Estates and Tenures.*)
Chambers, Sir Robert. *A Treatise on Estates and Tenures.* London: J. Butterworth, 1824.

(*Chandler. Land Title.*)
Chandler, Alfred N. *Land Title Origins, a Tale of Force and Fraud.* New York: Robert Schalkenbach Foundation, 1945.

(*Channing. William Penn.*)
Channing, Edward. "William Penn," *American Historical Association Annual Report for 1906,* pp. 193–97.

(*Chase. Haverhill.*)
Chase, George W. *The History of Haverhill, Massachusetts.* Haverhill, Mass., 1861.
(*Cherokee Nation v. Journeycoke, 155 U.S. 196* [*1894*].)
Cases Adjusted in Supreme Court, Oct. 1893–Oct. 1894. New York and Albany: Banks & Bros., 1895.
(*Chestnut. Ground Rents.*)
Chestnut, W. Calvin. "The Effect of Quia Emptores on Pennsylvania and Maryland Ground Rents," *University of Pennsylvania Law Review,* XCI (October, 1942), 137–52.
(*Chinard. Jefferson.*)
Chinard, Gilbert. *Thomas Jefferson, the Apostle of Americanism.* 2d ed. rev. Boston: Little, 1939.
(*Chitwood. Col. Amer.*)
Chitwood, Oliver P. *A History of Colonial America.* New York: Harper, 1931.
(*Coke. Three Law Tracts.*)
Coke, Sir Edward. *Three Law Tracts.* . . . London: printed for J. Worrall, 1764.
(*Com. and Ins. to S.C.*)
Commissions and Instructions From the Lord Proprietors of Carolina to Public Officials of South Carolina, 1685–1715, ed. A. S. Salley, Jr. Columbia, S.C., 1916.
(*Condon. Constitutional Freedom.*)
Condon, Peter. *Constitutional Freedom of Religion and the Revivals of Religious Intolerance.* ("Historical Records and Studies," Vol. IV.) United States Catholic Historical Society, 1906.
(*Conn. Hist. Soc. Coll.*)
Collections of the Connecticut Historical Society. 24 vols. Hartford, Conn., 1860–1916.
(*Conn. Pub. Rec.*)
The Public Records of the Colony of Connecticut [*1636–1776*]. . . . 15 vols. Hartford, Conn.: Case, Lockwood & Brainard, 1850–90.
(*Connor. N.C.*)
Connor, Robert D. W. *North Carolina — Rebuilding an Ancient Commonwealth, 1584–1925.* 4 vols. Chicago and New York: American Historical Society, 1929.
(*Conrad. Del.*)
Conrad, Henry C. *History of the State of Delaware.* 3 vols. Wilmington, Del.: Privately printed, 1908.
(*Coulter. Granville Dist.*)
Coulter, Ellis M. *Granville District.* ("James Sprunt Historical Publications," Vol. XIII.) Durham, N.C., 1913.
(*Craig. Collective Tenure.*)
Craig, Glenn H., and Loomer, Charles W. *Collective Tenure on Grazing Land in Montana.* (Montana Agricultural Experiment Station. Bulletin 406.) Bozeman, Mont., 1943.

(*Dalrymple. Feudal Property.*)
Dalrymple, Sir John. *An Essay Towards a General History of Feudal Property in Great Britain.* (2d ed. cor. and enl.) London: A. Millar, 1758.
(*Davis. N. Eng. States.*)
Davis, William T. (ed.). *The New England States.* . . . 4 vols. Boston: D. H. Hurd, 1897.
(*Davis. Wallingford.*)
Davis, Charles H. S. *History of Wallingford, Connecticut.* . . . Meriden, Conn.: Privately printed, 1870.
(*Dedham Rec.*)
The Early Records of the Town of Dedham, Massachusetts, 1636–1659, ed. D. G. Hill. 6 vols. Dedham, Mass., 1892.
(*Del. Acts.*)
Acts of the General Assembly at New Castle in the Government of the Counties of New Castle, Kent, and Suffex upon Delaware. October 1767–March 1775. (Title page missing.)
(*Del. Laws.*)
Laws of the Government of New Castle, Kent, and Suffex, upon Delawer. 2 vols. Philadelphia, 1752.
(*Del. Laws, 1829.*)
Laws of the State of Delaware . . . 1829 . . . , ed. Willard Hall. Rev. ed. Wilmington, Del.: R. Porter, 1829.
(*Del. Laws, 1827.*)
Laws of the State of Delaware, 1827. Dover, Del., 1827.
(*Dict. of Amer. Hist.*)
Adams, James T. (ed.). *Dictionary of American History.* 6 vols. New York: Scribner, 1940.
(*Digby. Real Property.*)
Digby, Kenelm E. *An Introduction to the History of the Law of Real Property.* London: Clarendon Press, 1897.
(*Dorchester Rec.*)
"Dorchester Town Records, 1632–1691," *Fourth Report of the Record Commissioners of the City of Boston, 1880.* Boston, 1896.

(*Dorr. R. I. Props.*)
Dorr, Henry C. *The Proprietors of Providence.* ("Publications of the Rhode Island Historical Society," New Series Vol. III.) Providence, R.I., 1895–96.

(*Driscoll. Charter of Liberties.*)
Driscoll, Rev. John T. *The Charter of Liberties and the New York Assembly of 1683.* ("Historical Records and Studies," Vol. IV, pts. 1 and 2.) United States Catholic Historical Society, 1906.

(*Driver. John Sevier.*)
Driver, Carl. *John Sevier, Pioneer of the Old Southwest.* Chapel Hill, N.C.: University of North Carolina Press, 1932.

(*Duke of York Rec.*)
Original Land Titles in Delaware . . . 1646 to 1679. [Commonly known as the *Duke of York Record.*] Wilmington, Del.: Sunday Star, [1903].

(*Edward I and III.*)
[*British*] *Statutes at Large from Magna Carta to 1761.* 8 vols. London, 1763.

(*Egleston. Land System.*)
Egleston, Melville. *The Land System of the New England Colonies.* ("Johns Hopkins University Studies in Historical and Political Science," 4th Ser., Vol. XI–XII.) Baltimore: N. Murray, Publication Agent, Johns Hopkins University, 1886.

(*Elizabethtown Bill.*)
Board of General Proprietors of the Eastern Division of New Jersey. *A Bill in the Chancery of New Jersey* [Elizabethtown Bill]. New York, 1747.

(*Elliott. N. Eng. Hist.*)
Elliott, Charles W. *The New England History From 986 to 1776.* 2 vols. New York, 1857.

(*Ely and Wehrwein. Land Economics.*)
Ely, Richard T., and Wehrwein, George S. *Land Economics.* New York: Macmillan, 1940.

(*Estill. Oglethorpe.*)
Estill, Eugene. *James Oglethorpe.* Charleston, S.C.: Southern Printing & Publishing Co., 1926.

(*Felt. Ipswich.*)
Felt, Joseph B. *History of Ipswich, Essex and Hamilton.* Cambridge, Mass.: C. Folsom, 1834.

(*Felt. Salem.*)
Felt, Joseph B. *Annals of Salem.* 2 vols. 2nd ed. Salem, Mass.: Ives, 1827; Boston: Munroe, 1845–49.

(*Ferree. Pa.*)
Ferree, Barr. "Pennsylvania, a Primer," *Year Book of the Pennsylvania Society.* New York, 1904.

(*Field. R.I. Hist.*)
Field, Edward (ed.). *State of Rhode Island and Providence Plantations at the End of the Century: A History.* 3 vols. Boston and Syracuse: Mason, 1902.

(*Flick. Loyalism in N.Y.*)
Flick, Alexander C. *Loyalism in New York During the American Revolution.* ("Columbia University Studies in History, Economics, and Public Law," Vol. XIV.) New York: Columbia University Press, 1901.

(*Flippin. Royal Gov. in Ga.*)
Flippin, Percy S. "The Royal Government in Georgia," *Georgia Historical Society Quarterly* (Savannah), X (1926).

(*Force. Tracts.*)
Force, Peter (comp.). *Tracts and Other Papers Relating Principally to the Origin, Settlement and Progress of the Colonies of North America.* 4 vols. Washington, 1836–46.

(*Ford. Colonial Precedents.*)
Ford, Amelia Clewley. *Colonial Precedents of our National Land System as It Existed in 1800.* (Bulletin of the University of Wisconsin, No. 352, "History Series," Vol. II, No. 2.) Madison, Wis.: University of Wisconsin Press, 1910.

(*Freeman. Cape Cod.*)
Freeman, Frederick. "The History of Cape Cod," *The Annals of the 13 Towns of Barnstable County.* 2 vols. Boston, 1858–62.

(*Fry. N.H.*)
Fry, William H. *New Hampshire as a Royal Province.* ("Columbia University Studies in History, Economics, and Public Law," Vol. XXIX.) New York: Columbia University Press, 1908.

(*George V.*)
The Public General Acts of 1922 Passed in the Twelfth and Thirteenth Years of the Reign of His Majesty; King George the Fifth. London, 1922.

(*George. Prog. and Pov.*)
George, Henry. *Progress and Poverty.* New York: Robert Schalkenbach Foundation, 1938.

(*Ga. Col. Rec.*)
The Colonial Records of the State of Georgia. 25 vols. Atlanta, Ga., 1904–10.

(*Ga. Hist. Soc. Coll.*)
Collections of Georgia Historical Society. Savannah: Morning News, 1873.

(*Gipson. Brit. Empire.*)
Gipson, Lawrence Henry. *The British Empire Before the American Revolution. . . .* 7 vols. (Vol. 1–3) Caldwell, Idaho: Caxton, 1936–; (Vol. 4–7) New York: Knopf, 1939–.

(*Gould. Land System Md.*)
Gould, Clarence P. *The Land System in Maryland.* ("Johns Hopkins University Studies in Historical and Political Science," Vol. XXXI.) Baltimore, 1913.

(*Gray. Perpetuities.*)
Gray, John C. *The Rule Against Perpetuities.* 3rd ed. Boston: Little, 1915.

(*Gray. South. Agr.*)
Gray, Lewis C. *History of Agriculture in the Southern United States to 1860.* 2 vols. Washington: Carnegie Institution, 1933.

(*G.B. Acts of Privy Coun., Col. Ser.*)
Great Britain. *Acts of the Privy Council, Colonial Series.* 6 vols. London, 1908–12.

(*Grubb. Judiciary of Del.*)
Grubb, Ignatius. *The Colonial Judiciary of Delaware.* ("Historical Society of Delaware," Vol. XVII.) Wilmington, Del., 1897.

(*Hale. Common Law.*)
Hale, Sir Matthew. *The History of the Common Law.* 2 vols. London: printed for G. G. and J. Robinson, 1794.

(*Hall. Narratives of Md.*)
Hall, C. C. (ed.). *Narratives of Early Maryland, 1633–1684.* New York: Scribner, 1910.

(*Hamor. Pres. Est. Va.*)
Hamor, Ralph. *A True Discourse of the Present Estate of Virginia . . . June 1614.* London, 1615.

(*Haney. Bus. Org.*)
Haney, Lewis H. *Business Organization and Combination.* New York: Macmillan, 1923.

(*Harris. Compensation.*)
Harris, Marshall. *Compensation as a Means of Improving the Farm Tenancy System.* ("Land Use Planning Publication," No. 14.) Washington: Department of Agriculture, 1937.

(*Harris. Legal Aspects.*)
Harris, Marshall. "Legal Aspects of Land Tenure," *Journal of Farm Economics* (Menasha, Wis.), XXIII (February, 1941), 173–84.

(*Harris and Ackerman. Agrarian Reform.*)
Harris, Marshall, and Ackerman, Joseph. *Agrarian Reform and Moral Responsibility.* New York: Agricultural Missions, 1949.

(*Harrison. Va. Land Grants.*)
Harrison, Fairfax. *Virginia Land Grants.* Richmond: Old Dominion Press, 1925.

(*Hartwell. Pres. State of Va.*)
Hartwell, Henry; Chilton, Edward; and Blair, James. *The Present State of Virginia and the College.* London: printed for J. Wyat, 1727.

(*Haskins. Inheritance.*)
Haskins, George L. "The Beginnings of Partible Inheritance in the American Colonies," *Yale Law Journal,* LI (June, 1942), 1280–1315.

(*Hazard. Annals of Pa.*)
Hazard, Samuel. *Annals of Pennsylvania From the Discovery of the Delaware, 1609–1682.* Philadelphia, 1850.

(*Hening. Stats.*)
Hening, William W. (ed.). *The Statutes at Large of Virginia, 1619–1792.* 13 vols. New York, Philadelphia, etc.: Bartow, 1809–23.

(*Hibbard. Land Policies.*)
Hibbard, Benjamin H. *A History of the Public Land Policies.* New York: Macmillan, 1924.

(*Hodge. Handbook of Amer. Indians.*)
Hodge, Frederick W. (ed.). *Handbook of American Indians North of Mexico.* (Bureau of American Ethnology, Smithsonian Institution. Bulletin No. 30.) Washington: Government Printing Office, 1907–10.

(*Holdsworth. English Law.*)
Holdsworth, Sir William. *History of English Law.* 12 vols. London: Methuen, 1925–.

(*Holland. West. Mass.*)
Holland, Josiah G. *History of Western Massachusetts.* 2 vols. Springfield, Mass.: Samuel Bowles, 1855.

(*Ingersoll v. Sargeant.*)
Wharton, Thomas I. *Reports of Cases Adjudged in Supreme Court of Pennsylvania.* Philadelphia: Johnson, 1870.

(*James. Laws of S.C.*)
James, Benjamin. *A Digest of the*

Laws of South-Carolina, containing the public statute law of the state, down to the year 1822. . . . Columbia, S.C.: Telescope Press, 1822.

(*Jefferson. Writings* [*Ford*].)
Ford, Paul L. (ed.). *The Writings of Thomas Jefferson.* 10 vols. New York and London: Putnam, 1892–99.

(*Jenks. English Law.*)
Jenks, Edward. *A Short History of English Law From the Earliest Times to the End of the Year 1933.* London: Methuen, [1934].

(*Johnson. Found. of Md.*)
Johnson, Bradley. *Foundation of Maryland.* ("Maryland Historical Society Publications," Vol. XVIII.) Baltimore, 1883.

(*Jones. Ga.*)
Jones, Charles C. *History of Georgia.* 2 vols. Boston: Houghton, 1883.

(*Jones. Va.*)
Jones, Hugh. *Present State of Virginia.* London: printed for J. Clarke, 1724.

(*Jour. of Congress.*)
Journals of Continental Congress, 1774–1789. 34 vols. Washington: Government Printing Office, 1928.

(*Judd. Hadley.*)
Judd, Sylvester. *History of Hadley, Massachusetts.* Northampton, Mass.: Metcalf, 1863.

(*Keith. Chron. of Pa.*)
Keith, Charles P. *Chronicles of Pennsylvania . . . 1688–1748.* 2 vols. Philadelphia: Patterson and White, 1917.

(*Kelso. Needed Research.*)
Kelso, Maurice M. "Needed Research in Farm Tenancy," *Journal of Farm Economics* (Menasha, Wis.), XXIII (February, 1941), 291–304.

(*Kilty. Land. Ass't.*)
Kilty, John. *The Landholder's Assistant and Land Office Guide.* Baltimore, 1808.

(*Kinney. Lost Continent.*)
Kinney, Jay P. *The Lost Continent.* Baltimore: Johns Hopkins University Press, 1937.

(*Lawler. Real Property.*)
Lawler, Joseph and Gail. *A Short Historical Introduction to the Law of Real Property.* Chicago: Foundation Press, 1940.

(*Lewis. Indiana Co.*)
Lewis, George E. *The Indiana Company, 1763–1798. . . .* Glendale, Calif.: Clark, 1941.

(*Livermore. Land Companies.*)
Livermore, Shaw. *Early American Land Companies, Their Influence on Corporate Development.* New York, 1939.

(*Liversage. Land Ten. in Col.*)
Liversage, Vincent. *Land Tenure in the Colonies.* Cambridge [Eng.]: Cambridge University Press, 1945.

(*Lucas. Charters.*)
Lucas, Samuel. *Charters of the Old English Colonies in America, with an introduction and notes.* (Published for the Society for the Reform of Colonial Government.) London: John W. Parker, 1850.

(*MacDonald. Charters.*)
MacDonald, William (ed.). *Select Charters Illustrative of American History, 1606–1775.* New York: Macmillan, 1899.

(*McElreath. Const. of Ga.*)
McElreath, Walter. *A Treatise on the Constitution of Georgia. . . .* Atlanta, Ga.: Harrison, 1912.

(*MacLear. N. Eng. Towns.*)
MacLear, Anne B. *Early New England Towns.* ("Columbia University Studies in History, Economics, and Public Law," Vol. XXIX.) New York: Columbia University Press, 1908.

(*MacLeod. Amer. Ind.*)
MacLeod, William Christie. *The American Indian Frontier.* London: Kegan Paul, Trench, Trubner and Co., New York: Knopf, 1928.

(*Maher. Looking Abroad.*)
Maher, Colin. *Looking Abroad, Looking Around, and Looking Ahead. . . .* Nairobi, Kenya Colony: East African Standard, [1943?].

(*Maine Doc. Hist.*)
Documentary History of the State of Maine. 24 vols. Portland, Me., 1869–1916.

(*Maine Hist. Soc. Coll.*)
Collections of Historical Society of Maine. 1st Ser., Vol. 1–10 (1831–84); 2nd Ser., Vol. 1–10 (1884–1919); 3rd Ser., Vol. 1–(1919–). Portland, Me.: Maine Historical Society, 1831–19–.

(*Md. Arch.*)
Archives of Maryland. 62 vols. Baltimore: Maryland Historical Society, 1883–19–.

(*Md. Laws, 1785–92.*)
Laws of Maryland Made and Passed at a Session of Assembly, 1785–92. Annapolis, 1786–92.

(*Md. Laws, 1785–99.*)
Kilty, William (ed.). *The Laws of Maryland, to Which Are Prefixed the Original Charter. . . .* 2 vols. Annapolis, 1799–1800.

(*Md. Laws Since 1763.*)
Contee, Alexander C. (ed.). *Laws of Maryland Made Since 1763.* Annapolis, 1787.

(*Md. Mag.*)
Maryland Historical Magazine. Baltimore, 1906–.

(*Mass. Bay Rec.*)
Records of the Governors and Company of the Massachusetts Bay in New England, ed. N. B. Shurtleff. 5 vols. Boston, 1853–54.

(*Mass. Charters.*)
The Charters and General Laws of Colony and Province of Massachusetts Bay. Boston: T. B. Wait, 1814.

(*Mass. Hist. Soc. Coll.*)
Collections of the Massachusetts Historical Society. 78 vols. (In 7 series of 10 volumes to each series.) Cambridge, Mass., 1792–19–.

(*Mayer. Ground Rent in Md.*)
Mayer, Lewis. *Ground Rent in Maryland.* Baltimore, 1883.

(*Mead. Conn. as Corp. Col.*)
Mead, Nelson P. *Connecticut as a Corporate Colony.* Lancaster, Pa., 1906.

(*Meek. Land Law.*)
Meek, Charles K. *Land Law and Customs in the Colonies.* London and New York: Oxford University Press, 1946.

(*Mereness. Md. as Prop. Prov.*)
Mereness, Newton D. *Maryland as a Proprietary Province.* New York: Macmillan, 1901.

(*Mershon. Staten Island.*)
Mershon, Stephen. *The Major and the Queen — The Grant of Staten Island.* New York: Beam, 1915.

(*Mitchell. Ga.*)
Mitchell, Frances L. *Georgia — Land and People.* Atlanta, Ga.: Franklin, 1900.

(*Myers. Narratives of Pa.*)
Myers, Albert C. (ed.). *Narratives of Pennsylvania, West Jersey and Delaware, 1630–1707.* New York: Scribner, 1912.

(*Nash. Weymouth.*)
Nash, Gilbert (ed.). *Historical Sketch of the Town of Weymouth.* ("Weymouth Historical Society Publication," No. 2.) Weymouth, Mass., 1885.

(*Neill. Va. Co.*)
Neill, Edward D. *History of the Virginia Company of London.* Albany: Munsell, 1869.

(*Neilson. Kent.*)
Neilson, Nellie (ed.). *The Cartulary and Terrier of the Priory of Bilsington, Kent.* Published for British Academy by Oxford University Press, 1928.

(*Nettels. Roots.*)
Nettels, Curtis P. *The Roots of American Civilization: A History of American Colonial Life.* New York: Crofts, 1938.

(*Nevins. Amer. States.*)
Nevins, Allan. *American States During and After the Revolution, 1775–1789.* New York: Macmillan, 1924.

(*N. Eng. Reg.*)
New England Historical and Genealogical Register. 93 vols. Boston, 1847–19–.

(*N. H. Doc. and Rec.*)
Documents and Records Relating to the Province and State of New Hampshire, 1623–1800. 34 vols. Concord, N. H., 1896–1907.

(*N. Haven Rec.*)
Hoadly, Charles (ed.). *Records of the Colony and Plantation of New Haven, 1638–1649.* Hartford, Conn.: Privately printed, 1857.

(*N.J. Acts.*)
Acts of the General Assembly of the Province of New Jersey, 1703–1730. Philadelphia, 1832.

(*N.J. Acts, 1703–61.*)
Acts of the General Assembly of the Province of New Jersey, 1703–1761, ed. Samuel Neville. 2 vols., [London], 1752–61.

(*N.J. Acts, 1765.*)
Acts of the General Assembly of Province of New Jersey, 1765. Philadelphia, 1830.

(*N.J. Arch.*)
New Jersey Archives. 34 vols. 1st Ser. Newark, N.J., 1800–1901.

(*N.J. Grants and Conc.*)
Grants, Concessions, and Original Constitutions of New Jersey, ed. Aaron Leaming and Jacob Spicer. Philadelphia, 1758.

(*N.J. Hist. Soc. Coll.*)
New Jersey Historical Society Collections. 7 vols. Newark, N.J., 1846–19–.

(*N.J. Laws.*)
Laws of the State of New Jersey. Trenton, N.J., 1821.

(*N. Neth. Laws.*)
Laws and Ordinances of New Netherland. Albany, 1868.

(*N. Plymouth Rec.*)
Records of the Colony of New Plymouth in New England. 12 vols., ed. Nathaniel Shurtleff (vol. 1–8) and David Pulsifer (vol. 9–12). Boston, 1855–61.

(*N.Y. Col. Hist.*)
O'Callaghan, E. B., and Brodhead, J. R. (eds.). *Documents Relative to the Colonial History of New York.* 15 vols. New York: Weed, Parsons, 1853–87.

(*N.Y. Col. Laws.*)
Colonial Laws of New York From 1664 to the Revolution. 5 vols. Albany, 1894–96.

(*N.Y. Col. Rec.*)
New York Colonial Records. (State Library Bulletin, History No. 2.) [Albany], 1899.

(*N.Y. Doc. Hist.*)
O'Callaghan, Edmund B. (comp.). *The Documentary History of the State of New York.* 4 vols. Albany: Weed, Parsons, 1849–50, 1850–51.

(*N.Y. Hist. Soc. Coll.*)
New York Historical Society Collections. 73 vols. New York, 1809–19–.

(*N.Y. Min. Exec. Coun.*)
Minutes of the Executive Council of New York. 2 vols. Albany, 1910.

(*N.Y. State Laws.*)
Laws of the State of New York, 1777–1789. 2 vols. New York, 1789.

(*Nissenson. Patroon's Domain.*)
Nissenson, Samuel G. *The Patroon's Domain.* New York: Columbia University Press, 1937.

(*N.C. Hist. and Gen. Reg.*)
Hathaway, J. R. B. (ed.). *The North Carolina Historical and Genealogical Register.* 3 vols. Edenton, N.C., 1900–1903.

(*N.C. Rec.*)
Colonial and State Records of North Carolina, 1662–1890. 30 vols. Raleigh and Winston-Salem, N.C., 1886–90, 1895–1907.

(*Noyes. Institution.*)
Noyes, Charles Reinold. *The Institution of Property; a Study of the Development, Substance and Arrangement of the System of Property in Modern Anglo-American Law.* New York, etc.: Longmans, 1936.

(*Nugent. Va. Land Patents.*)
Nugent, Nell M. *Cavaliers and Pioneers, Abstracts of the Virginia Land Patents and Grants, 1623–1666.* Richmond, Va., 1934.

(*O'Callaghan. N. Neth.*)
O'Callaghan, Edmund B. *History of New Netherland.* 2 vols. New York, 1845.

(*Osgood. Col. Gov.*)
Osgood, Herbert. "The Corporation as a Form of Colonial Government," *Political Science Quarterly,* XI (June, 1896), 259–77.

(*Osgood. 18th Cent.*)
Osgood, Herbert L. *The American Colonies in the Eighteenth Century.* 4 vols. New York: Columbia University Press, 1924.

(*Osgood. 17th Cent.*)
Osgood, Herbert L. *The American Colonies in the Seventeenth Century.* 3 vols. New York: Columbia University Press, 1904–7.

(*Palfrey. N. Eng.*)
Palfrey, John. *History of New England.* 5 vols. Boston: Little, 1860.

(*Paxson. Amer. Frontier.*)
Paxson, Frederic L. *History of the American Frontier, 1763–1893.* New York: Houghton, 1924.

(*Pelzer. Pioneer Settlement.*)
Pelzer, Karl Josef. *Pioneer Settlement in the Asiatic Tropics. . . .* New York: American Geographical Society, 1945.

(*Penn and Logan Correspondence.*)
Historical Society of Pennsylvania. *Correspondence Between William Penn and James Logan.* 2 vols. ("Pennsylvania Historical Society Memoirs," Vol. IX–X.) Philadelphia, 1870–72.

(*Pa. Arch.*)
Pennsylvania Archives. 1st Ser. 12 vols., 1852–56; 4th Ser. 12 vols., 1900–1902; 8th Ser. 8 vols., 1931–35. Harrisburg and Philadelphia, 1852–19–.

(*Pa. Col. Rec.*)
Colonial Records of Pennsylvania. Minutes of the Provincial Council and Public Safety Commission. 16 vols. Harrisburg, 1851–53.

(*Pa. Hist. Soc. Mem.*)
The Historical Society of Pennsyl-

vania Memoirs. 14 vols. Philadelphia: Lippincott, 1826–95.

(*Pa. Laws.*)
Laws of the Commonwealth of Pennsylvania. 4 vols. Philadelphia, 1810.

(*Pa. Stats.*)
Statutes at Large of Pennsylvania, 1682–1801. 16 vols. Harrisburg, 1896–1911.

(*Pennypacker. Germantown.*)
Pennypacker, Samuel W. *Settlement of Germantown, Pennsylvania.* Philadelphia, 1899.

(*Pim. Col. Agr. Prod.*)
Pim, Sir Alan. *Colonial Agricultural Production: the contribution made by native peasants and by foreign enterprise.* London and New York: Oxford University Press, 1946.

(*Pollock. Land Laws.*)
Pollock, Sir Frederick. *The Land Laws.* London and New York: Macmillan, 1887.

(*Pollock and Maitland. English Law.*)
Pollock, Sir Frederick, and Maitland, Frederick W. *The History of English Law Before the Time of Edward I.* 2 vols. Cambridge, Eng.: Cambridge University Press, 1923.

(*Porter. Hartford.*)
Porter, William S. *Hartford and West Hartford* ("Historical Notices of Connecticut," 2 vols. in 1.) Conn. Hist. Soc., Hartford, Conn.: E. Geer's Press, 1842.

(*Ramsay. Hist. of S.C.*)
Ramsay, David. *The History of South Carolina From Its First Settlement in 1670 to 1808.* 2 vols. Newbury, S.C.: Duffie, 1858.

(*Rand. Indians.*)
Rand, James H. *The North Carolina Indians.* ("James Sprunt Historical Publications," Vol. XII, No. 2.) Chapel Hill, N.C.: University of North Carolina Press, 1913.

(*Reinsch. Common Law.*)
Reinsch, Paul S. *English Common Law in the Early American Colonies.* (Bulletin of the University of Wisconsin, No. 31, "Economics, Political Science, and History Series," Vol. II, No. 4.) Madison, Wis.: University of Wisconsin Press, 1899.

(*Revolutionary Rec.*)
Candler, Allen D. (ed.). *The Revolutionary Records of the State of Georgia.* 3 vols. Atlanta, Ga.: Franklin-Turner, 1908.

(*R.I. Laws.*)
Laws of Rhode Island. Newport, R.I., 1730.

(*R.I. Rec.*)
Records of the Colony of Rhode Island. 10 vols. Providence, R.I., 1856–65.

(*R.I. Tracts.*)
Rhode Island Historical Tracts. 1st Ser., 20 Tracts; 2nd Ser., 1–; Providence, R.I., 1877–19–.

(*Rife. Land Ten. N. Neth.*)
Rife, Clarence W. *Land Tenure in New Netherland.* ("Essays in Colonial History Presented to Charles McLean Andrews by His Students.") New Haven, Conn.: Yale University Press, 1931.

(*Robbins. Our Landed Heritage.*)
Robbins, Roy M. *Our Landed Heritage; The Public Domain, 1776–1936.* Princeton, N.J.: Princeton University Press, 1942.

(*Roome. Early Days and Early Surveys.*)
Roome, William. *The Early Days and Early Surveys of East New Jersey.* Morristown, N.J., 1883.

(*Sakolski. Land Bubble.*)
Sakolski, A. M. *The Great American Land Bubble. . . .* New York and London: Harper, 1932.

(*Salem Rec.*)
Salem Town Records. ("Historical Collections of the Essex Institute," Vol. IX.) Salem, Mass.: Essex Institute, 1859–19–.

(*Salley. S.C. Land Warrants.*)
Salley, A. S. *Warrants for Land in South Carolina.* 3 vols. Columbia, S.C., 1915.

(*Savelle. Found. Civilization.*)
Savelle, Max. *The Foundations of American Civilization. . . .* New York: Holt, 1942.

(*Scharf. Hist. of Del.*)
Scharf, John T. *History of Delaware, 1609–1888.* Philadelphia: Richards, 1888.

(*Seebohm. Tribal Custom.*)
Seebohm, Frederick. *Tribal Custom in Anglo-Saxon Law.* London: Longmans, 1911.

(*Shepherd. Prop. Gov. in Pa.*)
Shepherd, William R. *History of Proprietary Government in Pennsylvania.* ("Columbia University Studies in History, Economics, and Public Law," Vol. VI.) New York: Columbia University Press, 1896.

(*Smith. Equality.*)
Smith, T. V. *The American Philosophy of Equality.* Chicago: University of Chicago Press, 1927.

(*Smith. Hist. of N.J.*)
Smith, Samuel. *History of the Colony of . . . New Jersey . . . to the Year 1721.* Burlington, N.J., 1765.

(*Smith. S.C. as Royal Prov.*)
Smith, William R. *South Carolina as a Royal Province.* New York: Macmillan, 1903.

(*Smith. Works.*)
Smith, John. *Travels and Works of Captain John Smith . . .*, ed. Edward Arber. 2 vols. Edinburgh: J. Grant, 1910.

(*S.C. Acts.*)
Acts and Ordinances of South Carolina, 1789. Charleston, S.C., 1789.

(*S.C. Hist. Soc. Coll.*)
South Carolina Historical Society Collections. 5 vols. Charleston, S.C., 1857.

(*S.C. Stats.*)
Statutes at Large of South Carolina, 1682–1786. 5 vols. Columbia, S.C., 1838.

(*Spelman. Relation of Va.*)
Spelman, Henry. "Relation of Virginia," *Complete Works . . . of Captain John Smith,* ed. Edward Arber (Birmingham, [Eng.] 1884), p. ci-cxiv.

(*Spotswood Letters.*)
Brock, R. A. (ed.). *The Official Letters of Alexander Spotswood, Lieutenant-governor of the Colony of Virginia, 1710–1722.* 2 vols. Richmond, Va.: Virginia Historical Society, 1882–85.

(*Steiner. Guilford.*)
Steiner, Bernard C. *History of the Plantation of Menunkatuck and the Original Town of Guilford.* Baltimore, 1897.

(*Steiner. Md. Charter.*)
Steiner, Bernard C. "The Maryland Charter and the Early Exploration of That Province," *Sewanee Review* (New York), XVI (April, 1908), 148–67.

(*Sullivan. Land Titles in Mass.*)
Sullivan, James. *History of Land Titles in Massachusetts.* Boston, 1801.

(*Sweet. Religion.*)
Sweet, William Warren. *Religion in Colonial America.* New York: Scribner, 1942.

(*Tanner. Prov. of N.J.*)
Tanner, Edwin P. *The Province of New Jersey, 1664–1738.* ("Columbia University Studies in History, Economics, and Public Law," Vol. XXX.) New York: Columbia University Press, 1908.

(*Thorpe. Charters.*)
Thorpe, Francis N. (ed.). *The Federal and State Constitutions, Colonial Charters, and Other Organic Laws. . . .* 7 vols. Washington: Government Printing Office, 1909.

(*Tiffany. Real Property.*)
Tiffany, Herbert Thorndyke. *The Law of Real Property,* ed. Basil Jones. 3rd ed. 6 vols. Chicago: Callaghan, 1939.

(*Tiffany. Treat. on Real Prop.*)
Tiffany, Herbert Thorndyke. *A Treatise on the Modern Law of Real Property.* Chicago: Callaghan, 1940.

(*Treat. Land System.*)
Treat, Payson J. *The National Land System, 1785–1820.* New York, 1910.

(*Trumbull. Northampton.*)
Trumbull, James R. *History of Northampton, Massachusetts.* 2 vols. Northampton, Mass., 1892.

(*Turner. Frontier.*)
Turner, Frederick J. *Frontier in American History.* New York: Holt, 1920.

(*Tyler's Quart.*)
Tyler's Quarterly Historical and Genealogical Magazine. 17 vols. Richmond, Va., 1919–.

(*U.S. v. Butler.*)
U.S. Reports. Vol. 297. "Cases Adjusted in the Supreme Court at October Term, 1935." Washington: Government Printing Office, 1936.

(*Van Rensselaer. City of N.Y.*)
Van Rensselaer, Mrs. Schuyler. *History of the City of New York in the Seventeenth Century.* 2 vols. New York: Macmillan, 1909.

(*Va. Col. Rec.*)
Colonial Records of Virginia. (State Senate Document Number 75.) Richmond, Va.: R. F. Walker, State Printer, 1874.

(*Va. Co. Abs.*)
Abstracts of the Proceedings of the Virginia Company of London, 1619–1624. 2 vols. ("Virginia Historical Society Collections," New Series Vol. VII–VIII.) Richmond, Va., 1888–89.

(*Va. Co. Rec.*)
Records of the Virginia Company of London, ed. Susan Kingsbury. 4 vols. Washington, 1906.

(*Va. Hist. Index.*)
Virginia Historical Index, ed. E. G. Swem. 2 vols. Roanoke, Va.: Stone, 1934.

(*Va. Hist. Reg.*)
Virginia Historical Register and Literary Companion, ed. William Maxwell. 6 vols. Richmond, Va., 1848–53.

(*Va. Jour. of Burgesses.*)
Journal of the House of Burgesses of Virginia, 1619–1776, ed. H. R. McIlwaine. 13 vols. Richmond, Va., 1905–15.

(*Va. Mag. of Hist.*)
Virginia Magazine of History and Biography. 57 vols. Richmond, Va.: Virginia Historical Society, 1893–19–.

(*Va. State Papers.*)
Calendar of Virginia State Papers, 1625–1869. 11 vols. Richmond, Va., 1875–1893.

(*Waterbury Rec.*)
Proprietors' Records of the Town of Waterbury, Connecticut, 1677–1761. Waterbury, Conn.: Mattatuck, 1911.

(*Watertown Rec.*)
Massachusetts Historical Society. *Proprietors' Records of Watertown, Massachusetts.* 4 vols. Watertown, Mass., 1894–1906.

(*Webster. Works.*)
Works of Daniel Webster. 6 vols. Boston: Little, 1860.

(*Wehrwein. Res. in Agr. Land Ten.*)
Wehrwein, George S. *Research in Agricultural Land Tenure — Scope and Method,* ed. John D. Black. (Social Science Research Council Bulletin 20.) New York, 1933.

(*Whitehead. East Jersey.*)
Whitehead, William. *East Jersey Under the Proprietary Government.* ("New Jersey Historical Society Collections," Vol. I.) Newark, N.J., 1846.

(*Wilhelm. Inst. of Md.*)
Wilhelm, Lewis W. *Local Institutions of Maryland.* ("Johns Hopkins University Studies in Historical and Political Science," Vol. III.) Baltimore, 1885.

(*William and Mary.*)
[*British*] *Statutes at Large from Magna Carta to 1761.* 8 vols. London, 1763.

(*W. and M. Quart.*)
William and Mary College Quarterly. Ser. 1, 27 vols., 1892–1919; Ser. 2, 19 vols., 1919–43; Ser. 3, 6 vols. to 1949, 1944–. Williamsburg, Va., 1892–19–.

(*Williamson. Me.*)
Williamson, William D. *History of the State of Maine.* 2 vols. Hallowell, Me.: Glazier, Masters & Co., 1832.

(*Winsor. Narra. and Crit. Hist.*)
Winsor, Justin (ed.). *Narrative and Critical History of America.* 8 vols. New York: Houghton, 1884–89.

(*Wright. Law of Tenures.*)
Wright, Martin. *Introduction to the Law of Tenures.* London: printed for F. Wingard, 1792.

Biographical Index

The Biographical Index includes the names of *persons* mentioned in this book. In numerous instances only the last name was available; in others, only an initial; while in others, only a part of the Christian name was available. National names, for example, the *Dutch, French, Swedes,* etc., are in the Subject Index.

Adams, John, 360
Aldworth, R., 277
Allen, Ethan, 308
Allen, Mrs. Graham, 395, 396
Andros, Edmund, 78, 79, 105, 106–7, 108, 112, 115, 116, 132, 143, 145
Anne, Queen, 137, 206, 244, 265
Archbishop of Canterbury, 40
Archdale, Governor, 230, 246
Argall (Argoll), Admiral Samuel, 184, 190, 193
Arlington, Lord, 89, 90
Ashley, Lord, 136
Atkinson, Theodore, 361
Attwood, Chief Justice, 361
Austin, Peter, 169

Bacon, Nathaniel, 368
Bailey, Captain John, 223, 225
Baker, 223
Baltimore, Lord, 76, 77, 78, 95, 102, 117, 118, 119, 120, 121, 122, 123, 124, 126, 133, 141, 143, 145, 147, 149, 153, 159, 168, 215, 216, 218, 219, 220, 248, 249, 325, 341, 342, 351, 358, 368, 396, 409
Barkham, 157
Beauchamp, John, 277
Belfield, John, 319
Belmont, Governor (Earl of), 214, 265
Berkeley, 45, 81, 95, 130, 131, 136, 222, 223, 225, 242, 243, 268, 269, 270, 325, 327, 335
Berringer, Simon, 232
Berry, Captain John, 225
Beverley, William, 208
Bishop of Durham, 38, 72, 119, 120, 121 133, 255

Blackwood, 244
Blathwayt, Auditor-General William, 329
Blunt, Chief, 175
Boone, Daniel, 301
Bourghalter, Michael, 272
Bracton, 50, 55
Bradford, William, 104–5, 116, 275
Bradshaw, Richard, 277
Brook, Lord, 113
Bryan, Morgan, 208
Buckly, Sir Richard, 187
Buckly, Thomas, 187
Budd, Thomas, 242
Burlington, Governor, 230
Byllynge, 131, 132
Byrd, Major, 260
Byrd, William III, 263

Cabot, John and Sebastian, 73, 146
Calvert, Secretary, 343
Calvert, Cecil; *See* Baltimore, Lord
Calvert, George; *See* Baltimore, Lord
Calvin, John, 349
Campbell, 244
Canonicus, Chief, 164
Canute, 23
Carr, Captain John, 266
Carr, Peter, 360
Carter, 187
Carteret, Sir George, 45, 81, 95, 130, 131, 132, 137, 222, 223, 225, 242, 243, 270, 325, 326, 327, 335
Carteret, Governor John, 327
Carteret, Sir Philip, 130, 225, 269
Chapeline, Joseph, 395
Chapman, 208
Charles I, 60, 100, 117, 128, 129, 137, 202, 351

Charles II, 34, 60, 89, 90, 94, 95, 111, 114, 122, 129, 130, 136, 137, 225, 244
Chew, John, 260
Church, Colonel Timothy, 269
Clapham, Joseph, 208
Clark, 386
Clark, Edward, 267
Clark, John, 111
Clay, Henry, 64
Clayborne (Claiborne), William, 168
Coddington, William, 109, 164
Codrington, Simon, 182
Colden, Cadwallader, 214, 361
Colleton, Sir John, 137
Colleton, Sir Peter, 232
Columbus, Christopher, 63, 146, 155
Constantine, Emperor, 348
Cooper, Anthony Ashley, 136
Cooper, William, 291, 308
Cornbury, Lord, 160, 244, 270
Cornwallis, General, 265
Cotton, John, 356
Cox, Colonel David, 242
Coxe, Daniel, 133
Cradock, Governor, 276
Craig, Andrew, 291, 308
Croghan, George, 308
Cromwell, Oliver, 78, 137
Culpeper, Lord Thomas, 89, 90, 91
Cumings, Archibald, 377

Dale, Sir Thomas, 172, 181, 182, 193, 196, 200, 267
Davenport, John, 113
Davidson, Nicholas, 277
Day, Stephen, 268
DeGraffenreid, Christopher (Christoph von Graffenreid), 247, 261
DeLancey, James, 370
DeLawar, Lady, 187
Delaware, Lord, 172, 267
Dinwiddie, Governor Robert, 263, 307, 378
Dobbs, Governor, 231
Dockwra, 268
Dongan, Governor, 167, 213
Duke of Albemarle, 136
Duke of York, 45, 77, 79, 81, 94–95, 114, 119, 121–22, 124, 125, 129, 130, 132, 136, 137, 166, 213, 222, 223, 225, 243, 244, 325, 326
Dunmore, Lord, 263, 301, 305
Durant, George, 169

Earl of Clarendon, 137
Earl of Craven, 137
Earl of Shaftesbury, 136, 232
Earle, Christopher, 267
Earle, Walter, 267
Eaton, 268
Eaton, Theophilus, 113
Edward I, 46, 47
Edward III, 43
Edward the Confessor, 23
Edwards, Governor, 247
Egremont, Lord, 295, 300
Elbridge, 241
Elbridge, G., 277
Elizabeth, Queen, 83, 157
Endicott, Governor John, 106, 163, 272
Evans, Major Henry, 269

Fairefax, William, 201
Fairfax, Lord, 89, 138, 148, 368, 369, 382
Fantleroy, Colonel, 169, 176
Fauconnier, Peter, 245
Fellow, Mistress, 283
Fenwick, 131
Finley, John, 301
Fitch, James, 165
Fletcher, Governor Benjamine, 165–66, 197, 213, 214
Fordham, Robert, 212
Foxton, Elias, 267
Frank, Martin, 247
Franklin, Benjamin, 353
Franklin, John, 298

Gage, General, 305
Galerius, Emperor, 348
Gates, Thomas, 267
George I, 138
George III, 133, 263, 372
Gibson, Chief Justice, 409
Gilbert, Sir Humphrey, 73, 146
Gooch, Lieutenant-Governor William, 299, 300
Goodkin, Captain Daniel, 268
Gorges and Mason, 79, 100, 101, 103, 106, 116, 127, 145, 148, 149; *see also* Gorges, Sir Ferdinando; Mason, Captain John
Gorges, Sir Ferdinando, 99, 100, 101, 102, 105, 127, 286, 326, 327; *see also* Gorges and Mason
Gorges, Robert, 101, 103, 106
Gosnold, 83
Goulding, William, 223
Graies, Thomas, 186
Granville, Lord, 79, 136, 137, 138, 139, 302, 368
Grayson, 389
Green, Roger, 260, 268
Grenville, Sir Richard, 83
Guest, Chief Justice, 361

Hackett, Edmond, 267
Halifax, Lord, 295
Hamilton, Alexander, 253, 400
Hamor, Captain Ralph, 184, 190
Hampton, William, 272
Harold, 23, 24
Harper, 187
Harquip Mangoi, Chief, 162
Harrison, Governor, 388

Harrison, Charles, 272
Harrison, George, 201
Harrison, James, 220, 238, 239
Harvey, Governor, 202, 203, 204
Harwell, Sir Edmund, 187
Harwell, Francis, 187
Hathersall, Thomas, 201
Hathorne, Captain William, 268
Hawthorne, Captain, 279
Haynes, 276
Heath, Sir Robert, 133
Henderson, Richard, 301, 302
Henrietta Maria, Queen, 120
Henry, Esther, 168
Henry III, 43, 50
Henry VII, 49
Henry VIII, 54
Heyd, Joost, 208
Hickford, Henry, 187
Hillsborough, Lord, 306, 307, 361
Hilton, Edward, 277
Hobbamock, 268
Hobson, Captain John, 186
Holmes, Thomas, 239
Homan, Benjamine, 225
Hooker, John, 280
Huddle, Andreas, 166
Hudson, Henry, 92
Hunter, Governor Robert, 165–66, 330
Hyde, Edward, 137

Jaffray, Judge, 361
James, I, 83, 85, 88, 202
James II, 95
Jefferies, 208
Jefferson, Thomas, 169, 296, 347, 348, 352, 353, 360, 365, 372, 373, 374, 375, 388, 389, 390
John I, 40
Johnson, Governor, 248, 325, 333
Johnson, Isaac, 276
Johnson, Sir William, 175
Johnstone, Dr. John, 244
Jone, Robert Jr., 173
Joshua, Thomas, 168
Julius Caesar, 22

Kercheval, 208
Ketelby, Able, 246
Kieft, Director-General William, 94, 96, 165, 212, 337

Lafayette, Marquis de, 373
Lane, Thomas, 232
Langton, Stephen, 40
Lawley, Edward, 267
Lawrie, 132
Leeds, Daniel, 242
Leverett, John, 277
Leverett, Thomas, 277
Levett, Christopher, 103
Livermore, Chief Justice, 356–57
Lucas, 132
Ludwell, Governor Phillip, 136, 230, 246
Lydius, John, 297
Lyman, General, 303

McKay, Robert, 208
Madison, James, 347, 353
Mallory, Philip, 162
Markham, Captain, 239
Marshall, Roger, 260
Martin, Governor, 301
Martin, Denny, 91
Martin, Captain John, 184, 187, 189
Mary, Queen, 137, 153
Mason, George, 300
Mason, Captain John, 79, 81, 101, 103, 127, 128, 129, 326, 327; *see also* Gorges and Mason
Mason, Robert, 101, 327
Mason's son, 129
Mather, Increase, 106–7
Mathews, Governor, 169, 170
Maynwaringe, Sir Henry, 187
Mees, Henry, 169
Miantonomo (Miantonomi), Chief, 164
Minge, James, 231
Minge, Ruth, 231
Minuit, Peter, 94
Mitchell, 247
Monck, General George, 136
Moore, Governor, 214
Moore, Maurice, 231
Moore, Tom, 283
More, Dr. Nicholas, 240
Morris, Governor, 261
Morris, Robert, 91
Morton, Thomas, 102–3
Mulberry, Henry, 168
Mulberry, Mary, 168
Murray, William, 305

Newport (e), Captain Christopher, 85, 170, 187, 267
Nicolls, Governor (Colonel), 95, 130, 166, 213, 223, 225
Norton, Captain, 271
Nowell, 276

Ogden, 223, 225
Oglethorpe, James, 138, 147, 171, 233
Opechancanough, Chief, 157, 170
Ousamiquin, Chief, 164

Palmer, Ed., 187
Pamunkey, King, 259
Parker, James, 250
Parrington, Sir Frauncis, 187
Paspehay, Chief, 169
Peachy, William, 242
Penn, Admiral, 122
Penn, William, 34, 76, 78, 119, 121, 122, 123, 124, 125, 126, 130, 132, 141, 143, 145, 147, 148, 149, 159, 160, 166, 167, 168, 220, 221, 237, 238, 239, 240, 241, 242, 243, 252, 262, 292, 297, 338, 350, 351, 357, 358, 359, 368, 379, 396, 409

Phetiplace, William, 186
Philip of France, 40
Pierce, Daniel, 225
Pierce, John, 104, 274, 275
Pike, Joseph, 240
Polland, William, 187
Pope, Alexander, 63
Popham, Sir John, 73, 99
Pott, Governor, 202
Powell, David, 240
Powhatan, Chief, 170, 175
Pricklove, Samuel, 169
Prim, Captain Martin, 263
Pugh, Thomas, 173
Purchase, Thomas, 276
Putnam, General, 303
Pynchon, William, 280

Raleigh, Sir Walter, 73, 83, 133, 146
Rawson, E., 272
Robert, Elias, 187
Robertson, William, 245
Robin, 231
Robinson, John, 299
Rolfe, John, 184
Rolfe, Thomas, 260
Ross, Alex, 208
Roswell, Sir Henry, 275
Russell, Richard, 269

Sackvill, Sir Edward, 187
St. Albans, Lord, 90
Salmon, John, 272
Saltonstall, Lieutenant-Governor, 276
Saye, Lord, 113
Sele, Lord, 113
Sharpe, Governor, 220, 343
Shattuck, Major William, 269
Shute, Governor, 108
Sixpence, Henry, 168
Sloughter, Henry, 213
Smith, Edward, 272
Smith, Captain John, 99
Smith, Joseph, 208
Smith, Major Lawrence, 260
Smith, Sir Thomas, 87, 184, 186, 188
Somers, Captain, 187
Somers, Sir George, 187
Sonmans, Peter, 244
Sothell, Seth, 232
Spotswood, Governor, 175, 206, 245, 329
Stephen, Governor Samuel, 229, 230, 246
Stone, Justice, 6
Stone, Governor William, 219
Story, Justice, 392
Stow, Goodman, 268
Strite, Samuel C., 395
Stuyvesant, Peter, 97, 130, 160
Symes, Major Lancaster, 265

Taylor, Reverend, 341
Thompson, 275
Thomson, David, 103, 277
Threr, 187
Throckmorton, Sir William, 190
Tilghman, Chief Justice, 409
Tom, William, 266
Tracy, William, 190
Tryon, Governor, 249
Turner, Richard, 231

Underhill, Captain, 97
Usher, John, 102
Usselinx, William, 125

Van Curler, Jacob, 166
Van Meter, Isaac, 208
Van Meter, John, 208
Van Rensselaer, Kileaen, 209, 212, 213
Van Swerring, Gerrett, 266
Van Twiller, 94, 166
Von Steuben, Major General Baron, 269

Waite, Jacob, 232
Waldo, Samuel, 277
Walkins, 208
Warner, 241
Washington, Bushrod, 291
Washington, George, 263, 291, 340, 353, 388, 389
Watson, Luke, 223, 225
Way, George, 276
Webster, Daniel, 365, 391
Webster, Pelatiah, 387
Werowance of Paspihe, 170
West, Governor, 202, 204
Weston, Thomas, 102–3
Wharton, Richard, 276
Wheelwright, 128
Whetcombe, 187
White, Father Andrew, 215
Wilkins, Governor, 305
Willard, Major Lyman, 268
Willaston, Richard, 187
William the Conqueror, 23, 24, 31, 38, 59, 69, 255, 394, 402, 407
William and Mary, 78, 107, 108, 270
Williams, Roger, 109, 110, 163, 164, 279, 349, 350
Williams, William, 173
Willocks, George, 244
Winslow, Governor, 163
Winthrop, 113, 272, 276, 278, 319
Wollaston, Captain, 102–3
Wollaston (Wallaston), John, 128
Wolstenholme, Sir John, 189
Wood, Captain Abraham, 260
Woodward, Thomas, 229
Wright, Governor, 236, 250, 370
Wyatt, Governor, 268
Wyatt, Sir Dudley, 89
Wyatt, Sir Francis, 201, 202

Yeardley, Governor George, 88, 157, 170, 182, 185, 190, 200, 201, 268, 269, 270, 332
Young, Arthur, 8

Geographic Index

The Geographic Index includes the names of *places* mentioned in this book. The names of geographic areas are included. State names shown do not include the thirteen original colonies; these are listed in the Subject Index.

Acadia; *see* Nova Scotia
Accomack Territory, 90
Acquedneck Island, 164
Alabama, 346
Alaska, 13
Albany, 167, 175, 208, 335
Albemarle County, 227, 229, 230, 246
Albemarle Sound, 230
Allegheny Mountains, 91, 264, 270, 309
Altamaha River, 138, 171
Androscoggin River, 276
Annapolis, 272, 334
Appalachian Mountain region, 17, 18
Appomattox River, 172, 260
Archer's Hope Creek, 259
Archurshope, 201
Argall's (Argoll's) Town, 190
Arkansas, 346
Ashby River, 231

Baltimore, 396
Baltimore County, 219
Bantam, 280
Barbados, Island of, 136, 137, 227
Barnegat Bay, 132
Barnegat Creek, 132
Barnstable, 283
Barrington, 281
Bath, 137
Beaufort, 248
Beaverbrook Plain, 283
Bennett's Creek, 174
Bergen County, 245
Berkeley's Hundred, 189
Berks, County of, 122, 147
Bermuda Islands; *see* Somers Islands
Bertie County, 171, 173
Black Point Grant, 277
Blackwater River, 172
Blue Ridge Mountains, 91, 137
Boonesborough, 302
Boston, 102, 129, 163, 278, 284, 377
Bristol, 83
Broad Creek, 174
Brown, 301
Brunswick County, 261
Bucks County, 313
Burlington, 308
Butlersburg, 270

Cambridge (Newtown), 113, 280, 282, 285
Camden, 277
Canada, 150
Cape Ann, 103, 106, 278
Cape Comfort; *see* Point Comfort
Cape Fear, 227, 247
Cape Fear River, 137
Cape Henlope (n), 119, 125, 129, 168
Cape May, 130
Cape Neuse, 247
Cape Porpoise, 102
Caroline County, 340
Charles City, 188, 332
Charles River, 106, 280
Charleston, 163
Charlestown, 280
Chenango River, 250
Chesapeake Bay, 68, 85, 117, 119, 166
Chester County, 313
Chicago, 18
Chickahominy Ridge, 260
Chickahominy River, 190
Choptico, 174
Claremont, 319
Clarendon County, 227, 229

Cohasset River, 104
Colchester, 279
Colleton County, 231
Connecticut River, 92, 113, 114
Connecticut Valley, 113, 165
Conway River, 91
Cooperstown, 308
Corn Belt, 17
Cotton Belt, 17
Cow Bay, 165
Craven County, 227, 231
Cull Bay, 166
Cumberland River, 266, 302

Dedham, 278, 279, 281, 282
Delaware Bay, 118, 119, 130, 218
Delaware River, 63, 66, 92, 93, 95, 119, 122, 124, 129, 130, 132, 156, 166, 167, 168, 239, 242
Delaware Valley, 129
Dismal Swamp, 291, 307
Dorchester, 113, 163, 278, 281, 283, 285
Dover, 128, 278
Duck Creek, 167
Durham, County of, 38, 39, 119

East Greenwich, Manor of; *see* Kent, County of
East River, 165
Edenton, 311
Elizabeth City, 203, 332
Elizabethtown, 225
Elizabethtown Purchase, 166, 223, 225, 244
Enfield, 281, 284
England, 11, 22, 24, 25, 33, 38, 44, 50, 55, 60, 61, 62, 69, 71, 73, 76, 83, 85, 86, 97, 106, 108, 127, 141, 142, 143, 144, 194, 253, 254, 255
Epsom, 281
Essex County, 245, 269
Europe, 13, 38, 58, 69, 194
Exeter, 83, 128

Fairfield, 114
Farmington, 114
Fenwick's Island; *see* Cape Henlope
Florida, 65, 134, 346, 393
Flushing, 211
Fort Charles, 172
Fort Christiana, 125
Fort Cumberland, 264
Fort Henry, 172, 260
Fort James, 260
Fort Lyttleton, 248
Fort Orange, 208
Fort Pitt, 306
Fort Royal, 260
Fort Stanwix, 168, 172, 306
France, 62, 127, 172, 347, 349
Frederick County, 220

Genesee River, 250
Germany, 293, 349

Granville District, 302
Gravesend, 211
Great Plains, 16, 17
Green River, 264, 302
Greenbrier River, 299
Groton, 279, 280
Guilford, 114, 281

Haddam, 114
Hadley, 278, 279, 281, 282, 284
Hagerstown, 395
Hampton, 128
Hard Labor, 172
Hartford, 113, 158, 278, 280, 285, 336
Hastings, 255
Hathersall Grant, 201
Haverhill, 280, 281–82
Hempstead, 211, 212
Henderson, 302
Henrico, 188, 203, 270
Henrico Plantation, 202
Hingham, 282
Holland, 94, 103, 210, 349
Holston, 301
Hope, 277
Housatonic River, 163
Hudson River, 62, 92, 93, 95, 130, 243, 364
Hudson Valley, 209, 341
Hungar's Parish, 269

Ipswich, 279, 281, 282
Italy, 349

Illinois River, 304
Intermountain region, 16
Iowa, 19

Jamaica, 223
James City, 203, 259, 332
James River, 85, 100, 169, 171, 172, 188, 189, 190, 260, 261
Jamestown, 63, 71, 85, 151, 170, 175, 188, 288, 291, 349, 394, 398, 399
Jersey, Island of, 137

Kaskaski, 305
Kenkokus Kill, 132
Kennebec Purchase, 275
Kennebec River, 73, 99, 100, 101, 105
Kent, County of, 30, 37, 38, 73, 83, 95, 99, 100, 107, 112, 114, 129, 135, 139, 147, 152, 153, 154, 184, 189, 198, 313
Kent Island, 168
Kentucky, 264, 301, 302, 308, 346, 386, 393
Keowee River, 266
Kequotan, 171
Kiccotan, 188
Killingworth, 114
King County, 269
King's River, 183
Kingswood, 281
Kittatinny Hills, 167

Lake Champlain, 265, 328
Lake Erie, 384, 386
Lancaster County, 313
Little Kanawah River, 306
Little Miami River, 386, 390
London, 83, 88, 185, 200, 242, 248, 290, 295, 300, 303, 304, 306, 329, 330
Long Island, 97, 130, 165, 166, 212, 223, 224, 343
Loqusquscit River, 164
Louisiana, 393
Lucke Island, 133
Lygonia Patent, 277

Maine, 95, 100, 101, 102, 103, 106, 107, 116, 173, 326, 327
Manakintown, 261
Manhattan Island, 92, 130, 165, 208, 209
Manor of
  Calverton, 174
  Cortlandt, 97
  Frank, 240
  Gilbert, 240
  Greenwich; *see* Kent, County of
  Growdon, 240
  Hampton Court, 139, 147
  Highland, 240
  Livingston, 97
  Pelham, 97
  Rockland, 240
Mansfield, 280
Marblehead, 281, 285
Marianna Grant, 103
Martin Gerritsen's Bay, 165
Martin Hundred, 189, 202, 203
Mason-Dixon Line, 119
Massachusetts Bay, 106, 112
Merrimac River, 100, 101, 106
Mespeachtes, 165
Middle West, 18
Middlesex, County of, 139, 147
Middletown, 114, 223
Milford, 114, 279
Mississippi River, 65, 263, 296, 300, 303, 304, 381
Mississippi Territory, 393
Monmouth Purchase, 223
Mooshausick River, 164
Moreland, 240
Muscle Shoals, 309
Muscongus River, 277

Narragansett Bay, 110, 111, 112, 115
Narragansett River, 104
Narragansett Territory, 291–92
Neshaminy Creek, 166, 167
Netherlands, 62
New Amsterdam, 96, 119
New Brittain, 245
New Castle, 122, 125, 270
New Haven, 113, 114, 158, 281, 283, 356
New Ireland Bay, 218
New London, 114
New Plymouth, 105, 274, 275, 283
New Sweden, 125
New York City, 18, 350
Newark, 223
Newbury, 279, 280
Newfoundland, 99, 117, 147
Newport, 109, 110, 280, 284–85
Newtown; *see* Cambridge
Ninecroft; *see* Nyantecutt
Normandy, 24
North Hampton, 278
North Tract, 292
Northampton, 280, 282, 283
Northampton County, 161, 269
Northern Ireland, 39
Northern Neck, 89, 90, 91, 138, 368, 382
Northumberland County, 170
Northwest Territory, 119, 380, 384, 391, 399
Norwalk, 114
Norwich, 114
Nottoway River, 162, 173
Nova Scotia, 107
Nyantecutt (Ninecroft), 158

Ohio River, 65, 172, 264, 296, 300, 304, 306, 393
Ohio Territory, 65, 263, 386
Ontario County, 250
Ossabaw Island, 171
Otsego tract, 308
Ozark Mountain region, 18

Pacific Coast states, 13, 74
Pamunkey, 172, 260
Panama Canal, 19
Pawcatuck River, 112
Pawtuckqut River, 164
Pejepscot, 276
Pemaquid tract, 277
Pemopeck Creek, 167
Penobscot River, 277
Pequot River, 110
Perquimans River, 169
Philadelphia, 91, 271, 292, 294, 298, 305, 391, 396
Philadelphia County, 313
Piedmont region, 352
Piscataqua River, 102, 103, 128
Piscataway, 225
Plymouth, 83, 103, 105, 109, 113, 159, 163, 164, 170, 192, 274, 275, 288, 335, 365, 398, 399
Point Comfort, 86
Pollawahna Island, 248
Port Royal Island, 248
Portsmouth, 109, 110, 128, 215, 278, 281, 284, 357
Portugal, 62, 63
Potomac River, 89, 90, 117, 118, 119, 168, 261, 364, 382
Providence, 109, 110, 112, 164, 279, 281, 357
Providence Plantations, 109, 110, 112, 164

Puerto Rico, 7
Putnam County, 370

Quebec, Province of, 296
Queene's Creek, 259

Rampo, 245
Rapidan River, 91
Rappahannock County, 161, 176
Rappahannock River, 89, 90, 171, 245, 260
Raritan River, 167, 223
Richmond, 331
Richmond's Island, 277
Ridgefield, 280
Roanoke, 83
Roanoke River, 174, 260
Roanoke Sound, 169
Rockaway, 165
Rocky River, 137
Roman Empire, 23
Rome, 15
Rowan County, 137
Roxbury, 113, 278, 280
Runnymede, 40

St. Anne's Parish, 269
St. Catherine Island, 171
St. George Parish, 269
St. Lawrence River, 65, 68
St. Marks Parish, 319
St. Mary's, 215
St. Matthias River, 133
Salem, 106, 109, 163, 278, 280–81, 283, 285, 287
Sandy Point, 223
Sapelo Island, 171
Savannah, 235
Savannah River, 138, 171, 172
Saybrook, 113, 114
Scandinavia, 349
Schuylkill River, 166, 167
Scioto River, 386, 390
Sewall's Creek, 168
Sharpsburg, 395
Shenandoah River, 261
Sicktewacky, 165
Simsbury, 114
Smith Island, 271
Smith's Hundred, 188
Somerset County, 119, 174
Somers Islands, 86, 87
South Farnham Parish, 269
South River, 208
South Tract, 292
Southampton Hundred, 188–89, 203
Southhold, 114
Southwest Territory, 393
Sowams, 284
Spain, 62, 63, 82, 127, 155, 349
Spartanburg, 171
Spotsylvania County, 261, 269
Springfield, 113, 279, 280, 282, 283, 285, 287
Stamford, 114
Staten Island, 165, 265
Stonington, 114
Stratford, 114
Stratford River, 165
Stratton Parish, 269
Suffield, 278
Susquehanna River, 166, 167, 168, 295, 297, 308, 342
Sussex County, 119
Sweden, 62, 125, 129

Tennessee, 266, 301, 386, 393
Tennessee River, 172, 264, 266, 309
Texas, 393
Thames River, 153
Thoms River, 132
Three Lower Counties, 119, 123, 125
Tidewater Virginia, 169, 352
Togolo River, 266
Trenton, 168, 297
Trumbull County, 384

Uchee Domains, 172

Van Meter, 261
Vermont, 102, 257, 269, 308
Virginia Military Reserve, 386, 390
Virginia, Valley of, 352

Wallingford, 281
Waldo Patent, 277
Wanasqutcket River, 164
Warwick, 110
Washington County, 264
Watauga, 301, 302
Waterbury, 279, 281, 283
Watertown, 113, 278, 281, 283, 284
Watkin's Point, 118, 119
Wayanoke, 170
Welsh Tract, 240
Western Reserve, 384, 386
Westminster, 41
Westmoreland County, 313
Westover Parish, 269
Wethersfield, 113, 278, 280, 336
Weymouth, 102, 282
Wiccocomico River, 174
Wilkes-Barre, 297
Wilmington, 125, 313
Windham, 297
Windsor, 113, 278, 280, 336
Windsor, Seigniory of, 123
Woodbridge, 225
Woodstock, 279
Wyoming Valley, 297, 384

Yamacraw Bluff, 171
Yao-Comoco, 168
Yazoo River, 303
York River, 171
Yorktown, 265

Subject Index

A

Absentee, 16, 198, 288, 298, 312
Accomack Indians, 173
Acquisition of land; *see* Indians' land, acquisition of
Adventurers, 69, 73, 85, 87, 112, 179, 181, 184, 200, 202, 229, 332
Aids, 25, 26, 40, 41, 60, 403, 410
Alaska, tenure laws of, 13
Albany Congress, 297
Alienation; *see also* Fine for alienation
  copyhold estates, 49
  forms of, 43–46, 324
  freehold estates, 42–49
  gavelkind, 37, 38
  New England, 276, 284–85, 287
  partial, 12, 15, 408
  patroons, 209
  public domain, 13, 20, 288, 291
  restrictions on, 5, 157–63, 166, 167, 168, 175, 196, 197, 216, 218, 234, 261, 265, 276, 284–85, 287, 288, 293, 318, 319, 379, 410
  right of, 53, 89, 158, 159, 209, 234, 244, 284–85, 310, 318–19
Aliens, rights of, 13, 317, 323
Allegiance, oath of, 117, 122, 134, 222, 223, 248, 312, 410
Allodial tenure, 15
  corporate colonies, 116
  and feudal tenure, contrasted, 3, 298
  royal colonies, 210, 211
Angles, 23
Articles of Confederation, 305, 367, 368, 381, 383, 384, 385
Articles of Surrender (New Jersey), 22

B

Bargain and sale, 43, 44, 251
Bequeath; *see* Inheritance; Wills
Bill of Rights
  England, 349
  Virginia, 373
Bishop of Durham, 37, 38–39, 72
Black Death, 36–37, 58, 59
Board of Common Council of Georgia, 233
Board of Nineteen, 92, 93
Bocland, 23–24, 53
Body of Liberties (Massachusetts), 109, 116, 145, 355, 356
Bondmen, rights of, 31, 36, 58–59
Boundary disputes; *see also* Territorial overlapping grants
  Connecticut-Rhode Island, 112
  Delaware-Maryland, 382
  Maryland-New York, 95, 119
  Maryland-Pennsylvania, 118–19, 122, 262
  Maryland-Virginia, 119, 121, 382
  Mason-Dixon line, 119
  Massachusetts-Rhode Island, 111
  Massachusetts towns, 280
  North Carolina-Virginia, 383–84
Brief Account (New Jersey), 225
Briefe Declaration . . . Virginia, 183
Bundle of rights, 4, 5
Burdens on land; *see* Feudal incidents
Burgage tenure, 27, 30, 147, 407–8

C

Camden-Yorke opinion, 295
Carolina (North and South), 75, 77, 79–81, 89–90, 127, 133–39, 143, 145, 147–49, 154, 162, 169–71, 173–74, 194, 196, 220, 226–33, 235, 246–48, 251, 266–67, 271–72, 295–96, 301–2, 309, 311–13, 316, 318–19, 321–25, 327–33, 337–43, 352, 358, 364, 368, 370, 372, 374, 377, 379–80, 383–85, 393, 406–8, 411
Caveat emptor, 9, 177, 178
Cayuga Indians, 265
Celts, 22, 38
Cessions to federal government, 267, 380–86, 388, 393
Charters
  Avalon; *see* Charters, Newfoundland
  Bermuda, 87, 147, 152
  Bishop of Durham, 72

Charters (*Continued*)
Carolina, 133–38, 148, 352
Connecticut, 113–16, 120, 129
Delaware, 95, 125–26
English, 71
Georgia, 138–40, 383
Gorges, 101–2, 103
Gorges and Mason, 100–101, 103, 127, 145
Guiana, 152
influence of, 73, 78, 108, 144–46
of Liberties (Pennsylvania), 124
Maine, 100–103, 128
Maryland, 37, 103, 117–21
Mason, 101, 103, 127
Massachusetts, 103–9, 116, 129, 141, 355
New England, Council for, 98, 99, 103–5, 147
New Hampshire, 100–103, 128
New Jersey, 129–32
New York, 91–97, 103, 106, 129
Newfoundland, 117, 146–47, 152, 351
Northern Neck, 89–91
of Pardons (England), 71
penalty, 145
Pennsylvania, 37, 121–25
presettlement, 72–73
of Privileges (Pennsylvania), 143, 358
of Privileges to Patroons, 92, 93, 96, 129
Rhode Island, 109–13, 120, 152
types of, 71–72
Virginia, 37, 77, 82–91, 103, 113, 133, 138, 185
first charter, 71, 73, 82–85, 91, 121, 129, 179, 180, 182, 184, 383
second charter, 86, 87, 88, 91, 146, 180, 182, 183
third charter, 86–89, 117, 186
West Indies
Carolana, 147
Montgomeria, 147
Cherokee Indians, 171–72, 174, 301, 302, 309
Chickahominy Indians, 162
Chinese, 13
Chivalry, tenure in; *see* Military tenures
Choptank Indians, 168, 174
Chopticon Indians, 175
Chowanoc Indians, 174
Churches, land for, 197, 216, 255, 257–58, 269–70, 271, 280, 397, 399, 400
Berkeley's Hundred, 189–90
by colonies, 216, 270
federal policies, 399, 400
land companies, 307
Martin's Hundred, 189
Virginia Company, 193, 339
Clothworkers' Company, 179–80
Collective use, 13, 16, 288
Colonies, types of
composite, 75–81, 127–40
corporate, 75–81, 98–116, 120, 126, 143, 145, 149, 354–55
proprietary, 75–81, 117–26, 143, 290–91
royal, 75–81, 82–97, 136, 290–91
Common fields, 278–79, 283–84, 287, 288
Common law, 143–44, 287, 310, 319, 322, 354–62
Communal tenures, 68, 87–88, 180, 183, 188, 192, 274, 286, 288, 398–99
Companies, land merchandising, 16, 289–309
alienation, 290
Atherton Company, 291–92, 293, 294
Burlington Company, 291, 308
churches, 298–99
Connecticut Land Company, 384
development of, 254
Dismal Swamp Adventurers, 307–8
fraudulent sales, 293, 297
free tenures, 290
Greenbrier Company, 299
Henderson, Richard and Company, 264
Illinois Company, 304–5
Illinois-Wabash Companies, 305, 306
Indian lands, 290, 291, 292, 297, 301, 304–5, 309
Indiana Company, 305–6
industry, 292
influence on tenure, 293–94
John Law's Mississippi Company, 293
Louisa Company, 301
Loyal Company, 295–96, 299, 300, 308
Military Adventurers, 302–4
military service, 302–4
Mississippi Company, 304
Ohio Associates, 391
Ohio Company, 295, 299–300, 304, 306, 308
Onion River Company, 308
post-Revolutionary, 289, 291, 309, 384
pre-Revolutionary, 289, 290, 291, 294–96, 297
purpose, 289, 290, 291
Quebec Act, 296, 305
sale of shares, 304
schools, 298–99
settlement regulations, 296, 308
Somers Islands Company, 87, 89, 291
speculation, 290–91, 293–96, 299, 309
Susquehannah Company, 167, 297–99, 384
Transylvania Company, 301–2
Vandalia Company, 289, 290, 304, 305, 306–7
Wabash Company, 305
West Jersey Society, 293
Companies, trading-settlement
Bermuda Company, 152
Dorchester Associates, 72
Dutch East India Company, 72–73, 92
Dutch West India Company, 82, 92, 97, 121, 125, 129, 160, 165, 191, 212, 213
Frankfort Company, 293
Free Society of Traders, 240, 292, 293

Friends of Yorkshire, 242
Guiana Company, 152
influence on tenure, 191–93
The Lincolnshire Company and Ten Associates, 277
London and Bristol Company, 99
London Company, 72, 73, 82, 83, 85, 86, 99, 108, 113, 117, 148, 149, 179, 199, 288
Massachusetts Bay Company, 106, 142, 273, 275–76, 280, 285, 286, 355
Merchants of the Staple, 72
Muscovy Company, 72–73
New England Company, 106
Newfoundland Company, 152
organizational difficulties, 150–52
Pemaquid Proprietors, 277
Plymouth Company, 72, 83, 86, 92, 98, 99, 100, 103, 108, 127, 128, 148, 273, 285, 291
settler inducement, 180–81
shares to adventurers, 87, 179–80
South Company, 125
Spiers and Company, 270
Swedish West India Company, 148, 156, 168, 191, 291
types of, 72, 82, 100
United New Netherland Company, 92
Virginia Company, 77, 86, 87, 88, 91, 99, 100, 103, 121, 145, 180, 182, 184, 185, 186, 187, 188, 192, 193, 200, 201, 203, 227, 263, 267, 269, 271, 275, 291, 318, 331, 339, 341; *see also* Virginia Company
Weston and associates, 72
Concentration, right of, 17–18, 178, 199, 204, 234–35, 253, 258, 284, 287, 405
Concessions and Agreements (Carolina), 134
Concessions and Agreements (New Jersey), 130, 132, 222, 223, 225, 241, 327, 335
Concessions to the Province of Pennsylvania, 124
Condemnation; *see* Eminent domain
Conditions of Plantation (Maryland), 215
Confirming Act, 298
Confiscation, 91, 95, 204, 213, 317, 367, 368–71
Congress, Continental, 367, 372, 391
confiscation urged, 368
land companies, 302, 305, 306
military lands, 257, 267, 382–83
western land, 381, 384, 385
Congress, United States, 7, 388, 389, 390
Connecticut, 75–76, 78, 80, 95, 97–98, 108, 112–16, 118, 120–21, 129, 143, 147–48, 153, 158, 164, 167, 172, 266, 278–81, 284, 292, 295, 297–98, 303, 315, 319, 336, 346, 356, 359, 380–81, 384–86, 388
Conservation, 6, 9
districts, 13
forest, 124, 221, 397
Consolidation; *see* Concentration
Constitution
federal, 5, 13, 374, 377, 385, 386, 389
state
Alabama, 346
Arkansas, 346
Connecticut, 76, 115, 346
Delaware, 352, 362
Florida, 346
Georgia, 352, 372
Kentucky, 346
Maryland, 121, 377, 379
Massachusetts, 372, 377
New Hampshire, 346, 372, 377, 378, 379
New York, 352, 379
North Carolina, 352, 377, 379, 383
Pennsylvania, 371, 372, 377, 379
Rhode Island, 76, 112
South Carolina, 352, 372, 377
Virginia, 377, 383–84
Continental Congress; *see* Congress, Continental
Conveyance; *see* Alienation
Co-operative grazing associations, 13, 16, 288
Co-operatives, 15
Copyhold tenure
alienation of, 49, 404
description of, 31–32, 406
elimination of, 32
inheritance of, 51–52
Statute of Tenures, 60, 95, 404
Copyholders, 31, 36, 37, 59, 147, 404, 406
Corporate landholding, 15, 16, 17, 20
Court of Assistants at the Hall, 179
Courts of assize, 41
Covenants, restrictive, 20
Credit transactions, 15
Creek Nations, 171, 172
Cropper; *see* Share-cropping
Curtesy, right of, 33–34, 374, 404, 407
Custom, 10

D

Daily News Building, 18
Danes, 23
Declaration and Proposal (Carolina), 227
Declaration of Independence, 267, 368, 380, 382, 384, 389
appropriation of land, 372, 383
equal protection, 346
human rights, 372
property, rights of, 372, 373
transfer of ownership, 367, 379–80
Declaration of Lord Baltimore's Plantation in Maryland, 215
Declaration of Rights (North Carolina), 331
Declaration on the Violation of Rights (Continental Congress), 372

Deficiency judgment, 14
Delaware, 63, 75, 78, 80, 95, 117, 119, 121, 125, 129, 143, 147, 149, 191, 194, 196, 220, 237, 266, 270, 313, 315, 322, 350, 352, 361–62, 382, 408, 411
Delaware Indians 167, 168
Descent; *see* Inheritance
De Viris Religiosis; *see* Statutes (Mortmain)
Devise; *see* Inheritance; Wills
Dickenson College, 271
Discovery, right of; *see* Land claims
Disposition, right of, 1, 2, 3, 8, 10, 13, 18; *see also* Alienation
Distraint, right of, 4, 326
Distress, right of, 56–58, 343–44, 404, 406, 411
Distribution; *see* Inheritance
Domesday investigation, 24
Dongan's deed, 167
Dower, right of
  colonial, 321–22, 374, 407
  copyhold, 32
  description, 33
  gavelkind, 37–38
  Ordinance of 1787, 392
  Statute of Tenures, 404
Due process concept, 6
Durham; *see* Bishop of Durham
Dutch, 62, 64, 66, 71, 82, 91, 92, 93, 97, 113, 119, 125, 131, 141, 146, 148, 149, 150, 156, 157, 159, 165, 177, 191, 208, 210, 211, 212, 213, 216, 239, 356

E

Easement, 2, 8, 9, 18, 20
Economic influence, 362–66
Egyptians, 22
Ejectment, 55, 56, 68
Elegit; *see* Writs
Elizabethtown Purchase, 166, 223, 225, 244
Emblements, right of, 32
Eminent domain, right of, 2, 6, 271, 312–14, 392
  improve tenure, 7
  incidence of, 11
  Indian tenure, 68
  Ordinance of 1787, 392
  practiced in colonies, 312–14, 411
  reserved by society, 5–7
Enclosures, 59
English, 22, 62, 64, 65, 66, 69, 71, 79, 82, 88, 92, 93, 95, 97, 114, 120, 124, 131, 141, 144, 148, 150, 156, 157, 160, 161, 162, 165, 171, 172, 173, 177, 200, 208, 212, 213, 237, 238, 239, 265, 288, 354, 355, 356, 360
Entails (fee tail), 5, 47, 49, 61, 123, 341, 410
  arguments for, 48, 374, 375
  barring of, 48–49, 323–24, 371, 373–76, 403
  disappearance of, 310, 376
  Georgia, 233–34, 323, 324
  headrights, 198
  influence of, 376
  Jefferson, 347, 365, 374, 375
  rule against, 19
Equal devolution; *see* Inheritance
Equality
  Fourteenth Amendment, 346
  influence on tenure, 345–48
  state constitutions, 346
Equity concept, 3
Escheat, right of, 8, 316–18, 411
  accidental death, 378
  church land, 46
  corruption of blood, 198, 221–22, 316, 371, 408
  feudal, 25, 27, 403
  gavelkind, 30, 37
  Indian tenure, 68
  lack of heirs, 221–22, 316, 317
  land, 89, 248, 252, 270, 317
  reserved by society, 7, 11, 15, 408, 410
  Statute of Tenures, 60, 404
  suicides, 316, 378
Escuage, 28–29
Exclusion, right of, 2, 3, 8, 10, 13, 84
Exeter Agreement, 104, 128
Expectancy, estate of, 5

F

Family-sized farm
  origin, 94, 97, 151, 192, 251, 253, 286, 400, 405
  policy objective, 13, 16, 18, 197, 199, 234, 287, 347, 380, 395
Fealty, 25, 189, 211, 403, 410, 411
Fee simple conditional tenure, 47–48, 404
Fee simple tenure (ownership), 251, 341, 373, 374, 404, 408
  alienation, 47–48
  corporate colonies, 116
  description, 5, 8, 13
  early charters, 146
  growth, 12, 32, 234, 310, 319, 324, 397
  headrights, 198, 200
  land companies, 304
  limitations on, 6
  Maryland, 121, 396
  New England, 276, 288
  New Jersey, 132
  Ordinance of 1785, 390–91
  origin of, 407–8
  Pennsylvania, 123
  trading companies, 191
  Virginia, 90, 91
Fee tail tenure; *see* Entails
Fencing requirements, 283–84, 287, 314–15
Feudal incidents; *see also* Aids; Escheat; Fealty; Fine for alienation; Homage; Marriage; Primer seisin; Relief; Wardship

abolition of many, 60, 410–11
abuse of, 40–41
decay of, 46, 54, 211
description of, 25–27
persistence, 408–9
Feudal tenure; *see also* specific type
abolition, 13, 395
adjustments, 406–11
and allodial tenure, contrasted, 3, 298–99
American, 3, 13
English, 258, 402–5
European, 13
manors, 149–50
Roman, 15
types of, 27–37, 43
Fidelity, oath of, 215, 219, 222, 223, 410
Financier's Plan, 388
Fine for alienation, 26–27
barring fee tail, 49
copyholder, 31, 49
description, 43, 44, 403
headrights, 198
Kentish tenure, 198
other restrictions, 287, 410
Statute of Tenures, 60
Statute of Wills, 54
tenants in capite, 43
Finns, 125
Fishing rights; *see* Hunting and fishing
Fishmongers Record, 179
Five Nations, 167, 172
Folcland, 23, 53
Foreclosure, 14, 16, 34
Forest land, 124, 221, 397
Frankalmoign, tenure by
description, 27, 30–31
Maryland, 407
not brought to America, 147, 407
Statute of Mortmain, 46–47
Franklin College, 258, 271
Free and common socage, 36, 149, 152, 198, 251, 407
adjustments, 406–8, 410
Carolina, 135, 229, 246, 247
Connecticut, 114
early charters, 146, 147
feudal, 27, 29–30, 60
Durham, 38–39
Kent, 37–38
Georgia, 139
Gorges, 100
London Company, 83
Maine, 102
Maryland, 120
Mason, 100, 129
Massachusetts, 107
military service, 256
Muscovy Company, 73
New England, 99, 278, 288
New Hampshire, 127, 129
New Jersey, 129, 222
New York, 95
Northern Neck, 89
Pennsylvania, 122, 221
Plymouth Company, 83
Rhode Island, 112
special purpose grants, 258
Statue of Marlborough, 42
Statute of Tenures, 60, 136, 404
Virginia, 184
Freedom of contract, 9, 20
Freedoms and Exemptions (New York), 94, 96, 129, 165, 209, 211
Freeholders, 36, 42–43, 56, 94, 97, 102, 191, 192, 198, 213, 219, 275, 277, 313
first in America, 181–83
French, 63, 65, 150, 156, 177, 198, 216, 257, 261, 362, 363
Frontier, 144, 199, 245, 246, 252, 302, 362–64, 365
Frontier protection, 65, 138, 183, 255, 257, 258, 259–62, 263, 311, 362, 397, 407
Fundamental Articles of New Haven, 114
Fundamental Constitutions, 135–36, 149, 231, 233, 358, 406, 407
Fundamental Orders of Connecticut, 113, 114, 356

G

Gavelkind tenure, 27, 30, 37–38, 51–52, 407–8
General welfare, 3, 6, 9, 14, 287, 302
Georgia, 65, 75, 77, 79–81, 127, 138–39, 141, 143, 147–49, 151, 162–63, 171–72, 174, 194, 197, 233–35, 250, 253–54, 256–57, 262, 266, 270, 272, 295–96, 309, 312, 317–18, 321, 323–26, 329–31, 333, 337, 340, 342, 352, 363, 370, 372, 380, 383–86, 393, 407, 410–11
German Lutheran Congregation, 271
Germans, 340
Good Speed to Virginia, 157
Government; *see* Power to govern
Government of Rhode Island, 110
Governor and Company . . . Rhode Island, 112
Grand Central Station, 18
Grand Deed of Albemarle (Great Deed of Grant), 229–30, 325, 327
Grant of Province of New Hampshire, 128
Grants; *see* Churches; Headrights; Industry; Meritorious service; Military service; New England, land system; Sale of land; Schools
Grants and Concessions (New Jersey), 357
Greeks, 22
Ground rent, 396

H

Hampden-Sydney College, 258, 270
Harvard University (College), 258, 270, 277

Headrights, 124, 131, 181, 194–236, 275, 397, 400, 405
abuses of, 195, 199, 207–8, 214, 231, 294
Carolina, 196, 226–33
Delaware, 220–22
early use of, 181, 194
feudal practices, 195, 198
Georgia, 197, 233–36, 251
and homsteading, compared, 195, 199, 401–2
inducements, 181, 196–97, 200, 210–11, 215, 216, 217, 221, 224, 225, 227, 228, 229, 233, 234, 274
Maryland, 196, 215–20
and New England system, compared, 274, 286
New Jersey, 222–26
New York, 197, 208–15
patroons, 209
Pennsylvania, 220–22
size of grants, 195, 196, 197, 201, 202, 203, 204, 205, 206, 207, 208, 213, 214, 218, 220, 232–33, 234–35, 274
trading companies, 199–202
unique features, 197
Virginia, 87, 91, 189, 196, 199, 208, 245, 246
Heath grant, 133, 148
Hebrews, 22, 347, 348
Hereditaments, 2, 83, 85, 334
Hired man, status of; *see* Laborer
Homage, 25, 60, 146, 211, 403, 410
Homestead Act; *see* Statutes
Homestead tax exemptions; *see* Taxation
Homesteading, 195, 199, 253, 401–2
Hoosac Mills, 6
House of Burgesses, 88, 161
Hudson Terminal, 18
Huguenots, 65, 349
Hunting and fishing, 2, 94, 100, 201, 210, 315–16

I

Improvements, 6, 9, 10, 11, 342
In capite, 27–28, 43, 407
Indentured servants, 181, 182–83, 195–96, 294, 405; *see also* Servants, land for
Indian tenure system, 66–70
effect on tenure, 144, 176–77
inheritance, 67
occupancy rights, 62, 67, 155, 163–64
ownership rights, 66–68, 109, 155
Indians
Accomack Indians, 173
Cayuga Indians, 265
Cherokee Indians, 171-72, 174, 301, 302, 309
Chickahominy Indians, 162
Choptank Indians, 168, 174
Chopticon Indians, 175
Chowanoc Indians, 174
Creek Nations, 171, 172
Delaware Indians, 167, 168
Five Nations, 167, 172
Iroquois Indians, 168, 171–72, 302, 380
Lower Creek Indians, 171
Mico Indians, 171
Nanticoke Indians, 174
Narragansett Indians, 110, 164, 292
Necotowance Indians, 171, 260
Nottoway Indians, 162, 173
Onondaga Indians, 265
Paukanawket Indians, 164
Pequot Indians, 173
Potomac Indians, 167
Shawnee Indians, 167
Six Nations, 167, 168, 174, 297
Susquehanna Indians, 167
Tuscarora Indians, 171, 174
Uchee Indians, 171, 172
Upper Creek Indians, 171
Wahanganoche Indians, 169
Wiccocomico Indians, 169, 170
Yeopim Indians, 169
Indians, land reserved for, 171, 173–75, 176, 297
Indians' land, acquisition of, 124, 125, 155–78, 250
by abandonment, 172
by gift, 170
by lease, 155, 173, 176
by purchase, 155, 176
Camden-Yorke opinion, 295
Dutch, 156, 159
Elizabethtown Purchase, 223
land companies, 290, 291, 292, 297, 301, 304–5, 309
Middle colonies, 165–70, 238, 242, 244, 297
Monmouth Purchase, 223
New England colonies, 110, 113–14, 163–65, 274, 276, 278
Ordinance of 1785, 390
price paid, 163, 164, 165, 166–68, 169, 177–78, 213
restrictions on, 157–63, 167, 379
Southern colonies, 169–70, 263, 309
Spanish, 156
Swedes, 125, 129, 156
by seizure, 155, 172–73, 176
by treaty, 166, 170–72, 176, 263, 302, 305–6
Industry, land for, 258, 259, 271–72, 397, 399–400
Ingle's rebellion, 268
Inheritance; *see also* Wills
aliens, 13
Baltimore, 117–18
bequeath, 2, 8, 186–88
in colonies, 319–24, 409–10
copyholds, 51, 52
descent
patroonships, 210
rules of, 234, 319, 320–23
distribution

right of, 3
rules of, 52–53
double portion, 319–20, 347, 348, 374, 375
earliest form, 23–24
equal devolution, 94, 211, 320, 347, 375, 376
failure of issue, 60, 408
females, 50, 51, 94, 320, 374, 404
feudal, 50–55
gavelkind (Kent), 30, 37, 38, 51–52
Indian, 67
lineal descent, 320
Magna Carta, 52–53
males preferred, 50, 404
Ordinance of 1787, 392
parcellation, 18, 114, 405
persons killed, 378
representation, 50, 51, 320, 321, 404
shares in company, 186–88, 267
Statute of Tenures, 60, 404
succession, 31, 50–53, 320–23, 392
suicides, 378
tax, 410
unborn child, 322
whole blood, 50–51, 320–21, 392, 404
Instructions for the Government of the Colonies (Virginia), 85, 180
Interstate commerce clause, 6
Iowa, termination of lease, 19
Irish, 340
Iroquois Indians, 168, 171–72, 302, 380
Isolation, 364
Italians, 216

J

Japanese, 13
Joint tenancy, 132
Jutes, 23

K

Kentish tenure, 30, 37–38, 152–54, 198; *see also* Kent, county of *in* Geographic Index
Knight service, 28, 29, 42, 54, 60, 101, 403, 407

L

Laborer, 11, 12, 14, 58, 59, 60–61, 294
Laissez faire, 9, 20, 197
Land Acts, Virginia, 204–6, 332, 355
Land claims, European
based on discovery, 62–66, 130, 156–57, 175
conflicting claims, 68–70
Land companies; *see* Companies, land merchandising; Companies, trading-settlement
Land grants; *see* Churches; Headrights; Industry; Meritorious service; Military service; New England, land system; Sale of land; Schools
Land offices, 232, 379–80, 397
Land policy, 197, 380–86, 388, 395, 399–402
Landlord; *see* Leasing
Law; *see* Common law
Lease and release, 43, 45, 130, 238–39, 392
Leasing (leaseholds), 3, 4, 5, 6, 8, 10, 11, 12, 14, 15, 17, 20, 32, 181–83, 324, 396, 397, 404–5, 406; *see also* Distress; Possession; Rent; Trespass; Waste
colonial, 339–44
early English, 55–58
first in America, 182, 192
Indian land, 155, 173
length of term, 1, 4, 5, 11, 19, 32, 218, 341–42, 396, 405
termination of, 19
Lesser estate; *see* specific type
Licensing, 14, 15, 17, 20
Lien, landlord's, 6, 9, 14
Life estate, 123, 276, 405, 406
Livery of seisin, 45, 332, 334, 336
London Bridge, 153
Lower Creek Indians, 171

M

Magna Carta, 28, 29, 33, 40–43, 46, 52–53, 71, 403
Manorial system, 35–37
Manors, colonial, 90, 97, 102, 120, 122, 126, 143, 149–50, 153, 213, 219–20, 240, 298, 341, 396
Marianna grant, 103
Marriage, 25, 26, 40, 46, 60, 286, 403, 410
Maryland, 37, 75–78, 80, 89, 103, 117–22, 124–26, 133, 143, 147–48, 153, 160, 168, 173–74, 194, 196–98, 215–17, 219, 229, 248, 256, 262, 264, 268, 271–72, 302, 313, 315, 318, 321, 325, 327–28, 330–31, 334, 338–39, 341, 343, 351, 358–59, 368, 370, 377, 379, 381–85, 395–96, 407
Maryland Toleration Act, 351
Massachusetts, 75, 78–80, 98, 101–3, 105–6, 108–13, 115, 128–29, 141–43, 146–48, 153, 159, 163–64, 266, 268, 270, 272, 278–81, 284–85, 295, 319–20, 335–36, 350, 352, 355–56, 359, 361, 372, 375, 377, 380, 382, 385
Mayflower Compact, 103–4, 105, 354, 398
Merchandise Mart, 18
Merchant Taylors' Records, 180
Meritorious service, land for, 257, 267–69, 397, 400
Mesopotamians, 22
Mico Indians, 171
Military service, land for, 259–67
army service, 246, 255, 256, 257, 258, 259–67, 370, 386, 388, 397, 399–400
Continental Congress, 257, 267, 382–83
frontier service, 229, 255, 257, 258, 259–62, 397, 399–400, 407

Military service, land for, (*Continued*)
land companies, 302–4
Land for Defense, 260–61
land office, 380
Ordinance of 1785, 390
Proclamation of 1763, 263, 265, 266, 296, 303
tax exempt, 260–61
Military tenures; *see also* Escuage; Knight service; Serjeanty
abolition, 54, 60, 404, 407
alienation, 43–46
charters, 147, 407
England, 24
forms of, 27, 28–29
Statute of Tenures, 403–4
Statute of Wills, 54
Mineral reservations, 20, 116, 196, 197–98, 376
Congress, 390, 393
Crown, 197, 311
Carolina, 133
charters, 146
Connecticut, 114
London Company, 83
Maryland, 120
Massachusetts, 107–8
New England, 99, 101, 114, 127–28
New Jersey, 131, 222
New York, 249–50
Pennsylvania, 122, 124
Plymouth Company, 83
Rhode Island, 112
Virginia, 83, 89, 90, 91, 181, 189, 201, 307
settlement agencies, 101, 104–5, 127–28, 189, 198
Monmouth Purchase, 223
Mortgages, 6, 8, 9, 13, 15, 16, 34, 331, 335, 404, 408
Mortmain; *see* Statutes
Mosaic law, 375

N

Nanticoke Indians, 174
Narragansett Indians, 110, 164, 292
Navigation Act, 132, 135, 136, 157
Necotowance Indians, 171, 260
Negroes, 225, 294, 333, 406
New England
land system, 273–88, 390, 397
alienation, 276, 284–85, 287, 288
beginning, 274
communal tenure, 274, 288
early settlement, 100–16
free tenures, 24, 116, 276, 288
grants, 275, 276, 277, 286, 287
influence on tenure, 388, 395
town system, 278–85, 294
arable-meadow land, 278–79, 282–83, 286, 287, 288
boundaries, 280
common fields, 278–79, 283–84, 287
government, 112, 114, 212
home lots, 278–82, 285, 286
proprietors, 278, 279, 281, 284, 285
New England, Council for, 114, 121, 277, 286
charter, 98, 99
dissolved, 101
land grants, 100, 101, 102–3, 104, 106, 113, 273, 274, 275
New Hampshire, 75, 77, 79–81, 98, 100–103, 106, 116, 127–29, 143, 147, 149, 153, 170, 265, 278, 281, 296, 308, 326–27, 336, 346, 350, 356, 361, 368, 372, 377–79
New Jersey, 45, 75, 77, 79–81, 95, 127, 129–33, 143, 147–49, 154, 160, 165–66, 194, 196, 198, 222–26, 237, 241–44, 252, 268–70, 272, 293, 311, 315, 322, 325–31, 335, 338, 350, 357, 359, 369, 396
New Netherland; *see* New York
New York, 63, 75, 77, 79–80, 82, 91–97, 103, 106, 114, 125, 130–32, 143, 146–50, 154, 157, 159–60, 165–67, 172, 191, 194, 197, 208–12, 214–15, 249–50, 256–58, 262, 265, 269–71, 294, 296, 308, 320–31, 337, 341–42, 344, 350, 352, 357, 361, 368–70, 379–81, 384–85, 387, 392, 395, 411
Norman Conquest, 3, 22, 30, 31, 35, 58
Normans, 22, 23, 24
North Carolina; *see* Carolina
Northwest Ordinance; *see* Ordinances
Nottoway Indians, 162, 173
Nova Brittania, 157, 180, 181

O

Oaths; *see* Allegiance; Fidelity
Occupancy, right of, 10, 125, 274
Onondaga Indians, 265
Oral agreements, 19
Orders and Constitutions and Instructions (Virginia), 185, 332
Ordinances
Northwest, 380, 397, 399, 400
Monroe's report, 391
Ordinance of 1785, 12, 309, 389–91, 407
Ordinance of 1787, 12, 309, 391–93, 407
Report of 1784, 388–89
Southwest, 309, 393
for Virginia, 88
Ownership; *see* Fee simple tenure

P

Parcellation; *see* Subdividing
Partido system, 11
Partnership, 15, 16
Patent, land, 12, 14
Patroons (patroonships), 93, 94, 96, 97, 150, 159, 209–10, 211, 341, 350, 368, 395, 409

Paukanawket Indians, 164
Pennsylvania, 37, 75, 78, 80, 117, 119, 121–26, 143, 147–48, 153, 160, 166–68, 172, 194, 196, 198, 220–22, 236–41, 251–52, 256–57, 261–62, 270, 292, 295, 297–98, 302, 305, 312–15, 318, 320, 322–23, 325–26, 330–31, 334, 337–38, 351, 359, 361, 368, 371–72, 377, 379, 382, 384, 386, 393, 396, 397, 408, 411
Pennsylvania Station, 18
Pequot Indians, 173
Percey's discourse, 175
Permit to use land, 17, 20
Perpetuity, 19
  Mason's 3,000 year grant, 128
Pilgrims, 72, 103, 104, 163, 274, 361, 398, 401
Piscataqua Combination, 104, 128
Pittsburgh Academy, 271
Plantations, origin of, 192
Plantations Agreement at Providence, 110, 357
Planters, 85, 142, 179, 181, 186, 198, 200, 201, 202, 208, 213, 262, 267, 335
Plymouth Colony, 103, 104–5, 106, 107, 109, 113, 163
Police power, 5, 6, 7, 9, 11, 68, 314
Political influence, 365–66
Possession, right of, 1, 10, 55, 342, 404
Potomac Indians, 167
Power to govern, 71, 73–81, 141–46, 151, 193, 289, 397
  Bishop of Durham, 38–39, 72
  Carolina, 75, 77, 80, 81, 133, 134–35, 138, 143, 145
  composite colonies, 127
  Connecticut, 75, 76, 78, 80, 113, 114, 143
  corporate colonies, 75, 76, 126, 288
  Delaware, 75, 78, 80, 124–25, 143
  feudal England, 258
  four eras, 141, 142, 143, 145
  Georgia, 75, 77, 80, 81, 139, 143
  influence of, 73–74, 141–46
  Maine, 102
  Maryland, 75, 76, 77, 78, 80, 120, 121, 126, 143, 145, 153, 220, 358
  Massachusetts, 75, 78, 80, 103, 104, 105, 106, 108–9, 142, 143, 145, 146, 354
  New England, 99–100, 101, 102, 103, 288
  New Hampshire, 75, 77, 80, 81, 101, 128–29, 143
  New Jersey, 75, 77, 80, 81, 130, 132, 143
  New York, 75, 77, 80, 93, 94, 95, 96–97, 103, 106–7, 143, 209, 212
  Pennsylvania, 75, 78, 80, 122, 123–24, 126, 143, 145, 153
  proprietary colonies, 75, 76
  Rhode Island, 75, 76, 78, 80, 109–10, 111, 112, 143, 152
  royal colonies, 75, 76
  Virginia, 75, 77, 80, 83, 84–85, 86, 88, 103, 106, 143, 188, 193
Pre-emption, 195, 253, 286, 348, 401
President's Committee on Farm Tenancy, 197
Price of land, 252
  Indian land, 163, 164, 165, 166, 167, 168, 169, 171, 177–78
  Georgia, 250, 251, 252, 253
  Maryland, 248, 249
  New England, 274, 275, 292
  New Jersey, 243, 244
  New York, 249, 250
  North Carolina, 246, 247, 370
  Pennsylvania, 238, 239, 241
  South Carolina, 247, 248
  Virginia, 245, 246
  western land, 390
Primer seisin, 25, 26, 54, 60, 403, 410
Primogeniture
  in America, 61, 198, 310
  description, 47, 50
  Jefferson on, 347
  Kentish tenure, 30, 37
  outlawed, 319, 370, 373–76, 400, 409–10
  problems, 198
  purpose, 48, 51
  Statute of Tenures, 404
Privity of contract, 57–58
Privity of estate, 57–58
Proclamation of 1763, 296, 300, 301, 303, 308, 367, 371, 383
Provincial colonies; *see* Colonies, types of, royal
Public domain
  alienation of, 13, 199, 245, 253, 288
  Army Plan, 388
  cession by states, 380–86, 393
  distribution, 309, 347, 386–93
Public land policies, 394–402
Pursuit of happiness, 371–79

Q

Quakers, 122, 132, 158, 242, 252–53, 326, 349, 350
Quebec Act, 296, 305, 367, 371, 383
Quia Emptores; *see* Statutes
Quintipartite deed, 132
Quitrents, 126, 131, 132, 137, 211, 215, 221–22, 227, 298, 302, 310, 324–31, 376–78, 397, 411
  abolition of, 91, 132, 198, 258, 327, 331, 378, 395–96, 400
  bought off, 198, 226, 253, 274, 395–96
  collection problems, 126, 132, 223, 225, 251, 258, 317–18, 327
  deferment of, 100, 196–97, 212, 229, 233, 256, 257, 258, 261, 262, 263, 300, 302, 304, 306, 327–28, 388
    military lands, 256–57, 261–62, 263, 265, 388
  effectiveness of, 205, 329–31
  feudal, 60, 153
  land companies, 290, 298, 300, 302, 304, 306, 307

Quitrents (*Continued*)
land free of, 116, 239, 253, 274, 278, 407
New England, 116, 198, 274, 276, 278, 288, 324, 326–27, 411
payment in kind, 90, 94, 210, 217, 328
penalty for nonpayment, 206, 216, 218, 316, 317–18, 328–29
rate of payment, 196, 296, 307, 325–27
Carolina, 230, 231, 246, 247, 248, 325–26, 327
Georgia, 233, 326
Maryland, 216–19, 248, 325
New England, 101, 274
New Jersey, 222, 226, 243, 326
New York, 212, 213, 214, 249, 265, 326
Pennsylvania, 220–21, 238, 239, 241, 326
Virginia, 89, 90, 91, 190, 201, 272, 300, 325

R

Reading Academy, 271
Recording, 132, 195, 331–36, 405
abuses, 199, 253
deeds, 131, 134, 331–36, 390
grants, 232, 331–36
Indian land, 160
leases, 131, 173, 334, 335
mortgages, 124, 331, 335, 336–37
Ordinance of 1785, 390
Ordinance of 1787, 392
patents, 227, 331–36
shares, 318
Statute of Tenures, 404
surveys, 337–38
titles, 110, 124, 131, 206, 331–36
transfer of shares, 318, 332
wills, 124, 322, 331, 332, 333, 337
Redemption, 14
Regulations, 6, 12
Relief, 25, 26, 40, 46, 54, 60, 403, 410
Religion, 258
Baltimore, 120, 121, 351
corporate colonies, 114, 116
freedom of, 106, 108, 109, 111, 112, 114, 122, 130–31, 133, 134, 294, 352–53, 397, 407
influence of, 59–60, 98, 109, 278, 319–20, 346, 348–54
intolerance, 117
law, 355–56
Penn, 122, 270
Reformation, 59, 63, 349, 354
Rent, 6, 9, 173, 343–44, 406
feudal, 31, 57–58
patroons, 210
share, 10, 182, 192, 210
standing, 10, 183
Statute of Tenures, 404
Replevin, right of, 57
Report of 1784, 388–89
Responsibility ignored, 8, 9, 145
Reversion, 9, 10, 68, 219, 234, 285
Rhode Island, 75–76, 78, 80, 98, 108–13, 115–16, 120, 143, 147, 152–53, 158, 164, 279–81, 284, 292, 295, 336–37, 349–50, 357, 359, 361
Right-of-way; *see* Easement
Rights in land, 21–24, 42, 64, 66–68, 73–74, 78–81, 84, 85, 86, 88, 90, 92, 93, 95, 106, 108–9, 110, 112, 120, 130, 132, 146–48, 149–50, 155, 182, 408; *see also* specific rights
Romans, 22, 33
Royal Council of Virginia, 84–85
Rules and Instructions for Granting Land (Carolina), 231

S

Sale of land
abuses, 245, 247, 253, 294, 297
Carolina, 231, 246–48, 251, 370
church land, 216, 269, 319
confiscated property, 370, 400
contract for, 9, 14, 17, 229
Delaware, 237–41,
escheated land, 248, 252
Georgia, 250–51
Maryland, 248–49
New Jersey, 241–45
New York, 249–50, 370
parcellation, 18, 253
Pennsylvania, 237–41, 251–52
public domain, 192, 199, 253, 392, 400
restrictions on, 212, 216, 234, 238–39, 247, 248, 252, 265, 267–68, 284–85, 287, 293, 304, 318–19
right of, 8, 318–19
settlement agencies, 397
speculation, 251, 253, 254, 293–94
Virginia, 245–46, 251–52
Saxons, 23, 24, 30, 33, 34, 35, 43, 360
Schools (colleges), land for, 193, 255, 256, 258, 259, 270–71, 299, 397, 399, 400
Berkeley's Hundred, 189–90
first grants, 193
Martin's Hundred, 189
Ordinance of 1785, 390
Virginia Company, 339
Scots, 39
Scutage, 40, 60
Seating and planting, 124, 195, 198, 215, 317
defined in Virginia, 204–5
military land, 260–61, 264–65, 266
penalty, 89, 101, 205, 211, 213, 216, 218–19, 226, 230–31, 235, 317, 368
requirement, 195–96, 253, 397
Carolina, 229, 230–31, 232, 272
Georgia, 234, 235–36
land companies, 299–300
Maryland, 216, 219
Massachusetts, 276
New England, 101, 145, 281–82

New Jersey, 131, 226–43
New York, 94, 210, 211, 212, 213, 214
Pennsylvania, 124, 221, 238–39
Virginia, 87, 181, 184, 204–5, 205–6
Serjeanty, 29, 43
Servants, land for, 200, 217, 221, 227, 239, 249, 275; *see also* Indentured servants
Share-cropping, 11, 12, 14, 19, 60–61, 340–41
Shawnee Indians, 167
Six Nations, 167, 168, 174, 297
Size of holdings, 251, 252, 395, 405–6
Carolina, 133, 135, 228–29, 231, 232–33, 246, 247, 248
churches, 189, 269, 270, 307
Georgia, 197, 233, 234, 235, 236, 250–51, 253–54
headrights, 195, 197
industry, 271–72
land companies, 300, 302, 304, 306, 307–8
limitation on, 196, 197, 205, 234, 252, 253–54, 287, 300
Maryland, 118, 217–20, 395
meritorious service, 267–69
military service, 256–57, 258, 259–66
New England, 99, 103, 104, 106, 275, 276, 277, 280–82, 286
New Jersey, 223, 224, 225
New York, 94, 97, 165, 197, 211, 213, 214, 249–50, 270
Ordinance of 1785, 390
Pennsylvania, 122, 221
Rhode Island, 112
schools, 270–71
Virginia, 91, 180, 181, 182, 183, 185, 189–90, 192, 200, 201, 202, 203, 204, 205, 206, 207, 208, 245, 246
Socage tenure; *see* Free and common socage
Social compact; *see* Exeter Agreement; Mayflower Compact; Piscataqua Combination
Soldiers; *see* Military service
South Carolina; *see* Carolina
Southwest Ordinance; *see* Ordinances
Space concept
above surface, 12, 14, 16, 18, 19
below surface, 16, 18
on surface, 16, 17, 18, 74
Spanish, 63, 64, 65, 138, 144, 155, 156, 198, 257, 362, 407
Speculation, 193, 251, 253, 254, 261–62, 293, 294; *see also* Companies, land merchandising
Spending power, 6, 7, 8
Spener's College of Pietists, 293
Spotsylvania and Brunswick Acts, 261
Squatter's rights, 68, 103, 109, 142, 152, 178, 195, 233, 278, 363, 400
State of Rhode Island and Providence Plantations, 112
Stationers' Records, 180
Statutes
of De Donis, 47–49, 403
of Enrollments, 44, 45, 54, 403
of Frauds, 54–55, 357, 406
of Gloucester, 42, 56
Homestead Act, 348
of Laborers, 58–59
Land for Defense, 260–61
Law of Property Act of 1922, 32
of Marlborough, 42
of Merchants, 34
of Mortmain, 41, 45, 46–47, 53, 216, 403, 407
Maryland, 47, 197, 216, 407
Pre-emption Act, 348, 401
of Quia Emptores, 41, 47, 49, 103, 121, 123, 396, 403, 407, 408
of 1776, 374
of Staples, 34
of Tenures, 40, 60, 95, 113, 116, 136, 403, 404–5
of Uses, 44, 54
of Westminster, 34
of Wills, 54, 55, 403
Subdividing, 8, 17, 18, 89, 90, 94, 131, 132, 242, 405
Subinfeudation
Baltimore, 121, 153
in colonies, 408
feudal, 43, 44, 143
Magna Carta, 41, 43, 403
Penn, 123, 396
Quia Emptores, Statute of, 47, 103, 409
Statute of Tenures, 404
Subleasing, 10
Substitution, alienation by, 43, 44, 47
Succession; *see* Inheritance; Wills
Suffers of 1754, 305–6
Supreme Court, United States, 7
Surveying, 195, 239, 252, 254, 269, 282, 307
abuses, 253,
agent's authority, 244
fraudulent, 208
headright grants, 201, 216–18
inaccuracy, 205, 230, 231, 233, 286, 337–39, 396
metes and bounds, 16, 395
Ordinance of 1785, 390, 392
processes, 310, 338–39
provided by law, 131, 132, 134, 213, 227, 245–46, 264, 296
rectangular survey, 16, 390, 399
Susquehanna Indians, 167
Swedes, 62, 64, 65, 66, 71, 119, 125, 129, 141, 156, 168, 191, 220, 239
Swiss, 247

T

Taxation (taxes), 9, 11, 132, 410
deferment, 100, 197, 209, 210, 250, 259, 260, 261, 272, 388
delinquency, 7, 14, 312, 317–18

Taxation (taxes) (*Continued*)
graduated inheritance, 5
graduated land, 5, 347
homestead exempt, 5, 347, 410
industry exempt, 197, 272
inheritance, 410
Jefferson on, 348
Ordinance of 1787, 392
poll tax, 311, 378
rates, 281–82, 286, 311–12
reserved right, 124
right to, 5, 7, 134, 311–12, 376–78, 411
Tenant (tenancy), 10, 11, 12, 19, 20, 137, 182–83, 339–44, 404; *see also* Distress; Leasing; Possession; Rent; Trespass; Waste
Tenancy agreement; *see* Leasing
Tenancy at sufferance, 5, 32–33, 405, 406
Tenancy at will, 5, 32, 405, 406
Tenancy in common, 67, 132, 307
Tenements, 2, 83, 85, 334
Tenure, types of; *see* Allodial tenure; Burgage tenure; Copyhold tenure; Curtesy; Dower; Entails; Escuage; Fee simple tenure; Fee simple conditional tenure; Feudal tenure; Frankalmoign; Free and common socage; Gavelkind tenure; In capite; Knight service; Military tenures; Serjeanty; Tenancy at sufferance; Tenancy at will; Villein tenures
Territorial overlapping grants, 148–49; *see also* Boundary disputes
in colonies, 148
Connecticut-Pennsylvania, 297
Connecticut-Rhode Island, 112, 292
Delaware-New Jersey, 129
Georgia-Carolina, 138
Maine, 101
Maryland-Pennsylvania, 125
Massachusetts-Virginia, 103
New England, 98–99, 106
New England-New Jersey, 129
New Hampshire, 106
Pennsylvania, 121
Plymouth-London, 83, 98–99, 148
Rhode Island, 109, 111
Virginia-Carolina, 133
Yazoo, 386
Title, land, 9, 13, 15, 202, 203, 206, 210, 244, 274, 287, 289, 302, 311
Trading companies; *see* Companies, trading-settlement
Transylvania Seminary (College), 258, 270
Treason; *see* Confiscation
Treasury right grants, 188–91, 246, 294
Treaties
of Breda, 130
of Fort Stanwix, 168, 172, 263, 302, 305–6
of Paris, 65
of Utrecht, 172
of Westminster, 95
Trenton Commission, 297
Trespass, 8, 10, 17, 56, 68, 84, 131
Trustees for Establishing the Colony of Georgia, 138
Trusts (trusteeship), 9, 112
Tuscarora Indians, 171, 174

U

Uchee Indians, 171, 172
Ultimogeniture, 48, 51
Undertakers for the Plantation of the Sommers Islands, 87
Unearned increment, 11
United Brethren, Society of, 270
Upper Creek Indians, 171
Use, right of, 1, 8, 10, 12, 13, 14, 15, 20
Uses, alienation by, 43, 45–46, 53–54, 130

V

Villein tenures, 27, 31–32, 36, 58–59, 404
Virginia, 37, 63, 65, 71, 73, 75, 77, 79, 80, 82–85, 87–91, 94, 96, 99, 102, 106, 109, 117–19, 121, 129, 133, 136, 138, 141, 143, 146–49, 153, 161, 169, 172–76, 179–90, 193–94, 196, 198–208, 229–30, 245–47, 252, 255–57, 259–64, 267–72, 275, 291, 295–96, 299–302, 304–8, 311–17, 319, 321–25, 327–29, 331–33, 336, 338–40, 343, 351–52, 358, 361, 365, 368–69, 372–75, 377–78, 380–86, 388
Virginia Company
chartered rights, 86, 180
dissolution of, 88, 91
first grant, 182
influence on tenure, 192–93, 341
land distribution, 181–82, 183–85, 186, 191, 192, 193, 200–2, 203, 277
land for separatists, 103
leasing, 182–83
objection to Baltimore grant, 121
origin of, 86
planters, 200
power to govern, 77, 86, 88
purpose, 191
rights in land, 79, 89, 180, 183, 184
settler inducements, 87, 180–81, 200
shares, 201–3
bequeathing, 186–88
number held, 185–86
selling of, 179, 180, 186–88, 318
tenants, 182, 340
Virginia toleration act, 352

W

Wahanganoche Indians, 169
Walpole-Wharton petition, 304
Wardship, 25, 40, 42, 46, 54, 60, 403, 410
Waste, 8, 10, 15, 32
Jefferson on, 360
Magna Carta, 42
Statute of Tenures, 404, 405
tenancy, 56, 342–43, 405

Water rights, 2, 124
Wiccocomico Indians, 169, 170
William and Mary College, 256, 258, 270
Wills, 2, 8, 374
  colonial, 322–23
  feudal, 53–55
  Indians, 159
  oral, 322–23
  Ordinance of 1787, 392
  Pennsylvania, 124
  shares in Virginia Company, 186–88
  Statute of Tenures, 404
  Statute of Wills, 54
Windsor, Castle of, 122, 147, 153
Women, 283
  headright grants for, 227
  sale of land by, 319
  signature of, 322, 336
  wills, 323
Writs
  of elegit, 34–35, 408
  of entry, 57
  of right, 57

Y

Yeopim Indians, 169

Z

Zoning, 13, 18

The Author

Marshall Harris, head of the Land Tenure Section of the Bureau of Agricultural Economics, has been in the United States Department of Agriculture since 1934. The present study was made under a grant from the General Education Board in recognition of his stature in this field.

In the USDA, his work has been principally research in land tenure, but additionally, he has served in the Tobacco Section of the AAA, as a technical consultant on the President's Committee on Farm Tenancy (1936–37), on the Inter-Agency Committee on Land Reform, and as a consultant on the Anglo-American Caribbean Commission (1944). He also has been technical consulant for numerous federal, regional, and state committees and technical adviser for a series of programs on land problems throughout the world produced at WOI-TV, the educational television station of Iowa State College.

He is editor or senior author of Family Farm Policy, Agrarian Reform and Moral Responsibility, Better Farm Leases, *and other similar writings. His article, "Land Tenure Policy Objectives," was published in* Readings on Agricultural Economics *(O. B. Jesness, editor).*

Author Harris has first-hand knowledge of farming and land tenancy. He grew up in the Bluegrass country with nine brothers and sisters on a 126-acre diversified farm, which his father purchased after having spent several years on the laborer and tenancy rungs of the agricultural ladder. Tobacco was one of the staple crops on the farm, and the family kept a herd of 30 milk cows in addition to their hogs and mules.

Marshall Harris received his bachelor of science degree from the University of Kentucky. He holds the master of science degree from the University of Illinois, and from the same institution received the first doctor of philosophy degree to be conferred in agricultural economics.

The Author